EMINENT GAN

Immigrants and the Birth of Organized Crime in America

James Fentress

University Press of America,® Inc.
Lanham · Boulder · New York · Toronto · Plymouth, UK

Copyright © 2010 by
University Press of America,® Inc.
4501 Forbes Boulevard
Suite 200
Lanham, Maryland 20706
UPA Acquisitions Department (301) 459-3366

Estover Road
Plymouth PL6 7PY
United Kingdom

Library of Congress Control Number: 2010927818
ISBN: 978-0-7618-5215-5 (paperback : alk. paper)
eISBN: 978-0-7618-5216-2

To

Denis Mack Smith, who taught me what it means to be a historian.

and to Lisa, who revived this book from the dead.

Love, James

Contents

Introduction
A New World

For the parents of Lucky Luciano, America was the land of dreams:

> All the time we was growing up, it seemed that all my old man ever talked about was going to America. We had a calendar that come from the steamship company in Palermo, which was where you got on the boat. My old man used to get a new one every year and hang it up on the wall, and my mother used to cross herself every time she walked past it. Sometimes we even went without enough to eat, because every cent my old man could lay his hands on would go into a big bottle he kept under his bed. It was his private bank and my mother would count it at the end of every month so we could figure how long it would take before we had enough to go to Palermo and make the boat.[1]

America seemed to beckon. And just as it was beckoning Luciano's parents, it was calling to countless others—share-croppers; tenant farmers; workers in the vineyards, groves, and gardens; clerks; and shopkeepers. In towns like Lercara Friddi where Luciano's family came from, deep in Sicily's Palermo Province, or Lauropoli, a hill town near the ancient city of Cosenza where Frank Costello was born, or the great city of Naples where Al Capone's father, Gabriele, plied his trade as a barber, whole families were pulling up stakes. There was always a story of some neighbor, cousin, or other family member who had made it in America. People listened to these stories, so even before they arrived, America had already unfolded itself in their imaginations.

The decades on either side of 1900 were the years of the great influx. It was then that immigrants came pouring in from Eastern and Southern Europe.

Their usual point of entry was the Port of New York, a primacy New York City had enjoyed for over a generation.[2] And thus, when the Luciano family boarded a ship in Palermo, it was a steamer bound for New York. As the end of the voyage approached, a tight little knot of passengers would have wedged themselves onto the bow, leaning out against the railings, braving the early morning chills, straining to see the first landfall. As the majestic bulk of the Statue of Liberty suddenly loomed over the horizon, there would have been whoops and shouts and a wave of commotion as the news spread sternward. Below decks, old men, women, and children would drop whatever they were doing and begin their scramble up to the decks where they would stand, wide-eyed. Occasionally there would be cheers. More often it seems, the assembled passengers simply stood there, silent and dumbfounded, as they gazed upwards.

It was difficult for the new immigrants to comprehend the magnitude of the vast continent on whose easternmost rim they were now standing.

There is a story dating from this time, a sort of running gag, no doubt tricked up into a little vaudeville number. It may well have sprung to life in vaudeville in the first place:

A family of poor Sicilians just off the boat walks up to a police officer. In broken English they endeavor to explain that they have a letter from their compari. This letter speaks of opportunities—a flourishing green grocery, fruit stand, or shoe repair shop. The letter bears an invitation to the friends back in Sicily. The family has taken up the invitation. So now if the good officer would be so kind as to direct the family to a place called McCleary.

Brave Officer O'Rooney takes off his helmet and scratches his head doubtfully before sending the family over to inquire at O'Houlihan's tavern. Perplexed in his turn, O'Houlihan sends them across the street to Schmidlapp the haberdasher, who buttonholes the passing Rabbi Silberstein, and on and on, the impossible names becoming more comically mangled with each successive encounter. All the while the poor Sicilian family grows ever more frantic.

In the end, one of the interlocutors has the good sense to take the letter and look at the post mark. Look here, he announces to them, your McCleary is in Ohio. The Sicilians are much relieved. And in what part of Manhattan might that be, they wish to know?

Perplexity is a good note to begin on, for turn-of-the-century America truly was a bewildering place. Already by the 1880s, reformer Jacob Riis wrote that the ethnic map of Manhattan would "show more stripes than a zebra and more colors than a rainbow."[3] Nevertheless, though they had no way of knowing it, the immigrants had picked a good time to arrive. For the thirty years before 1900, American growth had been, at best, uneven. These were decades that not only witnessed economic crises and recurring slumps, but also mounting tensions as workers organized themselves in trade unions to fight bad working conditions, lay-offs and wage reductions. Employers, in their turn, organized themselves to fight off these unwelcome innovations. By

1900, however, the clouds were lifting. The economy, especially the urban consumer economy, had begun to pick up, showing signs of a vitality not seen since the heady days of the post-Civil War railway boom. The economy was slowly gaining steam. America was about to embark on nearly thirty years of strong, uninterrupted growth. It was a swelling tide, a revival of economic buoyancy that boosted all ships, helping the new immigrants find jobs and opportunities, sweeping them forward along on the pathway towards assimilation.

Dynamism implied changes, however, changes that threatened the old order. Not everyone stood to benefit from change, nor would everyone welcome the immigrants with open arms. In 1900 many of the country's older residents associated the new immigrants with dirt, poverty, and crime, viewing them as a potential burden on the municipality. Nor could the Irish, German and Anglo-Saxon workers fail to perceive in the Southern Italians and Eastern European Jewish immigrants a threat to their own jobs and political clout. In fact, these Southern Italian and Eastern European Jewish immigrants were destined to be assimilated in a remarkably short time. But it would still be a struggle. The immigrants would have to fight their way up. Indeed, their fight is part of the story of American organized crime.

The following pages tell that story. In particular, they tell the tale of how the Sicilian-American mafia rose to a position of preeminence within the world of American organized crime. The story focuses on the eminent gangsters, a group of major underworld figures, either immigrants or the sons of immigrants, arriving in America during the turn-of-the-century years.

But is not this story all too familiar? Are not the names and faces of the eminent gangsters already celebrated in film and fiction? So are the places. There are now gangster tours in Chicago; the sites of the notorious deeds of the underworld are public landmarks in New York and New Orleans. There is a scholarly output as well. There are serious books, learned articles, and Websites, all devoted to the saga of organized crime. So why add another book to the pile, why in particular one focusing on the gangsters' own story?

Serious books on crime are not written by or for criminals. They are written instead by and for law-enforcement officials or by criminologists and other academics. The reasons are obvious enough. Officials, judges, and criminologists are serious, educated people, the sorts of people apt to write serious books. Criminals, by contrast, are, with certain interesting exceptions, very unlikely even to read such books, much less write them. For this reason it is easier to establish the perspective of the Law—the cop's view on things—rather than that of the criminals. Not that there is anything wrong with the Law's perspective; it is a fully legitimate way of approaching crime. Still, any book that adopts that perspective inevitably assumes the contours of an official history.

Such a book might even be called a typical "victors' version" of the story, except that, in our particular case, there never was much of a victory to crow over. The battlefield results are certainly meager enough—no triumphs for the forces of law and order in the 1920s, nothing before Capone's 1931 conviction for tax evasion. Several years later, Thomas E. Dewey in New York sent Waxy Gordon away on similar charges. Later, having failed to win a similar conviction against Dutch Schultz, he changed tactics and managed to convict Lucky Luciano for enforced prostitution. All in all, the Law did not bat so well in these years. The underworld was far more successful at punishing evil-doers and removing the thuggish element from America's streets than contemporary law-enforcement agencies were.

This raises a problem. We have no way of knowing how many gangsters and hoodlums were murdered during the 1920s and 1930s. Estimates for the mid-1920s Chicago Beer War alone are usually in the five hundred to seven hundred range. Assuming an estimate for the entire country of well over one thousand during the two interwar decades must certainly be highly conservative. So, of these thousand-plus murders, how many times were the perpetrators successfully brought to justice? At least as regards the major killings, the ones we can follow in the papers, the answer is none. That is our problem: without the gangsters' testimony, we do not know who killed whom or why.

Criminals are, of course, anything but reliable as sources. Were it possible to tell the story of organized crime in America without calling upon the gangsters, we probably would be happy to forego their testimony. Leaving them out of the story does, of course, leave questions of "why?" unanswered. Why did organized crime arise when it did and in the way that it did? Why indeed did it arise at all? But these are interpretative questions. Can we not simply tell the story, leaving interpretative questions aside? We cannot. Without the help of the underworld we simply do not know what happened.

There is a further problem with serious treatments. The rise of organized crime in America during the 1920s and 1930s was not a generic event. It is not something that can be explained solely in terms of general social causes—poverty, social breakdown, ethnic tensions, or the supposed criminal tendencies of certain groups. It was rather a set of specific historical events, events that occurred only once. Like all historical events, the rise of organized crime has to be understood in its proper setting and context.

This is a point that so much academic writing and studies from the perspective of law-enforcement agencies seem to miss. These represent crime as a sort of social malaise, a breakdown of social order to which impoverished, badly governed, and strife-torn communities are especially prone. From this perspective, crime is an exterior force, a form of chaos that normal, well-ordered communities can usually keep at bay, but to which they may fall victim in the event of social disruption. This view of crime as encroaching chaos is one that follows naturally when crime is viewed from the perspective of the Law. It is a view, indeed, that does seem to characterize certain types of crime, such as disorders which do indeed seem to emerge spontaneously in the wake of disasters and civil strife. But such a view hardly applies to organized crime, which, being *organized*, is anything but spontaneous.

Nor does the view of crime as an external force, preying upon otherwise peaceful and law-abiding communities, bear much historical scrutiny. As abnormal and dysfunctional as it may be, organized criminality has been part of America's social fabric for centuries. With the help of the big-city political machines, the urban underworld controlled prostitution, gambling, illicit drinking, and a whole range of other illegal businesses in nineteenth-century America. The passing of the Eighteenth Amendment ushering in Prohibition presented a golden opportunity, a new illegal market for the underworld to manage. Anyone with the entrepreneurial skills and connections to produce and distribute alcoholic drinks, together with the gumption and firepower to beat off all competitors, was set to make a killing. By the end of the 1920s, the bootlegging gangs that had survived the underworld wars were rich, powerful, and well-connected enough to step into the shoes of the older urban political rings, which now were everywhere in decline. With plenty of cash, connections, and muscle, they were able to extend their control over unions and small businesses.

Historically the underworld has been a force for illegality. Organized crime is violent and causes suffering and economic loss to countless individuals. This is not, however, the same as saying that criminality is necessarily a force for chaos or that criminality necessarily impinges on the community from the outside. Nor is it to say that the crimes criminals commit are irrational, random acts. Underworld members in the period covered here were businessmen, albeit businessmen in illegal markets.

These businessmen were willing to use violence to eliminate their rivals and intimidate their victims. They were criminals, but they were also businessmen in the sense of being economic agents who bought and sold goods and offered services (principally protection) to the community. Until we understand the business of crime, the network of complicity and intimidation which integrated this business to the rest of the community, organized crime will continue to appear to us simply as an enigma.

Among the many sources of confusion, we might add one final one—our own. It is not so easy to imagine the worlds of New York or Chicago or New Orleans as they existed a hundred, or even fifty years ago. America's historic cities dispose of their dead with an utter ruthlessness that is all the more impressive for being unconsidered. I am speaking here not of dead bodies but of dead landscapes. Where are the honky tonks of yesteryear--New Orleans' Storyville, Chicago's First Ward, old New York's Lower East Side or its Tenderloin District? Where indeed is dear old, seedy Times' Square of the 1950s and 1960s, the Village with the jazz clubs where Charlie Parker blew and the coffee houses and folk clubs where Simon and Garfunkel sang and Dylan played his harmonica "for 'bout a dollar a day?" America's urban landscapes seem forever in a state of fermentation, changing more rapidly than we would sometime wish. Change is relentless; the sheer dynamism of American commerce generates a demographic and economic pressure that consigns the old center-city honky tonks to oblivion. Not that we should really lament their passing all that much. The turn-of-the-century, big-city honky tonks were often true civic eyesores, unhealthy, over-crowded, crime-ridden districts set cheek by jowl beside the city's major financial, commercial or residential zones. We would not want them back.

But physical demolition is rarely the end of the process. Books and articles proliferate. Special exhibitions are mounted at the historical society or the public library or the city museum. New York, for example, has its museum of tenement dwelling, its museum at Ellis Island, etc. Indeed, having disposed of the bones, demolished the tenements and closed the sweat shops, the city is happy to re-admit the past as kitsch—gangster-themed restaurants, ersatz gaslight, old-fashioned oyster bars, authentic Irish pubs with sawdust on the floors, knick-knack stalls and tee-shirt vendors and the spumoni stands and grattachecca carts of New York's or Chicago's Little Italy. It is an assault on our senses and on our sentiments as well, and one that only adds to our confusion. What are we really looking at when we gaze at the grainy old black-and-white photographs that adorn the walls of an upscale bar at the South Street Seaport in New York's Lower East Side? There we see the faces of the old ones, the ones who have just landed, landed right here where we are now standing, a hundred or more years ago. Here before us is the cannon fodder of American history. Here are the peasants, the laborers, the shabby peddlers; here are their raggedy children, caught as they stepped off the boat from Ellis Island. They stare back at us dumbfounded, bewildered, and scared, straightening their jackets and wrapping their shawls around their shoulders. They never smile; they gape rather at the officious man, invisible to us, who has just ordered them to look at the camera and be still. Here we are beholding our great-grandparents as they beheld the reality of their American dream.

It was contemplating the faces of these ancestors as their improbable descendents flitted by, drinks in hand, that made me yearn for a more forthright dialogue. "Who are you really?" I wanted to ask them. "Are you the bedraggled victims you appear to be? Or are you prospective criminals? Are you filled with hope and high ideals? Or are you just plain scared?" Above all, I wanted to ask them, "What did you have to do to become us?" For it is not as if, after being caught in the act of stepping ashore on the Lower East Side, our ancestors quietly slipped down a rabbit hole, later to re-emerge, magically and immaculately transformed into us.

The immigrants never came to America to commit crimes; they came in search of a better life. Nevertheless, in the years that immigrants from Eastern and Southern Europe were flooding in, an older perception of crime in America, and of the urban underworld in particular, was beginning to change. Throughout the nineteenth century, it had typically been an Irish story. The Irish immigrants were popularly associated with crime and disorder. The Irish bore much of the blame for urban crime and political corruption. By 1900, however, the Irish were becoming respected citizens, typical Americans. Blame for the country's urban malaise was instead being pinned on the Jews and Italians. Something must have happened.

According to Daniel Bell, it was simply a case of "ethnic succession."

The latest immigrants, the Jews and Italians, were stepping into the shoes left vacant by the Irish. The previous immigrants had begun their ascent up the social ladder. The Irish were becoming indistinguishable from normal, mainstream Americans. Yet surely there is something awkward about this explanation. What is it about becoming a normal, mainstream American that makes an apprenticeship in criminality a necessary first step? Why is membership in the underworld an antechamber to a fuller participation in American life? Why, above all, is the underworld even necessary; what purpose does it serve? The assumption, almost never articulated but nonetheless almost universally held, was that the bottom rungs of the social ladder were firmly planted in criminality, and that these bottom rungs were necessarily occupied by blacks and recent immigrants. America's message to the new immigrants seemed to be, "You must start off in the underworld, and move up from there." It was a wish to go beyond the usual clichés and understood this bleak assumption that inspired me in this book.

Chapter One

Italian Crime comes to America:
Stoppaglieri and New Orleans

Origins of the Mafia in Sicily

In 1859, the police in Sicily uncovered a conspiracy deep in Agrigento Province in the southern part of the island. The conspirators met in taverns, where, according to the report, they laid plans to "set up a Government of Equality, which is their way of saying robbing the property of others, taking the possessions of the well-off, who, they say, ought all to be put to death, removing all distinctions of class, and dividing among themselves, brothers in equality and booty." The police estimated that the sect had about four hundred members.[1]

There was nothing new about conspiracies in Sicily. In the middle of the nineteenth century the island was struggling to free itself from the rule of the Bourbon kings of Naples. Conspiracies had been part of that struggle from the beginning. The conspirators formed themselves into clubs, secret societies with revolutionary political agendas. The clubs themselves were radical masonic off-shoots that had spread from Northern Europe, particularly from revolutionary France.

Radical free masonry had been carried into Italy with the invasion of Napoleon's *Grande Armée*. In Naples, the revolutionary societies were favored by Napoleon's boyhood friend, Camillo Saliceti, who served as the Neapolitan chief of police during the brief reign of Napoleon's son-in-law, Gioacchino Murat, as king of Naples.

Associated as it was with France's revolutionary ideals and favored by the chief of police, no less, radical free masonry became quite fashionable; and from the French army, the sects quickly spread among the Neapolitan nobility and Neapolitan military. As they did, they Italianized themselves. The original revolutionary sect of the French army in Italy had been called *Les Charbonniers*; as this sect adapted itself to the Italian south, it became known by the Italian name of *I Carbonari*.[2]

From Naples, the *Carbonari* spread into Sicily. Here the revolutionary agenda mutated, the sects were harnessed to wage Sicily's own gathering struggle against Neapolitan dominance. The Neapolitan government fought back, using their police and their army of spies and informers to try to nip the Sicilian independence movement in the bud. But the task proved impossible; for new conspiracies appeared faster than the government could suppress them. In 1853, the Neapolitan governor reported back to his government that the underground network of Sicily was "like the hundred-headed hydra—the more its heads are sliced off, the more they are born again."

With sects springing up all over the island, the news that yet another revolutionary plot had been uncovered in Agrigento would not, in itself, have alarmed the authorities. There was little they could do to stop it. What did alarm these officials, however, was their information about the new sects members. Revolutionary conspirators were typically students, sons of land-owners and minor nobles, young men with enough education to read the in-flammatory literature that the underground presses churned out and time on their hands to mix themselves up in revolutionary politics. As irritating as these student revolutionaries could be, they were not a real threat, at least by themselves. There were too few of them, and they lacked arms and military experience.

The 1859 plotters in Agrigento Province were not a handful a rich men's sons, however, but four hundred peasants and miners. The news that revolu-tionary enthusiasm was spreading further down the social scale was a matter for concern. Recent history had shown that when these classes heeded the call of the conspirators, the results could be mayhem.

In 1820, an uprising set off in Palermo by the *Carbonari* sects had ended in an orgy of violence, arson, and destruction when the lower classes had joined in. In January 1848, the revolutionary sects were at it again, igniting a fresh rebellion in Palermo. This one too would set the whole island ablaze. For a year and a half, an independent and freely-elected Sicilian government sought desperately for recognition and assistance from other European pow-ers while ordinary Sicilians took up arms to keep the Neapolitan army at bay.

As the people's representatives strove to keep their new state afloat, how-ever, the common people initiated a revolution of their own from below. The insurgents in Palermo sacked and burned virtually every police station in the city and murdered 340 policemen. Police officials incarcerated by the revolu-tionary government in the Santa Anna prison were at least given the benefit of summary trials before being shot. But when the crowds discovered the bones, teeth, and mutilated bodies of tortured victims in the central police stations at San Domenico and via del Celso, they hacked to pieces every official they found inside.

In the towns in the interior, peasants burned the census and tax records and opened the local jails, setting the prisoners free. Gangs of peasants sacked the houses of landowners and officials close to the Neapolitan regime, invading their fields, cutting down the crops, and planting their own instead.[3]

These rebellions had shown how violent and destructive the common people of Sicily could be. But this, the Neapolitan state told itself, was the limit of their political capacities: vengeance and a desire to loot and vandalize the goods and properties of their betters. The common people had joined the revolutionary societies, one police official wrote, simply because they knew that "political tumults" provided them with the best "means to satisfy their dark and brutal desires." Even when the common people fought on the side of the revolution, they were incapable of patriotism or political understanding. The common people were capable of destructive violence; they were not, the Neapolitan state assumed, capable of organizing an uprising on their own. They needed to be led by the gentry. It was this complacent assumption, however, that the news of a new sect in Agrigento Province seemed to throw into doubt.

In April 1860, the sects initiated a fresh uprising in Palermo. Heavily garrisoned and well-armed in the capital, the Neapolitan authorities managed to snuff out the insurgency in a matter of hours. Yet the plotters had prepared their ground. Revolutionary committees sprang up in towns throughout the western half of the island. These committees had been in contact with the sectarians in Palermo, promising to provide them with *squadre* of volunteers as they had in 1848. Unlike the capital, these towns were thinly garrisoned or billeted no troops at all. Even when they learned that the rebellion had failed in the capital, many of the plotters in the interior went ahead and, raising the flag, seized their towns in the name of the revolution. When Neapolitan authorities responded by dispatching flying columns into the interior, the plotters melted into the hills and waited for the troops to leave. In this way the rebellion hung on.[4]

Poorly armed and few in number, the insurgents had no hope of defeating the Neapolitan army in the field. Though they might skirmish and inflict casualties, they knew that they were too weak to risk battle. Yet help had been promised to them. In September 1859, Giuseppe Garibaldi, the hero of the short-lived Roman Republic in 1848–1849 and the revolution's charismatic military leader, wrote to the revolutionaries in Sicily that he "would come with pleasure, with joy." But first the Sicilians had to provide him with an excuse to intervene, "If you can do so with any chance of success," he added, "then rise." Even Count Cavour in Piedmont got into the act, providing secret financing to the revolutionary committees. But it was Giuseppe Mazzini, the revolutionaries' political leader and firey orator, writing on the eve of the uprising, who gave the plotters the final shove. "Dare and you will be followed," he wrote. "But dare in the name of National Unity; it is the condition *sine qua non*. Garibaldi is bound to come to your help."

By hanging on for over a month, the revolutionaries gave Garibaldi the

time he needed to organize an expedition. Slipping past Neapolitan block-
ades, Garibaldi and his thousand Red Shirts landed in Marsala on May 11,
1860. Assisted by Sicilian irregulars flocking to his colors, Garibaldi and his
volunteers defeated a superior Neapolitan force several days later in the battle
of Calatafimi. Then, sending the main body of Neapolitan troops off on a
wild goose chase, Garibaldi and his men slipped quietly into Palermo, bar-
ricading themselves in the center. When two weeks of bombardment failed
to dislodge them, the Neapolitans, wishing to avoid the carnage of 1820 and
1848, declared a ceasefire. Perhaps they reasoned that Garibaldi and his followers would eventually need to come out of Palermo; and when they did, the
Neapolitan army would wipe him out. After all, they still out-numbered the
insurgents by more than three to one.

But if this was their reasoning, they were wrong. Garibaldi did march out
of Palermo; but he defeated the Neapolitans in a string of battles that led him
from Palermo to Naples. Indeed, had not Victor Emanuele II of Piedmont arrived with his army to stop him, Garibaldi would have marched all the way to
Rome. It was Garibaldi who wiped the old Bourbon Kingdom of Naples off
the map. In October 1860, exactly six months after the landing in Marsala,
Sicily voted to unite itself to Piedmont under the House of Savoy. The modern
nation of Italy was born.

Garibaldi's success spared Sicily from the excesses of 1820 and 1848.
Palermo had suffered enormously from the Neapolitan bombardment; other
than that, however, violence and damage had been limited. Nevertheless, after
a half century of plotting, violence, and revolutionary adventurers, Sicily was
bound to be difficult to govern. Public administration had broken down. Brigands and armed bands were scouring the countryside. Families were divided
by blood feuds, villages torn by vendettas.

The government diagnosed Sicily as suffering from generations of Neapolitan misrule and from the after-effects of an almost fifty-year struggle for
independence. Authority, it decided, had broken down and needed to be firmly re-established. The diagnosis was true, but insufficient. Knitting a shattered
society back together would require time, patience, and political imagination.
It would also require gaining the confidence of Sicilians, a confidence that
could only be obtained by consultation and collaboration. But the government
was in a hurry. Nor did the ministers in the north fully trust their new subjects
in the south. Given a free choice, they suspected, Sicilians would elect the
men who had followed Mazzini and Garibaldi. These were hardly the men
that Count Cavour, Piedmont's prime minister, wished to see in office. There
was little consultation or collaboration. The northern government simply extended Piedmontese law to the new territories. They responded to brigandage
and civil unrest by dispatching the cavalry. The results were soon apparent.
Initially welcomed as liberators, the new officials and soldiers were soon re-
viled as conquerors. In 1865, the prefect of Palermo felt it his duty to inform
the government that public spirit in the island's capital was "gravely troubled"
by a "deep and prolonged misunderstanding between the Country and Author-

ity." It was a misunderstanding, he continued darkly, that was "helping to make it possible for the so-called *Maffia* or delinquent association to grow in audacity."

In 1866, Palermo rose up again, not against Naples this time, but against the government of the new, united Italy. Swooping down from the town of Monreale, a mob broke through the capital's western gate in the pre-dawn hours of September 16. Though the authorities were taken by surprise, the rest of the city was evidently expecting their entry, for, as soon as the news spread, sectarians from all over the city broke cover. As the sects rose up, the rest of the city arose in sympathy as well. A thousand or so sectarians with red caps or red scarves wound around their necks, handed out revolutionary pamphlets (sometimes printed on red paper) on the city's street corners. They were joined by fifteen thousand to twenty thousand from the city's lower classes, who were delighted to share in the revolutionary holiday. The atmosphere was that of a rowdy popular fiesta. There were few casualties, and, apart from the usual bonfires of police and tax records, little vandalism. The rebels managed to hold out for over a week, declaring the city an independent republic and even repulsing a government attack.[5]

Who were these men from Monreale, who broke through the Porta Nuova in September 1866? They were smallholders and workers in Monreale's citrus groves and vineyards. These same groups had risen up in the 1820, 1848, and 1860 rebellions; they were responsible for some of the arson and vandalism as well. They were, in the words of the last Neapolitan governor, part of that "audacious and trouble-making people who, in all times, have been the mighty arm of revolts in Palermo." By 1866, however, Italy had found a new and better name for these sorts of Sicilians. They were *mafiusi* or, in the Italian spelling, *mafiosi*.

The term *mafia* first appears in the Palermo area in the 1860s. The great Sicilian folklorist, Giuseppe Pitrè, remembered street peddlers hawking their wares in the 1860s with the cry *"haiu robba de mafia"* ("I've got *mafia* stuff!"). In its original context, the term referred to anything that was flashy, gaudy, or eye-catching. A hint of danger or provocation lurked in this eye-catching quality as well. It was a quality best summed up by the word *swagger*. Something *mafia* is a thing with swagger, something that struts its stuff and demands to be looked at. Here is another police description of a fashionable young mafioso, who "wears a brightly colored shirt, keeps his hat at a rakish angle, has his well-pomaded hair combed so that curl falls on his forehead; his mustache is well-trimmed. When he walks he swings his hips, and with his cigar in his mouth and his walking-stick in hand, he keeps his long knife well hidden [. . .] from the police."[6]

Today, of course, he would add a Rolex and Bally loafers.

In Sicily, peasants, workers, and the urban poor in general were supposed to be humble in front of their betters and obsequious to authority. They were not supposed to swagger. Yet the peasants, workers, and urban poor in the Palermo region had risen up, sacked the palaces of their betters, opened the prisons, and sent constituted authority running for help three times in less than two decades. They may have felt entitled to a little swagger.

Convicted of committing crimes during the 1866 uprising and sentenced to ten years' hard labor, one defendant rose and laughed in the judge's face. Don't you know, he said, that there's an uprising every ten years here. In a few years time they'll break open the prison gates, just like they've done all the other times, and I'll be a free man.[7] That was swaggering *mafia*-talk, and the authorities did not like it.

Swagger, however, was only one aspect of a *mafiusu*. The *mafia* equally embodied the Sicilian ideal of honor. A *mafiusu* was a man of honor whose manliness was expressed by his *omertà*. The term comes from *omu*, the dialect word for "man." Though it can be used to designate a whole range of manly virtues, in connection with the *mafiusu*, *omertà* usually means silence. A man of honor knows how to keep his tongue in check. He does not gossip or chatter idly. Above all, he keeps secrets, especially the secrets he has sworn an oath to keep. When interrogated by the *sbirri* (the Law), the man of honor invariably responds *"unni sacciu niente"* ("I know nothing about it.").

Honor was something you could almost see. It was bright and shining, clean. Dishonor was just as visible. Dishonor was a stain or mark, as visible as—the Sicilian saying goes—a fly on the tip of your nose. A man of honor was a man who refused to put up with a fly on the tip of his nose.

Sometimes the mark of dishonor could be placed there deliberately. In the 1880s, Calogero Sanfilipo Rinelli told his followers to avenge the murder of a member of his brotherhood by murdering a member of a rival association. He also told them to bring him back the victim's ear. Cutting off the ear of an enemy was deliberate mutilation. It conferred dishonor; it was what Sicilians called a *sfregio*. Rinelli was thus asking his followers to make a *sfregio* on the victim's corpse as a mark of dishonor and disdain. In 1897, at the close of a war between the Giammona and Siino clans, both families agreed to execute four of their members, evidently guilty of some offence (*sgarro*). The four men were duly executed, and afterwards their bodies were secreted (three were thrown down a well). This was another type of *sfregio*. By refusing to let the victims' families give them a proper burial or swear vengeance over their corpses, the clans were conferring dishonor on the victims; they were indicating that these victims were not casualties in an affair of honor, but rather were simply vermin.

Placing a mark of dishonor on an enemy in a just and honorable cause was itself honorable, an act typical of a man of honor. There were many varieties of such honorable acts, and many ways that honor thus acquired could be recognized and expressed. It all formed part of the traditional code of the *vendetta*. In 1885, the Sicilian sociologist Napoleone Colajanni defined the *mafia* as the code of the *vendetta* personified.[8]

There were many types of *sfregio* as well. Classically, a *sfregio* was a knife-slash on the face. Bearing such a mark was dishonorable, dishonorable not only to the victim, but dishonorable to the victim's family, friends, and associates. If these included men of honor, men who would not bear a fly on the tip of their nose, the *sfregio* was a collective dishonor that needed to be wiped clean. The only honorable way of expunging such a dishonor was through blood. In 1930, after announcing to the Castellammaresi in Brooklyn that the death of Sasa Parrino in Detroit had been no accident, Salvatore Maranzano stood up and proclaimed: "É una sporca macchia sull'onore di Castellammare" ("It's a black mark on the honor of Castellammare."). Every man at the meeting would have understood it as a call for blood vengeance.

As swaggering hoodlums, men of honor, and exponents of the code of the *vendetta,* Sicilian *mafiusi* resembled other groups in southern and central Italy, Sardinia, and Corsica. They were similar, for example, to Neapolitan *camorristi.* Yet there was a difference as well. Like the *mafia* in Palermo, the *camorra* in Naples ruled the urban underworld and prisons and maintained a complex set of back-channel understandings with the police and local politicians. Other than that, however, the *camorra* had no political allegiances. The *camorra* had played no role whatsoever in the epic political struggles leading to a united Italy.

The Sicilian *mafia,* by contrast, had. Even if their role had sometimes been a dubious one, *mafiusi* had fought against Naples in 1848 and had rallied to Garibaldi in 1860. The Sicilian underworld had sheltered sectarian leaders wanted by the Neapolitan police and protected them from mistreatment in the prisons they ran. Decades later, the respectable *Giornale di Sicilia* could still define the *mafia* as the 'chivalresque' side of Sicilian crime. Writers like Pitrè would later write of the *mafia* with a degree of sympathy, even pride. Certainly they were hoodlums; but they were honorable and patriotic hoodlums. Even their crimes could sometimes be forgiven. The *mafia,* wrote one author in 1901, "hated all despotic governments, all the instruments of such governments and all their laws, even those that were good. . . . Thus the *mafia* ought to be looked at as an excess of profound hatred towards the Bourbons, enlarged and sustained by the pride and punctiliousness of the Sicilian character."[9]

The *mafia* had thus played its own honorable role in Sicilian history. Even after 1860 it continued to play a role. By the end of the nineteenth century, the *mafia* had become deeply embedded in party politics throughout the western half of the island. There had formed, as the Sicilian political scientist, Gaetano Mosca, commented in 1905, chains of *ntisi* ("understandings," i.e. tacit agreements) linking town mayors, political leaders, and regional and even national deputies to *mafia* leaders.[10] As criminologist Henner Hess once observed, the *mafia's* political role in Sicily was not unlike that of the Ku Klux Klan in the American South.

Like the Ku Klux Klan, the *Carboneria* in Sicily sought precedents for themselves as patriots and fighters for independence. In 1890, imprisoned and waiting trial for the murder of Police Chief David Hennessy (see below), Manuele Polizzi told a fellow prisoner that the mafia was an honorable society, founded by patriotic Sicilian noblemen during the middle ages. This story had its roots in popular legends in nineteenth-century Sicily, about sects of noble avengers who struggled to free Sicily from foreign tyrants. In the 1862 dialect play *Li Mafiusi de la Vicaria,* the rough men of honor who come to the assistance of the imprisoned sectarian are specifically identified as *mafiusi.*

But the most popular account by far identified the origin of the mafia with the Sicilian Vespers uprising in Palermo in 1282, when the people of Palermo had risen up and massacred the French troops of the King of Naples, the French baron Charles of Anjou. It all started on a public holiday. On Easter Monday, peasants from surrounding villages were flocking to Palermo to enjoy the *festa.* As they passed through the city's gates, however, they were subject to searches for concealed weapons by troops from the French garrison. When certain of these soldiers took the order to search the incoming peasants as an excuse to take liberties with the breasts of a Sicilian woman, her enraged husband, drawing a sword that indeed had been concealed in his clothing, plunged it into the belly of an offending solider. As he did so, he supposedly shouted *Morte Ai Francesi, Italia Anela* ("Death To the French, Italy Yearns [or Pants]"). It was the spark that ignited the entire rebellion, and so, ever afterwards, the sects of noble avengers called themselves the "mafia from M-A-F-I-A, the acronym formed from the peasant's words.[11]

Whatever the legends, the original *Carbonari* had been a network of secret masonic societies, and thus it was free masonry that supplied the revolutionaries with an organizational model. This model would be retained by Sicilian political parties and by the *mafia* as well. As masonic-type societies, the sects were hierarchically organized; each member occupied a specific rank. New members entered at the lowest rank. Each new member would be instructed about the purpose and scope of the society, but only in a general way. Information about specific activities or even the identities of the higher-ranking members would not be revealed to him. Only at the end of a trial period, when the new member had proved himself capable and trustworthy, would he be nominated for initiation to a higher rank. At this point he would start to receive more specific instruction. The sects had thus a cellular organizational structure, and this structure protected the leaders and helped them keep the sects alive through periods of persecution. Low-ranking members could not reveal what they did not know. As long as low-ranking members remained ignorant of the leaders' true identities and knew little about the precise nature of the society, their arrest threatened neither the leaders nor the society.

Single societies were also cells in a much wider conspiratorial network. Once again, new members knew little about such connections. New members were initiated into such societies through a solemn rite. During their initiation, candidates were simply told that they were about to become members of a vast and powerful brotherhood, a brotherhood that knew how to protect and look after its members.

In 1880, Vittorio Urbani, a railway worker from Agrigento Province, was approached by a Giovanni Fanara, one of his workmates, and invited to attend "a meeting in a secret place." When Urbani, together with a stone mason, arrived at the spot, they found Fanara and three unknown men. Fanara led the new recruits to an abandoned lime kiln, and there invited them to join a republican brotherhood. The name of the sect was *La Fratellanza* ("the Brotherhood"). The Brotherhood, Urbani learned, would protect him from his enemies. Urbani later claimed that he tried to refuse, but, seeing that he was outnumbered, finally agreed to undergo the initiation ceremony. The police later discovered a description of this initiation ceremony in the house of the leader of the sect, Calogero Sanfilippo Rinelli:

The oath was sworn in the presence of three members, one of whom having bound the finger (of the candidate) with a thread, pricked it, and sprinkled a few drops of blood upon a sacred image (a picture of the Virgin). This image was then burned and the ashes thrown into the wind. The thread denoted the indissoluble bond that united each member to the others; the ashes signified that, just as it was impossible to give the paper back its original form, so was it impossible for a member to leave the society or to fail in the performance of his contracted obligations.

The holy image, moistened with the few drops of the candidate's blood, was placed in his cupped hands and set alight. The candidate cradled the burning image until it was entirely consumed by the flame. Then he would blow the ashes into the air while repeating the *Fratellanza* oath: "I swear on my honor to be faithful to the *Fratellanza*, just as the *Fratellanza* is faithful to me. And just as this Saint and these few drops of my blood burn, so will I pour out all my blood for the *Fratellanza*. And just as these ashes cannot return to their original state and this blood to its original state, so I may never leave the *Fratellanza*."[12]

This is close to the ritual described by Joe Valachi in New York in 1930, or to the one in which Jimmy Frattiano was later made a member of Joe Dagna's Family in Los Angeles. Indeed, the *Fratellanza* initiation seems the prototype of the initiation ritual used by the American Cosa Nostra. They stem from *Carbonari* rituals used more than a half century earlier. In these, the candidate swore an oath proclaiming that any member who revealed their secrets should die on the points of their daggers and be consumed in a hot furnace.

The original French *Charbonniers* called each other the *bons cousins* or "good cousins." This usage was sometimes retained in Italy—the *Carbonari* becoming *buoni cugini*. Yet Sicilians needed something stronger, something that indicated that members were like brothers to each other. Sometimes they used the word *fratuzzi* or "brothers." More often they used another term, *compare*.

An old tourist guide has a picture of two bewhiskered peasants standing in a field next to each other. They are smiling broadly and holding their clasped hands above their heads so the photographer can see. The caption reads *cumpari semu*, which is dialect for "We are *compari*." The reference is to the *comparaditico*, the tradition of god-siblinghood, one of the most important customs in traditional Sicilian society.

Sicilian men became *compari* to each other in a number of ways. The parents of a newly-born child might ask friends or patrons to act as sponsor at the baptism ceremony. It was an honorable position. The man to whom it was given would not only be godfather to the child. He would also be *compare* to the parents.[13] Similar requests might be made at the time of the child's first communion, graduation, wedding, or even birthday. By accepting to act as the sponsor, the godfather was implicitly agreeing to favor the child in later life. This made it important to choose someone of local importance. Nevertheless, despite the element of calculation in choosing a godfather, the *comparatico* was not about patronage but about friendship. True *compari* were friends and equals. The *comparatico* was thus dedicated to St. John, Jesus' true and beloved friend.

When Sicilian men became *compari di San Giovanni*, no issues of sponsorship were implied. It was simply an oath of friendship between two men, one that traditional Sicilian society regarded as holy and binding. This is what the two old men in the picture were trying convey: *cumpari semu, cumpari di San Iuuanni.*

Cumpare with a "u" is simply the Sicilian spelling of the Italian *compare*. But this is not what the term would necessarily sound like in a Sicilian dialect conversation. Here the "c" and "p" might be vocalized into a "g" and "b," while losing the "r" in the "*—are*" ending with a compensatory lengthening of the vowel. In spoken Sicilian, *compare* might easily sound something more like *goom-BAH*.

Those who reject the idea of mafia oaths and initiation rites as implausible miss this point. Certainly it would be odd for criminals joining an association whose purpose was solely that of committing crimes to undergo an initiation ceremony or swear an oath. What would be the necessity? What were these felons supposed to be swearing to? Yet, in their minds at least, these initiates were not joining a criminal enterprise; they were joining a brotherhood. This is abundantly clear from both the ceremony and the oath. There is not the slightest reference to crime or criminal intent in it. It is simply an oath of brotherhood together with the promise never to betray. Even if, as the 1859 Neapolitan police report put it, they were "brothers in equality and booty," the *compari* were still brothers to each other.

New Orleans

In the early 1880s, Sicily's leading newspaper, *Il Giornale di Sicilia*, published a novella written by Emanuele Scalici. Its title was *La Mafia Sicilana*, and its story was based on real events, events the paper had covered extensively. These concerned the activities of the Amoroso brothers, the leaders of a mafia association in Palermo's Orto Botanico district. An early scene finds two of the Amoroso brothers with their friends, Pippino Maraviglia and Totò Di Paolo, at the tavern, *Il Passarello*, just outside the walls of Palermo. They have come here to wine and dine Antonino and Carmelo Mendola, two young brothers they wish to initiate into their society and persuade to murder Giorgio Fanara. When the Mendola brothers arrive, Salvatore Amoroso greets them by exchanging the "kiss of the *Fratuzzi*," explaining that this is the way that they greet all their brothers. Then, to reassure their nervous recruits, the Amoroso brothers explain that their own society is only one branch of a greater society of forty-five thousand, centered in New Orleans.

> "In America!" exclaimed Salvatore Amoroso. "Who knows if one day I might end up in that world in the midst of that big-hearted people." . . .

> "In the golden land," said Gaetano Amoroso, "only the cowards go hungry. Anyone with a heart that beats in his breast knows how to get his way, even if he has to go to the house of the devil!"

> "Anyone can see that you're still green, Carmelo!" added Salvatore Amoroso, winking at Giuseppe Meraviglia seated in front of him, "Do you think that we don't have friends and brothers over there as well? Friends that wouldn't give us a hand in need? Brothers that would be glad to provide help as well as funds to new arrivals? I'm afraid that you still don't have any idea of just how strong and powerful our *society* really is." . . .

> "I'll let you into something else, my friends," murmured Salvatore from the corner of his mouth, leaning forward and fixing them straight in the eyes. "We've got a boss. One that leads us, helps us and protects us. This boss lives far away in America, in the city of New Orleans. And he knows every one of us, one by one, and every one of the members of all the other societies, because we've all bound ourselves together into a single brotherhood, even the *Stoppaglieri*. And we are in constant and continual contact with this boss of ours, and so, should any nosy flatfoot should ever try to pin anything on any of us, we know where we can get help quick. We can get whatever we want from the Land of the Free. Okay, enough said!"[14]

The real *Stoppaglieri* were members of a brotherhood/criminal association founded in Monreale at the beginning of the 1870s. Its members included landowners and agricultural workers, as well as municipal officials. The association had become involved in a war for control over Monreale's rich market gardens, citrus groves, and vineyards, a war that, inevitably, had local political repercussions. Their opponents, the "old mafia" of Monreale, were the *Giardinieri*, who were, it seems, the association that had supplied the men in red caps and scarves who had marched on Palermo in September 1866. The war between the *Stoppaglieri* and the *Giardinieri* had, by the mid 1870s, resulted in a string of murders, unsolved in part because both associations had allies on the police force. The decade ended with a series of inconclusive trials. Though never able to obtain convictions, the police and the state prosecutors were at least able to amass an impressive amount of information about the brotherhood.

In 1878, the state prosecutor in Palermo was informed of a new development. A certain Monrealese named Rosario La Mantia had walked into the office of the Italian Consul in Saragossa, Spain, with an interesting story and an even more intriguing set of documents. According to La Mantia, he had landed in New Orleans in 1878 knowing, or so he claimed, no one in that city. He nevertheless soon found a job working for a certain "Francesco Alessi." After several weeks, his employer confided that the name Alessi was, in reality, an alias. His actual name was Salvatore Marino. He was, he told La Mantia, the president of the Monreale *Stoppaglieri*, an organization with a membership of forty-five thousand.

During that summer, Marino caught yellow fever. Fearing that he would not survive the illness, he called La Mantia to his bedside and gave him a packet of secret papers. These he asked La Mantia to burn in front of him. La Mantia, however, surreptitiously switched the papers with a pile of unimportant bills, burning them instead. Evidently, the ruse worked, for when Marino died on September 29, 1878, La Mantia was able to depart with the papers.

According to La Mantia, when he left New Orleans he had intended to go to Marseilles. When he docked in La Harvre, however, he suddenly decided to go to Barcelona instead. From there he went to Saragossa where he contacted the Italian consul and showed him the documents in his possession. Eventually, La Mantia was taken to Rome for further interrrogation.[15]

La Mantia was certainly being less than candid with the police. A Monrealese with his own shadowy past, La Mantia would certainly have known who the *Stoppaglieri* of Monreale were. He also would have known that their president, Salvatore Marino, had, after arranging for the disappearance of documents regarding his indictment on a murder charge, obtained a false passport and emigrated clandestinely to New Orleans. La Mantia's claim that he just happened to be in New Orleans where he just happened to form an association with someone who later revealed himself to be the president of the *Stoppaglieri* is unconvincing. The Italian police believed that the Monreale *Stoppaglieri* had sent La Mantia to New Orleans as their emissary to Marino and to other *Stoppaglieri* hiding out in New Orleans. That would explain the two letters in his possession.

The first letter was not addressed to Marino. It was written instead to Salvatore Matranga, another Monreale *Stoppaglieri* in New Orleans. It was signed "Pippino," and was written by Giuseppe Maraviglia. The second letter was to Marino and was signed "Totò." Totò is short for Salvatore, and the police could not at first decide whether the writer was Salvatore Amoroso or Salvatore Di Paolo. Eventually, with the help of calligraphic experts, they decided it was Salvatore Di Paolo. Pippino Maraviglia and Totò Di Paolo, allies of the Amoroso brothers, were of course the two friends that Scalici put in the scene at the tavern *Il Passarello* when he wrote *La Mafia Sicilana*.

The two letters reported on turf wars currently raging in Palermo and Monreale. In his own report, the state prosecutor in Palermo observed that all four of the Monrealesi—Marino, Matranga, Maraviglia and Di Paolo—were dangerous criminals and that they were all members of the *Stoppagliere* association. Though the Italian police were naturally more interested in what these letters told them about the mafia in Sicily than about the mafia in New Orleans, the police still identified Salvatore Matranga as the head of the gang of Monrealesi operating in New Orleans.

The Italian authorities in Sicily initiated their campaign against the *Stoppaglieri* in 1877. They made out arrest warrants for some of the leading *Stoppaglieri* of Monreale. But these warrants proved hard to execute, for the leaders had gone into hiding. The *Stoppagliere* was a sect with affiliates throughout the Conca d'Oro. The Italian police in 1877 had no better luck against these well-connected sectarians than the Neapolitan police had had a generation earlier. We see the problem discussed in the reports that the police delegates of Monreale sent to the Palermo chief of police. The delegate told the police chief he had just discovered that one of the wanted men, a certain Pietro Parisi, had fled to America. He was currently working there as a carter for another Monrealese, Francesco Incontrera, who lived at number 205 St. Peter's Street in New Orleans.[16]

The Monreale police spent 1877 in a futile search for Salvatore Marino. A well-known figure in Monreale and Palermo, Marino had taken part in the 1860 rebellion against Naples. He was an important free mason and, as late as 1874, was in secret correspondence with Mazzini regarding a new scheme for a republican uprising, though he later betrayed Mazzini to the Palermo police. As a leading *Stoppagliere*, Marino was also accused of involvement in a long series of murders and other crimes. The prefect of Palermo had placed a large reward on his head. Unfortunately, both *Salvatore* and *Marino* were common names. When a certain bank robber named Salvatore Marino died in the late 1870s, one Palermo newspaper, confusing Marino the bank-robber with Marino the republican plotter and *Stoppagliere*, speculated that the death had probably been a suicide occasioned by the shame of having betrayed Mazzini. It was only a year later when Rosario La Mantia showed up at the consul's office in Saragossa that the police learn the true whereabouts of the Salvatore Marino they were looking for. They learned that Marino had fled to New Orleans where, under the name of Francesco "Cicciu" Alessi, he had established a prosperous business importing citrus fruits from Monreale. Among his employees were Rosario La Mantia and the fugitive Pietro Parisi.[17]

Marino had first landed in Boston. He made his way to New York. Later, when he arrived in New Orleans, he had the cash and connections to initiate his operations as a citrus importer. He had a contact with Matranga. Although the state prosecutor described Matranga as a "dangerous *Stoppagliere*," he does not call him a "fugitive" (*latitante*), which implies that Mantranga had emigrated before the arrest warrants were made out in 1877. If Marino and Matranga had taken the *Stoppaglieri* to New Orleans, could the war that, as we shall see, they waged on the docks of New Orleans against the Provenzano clan be a continuation of the war between the *Stoppaglieri* and the *Giardinieri* in Monreale? Both Amelia Cristantino, in her book on the Monreale *Stoppaglieri*, and the journalist Ed Reid writing on the history of the American mafia

1952 make this assertion, though it is not clear on what evidence.

The Provenzanos also came from Palermo Province; "Provenzano" is a well-known mafia surname in the region. It is indeed possible that the Provenzano family was from Monreale and had fought against the *Stoppaglieri* in the early 1870s. If so, at least one branch of the family must have immigrated to New Orleans earlier. The Matrangas are identified as interlopers and newcomers, but there is evidence of a Matranga presence in New Orleans as early as 1869.

Reid also informs us that three *Stoppaglieri* from New Orleans traveled to St. Louis, setting up a branch of the association in that city as well.[18]

Louisiana was one of the first American states to attract Sicilian immigrants. Sicilians had begun arriving well ahead of the great immigration waves to the northeastern states. In 1850, 915 Sicilians were recorded as living in New Orleans, as opposed to 835 in New York and much smaller numbers around the Eastern Seaboard and in California. By 1860, the number of Italians living in Louisiana was 1,134; the vast majority of them were Sicilians living in New Orleans. The community continued to grow after the Civil War. Official statistics speak of 3,622 Italians in New Orleans by 1890; but these official figures are underestimates. By now, the descendants of the original Sicilian settlers had become Americanized, and were no longer counted among the immigrants. Contemporaries believed that the true number of Italians in New Orleans was somewhere between twenty thousand and thirty thousand.[19] The majority of these were from Sicily.

What had made New Orleans the favored destination for these Sicilians? Despite all the political upheavals through which the island had passed, Sicilian agriculture had expanded through most of the nineteenth century. The pockets of fertile, well-watered land on Sicily's narrow coastal belt were ideally suited for specialized agriculture. The Arabs had introduced citrus trees here in the early Middle Ages. Later the British had pioneered vineyards in the Marsala region that produced a wine similar to Port. Sicily remained in British hands during the Napoleonic Wars, so exports of Marsala wine boomed. Peace in Europe meant more export opportunities for Sicilian fruits and wines. Tangerines from Sicily and a decanter full of Marsala wine became a traditional part of Yuletide celebrations in Britain. So rapid was the growth in exports that Sicilians were soon looking for new areas to cultivate. They started in Tunisia and Malta. By the middle of the century Sicilians were braving the Atlantic crossing to exploit their agricultural skills in the New World. They traveled to Rio de Janeiro, Buenos Aires, and Havana as these areas were suited to the type of agriculture Sicilians practiced. Enterprising Sicilians even sailed around Cape Horn. Settling in the San Francisco area, they were among the first to exploit California's wine-growing potential. They also sailed to New Orleans, as Louisiana also possessed the climate and soil necessary for specialized agriculture

New Orleans had another advantage as well: throughout most of the nineteenth century, the port of New Orleans acted as the hub for all maritime traffic between the Mediterranean Basin and the regions of Central America and the Gulf of Mexico. The corresponding hub on the Mediterranean side of this traffic was Marseilles. Before the days of steamship traffic, Sicilians had usually sailed to the New World from Marseilles, the biggest port in the Mediterranean. There had long been a Sicilian colony in Marseilles; Sicily's `French Connection' was established centuries before it was exploited for the drug trade. New Orleans too had a French Connection. French territory until the opening of the nineteenth century, the city remained a focal point for traffic between France and the New World. Whatever their final destination, Sicilians traveling to the New World before the 1880s often embarked in Marseilles and disembarked in New Orleans.

New Orleans was ideal for other reasons as well. It had regular connections to Central America, Cuba, Mexico, and Texas. New Orleans provided Sicilians with easy access to other potentially rich fruit-growing areas, and it connecting the Sicilian community of New Orleans to that in Cuba. Besides their enterprizes as specialized growers, Sicilians found work as fishermen, boat builders, and stonemasons. New Orleans was North America's most Mediterranean city, and Sicilians were the immigrants with the talents and skills that a Mediterranean city needed. They became merchants and grocers, hoteliers, restaurateurs and waiters, tailors and shoemakers, barbers and bootblacks, opera singers, violinists, and hurdy-gurdy players. Sicilians traveled up the Mississippi, opening restaurants, groceries, and dry-goods stores. Sicilians cooked for the lumber camps and kept accounts for the bargemen along the levees. In the barrel joints where the first bluesmen played, it was as often as not some Sicilian who owned the barrel. Unfortunately, the prosperity soon attracted Sicilians with different kinds of talent.

The first two decades after independence were chaotic years in Sicily. Brigand bands roamed the interior, stealing livestock, holding up stage coaches, and kidnapping landowners. The government dispatched cavalry units and mounted militia to hunt them down like vermin. Brigandage was a miserable life; most brigands survived about two years in the countryside before being shot by the law or betrayed by their companions. The best plan was to pile up enough loot to buy their way off the island. Malta and Tunisia were the traditional hideaways, but by the late 1860s the Italian consuls there were actively relaying reports about fugitives from justice to the local police and the leaders of the Sicilian immigrant communities. The trip to New Orleans was more hazardous and expensive, but once a brigand got across the Atlantic, he was safer.

At the end of the 1870s, the Italian consul in New Orleans was told to be on the lookout for ex-members of the band of Antonino Leone, particularly a certain Giuseppe Esposito. Esposito had been involved in the kidnapping of John Forrester Rose, a Presbyterian minister and British citizen, while he was on a visit to his Sicilian cousins. The British press had been outraged to learn that the brigands had sent the Rose family their loved one's blood-soaked ear as a token of their determination to do business. It was even more horrified when the first ear was followed by the second, together with a message that the next packet would contain the good curate's nose. With this, the Rose family, who had launched a public subscription, agreed to pay the ransom.[20]

The Rose kidnapping was discussed in the British papers, and Her Majesty's Government felt it could do no less than to lodge a formal protest with the Italian Government over the incident. The bad publicity prompted a seriously embarrassed Italian government into offering a 25,000 Lire (about $5,000) reward to anyone who might assist in the capture of the kidnappers.

According to the best, though incomplete, account, Esposito, along with six other Sicilian fugitives, landed in New York in late 1878. The men bought a dive on Thompson Street on the Lower East Side, which served as a hangout. After about six months, however, Esposito and his companions sailed to New Orleans. We do not know why. He settled in the New Orleans Italian colony in a house on Customhouse between Bourbon and Rampart streets with Sara (or Salle) Randazzo, a Sicilian widow and her two small children. He passed himself off as a fruit merchant under the name of Vincenzio Rebello (or Rabello).

Some time after his arrival, Esposito commissioned the building of a small lugger, which he christened the *Leone* after the leader of the band back in Sicily. He commissioned the boat from a Sicilian boatbuilder named Tony Labousse (Labruzzo). When the boat was finished, however, some sort of altercation seems to have occurred. Esposito refused to pay Labousse, who, in revenge possibly, may have revealed Esposito's real identity to the Italian consul.[21]

But how would Labousse have known Esposito's real identity? With a large reward on his head, Esposito had every reason to keep his mouth shut. Nor, it seems, was Tony Labousse the only Sicilian in New Orleans who knew who Esposito really was. It is possible that the indiscretion dropped in the ears of the Italian consul in New Orleans did not come from Tony Labousse; according to Tom Smith, Labousse accused another Sicilian, Gaetano Ardotta (or Arditto) of tipping the consul off, even threatening him with a gun. Three days after Esposito's arrest in the summer of 1881, Ardotta propped an old-fashioned blunderbuss loaded with a double handful of buckshot against a low iron railing on the corner of Exchange Alley and Bienville Street. The blast shattered Labousse's chest and riddled his lungs, though before succumbing Labousse, had the satisfaction of knowing that Ardotta himself had been shot in the back of the head by a certain Vincenzo Vasco. Ardotta was rushed to the hospital, where he asked for Tony Matranga.[22]

According to the Italian Consul in New Orleans, by 1890 there were about one hundred escaped Italians criminals in the New Orleans Italian community.[23] By the time of Esposito's arrival in New Orleans, there was already a flourishing community of Sicilian fugitives residing here. The reason that Esposito was unable to keep his identity a secret was probably that, within certain circles, there were just too many people who knew who he was. His notoriety might even have been an advantage for him within these circles. Here were people ready to give employment to a brigand and kidnapper as talented as Esposito. According to an article in the New Orleans *Picayune* at the time of his arrest, Esposito, "Arditto" and Labousse were all part of a gang specializing in extorting money from rich Italians in New Orleans under threat of kidnapping. The scheme was similar to the operations of the Black Hand two decades later. The leader of this early Black Hand gang was identified as Tony Matranga.[24]

The most plausible reconstruction is that in early 1881 Esposito had had a falling out with somebody, possibly with Labousse and Matranga. These two, seeking some way of getting rid of Esposito, revealed his identity, not to the New Orleans Police, but to the Italian consul—who was, after all, offering the reward.

We know that the Italian consul then asked the New Orleans police to obtain a picture of the man identified as Esposito so that he could confirm the identification. The consul subsequently sent this picture to New York, where the Italian consul there possessed another likeness of Esposito, drawn around the time of the Rose kidnapping. Satisfied that the two portraits represented the same person, the Italian consul in New York hired two detectives to travel to New Orleans and bring Esposito back to New York. Since the New Orleans police had nothing to charge him with, they had two of their own detectives tail Esposito. When the two detectives from New York arrived, they simply kidnapped Esposito and bundled him off to New York in chains.

On reaching New York, and before his deportation hearing began, Esposito sued his old confederates. He had learned that Labousse's friends had repossessed the lugger as well. He brought suit over this. Esposito, however, lost both actions. He lost his lugger and was deported to Italy where he was tried and convicted on eighteen counts of murder and one hundred counts of kidnapping and extortion, and sentenced to life with hard labor.

Throughout the 1880s, New Orleans fruit companies were expanding into Central America, introducing banana trees to the future banana republics. Sicilian fruit dealers were part of this expansion, controlling the unloading of the fruit boats at the New Orleans docks. New Orelans stevedores were usually blacks and Irish, but the fruit docks were an exception; they were controlled by two Sicilian groups, the Provenzanos and the Matrangas. The Provenzanos were the original group. They were employed by New Orleans's leading fruit merchants, the Oteris and the Machecas. They also enjoyed good relations with the New Orleans police and particularly with Police Chief Dave Hennessy. Hennessy, the Provenzano brothers, and Joseph Macheca were members, perhaps founding members, of a portside club known as the Red Lantern Club.

Both the Provenzanos and the Matrangas were also connected to Esposito. We know this because a group of Sicilians later went to New York to testify for Esposito during his deportation hearings. Among them was the leader of the Provenzano clan, Joe Provenzano, as well as Rocco Geraci, another Monrealese, who was later indicated as head of the *Stoppaglieri* association. It is thus possible that the Matrangas had originally worked for the Provenzanos. Some time in the 1880s, however, the Mantranga clan began encroaching on Provenzano territory. From 1886, there was a string of unsolved murders in the Sicilian community, troubles, and threats of violence on the docks.

Seeing a feud developing, both Police Chief Hennessy and the leaders of the Italian community stepped in and offered to mediate. Wouldn't it be better, they suggested, if the Provenzanos and Matrangas joined forces and formed one big stevedores' union. The Provenzanos, suffering from the incursions of the Matrangas, were agreeable to the compromise; but not the Matrangas. No Provenzano would ever be allowed to join the Matranga outfit, they declared. When informed of this rebuff, the Provenzanos remarked ominously that the docks would soon be awash in blood.

One day in May 1890, five of the Matrangas climbed into their wagon after a hard day's work and headed for home. They never got there. When their wagon reached the Esplanade, a volley of some twenty-five shots were fired in an ambush, severely wounding three of the riders. Though they all survived, Tony Matranga lost his left leg to the surgeon's knife.

Though the wounded Matrangas at first denied that they could identify their attackers, they later claimed that Peter and Joe Provenzano, Tony Pellegrini, and Nick Guillio had done the shooting. The accusations seemed logical. The Matrangas were slowly eating away at Provenzano territory. Already in 1888, many of New Orleans's larger fruit shippers had switched sides and agreed to deal exclusively with the Matranga outfit. It was the Provenzanos who had made dark mutterings about blood on the docks. No idle threat, it seemed.

Chief Hennessy arrested Peter and Joseph Provenzano along with the other two men accused by the Matrangas. They were bought to trial on July 15, 1889. The trial was quick. Leaders of the Italian community and members of the Matranga clan all came forward to testify against them. On July 19th, the jury returned a verdict of guilt on the charge of shooting and wounding with intent to kill members of the Matranga group. Their verdict was "guilt without capital punishment"—hard labor for life.

Joseph Macheca had appeared as a witness in the trial of the Provenzanos for the ambush of the Matrangas. He told the court that between 1878 and 1888 the Provenzano family "had the exclusive business of discharging fruit vessels." In 1886, however, a new company had appeared to challenge the Provenzano's monopoly—the firm of Matranga and Locascio. There followed two years of disagreements, at the end of which the shippers, forming their own association, decided to discharge the Provenzanos and do business exclusively with Matranga and Locascio. Although it is natural to suspect that the Matrangas had in some way put pressure on the shippers to switch stevedore firms, Macheca explicitly denied this in his testimony. The majority of stevedores on the New Orleans docks were blacks and Irish. During the 1880s, these stevedores had begun to agitate for their own trade union. The fruit shippers, Nelli speculates, may have preferred hiring their fellow Sicilians because they were more manageable.[25]

It is sometimes difficult to understand why a jury reaches its verdict, especially at the distance of over a century. The ambush against the Matrangas had taken place late at night in a wooded stretch of the outskirts of the city. It was dark, and the assailants were some distance away when they opened fire. Questioned immediately after the event, the members of the Matranga party had all agreed: it was too dark and the attackers were too far away; they could identify no one. Several hours later, however, they had all altered their stories. Now they all agreed that they had seen their attackers quite clearly; they identified them as Provenzanos. Surprisingly, the defence never made anything of this about-face, and never insisted on a re-enactment to test whether it was possible to identify four men across an unlighted plaza in the dead of night. The accused also had alibis. The prosecution kept repeating the old legal saw that an alibi is the felon's defence. In the Provenzano's case, however, the alibis were all corroborated, in the majority of cases, even corroborated by police officials.

Reporters later noted that there had been lots of police witnesses at the Provenzano trial, but that they had all testified for the defense. No police official testified for the prosecution. This struck the reporters as odd. It may have struck the jury as more than just odd. The New Orleans police, it seems, were just as much in the dock as the Provenzanos. By convicting the Provanzanos the jury was rejecting the police testimony, effectively calling the police witnesses liars. What made the jury think that? We do not really know, but it is possible that the citizens of New Orleans believed that the police and the Provenzanos were engaged in some sort of racket together. Some such thought seems to have been behind the recent falling out between Chief Hennessy and Joseph Macheca.

Having recently switched to the stevedoring firm of Matranga and Locascio, Macheca claimed that he was now being threatened by the Provenzanos. Unless he switched back again his life was in danger. He had relayed these threats to Chief Hennessy who did nothing, for, it turned out, he was protecting the Provenzanos. The failure of Chief Hennessy to investigate the esplanade shooting and the appearance of a number of police officers as defense witnesses may have struck the jury as evidence that the Provenzanos and the New Orleans police were indeed in cahoots. If so, police corroboration of the Provenzano alibis backfired, ending up giving a shot in the arm to what, objectively, was a very weak case for the prosecution.[26]

Still, New Orleans seemed satisfied with the verdict. According to the *Times-Democrat*, "When they found the better classes of their own community would come to their assistance, the victims of the ambuscade renounced the Mafia and appealed to the law." The Provenzanos, the editorial went on, had believed that "the trial, like those of the past, would be farcical, that Sicilians would never settle their differences in court."[27] We do not know to which trials "like those in the past," the *Times-Democrat* was referring. But already by 1886, New Orleans evidently knew something about the Sicilian mafia, their vendettas and their code of *omertà*.

The discrepancy between police evidence and the verdict could not remain unnoticed, however. Citing the police testimony in favor of the Provenzanos, opposition newspapers began accusing the police of shielding the mafia. Known as a friend of Joe Provenzano, Chief Hennessy had kept in the background during the investigations and did not testify at the trial. Hoping to dissipate the cloud of suspicion, Hennessy requested the Criminal District Court to conduct an investigation into the policemen's testimony. There is no way of knowing whether Hennessy really wanted to find out if his officers were lying, or was simply hoping to mollify public opinion with some officially-concocted whitewash. Whichever was on his mind, there is little doubt what the Criminal District Court took its job to be. Within one short week and without calling one hostile witness, the investigators had issued a report that thoroughly exonerated the police witnesses from any suspicion of perjury.

This may have avoided a police scandal, but, unfortunately, the matter could not rest here. Somebody had committed perjury, either the Sicilians who had testified against the Provenzanos or the police who provided them with alibis. If the police testimony were true, as the District Court seemed to have established, then the members of the Italian community who had testified against the Provenzanos must have been lying. In that case, the Provenzanos were innocent and should not be breaking rocks in the state penitentiary. The Provenzanos' lawyers demanded a retrial; and there was no way that, in justice, such a request could be denied.

The Provenzanos won the right to a re-trial at the beginning of August 1890, only a few days after the inquiry had exonerated the police witnesses. Their lawyers hoped for an immediate retrial, and bitterly complained when they were made to wait five months until January 1891. Yet the delay in their case can hardly be entirely attributed to official foot-dragging. A few months after the Provenzanos had won the right to a new trial, the entire New Orleans judicial system was thrown into turmoil by a far more clamorous event.

Around 11:30 p.m., October 15, 1890, Chief Hennessy was approaching his home at 274 Girod Street, just a few yards to the west of the intersection of Girod and Basin Streets. A cold, rainy night, the darkness was weakly penetrated by a low-hanging electric light above the intersection, about ten feet from where the shooting was about to take place. This light provided some illumination, even though, as the New Orleans *Picayune* later reported, "at the time of the shooting this [light] was nearly out."[28]

Two assassins were waiting under the eves of a shed on the opposite side of Girod. When they saw Hennessy nearing the light at the intersection, they fired a first volley. Wounded, Hennessy responded to their fire by pulling out his own service pistol and firing at his assailants. This was probably a mistake. He would have done better to have run, for he was now a clear target standing under the faint illumination of the light at the intersection. At this point three more armed assassins emerged from an alley on Girod Street, opposite where Hennessy was standing and fired the fatal second volley. Hennessy managed to stagger down Basin Street to the boarding house of a Mrs. Gillis, who summoned help.

After the shooting, the first two assassins ran down Girod Street, past Hennessy's house, and turning first left on Franklin Street then right, continued down Julia Street. The three assassins who had emerged from the alleyway, ran down Basin Street before they too turned right down Julia Street. All five seemed only interested in getting away as fast as they could. One of the group fleeing down Basin Street dropped his double-barreled shotgun in the process. The police later found it in the gutter. Two more shotguns were found on Julia Street where they had evidently been abandoned by the culprits as they fled. Two sawed-off shotguns were also found further down Julia Street. Had the murder taken place a half century later, these three guns would probably been all the evidence the police needed. Unfortunately, in the 1890s, forensic sciences were still in their infancy; the police could not take fingerprints or even trace ownership of the guns.

When they got him to the Charity Hospital, they found that Hennessy had been wounded several times. He was still alive, however, and managed to hang on for nearly ten hours. During this time, he was repeatedly asked if he could identify his attackers. He couldn't. The *Times-Democrat* reported: "When he was asked if he knew who shot him he shook his head from side to side in a negative way. [Police Sergeant] Walsh asked, 'Don't you know?' and a like answer was returned." Nevertheless, he had been heard to say, both right after the incident and later at the hospital, "the Dagoes shot me."

Had Hennessy recognized his murderers, he would certainly have identified them. The fact that he made no identifications is a strong argument that he did not know who they were. Many of the newspapers failed to mention that, except for his initial statement moments after the shooting, Hennessy repeatedly insisted that he had not recognized his assailants. Still, the initial statement seemed clear enough. With the Provenzano brothers still in prison waiting for a new trial, the statement about the Dagoes seemed an accusation against the Matrangas. Thus, despite the fact that Hennessy knew many of the Matrangas and would not have hesitated to identify them had he recognized them, and despite the fact that there was no material evidence linking the Matrangas to the shooting, suspicion fell upon them from the first.

The day after the murder, Mayor Shakespeare placed the entire New Orleans police force on duty. Assuming the murderers to be Italians, he told the police to "scour the whole neighborhood; arrest every Italian you come across if necessary." The police followed these orders enthusiastically, and soon the New Orleans jail was filled with more than one hundred Italian prisoners—"Sicilians, whose low, receding foreheads, repulsive countenances, and slovenly attire, proclaimed their brutal natures," as one reporter from the New Orleans *Times-Democratic* told his readers. In the same paper, an editorial proclaimed that, unless the assassins of Chief Hennessy are captured, tried, and punished, the victory is theirs, and they will hold a constant threat over the community that whoever interferes with them will be killed. New Orleans must surrender to the *mafia* and vendetta, unless it gets rid of these criminals, who have so openly defied its authority." The article concluded that the mafia "must be crushed and annihilated unless we wish to banish law and order and establish murder in its stead."[29]

Mayor Shakespeare would clearly have liked to bring the killers to justice, but this was not all he wanted. He wished, as he told reporters in a speech announcing the Hennessy murder to "teach these people a lesson that they will not forget for all time." He was determined to "crush and annihilate" the mafia.[30] Mayor Shakespeare spoke of the mafia as if it had declared war on the rest of the community, as if the Hennessy murder was an intentional provocation, slap in the face, and declaration that the mafia had no intention of recognizing the law. He was in no mood to distinguish the mafiosi from the rest of the "Dagoes." Solving the Hennessy murder would have called for careful police work; responding to the supposed challenge unfortunately did not. All that was needed was a demonstration of who was really calling the shots in New Orleans.

After approximately a month's investigation, the grand jury brought indictments against nineteen Italians as principles and accessories in the Hennessy murder. Included were the fruit importer Joseph P. Macheca and the shoemaker Pietro Monasterio, who had rented the stall under whose eves the assassins had waited for Hennessy. Indicted as well were Tony Matranga's brother, Charles Matranga, and a number of his friends and co-workers. These were more than were actually needed, so the prosecution had to quietly release ten of the prisoners before the trial started.

The idea that the Hennessy murder, like some of the other murders in New Orleans' Little Italy, had been committed by a secret order of assassins or "Stiletto Society" gave the whole affair a sinister allure. Still, despite a great deal of dark mutterings in the press, no one seemed to know much about this homicidal brotherhood, who they were or how they operated. During the Provenzano trial, the defense attorney had questioned Charles Matranga about this. But Matranga just brushed him away:

"Do you belong to any societies, Mr. Matranga?"

"I was grand marshal of the festival of the Italian community on the occasion of the celebration of the discovery of America by Christopher Columbus."

"Are you not president of an association of men joined together for the purpose of committing murder called 'The Stilettos'?"

"No, sir. I am not."[31]

This was all. Despite all the speculation whirling around, the issue of the mafia played almost no material role in either the Provenzano or the Matranga trials. There was nothing solid to go on. Still, the assassination of David Hen-

nessy had obviously been planned. It was organized and premeditated. Reporters came to interview Joe Provenzano, still in prison though about to be
released. Who do you think shot the chief, Joe, they wanted to know:

"I don't know."

"Nobody knows, but who do you think?"

"Matranga, sure."

"Why do you think so?"

"Because he [Hennessy] was going to be a witness for us and expose
them. He knew all about Matranga and Geraci. He got some things, from Italy
about them, and he was going to tell what he knew, and that would break them
up. Matranga was head of the Stopaglieri [sic] society."

"What's that?"

"They're the people who work for the Matrangas. There are about twenty
leaders of them. They're the committee and there are about three hundred
greenhorns who've got to do anything the leaders say. . . ."

Provenzano went on to explain that several years ago Matranga and Geraci had tried to extort $1,000 from them. A reporter than asked,

"Are there any Italians in the Mafia besides the people who work on the
ships?"

"I don't know. They've got a Mafia Society everywhere. They've got it in
San Francisco, St. Louis, Chicago, New York, and here. . . ."

Provenzano next explained that he and his brothers had formed an Italian
laborers association, which had acted like a trade union, keeping a closed shop
on the fruit docks for its members, who were assured a good weekly wage.
Then the Matrangas had moved in, shipping in a lot of greenhorns from Sicily
whom they paid less than a third as much as the Provenzanos had. They split
the difference with the shippers, half of it going in the Matrangas pockets and
the other half going to the shippers in the form of reduced labor costs. Shippers like Macheca, of course, were delighted with the new arrangements. Not
so the workers:

"Their own men hate them but have to do what they say or get killed.
They make the greenhorns do the killing. They pay them ten dollars, twenty
dollars, or hundred dollars to get a man out of the way, and if the man they
order to kill someone won't do it, they have him killed so he can't tell anyone
or go to the police."[32]

The argument that Hennessy had been murdered to prevent him from
giving damaging testimony during the Provenzanos new trial was, however,
merely a supposition. There was nothing in Hennessy's surviving papers to
back it up. Nor did the various eye-witnesses always help the prosecution's
case. An estimated eighteen to twenty blasts had startled the neighbors. Some
had to run to open their windows. Pietro Monesterio, the cobbler in the shanty
on Girod Street, had tumbled out onto the street in his underwear. Recognizing Hennessy, he began to shout in broken English about the shoes that Hennessy had left with him to repair for his mother. A number of policemen and

guards, hearing the shots, ran to the scene. The witnesses saw the running and confusion immediately after the attack. Some claimed to have seen the assailants fleeing the crime, yet their descriptions were contradictory. The defense attorneys attacked the credibility of the prosecution's eye-witnesses, none of whom could really place any of the accused at the fatal spot at the right moment.

Nor was the alleged motive entirely convincing. New Orleans was seething with rumors about the names that Hennessy was prepared to name and about the papers and dossiers that he was about to make public—a dossier on the Matrangas crimes. The dossier was said to be hidden in his house or given to a friend who had been instructed only to reveal the contents at a certain time. Given Hennessy's position and his manner of death, it would be surprising if such rumors had failed to spread. Nonetheless, despite extensive searches, no papers were ever found. Nor, it seems, had Hennessy even intended to use the Provenzanos' to make revelations about the Matrangas. He just wanted to get his police officers off the hook and put the whole embarrassing matter behind him as quickly and quietly as possible. This was the opinion of an old friend and confidant of Hennessy who was called as a defense witness.[33]

When, given the absence of hard evidence, the jury had no choice but to return a verdict of not guilty, the citizens of New Orleans were thunderstruck. They had been all set to witness some scene of collective vengeance. There were immediate rumors of jury-tampering. Yet the truth was probably more simple. As one of the jurors said, "I'm sorry I couldn't please the whole community, but I had to do what I thought was right."

On March 14, a crowd variously estimated from five thousand to twenty thousand gathered at the foot of the Henry Clay statue on Canal Street. They had been summoned by the "Committee of Fifty," a vigilante group of irate citizens, supporters of Mayor Shakespeare. The purpose of their assembly was, according to the committee's announcement, "to remedy the failure of justice in the Hennessy case." The organizers had foreseen from the first that this "remedy" they were proposing was likely to go beyond a mere formal protest, for the committee had also advised the citizens to "come prepared for action."

The mob was enraged to hear that the Italians were exultant. On the afternoon of the acquittal, it was reported that "the American flag was torn down, trodden under foot and spat upon" and the "Sicilians all over the city made the boast 'The *mafia* is on top now, and it will run the town to suit itself'." These latter details are contained in a letter to *Frank Leslie's Illustrated Newspaper*, written by John C. Wickliffe, the editor of the New Orleans paper the *New Delta*. By an odd coincidence, the day of the Hennessy acquittal fell on an Italian national holiday, the birthday of the king of Italy. The Italian community of New Orleans had traditionally celebrated the occasion, flying the Italian flag and making patriotic speeches. Since the speeches were in Italian, a language which none of the mob understood, it was easy for men like Wickliffe to interpret them any way they wanted.[34]

It was the presence of the Italian prisoners in Parish Prison waiting to be released that goaded the crowd into action. After they listened to the incendiary speeches of the Committee of Fifty, the mob set off for the prison. When the prison guards saw the angry men approaching, they knew what they wanted. Concluding with remarkably little hesitation that resistance would be useless, these guards told the Italians to hide as best they could. Thus a mob of prominent New Orleans citizens was allowed to break into the prison and hang, shoot or club to death eleven Italians that they found there. Four Italians who were in no way implicated in the events surrounding the Hennessy murder, but who were unlucky enough to find themselves in the Parish Prison, were murdered along with the rest.

After the murders, the mob's leader, Mayor Shakespeare's campaign manager in 1888, William S. Parkerson, emerged from the prison to the cheers of the crowd who carried him home on their shoulders.

The New Orleans Mafia

At first press comments were limited to the lynching. Characteristically, the northern press condemned such "pastoral scenes from the gallant South," while local papers defended them. The leader of the mob, Parkerson, wrote that, "When the mafia confined itself to killing its own members, we did not resort to violence;" when they killed a prominent American, however, the situation suddenly became "intolerable." The mafia had challenged New Orleans, and the city had risen in righteous response. "After the execution of the prisoners," wrote Wickliffe, "the Cotton Exchange, the Stock Exchange, the Sugar Exchange, the Mechanics', Lumbermen's, and Dealers' Exchange, and the Board of Trade held meetings, and each unanimously passed resolutions endorsing the act. Do the acts of these commercial bodies count for nothing with the world?"

Wickliffe went on to explain that "only the eleven whose guilt was clear were executed." But this last argument is clearly specious: the mob had burst into the prison and proceeded to shoot, hang or club to death the Italians they found inside. Four prisoners whose incarceration had nothing to do with the Hennessy assassination were among the murdered. Merely being Italian was evidently proof enough of guilt for these gentlemen.[35]

It was only later that writers began to wonder about the guilt of the mob victims in the Hennessy murder.[36] Humbert S. Nelli, for example, pointed out that the Hennessy slaying was not a typical mafia murder.[37] It certainly was not. The aim of the mafia, both in Sicily and in America, is always to establish a *modus vivendi* with the police. The mafia is usually happy to buy policemen; it tries very hard to avoid killing them, even by mistake. Killing police officers makes their friends on the force very angry, and angry policemen can cause problems. Organized criminals have enough problems with law enforcement agencies without making the police angry at them as well.

But does this mean that the Hennessy murder was typical of someone else? The answer is certainly "no." The slaying of a municipal police chief was an untypical crime. If it was untypical of the mafia, it was equally untypical of whoever actually committed it. Arguing that it was untypical of the mafia thus proves nothing.

Richard Gambino takes Nelli's argument a step further. Not only is there no evidence, he writes, that the mafia was involved in the Hennessy murder; there is not even any evidence that an association like the mafia existed in New Orleans at that time. Gambino is certainly right on the first count. No evidence connecting the Hennessy slaying with a mafia-type organization was ever presented. By itself, the murder hardly proves the existence of the mafia in New Orleans. Yet it hardly disproves it either. When Gambino writes of New Orleans that "there is not a shred of evidence that any large or powerful Italian criminal organization existed there, *at that time,*" he is ignoring the Italian sources that inform us that the Matranga family were *Stoppaglieri*.[38]

In fact, no one in New Orleans needed the Hennessy murder to prove that the mafia existed in New Orleans. They knew that already. The newspapers had been writing about mafia crimes for decades. As early as 1861, the *True Delta* had reported on a gang of Spanish and Sicilian thieves operating in New Orleans' Second and Third Districts. Two months later, there were reports of a Sicilian counterfeiting ring in the Second District. In 1869, the paper again reported on the "well-known and notorious Sicilian murderers and burglars, who, in the last month, have formed a sort of general co-partnership or stock company for the plunder and disturbance of the city."[39] The city's newspapers knew that Sicilian gangs had been operating in New Orleans for decades. They knew that the Sicilian community included a number of men who were fugitives from justice in their own country. Even if they knew nothing specifically about this mafia, there must still have been at least rumors that Charley Matranga put on a dark hood before he pricked the trigger fingers and administered the *Stoppagliere* oath to his greenhorns. Otherwise the Provenzanos' defence attorney would not have asked him whether he was the president of the Stiletto Society. But Charley replied with a flat "no," and there the matter had to rest.

During the subsequent Matranga trial, the lawyers called the father of Charley and Tony, Salvatore Matranga, to the stand. We saw that the Italian authorities had identified Salvatore Marino and Salvatore Matranga as the leaders of the New Orleans branch of the Monreal *Stoppaglieri* back in 1878, and that Salvatore Matranga was the addressee of the letter from Pippo Meravaglia. Either the Italian police had not bothered to tell the New Orleans police who Salvatore Matranga was, or if they had, the New Orleans police had forgotten all about it. By now a distinguished old gentleman with a cane and a flowing gray beard, the court politely asked Mr. Matranga whether he could help them get to the bottom of this mysterious business of secret societies, initiation rituals, and the *Stoppaglieri* from his native Monreale? No, Mr. Matranga gravely replied, I'm afraid I know nothing about it.

Nevertheless, the forced initiation ceremonies described by Joe Provenzano correspond to descriptions from Sicilian sources. One of these sources even concerns Monreale itself:

In 1876 the eighty-two year old Giuseppe Cavallaro was returning from Palermo on the Monreale road when he was stopped by six assailants and led down a solitary by-road. Here he was told to

> "go to the house of a certain P.D., there to take the oath of initiation into the society called the *Stoppaglieri,* who, being tired of the Italian government, had decided to launch a republic.

> Frightened as he was, and despite his eighty-two years, old Cavallaro plucked up enough courage to stall them a bit: 'Alright, I'll go tomorrow; but I can't tonight, I've been traveling and I'm too tired.'

> One of the assailants, dissatisfied with the answer, began to threaten the old man; another, however, stepped forward and said: 'Let it be. We'll talk about it tomorrow with Don Simone. But as for you, I'd advise you to show up. You'll be arriving at the same time as the *Gran Maestro* [the masonic grand master of the association] who is coming to administer the oath.'"[40]

In New Orleans the Matranga family played host to wanted men—Giuseppe Esposito, Salvatore Marino, Pietro Parisi and doubtless others. There were rumors that one hundred Italian fugitives were living in New Orleans at the time of the Hennessy murder, though there is no way of confirming this figure. Yet the usual number given for the New Orleans *Stoppaglieri* in 1890 is three hundred. Most were greenhorns. Some may have been in trouble with the police back in Sicily, but not all of them, perhaps not even that many. Caruso told Provenzano that the greenhorns were initiated only after their arrival in New Orleans; so few, presumably, would have criminal backgrounds. Why did the Matranga family force them to join their association? The answer is that they were not recruiting gangsters and criminals; they were recruiting workers. Like the *Stoppagliere* in Monreale, the *Stoppagliere* in New Orleans was not simply a criminal organization. It was rather a working men's organization, albeit one whose leaders did not hesitate to commit crimes.

Most of the three hundred *Stoppaglieri* in New Orleans were men who worked for the Matrangas, obeying their orders and paying them their dues. It is possible that they were indebted to the Matrangas in other ways as well. The Matranga family may have acted as *padroni*, advancing these immigrants money and tickets for the passage across the Atlantic. This would have made it easier for the Matrangas to recruit these men as laborers and as *Stoppaglieri* after they landed. They were men that the Matrangas owned anyway, men completely under their power: "Their own men hate them," Joe Provenzano had said of the Matrangas, "but have to do what they say or get killed."

We know that workers who refused to join the *Stoppaglieri* in Sicily were threatened; some were even killed. Those that acquiesced and agreed to join were administered the oath of *Stoppaglieri*, perhaps by some black-cloaked figure who played the role of *Gran Maestro*. The new members swore to secrecy and obedience; they also swore to obey the orders of their superiors in the association without question. They agreed to pay weekly or monthly membership dues. In return, they were promised protection and job security; they were also promised that if ever they fell into trouble with the law, their brothers would do all in their power to rescue them.

The *Stoppaglieri* in Monreale, the Amoroso brothers in Orto Botanico and other *cosche* (mafia associations) in Western Sicily all used these same methods. In this way, mafia leaders built up followings. These followings might act as factions in local politics or as gangs in local gang wars. Equally, the mafia might organize the workers in a particular sector or industry, their associations assuming the role of trade unions whose leaders could determine who got to work at what job and for what pay, collecting dues from one side and pay-offs from the other. This, we shall see, was standard operating procedure for the mafia in America. Despite its many faces, and despite the many and varied activities in which it involved itself, the mafia always remained, at base, a protection racket.

The Matrangas were acquitted in what Nelli calls a fair and proper trial. From Tom Hunt's more detailed description based on extensive archival research, however, shows that the prosecution's case was confused and inconclusive. The trial had been accompanied by corruption scandals, rumors of police pay-offs and accusations of jury tampering. It was also accompanied by the re-trial of the Provenzanos, where a guilty verdict, which, several month earlier the city's press has taken as a shining example of civic courage and justice done, was about to be overturned. It would be truer to say that the Matrangas won their acquittal because the case against them came apart at the seams, and the jury was left with no other choice. If this is the case, then what needs explaining is not the acquittal but the lynching.

According to what he later wrote, the leader of the Committee of Fifty, Parkerson, had intended a different outcome. Entirely convinced that the jury had been bribed, he had planned to storm the prison, seize the accused Sicilians, and give them public trials. Presuming that these trials would establish their guilt beyond the shadow of doubt, he intended to string them up publicly immediately thereafter. He assigned the task of escorting the Sicilians out of the prison to fifty marksmen armed with rifles, whom he called his Regulators.

If this is what Parkerson truly intended, then his plans went badly awry. The Regulators burst into the prison unopposed, and soon encountered a group of Sicilians who had run into the exercise yard looking for some place to hide. Ignoring their pleas, the Regulators simply opened fire, killing or wounding about seven inmates. They next picked up the wounded, though very much alive, Manuele Polizzi and dragged him in front of the prison, where, to the cheers of the spectators, they hanged him on the nearest tree. Curiously the excited mob included a number of blacks; thus the Parish Prison massacre represents an anomalous case of blacks participating in the lynching of whites. After dispatching Polizzi, the Regulators returned to the prison yard to select other wounded Sicilians for lynching.

Parkerson was thus either lying when he claimed that his intention was to try the Sicilian inmates in front of the prison or his Regulators never intended to follow his plan. In whichever case, there is a question of who really was the leader of the Regulators and what his intentions were. While the hangings were taking place outside, another party of Regulators went back in to search for other Sicilians. On the second floor, in the section reserved for prisoners with money, they found Joseph Macheca frantically trying to smash open a locked door. One of the Regulators smashed Macheca in the back of his head with a rifle butt, and Macheca fell dead upon the floor. A subsequent coroner's investigation, however, revealed a small pistol wound behind his left ear. Since the Regulators were only armed with rifles, the presence of the pistol wound seems to indicate that someone else had been active that day. Macheca may even have received the pistol wound before the Regulators found their way in. If this is what happened, then someone may have used the chaos created by Parkerson's mob as an opportunity to eliminate Joseph Macheca. No one took advantage of the same opportunity in the person of Charley Matranga. He remained quietly in his cell as the Regulators scoured the prison. He seemed to know that he was not on their list. The next day, the warden simply opened the door and told him to go home.

Mayor Shakespeare was out of office within a year. The Sicilians all voted against him, and his own supporters failed to mount a strong campaign on his behalf. Some may have felt a little ashamed of a mayor who had defended a lynching. The Parish Prison massacre did not enhance the reputation of the Reformist Democrats, and the faction soon disappeared.

The Provenzanos were soon released, and they tried to claw back their territory. Yet they failed. Their power had been broken. They later moved to Gretna across the river.

Tony Matranga had never been arrested. None of the witnesses said anything about a one-legged man at the scene of the crime. It was one compensation for the Provenzano attack.

Macheca and Son, Joseph Macheca's fruit company, did not long survive the death of its co-founder. It was soon swallowed up by the United Fruit Company.

Charlie Matranga remained in New Orleans. Officially he was a stevedore with the United Fruit Company. Unofficially, he was the leader of the New Orleans mafia until his death in the 1920s.

An 1869 article in the *True Delta* which spoke of Macheca's preeminence in the Sicilian community, also mentioned a "rendezvous on Royal Street," which served as Macheca's headquarters. This rendezvous was a saloon in a building owned by Macheca; it was managed by members of the Matranga family, recent immigrants from Sicily.[41] We do not know what happened to this Matranga rendezvous/clubhouse; but sometime after 1900, Matranga's son, Charles Matranga Jr., opened a honky-tonk dive on Perdido Street. He hired black musicians to play there, and Matranga's club was thus one of the first resorts featuring ragtime. Louie Armstrong had stopped by here to listen as a boy. There were prostitutes as well.

Matranga's club, along with the rest of Storeyville, was shuttered during the crackdown in New Orleans proceeding World War I. Around 1918, however, it opened again. The whores were gone but not the black music. There was a trio playing a new kind of black music. It was something they called jazz. The proprietor was now a certain Henry Matranga. When the trumpter couldn't make it one evening, a customers told Matranga that the sixteen-year-old kid that was always hanging around the place could "really blow the quail." So Henry Matranga gave Louie Armstrong a chance to show what he could do. And so it was that the *Stoppaglieri* gave the great Satchmo his first gig.[42]

Chapter Two
New York: Spoilsmen and Reformers

Mass Emigration

What America gained, other parts of the world lost. Massive immigration into America meant massive population losses elsewhere.

For the Eastern European Jews it was often a question of fleeing religious persecution. In 1881 a new czar ascended to the throne and almost immediately launched a wave of vicious anti-Semitism. These were years when the Russian authorities organized pogroms and unleashed the Black Hundreds on Jewish villages and urban ghettos. Jewish immigration to America followed the rhythms of these persecutions, increasing in the years when they intensified and falling whenever they relented. If Jewish immigration began to abate after 1900 it was because liberal opinion in Europe, which disapproved of these persecutions, was putting pressure on the czarist authorities.

The story behind southern Italian and Sicilian emigration is more complex. Southern Italian agriculture had expanded throughout the nineteenth century, especially in specialized crops grown in the pockets of richly productive lands around the coasts. The fertility of the soils around the Bay of Naples or Palermo's Conca d'Oro or the slopes of Mount Etna had been legendary since ancient times. In the 1880s, however, growth in export agriculture came to a halt. Pursuing a policy of autarky, Italian governments believed that rapid industrialization and agricultural self-sufficiency would transform Italy into a strong state and major power. Successive governments assigned to the south, Sicily in particular, the role of bread basket, just as it had been during the Roman Empire. Thus while northern Italy concentrated its capital and manpower on manufacturing, southerners were supposed to grow wheat on the plains of the interior. The government placed high tariffs on imported foodstuffs and refused all assistance to exporters along the coasts. When other European countries, particularly France, followed suit, embarking on a similar policy of agricultural self-sufficiency, southern Italians found that they could no longer export their specialized crops. The agrarian economy was devastated. To make matters worse, the phyloxera epidemic that was destroying vineyards in France spread to Italy. Indebted small-holders were wiped out, agricultural laborers lost their jobs, and many were forced to trek back into the interior to become shepherds and share-croppers on the wheat-producing estates. Others migrated to the cities and joined the ranks of the out-of-work. Neither was an attractive choice. Conditions in the interior were primitive, and the lives of shepherds and sharecroppers were hard indeed. Instead, the landless peasants, unemployed agricultural workers, and the bankrupt smallholders, artisans, and shopkeepers came flooding into the coastal cities in search of jobs.

Nor, unfortunately, was misguided government policy the only problem. The thick network of towns and villages specializing in export crops and market gardens in the province of Palermo had been the cradle of the Sicilian struggle for independence. It was also, however, the cradle of the mafia. In continual turmoil since the 1820 uprising, representatives of legitimate authority were rarely visible in Palermo Province as late as the 1870s. Even then the government visitors were usually in the company of an armed escort. Men of honor settled questions of land or family honor with a blast from a *lupara*, a sawed-off shotgun, lethal at close quarters and the ideal weapon for ambushes. In 1875, when Leopoldo Franchetti came to report on agrarian conditions in Sicily, he remarked that after hearing such tales, the fragrant orange groves of Palermo's Conca d'Oro seemed to stink of cadavers.[1]

There was, however, another, very different, factor behind the sudden upsurge in emigration. The first generations of settlers in the New World had been pioneers, many were commercial adventurers in search of new opportunities. They were young, able-bodied men, well able to bear the rigors of what was then still a chancy voyage on a wind-powered sailing ship. After 1880, however, steam was replacing sail as the usual means of crossing the Atlantic. Larger, faster, and independent of tides and winds, steamship crossings were cheaper and less hazardous than had been crossings by sail. Steamships also could carry many more passengers. North America-bound steamships began to leave from Palermo and even from the island's smaller ports, eliminating the necessity of a trip to Marseilles. As ticket prices fell, demand surged.

There was hope even for Sicilians too impoverished to afford the cheapest tickets. In village after village, recruiters appeared, offering people free passage to the New World and, what is more, a promise of a job and accommodation when they got there. And what was expected in return for all this generosity? The recruited laborers were required to work off their debts by laboring in the places and at the jobs the contractors specified, often living in work camps where the cost of food and lodging supplied by the contractors was added on to their original debt. The deal really amounted to a new form of indentured servitude. Even so, many Italians and Eastern Europeans were willing to sell themselves into virtual slavery to buy a new chance. They flocked to the bargain.

The figures speak for themselves. Some 12,354 Italians emigrated to the U.S. in 1880. In 1890, the number reached 52,003. By 1900, the number had climber to 100,135, mounting to 230,622 in 1903 and 285,731 in 1907. From 1903 to the outbreak of World War I, an average of around two hundred thousand Italians emigrated to the U.S. every year. The overwhelming majority of these were Southern Italians and Sicilians.[2] This was not emigration; this was flight. South Italians were fleeing a land that had failed them and putting their trust in a dubious bargain that would give them a new chance in a New World.

During these years, the U.S. did seem to have resources for everyone. It had room to grow in and jobs to offer. American industry was growing. It was particularly growing West of the Alleghenies in Western Pennsylvania where oil had been discovered; around the Great Lakes where rich iron deposits lay; and in Chicago whose stockyards served the entire nation. Earlier immigrants had often been skilled laborers, migrating to cities where their fellow country-men had set up enterprises requiring their skills. The new immigrants—Eastern European and Italian alike—simply went where their recruiters sent them. New immigration was concentrated in the new, labor-hungry areas. Italian and Eastern European communities seemed to mushroom from nowhere in oil and steel towns like Buffalo, Pittsburgh, Detroit, and Cleveland. And with the explosive growth of exotic communities—Jews, Italians, Greeks, Poles, Lebanese, and in the West, Japanese and Chinese—there arose tensions, ethnic and confessional hostilities, and sometimes feuds and gang wars.

There were internal migrations as well. Growth in the Northeast was sucking labor out of farming districts and into New England's mill towns and into the great emporia along the Atlantic Coast. Southern labor, both black and white, was heading up the Mississippi towards the growing industries in the Great Lakes region. Immigrants too were affected by these patterns. The New York Jewish community was expanding into Chicago and the rest of the Midwest or even heading straight to the West Coast. So were the Italians and the other immigrant communities. If one were to trace the patterns of diffusion of retail networks, especially in the garment, catering, and entertainment industries in the first decades of the twentieth century, it would probably closely resemble the patterns of diffusion of the Jewish and Italian immigrant communities. The geography of organized crime seemed to ride piggy-back on these changes.

It all started in New York, for New York was the immigrants' point of entry as well as the point of departure, the nodule from which further diffusion spread.

Here is where our story shall start as well.

NEW YORK, NEW YORK

In the first decades of the nineteenth century, visitors from the larger capitols of Europe were apt to be struck by the almost rural character of North America's cities. In the time of Monroe, these cities appeared as small, quietly prosperous and relatively egalitarian. Citizens expected little of their municipal administrations. City Hall provided legal services: it ran the courts where elected magistrates dispensed commercial and criminal law. The city itself provided few services or amenities. This, however, was soon to change. With economic growth and the influx of immigrants, America's cities began to grow, and, as they grew, they found themselves confronted by new challenges. Health problems were associated with overcrowding and the lack of public services; there were outbreaks of crime, ethnic, and religious animosities. There was a need for public transport and public education. By their very nature, these problems demanded a municipal approach.

"Unlike European cities," writes Robert Caro, "which also mushroomed in the Industrial Age but which had been built atop previous centuries strong administrative foundations, America's had sprung into gianthood relatively overnight, often organized around nothing but the factory or the mill, and had no such tested governmental framework."[3] Europe knew how to manage a large metropolis; it had been doing so for centuries. The U.S., by contrast, had not. Americans in fact had a tradition of hostility toward large metropolises. They implied inequality; they implied class differences, a yawning gap between a rich, well-educated, and privileged ruling classes on top and the poor, ignorant, marginalized masses on the bottom. There was something inherently un-American about so much inequality. Nevertheless, the traditional animosity notwithstanding, U.S. cities kept on growing. As they grew, they created precisely the unwanted manifestations of life in a great metropolis.

In the decades following the Civil War, larger U.S. cities were thus faced with problems of providing health, education, and public order for their growing populations. Finding solutions to these problems invariably meant enlarging the municipal bureaucracy. New departments needed to be created, and these departments needed to hire staff and workers. The city was embarking on a course that would rapidly transform it into a major provider of jobs, especially for unskilled labor. These changes would have a cost, of course. Someone was going to have to foot the bill for the new municipal services and for the wages of the men and women employed by the municipality. Who could this *someone* be? Logically, it could only be tax payers. And so it was that the transformation of the American city set off a perfect political storm.

Municipal growth and the necessity of finding ways to pay for this growth put nineteenth-century American cities on a collision course with their state legislatures. Though eloquent on the subject of states' rights, the U.S. Constitution has little to say about the shape and limits of municipal power. Threatened by the political clout of the growing municipalities, and jealous of their constitutional prerogatives, state legislatures fought back, trying to re-assert their own control, curtailing municipal spending programs and impeding municipal attempts to devise solutions to their problems independent of state oversight.

This conflict could be particularly acrimonious where state legislatures were in the hands of representatives from rural districts. These representatives traditionally espoused policies of low taxation, fiscal conservatism, and antagonism towards organized labor. Such policies put them at loggerheads with the cities, where industrial growth and immigration were necessitating tax hikes, fiscal experimentation, and a more accommodating attitude towards organized labor. It was a conflict of interests that often took on partisan, political colors. Since the Civil War, New England and the Mid-Atlantic and Middle Western states had consistently voted Republican in national elections; they had often elected Republican state legislatures as well. Nevertheless, in municipal elections, a different set of priorities prevailed, and the big cities frequently elected Democrat administrations. At the state level, the Republicans had a built-in advantage. Though the demography of the northern states had changed since the Civil War, these changes were not always reflected in the electoral rolls; nor were they expressed in the way the state was divided into congressional or legislative districts. Out-of-date districting tended to over-represent Republican voters in the rural districts while under-representing the Democrat voters of the cities, thus helping ensure Republican control at the state level. Despite this, since the cities, rather than rural districts, were the focus of demographic growth, the Democrat threat to Republican hegemony at the state level kept growing.

New York State was at the epicenter of this battle. With more electoral votes than any other state, New York was worth more than all the Western states put together. New York State was the key to national politics, and both the Republicans and the Democrats knew it. For the Republicans, holding onto the presidency required holding onto New York State. This meant mobilizing the small upstate towns that could be counted on to vote a straight Republican ticket, while containing the working-class in the big cities, which usually voted Democrat. The Democrat Party's strategy was a mirror image of that of the Republicans. Consolidating their hold on the larger cities, the New York State Democrat Party tried to nibble away at the bastions of Republican power, the state legislature and the governor's mansion in Albany. For such a strategy to succeed, however, it was crucial for the Democrats to ensure that the immigrants and working poor of Lower Manhattan showed up faithfully on election day and voted a straight Democrat ticket. Without the congressmen and state legislators elected with their vote, the Democrat Party would have been little more than a local party in New York State. This dependence upon New York City's working class and immigrant vote was something of a double-edged weapon for the Democrats, however. For these votes were organized and delivered to the Democrats courtesy of Tammany Hall. As the Republicans never tired of reminding the voters, Tammany was evil, the archetype of a corrupt and grafting political machine.

TAMMANY

Before the Civil War, Albany had begun to worry about the growth and activism of New York City. Even then, the behemoth on the Hudson was throwing its weight around, asserting its political independence. That independence included its right to initiate projects without proper—that is, state—approval and oversight. Hoping to nip this disquieting tendency in the bud, in 1857 the state legislature created a new County Board of Supervisors. The theory was that by creating a board with extensive oversight authority over municipal contracting and elections, graft could be eliminated. A young alderman, a certain William M. Tweed, however, perceived the defect in this scheme. The new Board of Supervisors was, in effect, a board of guardians. But who was going to guard the guardians? What the state legislature had actually done was to concentrate executive power conveniently in the hands of a small board and then tuck it inconspicuously into the folds of the municipal bureaucracy. Whoever controlled the County Board of Supervisors controlled the city.

Already as an alderman, Tweed had acted for the city in the acquisition of land for a new municipal cemetery. The land he bought was valued at $30,000; yet Tweed acquired it for $103,450, sharing out the difference with his cronies. It was but a small foretaste of the grand schemes to come. Tweed would seize control of the County Board of Supervisors, and in the next fifteen years swindled New York of $200 million in phony bond schemes, shake-downs, corruption and inflated construction costs.

It was a good time to be a Democrat in New York City. In 1857, the Republican state legislature had taken control of the Municipal Police Department out of the hands of City Hall. One of the first acts of the Democrat New York State governor in 1870 was to grab it back again. Appointments to the police department were now openly sold. Yet few officers complained about the venality, for it was understood that a policeman could re-coup the premium he had paid for his job in a matter of months in his share of the protection money he collected on saloons, brothels, and gambling dens. Corruption didn't seem so awful when everyone seemed to be profiting in it. In the spring of 1870, the Tweed's Black Horse Calvary in the state legislature granted the city a new charter giving the mayor's office unprecedented new powers. The Boss was the hero of the hour, the man who had freed New York from Albany's tyrannical grasp. Manhattan went into raptures. New Yorkers fell over each other to get on board his gravy train.

Good times never last forever, of course; and, when the bubble finally popped, it burst with an appalling abruptness. Nor was the sudden turnabout due to the diligence of a virtuous few who exposed the ring's evil ways. These had always been common knowledge. Tweed's downfall was due to the greed of his cronies, who fell to squabbling over the booty as scoundrels often do. Aggrieved grifters ratted on double-crossing kleptocrats, leaking incriminating tidbits to the city's press. What started as a series of isolated leaks swiftly turned into an indiscriminate feeding frenzy as Tammany placemen desperately sought to buy their own safety by revealing the misdeeds of their superiors. With this, the whole corroded pyramid imploded. By the fall of 1871, Godkin's usually staid *Nation* was suggesting that lynching Tweed would be no crime. On December 16, 1871, Tweed was arrested.[4]

As the full extent of the Tweed Ring's misdoings emerged in 1871, respectable opinion gasped in horror. Everyone knew that chicanery was part and parcel of municipal politics; but no one imagined that things could go this far. No one had imagined that a group of seemingly respectable public officials could sack an entire city. In Connecticut, the *Springfield Republican* expressed the bewilderment that many must have felt. Public office, its editorialist wrote, was a public trust. Most people would suppose that, before taking up the burden of public office, an aspiring candidate would carefully prepare himself. He would study law and constitutional theory, master the intricacies of public finance, and study the classics, reading the great political philosophers like Adam Smith, Jeremy Bentham and John Stuart Mill—"but not so with Tweed." Tweed had found another path. He had hit upon a science of government that, in its own earthy way, was as effective as any described by the political philosophers.[5]

The reality was less mysterious. The rail boom in the 1860s had created a financial bubble in New York City. Credit suddenly was plentiful and cheap, and, taking advantage of these conditions, New York City broke away from Albany's dour hand and embarked on a spending spree. Licenses for construction were granted, contracts were awarded, property was acquired, costs were estimated, and workers were given jobs. The functionaries who supervised the granting of licenses, the awarding of contracts, the acquisition of property, the estimating of costs, or the disbursement of public funds had ample opportunity to quietly dip their hands in and divert part of the funds into their own pockets.

Many seemed to have availed themselves of this opportunity. But how were they allowed to get away with it? Why did the tax-paying public allow itself to be fleeced, submitting meekly to what became a particularly brazen form of daylight robbery? Part of the answer is that the funds which ended up in the pockets of the Tweed Ring were funds generated by the credit bubble. Thus they did not at first seem to be coming out of anybody's pocket. Although the ways in which the Tweed Ring enriched itself were plainly illegal, as long as the money seemed to be coming out of thin air, no one was any the worse off. Stuffing some of the money into one's own pocket as it flowed by seemed an almost victimless crime. Some still objected, of course, but many who might have objected kept silent when they discovered that they too could climb aboard the gravy train. As Oliver E. Allen later observed, during the boom years, Tweed enjoyed the support and friendship of many men who ought to have known better.[6]

Nevertheless, despite the wide circle of complicity, Tweed and his ring could never have sucked up such vast sums of wealth and shared it out among a circle of cronies had they not had political cover. To obtain this cover, the ring had turned to the sachems of Tammany Hall and invited them in to share the feast. Tweed and his associates would manage the graft; Tammany would manage the patronage and run the elections. If Tweed bought political support by supplying the means for a vast golden shower of municipal benefices, it was Tammany that got to decide where this shower would fall.

It was a perfect fit. The Democrats were the natural majority party in New York City. By controlling the reservoir of voting power in the poor and immigrant districts of Lower Manhattan, Tammany could call the tune for the entire Democrat Party in the city. The alliance between the Tweed Ring and Tammany was not only logical; it was mutually beneficial. The ring engaged in profitable deals with individual speculators or concocted swindles and kickbacks from businessmen and politicians in both parties, while Tammany provided the means to control the popular vote. In Tammany, the ring discovered the ideal instrument to manage the redistribution of this largesse, the means of buying for itself the allegiance of a grateful electorate. If the ring wished to stay in power, it needed to keep throwing largesse Tammany's way.

Tweed himself proved adept at these wealth-recycling operations; indeed, it seems to have been part of his character. Weighing in at about three hundred pounds, Tweed was never a charismatic figure. With a poor speaking voice and bereft of that bearing, oratorical talent, and aptitude for theatrical flourishes essential for a successful political career in nineteenth-century America, Tweed impressed people as a bumbler, a not-too-bright fat boy who wanted everyone to like him. A modest-seeming person, embarrassed by his immense girth, Tweed appeared as happy to be of service, eager to accommodate his friends, always ready to express sympathy for the poor and needy. Even those who detected an element of cynical calculation behind these humble appearances admitted that it was hard not to like Bill Tweed. Under his rule, New York City became a veritable charity mill. The boss himself donated to hospitals, orphanages, and religious schools of various denominations, churches, cultural projects, and soldiers' homes. Years later, one newspaper editor could still comment, "Bill Tweed, to the world may have been a grafter, but to the poor people in the Bowery section . . . he was the greatest and most generous man in the world."[7] As Callow remarks, Tweed seemed to the world "as big in heart as he was in body."[8]

Charity on this scale was unprecedented. In the years between 1852 and 1869, the New York State Legislature appropriated a little over $2 million to private charities. In the period between 1869 and 1871, the two and a half years in which Tweed and Tammany dominated the State Legislature, the figure was $2.225 million, a figure that does not include municipal charitable expenditures or private donations from the boss himself. Conventional wisdom taught that large-scale charitable projects aimed at the poor were debilitating. The poor should be taught the virtues of hard work, thrift, and self-reliance; a ready availability of charitable relief would only reinforce bad habits of idleness and profligacy. When the Boss personally donated $50,000 to provide Christmas dinners to the poor, the *New York Times* was incensed, "This is conscience money, if Tweed has a conscience" it fumed.[9] But the poor were not the only beneficiaries. The Tweed Ring introduced acts which incorporated saving banks, hospitals and mutual assistance associations; it even introduced the act incorporating the Metropolitan Museum of Art.[10]

The real worry was not, of course, that all this charity was about to unravel the moral fiber of the city's working poor. The real worry was that Tweed and his cronies were changing the rules of the game and doing so to their own advantage. By supplying Tammany with the means to buy political loyalty, Tweed was turning it into a patronage mill capable of maintaining itself in power indefinitely. It was Tammany that decided who got what municipal job, who got what benefit and who paid what tax. Having the power to decide these things automatically gave Tammany the power to decide who got elected to what office. It was a virtuous (or, from another point of view, vicious) circle, in which patronage was translated into power and power was translated back into patronage.

Nevertheless, it is hard not to believe that the *Springfield Republican* quoted above was not being a little disingenuous. Admittedly, Tweed's system was not to be found in the works of Adam Smith, John Stuart Mill, or Jeremy Bentham. But that does not mean it was unprecedented. Had the *Springfield Republican's* editor bothered to browse through his library shelves, he would have discovered that just such a system is described by classical authors. He would have found lengthy discussion of it by English historian Edward Gibbon in his *Decline and Fall of the Roman Empire* (1776–89). Tweed had created nothing new; he had simply reproduced the classic spoils system. Possibly that is the Tweed Ring's true significance. A spoils system cannot exist unless there are sufficient spoils to distribute. This necessary precondition is typically met in cities whose administrations were influential local employers and whose functionaries dispensed a large enough array of licenses and benefits.

If spoils-system politics does not seem a salient feature of American history before the Civil War, it may be because the necessary preconditions did not yet exist. If such a system appeared in New York City—the largest city and commercial capital of the nation—in the 1860s, it may show that a critical mass had been achieved and that the times were now ripe. If this is the case, then the Tweed Ring is not so much of a historical aberration as a sign of things to come. Political machines using spoils-system strategies to entrench themselves in power would proliferate in late nineteenth and early twentieth-century American cities. They would, in short, become the norm. And this, as we shall see, will help explain the link between the immigrants and the urban underworld.

TAMMANY IN THE "IRISH ERA"

. . . Tall, fair and red-faced, terrible for the fierceness of their eyes, fond of
quarreling and of dreadful pride.

—Ammianus Marcellinus on the ancient Celts

In its struggle to keep power, it will prove helpful for the machine to present itself as governing with the consent and support of the common people. It is harder to contest the legitimacy of an authority exercising power in the name of the people and for the good of the people.

For more than a half century after the fall of the Tweed Ring, Tammany's hold over Lower Manhattan remained rock solid. Even the worst scandals failed to shake Tammany's core support. Loyalty of this sort was more than the result of a policy of bread and circuses. It was a genuine political identity. Tammany's core voters came from communities where voting a straight Tammany ticket had become a tradition and source of local pride. By then the political loyalties that the Tweed Ring created through large-scale benefactions had solidified into patron-client networks tying Tammany clubs on the Lower East Side to specific communities. Even if these local branches could provide only a fraction of the jobs and benefits these communities desired, the communities still regarded Tammany as their party. Tammany was their voice, their representatives, their connection, their advocates in the larger world.

Who were these core supporters?

Of the 1.5 million people recorded as living in Manhattan by the 1890 census, twenty-five thousand (one in sixty) are listed as Italian. Twenty-five thousand is a significant number, especially as Italian immigration was about to increase dramatically. Still, it was a drop in the bucket compared to the two other immigrants groups already there—the Germans and the Irish. The census figures are eloquent: alongside the twenty-five thousand Italians in Manhattan in 1890, the census reports the presence of a full three hundred thousand German immigrants. Many of these were second-generation Americans who, by now speaking English, were beginning to lose themselves in the native population. Yet even this German community was overshadowed by the Irish. Their number is recorded as more than four hundred thousand. The New York "Dutch," Italians, and all the other immigrant groups combined still numbered less than the New York Irish. According to the 1860 census, one out of four New Yorkers living in Manhattan was a first- or second-generation Irish immigrant. Nor were these proportions quick to change, for the Irish continued to arrive. The 1890 census still confirmed the old pattern—one out of four New Yorkers was Irish. If one were to include older Irish communities, the entire New York area was probably one third Irish in the 1890s.[11]

Tammany had begun before the Revolution as a political club open to all true-blue Americans. By calling themselves the "sons of 'St. Tammany," after the Indian chief who had supposedly granted lands to William Penn in the 1600s, the club was contrasting itself with other societies that linked their members to the Old World rather than to the New. This inclusiveness did not, however, always extend to religion. The outbreak of famine in Ireland in the 1840s had provoked an unprecedented wave of fresh immigration. Certainly the arrival of masses of wild-eyes, Gaelic-speaking, Irish peasants in ribbed woolen stocking and tight corduroy breeches did nothing to assuage the hostility of New York's working-class Protestants. Nevertheless, these Irish represented a reservoir of potential voting power, and that was something that Tammany's leaders could hardly ignore. An anti-Catholic policy would have made Tammany a politically marginal force in Lower Manhattan. In this sense, Tammany's decision to re-configure itself as the champion of the Irish in New York City was the only possible one.

Here was Tammany's core constituency. By the late 1850s, Daniel Patrick Moynihan remarks, Irish immigrants fresh off the boat were finding a new identity already awaiting them in New York. They were the "Irish-Catholic-Democrats." It was, Moynihan continues, a new sort of Holy Trinity—three in one, one in three, one which "could have been received from the hands of Finn McCool for the way the Irish clung to it."[12]

Between the 8th and the 23d of October 1868, during the run-up to the gubernatorial elections, the Tammany appointee to the State Supreme Court, George G. Barnard, naturalized 10,023 new immigrants, extracting from each of them a promise that they would vote a straight Tammany ticket in the forthcoming elections.[13] The majority of these immigrants were Irish. It was the massive recruitment of immigrant Irish voters in the Tweed years was that first gave Tammany its Irish character.[14] Moynihan called the years between 1870 and 1930 the Irish era in New York. Not everyone accepts this interpretation or concurs in the all-too-evident sympathy Moynihan shows towards Irish-dominated Tammany. Still, Moynihan surely gets the timing right. Moynihan gets the end right as well:

> The crash came suddenly. In June 1932 Smith was denied the Democrat renomination. The Tammany delegates left Chicago bitter and unreconciled. Two months later, Mayor Walker resigned in the face of mounting scandal and decided to leave the country with his English mistress. A few days before his departure, Franklin Roosevelt was elected president. The next man to be elected mayor of New York City was Fiorello La Guardia. Next came Max Baer, a heavyweight champion who was partly of Jewish heritage. Joe DiMaggio became the new name in baseball; Frank Sinatra the new crooner. So it went. The almost formal end came within a decade. In 1943 Tammany Hall itself, built while Walker was mayor at the cost of just under $1 million, was sold to Local 91 of the International Ladies Garment Workers' Union. Tammany and the New York County Democrat Committee went their separate ways. The oldest political organization on earth was finished. So was the Irish era.[15]

So the Irish fell in New York, but they were hardly effaced. Theirs was rather a death by absorption. While Tammany absorbed new waves of immigrants, their Irish constituents were quietly being absorbed into the middle class. By 1930 the Irish had ceased to be an underclass in New York. Nevertheless, their legacy lives on. New York still paints the center line down Fifth Avenue green on St. Patrick's Day. The Irish "Bowery Boy" remained the icon of Lower Manhattan life for generations of theatre goers. The Irish influence remained strong in the police, fire, and other municipal departments. It was a cultural tradition to which the newer immigrants were forced to adapt. Around 1900, we hear the first voices complaining about Jewish and Italian gangsters hiding behind their adopted "Mick" names.

RICHARD CROKER AND BIG TIM SULLIVAN

The Tweed Ring scandals put Tammany into comparative political quarantine in the later1870s and early 1880s. Boss Tweed was succeeded as Tammany Grand Sachem by the respectable "Honest John" Kelly. Though Kelly kept his head down and avoided scandal, he continued Tweed's work, organizing and consolidating Tammany, knocking it into shape and subjecting it to discipline. Kelly, wrote Werner, "found Tammany a horde and left it an army."[16] Still, during the Kelley years, the New York Democrats were led by groups of independent democrats from the rich Silk Stockings District uptown—the "Swallowtails," the Irving Hall Association, and County Democracy—tied to Midtown commercial interests. Tammany might control the vote and work its wiles upon the spoils system. Nevertheless, the public face of the New York County Democratic Association was Samuel Tilden and his respectable associates from uptown.

   Kelly had also expelled a number of corrupt, old-style bosses. These expelled bosses formed their own, independent factions. Some allied themselves to the Swallowtails, who, lacking a political base of their own, were glad to see some popular support come over to their side. When Kelly died in 1886, the new Grand Sachem, Richard Croker, re-united the New York Democrat Party by assimilating the Swallowtails and re-admitting the old bosses. With these bosses back in the wig-wam, the power of Croker's new, re-united Tammany extended far beyond the old Lower East Side to include Greenwich Village and much of the West Side as well as Harlem and the Bronx. Many of the bosses Kelly expelled were Irish. After they were re-admitted by Croker, they formed a self-perpetuating caste of leaders that maintained the Irish character of Tammany up to the 1940s.

   As Tammany Grand Sachem, Croker was *de facto* boss not only of the New York County Democrat Party, but of the entire city. His influence in the comptroller's office, the board of estimates and other key committees gave him unrivalled and unimpeded access to graft. With this, he became, in the words of historian Mark D. Hirsch, "the ablest and most ruthless marauder in [Tammany's] history."[17]

   The boss lived in a palatial mansion off Fifth Avenue where he was served by a retinue of liveried flunkies. He traveled in his own private Pullman car. He maintained stables and farms where he indulged his passion for stud horses. On his trip to England in 1894, Croker reportedly spent $700,000 on stud horses and racetrack betting. His style was an affront to the progressives, who denounced and investigated him throughout the 1890s. But reformist hostility only goaded Boss Croker to greater extravagances. He acted like royalty and demanded to be treated as such. He moved about the city with police escorts; his departures from New York for the country or for his summer trips to England were treated as state occasions: "his state rooms were filled with floral tributes and champagne and packed with dignitaries." Police craft and pleasure boats escorted his liner down the bay, and on one occasion a police launch fired a twenty-one gun salute as a farewell. The boss was pleased, "Why, that's the President's salute," he remarked. In 1899, he held a huge banquet in the Metropolitan Opera. The orchestra seats were removed and replaced by banqueting tables. Elaborate kitchens were set up on the side-walks outside who prepared food for the twelve hundred diners. Their wives, in evening dresses, filled the boxes. When Croker marched in, the band played "Hail to the Chief."

It was Tammany's resident sage, George Washington Plunkitt, who first coined a term for what Croker was doing; he called it "honest graft."

In the time of Boss Tweed, millions were made in straightforward bribes and kick-backs. By the 1890s, however, such primitive methods were no longer legally possible. So when Plunkitt said of Croker that he "never stole a penny from the city treasury. He just saw opportunities and took 'em," he was probably telling the literal truth. Croker never took bribes from the street-car companies to whom he awarded lucrative contracts. Instead, he accepted stock options, partnerships, and phony consultancies. This was an important difference. Tweed had never been involved in running the businesses he skimmed and milked. The Croker Ring worked through entrepreneurs and contractors. This made it more insidious. Once you paid off Tweed, he let you get on with your business. With Croker, you had a partner who never let you off the hook.

Even if we accept that Croker "never stole a penny from the city treasury" and that by serving as an intermediary between contractors and the municipal bureaucracy Croker was actually doing something for the graft he received, the sums involved still seem outrageous. Why was no one able to stop him? The answer is that, like Boss Tweed, Boss Croker had the power of Tammany behind him, and the power of Tammany meant the power of the solid bloc of immigrant votes, which by now included the Eastern and Southern Europeans. But such an answer simply moves the question to another level. What did the immigrants get out of supporting Tammany? Boss Croker, at least, could sometimes be quite candid about the role that the immigrants played in Tammany scheme. "Who else would do it [take care of them] if we did not?" Boss Richard Croker asked rhetorically when interviewed by the London *Review of Reviews* in 1897.

Think of the hundreds of thousands of foreigners dumped into our city. They are too old to go to school. There is not a mugwump [upper-class reformer] who would shake hands with them. They are alone, ignorant strangers, a prey to all manner of anarchical and wild notions. . . . Tammany looks after them for the sake of their vote, grafts them upon the Republic, makes citizens of them in short; and although you may not like our motives or our methods, what other agency is there by which so long a row could have been hoed so quickly or so well?

Croker's observations are self-serving, but they are also just, at least as far as they go. Economic growth had created a need for more labor. Overseas immigrants were arriving in America in response to this need. Many of the arriving laborers could not speak English, however, and were ill-prepared for American life. Someone needed to look after them, to align them properly and to set them along their road. In exchange for their votes, Tammany provided for them, gave them a start in life. Yet the answer is still incomplete. How did Tammany provide for them?

For the inhabitants of the Lower East Side in the years straddling 1900, the embodiment of Tammany's providence was not Boss Croker, but Big Tim Sullivan.

In 1889, a still unknown New York State assemblyman stood up to oppose a proposed new law giving the New York police the power to arrest anyone with a previous conviction as a suspicious person. The author of this proposal was New York City police chief, Thomas F. Byrnes. The young assemblyman was Tim Sullivan. Sullivan had personal reasons for speaking out—Byrnes had named him as the boon companion of thieves, burglars, and murderers. Worse, Byrnes had "pulled" two of Sullivan's saloons for excise law violations. Byrnes was trying to drive Sullivan out of politics, and, against the advice of his Tammany elders, Sullivan was counter-attacking.[18]

Born and raised in the slums of the Five Points area, Sullivan spoke of his impoverished and fatherless childhood to the Assembly. He described his saintly mother, who took in laundry to support a family of ten (five children of her own and five stepchildren). He spoke of starting work at the age of seven, and surviving the rough-and-tumble of the streets of the Lower East Side. With his choirboy good looks intact, Sullivan spoke for the tousle-haired Irish newsboys touting for trade along the Bowery. He was boastful and sentimental by turns, but always ready with a song or wry comment. It was a role that defined the persona of Big Tim Sullivan as a leading Tammany Boss for twenty-five stormy years.

Sullivan was a student of Boss George Washington Plunkitt, who expounded his views each morning while seated on a shoe-shine stand outside his clubhouse in Hell's Kitchen. A true leader, said Plunkitt, needs little formal education. A leader is someone who knows how to "study human nature and act accordin'." What Boss Tweed had shown was that a ward leader had to "go right down among the poor folks and help them in the different ways they need help." Helping the poor meant help with the municipal bureaucracy, help in finding relief and cheap housing, and help in getting a job. "I don't refer them to the Charity Organization Society, which would investigate their case in a month or two and decide they were worthy of help about the time they are dead from starvation." A true leader just goes ahead and does favors, letting the poor show their gratitude on election day. It was a virtuous circle: the gratitude of the poor, faithfully demonstrated in every election, gave the leader his political clout; the possession of this political clout gave the leader the power to perform even more favors. "I know every big employer in the district and in the whole city for that matter," Plunkitt explained, "and they ain't in the habit of sayin' no to me when I ask them for a job."[19]

Sullivan's speech before the State Assembly in 1889 was judged a success. It was a "manly" defense, and Boss Croker awarded the young assemblyman the leadership of the Fourth Assembly District—the world below 14th Street in the period of the Lower East Side's highest population density. In 1892, Sullivan was given the West Village to organize as well. Elected state senator the following year, he soon created for himself a tightly-knit political machine. It was run for him by his brothers, nephews, and cousins. Though nominally subordinate to Tammany's Grand Sachem, Boss Croker, Sullivan and his machine were in fact an independent power.

Big Tim presented Tammany as a vast club, a warm-hearted organization dedicated to helping people out. His yearly "chowders" or organized summer outings were remembered in successive decades with nostalgic affection. For the tenement-dwelling Lower East Siders, these outings were holiday treats, rare excursions into the greenery, something to look forward to the whole year around. As many as ten thousand tickets to these extravaganzas might be sold. Though the tickets could cost five dollars each, the great majority who obtained them, got them for free. Sullivan's agents would spend the weeks before the excursion canvassing saloonkeepers, grocers, and other businesses serving the tenement dwellers, persuading them to buy large batches of the tickets for distribution among their favored clients. In this way, poor families got free summer outings and local merchants earned the good will of their clients and the gratitude of the political bosses. Everyone seemed a winner; everyone got something in exchange. Such were the bonds of reciprocity that underlay Tammany control.

The day would start with Big Tim leading a street parade to an East River dock where steamboats would be waiting to ferry the eager picnickers up to Harlem River Park or out to College Point on Long Island. Here they would be treated to a clam fritter breakfast and a day of sporting events. There would be band concerts followed by a fish and chicken dinner, and dancing after sunset. A fireworks display would enchant the weary spectators as they settled back into the steamboats to chug back up the East River. A torch-light parade saw them back to their homes after they landed. There would be side-show entertainments, stalls and booths, pick-up baseball games, and pie-eating contests. There would be beautiful baby contests and prizes for the biggest and for the best turned-out families. There would, of course, be gambling as well, ranging from old staples like faro, poker, and craps to exotic newcomers like briscola, saginetto, stuss or fan tan.

Traditionally such summer outings had always been the occasion for much speechfying. But Sullivan disliked this tradition; Lower East Siders, he proclaimed, always distrusted a man who put on airs. He refused to turn his chowders into political rallies; he rarely spoke from a rostrum. He preferred mingling.

Mingling was what Big Tim did best. Picnics and excursions had always doubled as political fund-raisers, and Sullivan's were no exception. Like other Tammany bosses, he grew rich with no visible means of support. Yet wealth was always secondary to him, a means to the power and popularity rather than an end in itself. Big Tim cultivated his public image as the benefactor of the little guy, as a man always ready to stop and listen sympathetically to some tale of woe from the guy without the job or disability pension that was due to him. He was their channel into the municipal bureaucracy, ready to expedite requests for permits and licenses, to find a trustworthy bail bondsman for them, or to whisper a word into the ear of a sympathetic judge. This was the side of Big Tim Sullivan that the Lower East Siders were allowed to see; the other side, where he took his cut or pocketed the contribution, was more shielded from public view.

"Every community," Sullivan later explained to a reporter from the *New York World*, "has to have some man who can take the trouble to look out for the people's interest while the people are earning a living." . . .

> It doesn't make any difference whether he's tall, short, fat, lean, or hump-backed with only half his teeth. If he's willing to work harder than anyone else, he's the fellow who will hold the job. They're not always grateful by any means, and when they catch a man with a four-flush, no matter how good his excuse, it's "skidoo" back to the old home for him. . . . And so, after all, there isn't much to being a leader. It's just plenty of work, keep your temper or throw it away, be on the level and don't put on any airs, because God and the people hate a chesty man.[20]

The summer chowders were a political and financial success. They were widely covered by the local press, giving Big Tim ever greater public exposure. He responded by organizing even more charitable works. In the depression winter of 1894, Sullivan organized a Christmas dinner that fed thousands of poor New Yorkers. This became another of his traditions. Vaudeville celebrities were happy to come down to Big Tim's headquarters on the Bowery to provide free entertainment for the poor families as they ate their Christmas dinners.

In 1903, Sullivan invented a new tradition. He used to tell the story of an Irish elementary school teacher, Miss Murphy, who, one brutal winter day, noticed a poor little boy shivering at his desk. Miss Murphy gave the boy a note and told him to take to a Tammany ward heeler named Timothy Brennan. Not quite knowing what to make of it, the boy had gone to Brennan and handed him his teacher's note. The man read it, then, without saying a word, went and fetched the boy a pair of shoes and warm pair of woolen socks. "That little boy was me, the young Tim Sullivan," Sullivan would proclaim to his listeners. And Miss Murphy's gesture taught me something about true charity. "I never ask a hungry man about his past; I feed him not because he is good, but because he needs food. Help your neighbor, but keep your nose out of his affairs." This was Sullivan as he expounded his philosophy in front of the New York State Assembly in 1889. So every February from 1903 onward, on a day dedicated to the memory of Miss Murphy, thousands would line up outside Big Tim's Bowery office to receive their free pair of shoes and woolen socks.

Christmas turkeys and free woolen socks all cost money, however, and where was it all coming from? Capital might have flown easily in the freewheeling years of the Tweed Ring, remaining abundant as long as the speculative bubble lasted. But the speculative bubble lasted only until 1873. Then came years of municipal debt and retrenchment. Tammany could expect little succor from Albany, which now was safely back in Republican hands. Nor were they free to tax Wall Street and squeeze the folk uptown. Even had bosses Croker or Murphy been so inclined, a policy of soaking the rich would have upset the equilibrium within the Democrat Party. Forced loans and phony bond issues were out of the question; they would have undermined the city's creditworthiness. The sachems of Tammany Hall were forced to come up with money-raising schemes of their own.

As Grand Sachem and ruthless marauder, it was easier for Croker to make millions in graft. Yet Croker never posed as a man of the people, nor even, like Boss Tweed, as a philanthropist as big of heart as he was of girth. Big Tim, by contrast, was genuinely close to the people. He liked to be accessible, living on the Lower East Side, keeping the doors to his club open to all. Unlike Croker, he lacked direct influence on the committees and boards that handled appropriations and municipal contracting. Hence he lacked Croker's opportunities for graft. But Big Tim was still a rich man, not Croker-style rich, but rich enough to drop a few thousand dollars at the faro table without it breaking his stride. So where was Big Tim getting his money from?

According to one account, Tim Sullivan made his money by looking after the interests of the "horrible concert halls and gardens besprinkling the Bowery and other streets in the city," places where on Sundays, children who should be attending Sunday School might, for a few pennies, savor "Little Egypt" or other exotic delicacies. But this was not his only source of revenue. Big Tim Sullivan was also a member of the combine that looked after the interests of an estimated eleven hundred gambling establishments. This netted the combine an estimated $3.095 million annually.[21] Finally, though this was an accusation he vociferously denied, Big Tim was said to receive a cut from the bordellos in the Tenderloin District and a share of the profits in the "white-slavery" traffic.

THE HONKY TONKS, TAMMANY AND THE NYPD

Taverns, cheap theatres, gambling dens, and brothels: A common thread
linked all these establishments: they were all part of honky-tonk life. Theatres, taverns, bars, brothels, street-walkers, pool halls, gambling clubs, and
street-corner crap games were part of the city's leisure and entertainment industry. They were not perhaps the part of that industry that the city was most
proud of. For that reason, they tended to be confined to zones supposedly
unfrequented by respectable people—the honky tonks. Despite their confinement, however, and their insalubrious reputations notwithstanding, honky
tonks flourished in turn-of-the-century America; they flourished in New York
just as they flourished in Chicago's Levee, New Orleans's Storyville, and
San Francisco's Barbary Coast. Indeed, they flourished in most contemporary
American cities.

They were loud and raucous, and their presence was anathema to certain
segments of the citizenry. As George Ade, writing in 1931, said of Chicago's
Levee in the 1890s, it was "blaring and glaring and insolent," and it "held day
and night revelry on the very rim of the most highly respectable business section. Everything went, from pitch and toss to manslaughter."

But the honky tonks were not only centers of vice and sin; they were
profitable businesses as well. As Ade goes on to observe, "in order to keep the
good times rolling, enough money to settle Europe's war debts was passed in
bribes."[22] This made the honky tonk a mouth-watering target.

The existence of a highly-profitable vice industry concentrated in a few
city blocks represented, depending on how you looked at it, either a pressing
social problem or golden economic opportunity. Tammany certainly took the
latter view. The Midtown Tenderloin District and the Lower East Side honky
tonks from the Bowery to Second Avenue seemed to be honey pots far too
sweet for the Hall to ignore. By 1900, Tammany had been feeding on them
for over a generation.

Skimming the honky-tonks turned out, in fact, to be the ideal solution to
Tammany's financial problems. Honky tonks were filled with marginal, cash-
only enterprises whose proprietors and managers either kept few records or
kept them hidden from public scrutiny. They were also enterprises that needed
protection. The Sullivan organization extended its political protection to these
businesses in exchange for monthly payments. Sometimes, as in the case of
gambling, the Sullivan organization took money directly; sometimes, as in the
case of the brothels, the collections were made by the police and later shared
with Tammany.

Vice was business in New York, but, unlike other businesses, vice paid
little or no taxes. Some argued that the pay-offs were just an alternative form
of taxation, a way of evening up the score and making vice pay its proper dues.
Even the New York State Legislature's Lexow Commission on police corruption in the 1889Os described the pay-offs in these terms. The analogy between
protection and taxation was implicitly accepted. The "variety of vice" in the

city, Chairman Lexow wrote, "was regularly and systematically licensed by the police of the city. The system had reached such a perfection in detail that the inmates of the several houses [i.e. brothels] were numbered and classified and a rateable charge placed upon each proprietor in proportion to the number of inmates, or in cases of houses of assignation the number of rooms occupied and the prices charged, reduced to a monthly rate, which was collected within a few days of the first of each month during the year."[23]

Protection officials who argued the analogy of skimming to taxation also argued that the system actually brought distinct advantages to the public. Imposing regular cash tributes on the various shades of barely legal and plainly illegal activities going on in the honky tonks not only solved Tammany's pressing problem of finding cash to recycle as patronage. It also provided the New York Police Department, with a means of confining and controlling activities that, however offensive to certain members of the public, were in the opinion of many officials ineradicable. Protection, in this guise, represented a hidden form of social control and one that, by paying for itself, cost the public nothing. By paying protection money, the vice entrepreneurs were effectively paying the police to maintain good order in their resorts.

Or so the argument went. The reality was that, though police control did, to some extent, keep the vice industry confined and under control, this control never extended to what went on inside that industry. That was left strictly to the proprietors, who, in the case of the honky-tonk resorts, were invariably connected to the underworld. Indeed, considering the regularity with which Tammany bosses and police officials emerged as silent partners in the establishments, it seems apparent that, as long as they got their pay-offs, Tammany and the police did not really care what went on. They only intervened as a last resort or when a public outcry forced them to. Tammany and the police were happy to let the honky tonks run themselves in any way they wished.

In practice, this meant that the honky tonks were managed and run by the urban underworld, for the underworld had always controlled the honky-tonk vice industry. Thus, whatever the theoretical advantages of letting the police impose informal controls on the vice industry may have been, the actual results were always the same: a business partnership between the police and crime in which the police ended up working for the underworld rather than the public. By imposing protection on the vice industry, Tammany and the police ended up in the underworld's pocket.

The revelation that Big Tim Sullivan was part of a combine overseeing eleven hundred gambling dens and pocketing over $3 million per year, appeared in a *New York Times* article reporting on the Lexow Commission's inquiry. The article named the other two members of the combine as well. One was a well-known underworld-connected gambler. The other was New York Police Captain William "Big Bill" Devery. Readers were surely shocked by the extent and size of the grafting. They must have been less surprised to learn that their police were directly involved. They knew that already.

In the late 1860s, Boss Tweed increased the police force as well as the rest of the municipal employment rolls. Tweed's new "Shiny Hat Brigade" numbered twelve thousand to fifteen thousand, an increase in the budget that had helped triple the city's debt.[24] Their pay at first was miserable; the Boss was buying political loyalty rather than providing real jobs. He was packing the police force and other municipal departments with Tammany loyalists. Many looked at their measly pay and the derisory amount of prestige attached to their shiny new badge of office as an obligation merely to keep faith with Tammany on election day rather than a responsibility for actual work. Still, Tweed created a connection between Tammany and municipal employees that would last for generations.

His recruiting policy also helped give the New York police its traditional Irish coloration. Before Tweed, the police in New York were recruited from the older Anglo-Saxon and German immigrant communities. Especially in the case of the Germans, some of these traditions continued after Tweed. It was nevertheless the new Tammany-connected Irish recruits who now gave the force its character.

All in all, a career in the NYPD eventually became a decent enough prospect for a working man. Ill-paid in the early years, by 1890 a patrolman's wages had risen to those of a skilled worker. This was well above casual laborers who existed at starvation levels, and also above semi-skilled laborers like trolley drivers or construction workers. A patrolman could eke out a living, and, with expected promotions and accumulated seniority, buy a house and raise a family. There were other advantages as well. The city looked after its police. While unionization was firmly discouraged in other industries, the police were allowed to form a Policemen's Beneficial Association, which over the years grew and transformed itself into something very like a union, negotiating benefits for the rank and file. Policemen got free medical attention for injuries sustained in the line of duty, and, in the tragic eventuality, a funeral at the city's expense. They later won rights to disability pay and a pension. After 1900, Boss Charles Francis Murphy joked that the NYPD was the only Irish gang in the city with a pension plan.

There were other, less official, benefits. Uptown and in the financial district, the patrolman on the beat might be treated like the local postman, garbage collector, or doorman, receiving tips for special services and a little envelope at Christmas. All over the city patrolmen got free cups of coffee; it seems to have been a universal practice, and, especially during the winter months, there were few complaints.

Downtown patrolmen received gratuities as well, but these were apt to be of a much different nature. Contributions here were not always so spontaneous. Some were not even voluntary. Each precinct captain managed his own area here, dividing the graft among his men while providing Tammany with its share. There was a regular set of tariffs in each precinct: a certain amount for an illegal pushcart or an illegal street display, a sliding scale for protection for illegal gambling and brothels, a fee for approving a liquor license. There were also payments within the force: a captain's position cost $10,000, more for the Tenderloin precincts. A patrolman paid around $300 to get on the force. It was probably more than he could afford: but loans could be arranged on the understanding that part of the patrolman's take would go to the usurer. The amount of annual brothel contributions alone was reckoned at $8.12 million.[25]

The police, wrote Republican State Senator, Clarence Lexow, in his 1896 report, maintained "a partnership . . . in the traffic" of prostitution, thereby succeeding in "absorbing the largest part of the resulting profit."[26] Even in 1915, in a report to the police commissioner, it was reported that prostitution in New York City was still "controlled solely by the Police Department." In 1879, Police Commissioner, Joel B. Erhardt, admitted that numerous police captains and officers regularly received a "contribution" from gambling and vice resorts. This connection between the police and the gambling and vice resorts was confirmed by Theodore Roosevelt during his tenure as police commissioner in 1896. After 1900 it was further confirmed by commissioners William McAdoo and Bingham. Indeed, Bingham pointed out that, while mayors and police commissioners typically served in their posts for a short number of years, police captains spent their entire careers on the force and were therefore better able to rule their precincts independently, resisting the short-lived anti-vice campaigns emanating from City Hall or from the Commissioners' Office on Mulberry Street.[27]

As protectors of the honky tonks, Tammany and the NYPD had interlocking interests, so it is not surprising that senior police officials also held senior positions at the Hall or that Tammany looked after the patrolmen's interests. In 1886, the Central Labor Union, a militant, working class party in New York, launched the candidacy of labor reformer Henry George for the upcoming mayoral elections. George's candidacy enjoyed wide working-class support in Lower Manhattan. Faced with the prospect that, by cutting into their working-class support, an authentic radical might win the mayor's office, both factions of the New York City Democrat Party, the Swallowtail Democrats uptown, and Kelly's Tammany Hall downtown, agreed to bury their differences and unite behind Abraham Hewitt, a respected reformer and son-in-law of the industrial reformer, Peter Cooper. Shortly after winning the election, Mayor Hewitt summoned Police Commissioner William Murray to his office. The spread of vice, the new mayor gravely informed the police commissioner, was New York's number one problem. Vice in the city, he said, had reached monumental proportions. "Obviously," he went on in pointed tones, "such conditions prevailed because of police graft."

Unfazed, Commissioner Murray replied that this was most certainly the case.

Somewhat taken aback by the unexpected agreement, Mayor Hewitt asked whether the illegal joints—the dives, brothels and gambling dens—could be closed.

"Certainly," replied Murray, "it is only necessary to give the order."

Murray then paused and went on explain something to the mayor, "If the order goes out, you will be attacking the men who were your best supporters in the last election and who put you in the mayor's chair."

Taken aback once again, Hewitt reflected for a moment. He then asked Murray what his salary was. Three thousand five hundred dollars a year, Murray replied. But how much was he worth? Over $300,000, Murray replied without hesitation (a sum equal to over $6 million today). Mayor Hewitt might go on to observe at this juncture that, "If you're worth $300,000 you can afford to be honest." But Murray had made his point. The relationship between Tammany, vice, and police graft could not be reduced to the misdeeds of a few venal officers nor resolved by closing down the dives. Graft had become organic; it was now part of the system. Graft had entered into the bloodstream of both the NYPD and Tammany. Cut off graft, Murray was implying, and the whole system would buckle. Hewitt's subsequent crackdown on vice was half-hearted and short-lived.[28]

THE SLUMS

The immigrant in stories and fables arrives with nothing. He steps off the boat with little more than the clothes on his back. The reality of immigration in the 1890s was likely to be something less dramatic. Immigrants arrived in groups—family groups, neighborhood groups, or co-workers. They usually had a list of contacts in their new destination and often job offers as well. They arrived with a bit of saved-up capital to live on or, sometimes, even invest. Nor was the break between the Old World and the New as irrevocable as it sometimes seemed. Steamer traffic went both ways. Villagers in Eastern and Southern Europe became accustomed to seeing "Americans" with their shiny shoes and big-city suits come back to pay their respects and marry the brides their mothers had picked out for them. Sometimes they come home with their savings to spend the rest of their days in comfort where living was still cheap, the pace leisurely, and the locals spoke the old language.

Despite these exceptions, there was, nevertheless, still much truth in the popular image. The immigrants were, in general, poor. They were forced to work long hours at back-breaking or tedious jobs for little pay. They were packed into over-crowded tenements which lacked air and basic sanitary facilities. The districts where they lived were the parts of the city usually called the "slums."

Slums are perhaps best understood in relative rather than absolute terms. A slum is not simply a place of poverty. It is rather the area in which the city's impoverished and marginalized citizens—the ones at the bottom of the pile—live. Slum dwellers are not only poor; they are second-class citizens with little influence in the larger community. They are underprivileged, liable to be victimized, or ignored and forced to put up with abuses that even the poorest members of more established communities would never tolerate. Fresh off the boat, ignorant and unsophisticated, and often with little English language skill, the immigrants naturally slotted in as second-class citizens at the lowest rungs in the urban social hierarchy. They would, moreover, continue to be confined to the slums as long as they remained marginalized and disadvantaged second-class citizens.

The slums of Manhattan's Lower East Side were dominated by Tammany Hall. Here Tammany controlled the bureaucracy upon whose help and services the immigrants depended. Here Tammany controlled the police, and influenced local employers, who would not give an immigrant a job if they thought that, by doing so, they risked offending a Tammany boss or even a ward heeler. So it was here, in the immigrant slums, that the bonds or reciprocity and mutual dependence, the bonds on which Tammany's power was based, were forged. But Tammany was itself a hierarchical organization and one that, at its higher rungs, enjoyed wealth and power. For a young immigrant, it often seemed that the best way to overcome the disadvantages of poverty and second-class citizenship was to accommodate oneself to Tammany's system of power and seek to rise within its system. And this could mean working in the honky tonks.

Tammany was not just a machine that dispensed political patronage in exchange for voter loyalty; Tammany was also a protection racket that fed on the honky tonks. These two aspects of Tammany power—patronage and protection—were strictly complementary. It was Tammany's control of the municipal bureaucracy and, most particularly, the close and fraternal relations it enjoyed with the NYPD, that gave it the power and the means to systematically levy tributes upon the honky tonk resorts. Some of this tribute was transformed into the Christmas turkeys and woolen socks as well the barrels of whiskey and drinks on the house at election time that allowed Tweed and the Sullivan organization to present themselves to their slum-dwelling constituents as a big-hearted charitable institution. But much of the tribute simply went into the pockets of the Tammany sachems and NYPD captains and never came out again. Or, more precisely, it came out in the fine houses in Connecticut, thoroughbred race horses and sleek yachts that these so-called public servants owned. Public hearings and inquiries and newspapers investigations from the 1890s to the 1930s all uncovered the same pattern. Power meant patronage power, and patronage cost money. Vice and graft were where the money was. It surely must have seemed to many an ambitious young slum-dwelling immigrant around 1900 that vice and graft were the way to go. The alternative was a lifetime of tedious drudgery as an impoverished second-class slum dweller, or, as Lucky Luciano put it, life as a crumb.

Slums and the Street Gangs

How was an ambitious young immigrant boy, one perhaps not over-encumbered with moral inhibitions but possessed rather of that quality which Luciano referred to as "moxie," going to break into vice and graft? Neither Tammany nor the honky tonks organized training courses; nor could you enlist in the underworld. The answer is rather that crime at this initial level is opportunistic; you simply waited for the right opportunities to turn up. The best way, moreover, to make sure that you were drifting in the right direction was usually to join a street gang. It was here that the slum's potential for contact with the underworld was most likely to be realized.

"The greatest of the gangs that came into existence in New York after the Civil War," wrote Herbert Asbury, "was the Whyos, as vicious a collection of thugs, murderers, and thieves as ever operated in the metropolis." The Whyos were, among other things, pickpockets, sneak thieves, dive owners, pimps, brothel bouncers and panel-house thieves. Though they ranged throughout Lower Manhattan, they made their home in the area around Mulberry Bend to the north and east of the old Five Points, an old Irish area where the new Jewish and Italian immigrants had begun to settle in the last decades of the nineteenth century. Despite the changing demography, the Whyos themselves were a colorful bunch of hoodlums with Irish names: Hoggy Walsh, Fig Mc-Gerald, Bull Hurley, Googy Corcoran, Baboon Doyle, Red Rocks Farrell, Clops Connolly, Piker Ryan, Dorsey Doyle, and Big Josh Hynes. Among their associates in the early 1880s was the young Tim Sullivan, known at the time by his nick-name "Dry Dollar" Sullivan.

Piker Ryan owed his own brief fame to the circumstances of his arrest. He was caught handing out the following flyer advertising his gang's services:

Punching	*$2*
Both eyes blacked	*$4*
Nose and jaw broke	*$10*
Jacked out	*$15*
Ear chawed off	*$15*
Leg or arm broke	*$19*
Shot in leg	*$25*
Stab	*$25*
Doing the big job	*$100 and up*[29]

Although the Whyos' price list invariably appears in discussions of the gangs of old New York, it is still hard to know what to make of it. No mafia Family ever thought of sending their soldiers out to stand on street corners, handing out leaflets advertising their services to passing strangers. The Whyos seem more like contemporary New York Chinese restaurateurs whose take-out menus routinely clog up the city's letter slots. Indeed, the Whyos may have been employing a sort of take-out menu strategy: though like the Chinese restaurateurs, the Whyos could not predict exactly whom their publicity would attract, they were quietly confident that, somewhere out there were plenty of people disposed to pay for their services.

The event in question took place in the bad old days of the early 1880s, before successive police crack-downs. Lower Manhattan was still wide open, with prostitutes on every street corner and in every honky-tonk resort. The waiters in the concert halls still dispensed knock-out drops with a liberal hand. Low lifes ranged free in those days. So it is possible that Piker Ryan felt entitled to hawk the services of his Whyo associates like any other honest tradesman.

Unfortunately we possess very little precise information on the early days of the Whyos. Asbury and Harlow tell us that they arose after the Civil War and that they were a continuation of one of the original Five Points gangs, the Chichesters.[30] This latter detail seems appropriate; the Whyos do seem closer to the Plug Uglies or the Dead Rabbits than to any of the gangs that came afterwards.

By the 1880s, the Whyos were well enough established to employ the services of the era's paramount criminal lawyers, William Howe and Abraham Hummel, to whom Marm Mandelbaum, the city's leading fence, as well as many of the city's leading resort owners, paid an annual retainer. The gang made their headquarters in a succession of dives between the Bowery and Mulberry Bend, including an Italian saloon on the Bowery called The Morgue. Earlier, however, they had hung out in a saloon on Chrystie Street owned by Tim "Dry Dollar" Sullivan.[31]

Born in the Sixth Ward in 1863, by the mid-1880s Sullivan had become the proprietor of a string of dives and saloons. It was the invariable first step in a Lower Manhattan political career. One of the saloons that Police Chief Byrnes "pulled" in his 1889 attempt to nip Big Tim's political career in the bud was a dive on Doyers street, off the Bowery. The *Times* sent a reporter to investigate: "It is safe to say," he wrote, "that there are not a hundred people in this city who live above Canal Street who know where Doyers Street is, and if they did they would shun it as the plague. . . . It is narrow and dirty, and in the daytime is repulsive enough to keep anybody from trying to penetrates its mysteries, but at night, in addition to its ugliness, it looks dangerous."[32] Byrnes later defended his action, claiming that these dives served as hang-outs for notorious thieves, many of whom were Sullivan's "boon companions." He specifically mentioned members of the Whyo gangs, adding that Sullivan had tried to pressure the police in order to "make it light" for some of his friends.[33] Considering that one of these dives was the Whyo's headquarters, Byrnes probably knew what he was talking about.

In 1886, Sullivan was elected to the New York State Legislature. He ran as an anti-Tammany Democrat; indeed, he seems to have run as the Whyo candidate. His differences with Tammany were never more than circumstantial however. Once in Albany he fell under the influence of the Tammany assemblyman, Tom Foley, who remained one of his closest associates throughout his career. Foley persuaded Sullivan to enter the Hall, and to stand in the next elections as a Tammany candidate.

By 1890, the police had just about exterminated the Whyo gang. Two of their leaders, Danny Lyons and Danny Driscoll, both earlier mentioned by Byrnes as among Sullivan's boon companions, were convicted of murder and hanged in the yard at the Tombs. Sullivan had not been implicated; he successfully defended himself in the legislature in 1889. By now his former connection to the Whyos was nothing but a political encumbrance. Sullivan was intent on building up his own empire, one that, though semi-independent, would remain firmly allied with Croker's and, later, Murphy's Tammany. Still, even though his Whyo connections were no longer useful, he still needed underworld allies.

When the Whyo gang had first arisen in the 1870s, the Irish were still dominant in the area where Rynders' Five Points gangs had ruled a generation before. After 1890, however, they had become a minority. The old Five Points area had now become home to Eastern Europeans, both Jews and Catholics, and, increasingly South Italians. Big Tim Sullivan's new political organization below Fourteenth Street reflected these demographic shifts. His underworld allies would naturally come from these same groups.

The most important Lower East Side gang leaders in the years around 1900 were Monk Eastman and Paul Kelly. Monk Eastman was born Edward Osterman in 1873 in a respectable restaurant-owning Jewish family in the Williamsburg section of Brooklyn. Around 1890, his father bought Monk a small pet shop in Brooklyn which he managed for a few years. By the middle of the decade, however, Monk had crossed over into Manhattan. He became the bouncer at Silver Dollar Smith's Saloon, and later established himself as the sheriff, or chief bouncer, of the New Irving Dance Hall on Broome Street. Along with Tammany Hall itself, the New Irving Dance Hall was a favorite venue for rackets, the fund-raising balls that were such an important part of low-life society on the Lower East Side. Other favoured venues included Paul Kelly's New Brighton Dance Hall and the Walhalla Hall (better known as the Walla Walla) on Orchard Street near Grand. As a member of the Essex Market Courthouse gang and sheriff at the New Irving, Eastman had a full complement of underworld connections. By the Robert Van Wyck years as mayor, 1898 to 1901, he had emerged as the leader of a gang said to have around twelve hundred members. It had close connections to the Sullivan organization.

Much less is known about the early background of Eastman's rival, Kelly. Born of immigrant parents probably in the Lower East Side, he changed his name from Paolo Antonini Vaccarelli to Kelly when he became a professional boxer in the late 1880s. After a successful career as a bantamweight, he retired from the ring and acquired a stake in the New Brighton Dance Hall, making it the headquarters for his gang. This gang, which around 1900 may have numbered as many as fifteen hundred members, was called the Five Points Gang. Sante remarks that the name showed a nice feeling for underworld history, for the Five Points, along with the old Brewery and Paradise Square, had all disappeared thirty years before.

Most of our information about Eastman and Kelly derives from contemporary newspaper articles. These were the sources for both Asbury and Harlow. Asbury's description of Eastman is worth quoting at length:

> He began life with a bullet-shaped head, and during his turbulent career acquired a broken nose and a pair of cauliflower ears, which were not calculated to increase his beauty. He had heavily veined, sagging jowls, and a short, bull neck, plentifully scarred with battle marks, as were his cheeks. He seemed always to need a hair-cut, and accentuated his ferocious and unusual appearance by affecting a derby hat several sizes too small, which, perched precariously atop his shock of bristly, unruly hair. He could generally be found strutting about his kingdom very indifferently dressed, or lounging at his ease in the Chrystie Street rendezvous without shirt, collar or coat. His hobby was cats and pigeons—animals have always seemed to possess a fascination for gangsters; many of whom, after they have reformed, or had been compelled by the police to abandon the active practice of thuggery, opened bird and animal stores, and prospered. Monk Eastman is said to have owned, at one time, more than a hundred cats and five hundred pigeons, and although they were offered for sale in his bird and animal store in Broome street, it was seldom that he could be induced to part with any of them. He sometimes went abroad, on peaceful missions, with a cat under each arm, while several others trailed along in his wake. He also a great blue pigeon which he had tamed, and which perched on his shoulder as he walked.

> "I like de kits and boids," Eastman used to say, "I'll beat up any guy dat gets gay wit' a kit or boid in my neck of de woids."[34]

Paul Kelly, by contrast, appears as a gentleman of taste and refinement. He dressed well, spoke fluent French, Italian, and Spanish, and resembled, according to Asbury, "a bank clerk or theological student more than a gang chieftain, and his dive, the New Brighton, was one of the flashiest places of sin in the city."[35]

These sources also describe the war that broke out between the Eastmans and Kelly's Five Pointers during the years at the turn of the century. The formal cause was a territorial dispute. The Five Pointers ruled a slice of territory from Broadway east to the Bowery and from Fourteenth Street in the north to City Hall Park in the south. The Eastman gang controlled the adjacent strip to the east of the Bowery, all the way to the East River, including most of the Lower East Side's red light district. Disputed was a small section of the lower Bowery near Doyers and Pell Streets, immediately above Chatham Square. In a more general sense, however, the war was the logical outcome of each gang's habit of raiding the other's street-corner stuss games. Formal initiation of hostilities began in early 1901, when a gang of Five Pointers shot Monk Eastman in the stomach. Ambushes and shoot-outs followed, including perhaps the city's first drive-by shootings.

In August 1903, a group of Eastmans caught a group of Five Pointers preparing to raid an Eastman gang-protected stuss game under the Rivington Street arch of the Second Avenue El on Allen Street. Taking cover behind the huge elevated railroad trusses, the gangs began trading pot shots. Reinforcements soon arrived for both sides, who barricaded themselves behind the railroad arches. By midnight, the whole area resembled a battle zone. The police several times tried to rush the barricades, both inflicting casualties and suffering injuries themselves. It was not until well after midnight that, combining forces from near-by precincts, the police were finally able to disperse the rival gunmen. The number of dead and wounded could never be fully established. Among the arrested was Monk Eastman himself, who gave his name as 'Joseph Morris' and claimed that he was just passing by. He was arraigned the next morning before a Tammany magistrate and promptly released.[36]

The shoot-out under the Rivington Street arches made headlines in the morning papers, much to the annoyance of the gangs' political patrons. Representing Tammany, Tom Foley told both Eastman and Kelly that this sort of "Wild West" gunfighting on the East Side had to stop. He hosted a grand racket at the Palm Café on Chrystie Street at the edge of the disputed territory. Monk Eastman and Paul Kelly publicly shook hands on the dance floor and agreed to keep the truce. With this, the band struck up "Sweet Rosie O'Grady," and gang leaders from both sides gallantly danced with each others' molls.[37]

It was only months, however, before the two gangs fell to bickering and raiding again. Once more the politicians intervened. This time the dispute was to be settled by a boxing match between the two principles. They met in an unheated Bronx barn near the end of 1903. The two were closely matched; though Eastman had the advantage in brawn, Kelly had the advantage of professional skill. After two solid hours of slugging, they collapsed in each others' arms, and the match was called a draw. Seeing no way of settling the gang war peaceably, Tammany simply withdrew its support and let nature and the New York police take their course. Two months later, dodging the bullets of an angry Pinkerton detective, Eastman ran straight into the arms of a Midtown patrolman. This time there were no friendly bail bondsman or Tammany magistrate to put in the fix. Monk received ten years in Sing Sing. Tammany had decided to throw Monk away.[38]

Unfortunately, we know a good deal less about the specifically criminal activities of either the Eastman or the Kelly gangs. Both were involved in organizing and protecting gambling in their territories, contributing part of their takings to the Sullivan organization. Kibbe Turner reported that Eastman and Kelly both owned brothels and ran prostitutes. This is certainly true of Eastman, who was close to vice lord Marty Engels and to the Essex Market Courthouse gang. It is likely to be true of Kelly as well. Both were said to hire out thugs and goons in disputes between capital and labor, though most of these wars occurred after Eastman's fall.

Finally, both gangs were used by Tammany to organize repeater voters, intimidate enemies and stuff or otherwise dispose of ballot boxes. In the September 1901 election for Tammany District Leader in the Second Ward, Tim Sullivan's friend, Tom Foley, challenged Croker loyalist, Paddy Divver. Installing Foley as a district leader was crucial both to Big Tim Sullivan and to Charles F. Murphy; so Sullivan and Foley turned to Paul Kelly. Indeed, according to Thompson and Raymond, Foley turned directly to the Italian boss of the Second Ward, the future mafia *capo* Joe Masseria.[39] On the night of the elections, the Second Ward was filled with Italian thugs who, bloodying Divver supporters and stealing ballot boxes, insured Foley a landslide victory.[40]

It is tempting to interpret the war between Eastman and Kelly in ethnic terms—East Side Jews against Italians from Little Italy. It is true that that the Eastman gang's territory, east of the Bowery, was predominantly Jewish, while Kelly's Five Pointers were centred in the Little Italy around Mulberry Bend. Still, the interpretation is an over-simplification. Each gang was a master gang, or, perhaps even more accurately, an underworld faction. Either was a confederation of youth gangs, criminal groups, and other associations. The complexity of these arrangements was such that, at one point, the Eastmans even tried to get their members to turn in type-written reports of jobs completed in order to gain a better idea of what their far-flung confederation was up to. Even if the boundary between the Eastmans and the Five Pointers roughly corresponded to the boundary between the Eastern European Jews and the Italians, both gang leaders had allies in either community, as well as among the remaining Irish. Both gangs were also patronized by the Sullivan organization, which saw them as a source of hireable muscle and as a sort of grass-roots organization. Nor were their activities limited to crime and gang warfare.

Both the Five Pointers and the Eastman gang founded affiliates and youth clubs, a regular farm system, Sante remarks, often with patriotic booster names reminiscent of Young Republican Clubs. These included the Yankee Doodle Boys, the Go Aheads or the Liberty Social Club. There were also female auxiliaries, the Lady Locusts, Lady Truck Drivers, and the Lady Liberties of the Fourth Ward. The Eastman gang in particular, with their sponsored rackets, summer chowders, and baseball teams, seems to have been modelled like a Sullivan organization in miniature—into which it was indeed tucked— or even like the Police Athletic Leagues in Chicago. One of Eastman's gangs, the Midnight Terrors, had their own baseball team, complete with their own special uniforms. Crime was sometimes an adjunct to the fund-raising necessary to pay for the events on their busy social calendar. Like Big Tim, Monk Eastman was sometimes less a criminal than a criminal godfather.[41]

Kelly was also godfather to a number of gangs. A group in Brooklyn even called themselves the Five Points Juniors. One of its members was the teenaged Al Capone.[42]

As the tenements of the Lower East Side filled with fresh boatloads of Eastern European and Italian immigrants, the displaced Irish moved northwards, settling along the Hudson from the West Village to the lower Forties and in the Gashouse District along the East River. Hell's Kitchen, also

called the Slaughterhouse, was the Middle West Side between Eighth Avenue
and the Hudson. The area had been a center for Irish gangs since the early
1870s. Here were the famous "Battle Rows," where throughout the 1870s
Irish Catholics and Protestant Orangemen celebrated their animosities in the
time-honored manner, by fighting the bloody Battle of the Boyne on the street
each summer. "Boyne on the Hudson" screamed the headline in Godkin's
New York *Herald*.[43]

Besides the street-gang wars, there were feuds between Irish families
such as the Gallaghers, the Brennans, the Malarkeys and the Mulraneys. The
Battle Rows were found in the 20th Precinct where the police were as overwhelmingly Irish as the gangs. The most famous cop in the Slaughterhouse
Precinct, Patrick H. Diamond, nicknamed "the Iron Claw," carried, beside his
official-issue truncheon, an iron cargo hook. He claimed as a matter of pride
that he had never used his police-issue revolver.[44]

The West Side gangs preyed on local merchants. In particular, they ma-
rauded along the long stretch of railways and freight yards that ran from the
Battery to Seventy-second Street along Eleventh Avenue. Here there were almost nightly battles in the 1880s and 1890s. Police and railway guards might
choose to string themselves out along the entire stretch of track or to concentrate their forces at strategic points. Their deployment would depend on their
intelligence and how they anticipated that the gangs would attack that night.

The most famous West Side gang was the Gophers (pronounced *Goo-
fers* though with no connotation of goofyness). This name, which seems to
have been around since the 1870s, may well have been the invention of the
police or railway guards. It alluded to the custom of the freight yard thieves
to hide themselves in tunnels, cellars, and abandoned boxcars during the daylight hours, waiting for dark to emerge from their holes. For the police and
guards the object of the game was to knock the gopher on the head the second
he emerged from his hole. By the mid-1890s, the New York Central Railway
had grown seriously annoyed by the nightly thefts. It hired a large force of
guards. Some were ex-NYPD patrolmen with experience in the Battle Rows;
others, one imagines, were former Gophers attracted by a regular pay-check
and a pension at the end. "Platoons of railroad police clubbed, sapped and
kicked through Hell's Kitchen for several months. Every time a Gopher's
head popped up on the street he was run down and knocked senseless." In
this way, the gang was decimated, and rail yard theft ceased to be a serious
problem.[45]

In the 1870s, Gophers was the generic term for the Irish gangs in Hell's
Kitchen. By the 1890s, however, the Gophers had also begun to organize
themselves. Their headquarters was the tavern of Mallet Murphy on Thirty-
ninth Street near Tenth Avenue, in the heart of the Battle Rows. Murphy's
nickname derived from his weapon of choice; the wooden mallet he used
to pound the bung into beer barrels also served to pacify his boisterous clientele. By 1900, at their height, there were around five hundred Gophers.
Nevertheless, they remained relatively disorganized; Asbury remarks that the

"Gophers were so turbulent and so fickle in their allegiance that their leaders seldom retained their crowns more than a few months at a time." Despite their inability to produce leaders of the stature of Eastman or Kelly, many of their members did gain renown as fearsome street brawlers — Newburg Gallagher, Marty Brennan, Stumpy Malarky, and Goo Goo Knox.[46] The Gophers also imitated the Eastman and Kelly gangs in sponsoring rackets and other social activities. The formed their own ladies' auxiliary, called the Battle Row Ladies Social and Athletic Club, better known as the Lady Gophers. They also produced one of the era's few female gang leaders, Battle Annie, the queen of Hell's Kitchen, worthy heiress of the street-fighting tradition of Hell-Cat Maggie, Sadie the Goat, and Gallus Mag from the time of Ike Rynders. Battle Annie and her gang of furies later made themselves available for industrial disputes. There was scarcely a strike among the garment workers "that did not find Battle Annie and her gangsters enthusiastically biting and scratching both pickets and strike-breakers."[47]

Further south, in the West Village, began the territory of another Irish gang, the Hudson Dusters, named after their headquarters in a dive on Hudson Street near the pier where Old Smoke Morrissey had nearly been pounded to death by the Plug Uglies a half century earlier. The Hudson Dusters started as a faction of the Gophers led by Goo Goo Knox and friends expelled from Hell's Kitchen as a result of one of the Gophers interminable fracases. They owed their fame to their popularity with reporters, a fact which probably reflected the West Village's own emergence as the favored haunt of artists and writers in these same years. Serious artists and writers had discovered honkytonk culture in the 1890s, and began seeking ways of representing it in their works. Stephan Crane, for example, was arrested in a vice raid in 1896 while prowling the Tenderloin for material for a novel about life in the streets. Eugene O'Neill later numbered Hudson Dusters among his drinking buddies.

The Mid-town Tenderloin was traditionally Gopher territory. They were the bouncers and the muscle here. They were often the bagmen who collected the pay-offs for police officers like Clubber Williams and Big Bill Devery. An Eastman gang attempt to encroach on Gopher territory in the Tenderloin was angrily repulsed at the cost of at least one dead Eastmanite. This meant that, unless they were willing to venture into the impenetrably polyglot world from Mulberry Bend to the East river, the low lives that curious journalists, writers, and ashcan school painters were likely to encounter were prostitutes and showgirls, Irish gangsters, and Jewish gamblers. These are precisely the cast of characters in Damon Runyon's first stories.[48]

After Eastman was sent to Sing Sing in 1904, the most important members of his gang were Richie Fitzpatrick, Kid Twist (Max Zweibach), and Big Jack Zelig. Fitzpatrick and Kid Twist ruled jointly for about a year, until the Kid invited Fitzpatrick to the back room of the gang's Chrystie Street headquarters for a conference. As soon as Fitzpatrick entered the room, the lights went out and a revolver blazed. When the police arrived, Fitzpatrick lay on the floor with a bullet in his heart and his hands neatly folded over his chest. Kid

Twist lasted until the summer of 1908. Spending an evening in Coney Island with a friend called Cyclone Louie and a showgirl named Carroll Terry, Kid Twist ran into a nineteen-year-old Five Pointer named Louis Pioggi, better known as Louie the Lump. As a Five Pointer, Louie the Lump already had reason enough to dislike Kid Twist. The fact that the Kid was presently enjoying the company of Terry, the woman who had recently spurned his love, made the loathing all the more heartfelt. Unfortunately, both Kid Twist and Cyclone Louie were armed. They walked into the bar where Louie the Lump sat forlornly drinking, and when they saw him they mocked and derided him. They finally humiliated him by forcing him to jump out the window. With the advent of modern transport, however, Coney Island was no longer so far away from the Five Points. Controlling his rage, Louie phoned Five Points headquarters. An hour or so later, hearing someone on the outside shout his name, Kid Twist with Cyclone Louie walked out of the saloon and right into a Five Points fusillade. Hearing the shots, Terry rushed to the dying Kid, receiving for her loyalty a bullet in the shoulder. With this, the leadership of the Eastmanites passed to Big Jack Zelig.

Born in 1882 to the name William Alberts in a respectable Jewish family in Norfolk Street on the Lower East Side, Zelig led the remainder of the Eastman gang for approximately three years. It was a turbulent period full of internal feuding. As a result, Zelig spent much of 1911 and early 1912 in and out of the Tombs. It was during one of these periods inside that Zelig was allegedly contacted by Bald Jack Rose, the emissary of Police Lieutenant Charles Becker and asked to supply gunmen for the murder of the gambler Herman Rosenthal.

Kelly barely survived an attack by Razor Riley and Biff Ellison, two drunken gunmen who staggered into the New Brighton Dance Hall and, for motives that have not survived, opened fire on him in early 1905. He eventually recovered, and had sense enough to realize that this was no time to launch a new gang war. Tammany had withdrawn its protection from Monk Eastman the year before; it would not have hesitated to do the same to him were he to seek revenge. Kelly dissolved his association and laid low. Hence we lack the sort of colorful history that Asbury provides us for the later Eastmanites. Despite this, Kelly remained a key figure.

After the New Brighton shoot-out, Kelly's bodyguards transported him to East Harlem where he spent several months recuperating under the care of his friends, Ciro Terranova and the Morello family. Although his name would have meant nothing to newspaper readers in 1905, we shall see that the young Terranova, along with friends and relatives from the Sicilian town of Corleone, were among the founding fathers of the American mafia.

Even if Paul Kelly was no longer in the newspapers, he remained quietly influential. He assumed the role of *gran consigliere* or senior statesmen within the New York Italian underworld, a role he later bequeathed to his protégé, Johnny Torrio. As a respected underworld statesman, Kelly was valuable to Tammany, remaining close to Tom Foley, the Sullivan organization boss in charge of underworld connections. In 1910, Kelly opened the New Englander Social and Dramatic Club on the West Side just north of Hell's Kitchen. It was the headquarters for the remainder of his old gang, as well as a rendezvous for Italian underworld figures: "Detectives often raided Kelly's resort at the behest of the district attorney and the few honest officials of the police department, but never found evidence sufficient to warrant closing of place. Kelly, indeed, was of great aid to the raiding officers; he appeared always to know when a visit was in prospect, and met the detective at the front door or on the sidewalk, and ceremoniously conducted them through the establishment, but they never found anything more immoral than a dozen of his henchmen playing checkers or dominoes." In the 1920s, Kelly and Terranova expanded into trade unionism. Kelly first organized the Harlem ragpickers; later he became the leader of the powerful ILA, the International Longshoremen's Association, part of the AFL until it was thrown out for racketeering in 1953.[49]

Among the gangs that made up Kelly's Five Pointers was the James Street Gang led by Johnny Torrio. Born in Apulia in 1882 in Orsara di Puglia, Torrio had arrived in New York at the age of two. By the age of nineteen, under the name of J.T. McCarthy ('J.T.' would remain the nickname used by his underworld friends) Torrio was managing boxers. His fighters fought in what were billed as amateur exhibitions. Since the sport was illegal and unsupervised, fights were easy to fix. As a manager, Torrio earned money betting on fights whose outcomes he had already scripted. In 1904, Torrio invested his winnings in a saloon at James and Water streets, near the blind pig, owned by his step-father Salvatore Caputo. He also leased a near-by rooming-house, converting it into a brothel and a store which he turned into a pool hall. The back room served as headquarters for the James Street Association, the formal name of his gang.[50]

Torrio met Kelly around this time through Jack Sirocco, another saloon-keeper and an underworld power connected to both Kelly and Eastman, who owned a dive called the Pearl House. Torrio idolized Kelly and took him for a mentor. He was soon imitating Kelly's polished manners and conservative taste in clothes. For his part, Kelly took a shine to the young gangleader, so intelligent, capable, and quick to learn. The two of them would spend quiet evenings in the backroom of the New Brighton Dance Hall listening to Kelly's collection of Italian lyric opera recordings. When Tammany asked Kelly for help in the crucial 1905 mayoral election, Kelly turned to Torrio and his James Street gangsters. After Kelly left for East Harlem, Torrio remained behind briefly with Sirocco.[51] In 1908, on Kelly's advice, he sold his James Street resort, and, in search of a more tolerant atmosphere, crossed the bridge into Brooklyn.[52]

THE FOUR HORSEMEN

Like many Italian immigrants encumbered with the name of *Salvatore*, the young Salvatore Lucania, found himself tagged with the nickname *Sal* in

America. It was a name that he always hated— too much like *Sally* he thought. He didn't like his school either. The Lucania family had arrived on the Lower East Side in 1906 and enrolled the nine-year-old Salvatore in the local public school. But the teacher had forced him to sit in the back row of first grade until he could respond in proper English. He soon convinced himself that there was nothing that the "old broads" could teach him that he couldn't learn faster and better on the streets. There, he observed, "some people had money and some people didn't." If you wanted money yourself, you had to be where the change was. He ran errands, carrying packages from the neighboring ice-cream parlor and grocery store. He kept his eyes open; anything lying around loose and unguarded found its way into his pockets. He was everywhere, except in school where he was supposed to be. In 1911 the board of education sent him away for four months to truancy school in Brooklyn, an experience that resulted in a life-long aversion to Brooklyn.

Sal Lucania never returned to school after his release. Ignoring the pleas of his parents, he went back onto the streets, doing odd jobs for small change and pilfering whenever the opportunity presented itself. By now a small gang had formed around him, and Lucania discovered himself to be a natural organizer. He had been wrong, he decided; the old broads at elementary school had taught him something after all. They had told him about trade unions. Women on the Lower East Side worked in the rag trade. "Some of the mothers of guys I knew used to work on them sewing machines, and if they got up to get a glass of water or open their mouths to breath some air, some bastard foreman would fire 'em just like that." The elementary school teachers looked at Samuel Gompers, the leader of the fledgling International Ladies' Garment Workers Union, as a hero, and some of their enthusiasm rubbed off on Sal Lucania. It was the beginning, he later cheerfully remarked, of his life-long interest in trade unionism. What, he wondered later in life, would all those old broads have thought if they could have seen him as Lucky Luciano, managing unions with Lepke Buchalter and Gaetano "Tommy Brown" Lucchese.[53]

The garment workers' struggles taught young Sal the value of organization and discipline; it also taught him the wisdom of maintaining a centralized fund. These were lessons that Lucania applied to the gang of Sicilians that clustered about him. Lucania forced them to pool their resources, placing the proceeds of all their operations into a common fund, which he placed in a metal box that was carefully buried in a vacant lot.

Lucania's decision to organize his gang of Sicilian adolescents around trade union principles indicates a cerebral streak in his character. If he quit school in fifth grade, it was not because he lacked curiosity. He had decided that he was not learning what he wanted to learn. Elementary school, he thought, was preparing him for a life as a "crumb," a working stiff, a nine-to-fiver, a blinkered nobody who, sticking to the rules, would work like a dog for life and still end up with the short end of the stick. The future Lucky Luciano nominated himself into the party of people destined to be somebodies rather than crumbs.

Lucania saw a world divided into winners and losers, where the winners were a minority who didn't always play by the rules. Winners made their own rules. Lucania decided to make himself a winner too, so he set out to recast himself according to his own rules. This meant, in the first place, dressing the part. He had to be careful about this. The members of his gang were young Sicilians who still lived with their parents. Some of them were still in school. Showing up in new clothes was bound to arouse suspicion. Lucania decreed that the new clothes that the common fund allowed them to buy were only to be worn on the job. Being a winner also meant being well-spoken. Lucania was embarrassed by his bad English; he was to remain self-conscious about his speech for the rest of his life. Though self-deprecation was hardly a part of his character, when he dictated his memoirs in the 1960s, he apologized more than once about the thick, Lower East Side accent he continued to speak.

Above all, being a winner meant being an American. Americans were rich; they moved with ease and confidence. They feared no one. They walked as if they owned the city streets. Sicilian immigrants seemed servile by contrast. They had learned to bow their heads, fearful of anyone in power; they had learned to submit meekly and keep their mouths shut. The Sicilian immigrants were natural recruits to the class of crumbs that Lucania so despised. His decision to be a winner meant turning his back on his parents and the other Sicilian immigrants in Mulberry Bend and learning how to be an American.

By the time he was a teenager, Lucania had begun to explore the city, attracted by the bright lights of Broadway and the bustle of Times Square. "It was a Saturday night," he later reminisced, "and some of my guys and me went uptown to see what the action was. We liked to go to the movies because them silent pictures had titles and they helped us learn English." The little note of conscious self-improvement is very typical:

> Of course, we always sat in the balcony; it was cheaper and besides we could throw stuff down on the people in the orchestra and raise all kinds of hell. This particular night the manager threw us out, and at the same time he threw out some other guys who was sitting on the other side of the balcony. One of these guys was a little bit older than us and had an outfit called the 104th Street Gang. We got together and it turned out that this guy was not from Sicily; he was a Calabrian from Cosenza. His name was Francesco Castiglia; later on, though, he got famous under the name of Frank Costello.[54]

The young Costello was everything that the sixteen-year-old Sal Lucania admired. He was smart, and tough enough to have his own outfit. He knew how to get along. He was, to use the term Lucania so often used to indicate his approval, 'smooth.'

Castiglia in 1891 was born in Lauropoli in Calabria, the second son of Luigi Castiglia and Maria Saveria Aliose. His father, Luigi Castiglia, had emigrated to America in 1895, bringing his two daughters and Frank's older brother, Eddie, along with him. Six months later Luigi Castiglia sent for his wife and little Francesco. They arrived in 1896, and the re-united Castiglia family settled in East Harlem.

Young Frank did not stay in school long, dropping out to hang around the streets and get into trouble. He was arrested in 1908 and 1912 on charges of assault and robbery. By now he had a reputation as a local hoodlum. When he was picked up for carrying a gun in 1915, the judge, commenting that he "had the reputation of a gunman," sent him to prison for ten months on Welfare Island.[55]

Frank grew up in East Harlem with Willie Moretti. It was the beginning of a life-long friendship, one that lasted into the 1950s when Frank was the "prime minister," the *de facto* boss of bosses of the mafia Commission, on which Willie Moretti, the boss of Bergen County in New Jersey, sat as well. Young Frank was also friends with a certain Dudley Geigerman. Geigerman had a sister named Loretta, though everyone called her Bobbie. Shortly before his 1915 arrest, Frank married Bobbie. When he married in 1915, he gave his name as Costello not Castiglia. The marriage was a success, and for the next half-century people talked about Frank and Bobbie Costello. The names Francesco Castiglia and Loretta Geigerman were long forgotten.

We know comparatively little of Costello's early life. Luciano said that when they met at the movie theatre, Costello was twenty-four. Assuming that Costello was born in 1891, this would place the meeting in 1914 or 1915. By then, Costello had been arrested twice for robbery. He had left East Harlem, and had made friends with the Gopher leader, Owney Madden.

It was exceptional for a gang leader that Madden was neither Irish nor Jewish nor Italian. He was a Yorkshireman, though one who had spent much of his childhood in Liverpool. Then as now, Liverpool was home to one of the largest Irish populations in the British Isles. It was enough to establish Madden's Irish credentials with the Gophers; he was a Liverpool Mick. Tough and ruthless, though also clear-headed and intelligent, Madden was by far the most effective leader the Gophers ever knew. He organized the gang and did his best to curb its taste for mindless brawling. It probably helped when two of the Gophers leading hell-raisers—Marty Brennan and Newburgh Gallagher—were killed by the police during the 1911 crackdown in the Slaughterhouse District. Madden had married Dorothey "Loretta" Rogers that year. She was pregnant, about to produce a baby girl. The marriage, which lasted two years, had two consequences for Madden. First, it allowed Owney to absent himself during the troubles between the Gophers and the police. Other Gophers besides Brennan and Gallagher were killed in the affrays and many more were injured. There were scores of arrests. Madden did well to stay out of it. As Gopher leader, he risked at the very least arrest and a severe beating from the boys in the 20th Precinct.

The second consequence of marriage was less pleasant for Madden. Owney had married Loretta Rogers after leaving an earlier love, a girl named Freda Horn. After Madden abandoned her, Horn took up with one of Madden's enemies, a gangster named Paddy Doyle. When Paddy Doyle was murdered in 1912, Freda Horn told the police that Owney had done it. Madden always claimed that Freda Horn was acting out of spite. To the end of his days, he denied any involvement in the Doyle murder. Nevertheless, when he was convicted and sent to Sing Sing, he was philosophical enough to admit that the conviction on a bad rap probably compensated for all the other murders he had gotten away with.[57]

Madden and Costello were about the same age. They got on well together. Though both possessed a violent streak, neither was a simple brawler. They were intelligent, both looking for a chance to make some money. Katz mentions that Madden got Costello a job providing muscle for the stevedores' union on the Hudson Piers. This must have been before Madden's own trouble with the law in 1912. This was also the time, we shall see, that Kelly and Morellos were organizing laborers on the East Side docks. One wonders if Costello was not Kelly's emissary on the Hudson piers. Costello made friends easily, and soon established a network of cordial relations with the Irish underworld that would stand him in good stead during Prohibition.

Madden also introduced to him a young package thief named James Nolan, who would become better known as Legs Diamond. Joe Valachi remembered that, during the 1920s, the Diamond brothers often could be found at the Venezia Restaurant, a gangland hangout next to Ciro Terranova's house on East 116th Street—another link between the East Harlem mafia and the West Side Gophers.[57] Madden also introduced Costello to his Tammany connection, the district boss Jimmy Hines and his lawyer and speech-writer, Joe Shellack. Another of Owney's close friend was the actor George Raft. Raft became a close friend of Costello's as well, and went on to a successful career in the movies. Here he always played gangsters, and whatever gangster he was playing was modelled on his friends Owney Madden and Frank Costello.[58] Costello also met his future bootlegging connection, Bill Dwyer. It seems natural to assume that the metamorphosis of his name took place in these years as well. As soon as he became an honorary Gopher, Francesco Castiglia was reborn as Frank Costello.

For young Jewish boys, the worst bullies on the Lower East Side were the Irish gangs. They wandered through the immigrant quarters like marauders, stealing, tormenting passers-by and vandalizing property. Their favorite victims were the Jews:

> The Irish were our worst enemies. They hated Jews. They used to yell "Christ killers" at us. The cops were mainly Irish, and whenever there was a fight between Irish and Italians, or an incident involving Irish with Jews, the cops would always take the side of the Irish, even if they were known hoodlums. The Italians were Catholics too, but on the East Side the Irish considered them inferior.

> The Irish used to come into our area and jostle and stop the old men, pull their beards, and scream insults at them. Whole gangs of these Irish boys and young men used to come into our streets and stop boys like me and make them take down their trousers to see if they were circumcised. The Irish policemen used to laugh when Jewish shopkeepers complained about being

robbed by Irish boys. The Irish would walk into their shops and take what
they wanted without paying for anything.[59]

Meyer Suchowljansky was born in the Tsarist Polish town of Grodno in
1902. His grandfather, Benjamin Suchowljansky was a prosperous and well-
respected merchant. The town of Grodno was predominantly Jewish and a
center of rabbinical studies. It also became a center of Jewish resistance to
tsarist persecution, which increased dramatically throughout the 1880s. In
1911, the family patriarch Benjamin decided to retire, giving his goods to the
poor and sailing to Palestine, where he died shortly after disembarking. His
son, Max, together with his wife and two sons, decided to seek their fortunes
in American instead. Americanizing their name to Lansky, the family lived
for several years in the Brownsville district of Brooklyn, moving to the Lower
East Side in 1916.

In contrast to Frank Costello and Sal Lucania, Meyer Lansky loved
school, where he was an excellent student. He learned the Gettysburg Address
by heart, and, writing his projected memoirs in the 1970s, recorded as one of
his proudest accomplishments that he could still recite the entire *Merchant of
Venice* from memory.

Meyer also excelled at math, and, he later speculated, it may have been
this fascination for numbers that first awakened a passion for gambling that
had always lain dormant within him. He would stop and watch the street-
corner crap games along Delancy Street, experiencing a curious tingling sen-
sation in the pit of his stomach when he watched the little heaps of nickels,
dimes, and quarters wax and wane as players pushed them back and forth
across the sidewalk. He found himself mentally calculating the odds. It all
looked so easy, and little Meyer was itching to play.

It was Meyer's job in the Lansky family to take the *cholent* to and from
the neighborhood bakery. A sort of Kosher cassolet, a *cholent* is a mixture of
beans, beef, vegetables, and barley. The dish would first be assembled and
pre-cooked on Wednesday or Thursday; then, as work in the ghetto stopped
on Friday, the *cholent* would be borne to the baker's hot oven to simmer there
overnight so as to be hot and savory for the Sabbath midday meal.

Meyer's mother sent him out every Friday afternoon to take the *cholent*,
providing him with five cents for the baker. One Friday, stopping to watch
the crap game with the *cholent* in his hands, the temptation became too great.
Meyer handed over his nickel to the crap banker fully confidant that he was
about to win. Instead, he lost. "Nobody in the game paid any attention to me,
and I stumbled away. For a long time I didn't go home. I just couldn't face my
mother. I wandered around those streets carrying the *cholent* in total despair.
I felt worse that a criminal. I had let the family down."

"To tell the truth," he later admitted, "I was genuinely concerned at the
way I had upset my family. But what troubled me more than anything else was
the fact that I had lost that money." He had been taken for a sucker; that was
what really galled.

He returned to observe the game more closely, noticing things that he hadn't seen before. The men crowding around the crap shooters and faro dealers were idlers mostly, passers-by drawn in by the commotion. They stood there with their hands in their pockets like cautious animals sniffing at a baited trap, curious, but at the same time hesitant and suspicious. There was always one among them, however, who seemed to have no trepidations whatsoever. This man strode forward, and, as the other men stared, he boldly placed his bet upon the sidewalk. Usually he won, and there would be a gasp when his winning number or card came up, and the crowd pushed forward to see the banker hand him a pile of coins. As play continued, and as the first gambler continued to win, others were slowly lured in, overcome by excitement and greed. Reaching into their pockets, they fished out a single nickel or dime, cautiously placing them one by one upon the sidewalk. Sometimes they won, at least at first. In the heat of the game, however, when they no longer counted their bets, they always lost. Few if any of the suckers drawn into the game left it a winner.

After several weeks of observation, Meyer was convinced that he had understood the whole set up. The initial winner, the man whose confidence had emboldened the others, was the shill, the banker's partner. His job was to draw the suckers in. If some of these suckers won on their first few rolls, it was because the banker was letting them. The banker's skill lay in judging just how much bait to feed a sucker before reeling him in. The game was fixed, and the suckers never stood a chance.

Lansky observed something else as well;

> Slowly I began to notice that the men who actually ran the dice games and the street gambling with cards were only the pawns. Other men, well-dressed and looking much more prosperous, used to come and watch from time to time. I could see secret signs pass back and forth between the rich bosses and the men running the game. I used to follow them, making sure that they didn't notice me. I would see the banker pull out of his pockets all the money he had won from the suckers, as they called the gamblers, and hand it over to the man with the good suit and the nice clean shoes.

> Once down an alley I saw the man who collected the money hit the banker across the face and scream at him, "So you want to cheat us! Next time you'll get a bullet in the head." Two men with him pulled out knives and slashed the gambler across the face. As he fell to the ground pleading for his life, with the blood streaming all over his clothes, the one with the silk suit stepped back a shouted at him, "You pig! Your blood has stained my trousers." Then he kicked the bleeding man hard in the ribs and in the genitals. As the man on the ground coughed up blood, the silk-suited man and his two assistants laughed and walked away as if nothing in the world had happened. I was too frightened to come out from behind the garbage can where I was hiding until they had gone.

Meyer was itching to try again. He arrived the next Friday with the *cholent* in his hands and his mother's nickel in his pocket. He watched, staying carefully on the outskirts of the group, until he was sure that he had identified the shill. He watched where he placed his bet. "I waited for the second just before the banker threw the dice, and then suddenly bent down and placed my five-cent bet. I saw the banker give me a black look, but of course five cents wasn't very much and he didn't try to stop me. The suckers would have smelled a rat if the dice thrower had said something to me. My timing was perfect, but my hands were trembling so much that I thought that I was going to drop the *cholent* dish. But I won. I knew I would."

Lansky reflected on the experience:

> It's the fools who rush in unprepared, who try to get rich because they're greedy—they are life's suckers. . . . I gamble only when I know I can win, when the odds are stacked in my favor. And that's the only way you can win. There is no such thing as a lucky gambler; there are just the winners and the losers. The winners are those who control the game, the professionals who know what they're doing. All the rest are suckers.[60]

Crumbs or suckers, the twelve-year-old Meyer Lansky had recruited himself to become a member of the class of winners, of the people who stacked the odds, who made their own rules.

The victory, he later said, was a cautionary tale; it had taught him "a great lesson." Frank Costello was also learning his own great lesson. When he met him, Sal Lucania was impressed that Costello carried a gun. This, it turned out, was not as smart as Lucania may have thought. It was only a few months after their meeting that Costello was sent to Welfare Island for breaking the Sullivan Law prohibiting concealed weapons. It was his first and last time in prison. As soon as Costello got out, he put the hoodlum look in moth balls, exchanging it for the costume of a dapper man about town.

Lucania's turn to learn a great lesson came the following year. He had gotten a job as a runner for Goodman's Hat Company on West Twenty-fourth Street. His pay was six dollars a week. This was a dollar over the going rate, but Mr. Goodman saw Sal as bright and eager to please. He was also quick and ambitious, though just how ambitious Mr. Goodman was soon to learn. For some time Lucania had been watching George Scanlon move through the neighborhood:

"You couldn't miss Scanlon; he drove a big limousine and parked it wherever he wanted to—next to fire hydrants, even on the sidewalk—and nobody bothered him. He wore sharp clothes with wide stripes and he had a diamond ring on his pinky finger. He smelled like the United States mint."

Scanlon could behave like this because he was a drug pusher who paid off the local police. One day, when he noticed Scanlon's limousine was parked in front of his tenement, Sal rushed and got a rag and began polishing up the headlamps. When Scanlon came out, he stopped and watched the kid for a few minutes, then shouted, "here kid" and tossed him a quarter.

Sal caught the quarter and tossed it back. "Can I talk to you for a minute?" he asked.

He told Scanlon that he wanted to work for him. He explained that he went around delivering hats, and that the drugs could be easily concealed in the hatband.

With this, Sal was suddenly making good money. He could make in a week what he would have needed months to earn with Mr. Goodman. But the money was too easy; he was spotted by someone aware of his new earnings and jealous. The police tailed him as he went to a poolroom on East Fourteenth Street, a noted hangout for addicts and pushers. When he came out, he was stopped and searched and, in the hatband of one of the hats, a phial containing a half-dram of heroin was discovered. Lucania was sentenced to a year's imprisonment in the Special Session Court in 1916. He was nineteen years old. The prison was called Hampton Farms and he hated it. "I seen a movie," he later recalled, "called *Oliver Twist*. It was written by some English guy by the name of Charles Dickens, and the young kid in the picture used to remind me of myself, because they used to knock this little bastard around in the picture the way they did to me at Hampton Farms."[61]

He was out on parole after six months, and would not be convicted of another crime until he was almost forty and the most powerful gangster in America. The only other effect of his stay was to change his name. Instead of Salvatore Lucania, he now called himself Charlie Lucania.

Usually it was the Irish gangs that tormented the Jews, but sometimes the Sicilians joined in. Charlie Lucania later said that he admired his Jewish classmates because they were smart and did well in school. But this did not stop him from preying on them. He and his gang sold the Jews protection from the Irish. One day, Lucania tried to sell protection to Lansky. The meeting between Lansky and Lucania is part of gangland lore. It was a story that both Charlie and Meyer loved to tell. One cold January morning, shortly after the Lansky family had moved to the Lower East Side, Meyer found himself walking the streets alone. Suddenly, he was surrounded by a gang of young Sicilians. "If you want to stay alive, Jew boy," one of them said, "you've got to pay us five cents a week protection money."

Lansky, who never stood higher than five feet three inches—"seriously small" as one of his friends later put it—must have seemed an easy mark. The leader of the Sicilians, Charlie Lucania, was sure that the boy was so frightened that he was wetting his pants. Instead, the boy simply stared back at him and said, "Go fuck yourself."

The various gangland versions elaborate this initial encounter by inventing an exchange of rich and colorful invective that passed between the two future crime leaders. In some versions Lansky is even provided with another *cholent* dish, with which, at a certain point, he clobbers Charlie Lucania. The way that Lucania told it, however, is much simpler and probably much closer to the truth.

He stood there, just a little punk. I was five years or so older than him and could have smashed him to pieces in a few seconds. But he just stood there staring me straight in the face, just defying me and telling me to stick my protection up my ass. He was ready to fight. His fists were clenched at his sides. There were seven of us and any one could have given him the hiding of his life. In fact, one of my gang stepped forward to grab him and teach him a lesson he wouldn't forget.

For some reason I took a liking to the kid. He was very gutsy standing there and telling me to go fuck myself. Instead of being angry I wanted to laugh, but I didn't want to show my feelings because this would mean losing face in front of my gang. I told the boy that was going to beat him, "Forget it." Then I stood looking at this young Jew boy and I said to him, "We'll come back when the milk from your mother's tits has dried on your face."

There had been a kind of "instant understanding" between them, "it was something that never left us." It was a feeling that intrigued and almost troubled the cerebral Charlie Lucania:

In the later days, when I would think something, he would have the same thought at the same time. You know how it is with women sometimes, but of course we were men. The feeling was still the same though, it was as though we were twins and our minds were connected in some way. It may sound crazy, but if anyone wants to use the expression "blood brothers," then surely Meyer and I were like that, even though we had come from totally different backgrounds.[62]

By the time Charlie Lucania met him, Lansky had teamed up with Benny Siegel, whose parents had made the long journey from Kiev in the Ukraine to Delancy Street on the Lower East Side. Handsome and wild, Siegel was a *chaye*, an animal. Absolutely fearless, Siegel would charge into gang fights for the sheer excitement of it, a habit that troubled both Lansky and Lucania. Lansky remembered first seeing the adolescent Siegel rush in to pick up a revolver dropped by a gangster during a shoot-out on Delancy Street. As Lansky told it, Siegel stood there on the street, in plain view, with the gun in his outstretched hand, as if he was searching for the right person to shoot with his wonderful new toy. When he heard the sirens of an approaching police car, even the cautious Lansky jumped out of his hiding place to grab Siegel and yell, "You're crazy! Drop that gun and run!" A minute or two later, when the pair came to a panting halt after threading through the pushcarts, Siegel turned on Lansky; "Why didn't you let me kill that bastard. I needed that gun," he said. "Only an idiot, a *schlimazel,* would use a gun with the cops in sight," Lansky told him.[63]

Lucania's gang gave Lansky free protection against the Irish, and the two had become friends. When Charlie was released from Hampton Farms at the end of 1916, he was just short of twenty. Lansky, then working in a tool and die shop, was not yet fifteen. Lucania introduced Lansky to Costello, about twenty-four and, having recently been released from Welfare Island on a weapons charge, no longer carried a gun. Lansky brought along Benny Siegel, who, though four years' younger even than Lansky, charmed the two Italians.

"Everybody loved Benny," Charlie remembered. The youngest member of the group, Siegel was the only one who insisted on carrying a gun. Lucania decided that his two Jewish friends had all the qualities he admired. They were tough, smart and smooth; they had moxie, and they never lost their nerve. He proposed a partnership, a new experiment in Charlie's developing theory of organization and management. Understanding by now the inconveniences of tin boxes buried in vacant lots, Charlie even suggested that the four partners open up their own bank account.

Lucania picked a bank where Lansky's uncle knew one of the big shots. He sent Costello in to discuss the opening of an account. But while Frank was there "he couldn't help but kinda case the joint a little bit, and he sees that they only got one guard, an old guy that musta been about a hundred and four." Instead of opening an account, they decided to clean the whole place out. It was no more than they deserved, Meyer thought, "If that's the way they're goin' to protect our dough, the hell with 'em."[64]

This hadn't really solved the problem of what to with their war chest. The four of them were knocking off every thing they came across. One solution was to invest. Prospective gamblers usually bought into an already established game, paying either for a piece of the action or for permission to open up their own game in a specific territory. After licensing fees came the street tax. Gamblers had to kick back a certain percentage of their taking to the underworld group that controlled the area. Finally, gamblers had to "grease" the law. The foursome invested in a piece of one established book, and even bought shares in some smaller mid-town books.

Frank Costello looked after official arrangements. Affable and gregarious, he made friends with the police officials and magistrates he was greasing. "He had the style and the class of a guy twice his age," Charlie remembered, "and with that Irish-Italian name we hung on him, he was able to move in all circles. That's when we set up a private bank. Not a real bank. We called it our Buy-Money Bank." Starting out with a fund of five thousand dollars, Costello began judiciously spreading it around, handing it out to the police and politicians in the areas they were making book.

Costello was a born entrepreneur, a natural salesman with a feeling for what the market wanted. At the time, this happened to be novelties and gimmicks, especially anything connected with gambling. In 1919 he teamed up with Harry Horowitz to form Horowitz's Novelty Company. They made the punch boards used in penny-ante amusement arcade games and the kewpie dolls these games gave out as prizes. The company was successful, though perhaps not successful enough. Costello and Horowitz staged a fraudulent bankruptcy, lending large sums to their friends and then declaring themselves bankrupt when their friends defaulted on their debts. At the hearing, the judge wanted to know why they couldn't recover anything. Who were these debtors? "They're all East Side gangsters, your honor," Horowitz and Costello explained.[65]

There only remained one small difficulty for Lucania. What was he going to call his new partnership? The only name they could think of was the *Four Horsemen*, after the famous backs on the Notre Dame football team. "We were like the Four Horseman of Notre Dame," Charlie recalled, though he remembered wondering at the time, "What would two Jewish guys be doing at Notre Dame?" Still, what else were they going to call themselves, he thought, 'Two Jews, one Wop and a Mick?' Costello wasn't even a real Mick, though the Irishness of his name came in handy.[66]

By the time that Charlie Luciano, Meyer Lansky and Frank Costello gave interviews about their careers they were in retirement (semi-retirement in the case of Costello). They were obviously reticent about some events. There is no statute of limitations for murder, and so they were reluctant to say much about their personal involvement in specific acts of violence. Not wishing to incriminate their colleagues, they kept quiet about the current state of organized crime in America. For his part, Luciano continued to deny that he had ever had any dealings in drugs.

Yet about their early days and Prohibition, they were more open. The danger in their reminiscences is less reticence or deliberate prevarication then the usual misstatements when elderly men recall the glorious days of their youth. Stories are liable to become burnished in the retelling. Vain and socially insecure, Luciano in particular was inclined to boast and make up stories of his friendships with the rich and famous. He wanted to impress the journalists who were interviewing him. In Naples where he lived after his deportation, he told people that he had been a lieutenant in the U.S. Navy (keeping quiet about his real services to the Navy, described below). He liked to sit in his restaurant near the port and give autographed copies of his menu to American sailors. He was especially pleased when an officer asked him for one.

Though generous enough to admit that Lansky and Costello were sometimes the brains of his young gang, there was never any question in his mind who was the boss. Even the teen-aged Sal Lucania was the future *Capo di Tutti i Capi,* and, in his reminiscences, Charlie made sure that he represented himself in this way. The truth, however, is that, though the Four Horsemen remained friends and frequent collaborators, they often worked independently of each other. Lansky soon acquired his own gambling empire. Costello already had his own gambling operation and later a bootlegging empire as well. Luciano invested in Lansky's gambling houses, and in Arnold Rothstein's, but he remained a silent partner.

Charlie had his own concerns as well. According to underworld tradition, the young Luciano was a Five Pointer. Luciano grew up in the heart of Five Pointer territory. Although he never mentions Paul Kelly, who was before his time, he knew Johnnie Torrio, to whom he turned for advice at crucial points in his career. He also knew Al Capone and Frankie Yale. By the time he was released from Hampton Farms in 1916, Kelly's Five Pointers had dissolved into its component parts, though the name remained current on the Lower East Side into the 1920s.

As a young Sicilian, Charlie would at least have felt the influence of the reigning Sicilian boss, Joe Masseria. Charlie disliked Masseria; later he denied that he was ever a soldier in the Masseria organization. Strictly speaking, this is probably true. Were Charlie fully within the Masseria organization, he would not have been permitted to associate with Jews like Lansky and Siegel. Indeed, Masseria and later Salvatore Maranzano both tried to force Charlie to break with his Jewish friends. It was another thing that Charlie had against the traditional mafia. Nevertheless, Charlie and his young friends could never have prospered had they not acknowledged the authority of Masseria and known how to proffer him appropriate respect.

Lansky's reminiscences include another incident that would later become an underworld legend. In the summer of 1916, recalled Meyer, "I'd gone with my friends to the East River to swim. We put our clothes on the bank as usual and dived in. None of us could afford bathing suits in those days. We used to leave one boy on the bank to guard our clothes, because the Irish liked to find our things and throw them into the water. Or they would jump in with us and try to hold our heads under. While I was in the water, I saw the Irish gang leader on the bank. I knew there was going to be trouble. He and his friends took off their clothes and came in after us."

On this particular day, however, there was a group of Italian boys swimming nearby. Some were schoolmates of Lansky's friends. When the Italians saw the Irish wading in, they joined the fight on the side of the Jews. There was splashing followed by kicking and punching until suddenly a scream rang out. The water around the Irish gang leader was turning bright red. Frightened, the boys hurried out of the water, grabbed their clothes and ran off. Later that evening the body of the Irish gang leader was found washed up on the bank.

Lansky remembered Sal Lucania as the Italian who had knifed the Irish gang leader. He had only met him once before, the morning he had stood there defiantly shouting that he could shove his protection up his ass. Who else was there with them? Besides Benny Siegel, Meyer's own circle of close associates soon included Abner "Longie" Zwillman; Lepke Buchalter; Arthur Felgenheimer, later known as Dutch Schultz, Doc Stracher; and many others. Besides knowing Costello, Al Capone, and Frankie Yale, Charlie's circle of associates soon included other Italians like Vito Genovese, Joe Adonis, Willie Moretti, and others. The future *crème de la crème* of American organized crime, almost the entire cast, had now been assembled.

Gangland legend naturally likes to place them all there, swimming in the buff, in the East River on that hot summer day in 1916. It seems a little unlikely. Nevertheless, they were all contemporaries, New York Jews and Italians, all children of immigrants. Many of them knew each other since childhood. They could have all been there. This is the real point. Crime is opportunistic and, like all opportunities, may either come or not come by. As it was, in 1916 the opportunity for the greatest crime spree in American history happened to be just around the corner. It was an opportunity that would take a whole new generation of criminals to exploit, and it would make that generation. They would remain a close-knit generation, one whose roots remained in the immigrant slums of the larger cities. The moral of Lansky's story seems to be that this new generation was on its way.

Chapter Three

Italian Crime in America: Mano Nera, Camorra and Mafia

Prior to World War I, organized crime in New York was synonymous with Tammany. Tammany was the corrupt political machine; Tammany collected graft from the resorts in the honky tonks; Tammany protected gangs like the Five Pointers and Eastmanites on the Lower East Side and the Irish West Siders. Tammany was what organized crime meant to New Yorkers. It was what they read about in the *World* or the *American* or the *Herald* or the *Times* or any of the other major English-language newspapers. Tammany was the major league of New York criminality.

Charlie Lucania and Frank Costello were exceptional; though both Italians, they had broken out of their respective communities and spent their careers in this league. Yet there were other leagues too. Criminality existed in virtually every immigrant community in the city, often in the form of local extortion rings. We know comparatively little about these rings unfortunately, since they formed the minor leagues. So long as their activities remained confined to their own communities, they passed unnoticed by the English-language press and, to a large extent, by the police as well. Evidence for their presence, where such evidence exists at all, is often limited to reports in the little local newspapers written in the immigrants' own language. Italian crime was sometimes a partial exception, for Italian crime might sometimes be extensive enough or violent enough or grisly enough to merit the attention of the English-language press. This is fortunate (at least for us) for it allows us to observe something about the beginnings of organized Italian crime in America. For it was here, with the Italian community, rather than with the story of Lucky Luciano or Frank Costello, that the early history of the American mafia must be sought.

The Hennessy murder was not the case that introduced the idea of the mafia in America. There had been, we saw, earlier mafia cases in New Orleans. There were earlier examples in New York as well. The earliest known reference to the mafia in America is in fact in an article Nelli found in the San Francisco *Examiner* from 1878. It reported on a Sicilian crime ring that had been uncovered in the Bay area. It was called "La Maffia." The *Examiner* characterized it as a "neat little tea party of Sicilian brigands . . . attempting to bulldoze such of their countrymen who would stand their blackmailing tricks." The objective of this "villainous gang" was "the extortion of money from their countrymen by a system of blackmail which includes attacks on character and threats to kill." The center of their operations was Sausolito.[1]

California is literally about as far from Sicily as someone can get without leaving mother earth entirely. If the "neat little tea party of Sicilian brigands" contained men like Giuseppe Esposito, men wanted by the Italian police, they may have picked Sausolito precisely because they wished to put as much distance between themselves and Sicily as they could. But even if this explains the arrival of the mafia on the Barbary Coast, it does not explain the presence of their countrymen, the ones that the mafia was endeavoring to "bulldoze" with their "blackmailing tricks." Their presence is surely explained by something else—a soil and climate ideal for fruit and vines. These are what originally brought Sicilians both to New Orleans and California.

Was it in Sausolito then, rather than in New Orleans, where the mafia started in America? There is no reason to suppose the mafia traveled from Sicily to America on a single ship or arrived at an American port on a specific date and spread out from there. The American mafia did not grow from a single seed. Like the mafia in Sicily, indeed like the Sicilian sectarian tradition in which the mafia itself had its roots, the origins of the American mafia is multiple. The American mafia was probably founded a dozen or more times, and during the first generation witnessed endemic local warfare as start-up mafia groups battled each other, as well as with start-up camorra groups, for supremacy. It was only with the opportunities provided by Prohibition and with the Castellammarrese War at the end of the 1920s that the American mafia was able to consolidate their position and knit themselves together as a national crime syndicate.

The early reports remained vague; the mafia were extortionists. They were violent and were willing to murder anyone who refused to submit. The term *mafia* is never strictly defined. Although there were actual associations with actual members like the *Stoppaglieri*, the mafia remained a generic term. It never denoted an association that someone might join. For Sicilians in both Sicily and America, a *mafiusu* was a swaggering man of honor. The term *la mafia* or sometimes *la maffia* referred rather to swaggering men of honor in general, the, as it were, men-of-honor-element extorting the community.

SCROCCARE

By the nineteenth century in Sicily, extortion was more than endemic; it had become a something of a local custom as well.

The great barons of Sicilian history were noble lords of magnificence and bravado. Powerful and rich, they exercised a virtual life and death power over those below, laying claim to ownership rights over all that the island produced. Yet for all their almost unlimited pride and swagger, the behavior of the barons was circumscribed by custom and by the expectations of others. A true baron, Sicilians believed, showed his noble spirit through acts of liberality and charity. Liberality implied generosity. A true baron richly rewarded all those who loyally served him, showering them with honors, estates, and gold. A true baron also showed hospitality, greeting visitors and preserving places at his table for wayfarers and strangers. A true baron finally showed charity. He forgave the debts of his tenants, presented gifts to his servants, fed the hungry, clothed the naked, and gave rich endowments to the church, enabling it to carry out its mission.

In the sixteenth century, the great barons of Sicilian history lived up to these expectations. They celebrated their births and weddings with shows and spectacles and with feasts in which entire cities were fed. They made rich gifts and benefactions and showered the populace with silver thrown from their balconies or from their passing carriages.[2]

By the nineteenth century, with the island far poorer and the legal basis that had once underlain the barons' power was fast being dismantled, the deeds of the great barons were no more than distant legends. Nevertheless, something of the baronial ethos remained. The rich and powerful were still supposed to be motivated by paternalistic generosity and Christian charity rather than base economic calculation. By now, however, it was sometimes difficult to know where the line between noble generosity, on the one hand, and fear and self interest, on the other, might be drawn.

Conditions were persistently unsettled in Sicily throughout this century, with major uprisings following each other at a twenty years' interval. Nor were the years in between always peaceful, for they were marred by incessant factional struggles and endemic brigandage in the countryside. Wherever normal authority had temporarily broken down, groups of peasants were liable to form. These groups would break into storehouses and lightly guarded or isolated farm buildings, stealing whatever they found therein. Others armed with nothing but agricultural implements would appear at crossroads to try and stop the passing mail coaches, relieving the passengers of their valuables. Urban mobs would form in the *piazza* in front of the *palazzo*, angrily demanding jobs and money. At these times, the normal social order was temporarily overturned, and the rich and powerful were at the mercy of their social inferiors.

Despite this reversal, however, both sides kept up the pretence that nothing had really changed. The landowner who had discovered that 20 per cent of the grain in his stores had disappeared, would simply record the loss in his account books as "hospitalities." The brigands who robbed the mail coaches, stripping the passengers of their valuables, often treated their victims with exaggerated politeness, acting as if the money and goods they were taking were gifts rather than stolen loot. Both sides had an interest in maintaining this pretence. The show of deference tempered the humiliation felt by the upper classes at being victimized by those below. Lessening their humiliation it also lessened the bad blood that resulted, diminishing the chances that the perpetrators would be made to suffer the consequences of their deeds. As long the victims could pretend that an inversion of the social order had never really occurred, it was easier to forgive and forget. The victims would be less likely to pursue their victimizers when, as inevitably would happen, the normal social order came to be restored.

The police in nineteenth-century Sicily had a term for this ambiguous sort of criminality—*scroccaggio*. Normally the verb *scroccare* means "to scrounge," that is to beg or panhandle. In police usage, however, *scroccare* meant beg with menace or threats. Often in Sicily, the threats remained veiled. Increasingly in the Sicilian communities in America, the threat became explicit.

In both Sicily and America, the threats usually arrived as letters (*lettere di scrocco*). Some of the surviving specimens are crude and ungrammatical; others are polite and polished, clearly written by men of some education. Some were left unsigned; the cruder specimens might conclude with an "X" or sketched skull. In Sicily the letters sometimes bore the signatures of brigand leaders, leaving the police to wonder whether the sender was the actual leader or merely some pretender trying to strike terror in his prospective victim. Increasingly, however, extortion letters bore the signatures of vaguely-defined, sinister-sounding groups—the Association or the Committee. Others were more specific, signing themselves *La Società Cammoristica, La Mala Vita, I carbonari* or the *Maffia* or *Mafia*. Though the first to use the term *mafia* in California were its victims rather than the mafiosi themselves, the term had a sinister appeal. Following the Hennessy murder, newspapers wrote stories about a mysterious and clandestine order of Sicilian cutthroats known as the mafia. It was an opportunity too good to miss. Hoping to enhance on the persuasive power of their missive, extortionists made their threats in the name of *La Mafia*.

Calling the payments demanded by the authors of the *lettere di scrocco* gifts seems a contradiction in terms. Gifts are gestures of good will and, by definition, voluntary. If the gift is coerced, it is no longer really a gift. The contradiction in this case, however, was a deliberate one. By treating extortion as if it were a gift-giving relation, the extortionist obscured the criminal nature of the transaction. Nor was this the only ambiguity. By the 1870s armed brigand bands were infesting the mountains of Central Sicily's interior. The bands sent landowners *lettere di scrocco* demanding money and goods. Forced to comply, landowners instructed their custodians to open their storehouses when the bands appeared. They also allowed the brigands to graze and pasture their animals on the landowners' properties. Some of these animals, however, had been stolen, and were destined for resale on the black market. In the meantime, they were cared for on the landowners' property.

What did the landowners get in exchange for their hospitality and the care of the brigands' stolen animals? Nothing, these landowners invariably proclaimed. They had no choice; the brigands compelled them to open their storehouses and maintain these animals. They were acting under duress. The police were not so sure. The landowners would hardly be expected to admit to anything else, for anything else would imply that they were somehow beneficiaries in the transaction and therefore guilty of a serious felony. Still, an ambiguity persisted.

In principle, extortion is involuntary. The extortionist threatens his victim, telling him that if he fails to accede to the extortionist's demands, he will suffer the consequences. Protection, by contrast, is a longer term relationship, and it is this that opens up a possibility for reciprocal benefits. Even if the protected party may enter the arrangements unwillingly, simply as a victim, nothing prevents the relation between the protectors and their victims from developing into something beneficial to both parties. The police in Sicily were well aware of this possibility and frequently alleged that the relation between landowners and brigands went well beyond simple victimization. The landowners and the brigands had rather become partners in crime. In specific cases, the police were able to demonstrate that, in partnership with brigands, landowners had formed animal-theft rings or, on other occasions, used the brigands to terrorize or intimidate their enemies. Yet it was usually not possible to draw a firm line separating victimization from complicity. By treating all cases of protection in Sicily as *prima facie* cases of complicity moreover, the Italian government managed to alienate landowners, thus making them less willing to cooperate with the police. In this way, ambiguity set off a vicious circle that worked to the benefit of crime.

THE MANO NERA

By 1900, extortion was plaguing Italian communities everywhere in America. Extortion had become endemic. Charles Bacigalupo, the "Mayor of Mulberry Bend," the Lower East Side's Italian community spoke of the problem in an interview with the New York *Herald* in 1902. whatever they called themselves, these extortionists were "bad people to work with, and are, I believe, working in all cities in this country where there are Italian colonies." In New York, he reported, "a great many doctors, bankers and others have received blackmailing letters in the last few months."[3]

Giovanni Branchi, the Italian consul general in New York City from 1895 to 1905, later gave an interview with the London *Times*. The Italian population in the New York area, he reported, was by then between two hundred fifty thousand and three hundred thousand. On entire blocks, only Italian was spoken. This area was virtually unpoliced, "with the exception of the regular Irish policeman at the corner, who did not care a rap what the Italians did among themselves so long as they did not interfere with other people and so long as they voted the regular [Tammany] ticket." There were, he continued, only two or three Italian speakers among the New York police anyway. The result was that in the Italian areas, most crime went unreported and unpunished.[4]

In 1903, however, a change took place; extortionists ceased delivering their threats in the name of the mafia or camorra. A new association seems suddenly to have appeared. Letters were now written in the name of the *Mano Nera* or "Black Hand."[5] Over the next fifteen years an epidemic of Black Hand threats spread to Italian communities throughout the country. Writing in 1913, the Chicago *Daily News* reported:

> In the first ninety-three days of this year, 55 bombs were detonated in the spaghetti zone. Not one of the 55, as far as can be determined, was set for any reason other than the extraction of blackmail. A detective of experience in the Italian quarter, estimates that ten pay tribute to one who is sturdy enough to resist until he is warned by a bomb. Freely conceding that this is all guess work, then 550 men will have paid the Mano Nera since January 1. The Dirty Mitt never asks for less then $1,000. If a compromise of $200 was reached in each of the 550 cases, "Black Handers" profited $110,000 in 93 days. . . . Well informed Italians have never put the year's tribute of the "Black Hand" at less than half a million dollars."[6]

Newspapers, we see, quickly adapted themselves to the change. Extortion in the Italian districts was called the Black Hand (*Dirty Mitt* being a Chicago-ism), and extortionists were generically "Black Handers."

The figures for New York were similar. In a 1909 article concerning Commissioner Bingham's report on New York crime statistics, *Cosmopolitan* reported that the police estimated that for every extortion attempt reported to the police there were 250 that went unreported.[7] There is no indication how the police arrived at this figure, which is possibly an exaggeration. It is also true that many, perhaps the majority, of these letters were simply dismissed by their recipients. Nevertheless, 424 Black Hand threats were reported in 1908 alone. Even if the true figure was only several times the reported figure, the Black Hand was clearly menacing the entire New York Italian community.

What was this Black Hand anyway? Both John S. Kendall and David Chandler claim that the Black Hand started as a Spanish secret society called *La Mano Negra*. This was also the opinion of the journalist Lindsay Denison, who wrote in 1908 that the Mano Negra was "a secret society which fought the government and the church" during the Spanish Inquisition.

Many scholars have doubted that any such sect ever existed. Nevertheless, nineteenth-century Spanish history is filled with sects and conspiracies. There is nothing inherently unlikely about the idea that a secret society called *La Mano Negra* existed. The real question is not whether such a society existed, but whether and in what sense the innumerable Black Hand gangs operating in America were ever part of it. That seems more unlikely. There is nothing sophisticated about extortion. It is one of the most primitive types of criminality imaginable, not one that presupposes arcane knowledge or complex tools. It is certainly not necessary to join a mysterious sect in order to practice it. There is nothing, however, to prevent a would-be extortionist from pretending that he is a member of such a powerful and mysterious sect, one that is all-seeing and employs fearsome tools and techniques of persuasion. The extortionist might understandably believe that presenting his extortionate demands in the name of such a sect would enhance his claim and maybe terrorize his intended victim into submission. In this sense, the fact that Italians all over America were receiving *lettere di scrocco* in the name of *La Mano Nera* neither proves nor disproves that such a society ever existed. It simply shows that rumors of some sort of Black Hand society were circulating at the time.

It often turned out that the writers of threatening and extortionate letters were vagrants and petty criminals. Some letters reflected class animosity. Workers in the mines in the Mahoning Valley, stretching from Western Pennsylvania to Eastern Ohio, were often first-generation South Italian immigrants. In 1906, Pinkerton detectives were called in to investigate suspicions that a Black Hand gang had been responsible for two local murders—the first of a game warden and the second of an elderly farmer. After spending several weeks under cover in the mines, the Pinkertons had gathered enough evidence to warrant the arrest of twenty-two miners on the charge of being part of a gang that preyed upon other Italians, threatening them and forcing them to join their society and pay their dues. The *modus operandi* was familiar; it was identical to that used by groups in sulfur-mining areas of south-central Sicily. Indeed, one witness later testified that the Black Hand Societies of the Mahoning Valley were an extension of the mafia brotherhoods already existing in Sicily.

Humbert Nelli made a statistical analysis of Black Hand cases reported in the American press in 1908.[8] As might be expected, the lion's share of these cases occurred in New York. They were also frequent in Eastern ports where immigrants landed—Boston, Philadelphia, Baltimore, and, of course, New Orleans. They were increasingly frequent in Chicago, where the Italian community grew rapidly in the years after 1900. After this, however, the geography becomes rather ambiguous: there was significant Black Hand activity in Cleveland, Pittsburgh and Kansas City; there were also cases in Pottsville, Pennsylvania; Export, Pennsylvania; Richmond, Virginia; Elkins, West Virginia; Punxsutawney, Pennsylvania; and Berkeley, California. The table is nothing more than a random snapshot of a form of crime that everyone agreed was mostly unreported. Had Nelli chosen another year, other cities—Detroit, Buffalo, and St. Louis among them—might have shown up on his lists. Still, the geographical spread is suggestive. A Black Hand gang could arise in any Italian immigrant community, large or small. Gangs had arisen in the oil towns of Western Pennsylvania or the coal towns of West Virginia just as they had arisen in the sulfur mining towns in Central Sicily twenty years earlier. All that was necessary was the organization of a handful of men who knew how to exploit poor, disorganized workers. It helped if the area was poorly policed, or if the non-Italian speaking local police did not care a whit what the Italian workers got up to. That might easily have been the case in Punxsutawney, Pennsylvania, in 1908. It also helped if a significant number of the Italian immigrants had come from the same region and spoke the same dialect. This made it easier for one "neat little tea party of Sicilian brigands . . . to bulldoze such of their countrymen who would stand their blackmailing tricks."

Nelli's point of departure are the 424 Black Hand cases reported by Commissioner Bingham in 1908 and the subsequent article in *Cosmopolitan*. These were just the tip of the iceberg. If we had a fuller picture, rather than just a random snapshot taken for one year, we might well discover that the problems of Sausolito, California, in 1878 or Pottsville, Pennsylvania, in 1908 had been plaguing Italian immigrant communities wherever they found themselves.

In Italy, *scroccaggio* had been endemic in poverty-stricken areas for centuries, if not millennia. It was less a crime than part of the relations between the rich and the poor. Normally the rich soaked the poor, carrying away in rents and taxes all but the bare minimum necessary for survival. Sometimes, however, in times of chaos, the poor got their own back. In these moments, the normal flow of expropriation would temporarily be thrust into reverse gear. Gangs of peasants or *lazzaroni* would break into the storehouses and *palazzi* to loot and pillage. The poor had memories. When Joe Petrosino referred to the Black Hand trade and its punishments and outrages, he was referring to a code that every Italian immigrant in America intuitively grasped. You are always vulnerable. However, even if he is a criminal and is trying to blackmail you, you do not turn your neighbor over to the police. Your neighbor has friends and family, and these will remember, and you will always be vulnerable. You do not go to the police unless you have exhausted every other means.

Within Italian communities, Black Hand threats tended to peak during the winter months. Lieutenant Joseph Petrosino of New York police Italian Squad explained that: "The winter is a hard time of year for all Italians, and naturally the collections come harder." In other words, "men who have given up a few dollars [to the Black Handers] for months suddenly decide that, come what may, they will pay no more. According to the laws of the trade, this means punishment, and there you have your outrages."[9] Many of the threats were pure *scroccaggio*; the letters were written by poor men; men, Nelli remarks, probably employed as seasonal laborers in construction projects and forced to live through the winter on the meager savings from their fair-weather jobs. The truly destitute, however, rarely constitute a physical threat to the better off, especially when they are acting on their own. Recipients usually ignored letters if the threat seemed empty. Occasionally, as in Sicily, they might even pay a few dollars more out of charity than from fear. Yet extortion is a potentially profitable line of business. In Sicily, disorganized *scroccaggio* had evolved into organized *brigantaggio*.

At first the threat was usually murder. Yet as awesome as murder may be as a threat, it is less effective as a negotiating technique. It is difficult to extort money from the man you have murdered. Since money rather than murder was what they were really after, the professional Black Hand gangs soon began using different threats. Sometimes they threatened to murder a family member; increasingly, however, the threat was dynamite. In the first decade and a half of the new century there was a spate of Black Hand bombings in America. There were eight such incidents in New York alone; involving, in the most serious cases, multiple bombings. In May 1908, a rich tenement owner named Francesco Spinella received a letter telling him that unless he paid $7,000 his "entire property" would be destroyed. Spinella refused to pay, and less than two weeks later, a bomb exploded in front of one of his properties. In the weeks that followed, the original letter was followed by twenty more, each repeating the same demands. Spinella still refused to give in, and in this same period ten explosions ripped through his and surrounding buildings, driving away all his tenants. In less than three month, the extensive patrimony of the Spinella family was leveled to the ground and the family left penniless. If, as the police reported, Italian communities throughout the country were becoming panicked, it is easy to understand why.[10]

Not all threats were symptoms of class tensions or the work of professional criminals; others were expressions of *invidia* (envy). On September 13, 1903, the New York *Herald* carried a story about a Black Hand extortion plot against a wealthy Brooklyn contractor and dock builder named Nicola Cappiello. Cappiello ignored a note threatening to dynamite his home and kill his family. Two days later he received a second note saying that he could still save his family if he agreed to pay the Black Hand $10,000 and sacrifice his own life. Several days thereafter, he was paid a visit by three of his oldest friends and a fourth man whom he did not know. Having learned of his plight, these friends had come to his assistance. If Cappiello agreed to hand over $1,000, they thought they could persuade the Black Handers to back off. Cappiello consented and paid $1,000. But after several days his friends returned. The Black Hand was still not satisfied, they told him; they wanted $3,000 more. Convinced now that the Black Hand simply intended to bleed him for all they could, Cappiello took the unusual step of enlisting the aid of the Brooklyn police. The police instructed him to arrange a meeting to hand over the money. The meeting was a set up, and when the police arrested the men with Cappiello's money on them, they turned out to be his three best friends along with two thugs enlisted for the occasion.

Cappiello's tormentors were not the envious poor, but disgruntled rivals who wanted to drive him out of business or, by terrorizing him, milk him of his assets. These could be more dangerous, for they could afford to hire the specialists able to dynamite the intended victim's home or store or even kill him. Usually these specialists were out-of-towners. In 1907, the house of a successful Baltimore fruit merchant and immigrant from Sicily, Joseph Di Giorgio, was bombed. In the months before the incident, Di Giorgio had received three letters each demanding $10,000. The letters were all postmarked from Pittsburgh. The police in Baltimore and Pittsburgh traced the letters and the dynamiting to Di Giorgio's principal rival in Baltimore, Antonio Lanasa. Earlier in the decade, Lanasa had seen his own business ruined by Black Hand gangs. Unable to bear the spectacle of Di Giorgio succeeding where he had failed, Lanasa had contacted specialists from Pittsburgh and Cleveland, hiring them to destroy his rival.

Although police officials were often skeptical about claims that a Black Hand extortion ring ever existed in America, they well understood that extortion was real and widely spread and that much of this extortion was being perpetrated in the name of the Black Hand. New York Commissioner William McAdoo wrote in 1906 that he never saw any evidence that there was any such thing as "a thoroughly organized, widely separated secret society which directs its operations in all part of the United States from some great head center, such as the Mafia or Black Hand is pictured." Nevertheless, McAdoo was right to emphasize how terrorized the Italian and even the Jewish communities were growing. The Italian community believed the Black Hand stories; and this, as McAdoo understood, was a relevant point. It was McAdoo who, meeting the criticism of the Italian consul-general in New York, first recruited a squad of Italian-speaking detectives.[11]

THE MORELLO GANG

Giuseppe Morello emigrated to America in 1892. He came from Corleone, a large agrarian town in the interior of Palermo Province where he belonged to a numerous and well-connected family. Members of the Morello family owned land and even sat on the town council. Giuseppe Morello was not, it seems, a scion of the wealthier branches however. Morello had not arrived in America with much money in his pockets. After disembarking in New York, he made his way to New Orleans where he worked as a fruit picker, later migrating to Texas to work as a sugar planter and cotton picker.

Conditions for Texas cotton pickers were either very favorable at the time, or else Morello had hit upon an alternative source of income. Within a year, he acquired enough money to summon the rest of his family to join him. His mother, step-father Antonio, four sisters and brother Nicolo soon arrived, to be followed by cousins and step-cousins from the Terranova family. In 1896, Giuseppe gathered the entire clan and moved them back to New York. He and his step-father began working there as plasterers. Though not notably successful at this line of work, they nonetheless somehow acquired enough money to launch other businesses—coal hauling and two saloons. Though none of their businesses seemed very profitable either, the Morello family was still growing steadily richer.

The mother of Ciro and Vincenzo Terranova, Rosalia Morello was the daughter of another member of the extensive Morello clan, a man who had served on the Corleone Town Council. Sometime in the 1880s, Rosalia married one of her cousins in the related Terranova family, also from Corleone, later giving birth to Vincenzo and Ciro and a daughter. In the mid-1890s, however, Rosalia's husband was gunned down, an accidental victim, she claimed, in a mafia a turf war. The Morello-Terranova family decided that the young widow should marry Antonio Morello, whose oldest son, Giuseppe, was currently laboring in the Texas cotton fields. Antonio was a widower; one who had already visited America. He had married a girl from back home, leaving, as was the custom, his wife to wait until he had settled in America and could send for her. But Antonio's first wife had died while he was still in America, forcing him to return to Corleone to marry his cousin, the widow Rosalia Terranova. Then, accompanied by her three children, Antonio returned to America to form part of the growing Morello clan, by now resettled on New York's Lower East Side under the leadership of his step-son Giuseppe.

In their native Corleone, Antonio and Giuseppe Morello had both been members of an unnamed sectarian organization outlawed by the police. We know this because each time Giuseppe's home in New York were raided (1903 and 1909), the police found documents and letters linking Morello to sects in both America and Sicily. It is even possible that Antonio and Giuseppe Morello's decision to emigrate had been prompted neither by desperate poverty nor by a desire to escape an arrest warrant, but rather by struggles within the sectarian underworld of Sicily's interior.

Soon a new member joined the growing clan. In 1898, Ignazio Saietta arrived from Corleone fleeing an arrest warrant. He was wanted in connection with the killing of another Morello cousin, Salvatore Morello. Evidently there was a feud within the Morello family, for when Saietta arrived in New York he was welcomed by the New York Morellos. Saietta, who became better known in New York as Ignazio Lupo, and, inevitably, Ignazio the Wolf or even Lupo the Wolf, opened a store on Seventy-second Street with some of his Saietta cousins. There may have been a falling out with these cousins, for Ignazio soon sold his Manhattan business, opening an Italian food import store in Brooklyn. It was the first of a string of businesses.

By 1900, both Giuseppe and Ignazio seemed business failures. Singly and together they had invested in building and decorating firms, coal haulage businesses, feed businesses, dry-goods businesses, a date factory, a food-import store and saloons. None of these enterprises seemed to prosper, however, and Morello and Lupo usually sold out within months, often at a loss, before moving on to something new. Yet at the same time, the two men were growing richer and more powerful. Clearly they had an alternative source of capital. On June 11, 1900, Giuseppe Morello and Calogero Meggiore were arrested for selling counterfeit money.

The arrests were the result of Secret Service investigation into a new set of counterfeit five dollar bills that were being circulated in Brooklyn. The bills were of poor quality and easy to identify, and the agents believed they had could trace them all to Morello and Meggiore. Morello denied everything, however, and the prosecution lacked sufficient evidence to prove that he was the bills' source. Thus Morello was soon released. Lupo was never implicated in the counterfeiting ring; nevertheless, the counterfeit bills were being circulated in Brooklyn near the area where he had just opened his Italian food import business. It was a useful cover for a smuggling ring; several years later, Lupo was caught using macaroni boxes to smuggle in his counterfeit notes. Six months after Morello's arrest, Lupo sold his food import business in Brooklyn. He returned to the Lower East Side where he bought a saloon of 8 Prince Street, opening another import store at number 9 next door.[12]

In the late 1890s, the Italian police in Sicily broke up a counterfeiting ring whose operations extended throughout the island and as far away as Venice. Following a tip-off from a member of a rival gang, the Palermo police discovered a printing press and counterfeit plates in a farm building on the outskirts of a small town deep in the interior. The police believed the Palermo Province counterfeiters were linked to Sicilian gangs operating in America. Although the printing press the police discovered had been brought out from Palermo, the plates from which the false notes were printed had been commissioned in New York and cut by forgers working in Buffalo and Pittsburgh. Others plates had been stolen from a U.S. Government printing office in Morristown, New Jersey. The forged five dollar and two dollar notes were smuggled back into America, some of them in macaroni boxes.

The Italian police had evidently known of the existence of a counterfeiting ring for some time, and had shared their information with American authorities. Investigating counterfeiting cases falls to the United States Secret Service, and, since the counterfeit notes were entering through the Port of New York, the information was passed to the New York Bureau. Its chief, William J. Flynn, later wrote that the Secret Service had begun assembling dossiers on counterfeit bills arriving from Italy as early as 1884.

Already in 1889, Chief Detective Byrnes had picked up two Palermitans in connection with the murder of Antonio Flaccomio. Though unable to speak English, the two men were educated. Through interpreters, they both admitted to being members of a secret society involved in criminal activity. They had fled to America, they said, as a result of a feud within their society. It was a society that now had branches in America, they claimed. The headquarters were in New York City and New Orleans. The murdered man, Antonio Flaccomio, had also been a member of this society, they went on to explain. He had obviously committed some sort of *sgarro,* an offence or breach of code, and had paid for it with his life. The actual murder, they said, was the work of a certain Carlo Quarteraro, since returned to Sicily. His brother, and an accomplice in the murder, Vincenzo Quarteraro, however, was still in New York. Byrnes had Vincenzo arrested and arraigned for murder. At his trial, however, witnesses came forward and provided him with an unbreakable alibi. Frustrated at this show of *omertà,* Chief Detective Byrnes threw up his hands, saying that mafiosi from Sicily were welcome to go ahead and kill each other as far as he was concerned. Commenting later on the Flaccomio murder, Agent Flynn wrote that what Chief Detective Byrnes had been unable to discover was that Flaccomio had been murdered for cheating the other members of the counterfeiting ring.[13]

In 1903, a fresh sectarian killing took place in New York. Shortly after dawn on April 14, a body was discovered jammed into a barrel and placed on East Eleventh Street near Avenue D on the Lower East Side. The body bore seventeen stab wounds. According to Arrigo Petacco, the victim's head had been cut off and had been placed on a filthy pile of sawdust at the top of the barrel. His penis had also been severed and stuffed into his mouth.[14]

According to the coroner's report, the victim's death had not been caused by the stabbings, but rather by the severance of the jugular vein as his head was being cut off. This led the coroner to suspect that the victim had been tortured before being murdered.[15] This, and the gruesome nature of killing and the subsequent mutilation of the corpse, seemed to indicate a killing at the hands of some sort of underworld sect. The placing of the barrel in plain sight on Eleventh Street further indicated that the killers had intended the murder to be discovered. Indeed, when the police first examined the corpse, it was still warm. Given that the barrel was found a short distance from Little Italy, the police naturally linked it to the Italian underworld. With this conclusion, the police at the Second Precinct, where the body had been taken, summoned the New York Police Department's expert on the Italian underworld, Detective Sergeant Joe Petrosino.

Born in Padula in the province of Salerno in 1860, Joe Petrosino had immigrated with his family in 1873. In 1878 he had obtained a job as a municipal street cleaner, quickly rising to crew foreman. Evidently he possessed a good ear and talent for languages, for Petrosino not only picked up English very quickly; he also became fluent in the various Italian dialects spoken in Lower Manhattan. Working in the Midtown Tenderloin district, by 1880 the talented and observant young Italian had attracted the attention of no less than Alexander "Clubber" Williams. Williams recruited him as an informer and translator, three years later rewarding him with a regular job on the force. He was the first Italian to join the New York Police. In 1890, Petrosino joined the Detective Bureau, and was later promoted by Commissioner Roosevelt to the rank of detective sergeant.

Petrosino proved a model detective, brave, honest, and hardworking. Methodical and painstaking rather than brilliant, he got results. Though inclined to be taciturn, he was inevitably the first person reporters came to for comments on Italian crime stories. Though hardly eloquent—his statements read like official reports—he was immensely well-informed. There were, he told the assistant district attorney, five thousand Italian ex-convicts in New York City alone, a large proportion of which he knew by sight and name.[16]

Though the victim's identity was unknown, his face was familiar. As part of their continuing efforts to stem the influx of counterfeit U.S. notes from Italy, the New York Bureau of the Secret Service had been keeping Morello, Lupo and their associates under surveillance. Agents had noted the victim in the company of Morello gang members in the days immediately before his murder. The murder also reminded the police of a similar case. The year before, four boys swimming off the Bay Bridge on Seventy-third Street had found a body stuffed into a potato sack The body was eventually identified as that of Giuseppe Catania, a Brooklyn grocer believed to have been part of the Brooklyn counterfeiting gang and associate of the Morello gang. Indeed Catania had married one of the four Morello sisters in 1899. As a grocer, Catania had presumably bought the Morello counterfeit bills. Shortly before his murder, he had been seen in the company of Lupo.

Police suspicions against Morello and Lupo in the Catania murder were based on nothing more than supposition. Catania had been close to both Morello and Lupo; had he been murdered by a rival gang, Morello and Lupo should have declared a vendetta. Instead, they did nothing. It seemed, therefore, logical to suppose that Morello and Lupo had murdered Catania themselves. Though there was no material evidence, the suspicions were strong enough to redouble police surveillance. Giuseppe's brother and step-brothers, Nicolo Morello and Vincenzo and Ciro Terranova were repeatedly pulled in for questioning. Ciro at this time was working as a waiter in Lupo's Prince Street saloon.

Sifting through the barrel into which the body had been stuffed, Petrosino found enough clues to establish that the barrel had come from a nearby pastry shop, La Stella d'Italia, on Elizabeth Street. La Stella d'Italia was on the list of known Morello gang hang-outs that the Secret Service provided. Others included a butcher shop on Stanton Street and the saloons and restaurants on Prince Street owned by Giuseppe Morello and Lupo.

With this information, the New York police decided to pull in the entire Morello gang. The arrests took place on the evening of April 15, about thirty-six hours after the body had been discovered, and included Giuseppe Morello, Tommaso Petto, Joseph Danaro, Antonio Messina Genova, Lorenzo LoBaido, Vito LoBaido, Demonico Peccoraro and the owner of the pastry shop, Pietro Inzerillo. The next day, the police made four more arrests: Ignazio Lupo, Vito Laduca, Nicola Testa and Giuseppe Lalamia. All were armed with guns or knives, though Morello and Petto had gun permits. The Secret Service estimated that the Morello gang once had as many as thirty members, though a series of raids had much reduced their numbers. In 1902, the police had arrested a number of gang members in Morristown, New Jersey, for trafficking in counterfeit five dollar notes. Shortly thereafter there had been another raid in Hackensack.

Still, Agent Flynn was convinced that the Morello gang was closely associated with other gangs working in New Orleans, Chicago, Pittsburgh, Baltimore, and Buffalo, as well as some smaller cities and towns. The police searched Morello's house, finding letters that confirmed that he was part of an association with branches in a number of U.S. cities; they searched Lupo's house and found evidence that he was connected to the murdered Catania; they also found evidence that other members of the gang were engaged in Black Hand extortion.

The twelve arrested men were arraigned but not formally charged. Indeed, with no identification of the victim there was little prospect of formal charges or even holding them in prison for long. Petrosino spent a futile few days showing the corpse or a photograph to hundreds of Italians. No one recognized it; and Petrosino began to suspect that the victim had come from out of town. Flynn told Petrosino that there were around twenty other Italians currently serving sentences in American prisons for counterfeiting offences. He suggested that the New York police show the victim's photograph to these men. He added that there was one Sicilian gang member, Giuseppe De Priemo (or De Primo), who was currently serving a sentence in Sing Sing. He had been there three months on charges arising from the Morristown raid. De Priemo, Flynn observed, felt that the gang had let him down, and so might prove cooperative. When Petrosino arrived to interview De Priemo, showing him the victim's photograph, De Priemo immediately exclaimed; "Why that's my brother-in-law!" The victim's name was Benedetto Madonia. He lived in Buffalo, but was making a visit to New York in the company of a friend named Tommaso "The Ox" Petto. The name Tommaso Petto rang a bell; he was one of the Morello gang members that the police were holding in custody. He was, moreover, the gang member observed by Secret Service agents in the company of the victim in the days before the murder.

The identification and incriminating evidence was enough to obtain the re-arrest and re-arraigning of the prisoners, some of whom had by now been released. Petrosino traveled to Buffalo to confirm the identification with Madonia's family. The family also told Petrosino that Benedetto Madonia always carried a pocket watch with him, providing a description of the object. At the time of his arrest, Petto had been searched and a pawn ticket had been found in his pocket. When the police went to the pawn shop indicated on the ticket, they discovered that the ticket's number corresponded to Madonia's watch which, the pawn shop owner recalled, Petto had brought in on the day after the murder. Although neither De Priemo nor the Madonia family would say anything that might incriminate Benedetto Madonia or associate him with the Morello gang, it seemed clear to Petrosino and Flynn that Benedetto Madonia was indeed a member of the gang, and that he had traveled from Buffalo to New York on gang business. The gang, however, became convinced that Madonia had committed a *sgarro*. Shortly after he had arrived, they murdered him, then, mutilating his body and dumping it in a barrel, they placed the whole grisly package on Eleventh Street as an *avvertimento* (warning).

With the additional evidence, the assistant district attorney was able to obtain an indictment for first-degree murder against Tommaso Petto. He was also able to keep other members of the gang in prison as accomplices or material witnesses. Though the police were convinced that the murder had been ordered by Ignazio Lupo and carried out in the Stella d'Italia, they lacked sufficient evidence to bring charges either against Lupo or the pastry shop owner, Pietro Inzerillo, and the two men were set free. Still, the case against Petto, at least, seemed strong. Nevertheless, the police had made one slip-up. To prevent the release of the gang in the week immediately following the murder, the police had used the expedient of re-arraigning them. The police, in other words, had released the prisoners and then immediately re-arrested them and re-arraigned them for another forty-eight hour stretch. The re-arraigning procedure took place in a confused courtroom, however, filled with Italians shouting and with defense lawyers trying to obtain writs of *habeas corpus*. At some point during these proceedings, Petto had evidently faded back into the crowd letting another man step forward to take his place. No one had noticed it at the time. At the moment of the formal indictment, however, the new man entered a plea of 'not guilty' on the grounds that he was not Tommaso Petto at all but Carlo Constantino. The real Petto had vanished. All of the Sicilians, including the victim's family, observed *omertà;* and all of the accused were acquitted.[17]

Why had Madonia been murdered and what was the reason for the brutal mutilation? It is the Italian author, Petacco, who provides the detail of the penis stuffed into the victim's mouth. According to him, Madonia had come to New York to collect some money that Morello had owed him. But Morello refused to recognize the debt. At this refusal, writes Petacco, Madonia threatened to go to the police and tell them all he knew. Hearing this threat, Morello ordered his gang members to murder and mutilate Madonia as a warning to all would-be squealers. Petacco's reconstruction seems unlikely. It is hard to believe that anyone could be so stupid as to tell a mafia boss to his face that he intended to spill his guts to the police and expect to get out of the room, much less to the police station, with body and soul still connected to each other. The police found evidence supporting a different reconstruction. Earlier in the year, Morello had sent Madonia on a mission to Pittsburgh where some of Morello's counterfeit bills had been disappearing without a trace. Madonia was supposed to straighten things out. He had not, evidently, straightened them out to Morello's satisfaction, and there was a disagreement. Searching the Morello home, the police found a letter from Madonia saying that he was fed up with Morello's complaints and was going back home to Buffalo. Morello summoned him to New York for some sort of show down, and this eventually resulted in the murder.

Alternatively, it is possible that Madonia's murder and mutilation was indeed a reprisal for squealing, even though it was not Benedetto Madonia who had been the squealer. Giuseppe De Priemo had been among those arrested in Morristown, New Jersey. Later he had later turned state's evidence and received a reduced sentence. De Priemo was an important witness in the counterfeiting trial as well as Benedetto Madonia's brother-in-law. De Priemo was, however, behind bars, and therefore safe from the Morellos' revenge. The Morellos may have decided to eke out their revenge by killing Madonia in his place. In Sicily, the practice is known as a *vendetta traversale.*

Finally, though the barrel murder was unquestionably an *avvertimento*, contrary to Petacco's assertion, there was no coded reference to squealing in the mutilation. The Morello gang were men of honor, followers of a code much older than the mafia itself. A gang war is a blood feud, and therefore an affair of honor. Those who fall in such an affair die with their honor intact.

They are casualties of war, guilty of nothing more than fighting on the wrong side. They are deserving of respect, and in America, the mafia sometimes pays the funeral expenses of its own victims or at least sends wreaths for their funeral. The practice may seem macabre and hypocritical to outsiders; but within the mafia's code of honor it makes sense. It would be unthinkable to mutilate the corpse of a man who had died honourably. Mutilation is rather a way of *dishonouring* the victim. It is close up and personal, the revenge of the offended party. It is the right and duty of the offended man of honor to inflict this sort of punishment himself; or, where this is no longer possible, it is the right and duty of his surviving brothers or sons. As a mark of dishonor, cutting off a man's penis and stuffing it into his mouth is the ultimate humiliation. Sometimes this particular form of mutilation indicates that the victim's offense was of a sexual nature, though this is by no means always the case. It does not, however, indicate that the victim was a squealer. The mafia have another symbol for that—a stone in the victim's mouth.

For a time, the barrel murder made headlines in New York. Though descriptions remained decorously elusive, enough juicy detail seeped through to keep the reader's interest whetted. The case also introduced the newspaper-reading public to Joe Petrosino, who would be kept busy for the six remaining years of his life fielding reporters' questions about Italian crime. The barrel murder popularized the term *Black Hand*, which, for a decade or more in New York would eclipse *mafia* as the name for Italian organized crime in America. The gruesome murder produced a spate of articles on crime and extortion in the Italian communities, as well as hand-wringing editorials such as that of the *Times* quoted earlier. According to the *Tribune*, "The city is confronted with an Italian problem with which at present it seems unable to cope. Citizens are waking up mornings to read "Black Hand" letters demanding extortionate sums of money, to be deposited in some out of the way rendezvous or else a pistol shot or dynamite bomb will end their days."

The city seemed overwhelmed by a Black Hand epidemic; and the police seemed powerless:

Officers, the *Tribune* continued, make a series of theatrical arrests, only to be compelled to let their prisoners go. Mysterious witnesses are unearthed, who, after many dark hints, leave Police Headquarters as mysteriously as they went there. In the case of the "barrel murder," after the city had gone to great cost in "scouring the East Side," in arresting "alleged cutthroats" and in "giving them the third degree," it was at last required to set the whole gang free.[18]

Police Commissioner at the time of the barrel murder, William McAdoo later wrote that the policeman was not a naturally sympathetic figure. Constantly accused of corruption and suspected of brutality, confronted with feuds inside the Italian-speaking underworld, the New York police must have been tempted to simply look the other way, hoping, like Chief Detective Byrnes, that the mafia would simply kill each other off. Yet if the violence hit a critical level, there was bound to be an outcry. The police were lazy and incompetent, the papers would cry; they were unable to protect the public, unable to bring criminals to justice. The Morello gang had made fools of the NYPD and the Secret Service, spiriting away Tommaso the Ox from under their very noses. The police and Secret Service were bound to resent this. Though they had been unable to obtain indictments against either Morello or Lupo for their involvement in the Madonia murder, they immediately re-arrested both of them on counterfeiting charges. Once again, however, they were unable to make their charges stick. The police and Secret Service redoubled their efforts, determined to drive the gang out of business. Giuseppe Morello and Ignazio Lupo responded by moving out of Lower Manhattan.

By 1900 New York had surpassed New Orleans as the capital of the Italian community in America. The city contained the largest number of Italian immigrants in the country. Indeed, second only to Naples, New York now contained more Italians than any other city on the face of the earth. Within New York, the largest Italian community remained on the Lower East Side. Despite this predominance, however, the Lower East Side was not ideal territory for the Morello gang. It was overcrowded. There were immigrant communities here from Naples and Palermo and from the mafia-ridden towns in Sicily's interior and west. But there were also immigrants from Eastern Sicily, Calabria, Campania, Basilicata, Apulia, and the Abbruzzo, as well as smaller communities from Central and Northern Italy. Protection rackets preyed on their own communities; the mafia imposed the *pizzu* (protection money) on Sicilian businesses, leaving Neapolitan businesses to the camorra. In the first decades of the new century, no Italian gang was strong enough to establish any sort of prominence over the ethnic diversity of the Lower East Side's Little Italy. Nor were ethnic Italian gangs the only competitors; there was also Jewish organized crime and the remains of the Irish gangs. Finally, there was Tammany.

The Morello gang was operating in Big Tim Sullivan's backyard. It is likely that Giuseppe and Nicolo Morello and Ciro and Vincenzo Terranova had by now made friends with Paul Kelly and his Five Pointers on the Lower East Side. These friendships may have provided them with some respite from official pressure. Still, with the police and the Secret Service making things uncomfortable for them, Morello and Lupo began to feel cramped.

In 1904, the bond between Morello and Lupo was sanctified when Lupo married one of the Morello sisters. The new brother-in-laws celebrated their union by launching the Ignazio Florio Association, a construction and property development company centered in East Harlem and the Bronx. Ignazio Florio was the name of Sicily's leading industrialist and shipbuilder. By naming their company after him, Morello and Lupo may have wished to render wry homage to a man whose ships had been bringing them a steady supply of counterfeit U.S. banknotes secreted in macaroni boxes. Morello and Lupo listed themselves as joint presidents and largest stockholders of the new company. They acquired a vacant lot at 630 East 138th Street, upon which they built the association's offices and a large residence for the growing Morello family.

Although Lupo and Morello sold their groceries and restaurants on Prince Street, Lupo opened a new Lower East Side emporium in a seven-story building at 210–214 Mott Street. It was his most luxurious venture. As "one of the most impressive stores in the neighborhood, many of the locals could only dream of shopping there."[19]

In 1908, however, Lupo suddenly filed for bankruptcy. He claimed $100,000 worth of debts on a store inventory worth only $1,500. The bankruptcy was certainly fraudulent. Investigators discovered that much of the $100,000 debt was on goods that Lupo had recently purchased, but whose whereabouts he could not account for. They later discovered that most of these unaccounted-for goods were American foodstuffs hidden on a transatlantic pier where they were due to be shipped to Italy. Lupo was evidently preparing to skip the country.

In 1905 Lupo was arrested for the murder of Brooklyn butcher Gaetano Costa, who had been resisting his demands for protection. He was arrested on a kidnapping charge the following year. Though he eventually beat both raps, he was forced to spend some time in the Tombs. The police were keeping him quite busy. The Secret Service was also breathing down his neck, forcing him to be constantly on the move. The Morello gang had added heroin smuggling to its repertoire. They had always been Black Handers. When members of the gang were finally charged in connection with the barrel murder, the judge set bail at $16,000, an extremely high figure at the time. The following morning, however, the Morello gang's lawyer appeared in the company of a Mott Street barber named Macaluso. The barber was carrying a packet made out of a large, knotted pocket handkerchief. It contained a pile of bills amounting to $16,000. The money, he explained, was the result of a collection taken in the Italian neighborhoods the night before. Some sort of collection had obviously been made, but it is unlikely that the contributions were entirely voluntary. Shortly before declaring bankruptcy, Lupo had made a special collection, one just for himself. The police surmised that, before fleeing to Italy, Lupo had planned to fill his pockets with extortion money and amass fifty thousand dollars worth of American goods to sell in Italy. By the time the police reached these conclusions, however, Lupo had disappeared.

Lupo's aborted bankruptcy fraud had implications for his brother-in-law Giuseppe. The Morello house on 138th Street was property of the Ignazio Florio Associaton, of which Lupo was joint president. The house was sold to meet Lupo's debts, and Morello was forced to move. He bought a large new building at 231 East 107th Street in the middle of East Harlem. The house soon became a headquarters for the Italian underworld in New York; Steve La Salle lived there and Giovanni Rao, the father of Joey Rao, ran a shop on the ground floor. Nearby, at 277 East 107th Street, there was the saloon owned by Angelo Gagliano and Ippolito Greco.

In late 1909, Lupo suddenly re-appeared, walking into the offices of the receivers dealing with his bankrupt properties. He had not been hiding out from the law, he disingenuously claimed; he had been hounded by Black

Handers who had forced him to flee first to Baltimore and then to Buffalo.
Dubious to say the least, the investigators had Lupo arrested on an old extortion warrant. Yet, typically, the police were unable to obtain a conviction for
any of the extortion charges—all those victims willing to swore out statements to the police when the fearsome Lupo was in hiding suffered from
bouts of amnesia as soon as he reappeared. Nevertheless, the Secret Service's
own investigations were now beginning to bear fruit.

In 1907, Antonio Comito, a trained printer who had emigrated to New
York from Catanazaro, found himself approached by a certain Antonio Cecala, who asked him if he needed work. It soon became evident to Comito
that the work Cecala contemplated consisted of printing U.S. and Canadian
bank notes. At first Comito hesitated. By the end of 1908, however, he had
overcome his scruples. Together with Cecala and Cecala's godson, Salvatore
Cina, they travelled up the Hudson to a farm in Highland New York. Here
they were met by Nicky Silvester, a friend of the two Terranova brothers
and former employee in Lupo's Mott Street grocery, and Cina's brother-in-
law Vincenzo Giglio. They began printing Canadian five dollar bills in January 1909. By the end of the month they had printed sixteen thousand dollars
worth. They next started on a run of U.S. two dollar bills.

Comito, Cecala and Giglio kept working on the U.S. bills throughout the
winter of 1908–1909. Ignazio Lupo later visited the farm, staying a few days.
He had brought revolvers and hunting rifles, and spent the morning shooting on the farm. In the afternoons he went to a drugstore in a nearby village,
where, imagining himself unobserved, he made phone calls to Baltimore,
New York, and Hoboken. By the end of February the gang had finished the
first batches of U.S. two dollar notes, and Cecala and Cina travelled to Chicago, Pittsburgh, and Buffalo to sell them. Although they had printed twenty
thousand dollars worth of notes, they were of poor quality; and the gang only
got $800 for their labors. Lupo told him that he had made a "shit-like material
of no use." They burned the remainder of the notes and split the $800.

At this point, Comito was ready to quit. He was being held a virtual prisoner at a series of isolated farms. The poor quality of the work was not his
fault, he said; the plates were bad, and the ink was the wrong color. He asked
at least to return to the city to buy some good ink, but Cecala and Cina told
him to stay put. In March, the gang hired another printer, Giuseppe Calicchio,
to help Comito out, paying him twenty dollars. With new help, and with better
plates and ink, Comito quickly succeeded in printing about thirty-two thousand dollars in phoney two dollar notes. The quality was much better. But by
now, the quality of the counterfeit bills was only one of the gang's problems.

Lupo was supposedly in hiding, but the Secret Service had learned of his
presence in Highland and had sent out investigators. The gang noticed strangers in the area and became jittery. Several times they bundled up their operations, destroyed the evidence and moved off to another isolated location—a
sort of dress rehearsal for the cat and mouse games played in the Catskills
during Prohibition. Agents had now identified Cecala as the liaison between

the Morello and Lupo and the printers. Cecala also had the job of delivering the counterfeit notes to storeowners and businessmen. By following Cecala on his rounds, the agents were able to make a list of businesses involved in circulating counterfeit money in Manhattan and Brooklyn. The police and Secret Service finally arrested Cecala and Morello in mid-November 1909. They arrested Lupo several days later.

When Cecala failed to return from his regular trip from the city and there was no word from the bosses, the men in the printing operations panicked. They decided to pack up operations, split up and return to the city. Unwisely, some immediately visited the Morello house on East 107th Street, which was under police surveillance. Calicchio was spotted in the area and later arrested on Bleeker Street. Comito had simply gone home, however, and he was arrested there at the beginning of January 1910. Comito was not a professional criminal. The whole affair had turned into a nightmare for him. He immediately agreed to cooperate with Captain Flynn of the Secret Service. A month later, Comito was the lead witness for the prosecution. Morello, Lupo, Cecala and the rest were found guilty on all counts and sentenced to fifteen years hard labor. The minor gang members were paroled between 1913 and 1916. Giusppe Morello and Ignazio Lupo were paroled in the 1920s, still in time, Nelli comments, to celebrate Prohibition's many opportunities.

"Good People"

Giuseppe Morello and Ignazio Lupo ran a counterfeiting ring; they were Black Handers, and they were sectarians. What is the connection between these activities?

The Black Hand legends were not only believed by the victims; they were at least half believed by the Black Handers themselves. Just as Charles Matranga donned a black domino to impress the greenhorns when he solemnly inducted them into the *Società Onorata* of the *Stoppaglieri,* so Black Hand associations developed their own pseudo-masonic initiation ceremonies complete with oaths and passwords. Indeed, if a clandestine sect called *La Mano Negra* did in fact originate in nineteenth-century Spain, it seems far more likely that, at least at its point of origin, it more closely resembled the original *Stoppaglieri* of Monreale that anything it became later. It would, in short, have originated as one of the many revolutionary or anarchic political societies current in these years rather as a group dedicated to crime. It might even have arrived in America as a political sect. This would help explain why, like the first generation of the *Stoppaglieri,* the early Black Handers seemed so obsessed with initiation ceremonies, secret passwords, and cryptic codes.

The New World has always attracted political refugees of all stripes. By 1900 there were anarchist and socialist groups active in the Italian and the Eastern European immigrant communities all over the country, some of whose members were fleeing from arrest warrants back home. If they were wise, once the got to America they kept to themselves. As long as they conspired in a foreign tongue and limited their plotting to the death of tyrants back home, the American police took little notice. In July 1900, however, the Italian community in America was horrified to read that the king of Italy had been assassinated. Their consternation was all the greater when they learned that the assassination had been organized by an anarchist group in Paterson, New Jersey. The regicide, Gaetano Bresci, had left Paterson for Rome with the express purpose of murdering the king. Outraged, the Italian government demanded that the American police round up the entire gang and extradite them to Italy. But the Paterson police chief politely demurred. None of them had broken any laws in Paterson, he said; he had no grounds for arresting any of them.[20] It was a tradition of benign indifference that would last until the Palmer Raids and the Sacco and Vanzetti case at the beginning of the 1920s.

In the years around 1910, the United States Secret Service were completing its investigations of a Sicilian counterfeiting and smuggling ring centered in the East Harlem/Bronx area in the Morello gang territory. On one of the gang's members, a certain Rudolfo Palermo, they found a little book with the rules of the Black-Hand Society. These rules and solemn oaths were similar to those of the *Fratellanza* in the Agrigento mining districts in the early 1880s.[21] The Secret Service also recovered a number of letters. One of these was written to associates in Chicago; it gave New York's ruling over the correct procedures that the society was to follow, particularly in the relations between the "Council" (seemingly a sort of governing body) and the "Assembly" (the members at large). Another letter to Chicago was a complaint on behalf of a certain Calogero Constantino, a member in good standing. It seems that Costantino had been arrested in Bacaluse, Louisiana, and had been promised help from the Chicago branch; but this help had not been forthcoming. New York wanted to know why.[22]

During the 1890s, Vito Cascio Ferro, born in the interior of Palermo Province, kept company with the local anarchists and radicals. In the early 1890s he is listed by the police as one of the leaders of the socialist peasant leagues in Sicily's interior. His activities as a political radical and organizer were abruptly cut short by an Italian government crackdown in 1893. This forced Ferro to flee to Tunisia to avoid arrest. But Ferro had a far wider circle of associates. His father Accursio had been an estate guard and *uomo di fiducia* of the Inglese family, members of Sicily's landowning baronage. It was a position that Vito inherited. With the support of the Inglese family, Vito was able to return from exile some time later in the 1890s. Publicly at least, he had severed all ties with the radical left. He began to frequent Palermo society, wearing stylish and expensive clothes, going to the best restaurants and clubs. He was constantly on the move between Palermo and the towns of the interior. Though he spent money freely, he had no visible means of support. The police strongly suspected that his wealth came from mafia-connected protection rackets. When the police proposed placing him under special surveillance, he obtained a passport and, in 1901, emigrated to New York.

Once in America, he contacted Giuseppe Morello, members of whose family he already knew in Corleone.[23] An advantage of a masonic-type organization is that it tied the mafia into a network of other fraternal societies. Mafiosi are, by definition, "connected guys." Cascio Ferro had connections with the Morello family. He had kept up his old anarchist connections as well. During his stay in New York he traveled to Paterson, New Jersey, becoming friends with Sophie Knieland, the lover of Gaetano Brescio, the assassin of King Umberto. The two friends continued to exchange letters even after Ferro had returned to Sicily.[24]

In the days after the barrel murder, Ferrro left New York for New Orleans. Petacco and others try to connect him to the 1903 murder, interpreting his disappearance shortly thereafter as flight. It seems more likely that he was planning to travel to New Orleans anyway. He may have wished to avoid the dragnets of Italian gangsters that followed in the days after the murder, but there is no evidence to link him with the murder itself. In whatever case, he left with another Morello gang member, Paolo Marchese, and stayed in New Orleans for over a year. He was intending to stay longer. In late 1904, however, his application for U.S. citizenship was turned down after the Immigration Service received an unfavorable report from the Italian government. In September 1904 he returned to Sicily. The day he left he received a telegram from New York: "Very upset over your misfortune. Have no worries on my account or on account of the others. We wish you all the best. Courage. Write on arrival. Giuseppe." The author was probably Giuseppe Morello.[25]

Cascio Ferro probably went to New Orleans on sectarian business. He and Marchese were in contact with Nick Favia, a local boss. Marchese remained in New Orleans where he was later involved in Black Hand war. A regular New York–New Orleans axis in the Italian underworld had existed for years. Connections to Sicily were also scrupulously kept up. One of the men arrested in connection with the barrel murder, Vito LaDuca, returned to Corleone at the end of 1903, where he became Giuseppe Morello's representative. After his release from Sing Sing, Benedetto Madonia's brother-in-law, Giuseppe DePriemo, traced him there in 1908 and shot him in revenge for the Madonia slaying.

The letter recommending Calogero Constantino that the Secret Service found at the Morello house in 1903 is very badly translated and thus obscure in a number of places; but it fits clearly into a larger network. Morello writes that though "We of Corleone have never had any dealings with them [the Constantino family] . . . I and my townsmen have always known the Constantino family as a good family, and none other but very good, and the boss of my town, I am sure, cannot give you better details, though I doubt if they knew this family just because they were not to our bearing, but nevertheless leaning towards good people; have you seen 'the ox, neither white nor black,' this is their bearing."[26]

If "town" translates *borgata,* Morello was using an Italian term which not only means a town or a part of a town, but a term which, in the American mafia, means an area dominated by a single mafia group. In the Sicilian mafia, moreover, phrases such "of good family" or "good people" are very often used to mean "one of us," members of the sect. In such case, the opening part of the letter becomes much clearer: 'We of the Brotherhood in Corleone and in its branches in America have never had any dealing with them [the Constantino family who came from Partinico]. . . . But I and the members of the Corleone brotherhood here in New York have always known the Constantino family as a good family, entirely loyal to the brotherhood, and the head of the brotherhood back in Corleone, I am sure, cannot give you better information, though I doubt whether the Corleone brotherhood knew much about the Constantino family because they were not in the same branch of the brotherhood as ours, though they were still in a branch that was leaning towards the true brotherhood." The reference to "the ox neither white nor black" is more mysterious; though it seems to indicate the branch of the brotherhood to which the Constanino family belonged.

We do not know what became of Calogero Constantino; there was, however, a lieutenant in Morello's gang named Carlo Constantino. Given Morello's endorsement of the Constantino family, it seems likely that Carlo Constantino and Calogero Constantino were related, perhaps even the same person. It also seems significant that a mafia boss like Morello regularly corresponded with members of his sect in Chicago, New Orleans, and Sicily, discussing official business, endorsing members or introducing them into fraternal branches in new cities. The overwhelming majority of Sicilian immigrants were officially illiterate, though the official statistics were probably an exaggeration. Petacco quotes letters to Italian police officials sent from New York. The letters are written in a mixture of dialect and formal but ungrammatical Italian, supporting an inference that the writers were dialect speakers who had picked up literacy through reading the papers.[27] Cascio Ferro, who was certainly literate and even passed for a gentleman of a certain refinement, obtained his education by the simple expedient of eloping with the local school mistress. Giuseppe Morello and Vito Cascio Ferro were criminals certainly, but they were not brute thugs. However they picked it up, they were better educated than most of their countrymen.

They were also the leaders of a powerful, if also obscure and sinister, brotherhood. Most immigrants had heard rumors about these brotherhoods, knew that they were supposed to be powerful, well-connected, and ancient and so concluded that they needed to be respected. It was a useful attitude for the sects to foster. Flynn suspected that the Morello family was deliberating creating branches of the sect in Western Pennsylvania as outlets for counterfeit bills. The truth may have been a little more complex. Branches were certainly a convenient way of putting more counterfeit bills into circulation. But Morello would, in any event, have wanted to create as many branches as he could; the more franchises he opened, the better connected and thus more powerful his own branch became. In the chain of Italian underworld wars which were about to explode, it was not always the biggest or best armed or most ruthless group that came out on top, but rather the best connected (or, on occasions, the luckiest).

THE MURDER STABLE

Whether it was true, as the Italian consul general charged, that "the regular Irish policeman at the corner . . . did not care a rap what the Italians did among themselves" Mayor McClellan and the upper echelons of the New York Police Department were growing alarmed. Crime and Black Hand extortion was spooking the immigrant communities, and Commissioners McAdoo and Bingham both recruited Italian-speaking detectives to combat it. Italian detectives helped; but they were not enough to overcome the traditional reluctance South Italians felt about approaching the police. It was an uphill battle.

The *Times* wrote that the identities of the extortionists were well known to prominent Italian citizens; but these citizens hesitated to bring complaints to the police, fearing that doing so would only draw the attention of these criminals upon their own families. "We have too many bad Italians here already," complained the *Times* editorial, "and since the good Italians so generally refuse to give any information to the police which might assist them to run down criminals of their race, we may be unable in any protective measure we adopt to distinguish the good Italian immigrant from the bad Italian immigrant." If this non-cooperation continued, the editorial concluded, the government might be forced consider banning the South Italian and Sicilian immigration altogether.

The editorial was titled "There is Another Way." The expression seems deliberately allusive, coming in the wake of a series of articles in which the *Times* and the *Tribune* began hinting that the Italian communities were indeed evolving "another way" of dealing with free-lance extortionists. The Italian community was taking matters into their own hands. Italians were buying guns:

> Many Italians of Newark have bought second-hand revolvers and guns in the last few days, and about every house in the several Italian colonies there now looks like an arsenal. The Italians, it is said, have armed themselves in fear of the Mafia, for which they refused to contribute to the defence fund of those men held in the city in connections with the "barrel murder mystery."[28]

It was to East Harlem that, after the shoot-out at the New Brighton Dance Hall in 1904, the Morellos and Terranovas brought Paul Kelly to recover from his wounds. He stayed only a block or so away from the house of a more recent immigrant, Francesco Castiglia, better known as Frank Costello. In the 1950s an old resident of East Harlem and acquaintance of Frank Costello, Giuseppe Selvaggi, published his reminiscences. He included a long account from Zi Trestelle, ("Uncle Threestars") a Neapolitan who had arrived in East Harlem in 1912. Zi Trestelle had a high-school diploma and worked as an accountant in the Italian community. Zi Trestelle's account of the beginnings of organized crime in East Harlem is worth retelling, at least in part. Even where it is inaccurate, it probably gives some idea of this story as Italians of the time experienced it. Indeed, the story seems taken from the pages of Verga's *Cavallaria Rusticana*.

In the years after the turn of the century, there was a stable on Second Avenue that stretched along East 108th Street. Everyone in East Harlem knew this stable, for it looked after of the horses for the area's delivery vans. The stable itself was, in the words of one newspaper description, "A rambling one-storey structure, built impartially of sheet-iron, packing boxes, discarded odds and ends of house wreckage—doors for instance with hinges still on them. It is a rabbit warren which shelters two or three junk shops, a wheelwrights, a blacksmiths, a ... boarding stable and a hay and grain store."[29] It resembled, Zi Trestelle remarked, one of those large maintenance garages that a modern trucking company might keep on the outskirts of a city. Like a maintenance garage, the stable did much of its work at night so that the horses and carts could be ready for the morning's round of deliveries. Thus, like other maintenance garages on the outskirts of big cities operating through the wee hours of the night, the stable on 108th Street became a hang-out for East Harlem's low life.

The owner of the stable was a widow from the Abruzzo named Pasquarella. Though she and her family lived a block away, she kept her office just inside the 108th Street entrance. Here were her table and chairs, and here she covered the wall with mysterious black lines drawn in charcoal. The police later wondered about these charcoal lines, speculating that they might be some arcane criminal code. The real explanation was much simpler. Pasquarella was illiterate, and the lines on the walls were her way of keeping accounts. The secret was less in the accounting itself than in what those lines on the wall were keeping accounts of. Along with her other occupations, Pasquarella was a *strozzina* or loan shark.

Usury exists all over the globe, where it is often the only form of credit available to the poor. The principle is simple: a client "rents" a sum of money and agrees that, until the loan is repaid in full, he or she will pay a fixed amount to the usurer every week. Where the amounts are small or where the loans are informal and between friends, the system functions well enough. Indeed, shopkeepers have used these sorts of arrangements for centuries to see their poorer customers through bad patches. Yet the weekly payments, the "vigorish" as they are called, are liable to mount up fast. If someone borrowed $100 and agreed to pay five dollars a week in vigorish, they would be agreeing to an interest of 5 percent per week, 20 percent per month and 240 percent per year. The illiterate rarely understood rates of interest. They were renting the usurer's money just as they were renting their rooms. They simply accepted that they would have to pay their rent until they were able to make repayment. They rarely calculated that, by the time it did, they would have already paid several times the original amount in vigorish.

Unlike occasional usurers like merchants, professional loan sharks are a predatory species. Gamblers are not only liable to fall recklessly into debt;

they are liable to nurture vain hopes that, if only someone will stake them to one more throw, their luck will turn and everything will come out right for them. The stable hands and small-time crooks in Pasquarella's stable whiled away their spare time drinking and playing at cards and dice. This was probably the beginning of her career as a loan shark.

One of the activities of the boys in Pasquarella's stable was rustling horses from the vegetable and meat sellers of East Harlem. Pasquarella would then ransom these horses back to their rightful owners, explaining that one of her boys had just happened to find the animal. She would suggest that the owner might wish to show his gratitude by leaving a substantial tip. No one was fooled, and the cart-owners of East Harlem began to feel that the continual disappearance of their horses and the necessity of ransoming them back again constituted a serious impediment to their businesses. They did not bring their complaints to the police, however, but to the man they were paying to protect them against just such inconveniences—the owner of a bakery at 318 East 109th Street near First Avenue.

Selvaggi identifies this man as a Neapolitan named don Giosuele, zio Mico to his friends. Don Giosuele seems the picture of elegance. He washed himself with scented soaps and carefully waxed and dyed the tips of his mustache. He wore highly-polished boots that came up to his knees, and, as he strode about in his bakery he brandished a black leather whip into whose handle he had had inserted a large turquoise of the most delicate dove's egg blue. He and his band of *guagliuni*, the Neapolitan equivalent of *mafiosi*, were East Harlem's leading *cammoristi*, Neapolitan for "racketeers". This in itself would have made inevitable a showdown between him and Pasquarella. What made matters worse was that don Giosuele ran the *cammora* ("racket") that was taxing East Harlem's cartowners a dollar a week for a protection that they were emphatically not receiving. Yet even this might have been borne if it were not for Pasquarella's carriage.

Pasquarella was a burly giant of a country woman. There was dirt and straw in her unkempt red hair. Despite her wealth, she dressed poorly. Nevertheless, with her stable business, her loan sharking and other activities, Pasquarella had grown immensely rich. Unwisely, Pasquarella chose to flaunt her new-found wealth, bragging that she was the richest woman on 108th Street. She made expensive gifts to her three children and gave lavish offerings to the Madonna del Carmine in her church on 115th Street. She organized trips downtown to the Bowery to see the Italian theatre and the puppet shows. She drove her own personal carriage.

Shortly after his arrival in America, don Giosuele had become infatuated with a charming *entretaineuse* some years younger than himself, whom, in his passion, he had married. As years passed, however, don Giosuele found the performance of his nuptial duties ever more arduous. To console herself for the frigidity of her marital bed, his wife had taken to wrapping herself in luxurious white furs. In compensation for a union unblessed with issue, she had acquired a small, white lap-dog, affectionately naming him "Gioseulino."

Desirous of enhancing her fading charms, she had accessorized her fur and lap-dog combination with gold and pearls and a large-brimmed hat with a trailing white veil. Thus attired, she would ascend into the back seat of the ostentatious carriage that her husband had bought for her and prevail upon one of her husband's *guagliuni* to drive her about the streets of East Harlem. In this way, she at least might have the solace of appearing to be a happy princess in the eyes of the common herd. Imagine her chagrin when, while riding about one fine day intent on soaking up the envy of all who beheld her, she passed the carriage of Pasquarella. The facts that Pasquarella lacked her jewels and fine apparel, that her driver was a common stablehand and that the whole contraption reeked, was as nothing compared to the fact that Pasquarella had the larger carriage. The wife scanned the faces of the passers-by; they were smiling at each other and nodding knowingly. It was a public humiliation too much to bear.

Compelled to pay a call at Pasquarella's stable the following morning, don Giosuele was the picture of gallantry. *Commare* Pasquarella, he began, it has been too long since I paid you a neighborly visit. For we are neighbors after all, and thus people who, in the neighborly way, might perform services for each other. I for my part would be honored if I could be of service to you in any way. Indeed, I hope that we may come to regard each other not simply as neighbors but as part of a single family, always ready to defend each other and shoulder each other's burdens. Truly is it said that when a family is united it is strong, but when it is divided against itself it is weak and vulnerable.

Taken aback by this unwonted burst of fine speech in her stable, Pasquarella paused. Yes, she conceded, they were neighbors and it would be better to work as friends than as enemies. Still, it must be clearly understood that theirs would be a friendship of equals. Neither of them would be boss.

But of course! expostulated don Giosuele. He would not dream of giving orders to Pasquarella. There was one minor point, however, a mere matter of professional courtesy really. Given his rank and seniority and given his long association with venerable Neapolitan confraternities, it would only be fitting if Pasquarella were to pay a small percentage of her earnings to him.

On hearing this, Pasquarella turned to confer with her boys. Then she turned back to don Giosuele and replied, "Don Giosuele, I thank you for your offer. But my boys think that I am as good as any man in this city, and they don't see why I should have to pay tax to you."

With these words, don Giosuele bowed and left the stable.

Pasquarella doted upon her three children, two girls and a boy. Her eldest daughter was of marriageable age, and Pasquarella was already on the look-out for a suitable match. One evening several days after the meeting with don Giosuele, however, the daughter did not return home at her usual hour. As the time for the evening meal came and went, Pasquarella grew more agitated. She sent her boys looking for her, she even asked the police. Around midnight, Pasquarella and her boys went out to look for the daughter themselves. They found her shortly before dawn swaying back and forth as she grasped the parapet of the Bronx River Bridge. She was moaning softly to herself as she stared down at the water below. At first she refused to even acknowledge the presence of her mother, who quickly understood what had happened. Her daughter had been kidnapped and dishonored by a pack of *guagliuni*, sent out for that express purpose by don Giosuele.

It is probably well to interrupt Zi Trestelle's account at this juncture. On October 29, 1911, Pasquarella Spinelli's daughter, Nellie Lenere, visited the police station on East 104th Street and told the police that a man had just met with an accident in her home. When the police arrived to investigate, the police discovered a man, whom they immediately recognized as the gangster Frank "Chick" Monaco, pinned to the floor by a large safe on his chest. Monaco was dead. Though Nellie Lenere first claimed that Monaco had died because the safe had accidentally fallen on him, she was forced to reconsider her evidence when a cursory examination revealed that Monaco had been stabbed twenty-five times and was probably dead by the time someone had added insult to injury by dropping the safe on him. Confronted with the improbability of her initial account, Nellie Lenere now described how she had killed Monaco herself when she had caught him trying to steal the safe. But whoever had killed Monaco had given him a good going-over. When Nellie Lenere had come to the police, however, neither her clothes nor her hair gave the slightest indication of a violent struggle. Someone had killed Monaco; but it had not been Nellie Lenere. Arrested and sent to the Tombs on suspicion of being an accomplice to murder, Lenere began to recount a more complex, and probably more truthful, account.

Two years earlier, she said, she had married a certain Gaetano Napolitano in a civil ceremony. She and Napolitano had planned to hold a religious ceremony, but Napolitano had mysteriously disappeared before the church ceremony could be arranged. Monaco, who was connected to the stable, was well known to both Pasquarella and Nellie. He recently told Nellie that he had discovered her missing husband's whereabouts. He lured her to a cottage in Westchester, where he robbed her and held her prisoner for two days, possibly raping her as well. Zi Trestelle's account of the dishonoring of Pasquarella's daughter at the hands of don Giosuele's *guagliuni* seems a reference to Monaco's abduction of Nellie Lenere. Indeed, according to the police reconstruction, it was Monaco that had been trying to blackmail Pasquarella.

With Morello and Lupo in prison on counterfeiting charges, leadership of the Italian underworld in East Harlem passed to Giosue Gallucci—the "Don Giosuele" of Zi Trestelle's account. Gallucci was indeed a Neapolitan. He had immigrated in 1899 with his brother, Gennaro, who had recently escaped from a Neapolitan prison where he was serving a life sentence for a double murder. There is thus reason to accept Zi Trestelle's claim that Gallucci was connected to the camorra.[30]

Several hours after finding her dishonored daughter—to resume Zi Trestelle's story—Pasquarella was standing outside don Giosuele's bakery.

"*Vendetta!*" she yelled, "*Vendetta eterna!*" She stayed there proclaiming vendetta for the entire morning until everyone in the bakery and everyone in East
Harlem knew. Then adding that don Giosuele and his crew should now begin
to dig their own graves, she turned on her heels and went back to her stable.

Everyone expected Pasquarella to enact some deed of terrible vengeance.
Don Giosuele and his crew barricaded themselves in their bakery, too frightened to leave. Yet nothing happened. The street remained quiet. After a week,
don Giosuele sent out his crew to scout out the area. When they came back,
they reported that after crying vengeance, Pasquarella had returned to her
stable and fallen into a state of lethargy. She sat in her old chair and stared
dumbly at the wall. Timidly at first, don Giosuele's crew began to leave the
bakery and take up their old activities. Soon they were back in business as
usual.

After several months, don Giosuele had grown confidant enough to send
an assassin to Pasquarella's stable. To escape the summer heat, Pasquarella
had had her easy-chair moved outside and placed under a shade tree. As she
sat there half-asleep, fanning herself, the assassin walked up before her and
planted five shots into her belly before walking away.

As Zi Trestelle tells it, determined to punish Pasquarella for her public defiance of him and her refusal to pay him protection, "don Giosuele" Gallucci
had been responsible for the dishonoring of the daughter and the subsequent
murder of Pasquarella. Yet it was Monaco who had attempted to blackmail
Pasquarella; it was Monaco who had abducted and possibly raped her daughter, ending his days pinned under a large safe. But Chick Monaco had no
apparent connection with Gallucci. Instead, he was connected to "Zoppo the
Gimp," the nick-name of a much-feared Black Hander named Aniello Prisco.
Zoppo was said to have sworn vendetta for the murder of his friend Chick Monaco; and so it was Zoppo whom the police suspected of killing Pasquarella
Spinelli in 1912.[31]

The murders of Chick Monaco and Pasquarella Spinelli initiated a chain
of vendetta slayings in East Harlem. Whether Gallucci was involved in either
of the initial killings, as the rising power in the East Harlem underworld, it
was inevitable that he would eventually be sucked in. Whatever his connection
with the camorra, Gallucci was principally a businessman. Unlike Morello
and Lupo, who used their store-fronts merely as a means of putting counterfeit
notes into circulation and who let their businesses fail once they had achieved
their purposes, Gallucci was a successful entrepreneur. After the conviction
of Morello and Lupo in 1910, Gallucci enlarged his empire, acquiring bakeries, ice hauling firms, coal firms, timber yards, Italian import stores and
commercial and residential properties in both East Harlem and Little Italy.
By 1912, Gallucci was becoming "the most powerful Italian politically in the
city," one that was "exceptionally active" in municipal political campaigns.
So politically active had he become that he had acquired "a certain measure of
immunity from police interference."[32] As the Gallucci empire in East Harlem
expanded, however, it began to encroach into Morello territory.

The Italian lottery (*lotteria*), also called "policy," or, today, the "numbers racket" is a type of gambling that, in Italy, is at least as old as the Renaissance. Though the church and municipal authorities frowned on all types of gambling, the lottery was considered a relatively innocuous pastime. Indeed, it became part of the traditional culture of the urban poor in South Italy, supporting an elaborate and arcane pseudo-science devoted to assigning numerical values to dreams and incidents in order to predict the winning number. In Naples, protection of the lottery as well as other games of chance naturally fell to the underworld—the *camorra*. The word *camorra* itself is usually derived from *capo e morra* or the boss or *capo* of the game of *morra,* another traditional game of chance.

Gambling and protection rackets developed in a natural symbiosis. Even when the stakes were small, a game of chance was like a honey pot, attracting the unwanted attentions of any half-witted thug who might consider knocking it off. Gambling was profitable and protection was always necessary; and thus the men who ran the games of chance in the cities of the Italian South were likely to be connected to the urban underworld. This was true in Italy and America. In September 1908, Vincenzo Terranova was indicated as the killer of "Diamond Sam" Sicco, an "Italian lottery" owner in East Harlem. By 1912, however, East Harlem had a new policy king—Giosue Gallucci.

One of Gallucci's bodyguards was a boxer named Antonio Saraca, who fought under the name of Young Sharkey. Suspected of involvement in several murders and under police surveillance, Saraca rarely strayed from the area around the Gallucci bakery. In September 1912, while playing cards in Jacko's café on East 109th Street, he was shot in the head. The police suspected Aniello "Zoppo" Prisco. Prisco had already been linked to four killings in 1912. According to the press, he was the most vicious Black Hander in East Harlem. The four killings attributed to him had been intended as punishments to clients who had refused to pay their protection money and to encourage cooperation and prompt payments in all future clients. In December 1912, however, Prisco's own turn came up.

Gallucci had been a Black Hand target for years. Prisco had arranged a meeting with Gallucci at a barber shop on East 104th. But Prisco decided not to show up, sending a message that he would meet Gallucci at the bakery on 109th Street instead. He turned up there around midnight and was shot twice in the head by Gallucci's nephew and bodyguard, John Russomano. Gallucci later explained that Prisco had been armed and that Russomano had shot him in self-defence. Given Prisco's violent precedents, the police were inclined to credit Gallucci's version: the notorious Aniello Prisco alias Zoppo the Gimp, the infamous Black Hander, had been attempting to blackmail Gallucci but had been shot instead. If that were all there was to it, it should have been the end of the story. But it was not. The killings continued.

Less than three months later, Russomano and his own bodyguard were shot while standing at the doorway of Russomano's house opposite the Gallucci bakery. The bodyguard was killed instantly, though Russomano suffered only a fractured arm. Whoever had done the shooting had been hiding nearby, waiting for Russomano to show up. They had even put silencers on their guns. The ambush was attributed to Prisco's partner, Amadio Buonomo. Buonomo however denied involvement. Whoever had shot Russomano was now after him as well, he told a *Herald* reporter. He was afraid to go east of Third Avenue, afraid even to visit his own coffee shop; "I very seldom leave my flat, and then I am closely guarded. The men who are to kill me are always near the house. I see them, but with my guard they are afraid to attack me." Buonomo was fatally shot in April 1913. Before expiring he was quoted as saying; "I knew they would get me, but my friends will get them, and this feud will go on until all of them are wiped out of existence. They killed my friend Prisco, the cripple." There was no indication of who the *they* were.

These murders took place against the background of the police crackdown against hoodlums and gamblers ordered by Commissioner Waldo. Up to now, the three police flying squads had concentrated their activities in Midtown and Downtown Manhattan. In the Spring of 1913, Deputy Commissioner Dougherty ordered the squads into Harlem. Thirty-five Italians were arrested in late July either in gambling raids or for Sullivan Law violations. Among those arrested on concealed weapons charges were Giosue Gallucci and two of his bodyguards, his nephew John Russomano and Joseph "Chuck" Nazzaro. Considering how politically well connected Gallucci was reputed to be, it seems odd that he lacked a proper gun permit. Even these arrests did not halt the chain of killings. After Pasquarella's murder, ownership of her stable had passed to her partner, the elderly Luigi Lazzazara. Lazzazara had also been close to both Monaco and Prisco and was rumored to have a part in the scheme to blackmail Pasquarella. He was stabbed to death in an altercation in February 1914. Angelo Losco, a saloon keeper on East 108th Street, was later arrested in connection with the murder. In May, Charles Lomonte, who ran a hay and grain business a few doors away from the stable, was shot three times in the back. In early 1915, Carmine Mollica was ambushed and killed. In May of 1915, the killers finally got to Gallucci.

According to Zi Trestelle, after Pasquarella's death, don Giosuele had taken over her loan-sharking business. He announced that all of Pasquarella's debts were now owing to him, and that he would expect to receive the vigorish in full. It was not a popular move. There is a saying that the capo should not eat alone. He should take care of those below. But don Giosuele was a greedy old miser. When someone spoke up for the members of Pasquarella's crew, don Giosuele had him murdered.

In May 1915 don Giosuele was hosting a banquet in a restaurant next to his bakery. Two unknown men suddenly appeared at the door. They bowed courteously to the company seated at the banqueting table, then pulled out revolvers and pointed them at don Giosuele, shouting to those seated around him to "Get away from those two." By `those two' they meant don Giosuele and his son, a young man returned from Naples to visit his father. Don Giosuele implored the men to spare at least his son, innocent of any involvement in their quarrel. But they had chosen this moment. To avenge all the hardships that don Giosuele and his band of Neapolitans had visited upon the Sicilians and Calabrians of East Harlem, it was not enough to kill him. They needed to dishonor him as well. The two men fired their guns in unison, each bullet passing through their victim's heart. Two master shots, Zio Trestelle commented, the marksmen were in no way disturbed by the large, white dinner napkins hanging from the victims' collars.

In fact, Giosue Gallucci and his son Luca were murdered around 10 a.m. in a coffee shop that Gallucci had just acquired a few doors away from the bakery. There were four killers rather than two, and they fired a total of seven shots. None of them were master shots; Luca Gallucci died the evening of the shooting while his father hung on for three days, dying to the sound of church bells as his son's funeral cortege was passing by. There were about fifteen people in the coffee shop when the shooting took place, but no one "saw" anything, nor could anyone identify the shooters. Nor was even this the end of the killing. In October 1915, Charles Lomonte's brother Thomas was shot in the back. In the same month, the new owner of Pasquarella's stable, Ippolito Greco, was also shot and killed.

Beyond the embellishments and factual errors, what is striking about Zi Trestelle's account is what it does not say. Zi Trestelle does not come out and say that don Giosuele had been killed by the Morello–Terranova family. He does, however, strongly imply it. In newspaper accounts, the East Harlem killings were Black Hand murders and little more. The fact that three successive owners of the stables on East 108th Street—Pasquarella, Luigi Lazzazara and Ippolito Greco—had been assassinated implied that some sort of turf struggle was going on as well. Still, the newspapers did not interpret the killings as a gang war, much less an ethnic war between the Neapolitan camorra and the rest of the Italian underworld. This, however, was Zi Trestelle's version of the events.

Maybe Zi Trestelle was frightened. When he told his story to Selvaggi, probably some time in the 1930s, Ciro Terranova was still alive and dangerous. Zi Trestelle may have been reluctant to tell the world everything he knew, especially that Ciro had taken part in the Gallucci murders. Or maybe Zi Trestelle just did not know.

If Zi Trestelle interpreted the murder stable killings in the context of a struggle between the Neapolitan camorra and the Sicilian mafia, it was surely because this was the way the Italians living in East Harlem at the time interpreted the events. The real explanation, however, would have been known only to a handful of men, the very men who had the least motive for providing us with full and correct explanations. We have no way of knowing whether contemporary Italians had it right. The meaning of historical events can be lost when their context is lost. This is a sort of knowledge that exists only in people's heads, and it is just this sort of contextual knowledge that is liable to deteriorate as the older community breaks up.

The murder stable killings left a tradition of confusion behind them. The term *murder stable* was invented by the newspapers to refer, appropriately enough, to Pasquarella's stable on East 108th Street. Eventually, however, the name began to be applied to the nearby Morello house on East 107th Street. The usually well-informed Virgil Peterson writes; "[Ciro] Terranova and his allies brought mobsters to this place; there the guests either agreed to the demands of the Terranova forces or were eliminated. The police asserted that at least twenty-three men were put to death in the murder stable between 1900 and 1917." Carl Sifakas ups the ante, informing us that on some unspecified occasion, "The authorities dug up the premises, unearthing the remains of about 60 murder victims." But Morello and Lupo only acquired the East 107th Street property in 1904, and it became the Morello family residence only after the bankruptcy of the Ignazio Florio Association in 1908. After 1904, Lupo, though undoubtedly committing crimes, was often in hiding; after 1910, he was in jail. For his part, Asbury, adds that the murder stable was "the scene of more killing than any other spot in America, with the exception of the Bloody Angle of Doyers Street in Chinatown." For some unknown reason, however, Asbury locates the murder stable even further away, on East 125th Street. He finally relates that Lupo the Wolf and his followers "were reputed to be able to cast the evil eye, and to possess other magical powers."[33]

The sudden epidemic of Black Hand extortion in the new century not only terrorized ordinary Italians. It threatened the Italian underworld as well. Shortly before his own murder, the East Harlem Black Hander Aniello Prisco had agreed to meet Giosue Gallucci at the barbershop of the Del Gaudio brothers. Nicolo and Gaetano Del Gaudio were Neapolitan immigrants and friends of Gallucci. They were also member of the East Harlem camorra, involved in gambling and connected to Neapolitan gangs in Brooklyn. Suspecting that he would be putting himself in an exposed position at the barbershop, Prisco later cancelled the meeting. Perhaps he suspected that Gallucci was planning to ambush him. It is even possible that he was right. With the help of the Del Gaudio brothers, Gallucci was indeed contemplating Prisco's elimination. In whichever case, when Prisco approached the Gallucci bakery later that evening, he was angry. Gallucci gang member John Russoman claimed that he had shot Prisco in self-defense, given Zoppo the Gimp's unsavory reputation, the police were willing to give him the benefit of the doubt.[34]

The citizens of East Harlem were probably relieved that Prisco was no longer among them. Nevertheless, even though he was hardly popular, he had his own supporters. Within a few years, the two Del Gaudio brothers as well as Gallucci had been murdered. Even for well-protected gangsters, Black Handers still represented a menace.

The Black Hand gangs sowed terror in Italian communities. They even threatened the Italian underworld. But for the underworld, they also represented an opportunity. As Petacco relates it, in 1904 a small shopkeeper from Elizabeth Street on the Lower East Side described the following scene to the New York police:

There were three of them, tough-looking guys, but well-dressed and very polite. They knew that I had been receiving "*lettere di scrocco*" and so they came to offer me their protection. "You've got to trust us, don Vincenzo," they told me putting their hands on their hearts, "from today on, no one is going to touch a hair on your or on anybody in your family's head." So I asked them why they should do this for me, and what they were asking in return, because I could see that they weren't the types that were going to give you something for nothing. *Fateci vagnari lu pizzu*, was all they replied.[35]

Though the literal meaning the dialect word *pizzu* was "beak," the term also referred to a coal-scuttle-like implement used in Sicily to scoop up grain. Estate guards and other officials customarily had the right to take one scuttle-full or beak-full of grain from each share-cropper's share of the harvest each year. They were, that is, allowed to wet their beak (*vagnari lu pizzu*) at the share-cropper's expense. In this way the term came to stand for any sort of imposed tribute: corrupt officials after bribes, gangsters selling protection—they all wished to wet their beaks at someone else's expence. Ordinary Sicilians naturally resented the custom. Why should share-croppers be required to pay a tribute to the landowner's men? Why should shopkeepers be forced to pay protection to gangsters? But conditions in immigrant communities in the first years of the new century changed this attitude. The Black Hand panic had created a seller's market in protection. The underworld was offering a service that ordinary citizens wanted to buy.

In its obituary, the *Herald* spoke of Giosue Galllucci as "the most powerful Italian politically in the city." The article went on to mention Gallucci's many and varied business interests, his political influence, and his "immunity from police interference." Clearly Gallucci had been a power in the Italian underworld. He seems, however, to have been an elder statesman, intermediary, and fixer. He was the "Boss" or "King of Little Italy" in the way that Big Tim Sullivan had been the "Boss" of the Lower East Side or "King of the Underworld," rather than the way Giuseppe Morello or Ignazio Lupo had each been an active Italian underworld *capo*. This had made Gallucci a target for Black Handers. He received threats for years and surrounded himself with bodyguards. It was not salubrious work; ten of Gallucci's bodyguards were murdered in ambushes. Gallucci was repeatedly shot at and "wounded many times." He grew fatalistic. A week before his murder, The Boss had predicted, "I know they will get me yet." He did not specify who. Perhaps he did not event know himself.[36]

Under Gallucci's leadership, a gradual shake-out in the Italian underworld was taking place. Strong gangs, like the Morello gang, consolidated their power. As they did so, they drove the independent Black Hand gangs out of business, sometimes eliminating them physically. But Gallucci himself was eliminated in 1915. The immediate beneficiaries were the Morello-Terranova brothers. The convictions of Giuseppe Morello and Ignazio Lupo in a federal court in 1910 had crippled the Morello gang. The three remaining brothers had needed to fight to keep their control of rackets in East Harlem and Lower

Manhattan. The elimination of Gallucci helped them tighten their grip on East Harlem and the Bronx and removed an obstacle to their further expansion.

But the murder of Gallucci also made their lives more precarious. Within the Italian underworld, the powerful, highly respected, and well connected Gallucci was a moderating influence. Without that influence there was little to prevent a large-scale gang war from developing.

THE FIRST MAFIA-CAMORRA WAR

With Gallucci's death, the most important Italian gangs in New York City were the Morello gang in East Harlem and a set of Neapolitan gangs in Brooklyn centered in Navy Street and in Coney Island. The Navy Street gang was led by Alessandro Vollere and Leo Lauritano, and their headquarters was Lauritano's coffee shop on Navy Street in South Brooklyn. The Coney Island gang was headed by Pelligrino Morano, who ran it from his Santa Lucia restaurant. Up to now, the gangs had behaved with proper respect towards each other, avoiding antagonizing the others or encroaching on their territories. Every year, at the invitation of Andrea Ricci, a respected elder statesmen in the Brooklyn camorra, the Morello-Terranova brothers went to Brooklyn for a smoker (a festivity) held in their honor.

On June 24, 1916, Pelligrino Morano invited the East Harlem Sicilians to his Coney Island restaurant to discuss a new project. Morano explained that the Brooklyn gangs wished to expand into Manhattan. They wanted to set up gambling parlors and sell drugs and protection there. They were particularly interested in taking control of the Italian policy rackets and the numerous *zicchinetta* card games in Little Italy. Before making any moves, however, etiquette and elementary common sense counseled that they should discuss their project with the Morello gang. Morano offered to cut the Morellos in on both the numbers racket and the *zicchinetta* games. The details of the split could be worked out among themselves. The Morellos were represented by Nicolo Morello and his number two, Steve LaSalle. Nicolo replied that he would happy to agree to the Brooklyn gangs' offer. Before he could accept, however, he needed the Neapolitans to do him a special favor—kill Joe DeMarco.

Nicolo Morello had two reasons to want DeMarco (or DiMarco) dead. The first was straightforward: DeMarco had run a rival gambling operation in East Harlem. When the Morellos had tried to take it over, DeMarco tried to have Nicolo Morello killed. Morello responded by sending his own guns after DeMarco. After the two failed attempts on his life, DeMarco had relocated his operations Downtown, first on Mott Street and later at a club at 54 James Street.

The second motive was more complex: DeMarco had tried to block Morello's control of the *Unione Siciliana* in East Harlem. Both the Morello gang and the Brooklyn gangs were sectarians; in a trial the following year, witnesses gave detailed accounts of the organization and initiation rites of both the East Harlem mafia and the Brooklyn camorra.[37] The *Unione Siciliana* was a large Sicilian immigrant fraternal society founded in New York near the end of the nineteenth century. Shortly after 1900, the mafia, specifically perhaps the Morellos, began to insinuate themselves into the association. Although the large majority of its members in both New York and Chicago were not gangsters, by 1920 the *Unione* in both cities was underworld controlled.[38]

In their 1940 *Gang Rule in New York* , Craig Thompson and Allen Raymond state that Ciro Terranova was head of *Unione Siciliana*, and its headquarters was on East 108th Street.[39] Neither piece of information is quite exact. It seems likely that, before 1910, Giuseppe Morello and/or Ignazio Lupo were president of the *Unione*. After their incarceration, however, the president became Salvatore D'Aquilo, a cheese importer. It is not clear whether D'Aquila was also an underworld power; but the fact that he was murdered on the orders of Joe "the Boss" Masseria at the beginning of the Castellammarese War in 1928 suggests that he was. Nicolo Morello and Ciro Terranova became the new leaders of the Morello gang, though we do not know what position either held in the *Unione Siciliana*.

Giuseppe Morello's home on East 107th might have doubled as the *Unione Siciliana* clubhouse; but it is not certain. The mafia embedded themselves in otherwise legitimate associations like the *Unione Siciliana* in order to provide a cover and a means of extending their influence in the rest of the community. Using as the association headquarters Giuseppe Morello's old home, under whose floorboards the remains of an unknown number of the gang's victims supposedly lay rotting, would hardly have contributed to the picture of the *Unione Siciliana* as an innocuous beneficent brotherhood. It would be like putting a torture chamber in the Elks Club basement.

There were, in any case, more than one association in New York City calling itself the *Unione Siciliana,* and there may even have been rival branches in East Harlem itself. One of the Brooklyn gunmen, "Johnny Lefty" Esposito, later testified that Morello wanted DeMarco killed because he was trying to set up a rival branch.[40]

When he heard that the price of Nicolo Morello's cooperation was the murder of DeMarco, Morano stalled for time. DeMarco had the rank of a boss, and Morano was afraid to agree to the murder on his authority alone. He told Morello that he would first have to discuss the matter with the other Brooklyn gang leaders. Later, after discussing the matter with Lauritano and possibly Vollero, he sent word to Morello that they would agree to the hit.

Three weeks later, Morello, LaSalle and Terranova returned to Brooklyn to plan the murder with Leo Lauritano. With them they brought Giuseppe Verizzano (or Verazzano). Verizzano was an important Lower East Side gambling operator, who had worked with DeMarco in his East Harlem days. Verizzano and DeMarco were still on good terms, and Verizzano would easily be able to get past the guards outside DeMarco's James Street club. Once inside, he would point out DeMarco to the gunmen. Since DeMarco's men knew who the Morello gunmen were, it was essential that they use men from Brooklyn instead.

Lauritano gave the job to John "The Painter" Fetto. But Fetto had never been to Manhattan. He crossed the Brooklyn Bridge only to get lost in the labyrinth of Little Italy. By the time he found DeMarco's James Street club, it was too late. DeMarco had already left.

The failure of the first attempt made the Morellos jumpy. DeMarco suspected that the Morellos were planning something, and had begun bringing down bodyguards from East Harlem. Lauritano and Fetto got into a shouting match, and Lauritano assigned two more men to the shooting party— Johnny Lefty Esposito and Tom Pagano. He also assigned Rocco Valente to stay outside and act as look-out. Lauritano also bribed the club's doorman, Nick Sassi, to let the killers in through the kitchen. The killing of DeMarco was being planned as a major hit, an indication of the importance that Nicolo Morello attached to it.

The shooting party met up for lunch at a restaurant on Elizabeth Street on the Lower East Side. They then walked to the James Street club where Sassi let them in through the kitchen as planned. When they got inside the club, Fetto, Esposito, and Pagano found Verizzano seated at a gambling table playing cards. Directly opposite him were two other players. Misreading Verizzano's signals, and perhaps nervous over his earlier failure, Fetto pulled out his revolver and killed Charles Lombardi—a man who had the misfortune to be seated next to DeMarco at the time. In the confusion that followed, Verizzano picked up a revolver and killed DeMarco himself. Then Verizzano fled upstairs and, with the other three and escaped through a bedroom window.

DeMarco was murdered in his James Street club on the afternoon of July 20, 1916. That morning, Terranova and LaSalle had arrived at Lauritano's to make the final arrangements. After that, they simply stayed in Brooklyn awaiting the news. As soon as they heard DeMarco was dead, they called Nicolo Morello and Vincenzo Terranova, telling them to come down to Brooklyn. Together with other members of their gang, they assembled at the Navy Street clubhouse to celebrate with Lauritano. Verizzano, who had actually pulled the trigger, was there as well, and was no doubt roundly congratulated by all for his presence of mind. The Morellos presented Lauritano with a fifty-dollar honorarium, telling him to spread it among his gunmen. The only matter casting a pall over the festivities was the fact that the man Johnny Lefty had murdered by mistake, Charles Lombardi, had been a good friend of Lauritano's. Annoyed at the loss of his friend, Lauritano docked Johnny Lefty's pay from fifteen dollars to ten dollars a week. This left Esposito feeling aggrieved. Why, he complained, should he be forced to suffer for what had, after all, been an innocent mistake?

Despite the jubilation of the Morellos, the immediate beneficiaries of the DeMarco hit were the Navy Streeters. There was nothing now to stop them setting up their games in Lower Manhattan.

When Pelligrino Morano told Nicolo Morello that he first needed the assent of the other Brooklyn leaders before killing DeMarco, he had either failed to contact Alessandro Vollero, or else, at some point, Vollero changed his mind. Vollero had been an associate of DeMarco; he had never been an associate of the Morellos. He had taken no part in the DeMarco hit, and, afterwards, told Morano and Lauritano that, having gotten rid of DeMarco, the Brooklyn gangs ought to get rid of the Morellos as well.

He arranged a meeting Downtown. On September 7, Nicolo Morello and Charles Ubriaco arrived at a club in Little Italy. They were served drinks by a Navy Street gang member named Ralph Daniello. At a certain point, Tom Pagano showed up and told them that the meeting had been changed. He was supposed to take them over to Brooklyn instead. Suspecting nothing, Morello and Ubriaco let Pagano drive them into Brooklyn where, as they got out of the car and were walking towards Myrtle Avenue, they were ambushed. Pagano shot and killed Nicolo Morello. His bodyguard, Ubriaco, was killed by another Navy Streeter, Thomas Carillo.

A month later, Verizzano was murdered. Perhaps as a reward for his part in the DeMarco murder, Verizzano was allowed to extend his operations on the Lower East Side. On October 6, a party of five men led by Charles Giordano from Staten Island, burst into the Italian Gardens restaurant at the Occidental Hotel, the old Sullivan headquarters, and murdered Verizzano.

In the final months of 1916, full-scale war between the Navy Streeters from Brooklyn and the Morellos from East Harlem broke out. Though the war was over control of gambling, drugs, and other rackets on the Lower East Side, the fighting itself was city-wide. The Morellos were particularly mobile. Ciro Terranova drove a modern, black open-body Packard, while his brother Vincenzo had a red Hudson. The Morellos seem to have used the war to clean the last remnants of the Gallucci gang from East Harlem. It was during this period that the nick-name *murder stable* moved from Paquarella's stable on East 107th Street to the Morello home on East 108th. The stories of piles of dead bodies rotting underneath the floorboards dates from this period as well. The war even spread outside the city. Andrea Ricci, the camorra's elder statesman, paid a visit to Philadelphia, and, as a consequence, four Philadelphia gangsters from Sicily were murdered.

Before launching his attack on the Morellos, Alessandro Vollero had made careful preparations. He had recruited a regular army of Brooklyn Neapolitans: married members of his gang were paid twenty dollars a week; single members received ten dollars. Even occasional members or those not engaged in the fighting were supposed to receive seven dollars. Such payments rapidly depleted the gang's war chest, and Vollero foresaw that he would need to establish new sources of income. He planned to cover his war costs by looting the Lower East Side underworld and honky tonks. He taxed the gamblers and moved in on the protection rackets over ice and coal haulage. He tried to take over the Morellos' artichoke racket, demanding that wholesalers pay the gang fifty dollars for each railcar load of artichokes arriving in the city from California. The demand was exorbitant, and, forming their own organization, Italian food wholesalers in Brooklyn and Manhattan made a counter-offer of fifteen dollars a load.[41] Eventually the two sides compromised at the figure of twenty-five dollars.

The Brooklyn camorra's onslaught into the Lower East Side had set the Morellos reeling. Vollero had hoped to catch the entire Morello leadership in the September 7 ambush, though he had to be content with the murder of Nicolo Morello. Ciro and Vincenzo Terranova had not come to the meeting. Steve LaSalle was temporarily in prison. Still, after the ambush, Vollero held the upper hand. In the subsequent trial, a East Harlem gambler testified that during this period he had to travel every week to Brooklyn and submit his books to the examination of the Neapolitans. It was a total inversion of the natural order; Manhattan was paying tribute to Brooklyn.

Vollero and the Neapolitans tried to move the war uptown. The Terranova brothers survived a series of assassination attempts in November 1916. They also foiled attempts of Brooklyn gunmen to rent rooms across the street from their home on East 116th Street. Still, the Morellos were on the defensive, desperately scrambling to defend their East Harlem territories from the Brooklyn attack.

In May 1917, however, an event occurred that led to a sudden unraveling of the whole war. Ralph Daniello, who had been involved in the Morello, Ubriaco, and Verizzano murders, suddenly eloped to Reno with a Miss Amelia Valve from Prospect Street in South Brooklyn. It had all been rather sudden, and Daniello soon found himself short of cash. He sent letters to his friends at Navy Street asking them to forward him his pay. But romantic escapes to the Nevada desert were not among the benefits that the Brooklyn gang offered its gunmen, and the gang simply ignored his requests. When the Brooklyn police discovered these letters in a raid on camorra headquarters, they wired the police in Reno asking them to bring Daniello in. Surprisingly perhaps, the Reno police found Daniello just where he said he would be.

The Navy Street gangs had been making ample pay-offs to the police in Brooklyn, who, in turn, had allowed them to operate almost openly. The gangs had, in consequence, become lax over security, leaving all sorts of incriminating evidence lying around, happy to believe that their friends on the force would never do anything so rude as to search their premises. Yet gambling and protection rackets were one thing, a city-wide gangland war was quite another. The Brooklyn police soon began to feel a pressure bearing down upon their heads so intense that it overcame their sense of camaraderie with their gangland friends. When Daniello arrived back in New York, he was arrested and dismayed to be told that the police intended to indict him on first-degree murder charges in the murders of Morello, Ubriaco and Verizzano. He was sure to get the chair. Impressed by the prospect, Daniello began to cooperate fully.[42]

The arrest of Daniello in May 1917 changed everything. When the Brooklyn police realized the implications of Daniello's confession, they brought him to the office of King's County (Brooklyn) District Attorney, Edward Swann. For the next ten days, Daniello told Swann all he knew about the Brooklyn camorra—the organization and ceremonies, the rackets and activities of the recent murders. The Brooklyn police and the New York criminal justice system was soon doing what the Morellos could not do themselves, snatching victory from the jaws of defeat.

In Daniello's confession, the Morellos were featured only as adversaries and victims. Nicolo Morello now being dead, the best the authorities could do was to indict Ciro Terranova as an accessory in the DeMarco murder. He had been charged on the testimony of Johnny Lefty; but he was later acquitted when that testimony could not be corroborated. The Neapolitan gunmen were, by contrast, convicted of manslaughter, receiving from six to ten year sentences. Though clearly guilty in the DeMarco murder, Leo Lauritano had played a minor role in the subsequent mafia-camorra war. He received a twenty-one year sentence, though he was paroled after serving only seven years. He was than re-arrested in connection with the Verizzano murder and served an additional five. The Coney Island gang leader, Pelligrino Morano was convicted of murder in the second degree and sentenced to twenty years in Sing Sing. The leader of the Brooklyn Neapolitans, Alessandro Vollero received a life sentence in Sing Sing. Daniello got a suspended sentence. By 1918 the Neapolitan camorra had been decimated, and its leaders were all behind bars. Fortune had smiled upon the Sicilian mafia.[43]

Chapter Four
Expanding Immigration: Chicago and the Levee

For many, the port of entry was no more than their starting point. New Orleans' Sicilian community had soon begun to travel upstream, heading north along the Mississippi. Those landing in New York and other Atlantic Seaboard ports often headed west where new settlements were being created and new jobs offered. Turn-of-the-century America still had something of the aspect of an unfinished rag doll. Though its basic contours were by now fully delineated, its shape still lacked volume, still needed filling out. The immigrants played their part in this filling out process. At the confluence of all this traffic, north-bound and west-bound, however, stood the booming new heart of Industrial America—Chicago: Queen of the Prairies, Capitol of the Midwest.

In truth, Chicago had always possessed another qualification as well. It had a reputation for special wickedness. In the 1830s, when the city was still but a portage on the Chicago River, "The portage's single hotel was a barracks, its streets were pig-wallows, and all the long summer night the Pottawattomies mourned beside that river: down in the barracks the horse-dealers and horse-stealers were making a night of it again. Whiskey-and-vermilion hustlers painting the night vermilion."[1] The passage, as true Chicagoans will no doubt recognize, comes from the opening pages of Nelson Algren's *Chicago: City on the Make*. Nor do things get better in the pages that follow.

The Pottawattomies may have been first to mourn at the banks of the Chicago River, but they were far from the last. They would be joined by ranks of revivalist preachers, vice crusaders and civic reformers, those whom Algren simply refers to as the "Do-Gooders." The Do-Gooders rarely had anything good to say about Chicago. "The sovereign people may govern Chicago in theory," declared the English moral reformer William T. Stead in the 1890s "[but] as a matter of fact King Boodle is monarch of all he surveys."[2] Nor was it simply a matter of graft, corruption, hard-drinking, and painted ladies. The East Coast papers also poured ridicule on Chicago's cultural pretensions during the Columbian Exposition. In 1902, a British journalist visiting Chicago commented, "Having seen it, I urgently desire never to see it again. It is inhabited by savages."[3] Arriving from London to drum up war support, Rudyard Kipling found the Palmer House, Chicago's most sumptuous hotel, ugly and vulgar, "a gilded and mirrored rabbit warren . . . a huge hall of tessellated marble, crammed with people talking about money and spitting about everywhere." He too hoped that he would never be required to visit the city again.[4]

Even before Prohibition, Chicago had acquired its own black legend; it was a city on the make, a city of hustlers and swindlers, of hard drinking and dirty fighting. It was the city of Tyson Yerkes, the Black Sox, of the Levee with its black and tans and the Everleigh sisters. It was as if destiny was carefully preparing the ground for Al Capone.

The notoriety was perhaps unavoidable. Sitting on the southern shore of Lake Michigan, and with a rapidly expanding rail network connecting it to the entire continent, Chicago was not only uniquely placed to take advantage of industrial growth; it stuck out like a sore thumb. An upstart town to begin with, Chicago was born again when it arose from the ashes of the Great Fire of 1871. As the city sprang to life for a second time, immigrants seemed to pour in. And what an indigestible lump of newcomers it was. Between 1890 and 1910, Chicago became, after New York, America's largest city. Displacing earlier Yankee and Irish settlements, immigrants eventually formed the largest communities of Poles, Swedes, Norwegians, Danes, Bohemians, Dutch, Croats, Slovaks, Lithuanians, and Greeks in all of America. Chicago became the second largest Bohemian city in the world, the third largest Swedish, the third largest Norwegian, the forth Polish, and fifth German. There were growing Jewish, Southern Italian, and Sicilian communities.

Arriving too suddenly and from too many different places, Chicago's immigrants brought a full complement of Old World animosities along with them. Divided by language, religion, ethnicity, and history, immigrant political affiliation in immigrant Chicago was often simply an expression of the venerable principle that the enemy of my enemy is my friend. The Chicago Germans, resenting the influence of the Irish Mike McDonald and his successor, Roger Sullivan, in the Chicago Democrat Party, turned to the Republicans. But the city's growing Polish community, apt to view the Germans, especially German Protestants, as their historic enemies, viewed the Catholic Irish as potential allies and joined the Democrat Party. Yet the Poles had their own enemies. In 1919 the Lithuanian National Congress, meeting in Chicago, accused the Polish army of oppressing Lithuania. In that same year, Chicago's Jewish community protested against Polish pogroms; there was a large protest demonstration in the Loop. Shortly after this, the Poles took to the street over a rumor that a Polish child had been murdered by a Jewish grocer.[5] Such internal division made it impossible for either the Democrats or the Republicans in Chicago to establish themselves as the champions of immigrants in general.

The 1890 census revealed that Chicago's population stood at a little over 1 million. The population had doubled in ten years, and it would soon double again. By 1900, the figure was almost 1.7 million. The crossroads of the nations was expanding at an almost unimaginable clip. As it expanded, it sucked in workers from the old East Coast and Midwest, the Old South and from Europe and Asia as well. There were jobs at the stockyards or in the meat-packing plants. Other industries sprang up. Little farming towns in Cook County suddenly found themselves transformed by the erection of a factory and the arrival of a horde of foreign-speaking workers. The village would blossom into a boom town, and then, just as quickly, be engulfed by the expanding metropolis itself.

With this sort of growth, it proved impossible to establish the sort of city-wide network of municipal patronage that Tammany had built up in New York. Jealous of the growing power of the colossus on the shores of Lake Michigan, the Illinois General Assembly had divided administrative authority among the Chicago City Council, Cook County and various semi-autonomous authorities. The result was that Chicago municipal services were "in the city but not of it." Chicago was an administrative nightmare, a jumble of neighborhoods, ethnic communities, rotten boroughs, half-incorporated suburban towns and authorities with ill-drawn or overlapping jurisdictions.[6] Chicago's fifty-four wards each had nearly as much political autonomy as a New York borough. Important decisions were taken at ward level, and politics and administrative policies could vary from ward to ward. Even though Cook County as a whole tended to vote Republican, the central wards where the immigrants first settled were often solidly Democrat. The powerful First Ward never voted any other way. When the First Ward boss, alderman and saloon-keeper Hinky Dink Kenna bragged that he had never lost an election in his career, he did not need to specify that he was referring to Democrat primary elections in the First Ward—the only elections that counted.

The 1870s and 1880s had been the lean decades for the American working man, the bleakest years in the history of American labor. Although growth created jobs, a high birth-rate and constant stream of immigrants kept the price of labor low. Immigrant labor was cheap and easy to exploit. Why negotiate with your work force over pay and conditions, factory owners reasoned, when boatloads of workers were arriving every day, willing to do the same job at an even lower wage? Although the national economy did expand in these decades, few of the benefits fell to labor. Workers who complained were fired or locked out, often evicted from their homes as well. Workers who tried to organize protests were harassed by the local police or roughed up by the Pinkerton men. When things turned nasty, as they too often did, the troops could be brought in. The deck was stacked in the employers' favor.

Devout Christians, the city's industrial and mercantile elite, men like Marshal Field, Cyrus McCormack, Philip Armour and George Pullman, were hardworking, intelligent men by no means devoid of public spirit, charity, and, by their own standards, humanity. Yet they were old-fashioned social conservatives who had no scruples whatsoever about firing on their workers. In 1885, Marshall Field had grown so alarmed at labor unrest that he proposed that the members of the exclusive Commercial Club, at their own expense, should acquire sufficient land to hold a U.S. military base. Federal troops had shown themselves effective against the strikers at the McCormick-Harvester plant the year before. Field's proposal was accepted, and Chicago's Fort Sherman was later inaugurated. The rival Merchants' Club responded by donating a stretch of lakefront property as a Naval Training Station. Had they had it their way, Chicago's leading citizens would have turned the city into a citadel where workers labored at gunpoint.[7]

In May 1886, the tensions exploded. It was late in the evening, and a large rally, called to show solidarity with the workers locked out of the McCormick Harvester plant, was slowly breaking up. Then someone hurled a bomb into the police ranks, severely injuring many officers. The explosion of smoke and blood and broken glass in the gathering darkness set off a pandemonium. The police, dazed and confused, opened fire, shooting blindly into the crowd. Seven policemen were killed and at least twenty-five wounded before Captain Black Jack Bonfield ordered a cease fire. Though some of the dead and injured were victims of the original blast, the majority of injuries were from bullet wounds. The Chicago police had shot their fellow officers. The number of civilian dead and wounded was never established. By the following morning the city was in the throes of a Red Terror. For eight weeks the police rounded up socialists and anarchists, closed down their societies and smashed their presses. Two hundred were arrested, though the grand jury only handed down ten indictments. After a short, vituperative trial, seven were convicted and sentenced to be hanged.

Shortly after the bombing, Marshall Field, approached the mayor. He was determined to see the perpetrators of the outrage executed and demanded that, in the interests of public safety, the mayor repress free speech. When Mayor Carter Harrison demurred, Marshal Field is supposed to have replied, "Mr. Harrison, we represent great interests in Chicago."

Field was speaking for Chicago's commercial and industrial leaders. They formed the backbone of the Cook County Republican Party, which had dominated Chicago during the Civil War years, passing laws outlawing prostitution, gambling, and Sunday drinking. These vice laws remained on the books for decades after the fire, even though, as was universally admitted, they had proved impossible to enforce. Chicago was and always would be a wide-open city. The most notable effect of these Blue Laws was, instead, to provide every opportunity for Chicago's acrimonious and partisan, though very lively, press to sling mud.

A second result, fully predictable though still undesirable, of keeping the blue laws on the books while refusing to enforce them was to help introduce rampant grafting and corruption into Chicago municipal politics. In the middle of the decade, Mike McDonald, one of the city's leading gamblers, brought together the city's saloonkeepers to fight for the repeal of the Sunday closing law. He called his alliance the People's Party. Several years later, merging his People's Party with the Chicago Democrats, McDonald became Chicago's Democrat boss, a role he continued to exercise for almost forty years.[8] In 1877, the conservative and salacious Chicago *Times* had pointed out that among the properties of Carter Harrison were saloons, tobacco shops, and hotels where gambling flourished and where "gay damsels" were allowed to "nestle down."[9] It was a charge that could probably have been truthfully levelled against anyone who, like Harrison, had made money in property speculation and the building boom during the post-fire years. Nevertheless, when Harrison entered municipal politics two years later, it was natural that he did so with McDonald's backing.

Carter Harrison Sr. won four consecutive terms as mayor between 1879 and 1887; in 1893 he was elected to a fifth term. His son, Carter Harrison Jr., also would later be elected to five terms. The father's relations with McDonald remained cordial; Harrison allowed McDonald and his associates a free hand in the levee, and McDonald and his friends reciprocated by funding his campaigns and bringing out the Democrat vote. The Republican press naturally labelled Harrison a corrupt boodler. But the Yale-educated Harrison was his own man and an astute politician, with an intuitive sense of what the voters in Chicago wanted. Despite the claims of the moneyed elite, the fervent prayers of the various temperance, women's, and Protestant groups, the demands of the Republican Party, and the ringing editorials of the *Times* and the *Tribune,* Carter Harrison knew that the voters did not want workers to be forced to work at gunpoint. Nor did they wish to see the city's blue laws seriously enforced. Chicago's voters wanted to keep their city open.

An instinctive populist, Harrison represented himself alternatively as the "workingman's friend" or "the immigrant's friend," whichever best suited his particular circumstances. In this he resembled Chicago's other two famous wheeler-dealer mayors, Big Bill Thompson and Richard Daly. Each was, in consequence, forced to endure their share of bad press, not all of which was undeserved. In 1893, the *Illustrated American,* while acknowledging that Harrison was held in great affection by "the lower classes of Chicago," called him an "unspeakable rogue and demagogue." His populism and feigned patriotism were "rank hypocrisy performed by the very man who was the chief agent in securing the release from prison of the guzzling, unwashed foreigners who lately took up arms against the peace and order of an American community." The reference was to Harrison's behavior during and after the 1886 Haymarket Riot. He had issued the original permit for the rally. Later he ignored Marshall Field's demands for a clampdown and even signed petitions to the Illinois governor asking for clemency and new trials for the condemned prisoners. The conservatives never forgave him; the 1893 article went on to say that, during the Haymarket riot, Carter Harrison not only revealed himself as "an unblushing demagogue, but a cowardly, sneaking traitor." He was made to pay for his courage; terrified at the spectre of a red insurrection, Chicago turned him out of office in 1886.[10]

In 1879, McDonald had persuaded the newly-elected Mayor Harrison to appoint his friend, the twenty-nine-year-old William McGarigle, as Chicago police chief. It was the first in a series of municipal offices that McDonald and Harrison secured for him. McGarigle supplied McDonald with an array of strategic allies in the municipal bureaucracy, which allowed McGarigle and McDonald to bilk the city in a series of Tweed-style frauds. Friends on the police force helped ensure that McDonald's bail bonding business remained in the black. Though no doubt aware of what was going on, Harrison kept to the sidelines. McDonald and Harrison also consolidated their grip on the Chicago Democrats, securing the election of loyal friends on the Board of Aldermen or on the ward committees such as Tom McGinnis, Pat O'Malley, John F. O'Malley, Johnnie Rogers, and Jim O'Leary.[11] In 1889, John Powers was elected alderman for the Nineteenth Ward, an area about to become home to Chicago's Italian community. In 1892, McDonald had Bathhouse John Coughlin elected alderman for the First Ward.

Born in County Roscommon in Ireland, the seven-year-old Coughlin had sailed to America with his family in 1867, settling in Chicago's First Ward, where he would remain happily for the rest of his life. The Coughlin family, he proudly proclaimed, were part of the "bare-arsed-poor." His father's little store burned in the 1871 fire, forcing the Coughlin family to start again from scratch. He acquired his name "Bathhouse John" from his first job as a rubber in a Turkish bathhouse. Later he became chief rubber in the Palmer House baths, where, as he later loved to relate, he got to pound the flesh of the great Marshall Field. Affable and immensely gregarious, Coughlin made friends with the politicians and officials he massaged. He joined the Democrat Party, in which he made himself so useful as a ward heeler and campaign worker that, in 1882, the Democrat First Ward captain loaned him the money to open his own bathhouse. The venture was a success, and with money and increased influence, Bathhouse soon became a precinct captain in the First Ward Democratic Club. By 1886, Bathhouse John had become a familiar figure at the Washington Park race track, where he attracted the attention of Prince Hal Varnell. Close to both McDonald and Harrison, Varnell was a gambling-house operator with a syndicate of bookmakers who controlled betting on race tracks in Illinois and Indiana. In the years after the Haymarket Riot, Republican administrations tried to crack down on race-track betting, and Varnell was looking for political help. With the help of McDonald, Varnell had Coughlin elected alderman.

Varnell was not the only one in search of protection in the early 1890s. Mike "Hinky Dink" Kenna was a saloon keeper and another rising star in the Democratic Party. As in New York, saloon-keeping was often a first step in a Chicago political career. Kenna, a precinct captain and member of the ward's Democratic Club, had recently seen his club raided. He responded by creating an alliance of Levee saloon owners. Leadership of this group of lucrative and politically-strategic concerns automatically made Kenna an influential figure in the Chicago Democrat Party. It also, as in the case of McDonald a generation earlier, gave him access to large amounts of cash which he could use in defense of his associates. In 1898, Kenna opened the Workingman's Exchange on Clark Street. Its one-hundred-foot bar was, he bragged, the longest in the world. Here Kenna offered "The Largest and Coolest Schooner of Beer in the City" for a nickel and with it, the best free lunch in town. For the next twenty years the working men of the First Ward ate and drank at Kenna's bar, and voted for whomever Kenna told them to vote for.[12]

With the consolidation of the rail network in the last decades of the nineteenth century the nation's crossroads became the nation's host as well. Conventioneers, vacationers, company representatives, traveling salesmen, transient workers, new immigrants, farmers selling their pigs and wheat in the agricultural markets, and others all stepped from Chicago's station platforms into the city's milling crowds. In their plentitude, they formed a rich and variegated fauna for the local predator species to sup upon. "Pickpockets," writes Perry Duis, "worked the endless crowds, confident that visitors would never recognize them. Evil cabbies delivered loads of the innocent to their doom: immigrants to exploitative hotels, young women to brothel recruiters, and prosperous-looking marks to thieves. The booming hotel business provided rich opportunities for hotel thieves, while con men cruised the bars, lobbies, dining rooms, and barber shops in search of potential victims."[13] Legions of traveling men were systematically fleeced by the armies of thieving gamblers or by the prostitutes in the panel houses, cribs, and concert saloons in Bed Bug Row down on the South Side Levee.

At the center of all the hubbub, facing Lake Michigan, was the Loop, where imposing granite, beaux-artes style buildings were now beginning to sprout. The Loop was the financial and commercial capital of the Midwest. Just south, however, from Clark Street to Wabash Avenue, and from Eighteenth to Twenty-second streets, was another center of business and commerce, though of a different kind. By the 1890s, the Levee had become Chicago's honky tonk, its red light district, where gambling halls, dives, cheap eateries, popular theatres, lodging houses, pawn shops, and flea-bag hotels were concentrated. The police strove to keep both business communities happy, ensuring that all their enterprises ran smoothly.

Unlike New York, where the Lower East Side and the Wall Street District Downtown were distinct geographical features in Manhattan's original topography, early Chicago lacked definition. Vice and crime were spread throughout the early city, and no single area could be defined as early Chicago's 'red-light district' or rough area. The Loop and Levee were new creations, side-effects of the concentration of new rail ties and the re-building of Chicago after the Great Fire in 1871. As the city emerged from the ashes, and became centered on the lakeside First Ward, big business and vice began to part company. Finance and business congregated in the northern half of the ward, vice in the southern.

The districts encircling the city's lakeside heart had originally been working-class Irish suburbs. Largely spared by the Great Fire, this inner ring of suburbs to the south and the west now became the homes of new communities arriving from Eastern Europe and Italy. As in New York, vice flourished in these immigrant districts. It was the association between vice and the immigrants that led Protestant church leaders and other reformers to claim that it was the immigrants—the Jews and the Catholic Italians and Slavs—that were bringing foreign vice to America's shores. The accusation was inherently absurd. From its very founding, Chicago had been known as a wicked city. There had never been anything foreign about vice in Chicago.

In nineteenth-century America, vice flourished wherever middle-class social control did not extend its reach. Vice was thus associated with the frontier; in the large cities, by contrast, it was associated with the poor in the urban slums. This helps explain the real connection between vice and the immigrants. It was not that the immigrants introduced vice to America; vice was already well established when they arrived. It is rather that the immigrant communities became concentrated in the disreputable districts where vice was already present. With vice on their very doorstep, moreover, the hoodlums, fugitives from justice, and criminals within the immigrant communities soon found rich pickings.

Prostitution is never respectable and rarely legal; that makes it hard to measure. Street walkers and brothels rarely appear as such in census reports. How can we estimate the number of brothels, concert halls and street walkers that a city like Chicago needed to fulfill its demand? In 1911 the Chicago Vice Commission eventually concluded that the real demand was far higher than anyone had ever imagined. Sex was a big business in Chicago. Still, it was just as hard to specify where this demand was coming from, since few respectable men would admit to frequenting prostitutes. This reticence had allowed an earlier generation of reformers to nurture the comforting illusion that only low-lifes, the hopelessly besodden, the degenerate, and the morally bankrupt paid for sex. The Chicago Vice Commission's estimates confirmed what many had long suspected: the demand for vice was far greater than that. Vice was not only a big business; it was a very popular one in Chicago.[14]

Vice may have been a big and popular business in Chicago; but it was never an open business. Brothels, concert halls, and street walkers could not practice their trade openly in respectable neighborhoods. Vice inhabited Chicago's inner ring of poor suburbs, also the homes of the city's growing immigrant population. It was convenient to operate brothels alongside the cheaper clubs and drinking and gambling establishments in the slums.

The blocks from Adams to Twelfth Streets and west from Wabash to the river comprised the Old Levee, also named Little Cheyenne, as Cheyenne, Wyoming, was suppose to be a very wicked place. By the end of the 1880s there were thirty-seven brothels and forty-six saloons here, along with numerous pawn shops and peep shows. The resorts ran the gamut from twenty-five-cent dipping houses to the luxurious brothels of Carrie Watson and Vina Fields. Fields was a large black woman who fed the poor during the Panic of 1893. After the Columbia Exposition, the red light district expanded a quarter mile further southwards. So as not to lose this valuable source of graft, the Democrats of the First Ward arranged to have boundaries redrawn so that the

First Ward included both the Old and the New levees.[15]

Chicago's reformers had originally agreed to establish a red-light district in the southern half of the First Ward in the hopes that there vice would be confined and segregated. In their 1911 report, the Chicago Vice Commission discovered that the results were not what they had hoped. The presence of a red-light district, they found, had a corrupting influence on the surrounding areas. The agents of corruption, moreover, were not so much the resort owners and prostitutes themselves as the high-handed and venal Chicago Police Department. After listing the various ways in which disregard for the law was spreading, the Commission concluded, "In addition officers on the beat are bold and open in their neglect of duty, drinking in saloons while in uniform, ignoring the solicitations of prostitutes in rear rooms and on the streets, selling tickets at dances frequented by professional and semi-professional prostitutes; protecting 'cadets,' prostitutes and saloon keepers of disorderly places."[16]

Like their colleagues in New York, the police in Chicago had no reason or desire to bite the hands that were feeding them. They were glad to sell tickets to the fund raisers sponsored by Bathhouse John and Hinky Dink Kenna for the First Ward Democrat Party, events to which the saloon keepers and madams of the Levee were expected to contribute and attend.

Tourists and business travelers in Chicago during the Columbian Exposition in 1893–1894 created a boom for the vice business. The New Levee became Chicago's Tenderloin—an up-market honky tonk. Indeed, the New Levee was even nicknamed the Tenderloin. The inadvertent result of segregation was thus to make Chicago a world class and world-renowned center for drinking, dining, gambling and recreational sex. "French Em's" as Madame Emma Duvall's brothel on Dearborn Street was known, became America's first resort to install all-mirrored bedrooms. Several doors down, Ada and Minna Lester opened the Everleigh Club in 1900, the most notorious, luxurious, and, according to Asbury, the most consistently profitable brothel in America, if not the world. It was here, during a banquet held in his honor, that Prince Henry of Prussia initiated the gallant custom of sipping champagne from his companion's slipper.[17]

With business booming, and the Levee becoming so rich that it was almost respectable, its weight in municipal politics naturally grew. The price of prosperity and tolerance was thus an increased underworld presence in municipal politics. Harrison Carter Sr. had calculated that by keeping the town open he was giving the working man what he wanted, thereby ensuring social peace and the predominance of the Democrat Party. What he did not foresee was that a policy of toleration and segregation gave the Levee the opportunity to organize itself politically. Writing of the 1920s, John Landesco observed, "For many years Chicago has been under the domination of the underworld. For many years Chicago has tolerated vice, and now the underworld and vice have it by the throat."[18]

The Levee Lords now lived in a profitable symbiosis with complicit police forces and cooperative political protectors. There emerged an important class of intermediaries who administered what, in turn-of-the-century Chicago, was called the "grease," the money that flowed from the resort owners to their friends and protectors. There were greasers who gave and greases who received. On the West Side around 1900, Jim Cross channeled the flow of grease from a zone of cheap brothels called "the Jungle," into the expectant hands of the Maxwell Street police station and elsewhere. He was aided by Mike "de Pike" Heitler, who later served the same function under Capone and concert hall owner Mike Fewer.

But most of the grease came from the Levee. Foremost among the greasers here was Ike Bloom, who managed Freiberg's Dance Hall on Twenty-Second Street between Wabash Avenue and State Street. Outside of Ada and Minna Everleigh's (as the Lester sisters were usually known) expensive and socially-exclusive club, the Freiberg Dance Hall was Chicago's most renowned sex emporium. It was here that the B-girl was invented—entertainers who forced their customers to ply them with drinks of colored water at forty cents a shot. In the first decade of the Twentieth Century, Bloom was known as Chicago's vice king. Whenever new reformist political administrations sought to show their voters that they meant business, they started by taking Bloom's liquor license away. This did not seem to bother Bloom too much, for he usually managed to get it back in a month or two. Bloom was a hero at the 22nd Precinct station, whose monthly visits were eagerly awaited and whose photograph, elaborately framed, hung in a place of honor in the squad room until the reformist captain Max Nootbaar took it down. Bloom's excellent standing in the 22nd Precinct meant that he could terrorize the lesser crib and dive owners with impunity. It was from these unprotected bits of low life, rather than from his friends and partners, that he collected his grease money. Indeed, Minna Everleigh remarked that the lower sort of Levee businessman feared Ike Bloom far more than he did any 22nd Precinct captain.

Graft in the Levee was dominated by Bathhouse John Coughlin and Hinky Dink Kenna. Bathhouse John and Hinky Dink not only took pay-offs, but forced all brothel-owners to buy their insurance from Bathhouse John's company. They also forced them to buy their liquor at Freiberg's, which Bloom and Bathhouse John jointly controlled. They also were forced to buy their provisions from the four grocery stores favored by Bathhouse John and Hinky Dink. Coughlin was the public face of Levee politics. Asbury called him . . .

a bombastic jackass who attempted to conceal his political shenanigans behind a plethora of meaningless words about democracy and the rights of the working man. He was pompous and willing to perform any antic that would get his name into the newspapers, and addicted to the use of big words without the slightest idea of their meaning. . . . He customarily wrapped his heavy frame in a long, green frock coat and a vest of thick plush under which, in cold weather, were two suits of heavy underwear, one of wool and the other of balbriggan. On formal occasions he sometimes wore formal clothes, but more often he would appear wondrously arrayed in silk hat, pink gloves, yellow shoes, a swallow-tail coat of bottle green, lavender pants, and a cream-colored vest gleaming with diamond studs and embroidered with roses and carnations. . . . In 1899 Bathhouse John wrote a poem called "Dear Midnight of Love," which had all the literary quality of a first-grade essay on "Oh See the Cat." Nevertheless, it was set to a sort of music and sung at the Chicago Opera house, with some difficulty, by May de Sousa, a popular songstress of the period.[19]

Carter Harrison Jr. once asked Kenna if the Bathhouse was crazy or just full of dope. "No," Hinky Dink responded, "John ain't dotty and he ain't full of dope. To tell you God's truth, Mr. Mayor, they ain't found a name for it yet."[20]

The two aldermen organized the First Ward Democratic Club Annual Ball at the Chicago Coliseum during the Christmas holidays. The ball, characterized by the Illinois Crime Survey as an "annual underworld orgy," served as Coughlin's and Kenna's fundraiser. Asbury is once again irresistible:

> Every harlot, every pimp, every streetwalker and pickpocket, every burglar and footpad, was expected to buy at least one ticket, and the keepers of the brothels, saloons, and other resorts had to take large blocks. The most important madams brought boxes, where they sat in state amidst their strumpets, guzzling champagne by the case and rubbing elbows with city officials and prominent politicians. On the dance floor swarmed the riff-raff of the city, all masked, most of them drunk, and many of the ladies wearing what the newspapers delicately called "abbreviated costumes." As the *Record-Herald* said in 1903, "Disreputables from every levee resort in the throng, blackmailers and thugs paraded arm-in-arm with the police sent to guard pleasure-seekers from the loss of jewelry."[21]

It's hard not to believe that some folks did not buy tickets just to see the show.

The First Ward Annual Ball began at Freiberg's in the 1880s. It was in honor of "Lame Jimmy," the crippled Irish fiddler and pianist who played in Carrie Watson's resort. The first years they were largely spontaneous affairs rather than a money-raising scheme. This ended in 1895 when one Harrison Street police detective shot another in a drunken dispute over money. The next year it was taken over by Kenna and Coughlin. Since Freiberg's could only hold three hundred guests, the duo rented the Seventh Regiment Armory. Later it moved to the Chicago Coliseum. It was something of a low-life trade fair. Private boxes were set up and sold to prominent Levee citizens—politicians, police officials, madams, saloon owners, brewery owners, whiskey and beer salesmen, a veritible Who's Who of Chicago vice, Lindberg calls it. Each box was decorated as ostentatiously as possible. There were out-of-towners as well. At the 1907 ball, the guest of honor was New York's Big Tim Sullivan. Two congressmen and the mayor of Kewanee, Illinois, were present as well. At midnight came the Grand March, led by Coughlin with the two Everleigh sisters on his arm. The band would strike up "Dear Midnight of Love." It was also something of a potlatch; Levee big-shots were known as big tippers and big entertainers. People buying the dollar tickets could often consume the price of entrance back in free drinks and grub. Even the waiters paid a dollar a head to serve at the event. Even with all these freebies, the Annual Ball still cleared $25,000 for the duo for over ten straight years. It was what Hinky Dink called a "lalapalooza."

Respectable opinion was appalled. In 1907 the *Tribune* sourly commented that it was a shame that the Coliseum's roof hadn't fallen in. If that had happened there wouldn't have been "a second-story worker, a dip or plugugly, porch-climber, dope fiend or scarlet woman" left in the city.[22]

THE SCOURGING OF THE LEVEE

In New York in the 1890s, anti-vice crusades had rapidly evolved into campaigns against municipal graft and police corruption. Reformers fastened their attention on Tammany as their principle adversary and as a convenient symbol for the city's social and political ills. Chicago, by contrast, lacked the equivalent of a Tammany. Chicago voters were also concerned about graft and police corruption, But Chicago lacked a visible target upon which voters might vent their ire. Lacking a convenient political focus, vice reformers in Chicago kept to the original agenda of Anthony Comstock and Frances Willard—the total suppression of vice.

In 1908, the elders of the Grace Episcopal Church asked the Superior Court for an injunction closing down Coughlin's and Kenna's Annual Ball. When the court responded that it lacked the jurisdiction, certain reformers took matters into their own hands. Two weeks before Christmas a bomb exploded in the Coliseum, wrecking a two-story building and breaking windows in a radius of two blocks. But the "Derby," as Bathhouse John affectionately called the soiree, went ahead as usual. And though the pastor of the Lexington Avenue Baptist Church called it "unspeakably low, vulgar and immoral," Bathhouse John said it "was the nicest Derby we ever had."

Still, Bathhouse John's and Hinky Dink's 1908 Derby somehow breached a threshold. Reformist groups were becoming increasingly agitated. In 1909, Mayor Fred Busse refused to issue a liquor license for the annual do. Although it went ahead as usual, the liquor-free derby of 1909 was a dismal, ill-attended affair, failing to bring the expected money ringing into Bathhouse John's and Hinky Dink's coffers. It was to be their last one. The following October, the Levee was scourged.

What Chicago's anti-vice groups lacked in political focus they made up for in messianic zeal. Twenty thousand men, women, and children followed the English revivalist preacher Rodney "Gypsy" Smith out of the Seventh Regiment Armory on Wentworth Avenue. Invoking divine aid against the cohorts of evil, the evangelist had commenced his campaign with a prayer meeting and blessed his "Army of Christians." Instead of "abbreviated costumes," the women paraded out of the Wentworth Avenue Armory in flowing gowns of somber black material. They carried unlit torches. The throng followed Preacher Smith from the Armory to the Levee in a silence broken only by the sound of the drums of three brass bands slowly beating out a solemn march.

When the crowd reached the edge of the Levee on Twenty-second Street,

Gypsy Smith stretched up his hands before him. At this signal, the crowd lit their torches and the brass bands struck up "Where He Leads Me I Will Follow." Still proceeding at the funeral rhythm beat out by the drums, the crowd slowly surged forward across Twenty-second Street and into the Levee. For the next hour they marched back and forth through the Levee, singing hymns and stationing little prayer groups in front of some of the most notorious resorts, kneeling and earnestly intoning the Lord's Prayer and the Twenty-third Psalm or singing "Where is My Wandering Boy Tonight?" Finally, re-assembling his scattered crusaders and leading them in the hymn, "Nearer, My God, to Thee," Gypsy Smith turned and marched them off to Alhambra Theatre for a prayer service for the fallen.

The almost military precision of Gypsy Smith's black-clad, hymn-singing Army of torch-bearing Christians neatly maneuvering their way through the Levee left its denizens mesmerized. They watched in complete silence, from parlor or upstairs bedroom windows or huddled together in the doorways, staring out as the disturbing apparition passed them by. They hardly dared breathe. The eerie silence lasted several minutes after the army had departed. Then, suddenly, as the piano and banjo music rolled back out onto the street, the Levee exploded back to life. The crusading army, it was later discovered, had left some of its soldiers behind. More had gone in than had come out, and the Levee went on to enjoy one of the biggest nights in its history. "We were certainly glad to get all this business," said Ada Everleigh, "but I was sorry to see so many nice young men down here for the first time."

Reformist attacks were nonetheless increasing. In January 1910, the head of the Cook County chapter of the Women's Christian Temperance Union, Mrs. Emily C. Hill, led three thousand marchers to City Hall. They had come to petition Mayor Busse to close down the segregated district. Rather curtly, Mayor Busse told the good ladies that he would put the matter "under investigation." Undaunted by the official brush-off, Mrs. Hill said that she and her party would remain outside praying to the Lord that He might provide the mayor with divine guidance. It was an old prohibition tactic later adopted by the Anti-Saloon League; women in mourning dresses and black veils singing hymns or kneeling in prayer outside the saloon doors. It discouraged customers and unnerved the clientele inside. It soon began to unman Mayor Busse. The following week the Federation of Protestant Churches met as well and passed a resolution asking the mayor to appoint a Commission of Inquiry. With this, Mayor Busse threw in the towel. In March he announced the formation of a Vice Commission, which began its work in July.

CHICAGO'S ITALIANS

Arriving in port cities on the Atlantic seaboard or along the Gulf of Mexico, Italian immigrants were disembarking in places where Italian communities were already established. There were thriving communities in both New York and New Orleans before the Civil War. The Italians who flooded into the Midwest and the Western Alleghenies in the latter part of the 1890s, by contrast, were arriving in regions where few of their fellow countrymen had previously settled.

Often they came as contract laborers. Recruited in the towns and villages where they were born, potential recruits heard fabulous tales of the wealth that might soon be theirs. They were offered free passage and a guaranteed job in the fabled land of opportunity. Even if they suspected that the stories were so much smoke, it was still a tempting offer.[23]

They arrived in the promised land already indebted. Here they began a life of hard work and hard conditions. They were often confined to work camps where, already over-worked and under-paid, they would also be over-charged for their food and lodgings. In the winter when outdoor work was no longer possible, they might be housed in unheated boxcars, twelve or fourteen men to a car. The rent for these luxurious winter accommodations was deducted from their future wages. But the truth was that these dismal conditions were scarcely worse than what many had left behind. Life was hard, but they ate. In the Sicilian interior, in Basilicata, Calabria, Lucania, or Molise, a bad harvest could mean starvation. There were no famines in America. In America there was also hard cash. So impoverished were the interiors of Southern Italy and Sicily that cash had virtually stopped circulating in many villages; families paid their rents and taxes in kind, and lived off what they grew or bartered. Employers in America may have conspired to squeeze every last ounce of sweated labor from their workers in exchange for derisory wages they paid; but at the end of the month, the worker still got something; and however small this pittance may have been, the coins jingling in the immigrant worker's pocket were what kept the whole system going.

The basic wage of a new Italian immigrant in turn-of-the-century Chicago seems to have been in the range of twenty dollars to twenty-five dollars per month.[24] The customary exactions and tributes having been deducted, this left the immigrant with a disposable annual income of about $150. The immigrant, in other words, received about $150 every year in cash which he could spend, save or send home as he chose. The temptation to spend it all must have been great. On the Far South Side and in the Nineteenth Ward, working men's wages were what kept the beer flowing, the dice rolling and the painted ladies flashing their smiles. Despite these temptations, however, many immigrants did manage to save a proportion of their wages. They were usually younger men, men who believed in their futures. Often their belief was justified. Chicago's economy was expanding and its job market remained fluid and dynamic. Italians with special skills or with at least rudimentary English often found better jobs. Others, more disciplined, more industrious or more ambitious worked their way up, starting their own small businesses. Still others, the most ruthless and violent, discovered that there were alternative routes. What united them all was a common need of special friends—connections. To escape the *padrone* system, the immigrant needed the help of intermediaries who would give introduction to new employers or to money lenders who would finance projects on reasonable terms or to those who could give him other types of help and protection.

These intermediaries were the patrons of the Italian communities, powerful men who dispensed favors in return for loyalty. What the rising immigrant was doing when he attached himself to these important figures was not so much leaving the *padrone* system as exchanging one *padrone* for a better one.

But in a town like turn-of-the-century Chicago, without an established Italian community, where could these *padroni* be found? Chicago Sicilians might join the *Unione Siciliana*, which had been founded in 1895. Neapolitans could join the *Amici di Acerra*, named after the ancient town on the Bay of Naples, birthplace of Diamond Joe Esposito. These were just two of the many clubs and fraternal societies started by Chicago's Italian immigrants.

Many of these societies were connected to municipal unions. *Unione* president Anthony D'Andrea's older brother, Joey, was head of the Sewer Diggers' and Tunnel Miners' Union. Esposito had a far wider range of union connections. As unofficial mayor of Chicago's Little Italy, the keg-shaped Esposito sat at the apex of a vast patronage network. The connection between the patronage and trade unions was far from casual. Most of the immigrants worked as common laborers; for them, a regular union job represented a step up. A union job delivered the immigrant from some of the worst aspects of the old *padrone* system; he was no longer entrapped in systematic debt but a free man selling his labor at the market price. But to obtain his freedom he needed a union card.

In principle, unions existed to help workers in their relations with their employers; the reality, however, was somewhat more complex. Where unions succeeded in imposing their demand that access to certain jobs be limited to their members, it was the unions, rather than management, that become the true employers. Where union membership was open to all, this did not matter; where union membership was not open, however, but at the discretion of the union's leaders, it mattered a great deal. Whatever the occupation and connection to the industry, it was the union leaders who had the power to hire and fire.

As mayor of the "Valley," as Chicago's Little Italy was often called, Esposito played a role similar to that of Big Tim Sullivan; he doled out patronage in exchange for power and influence. Diamond Joe exercised his power over the Valley's Italians by controlling their access to jobs and other benefits. This power gave him political clout with Chicago's Republican Party and with Republican U.S. Senator Charles S. Deneen in particular. Esposito was thus himself an intermediary; the point of contact between Chicago's Republicans and Chicago's Italians.

To many, intermediaries like Espositio were an aberration. What was the use of them? Why could the newly arriving immigrant laborers not sell their labor directly to their future employers? Why did they need to first be organized by intermediaries such as Esposito? The answer was the one that we saw Boss Croker providing the London *Review of Reviews* in 1897. The immigrants, Croker had said, were "ignorant strangers, a prey to all manner of anarchical and wild notions." Although they needed jobs, had indeed come to America is search of such jobs, they were incapable of finding their way to them on their own. Someone with local knowledge needed to befriend the immigrants, provide for them, and guide them to their future jobs. Someone had to effect the connection. According to Croker it was simply a matter of politics, "Tammany looks after them for the sake of their vote, grafts them upon the Republic, makes citizens of them in short." It was more than that, of course. Whoever was able to make the connection was in a powerful position: by keeping the bosses supplied with new workers and keeping the immigrants supplied with jobs, he stood in the right place; he had made himself necessary to both sides of the economic equation, and though Croker neglected to mention this fact, could exploit his position to make himself immensely rich. Croker and his fellow Tammany sachems had little scruples over using their power; nor did Diamond Jim in Chicago.

By the end of the 1890s, Italians were arriving in Chicago at the rate of thirty thousand to thirty-five thousand a year. The rate would increase in the following decade.[25] Here were the workers that Chicago's capitalists were seeking. But they needed shepherding. The immigrant workers represented an economic asset; they were a potential political asset as well. But for these assets to be realized, someone would have to mediate, organize the workers and feed them to the employers. It was this necessity that threw up intermediaries like Diamond Joe. Captialists need laborers and laborers need capitalists; but in turn-of-the-century Chicago, *both* capitalists and laborers needed Diamond Joe. This mutual dependency, a necessary reciprocity, lies at the heart of a patronage system.

ANTHONY D'ANDREA AND THE ALDERMEN'S WAR

Many of the Italians pouring into Chicago in the last years of the nineteenth century made their homes on the city's Near West Side. Chicago's Little Italy comprised an area immediately to the west of the Loop, encompassing Sedgewick west to the river and from Chicago Avenue north to Division. Its center was on Taylor Street. Like East Harlem, Chicago's new Italian immigrants typically settled where family and fellow townsmen had gone before. Here they found people who spoke their dialect and local patrons to help them find jobs and housing. The spirit of *campanalismo* or local rivalries was alive and well in Chicago's Little Italy.

As in East Harlem, Neapolitans and Sicilians formed separate communities; even streets were associated with particular towns in Sicily—those from Altavilla, a village on the outskirts of Palermo, settled on Larrabee Street; those from Alimena and Chiusa Sclafani in the wheat-growing plains went to Cambridge Street; families from Bagheria on the northern coast lived along Townsend Street; while those from Sambuca deep in the island's western interior made their homes on Milton Street.

Politically, Chicago's Near West Side formed the heart of the city's Nineteenth Ward. Originally home to a working-class Swedish and Irish population, the Nineteenth Ward had been long been the personal domain of Democrat Alderman John Powers. Elected alderman in 1888, Powers had been part of Mike McDonald's association of gamblers that dominated the Democrat Party in Chicago and provided Carter Harrison Sr. with his core of supporters and contributors. Acting as Harrison's campaign manager in 1893, Powers had made a killing from contracting and permits for Chicago's Columbian Exposition. Powers was also one of the Democrat aldermen who helped street-car tycoon Charles Tyson Yerkes embezzle millions from the city, an association that earned him the epithet of "Prince of Boodlers."

Powers was a wily old boss. Never a paper much inclined to show charity to Democrats, especially Democrats associated with the Harrisons, the Chicago *Times* informed its readers in 1918 that Alderman Powers was "bloodless, personally unattractive. His demeanor is one of timid alertness and anxiety to please, but he is actually autocratic, arrogant and insolent." He owed his continuing political success to his assiduous attendance at his constituents' funerals; "he has bowed with aldermanic grief at thousands of biers." Despite this "bloodless, personally unattractive" demeanor, Powers's hegemony was so entrenched that the demographic transformation of the Nineteenth Ward from predominantly Swedish and Irish to overwhelmingly Italian failed to dent it in the slightest. He acquired new nicknames; the Italians called him "Johnny De Pow" or "Gianni Pauli." Beyond that, John Powers's position remained unchallenged until 1916.

Anthony D'Andrea was described by the Chicago *Tribune* as "an unfrocked priest . . . former power in the old 'red-light district' . . . released from penitentiary after . . . thirteen months on a counterfeiting charge . . . also connected with a gang of Italian forgers and bank thieves."[26] No more inclined than the *Times* to say complimentary things about the city's Democrats, the *Tribune* clearly regarded D'Andrea as spawn of the Italian underworld. It was only half right.

D'Andrea was not an unfrocked priest; he had graduated instead from the University of Palermo. He might at one time have been a seminary student. Seminaries in the Italian South provided secondary education, and, especially in areas where good state schools were lacking, ambitious parents often chose to send their sons to the local seminary. Two of Anthony D'Andrea's brothers, Horace and Louis, did become priests. The most academically gifted of the D'Andrea brothers, Anthony, was allowed to go on to university. He would almost certainly have studied law in Palermo, for a law degree was the usual first step toward a career in politics, the judiciary, or the civil service. The four D'Andrea brothers chose, however, to emigrate. We do not know why they left Sicily nor even when and where they reached America. It must have been before 1902, however; for in that year, Anthony and the Milano brothers of Cleveland, Frank and Tony, were convicted of passing counterfeit money and sent to Joliet Prison.

The counterfeit bills had been supplied by Ignazio Lupo and sent from New York. Besides Cleveland and Chicago, the Sicilian counterfeiting ring had connections in Buffalo, Pittsburgh, and, Western Pennsylvania. In 1908, the Boston police traced the counterfeit coins circulating in the city to the Italian immigrants. In New Orleans the counterfeiters were led by another Sicilian, Sam Geraci. The association between Sicilians and the appearance of counterfeit money was no coincidence. A Sicilian counterfeiting ring had been active in America since at least the 1880s. During Prohibition these same gangs even faked whiskey labels.[27] In certain parts of the Sicilian community, counterfeiting had become a cottage industry. In New York, we saw that counterfeiting was organized by Lupo and Morello's *Unione Siciliana*. It thus seems significant that in 1919 the new president of Chicago's *Unione Siciliana di Mutuo Socorso negli Stati Uniti* (to give it its full title) was Anthony D'Andrea.

According to historian Giovanni Schiavo, the *Unione Siciliana* remained largely a fraternal, beneficent society until the 1920s when, seduced by the profits from illegal distilling, it became increasingly criminalized.[28] There is some confusion over the *Unione Siciliana*. All sources agree that it was founded in 1895. Some sources, however, follow mafia boss Nick Gentile in claiming that the founder and first president of the *Unione* was Anthony D'Andrea. John Landesco, by contrast, dates D'Andrea's election to the *Unione* presidency to 1919. If Landesco is correct, then the beginning of the *Unione*'s close association with organized crime would coincide with D'Andrea's presidency. In this case, Schiavo's claim that, before 1920, the *Unione Siciliana* was still a fraternal society gains plausibility. Nevertheless, Schiavo's claim that the *Unione* had no connection to organized crime before the 1920s is certainly an exaggeration. In both New York and Chicago, the *Unione Siciliana* had served as a vehicle for organized counterfeiting from its inception.

Despite this, Schiavo is still making a valid point that the *Unione Siciliana* was indeed "one of the thousands of fraternal organizations which the Italians established in America along the lines of mutual benefit societies." Fraternal organizations, often organized as mutual benefit societies and often with links to local politicians, had been part of the social fabric of any South Italian or Sicilian town.

"Italian Harlem," writes Orsi, "was a private matriarchy." In the Italian home, it was "in a woman's power to define who belonged . . . and who did not, who was to be excluded. They identified the *comari* and the "cousins" to be respected by their husbands and children. A woman's relatives were always closer to her domus than her husband's relatives. Women tended to live close by their mothers after they married, for example, and a woman's oldest brother was a recognized authority in her household because he was related to her." The Italian home was thus a women's domain; and husbands and adult sons felt distinctly uncomfortable hanging about the house during daytime hours.

Orsi more than once observes that street gangs and clubs served as male refuges, places where, in the words of one of his informants, "the acting was unnecessary, the father went out into the street and behaved as his real self."[29] In

Sicily, the men passed long afternoons at the *Circolo* (club), gossiping, playing cards, reading newspapers or staring vacantly off into space. The only alternatives were the cafés or, for those too poor to afford a cup of coffee, the park benches. As local parties and workers leagues arose in Sicily in the last decades of the nineteenth century, they naturally formed themselves as male clubs, sometimes offering benefits to their dues-paying members. Such political clubs and workers' leagues might be articulated into larger federations; some might preserve Masonic grades and initiation ceremonies. There was, in short, a well-established tradition of men's clubs in South Italian communities in both the Old World and the New. The *Unione Siciliana* was an example of such a club, and Schiavo's description is therefore justified—at least in part. The qualification is important, however, for, as we shall see, the *Unione Siciliana* was, in certain ways, anything but a typical South Italian men's club.

The question of whether the *Unione Siciliana* was a legitimate mutual aid society or a front for organized crime is perhaps a false alternative. The same question could after all be asked of the Teamsters Union. In their case the answer would surely be both: the Teamsters provided real services for its members; yet for decades the Chicago outfit treated the Teamster Pension Fund as its own private savings and loan association.

Giuseppe Morello and Ignazio Lupo were professional criminals; it seems likely that when they opened a *Unione Siciliana* in East Harlem, it was, among other things, to facilitate their counterfeiting ring. Anthony D'Andrea, by contrast, was not a professional criminal; he was aspiring politician. If he became president of the Chicago *Unione Siciliana*, it was probably, in part at least, in the hopes of attracting and organizing prospective voters. D'Andrea was an ambitious young lawyer from Palermo organizing his political base, and may not have known about the Sicilian counterfeiting ring before he joined the *Unione*. He found out soon enough, however, and was soon availing himself of a marvelous service that the *Unione* offered to a select group of its members—turning worthless paper into money. Yet D'Andrea was also a well-educated and cultured man. He gave Italian lessons to fashionable ladies from Chicago's Gold Coast. So impressed were these good ladies with D'Andrea's sincerity and good manners that they petitioned that President Theodore Roosevelt pardon him after his counterfeiting conviction. Roosevelt did pardon him in 1903.[30]

In 1916, D'Andrea felt strong enough and rehabilitated enough to challenge John Powers for the Democrat leadership of Chicago's Nineteenth Ward. Infuriated by what he took to be the *Tribune*'s attempts to smear him, he publicly stated: "I have been, since my pardon, the president of one of the largest Italian societies in Chicago, and three or four year ago was elected president of the Italian Colonial Committee of the Italian Societies of Chicago, and am now enjoying the proud distinction of being president of the International Hod Carriers' Union."[31] By now, D'Andrea was a practicing lawyer; two of his daughters had graduated from the University of Chicago, and a third was starting her freshman year. He was also president of Chicago's Macaroni Makers Association. D'Andrea was a successful, well-connected, and extremely respected lawyer in Chicago's Little Italy.

After his release from Joliet, Anthony also worked closely with his brother, Joey. Anthony served as business manager of Joey's unions. Joey was also an associate of Big Jim Colosimo, who represented Italian interests in the Levee. No doubt his brother Anthony was connected to Colosimo as well, and it was probably the brothers' Colosimo connection that led the *Tribune* to call Anthony D'Andrea a power in the old red-light district. But neither of the D'Andrea brothers is mentioned in the 1911 Chicago Vice Commission report; nor do either Landesco or Asbury identify either of them as involved in prostitution. When, in 1914, Joey D'Andrea was murdered in a fight over municipal contracting, Anthony took over as union boss as well. He became co-president of the Sewer Diggers' and Tunnel Miners' Union; the co-president was Diamond Joe Esposito. In 1915, D'Andrea ran against Powers's choice for county commissioner. He was defeated.

Like Big Tim Sullivan, John Powers had been careful to cultivate the new immigrants in his district. He had built up his own following in Little Italy. Anthony D'Andrea's challenge split the nineteenth-ward Italians into two warring factions.

In February 1916, D'Andrea announced that he would run for the Democrat alderman nomination against James B. Bowler, the Powers candidate. Several days later, one of Powers's ward heelers, an Italian saloon owner named Frank Lombardi, was murdered. Two Italians walked into his saloon and asked Lombardi to join them in a toast. "Long life and happiness to you," said one of the men in Italian. The three men drank; then one of the men put down his glass, pulled out a revolver and shot Lombardi twice, killing him. Lombardi's eighteen-year-old daughter told the police that her father had been murdered "because he had dared to head a determined fight against D'Andrea, who had lorded it over a fear-stricken ward, too afraid of his power to cross him." There is some confusion over the identity of this victim, however. Landesco identifies the victim as Frank Lombardi; Kobler however identifies him as Frank Raimondi. Kobler adds the significant detail that, as to the actual killers, "the name most frequently whispered was 'Genna.'"[32]

D'Andrea was again defeated by the Powers backed candidate. In 1919, he ran for the Democratic nomination for representative in the Constitutional Convention from the Democrat Second District against Senator Francis A. Hurley. Though initially victorious, he was accused of electoral fraud in the Nineteenth Ward. As a result, the election was given to Hurley. By now, however, D'Andrea was strong enough to impose a deal on Powers. If Powers would relinquish his control of the important nineteenth-ward committee, D'Andrea would support his campaign for re-election as alderman. Though permitting Powers to retain his personal power, the arrangement cut out Powers's followers. These followers naturally denounced the arrangement as a sordid deal and arranged for it to be voided by the Illinois Supreme Court. They switched their allegiance to James Bowler. The result was that, when fresh elections were called in 1920, Democrats on both sides of the factional dispute were feeling aggrieved and looking for revenge.

In September 1920, a bomb blast at the Powers home on McAllister Place knocked five people out of bed and shattered the windows of the surrounding houses, though, fortunately, causing no injuries. The following February a powerful bomb exploded during a D'Andrea rally on Blue Island Avenue. The bomb consisted of three sticks of dynamite in a wooden box attached to the outside wall of the home of a D'Andrea supporter who was hosting the rally. It blew a three foot hole in the wall and sent bricks flying into the interior, injuring seventeen people. Powers immediately disclaimed any responsibility, deploring the incident and expressing his sympathy for the injured; "only last Saturday," he continued, "D'Andrea and I sat down together for two hours in the Sherman House and agreed to conduct a clean campaign. There would be no mud slinging and absolutely no gunmen on election day, or any other time. We shook hands and parted best of friends."

Despite their accord, two more bombs were detonated, each one aimed at D'Andrea supporters. On election day, February 22, 1921, the Chicago police picked up 150 men, including Spike O'Donnell, discovering two hundred pounds of dynamite and a large sack of blasting powder hidden in a cache. During the elections themselves, more than fifty people were under arrest before noon. Whatever the effect of the violence may have been, when the votes were all finally tallied, Powers retained his seat by a slim 435-vote margin. But the end of the elections was not the end of the violence. It was merely the prelude.

Several days after the elections, Court Deputy Bailiff Paul A. Labriola, a Powers stalwart, was gunned down on the corner of Halstead and Congress streets by a party of Sicilians: Angelo Genna, Samoots Amatuna, Frank "Don Chick" Gambino, and "Two Gun Johnny" Guardino. After the initial volley, Genna was seen walking up to and inspecting the body srawled on the pavement. Then, positioning himself straddle-wise above his victim, Genna fired three more bullets into his body to make sure. After that, he and his companions walked over to a waiting car and drove off.

On the same day, four men gunned down Harry Raymond (or Raimondi) in his cigar store on Taylor Street. Raymond was a renegade D'Andrea supporter, suspected of having told the press details about D'Andrea's past arrest. Two more Powers supporters died shortly therafter—Gaetano Esposito and Nicolo Adamo. Adamo's wife identified Genna as one of the killers. The next Powers supporter to be murdered was Paul Notte. In a deathbed statement, he named Genna as one of his assassins. Genna's lawyers managed to have the statement disqualified, however, on the ground that Notte made it while under the influence of opiates.

What was behind these killings? The five murdered men—Labriola, Raimondi, Esposito, Adamao, and Notte—had all belonged to the Powers faction. But Powers's candidate had won the election. Both Powers and Bowler had naturally denied any part in the bombings. Yet, even if one of them had invited

Spike O'Donnell in to bomb the homes of D'Andrea supporters, they would have called him off as soon as their victory had been declared. After the MacAllister Place bombing, Bowler claimed that imported gunmen were conducting a systematic campaign of terrorism in the Nineteenth Ward: they had threatened the lives of municipal officials and slugged campaign workers and labor leaders. Bowler continued:

> Gunmen are patrolling the streets. I have received threats that I was to be "bumped off" or kidnapped. Alderman Powers' house is guarded night and day. Our men have been met, threatened and slugged. Gunmen and cutthroats have been imported from New York and Buffalo for this campaign of intimidation. Alderman Powers' forces can't hold meeting except under heavy guard. Owners of halls have been threatened with death or destruction of their buildings if they rent their places to us. It is worse than the middle ages.[33]

The reference to New York and Buffalo is significant. With Cleveland and Detroit as well as Chicago itself, they delineate a network of growing *Unione Siciliana* power that would prove their importance in the coming Castellammarese War.

The Powers faction were not, however, the only victims. In the days before the 1921 election, three houses of D'Andrea lieutenants were bombed. Shortly after the funerals of Labriola and Raimondi, a gang in a stolen car peppered a crowd in front of a pool-room with sawed-off shotguns. The police thought that the gang was targeting D'Andrea supporters in the crowd. A week later there was another shoot-out at a grocery owned by friends of Powers.

D'Andrea angrily denied any involvement in these shooting. He had earlier announced his withdrawal from politics "rather than have it thought my political ambitions caused bloodshed." On May 11, 1921, he was the target of an attack with a sawed-off shotgun. Anthony D'Andrea was now frightened for his own life. He had begun carrying a concealed weapon.

Soon after D'Andrea announced his political retirement, Abraham Wolfson, who lived across from D'Andrea's ground floor apartment, began receiving a series of Black Hand-like notes. "He killed others. We are going to do the same." the first message read. Finally, "You are to move in fifteen days. We are going to blow up the building and kill the whole D'Andrea family. He killed others and we are going to do the same thing. We mean business. You better move and save lives." Terrified, the Wolfson family moved out and let the killers moved in.

On the night of May 11, 1921, two men snuck into the now-abandoned Wolfson apartment. As D'Andrea entered his apartment after a late-night dinner at "Diamond Joe's" Neapolitan Café, he took two shotgun blasts full in the chest. He pulled out his revolver and manged to get off five wild shots before he collapsed in the doorway, shouting to his wife, "Lena, I'm dying!." He died in Jefferson Park Hospital murmuring to his wife and daughters, "God bless you."

In the empty Wolfson apartment, the police found along with the usual pile of cigarette butts, a two-dollar bill pinned to a note. "This will buy flowers for that *figlio di un cane* ["son of a dog"]," the note said.

The Catholic Archdiocese of Chicago refused to allow the corpse of D'Andrea to be brought into a church or to be buried in consecrated ground. D'Andrea, the church said, "had not lived as a Catholic, therefore he should not be buried as one . . . as he lived so shall he be buried." The service was held on the sidewalk outside his house, the spot where he had been murdered. The prayers were offered by two priests, Horace and Louis D'Andrea. An estimated crowd of eight thousand mourners filled the street. The funeral cortege that carried the casket to Mount Greenwood Cemetery was two and a half miles long. There were thirty-nine honorary pallbearers, twenty-one of whom were judges. Also present, according to the *Tribune,* were representatives of thirty branches of the *Unione Siciliana.*

All told, there were more than thirty murders in the so-called "Aldermen's War" in Chicago's Nineteenth Ward. Paradoxically, the most brutal of these murders all occurred after D'Andrea's slaying. In its initial stages, the Aldermen's War had consisted of political infighting, threats, beatings, and sporadic bombings. It culminated in a few short months of concentrated brutality. Even by Chicago standards, these final stages were loathsome. The final stage of the Aldermen's War unfolded as a series of cold-blooded assassinations and bombings, often in the victim's own homes or shops.

At the funeral, D'Andrea's chauffer, Joe Lapisa, and his Sicilian blood brother, Joe Sinacola, swore they would avenge the killing. They never got the chance. Lapisa died behind the wheel of his car on Dead Man's Corner in front of the Church of San Felipo Benzi. Sinacola was shot as he was walking with his thirteen-year-old daughter, Josephine. As the daughter watched in horror, an automobile pulled up alongside them and two men got out. One pulled a gun from his coat pocket and shot her father through the head. Miraculously, Sinancola survived, but refused to talk about the attack. Nevertheless, having surviving one attack, Sinacola was murdered on his front porch in front of his wife and children. Two other D'Andrea loyalists, Andrew Orlando and "Two Gun Johnny" Guardino were murdered. In May 1921, Michael Laccari, another friend and supporter of D'Andrea was shot. In June, another D'Andrea supporter, Clemente Basile, was shot dead by two men while sitting outside his fruit and candy store watching children play in the street in front of him. On May 14, sanitary workers discovered the body of an unidentified man in a drainage canal. His head had been crushed and mutilated and a grain sack had been placed over his head and secured by wire. Another sack filled with cobblestones had been wired to his feet. These were not the victims of a political brawl; they had been executed.

Yet only Angelo Genna ever came to trial. This was in connection with the murder of Paul Labriola, which had occurred in broad daylight and in front of witnesses. Even so, the trial resulted in an acquittal. As Dion O'Banion later remarked, "we have a new disease in town. It's called Chicago amnesia."[34]

Nobody really understood these killings. Powers and D'Andrea may have had blood on their hands, at least in the earlier stages. "Two Gun Johnny" Guardino, one of the killers of Paul Labriola, was a close associate of D'Andrea. He was later murdered himself. Still, even though it was D'Andrea's challenge to Powers that triggered the hostilities, the war eventually developed a particular ferocity and a mysterious and brutal logic of its own. By the end, both Powers and D'Andrea seemed cowed, fearful for their own lives and perhaps as bewildered as the rest of their community. What alderman's seat could possibly be worth this mountain of corpses?

JIM COLOSIMO

Jim Colosimo was born near Cosenza in 1872 or 1873 (he was forty-seven when he died in 1920). His father, Luigi Colosimo, brought him to Chicago some time in the early 1890s. Like Charlie Lucania in New York, the young Jim Colosimo was a bright, active boy who picked up his education on the streets. He blacked boots, sold newspapers, and often slept rough. He became an expert pickpocket. He was water boy for a crew laying railway tracks through Chicago's First Ward. He was good with his fists. At eighteen, he tried working as a pimp, protecting two girls; but a brush with the law made him return to legitimate work. So he became a municipal street sweeper. Soon Colosimo had organized his fellow street sweepers into a social and athletic club which pledged its political loyalties to Dink Kenna's First Ward Democratic Club. It was a gesture Bathhouse John and Hinky Dink readily understood; they responded by appointing the young Italian as Democrat precinct captain. Not only did this appointment confer virtual immunity from arrest; it served as a necessary prerequisite for anyone wishing to open or manage a saloon, poolroom, or brothel in the Levee. Colosimo had gotten his union card.

Resort management was precisely the direction the Jim Colosimo wanted to take. He managed a string of poolrooms and saloons for Coughlin and Kenna. Rising quickly in their organization, he was soon trusted enough to work as a bagman, collecting protection money from the brothels. Minna Everleigh later said that she had funneled over $100,000 through Big Jim.[35] Working as a bagman he also met a certain Victoria Moresco, whom Kobler describes as "a fat, homely, middle-aged bawd who operated a second-rate brothel on Armour Street." Bowled over by what Kobler describes as Colosimo's "dark, Latin virility," Moresco offered to hire him as private manager. Colosimo eagerly accepted, and two weeks later, in 1902, the pair married. Under Colosimo's energetic management, and with political protection assured, the Moresco brothel prospered. Soon Colosimo renovated it, renaming it "The Victoria" in honor of his bride. It became one of the swankiest and most profitable resorts on the Levee. Colosimo invested his profits in new saloons and cribs. To insure a constant supply of fresh, new faces at his flagship operation, he began to traffick in women as well.[36]

Big Jim Colosimo's first partner was a Frenchman—Maurice Van Bever.

"French Em" Duvall and Alphonse and Eva Dufour all ran French brothels. The neighboring Russian Jewish syndicate was centered around Julius and Charlie Maibaum, who worked with Ed Weiss, Jakie Adler, Harry Hopkins and Jakie Wolfsohn. There were also a number of independents, Joe "Jew Kid" Grabiner and Harry Guzik and his brother, the famous "Greasy Thumb" Jake Guzik. The French and Russian rings cooperated, doing business with each other and with independent rings such as the organization run by the Marshall brothers. The Vice Commission specifically investigated the Colosimo-Van Bever ring, discovering that it had connections with gangs in Chicago, New York, Milwaukee, and St. Louis.

The capture of one of the Colosimo-Van Bever lieutenants, Joe Bovo, brought this network to light. Bovo was bringing two prostitutes, Pearl Henderson and Hazel Elbe, from St Louis to work in the Levee. Colosimo did everything he could for his lieutenant, supplying his own lawyer, Rocco De Stefano, to represent him at his trial. Nevertheless Bovo was nailed by the direct testimony of the two prostitutes; he was convicted of pandering and given a six-month prison term with a $300 fine. There was evidence against Van Bever as well, and he and his wife Julia were each given a year's imprisonment and fined $1000. Though Colosimo's name was frequently mentioned in the proceedings, Bovo kept silent, and there were no other witnesses. So Colosimo was never even charged. Two more of his lieutenants, however, Johnny Torrio, who ran the Saratoga brothel for Colosimo, and the manager of the Victoria House, Sam Hare, were also indicted. The charge depended on Bovo's testimony, and, once again, Bovo decided to keep his mouth shut. Thus Torrio and Hare were released. Newspaper reports of the indictments appeared in 1909, and served as Chicago's public introduction to Torrio.[37]

According to Curt Johnson, Big Jim was earning $50,000 a month, all of it untaxed, off vice.[38] The figure is just a reporter's guess. We have no way of actually knowing how much Colosimo was earning. Nor do we know how much he was paying to the police, the First Ward Democrats or to other politicians, officials, or underworld bosses whose position in the patronage network entitled them to take a *pizzu* from Big Jim's ample share of the harvest. Big Jim was just another cog in the machine that transformed vice and labor into money, power, and influence. What we do know is that Big Jim was rich. He built a large house for his papa Luigi and an even larger one for himself and Victoria. He filled it with costly antiques, rare Turkish carpets, *objects d'art* and costly bibelots. Everyone seemed to agree that Colosimo had loads of taste, and that all of it was bad. Walter Noble Burns remembered in 1931 that . . .

> he lived without taste or refinement but on a scale of barbaric magnificence. He plastered his home with gaudy wallpaper, adorned it with expensive daubs masquerading as art, and cluttered it in grotesqueries of bronze and marble until it resembled a junk yard, in spite of its deep rugs and costly furniture. He had servants, a liveried chauffeur, the most glittering automobiles money could buy, and diamonds by the hundred. Diamonds were his passion. He had obtained most of his gems from thieves or from broken

gamblers who had pawned them to him. He blazed with the precious stones. He wore diamonds on his fingers, in his shirt front, on his watch chain, in his cuffs, on his suspenders, on his garters. He carried them in a buckskin pouch in his pocket. He delighted to finger them and to pour them in a glittering cascade from one palm to the other. He sometimes heaped them on a white tablecloth and gazed at them in rapt admiration.

Did Big Jim care what the art critics thought of his collections? Still Ada and Minna Everleigh must have shuddered whenever they thought of it, politely declining invitations to take tea at the Colosimo residence.

All this money bought influence too. Colosimo was allowed to buy a piece of the profitable Italian lottery. His first political contact had been "Dago Mike" Carrozzo, a labor organizer/racketeer connected to the Chicago Department of Sanitation. With Colosimo's backing, Carrozzo rose to become leader of both the Chicago Street Laborers Union and the Chicago City Street Repairers Union. These two unions worked closely with Joey D'Angelo's Sewer Diggers' and Tunnel Miners' Unions.[39] In reality, of course, these were not unions at all, but organized patronage networks. Already by the first years of the new century, the Chicago Italians were staking out their claims to these lower-paid municipal jobs. These became the new fiefdom, their own slice of the municipal pie. The unions did whatever it took to make sure that this small slice of municipal patronage remained firmly in their grasp. Access to such sources of municipal patronage gave Colosimo, Carrozzo, D'Andrea and Esposito a power like that of Saint Peter at the heavenly gates. Those admitted got the right to dig out Chicago's sewers at regular union rates; those excluded did not even get that far.

The End of the Levee

In 1911, Carter Harrison Jr., was narrowly elected for a fifth term. He owed his election to Aldermen Kenna and Coughlin, who brought in the First Ward Democrat vote in for him just as Mike McDonald had so often done for his father years before. Hinky Dink and the Bath had been Carter Harrison Jr.'s political allies since his first election in 1897. He referred to them somewhat incoherently as the "Two Rocks of Gibraltar."[40] But by 1911 they were his chief political embarrassment since Mayor Busse had convened the Chicago Vice Commission in 1910. Their report came out in 1911, and when its findings were trumpeted by the reformist and Republican press, the newly-elected Harrison realized that he had to do something.

He had no wish to alienate his friends and supporters in the First Ward Democratic Club, and thus refrained from attacking the Levee with conspicuous vigor. He concentrated his initial efforts inside the Loop, telling the police to chase the street walkers off Michigan Avenue. He closed down pool rooms and bookmaking establishments. He closed down a number of cheap cribs and hot-sheet hotels from Twelfth Street south. The Chicago police had published a set of rules a year earlier. Males under the age of eighteen were forbidden in segregated houses, as were females under legal age. Public soliciting and street walking were also forbidden, and unaccompanied women were banned from saloons. The advertising of Levee resorts was forbidden, as was the wearing of indecent clothes in their public rooms. Most important, the serving of liquor in such resorts was forbidden as well. Such rules had always existed, though they had never been more than intermittently enforced. Their main function was to provide the police with legal grounds for closing down any place that annoyed them. From now on, Harrison proclaimed, the police would ensure that these rules were strictly adhered to. It was an impossible task; the police knew that vice was big business, too big for them to supervise.

The police concentrated their efforts in the down-scale sector, especially in the predominantly black southern part of the New Levee. Here the cheapest cribs and most notorious saloons were found. They laid off the up-scale, white brothels and clubs in the Tenderloin section of the Levee. The Vice Commission noted that well-mannered, respectably dressed white prostitutes were almost never bothered by the police. Late in 1911, however, having just delivered a speech extolling Chicago as a city full of marvelous commercial opportunities at a convention for out-of-state businessmen, a waggish conventioneer from Missouri handed Mayor Harrison a glossy, full-colored brochure. Was this an example of the sort of marvellous commercial opportunities that the mayor speaking of? The brochure informed visitors to the city of the good taste, elegance, and luxury awaiting them at the Everleigh Club. Offended, or perhaps out of pique for the public humiliation, Harrison ordered Police Chief John McWeeney to close the place down. He even wrote the order out himself. And so, on 12:45 a.m., October 25, 1911, appeals denied and legal manoeuvres finally exhausted, the Chicago police arrived to padlock the Everleigh Club. Despite the lateness of the hour, a crowd had gathered to watch the spectacle. Silk-hatted gentlemen bid their elegant companions a last, fond adieu, and, tipping their hats, departed in their carriages or chauffeured automobiles. Gracious to the last, the sisters handed out free champagne. As the police arrived with the padlock and judicial seal, Minna proposed one last toast; "The ship has sunk. She was a good one. Let's all give her a last hurrah."[41]

By now the red-light districts were being "slummed" almost every week by official visitors, journalists or mission workers striving to rescue the fallen. In September 1912, Virginia Brooks arrived in Chicago from Hammond, Indiana, where she had closed down around fifty taverns by threatening to hatchet them Carry Nation style. She led a group of preachers on a new march through the Levee. These marchers were accompanied by a squad of mounted police as well as platoons of Girl Scouts, Boy Scouts, the Epworth Leaguers, the Women's Temperance Union, the Catholic Temperance Union, the Baptist Missionary Training School, and the Garrett and Moody Bible Institutes. There were floats, and a brass band repeatedly played "Onward Christian Soldiers." The Levee had by now turned into the established target of anti-vice crusaders of all types and from all places.

"The aims of [Virginia Brooks's] crusaders seem rather diverse," reported the *Record-Herald,* One of the floats bore a huge sign declaring that the Chicago Cubs baseball team "must cut out cigarettes." The Norwegian churches had dressed twelve men as medieval knights, and a thirteenth in pink tights as the god Thor. Around his neck he wore a placard that read: "The Great God Thor with his hammer. The Norwegians will help smite the saloons."[42]

Officially, Harrison's attitude was still pro-segregation. Even politicians who condemned the Levee argued that, though vice could not be eradicated, it still might be confined. The Chicago Vice Commission had taken the opposite attitude. It announced that its program was, "Constant and persistent repression of prostitution the immediate method; absolute annihilation the ultimate ideal." It was a slogan that became a war-cry for anti-vice crusaders as far away as California.[43] Through late 1911 and most of 1912, reformers hammered away at Harrison and Chief McWeeney, accusing them of dragging their feet. They also attacked the state's attorney for Cook County, John E. Wayman. The handsome, well-educated Wayman had been elected by the Republicans in 1908, but his initial efforts had been stymied by under-the-table agreements between the city's Democrats and Republicans and by a general reluctance on the part of either party to dismantle such a profitable source of graft and campaign funds. Outraged by his lack of action, the anti-vice leagues forced the Republicans to drop Wayman from the ticket for the elections due in 1912. Stung, and with nothing now to lose, Wayman suddenly swung into action. Beginning on October 4, he launched a week-long series of raids. He set up a "Levee Court" in the Criminal Courts Building and kept it in operation until ten o'clock every night. Gypsy Smith had been an apparition, a mere warning; the scourging of the Levee by John E. Wayman two and a half years later was the real thing. Wrote the *Record-Herald,*

> Electric pianos stopped as if paralyzed. Bright lights went glimmering. Into the streets poured a crowd of half-dressed women, some with treasured possession tied in tablecloths. Others were packing suitcases as they moved, and most of them were running, a majority not knowing where they were going, but anywhere to get out of the district. In front of a few of the more pretentious establishments automobiles suddenly appeared. Women soon loaded them down, and they raced away.[44]

Thousands rushed into the Levee to view the auto-da-fé. The Salvation Army sent in their brass bands; the missions alerted volunteers to hasten in to save the souls of the confused and terrified harlots wandering the street. There were violent confrontations when gangs of vandals, appearing on the scene to strip the abandoned bordellos of their costly fittings, encountered church groups trying to hold services of thanksgiving on the same premises. By the end of October 1912, the infamous Chicago Levee was, officially at least, shut down.

The day after the Wayman raids began, a group of alarmed vice entrepreneurs assembled to consider what to do next. They met at the restaurant of Big Jim Colosimo.

Colosimo's arrest on pandering charges had occurred in 1908. It was his first run-in with the law since his adolescence. Though his name appears in the Vice Commission report and in the newspapers, he was never seriously inconvenienced by the police thereafter. He was leaving the brothel business. In 1910, Colosimo opened Colosimo's Café, on 2126 South Wabash, which rapidly surpassed Diamond Joe's Esposito's Bella Napoli as the Windy City's best Italian restaurant. It was also the most extravagant,

> from its gilded portals to its immense mahogany and glass bar. Green velvet covered the walls. Gold and crystal chandeliers hung from a sky-blue ceiling where rosy, dimpled seraphim gamboled on cotton-candy clouds. Wherever the eye fell, it was dazzled by gold-framed mirrors, murals depicting tropical vistas, tapestries. At the flick of a switch hydraulic lifts raised or lowered the dance floor on which bobbed-haired women with calf-length skirts and their tuxedoed escorts performed whatever gyrations the current fad dictated—one-step, two-step, Boston, turkey trot, grizzly bear, bunny hug, Castle walk—to the beat of "Tiger Rag," "Ja-da," "Pretty Baby," Dardenella," "Oh! How She Could Yacki, Hacki, Wicki, Wacki, Woo."[45]

As in New York, the desire of fashionable North Side couples to spend an evening out on the town also helped to drive overt commercial sex out of the Levee. The members of the Chicago Vice Commission who considered dancing, especially dancing to Negro music, as only marginally less sinful than paid sex, may not have thought the new situation much of an improvement. But Colosimo basked in it all. Despite his lack of social refinement, and despite a taste in décor that echoed that of *chez Colosimo* a few blocks away, Colosimo was becoming a local celebrity. His café also featured opera nights; and when the great Italian sopranos and tenors sang at the Chicago Opera they were treated as Big Jim's special guests. After 1910, most of Chicago knew Colosimo as the proprietor of one of the city's favorite night spots. Fewer Chicagoans knew or remembered or even cared that the portly man in the white suit with the buckskin bag full of diamonds had also been one of the city leading vice lords and white slavers.

After the Wayman raids, some of the Levee vice lords followed the Everleigh sisters' example; they retired on their accumulated earnings or went off in search of better pastures. Others fought the reformers to the bitter end. As their political boss, Hinky Dink Kenna naturally led the way. Kenna secured the appointment of Michael F. "White Alley" Ryan as police captain of the Twenty-second Street Precinct. Ryan was entirely Kenna's creature, and fought to defend Kenna's and Bloom's interests.

Over time, the pace of raiding began to slacken. In part, this was the result of the efforts of men like Colosimo, Bloom, and Van Bever. Raising colossal sums to disperse to influential friends, they set new standards in the history of bribery in Chicago. Yet the slackening was probably a natural effect as well. The campaign to close down the Levee was simply running out of steam. Concluding that the campaign had been a success, newspapers let other issues crowd the Levee out of the headlines. Governor Edward F. Dunne gave Illinois women the vote in 1914, and the president of the Cook County Suffrage Alliance, Marion Drake, promptly presented herself as candidate for First Ward Alderman, rallying reformers and the newly-enfranchised women voters against Bathhouse John Coughlin. Despite inevitable, and no doubt well-founded, accusations of ballot-box stuffing and electoral fraud, The Bath held onto his seat.

Accusing Mayor Harrison and the Chicago Police of lacking sincere zeal, foot dragging, and perhaps even complicity, the anti-vice leagues demanded the sacking of Police Chief McWeeney. Harrison must surely have known that the source of the problem was not Chief McWeeney but Captain Ryan of Twenty-second Street. Nevertheless, the demand presented him with the opportunity to indulge in a little political grandstanding. By sacking McWeeney he burnished his anti-vice credentials; by refusing to sack Captain Ryan, he preserved his tenuous alliance with Kenna, whose political support he still needed. The new police chief, James Gleason, however, came up with a new angle. Acting on a suggestion from the reformist Committee of Fifteen, Gleason agreed to set up a separate Morals Squad to police the red-light district. To lead this new force he appointed an Illinois National Guard Major named Metellius C. Funkhouser and William C. Dannenberg, a former Federal agent who had helped break up Maurice and Julia Van Bever's white-slaving ring. Significantly, and no doubt deliberately, neither Dannenberg nor Funkhouser had any previous contact with the Chicago Police Department. The troublesome Captain Ryan was being outflanked, a manoeuvre greeted with glee by the vice campaigners and with rage and consternation by the Chicago police. "This whole nasty affair can be placed at the door of politics," Captain Ryan told the reporters. The Levee now had two separate and opposed police forces.

In late 1914, the raids resumed in earnest. The vice lords and their Twenty-second Street police allies mobilized in defence. On the suggestion of two Precinct detectives, Colosimo and Van Bever dispatched Chicken Harry Gullet to offer Dannenberg $2,000 a month to lay off. The plan backfired when Dannenberg simply arrested Chicken Harry. As raiding continued, the resort owners' costs in pay-offs and fines mounted steadily. Still, Captain Ryan's troops enjoyed the support of the Levee's low-life denizens, and this gave them the advantage of a guerrilla force; the jungle telegraph worked in their favor, keeping them well informed. So as not to give advance warning, the Morals Squad men began working in plainclothes. Still by the time they made their appearance, incriminating evidence often had been spirited away. To counter-balance this disadvantage, the Morals Squad began to form their own network of stool pigeons. Not only were there now two warring police factions in the Levee; either faction allied itself with a set of underworld clients. The predictable result was to set off a war in the underworld itself. The Twenty-second Street boys had circulated photographs of Dannenberg's men and the stool pigeons to resort owners. There were rumors that the underworld was out to hunt stool pigeons.

On July 16, Dannenberg and his men launched another raid. At first the raiders came up empty handed. When they got to The Turf Inn, a three-storey resort on West Twenty-second Street with bedrooms on top, they found it still open. Dannenberg arrested two men and a woman, then, leaving two officers to guard them until a patrol wagon arrived, carried on raiding. Word of the arrests soon spread. By the time the patrol wagon had pulled up, The Turf was surrounded by a large and angry crowd. When the police led the trio out of the resort, they were greeted by jeers and insults, followed by a rain of rocks and bricks. Surrounded by the hostile crowd, the two officers drew their guns.

At this point, as Lindberg writes, the story now becomes "somewhat confused." Hearing the commotion, two Twenty-second Street detectives raced to the scene. According to their version, when they saw the mob closing in on two armed men, they assumed that the men were hoodlums threatening the crowd. They drew their own pistols and opened fire. The two Morals Squad officers returned the fire. For certain men in the crowd, the sight of policemen shooting at other policemen presented a once-in-a-lifetime opportunity. They pulled out their own guns, and began shooting at the policemen too. Among the spectators were now Johnnie Torrio, Rocco Vanelli (better known as Roxy Vanilla) and Mac Fitzpatrick. When they arrived in Torrio's big red touring car, Roxy Vanilla impulsively jumped out and charged into the crowd.

When the shooting finally stopped, one of the Twenty-second Street detectives lay dead on the pavement while the other was seriously wounded. The two Morals Squad men were both shot in the leg. Vanilla had been wounded as well; but Torrio and Fitzpatrick had scooped him up and sped him off to Padua Hospital.

By the time the news hit the morning dailies, the two police factions were already pointing accusing fingers at each other. Had the Moral Squad men not returned the fire, Captain Ryan, proclaimed, the whole tragedy could have been avoided. But it had been the two Twenty-second Street detectives who had started the shooting. They had done so on purpose, the reformist papers angrily charged, knowing full well that the men were Morals Squad officers. The Twenty-second Street detectives had been sent out gunning for the Morals Squad by Hinky Dink and Bathhouse John themselves. The acrimonious exchanges and accusations of treachery were cut somewhat short by the news that the murdered Twenty-second Street Police detective, Detective Sergeant Birns, had been killed by a dum-dum shell. The Morals Squad used .38 calibre bullets. Whoever had killed Detective Sergeant Birns, it had not been the Morals Squad.

In books, articles, and websites devoted to the history of organized crime, the curious reader is often informed that Detective Sergeant Birns was murdered by Roxy Vanilla.[46] This is possible, but it is anything but an established fact. There were other guns in the crowd and other hoodlums firing them. There may have been other wounded as well. That the police did not even interrogate Vanilla shows that they did not consider him a prime suspect. Some accounts go on to claim that the shooting had taken place on the orders of Colosimo. That claim is frankly absurd. Colosimo was a vice lord who paid Captain Ryan large sums to protect him from the Morals Squad. The last thing he would have wanted was to kill a detective sergeant from Ryan's force.

Besides, it seems clear that the murder of Detective Sergeant Birns was not a planned assassination but a monumental foul-up. There were too many guns on the street and too many police forces working at cross purposes. It probably did not help that the two Morals Squad men assigned to escort the prisoners to the patrol wagon were rookie cops. When Captain Ryan's friends began to circulate photographs of the members of the Moral Squad, Dannenberg may have countered by recruiting new, and previously unknown, faces. The unforeseen result of this manoever, however, was to give Captain Ryan a certain plausibility when he asserted that his boys had no way of knowing that the two men in plainclothes pointing their guns at the crowd were Morals Squad officers.[47]

"As an organizer and administrator of underworld affairs," Herbert Asbury wrote, "Johnnie Torrio is unsurpassed in the annals of American crime; he was probably the nearest thing to a real mastermind that this country has yet produced. He conducted his evil enterprises as if they had been legitimate businesses." Elmer L. Irey, the U.S. Treasury Agent who nailed Capone for tax evasion, called him "the father of American gangsterism."

In 1914, however, Torrio's greatness still lay in the future. Ignorant of the august destiny awaiting him, the Chicago papers had no reason to pay him special attention. What the press did know was that Torrio, Vanilla, and Fitzpatrick all worked for Big Jim Colosimo. At the time, this was more interesting information, for in 1914 everybody knew who Big Jim was. The question that reporters naturally asked themselves was, What was Big Jim's role in the Turf Inn shoot-out? State's Attorney Maclay Hoyne speculated that Colosimo had sent Torrio out to kill Dannenberg.[48] This version at least makes sense. Dannenberg was chief of the Morals Squad, someone to whom even a retired brothel owner might take exception. Yet it still seems very unlikely. As one of the lords of the Levee, Colosimo would surely have understood that murdering Dannenberg in cold blood while in the line of duty would have brought the wrath of God down upon him. Besides, even if Hoynes's speculation was correct, by the time Torrio and friends had arrived, Dannenberg was gone. Hoynes's speculation has no bearing on the murder of Detective Sergeant Birns. The truth is that we really do not know who killed Birns. Nor, for that matter, do we know who shot Vanilla.

It is tempting to write history with hindsight, treating events as portents for the future. It is tempting to make Torrio the leading protagonist in the shoot-out at The Turf. The sad truth, however, is that our knowledge of Torrio's career at this juncture is at best patchy.

COUSIN JOHNNIE

That Torrio was Victoria Moresco's cousin seems certain. Torrio arrived in

Chicago with his mother, Maria Caputo, who remained for a time as a guest in the Colosimo house. Torrio was therefore probably related to Moresco on his mother's side. That Torrio arrived to help Colosimo fight the Black Hand is also probable, at least as far as it goes. Colosimo certainly was having his difficulties in that sphere.

In 1909, Big Jim Colosimo was a still prosperous brothel keeper and white slaver, as well as a union racketeer with gambling interests. He was also publicly and ostentatiously and vulgarly rich. Colosimo, in short, was a just the sort to attract the attentions of a Black Hand gang.

The first to try his hand was Vincenzo "Sunny Jim" Cosmano, a labor racketeer and Black Hand extortionist. He asked for $10,000, but got a shotgun blast in the stomach instead. The police never got very far on this case. While the police were waiting for Cosmano to recover enough to question him, his own gang members paid him a hospital visit. They bore flowers and candy in their hands; but they carried guns in their pockets. Overpowering the two policemen set there to guard him, the gang bundled Sunny Jim up, wheeled him out and bore him away. The incident seems to have left little bad feeling on either side. Kobler notes that Cosamano later became a regular client at Colosimo's Café.[49]

When the next demand came, Colosimo decided to play the Black Handers along. He agreed to make an initial payment, agreeing on a deserted spot in which to make the deposit. Though probably told to come alone and unarmed and to leave as soon as he had deposited his packet, either the Black Handers were very stupid or overcome by their greed (or both). As three men impulsively raced towards the worthless paper bundled inside a white handkerchief, Colosimo's friends stepped out from the shadows and blew them all away. Johnson adds that Colosimo strangled two of them himself—under the circumstances perhaps it was a mercy killing.[50] But still the demands kept coming. So Victoria wrote a letter to her cousin in Brooklyn, asking for a hand.

Shortly after Torrio's arrival in Chicago, Colosimo sent him to meet with three more Black Handers. The meeting took place under the Rock Island Railway viaduct over Archer Street. After negotiating, Torrio and the trio agreed to a figure which Torrio promised he would bring the following evening. At the agreed hour Torrio arrived in a carriage. He stepped out under a street light and, as he did, he held a satchel aloft. Advancing towards the viaduct, he saw the three Black Handers come out of their hiding place. Their eyes were fixed on the satchel, as he knew they would be. By the time they noticed Joey D'Andrea and Mac Fitzpatrick materializing out of nowhere on their right and their left, it was too late. They had fallen into the same trap. Colosimo later asked Torrio if the three were dead; "Well, I looked back, and they didn't wave good-bye," Torrio is supposed to have replied.[51]

There is, however, a problem about this account of Torrio's move to Chicago. Colosimo was certainly a natural target for Chicago's Black Hand gangs; but Colosimo had many friends in the Chicago underworld. Why did he not ask some of these friends for help? Why did have to send for his wife's cousin in Brooklyn, someone who had never set foot in Chicago before?

Soon after Torrio arrived in Chicago, he summoned his mother, Maria, to join him. At first, both Torrio and his mother stayed at the Colosimo house, remaining there until Torrio's marriage in 1912. Maria may have remained a guest at the Colosimos even longer. When Big Jim bought the property for *Colosimo's Café* in 1910, he made out the deeds in Maria Torrio's name. Big Jim Colosimo, in short, never treated Johnnie Torrio as a gunmen hired to do a piece of work for him. From the start, Cousin Johnnie was the heir apparent.

But this solution only deepens the original mystery. Why, with all his connections on the Levee, would Big Jim have summoned his wife's cousin from Brooklyn and groomed him as his heir? And if Colosimo was intent on launching Torrio in Levee vice, why did he first ask him to take care of the trio of Black Handers? It was a dangerous mission. Why did he not ask some of his Italian associates to handle it?

The answer may be that all of Colosimo's connections were in the vice business. He was a Levee Lord, the only Italian of any prominence in the vice business at the time. He was not a prominent figure in Chicago's Italian underworld, however, and thus may not have had many Italian underworld associates. Since he may not have been sure exactly from where in the Italian underworld the Black Hand threats were coming; he might have been reluctant to entrust his own personal safety to the Chicago Italians.

Nevertheless, Colosimo was never totally without Italian underworld connections. He employed Joey D'Andrea, whose brother, Anthony, would become president of the Chicago *Unione Siciliana*. These Sicilians would certainly have provided Colosimo with all the protection he needed. But what would they ask in return? If the Sicilians agreed to give Colosimo protection, their price might have been a slice of Colosimo's profitable vice business, and that might have been a price that Colosimo did not wish to pay. Indeed, Colosimo may even have suspected that behind the sudden rash of Black Hand demands lay an attempt to force him to accept Sicilian protection.

Admittedly, this is speculation. We know very little about Colosimo's connections outside of the vice business. Still, the speculation provides a fresh angle on the question of why Colosimo sent for Torrio. Cousin Johnnie was well acquainted with the Morello-Terranova gang and Frankie Yale, important members of the *Unione Siciliana* in New York. Big Jim was associated with Joey D'Andrea, the brother of Anthony, in his turn a member of the Chicago *Unione Siciliana* from at least 1903. If Colosimo was trying to negotiate protection from the Sicilians, this would have been a key asset. It is even possible that Colosimo put Torrio in charge of negotiations, working out the arrangements that governed relations between Colosimo's vice empire and the Italian underworld. Though we have no details, we can surely infer that some sort of deal was eventually made. One of the two gunmen who Torrio brought to kill the Black Handers under the Rock Island Railway viaduct was, after all, Joey D'Andrea. Soon afterwards, Mike Merlo, another important figure in the Chicago *Unione Siciliana* appears as a member of Torrio's gang. Torrio, it seems, had secured for his uncle a good working relation with certain Sicilians.

The Death of Colosimo

With his business interests increasingly in the hands of his capable and inno-
vative lieutenant, Johnnie Torrio, Big Jim Colosimo felt free to pursue other
interests.

After The Saratoga and The Victoria were raided, along with Colosimo's
other Levee brothels during the years of the Vice Commission, Big Jim simply sold them off. By now they were so much bad publicity to get rid of. The
only resort he was publicly associated with was Colosimo's Café. It was a
fashionable night club. Few of Big Jim's clients there may have suspected, or
have wished to know, how their host had made his original stake. Colosimo's
Café was one of the few Levee resorts that was allowed to flourish relatively
unmolested after 1915. There was the gambling on the second floor, but there
was little else to attract the attention of the law. In its final months, Mayor
Harrison revoked Colosimo's liquor license, probably as a reprisal for Colosimo's switch in political allegiance. In 1914, Colosimo had abandoned Hinky
Dink and the Chicago Democrats for the Republicans under William Hale
"Big Bill" Thompson. When Big Bill took office in 1915, he immediately
restored Colosimo's license.

A jovial, portly millionaire, Big Jim himself was instantly recognizable,
with his liquid Latin eyes, brush mustache, girth, and immaculate white-linen
suit. The Colosimo Café was his toy, his pride and joy. No expense was ever
spared. No imported wine or delicacy was ever too good for his clientele. It
was also his way of providing jobs for the hungry Colosimo and Moresco
relatives whom he could not otherwise employ.

With his famous resort prospering and filled with his celebrity friends,
with his servants, liveried chauffeur, glittering automobiles, and diamonds
by the hundred, Big Jim's cup was almost full to the brim. In 1913, a Chicago *News* reporter prevailed on him to give a young singer from the South
Park Avenue Methodist Church choir a shot in his floor show. The girl was a
nineteen-year-old, blue-eyed ingénue from Ohio, with skin like the petals of a
white rose. Her name was Dale Winter. Just looking at her made Big Jim go
weak in the knees. When Dale Winter walked into his life, Big Jim knew he
was staring total fulfillment in the face—the final, missing piece. For the next
seven years, Big Jim's full-time occupation was that of sugar daddy. He supported Dale's singing career, paying for her lessons. He changed his tailor and
left his diamond garters and suspenders lying in the bedroom safe. He went
horse-back riding to please his lady love and wore well-cut English tweeds; he
stood by her side meekly in public museums letting clever people explain the
works of art he was supposed to admire. Samson had finally met his Delilah;
Beauty had subdued the Beast.

Victoria Moresco, as can well be imagined, never took kindly to any of
this. But Colosimo divorced Victoria Moresco in 1919, and, in early 1920,
Jim and Winter were wed. "This is the real thing," he told Johnnie Torrio.
"It's your funeral," Torrio is reported to have replied.[52]

On May 11, 1920, less than a month after the wedding, Colosimo was shot dead by an unknown assailant in the vestibule of Colosimo's Café.

The most detailed modern account of Colosimo's murder is provided by John Kobler. On the morning of May 11, Torrio had called Colosimo to tell him that two truckloads of whiskey would be arriving at the Café at 4 p.m. Colosimo arrived in his office at the back some time before the appointment. He talked business awhile with his secretary, Frank Camilla, and his chef, Caesarino, and tried unsuccessfully to phone his lawyer. At 4:25, Colosimo walked out of the office. Camilla and Caesarino had the impression that he was going out to meet someone on the sidewalk. A moment later they heard two sharp reports. When Camilla came out to investigate, he found Colosimo lying face down on the vestibule floor. There was a bullet hole behind his right ear. A second bullet had cracked the cashier's window and buried itself in the plaster wall opposite.[53]

As the police reconstructed the killing, the assassin had been waiting for Colosimo in the cloakroom.

The police naturally questioned all of Colosimo's known associates. They wondered if one of Moresco's brothers had killed Colosimo in revenge for his treatment of their sister. It was unlikely; Big Jim had given Victoria $50,000 not to contest the divorce. She took the money, and three weeks after the divorce decree, married a Sicilian twenty years her junior and took off for the West Coast. In any case, the most likely Moresco, Joe, had a good alibi. Torrio was also questioned; he too had a good alibi. The case was getting nowhere. Kobler continues:

> Yet there were developments that suggested the solution. Chance, underworld rumor and the testimony of the café porter produced them. Into a police dragnet the day of the murder blundered the veteran Five Pointer and executioner, Frankie Yale. He had been in town a week and had been about to board an eastbound train when the police stopped him. They could not connect him with the murder at the time, however, and they let him go to New York. Then the porter came forward with a description of the stranger he saw enter the café at Colosimo's heels. It fitted Yale. Finally, an underworld stool pigeon passed along an underworld rumor that Torrio had paid Yale $10,000 to rid him of Colosimo. At the request of the Chicago authorities the New York police picked up Yale, and the porter was brought to New York. Face-to-face with the killer, the witness froze. He swore he could not identify him. The investigation foundered there, but the police of both cities doubted neither Yale's guilt nor Torrio's.[54]

But why would Johnnie Torrio want to kill Colosimo? According to another, even more recent, Capone biographer, Robert J. Schoenberg, Colosimo was reluctant to become deeply involved in bootlegging. By now he had enough money and simply wished to run his café and enjoy life with Dale. Torrio had persuaded him to back Jake Guzik's investment in a brewery; but this was as far as Big Jim wished to go. Torrio had much bigger ambitions, however. He wanted to get into bootlegging. For this he needed Big Jim's permission. But "whatever hope Torrio might have cherished of changing Colosimo's mind when the big man confided his intention of divorcing Victoria and marrying Dale."

Schoenberg adds that, "The highly improbable story has survived that Torrio replied, 'It's your funeral.'" In this, Schoenberg is right; the "It's your funeral" line is certainly a later interpolation. Nonetheless, the story is widely credited; the line appears in Kobler, Johnson, Tuohy, and other recent accounts. It does not appear, however, in Asbury writing in 1940 or even in McPhaul's long and highly imaginative account written in 1970. It is clearly a recent invention. Schoenberg, however, then continues:

> Meanwhile, Torrio prepared. He consulted his rising young lieutenant, Capone, on the choice of the right to do the job, and then left him to make the arrangements. A lot might turn on the choice made. This would be no routine "crime-wave" murder; Torrio knew that the police would exert themselves in this one, so he and Capone could afford no clues and no trail. No matter how carefully plotted and mounted, the action might develop snags. If everything was not exactly right, the killer would need the judgment to postpone. Such cool heads were not easily found. While Colosimo honeymooned, Capone put in a call to Frankie Yale. It was the sort of favor that would not be refused, and indeed would be returned less than a year later.[55]

Well, Schoenberg is writing a biography of Capone. He needs to squeeze his hero in some way, to display him as a protagonist. The story, however, lacks any shred of credibility. In 1920, Capone was a young punk from Brooklyn still struggling to find his way around Chicago with a street map. Yale was Torrio's boyhood friend; Yale, as we shall soon see, was, by contrast, Capone's former employer. He was very much Capone's senior at the time. Capone could not pick up the phone and make Yale an offer he couldn't refuse. Schoenberg is just confabulating.

What about the motive? All accounts agree that Torrio killed Colosimo because he was going soft. Colosimo wanted no part in the rough stuff. Colosimo was indeed a softy; he had earned his stake in prostitution. When political pressure had mounted against the Levee, however, he closed down and sold out, opening Colosimo's Café instead. Describing the murder, the Chicago papers identified Colosimo as the proprietor of a popular night spot, not a well-known gangster. By 1920, this was the simple truth. But Colosimo had gone soft a decade earlier. If Torrio wanted to kill him for being a softy, he should have killed him in 1910.

Torrio certainly had plans for the future. Since his arrival, Torrio was Colosimo's connection to Chicago's Italian underworld. By 1918, he was establishing a string of road house brothels and gambling joints on the Illinois-Indiana border. After 1920, he moved into beer-making. Torrio was independent, running his own operations. Even had Colosimo wished to, he could hardly have stopped Cousin Johnnie. But why would he have even wished to? Colosimo might not have wanted to get into bootlegging himself. He might have thought it too dangerous. He might have thought that, as a popular, if notorious, Chicago celebrity, his position was too exposed. But he could hardly have objected to bootlegging in principle. Colosimo ran a night-club for heaven's sake.

There are other considerations as well. Colosimo's was the first of Chicago's great underworld funerals. Ike Bloom, who stood up to deliver the eulogy, declared that "There wasn't a piker's hair in Big Jim's head. . . . Big Jim never bilked a pal or turned down a good guy and he always kept his mouth shut." Dink Kenna and Colosimo's lawyer, Rocco De Stefano, supported the distraught widow as Bathhouse John Coughlin led the prayers for the soul of the departed.

Colosimo had powerful political friends in the First Ward. With Colosimo's murder, Torrio had not only lost his uncle; he had lost his godfather as well. Torrio now had to knit back together the complex web of political connections that Colosimo had provided. The First Ward Democrats did not need Johnnie Torrio, at least not yet. But Torrio needed them. If Bloom or Kenna or Coughlin even suspected that Torrio had arranged the murder of their old crony, Jim Colosimo, they would have shunned him like the plague. Yet relations rolled on serene and untroubled. Kenna and Couglin gathered Johnnie Torrio to their collective bosoms like a bereaved orphan in need of comfort.

In his own account, Kobler is probably drawing on Herbert Asbury and Thompson and Raymond, as both associated Torrio with the Colosimo murder. Both, however, published their versions in 1940, twenty years after the event. Contrary to what Asbury and later Kobler assert, moreover, the Chicago police did not "always" believe that Torrio was responsible for Colosimo's murder. At first, the Chicago police connected the murder to Black Hand gangs. This was also the opinion of John Landesco writing for the Illinois Crime Commission in 1928. Landesco also mentions the theory that Colosimo was murdered on the orders of Hinky Dink Kenna in revenge for his switch to the Republican Party in the 1915 mayoral elections. In his 1929 exposé on Chicago crime, reporter Edward D. Sullivan mixes up some of his facts; yet he still provides what, at that time, was the accepted opinion—Colosimo was killed by Black Handers. Nor does he alter this interpretation in his 1930 sequel.

In 1930, Capone's earliest biographer, Fred D. Pasley simply wrote: "In the meantime Colosimo had died, in a murder mystery never solved. A lone assassin secreting himself in the check-room of the café, in the morning hours when it was empty save for the help, had shot him and slipped away." Pasley has gotten the time of the murder wrong. He continues however; "His funeral was impressive for the number of State legislators, judges, and city and county officials attending. Torrio was a pallbearer, as also were Anthony D'Andrea and Diamond Joe Esposito, Democratic and Republican committeemen from the old Nineteenth Ward, who were to die by the sawed-off shotgun." If Pasley was implying that Colosimo was killed by a sawed-off shotgun, he got that detail wrong. Still, the reference to D'Andrea and Esposito is significant. Along with Colosimo, they were rich, politically-connected and underworld-connected Italians. All were later murdered (Esposito in 1928). All their murders were unsolved. Pasley is surely suggesting the existence of a common thread.

The "underworld stool pigeon" who, according to Kobler, passed along the rumor that Torrio had paid Yale $10,000 to rid him of Colosimo could not have passed this rumor along before 1930. Had he done so, it would surely have been picked up by one of Chicago's many crime reporters. The earliest reference in fact comes from Burns in 1931: "an underworld rumor, quite definite and insistent, reached the police that Torrio had plotted Big Jim's murder and had paid Frankie Uale of Brooklyn $10,000 to commit the crime." Burns sagely observes, however, that "suspicion is not evidence." Unfortunately, the underworld stool pigeon is nowhere identified. We do not know when he passed this rumor along or where he got it. There is, however, one possibility. Maybe he got it at the movies.

Had it appeared in 1930 as planned, Howard Hawks' *Scarface* , co-produced by Howard Hughes and written by Ben Hecht, would have been America's first gangster film. Unfortunately, its content was deemed too violent, and the release was delayed until 1932, by which time *Public Enemy* and *Little Caesar* had already appeared. In 1929, the St. Valentine's Day Massacre had made Al Capone America's most well-known criminal; in March of 1930 his face even appeared on the cover of *Time*. Interest in him was now enormous. Damon Runyon covered his 1931 trial and Walter Winchell interviewed him three times. Accounts of his life appeared in *Collier's*, *The Outlook* and *Master Detective*. Hecht had based his own script on a thriller that had appeared earlier in 1930, also called *Scarface*, and written by one Armitage Trail. In 1932, Capone had begun his eleven-year sentence for income-tax evasion. With the bogeyman safely behind bars, the studios felt they could cash in on Capone's undoubted appeal without arousing undue public anxiety.

The opening shot of *Scarface* shows the shadow of the Capone character—Tony Camonte, played by Paul Muni—as he murders the crime boss and bootleg king, "Big Louie" Costillo (Big Jim Colosimo). He does so, we learn, on the orders of his mentor, Johnny Lovo (Johnny Torrio). For anyone in the know, the reference was clear: *Scarface* was saying that Capone had killed Colosimo on Torrio's orders.

Somehow, the Capone outfit had gotten a copy of the screenplay before the release. As Hecht liked to tell the story, two men came knocking on his hotel-room door in Los Angles.

"You the guy who wrote this?" said the man who was carrying the script.

Hecht admitted he was.

"We read it."

"How did you like it?"

"Is this stuff about Al Capone?"

"God, no!" said Hecht. "I don't even know Al." He named a few gangsters he had known as a reporter in Chicago—Colosimo, O'Banion, Hymie Weiss.

"OK, then. We'll tell Al this stuff you wrote is about them other guys." But then, as they were leaving, one of the duo asked Hecht, "If this stuff isn't about Al Capone, why are you calling it *Scarface?* Everybody'll think it's him."

"That's the reason. Al is one of the most famous and fascinating men of our times. If you call the movie *Scarface*, everybody will want to see it. That's part of the racket we call showmanship."

"I'll tell Al. Who's this fella Howard Hughes?"

"He's got nothing to do with it. He's the sucker with the money."

"OK. The hell with him."

Though the names were all changed, the publicists at Universal Studios agreed with Hecht that the title *Scarface* was box-office magic. Everyone understood the connection with Capone. The publicists claimed their film was "snatched from the headlines." In a sense it was. The film referred to real people and to real events, though in no particular order or with little concern to attach the events to the right character. After rubbing out Big Louis Costillo, for example, Tony Camonte takes his girlfriend Poppy. Al Capone, by contrast, had no connection to Dale Winter. Tony Camonte's killing spree included references to the murders of O'Banion and Weiss. It included as well a reference to the murder of Legs Diamond, with which Capone had no conceivable connection. The characters and events were real; but the plot was pure invention. Capone saw *Scarface,* and loved it so much that he bought his own print. Capone, at least, knew the real story. Other gangsters no doubt enjoyed it as well, though, unlike Capone, they were in no position to distinguish fact from fiction. It is possible that the unnamed underworld source who told the police that Capone killed Colosimo on the orders of Torrio had gotten the tip-off from none other than Hecht.[56]

The history of organized crime in America is in many places deeply obscure. There are too many unsolved murders, too many inexplicable shoot-outs, too many questions and not enough facts. Lacking facts, policemen, crime reporters and even the underworld itself filled in the blanks by confabulating the answers. They picked out the big names, the ones everybody knows, and inserted them into the unsolved mysteries, inventing a plausible story line. Thus McPhaul confabulates the missing details in the life of Johnnie Torrio as Schoenberg confabulates the life of Al Capone. Little details, like Torrio's "It's your funeral" line, emerge as burnished nuggets, and by dint of constant repetition, assume the patina of undoubted truths. It is only natural; no one likes an unfinished story, and the guy who confidently asserts that he knows all the answers seems the clever one, the one in the know.

The truth is, however, that we do not know who killed Big Jim Colosimo, just as we do not know who killed Detective Birns. Not knowing the answers may be unsatisfying, but it is better than closing the door with a false conclusion. In the course of his discussion of the end of the aldermen's war, Landesco cites a certain William Navigato, a former member of the Illinois Legislature and a personal friend of D'Andrea. After the first attempt on D'Andrea's life in May 1921, he said, "If they find the men who tried to murder D'Andrea, they may find the same gunmen who murdered Jim Colosimo."[55] Like Pasley, like indeed many in Chicago at the time, Navigato connected the Colosimo murder with the violence in the Nineteenth Ward. There was a war going on in the Italian underworld on the West Side, some sort of struggle for control that we do not fully understand. It was a struggle, moreover, which, besides Colosimo, D'Andrea, and Esposito, would claim the lives of many others. Nor did the internecine war end with the murder of Colosimo. It would be resumed in a few short years and claim successive *Unione Siciliana* presidents as well. Capone would find himself sucked in. Colosimo had good reason to try and keep clear of Italian underworld politics in Chicago. Torrio would have been the first to agree. In 1925, Johnnie and Anna Torrio left Chicago for a long vacation. It was neither the first nor the last time that Torrio judged that the war in Chicago had spun out of control, and that he had better go somewhere else.

Chapter Five
Prohibition: The New Gold Rush

"We can't suppress an ironical snicker, when we think that all [the prohibitionists] succeeded in doing was transporting women from the drawing room into the speakeasy."

—Alicia-Leone Moats[1]

We are now in the late 1920s. Prohibition has been on the statutes for nearly a decade. Ten years earlier the debate had still been largely hypothetical. What would be the effect of banning alcohol? Was it a good idea? Could such a ban ever work? Ten years on now, and the newspapers felt it was time to supply some answers to these question. Most agreed that prohibition was not working and indeed could not be made to work. There was not really much debate over this. Even the Bureau of Prohibition publicly admitted that enforcement had been woefully ineffective. The failure suggested some fresh questions.

For prohibition's supporters, the relevant question seemed to be: should we redouble our efforts? Redoubling the effort would entail increasing the government funds available to the Bureau of Prohibition. It would also mean introducing legislation giving the federal government power to compel reluctant state and local police forces to enforce the federal Prohibition statutes. There were drawbacks in both these proposals. Enlarging the Bureau of Prohibition and reshaping it into an effective national police force dealing in Prohibition violations was bound to be a slow process and one that would prove costly in tax dollars. Making state and local police subordinate to the federal government in all matters concerning Prohibition was bound to be resented by state and local governments. There was likely to be collateral damage as well. Prohibition already was increasing the nation's prison population dramatically; redoubling enforcement efforts would inevitably place thousands more behind bars. Then there was the problem of the cities; in many, Prohibition was simply a dead letter. How many agents would it take to force compliance upon a reluctant New York, Boston, Philadelphia, Chicago, Detroit, St. Louis, and Kansas City? What would be the reaction of the voters there who woke up to find their towns under siege by federal agents? Finally, and perhaps most disturbing, there was no guarantee that even redoubling the effort would actually produce the desired results. The Bureau of Prohibition had recently taken steps to beef up enforcement and to shake out the rampant corruption in their agency; other measures were in the pipe line. Yet the public was growing unsure; the cost of enforcement was high, and the damage it was inflicting on the nation great. Many of prohibition's original supporters had begun to waver.

For Prohibition's opponents, or for those merely inclined to skepticism, there were other issues. Critics had always argued that, regardless of whether prohibition was desirable in principle, it was not enforceable in practice. There were areas in the South and the Plains States that had been dry for decades: here prohibition would work, or at least would work as well as it had before national prohibition had come into effect. But the rest of the country was not dry and, especially in the big cities, showed not the slightest inclination of becoming so. Here, they had predicted, prohibition simply would never work. Experience was now proving these critics right.

Also, why a constitutional amendment? America's churches had long preached sobriety; they had preached it along with chastity, piety, filial obedience, and personal cleanliness. These were the things people expected their churches to preach. But preaching was one thing, the U.S. Constitution was another. People had never expected to see these beliefs enshrined in the Constitution, or at least not until recently. Writing prohibition into the Constitution turned out to be more than just a radical departure in America's social history; it was a new departure in the country's legal and political history. The Eighteenth Amendment did more than just prohibit something. It changed the way America governed itself.

Prohibition, wrote H. McBain in 1928, "withdrew power from the states and from the people. It did not merely grant power but attempted to fix an implacable policy. It vastly increased the hitherto limited police power of Congress. It vastly curtailed the police power of the states. Unlike most other constitutional prohibitions, it was directed not to the national or the state governments but to individuals. It was a sumptuary fiat quite different from anything else found in the constitution."[2]

Among those who were now asking these questions was the columnist Walter Lippmann. In its simplest sense, Lippmann began, the Volstead Act might seem simply an attempt at "regulating the liquor traffic." The Volstead Act flatly forbade it. With the Eighteenth Amendment, however, Prohibition was also enshrined in the Constitution; it became the basic law of the land. Prohibition thereby took its place with liberty and the right to bear arms as defining features of the American polity. Lippmann wondered why the traffic in liquor needed to be regulated by a Constitutional Amendment. America was after all a vast free-trade zone; commerce might be regulated at state and local levels, but regulating retail commerce had never been part of constitutional law. If someone were to propose amending the Constitutional to regulate the trade in sweet potatoes or the creation of a national police force to prohibit the buying and selling of roller skates, they would be heaped with ridicule. Why was the liquor traffic so different? It was special, Lippmann observed, because that traffic stood as a symbol of the "evil which old-fashioned preachers ascribe to the Pope, to Babylon, to atheists and to the devil." The Eighteenth Amendment was not about the regulation of commerce at all; it was rather a challenge. It "involves a test between social orders." Prohibition was meant to define America, to lay down once and for all what it meant to be an American; "The Eighteenth Amendment is the rock upon which the evangelical church militant is founded, and with it are involved a whole way of life and an ancient tradition. The overturning of the Eighteenth Amendment would mean the emergence of the cities as the dominant force in America, dominant politically and socially as they are already dominant economically."[3]

THE POLITICS OF PROHIBITION

It had all happened so quickly, however. Why, brushing reasonable objections aside, had Congress and the state legislatures fallen over themselves in passing unenforceable laws? Why had so few seen the implications in all this? By the late Twenties, as Americans began to wake up to the enormity of what they had wrought upon themselves, they began to wonder how it had all come about.

Progressivism in America had never been a unified movement. It was made up rather of contemporary or nearly contemporary movements—for good government, vice reform, workers' rights, public health and safety, prohibition, and women's suffrage. Each of these was, in itself, a minority issue, and to make political headway on any one of them it was necessary for reformers to form alliances. Yet even broad reformist alliances were politically weak. Republican and Democrat bosses sometimes found it expedient to ally with the progressives, presenting progressive candidates for elections; yet, even at local levels, progressives were rarely able to dominate either of the major parties on their own. Nor were the progressives always united among themselves. Progressives were often—out of moral conviction or mere expediency—willing to make common cause with supporters of other causes, but not always. Workers' rights, prohibition, and women's suffrage were all issues that divided progressives as often as they united them.

The progressive movement also suffered from a deeper cleavage; it was geographically divided into urban and rural wings. During the early years, from the 1890s to 1910, Progressives were more apt to be defined by what they stood against than what they stood for, and thus, in the turn-of-the-century years, progressives of all shades and hues could unite against the corrupt, urban machines. Opposition to Boss Croker's Tammany and Harrison Carter Sr.'s administration in Chicago brought the vice reformers and the champions of good government into the same fold. Overthrowing the corrupt machines, grafting police forces, and compliant, politically-appointed magistrates was a priority for all progressives. Nevertheless, even in the 1890s, the division between the urban and the rural progressives could still rise to the surface.

In an emotional outburst following his "Cross of Gold" speech at the 1896 Democratic Party Convention, the party nominated as its presidential candidate an obscure congressman from Nebraska, William Jennings Bryan. Bryan advocated the free coinage of silver, a position that he had adopted from the old Populist Party. For over a decade, Western reformers had advocated free silver as a panacea for workers suffering from low wages and Western farmers suffering from declining farm prices. Farmers especially had been caught in a cycle of mounting debts. With declining farm prices, a debt that could have been paid in 1865 with one thousand bushels of wheat, needed three thousand bushels to repay in 1896. The Populists had argued that the decline in farm prices was caused by a shortage of money, a shortage that could be remedied simply by increasing the money supply through the free coinage of silver. Speaking for the workers and the farmers, Bryan represented free silver not as a rational economic policy but as a moral imperative; the farmers were the backbone of America and the government had a duty to come to their aid.

Despite this, writes Richard Hofstadter, "in 1896 free silver ranked among the heresies with free love. Except in the farm country, wherever men of education and substance gathered it was held to be beneath discussion."[4] Free silver was roundly rejected in the commercial and financial centers on the East Coast. Economists and editorial writers, both Republicans and Democrats, regarded it as pure demagoguery, an attempt to debauch monetary sanity. The Democratic ticket fared poorly in the populous East, allowing the Republican ticket of McKinley and Roosevelt to win in a romp. Nevertheless, Bryan's campaign had uncovered a nerve, demonstrating that the rural West and the urban East conceived of the reformist undertaking in radically different lights. Bryan summed up the feelings of much of rural America when he referred to New York as "the enemy's country."

The divisions between urban and rural progressivism reflected different experiences. Writes Stephen Fox,

> From the mid-1880s, American life was modernized by three overlapping social revolutions. Industrialization turned a slower agricultural society powered by muscle and wind into a factory world racing on steam, electricity and fossil fuels. Urbanization took farmers and others from their isolated, homogenous island communities, and deposited them in heterogeneous cities and towns. Immigration from abroad, in its ethnic diversity, challenged the easy domination by British-descended Protestants who had originally settled their portion of North America and run things for two centuries.[5]

By the mid-1880s, America's factories and workshops were churning out an ever-increasing variety of goods for the consumer, everything from canned peaches to bustles and ostrich-feather hats to bicycles for the new cycling craze. After 1900, Americans could boast that they walked on more carpets than all of Europe's nations combined. Cars and radio sets were being mass-produced. Prosperity was creating a consumer heaven, but it was a paradise that belonged to the cities far more than to the countryside. The cities were growing in size and prosperity while rural townships stagnated or fell into decline. Urban households indulged in new fashions while rural housewives looked at the "wishing books," the mail-order catalogues, and dreamed, per-haps experiencing more than a twinge of envious resentment. Urban workers went to baseball games on Sundays and cheap theatres on Saturday nights. Everyone could afford a half-hour at the nickelodeon. For farming-town fami-lies the choice of entertainment was far more restricted; for men there were saloons, political clubs, and the churches; for women there were often only sewing circles and churches.

Rural America was bewildered at this turn of events. Nineteenth-century America had celebrated its farmers and pioneers, the hearty, self-sufficient yeomen of the Jeffersonian and Jacksonian tradition — Indian-fighters like Wil-liam Henry Harrison and rail-splitters like Abraham Lincoln. These were the true Americans. By the end of the century, however, these true Americans had fallen into eclipse. Rural America felt by-passed. Bryan's electoral campaign in 1896, writes Andrew Sinclair, "was less an economic matter than an expres-sion of rural hatred of Eastern financiers who waxed fat under the mysterious protection of the devilish gold standard."[6]

As prosperity's beneficiaries, urban America was apt to regard the social changes that growth had brought in a positive light. These changes included the emergence of a new consumer society and the birth of new forms of popu-lar culture. Economic growth was emancipating urban women, turning them into salaried employees and independent consumers. Urban prosperity brought tolerance towards the immigrants and their foreign ways. These immigrants were, after all, workers and voters. Rural America, by contrast, especially in the West and South, regarded the new consumer society, with its ridiculous fashions and styles, its primitive jazz and rag-time music, and its nickelodeons with deep suspicion. It looked on the crowds of unchaperoned young working women going to dance halls, amusement parks, and theatres with horror. It wor-ried too that the cities, now overflowing with new immigrants, had lost their American character. Rural white America had shunned the immigrants, just as it had segregated itself from the Blacks. Yet it was still impossible to keep the cities out of their lives. Even after farm prices began to rise in the 1890s, the old self-sufficiency of the rural townships was undercut by the appearance of cheap, mass-produced consumer goods. Farmers were forced to depend on the mail-order houses for the clothing and implements they had once proudly made themselves. Radios and motor cars only served to highlight the isolation of rural America. The city, Bryan's "enemy's country," was forcing itself on the township.

The two wings of American progressivism continued to collaborate through the presidency of Woodrow Wilson, though their partnership was growing increasingly strained.[7] The divisions finally came to a head during the 1924 Democratic National Convention in Manhattan. The Western and Southern Democrats supported William Gibbs McAdoo, standing, in the caustic words of Arthur Schlesinger Jr., for "economic pseudo-radicalism, prickling with fulminations against Wall Street and monopoly." The Eastern Democrats supported New York Governor, Al Smith.

The two opposing candidates were, as Schlesinger continues, "antagonistic symbols for the emotions of agrarianism, prohibitionism, fundamentalism and xenophobia." For months the Eastern Democrats had demanded that McAdoo publicly renounce the support of the Ku Klux Klan. When the convention introduced a resolution denouncing the Klan by name, McAdoo replied with his own conspiratorial denunciation of the "sinister, unscrupulous invisible government which has its seat in the citadel of privilege and finance in New York City." Bryan, in his last major political appearance, weakly appealed for party unity. Knowing that many of his own supporters were Klansmen, Bryan told the convention, "We can exterminate Ku Kluxism better by recognizing their honesty and teaching them that they are wrong." His speech was nearly drowned out by cat-calls from Tammany hecklers in the balconies of Madison Square Garden. The resolution to denounce the Klan by name was defeated by one vote; and after 103 gruelling ballots, the party settled on the West Virginian John W. Davis as a compromise candidate. In the end, the Democrats had torn themselves apart for nothing. Davis went on to be handily defeated by Republican incumbent Calvin Coolidge.[8]

Only a small minority of rural America joined or even supported the Ku Klux Klan; yet many broadly sympathized with its program of agrarianism, fundamentalism, and xenophobia and shared its hostility towards Wall Street and the older Eastern elites. These were the Americans who embraced prohibition. The issues were as symbolic as they were economic. What did it mean to be American? Whose country was it anyway? The 1924 Democrat Convention only sanctioned a breach that had been quietly festering for years. Rural America's assault on the citadels of the privileged elites and the immoral and un-American cities had started over a decade earlier in 1913, when the Anti-Saloon League had decided that the time had come to write prohibition into the American Constitution.

In 1893 a new temperance organization had been founded—the Anti-Saloon League. From the start, the League pursued a new tack: the old prohibitionists had been a political party; the new Anti-Saloon League was a pressure group. Founded in Oberlin, Ohio, the Anti-Saloon League was founded to organize local Protestant churches in their struggle to ensure the election of dry candidates. As Oberlin was in Republican territory, the League naturally began its work with the Republican Party. Yet as the League leaders realized, the tactic worked just as well with the Democratic Party, especially in the South. It soon became League policy to support the dry candidate, irrespective of his party affiliation. It was a new and effective tactic, and two years' later in 1895, other temperance and prohibition merged with the Ohio Anti-Saloon League, forming a new national Anti-Saloon League.

Adherents of the old Prohibition Party asked how the League could support individual dry Republicans and dry Democrats when they knew that both the Republican and the Democratic parties remained in the hands of the wets? The Anti-Saloon League replied that, while the old Prohibition Party was doomed to electoral irrelevancy, their tactics worked. As a national association, the League was well organized and methodical. Between 1911 and 1925, from thirty thousand to sixty thousand churches all over the country were affiliated with the Anti-Saloon League. Affiliation meant that Anti-Saloon League speakers spoke from the pulpit and shared in the collection. This alone gave the League millions of dollars in funds. The League also had tens of thousands of private affiliates, each of which paid a monthly subscription fee. With money and grass-roots support, the League grew increasingly active. Whenever a dry option was on the ballot, the Anti-Saloon League was there, sending in their speakers to rouse the faithful. The League turned the pulpits "into a battery of Krupp guns, from which to hurl the bursting shells and solid shot against the saloon and its defenders."[9] The League taught the churches how to denounce wet candidates. It provided political organizers. From its printing plant in Westerville Ohio poured out forty tons of dry propaganda every month.

The League's policy was to pick off wets one by one. No election was too insignificant. The League campaigned in town council elections and for dry option ballots at the local level. From here the League set its sights on the state legislatures, picking off wet assemblymen. Nothing delighted the League more than writing the political epitaph of a prominent wet politician. By the mid-1890s, the Anti-Saloon League had been able to write such epitaphs for seventy wet state legislators in the state of Ohio. The League went on to unseat the incumbent wet governor in Ohio in 1905, replacing him with a dry. By now the League was a significant force in national politics; even Washington was sitting up to take notice.

Regardless of their views on drinking, saloons, and the traffic in alcohol, most politicians detested the League. Dry politicians resented having to toe the Anti-Saloon League line; wet politicians disliked finding themselves in the Anti-Saloon League's sights. Still, the League strove to make capitulation as painless as possible. It was usually enough for a politician to declare his sympathies for the League and his support for their policies. The League did not press state legislatures to enact specific policies. It became very easy for politicians to comply with the League's demands, since a *pro-forma* submission was all that was required. The League was not asking these politicians to offend their wet supporters by enforcing dry policies. Indeed the League did not even demand that the politicians give up drinking themselves. The League's enemies accused it of blatant hypocrisy; the League was eliminating the wets, only to replace them with an army of stooges. But the League was biding its time, fostering the impression that a dry tide was sweeping the country. It was growing steadily more powerful. Enforcement could wait until the League was truly in the driver's seat.

The immediate objective was control over the nation's political classes. In this, they were increasingly successful. The Anti-Saloon League proclaimed itself to be the political voice of the church, the voice of the real America. It was an awesome claim, enough to make all but representatives of the most irredeemably wet cities tremble with fear. Congress, wrote the dyspeptic H. L. Mencken, was made up of "petty scoundrels, pusillanimous poltroons, highly vulnerable and cowardly men," who dared not do anything that might provoked the "full fire of the Anti-Saloon League."[10] After 1910, wrote Louis Seibold, the average United States Congressman was more frightened of the Anti-Saloon League than he was of the president.[11]

National campaigns need powerful symbols to serve as rallying points. Reformist campaigns in particular need negative symbols. Reformers need to demonize someone, depict for their followers exactly who it is that they are combating. The earliest temperance campaigns had been aimed at the drunkard; the League fixed its attentions on the saloons instead. The choice was inspired, though, in context, quite natural as well. Never a highly esteemed part of American culture, by 1900 the reputation of the saloon had fallen to new lows.

In January 1892, a year before the founding of the League, the Rev. Dr. Parkhurst, a reformist leader in New York, had voiced his opinion that the worst consequence of vice was not its effect on individual sinners but its capacity to corrupt public life. It was an argument that re-aligned the reformist outlook. Vice and sin were no longer private matters, matters between God and the sinner. Nor was the danger of vice limited to the possibility that vicious habits endangered wives, children and the scions of pious and well-regulated families, as Anthony Comstock and Frances Willard had constantly warned. Parkhurst took the anti-vice rationale a step further, arguing that since political corruption fed on vice, anyone who indulged in vice was *ipso facto* guilty of abetting corruption. Those who indulged were not only endangering themselves and their families; they were damaging the whole community.

In this interpretation, the prostitutes, gamblers, and drunks, those who had fallen into vice, were no longer the real dangers. The true threat came from the nexus of commercial and political interests that held the cities in their grip. It was their unbridled greed and rapacity that had reduced the unfortunates to their miserable state. The prostitute became progressively reconfigured, less and less of a sinful temptress and more an innocent victim forced by circumstance, or even compelled against her will, into a life of sin. It was easier to rally public opinion against the vice trade when prostitutes could be represented as victims of squalid commercial and political interests. The white slaver, particularly the foreign white slaver, was an effective cardboard villain. In the same way, the Anti-Saloon League represented the drinker as the victim of an unholy alliance of saloon owners, brewers, spirits manufacturers, and the politicians whom the liquor trade bought and sold. The difference here is that these were not mere cardboard villains; saloon owners and liquor dealers had long had it coming to them.

In 1862 a new Internal Revenue Act placed a license fee of twenty dollars on retail liquor dealers and a tax of one dollar a barrel on beer and twenty cents a gallon on spirits. In that same year a new organization, the United States Brewers' Association, was formed, to fight these taxes. By 1866 the brewers and their allies had established a "permanent committee," a permanent staff of well-heeled lobbyists in Washington to protect the interests of the industry. Other associations soon followed, and by end of the decade Congress and the liquor business had established a cosy and mutually profitable relationship. Whiskey was cheap to produce and, if taxes were kept low, immensely profitable to sell. The Whiskey Ring scandals under President Grant and the Whiskey Trust scandal in 1887 showed that the distillers were willing to provide handsomely for any politician endeavouring to keep things that way. Scandals concerning the Texas brewers followed. The final indictment of decades of bribery and corruption appeared in a 1919 Senate report. The report disclosed that brewers controlled large segments of the local press in America. They had interfered in elections and made candidates sign pledges of support in exchange for funding. They had organized boycotts of dry-owned businesses. On the assumption that women would use the vote in favor of prohibition, brewers had also organized the saloon-keepers to campaign against women's suffrage. During the war, the brewers had maintained contact with the outlawed German-American Alliance, "many of the members of which were disloyal and unpatriotic."

On a local scale, the liquor trade had begun buying politicians and political protection before the Civil War, forming alliances with Tammany in New York and other urban machines. Brewers and distillers paved the way for aspirant local politicians, setting them up in saloons and providing free beer and whiskey for political campaigns and the inevitable election day brawls. An already bad situation seemed to worsen in the 1880s; economic growth was creating raucous honky-tonks in the city centers. By the 1890s, the Chicago Levee had grown "blaring and glaring and insolent," while "enough money to settle Europe's war debts was passed in bribes."[12]

Like prostitution, beer sales became even more profitable as the industry organized and became vertically integrated. Traditionally, brewing was a small-scale local industry. By the last half of the nineteenth century, however, the brewing industry had begun to consolidate, with the German-dominated Milwaukee breweries gaining a commanding position. These breweries invested their profits in urban property, buying up old saloons and taverns and opening as many new ones as they could. In so doing, they drove the old, independent saloon proprietor to the wall. The brewers hired the old proprietors as tenant-managers, tied to the brewery and required to sell only their products. Investing their profits in urban real estate, rival brewers bought up corner sites and expanded into the new suburbs in the manner of fast-food chains in our own epoch. Local residents complained: there were too many saloons. Rival breweries erected saloons on opposite street corners, saloons were invading residential districts, saloons were being built in front of churches and schools, and saloons were increasing prostitution.

Echoing the Chicago Vice Commission, the Wisconsin Vice Commission concluded that "the chief direct cause of the downfall of women and girls is the close connection between alcoholic drink and commercialised vice."[13] The brewers', distillers', and saloon-keepers' associations were told to clean up their houses lest an enraged public force the government to clean them up for them. Locked in cut-throat competition and seduced by a vision of a never-ending stream of profits, they ignored this sound advice. Though Prohibition failed to stop drinking in America, it did kill off the old saloon. As journalist George Ade put it in 1931, *The Olde Time Saloon, not wet, not dry, just history.* Few mourned its demise.

In its struggle against the saloon, the Anti-Saloon League assumed the high moral ground with such assured confidence that few politicians dared raise their voices against them publicly. Congressional wets no longer contested that national prohibition was a high ideal; they had fallen back to arguing that this ideal was neither necessary nor realizable. America's entry into World War I stripped the wets of these last arguments. With the outbreak of war, the drys claimed that, in a time of national emergency, using grains to produce whiskey and beer instead of bread, was immoral, selfish, and unpatriotic. The public was told that every time the drinker drained a schooner of beer or a glass of spirits, he was depriving a starving child of a loaf of bread. The argument was specious; the making of spirits and beer had never caused bread shortages. Nevertheless, in the national mood of Spartan idealism created by the war, the dry argument spoke to a desire for solidarity and self-sacrifice in the face of a common peril. Self-indulgence betokened moral indifference, and moral indifference was unpatriotic. Men who idly drank or smoked while the nation was in peril were behaving unworthily. The war also created high expectations; people wanted and expected something apocryphal to happen. The House and the Senate sensed the new mood. Bullied, blackmailed, browbeaten and by now rather awed, Congress passed Prohibition. Wrote Frederick Lewis Allen in 1931,

Nothing in recent American history is more extraordinary, as one looks back from the nineteen-thirties, than the ease with which—after generations of uphill fighting by the drys—prohibition was finally written upon the statute books. The country accepted it not only willingly, but almost absentmindedly. When the Eighteenth Amendment came before the Senate in 1917, it was passed by a one-sided vote after only thirteen hours of debate, part of which was conducted under the ten-minute rule. When the House of Representatives accepted it a few months later, the debate upon the amendment as a whole occupied only a single day. The State Legislatures ratified it in short order; in January 1919, some two months after the Armistice, the necessary three-quarters of the states had fallen into line and the Amendment was part of the Constitution. (All the rest of the states but two subsequently added their ratifications—only Connecticut and Rhode Island remained outside the pale.)[14]

It was more of a surrender then a debate. But by 1919 most of Congressmen and Senators were undoubtedly happy to see the back of the issue that had been plaguing and vexing them for decades.

The Problem of Enforcement

Be a good sport about it. No more falling off the water wagon. Uncle Sam will help you keep your pledge.

—William H. Anderson, Superintendent of New York State Anti-Saloon League[15]

The drys were the revolutionaries. Like Oliver Cromwell and his Ironsides, they had put the dissolute old cavalier army to flight. By passing the Eighteenth Amendment, the drys had won the war. Many of them, writes Andrew Barr, thought that this was enough.[16]

The struggle for prohibition had been a struggle over values and definitions. Was America a nation that simply supinely accepted the presence of sin, dissolution, and ungodliness in its midst, or was it prepared to stand up and fight these challenges? As a matter of principle, the Eighteenth Amendment seemed to have resolved this question definitively. As a matter of fact, however, it had resolved nothing.

Though the drys were no doubt the revolutionaries, they were a revolutionary army with only one objective—prohibition. Having achieved that objective, many of the drys simply decamped; they packed up their armor and returned home. The drys had never given much consideration to the question of what came next, of how prohibition was to be politically managed and enforced. Compared to the moral issue, the problem of enforcement had always seemed secondary. Some even thought that if there were those in the country who persisted in their error, it was not really a concern of the righteous at all. The evil-doers would surely get their just deserts at the hands of a Higher Power. Committed drys were happy enough to see Prohibition violators behind bars; many would have been happy to see the godless immigrants, with whom the drys associated the liquor traffic, sent back to where they came from. The drys just had not considered how it was all going to be worked out.

Enforcement, they felt, could not simply be left in the hands of the politicians. The rural drys hated government and deeply distrusted the politicians. These were the same corrupt, spineless men who had needed to be bullied, bludgeoned, threatened, and cajoled for decades before they would do their duty and outlaw alcohol. Sure to backslide or sell out at the first opportunity, the politicians could not be trusted to enforce Prohibition on their own. Someone needed to remain in Washington and keep an eye on the unprincipled politicians. Thus the dry army was grateful that Anti-Saloon League strategist Wayne B. Wheeler had agreed to remain behind. Wheeler had been the principle author of the bill that was later named after Andrew Volstead of Minnesota.

Wheeler would see to it that there would be no backsliding. Nevertheless, all of Wheeler's efforts notwithstanding, the politicians, restive and resentful under League control and aware of Prohibition's unpopularity in parts of the country, let enforcement of the Eighteenth Amendment languish.[17]

The continental United States has over eighteen thousand miles of coast-line and frontier. No one considering this fact could seriously have imagined that all of these frontiers and coasts could be secured from the determined efforts of smugglers, especially if the smugglers' efforts were seconded by local allies, confederates, and thirsty customers. Smuggling was going to take place whatever the government did; but smuggling was hardly the only problem. Alcohol could still be produced for a variety of industrial and medical purposes. Doctors could prescribe and druggists could dispense as much alcohol as they wished. Before Prohibition this had never been a problem. Who was going to drink medicinal or industrial alcohol when much more palatable stuff was readily available? Prohibition changed all this; Prohibition made doctors and druggists the licensed purveyors of prohibited substances. Drys failed to foresee that some doctors and druggists might—out of venality, wet sympathies or sheer cussedness—prove less than wholly compliant. Prohibition also allowed the production of near-beer, of beer, that is, without alcohol. But it was impossible to brew non-alcoholic beer. Normal, that is alcoholic, beer had to be brewed first and then have its alcohol removed. Again, it was easy to foresee that many honest beer-makers might object to this, might regard the subjection of their product to this sort of treatment as an insult to their professional skill. Rather than see all their good beer ruined, many brewers were happy if someone mislaid or diverted the beer on the way to the de-alcoholization plants, even if this were not strictly legal.

An even bigger failure of the imagination concerned illicit distilling—moonshining. Whiskey had always been subject to tax. It was a tax, however, that certain Americans had always tried to avoid paying. Moonshining was the proverbial oldest crime in the book. Prohibition had not changed anything here; moonshining was just as illegal in the 1920s as it had been a decade before. It was just that now moonshining was in more convivial company. The demand for the moonshiner's product suddenly grew exponentially. That demand indeed was far greater than all red-necked old hillbillies hidden in the mountains with their copper kettles could possibly supply. Enterprising new businessmen would soon arise in the cities themselves to meet the new demand. A home distillery kit, after all, could be ordered from the Sears-Roebuck catalogue for a mere five dollars, and it was perfectly legal.

The Constitution vests police powers in the hands of the states; in 1919 few branches of the federal government had enforcement arms. One that did was the Department of the Treasury, whose commissioner of internal revenue had the power to investigate income tax avoidance. This was the agency that Wheeler picked to enforce Prohibition. As its principle author, Wheeler had put himself in charge of interpreting and enforcing the complex and contradictory Volstead Act. He would remain the effective, though informal, czar of Prohibition until his death nine years later. Sinclair suggests that Wheeler chose the Internal Revenue Service because it was filled with Anti-Saloon League allies from Ohio.

These were good years to be an Ohio Republican, especially an Ohio Republican in good graces with the Anti-Saloon League. In 1917, the Republican Senator from Ohio, Warren G. Harding, performed his own obeisance to the League. Though a drinking man himself, Harding foresaw that the storm of patriotism accompanying America's entry into the war made the Anti-Saloon League impossible to withstand. After Harding switched sides, the League came out in his support and later helped ensure his election as president in 1920. Harding packed his cabinet with old Ohio cronies, while Wheeler gave out jobs on the new Bureau of Prohibition to Anti-Saloon League members from his home state.[18] The first prohibition commissioner, an Ohio lawyer named John F. Kramer, served for a year and a half, and was best known for his public statement that, "This law will be obeyed in cities, large and small, and in villages, and where it is not obeyed, it will be enforced." He was replaced by Roy Asa Haynes, former mayor of Hillsboro, Ohio, the birthplace of the Women's Crusade. Haynes was an active member of the Methodist Episcopal Church, Ohio Republican Party, and Anti-Saloon League. Wayne B. Wheeler personally nominated him. It was courtesy of Haynes, writes Kobler, that "liquor for [Harding's] Ohio gang's K Street jollifications was delivered to the front door in Wells Fargo express wagons with armed dry agents on guard."[19]

The first duty of a revolutionary party following a successful *coup d'etat*, is to fill the state aparat with the revolution's loyal supporters. Wheeler understood this well. Though undoubtedly a sincere dry, Wheeler's behavior was no different than that of Boss Tweed after his success in the 1868 elections. Each put loyalists on the payroll. Bureau of Prohibition agents and employees were exempted from the Civil Service rules; this meant that men could be appointed as Prohibition agents without regard to their qualifications or previous conduct. During the Harding and Coolidge years, Wheeler, working through Haynes, vetted most nominations for Prohibition Bureau jobs. He found himself however deluged by requests from dry politicians to give jobs to their supporters. Being outside the Civil Service rules, the agents were not only often underqualified; they were also under-paid. Wheeler could only hope that, as clients of dry politicians, he could at least count on their political loyalty. What he could not count upon, however, was their incorruptibility. In 1920, a dry agent's pay ranged from a miserly twelve hundred to two thousand dollars a year. Even in 1930, when the problems of lack of qualifications had been acknowledged, pay scales had only risen to between twenty-three hundred and twenty-eight hundred dollars. These were not living wages. As F.L. Allen commented,

> Anyone who believed that men employable at thirty-five or fifty dollars a week would surely have the expert technical knowledge and the diligence to supervise successfully the complicated chemical operations of industrial-alcohol plants or to out-wit the craftiest devices of smugglers and bootleggers, and that they would surely have the force of character to resist corruption by

men whose pockets were bulging with money, would be ready to believe in
Santa Claus, perpetual motion, and pixies.[20]

Throughout the war years, the League had associated prohibition with patriotism; anyone declining to support prohibition was suspected of being anti-
patriotic. After 1920, however, the argument cut the other way. Politicians
had done their patriotic duty in supporting Prohibition; they were now doing their patriotic duty in refusing to waste their constituents' tax dollars. It
was an attitude that chimed in well with the political philosophy of Calvin
Coolidge. As a teetotaler, Coolidge had always enjoyed friendly relations
with the Anti-Saloon League. Yet, though Coolidge's repeated declarations
that Prohibition was the law of the land and that every citizen had a duty to
obey the law were undoubtedly sincere, they never amounted to more than
exhortations. Coolidge was merely telling Americans that they had a duty
to obey the law; he was not recommending a large-scale policy of federal
government intervention to enforce Prohibition. As a traditional Republican,
large-scale policies of federal intervention were anathema to him. Coolidge
opposed high taxes and interventionist government as a matter of principle,
believing that the role of the federal government in internal affairs should be
that of arbitrating disputes. Prohibition, he believed, was up to the states to
enforce. Yet most state legislatures were no more inclined to support programs of enforcement than was the congress. No matter what the Anti-Saloon
League might claim, politicians knew that Prohibition was divisive. They
straddled the issue, paying lip service to the dry argument and to the citizen's
duty to obey the law while carefully doing nothing that might rile their wet
constituents. "The state governments were supposed to help the Prohibition
Bureau," wrote Allen, "but by 1927 their financial contributions to the cause
was about one-eighth of the sum they spent enforcing their own fish and game
laws. Some legislatures withdrew their aid entirely, and even the driest states
were inclined to let Uncle Sam bear the brunt of the Volstead job."[21]

Prohibition Commissioner Kramer had predicted that enforcement would
prove "quick and cheap." Yet it was only quick and cheap in areas that were dry
already; and even in these it was only partially effective. In other areas, Prohibition quickly proved unenforceable. It was what the wets had predicted all along.

In the three months leading up to the Eighteenth Amendment, over half
a million dollars of liquor was stolen from government bonded warehouses.
Authorities redoubled the guards, but the liquor kept disappearing. With a
fifth of whiskey now selling on the black market for between ten and fifteen
dollars and a gallon of moonshine from the stills at twenty dollars, thieves,
bootleggers and moonshiners not only had an incentive to steal and produce;
they had the money to bribe officials. In February 1920, less than a month after the Volstead Act had gone into effect, two prohibition agents in Baltimore
were indicted on corruption charges. By the late spring, the federal courts in
Chicago were hopelessly congested with Prohibition violations. Indicative of
the basic problem, liquor flowed freely during the Republican and Demo-

crat Conventions that summer, and many of the delegates were staggeringly drunk.[22]

The drys were hoisted on their own petard. Having proclaimed that Prohibition would be the start of a new era, that the Eighteenth Amendment had overwhelming support in every part of the country, and that enforcement would be quick and cheap, it was hard for them to admit that Prohibition was not working. It was harder still for them to recommend a costly and invasive program of federal enforcement.

Wheeler's hand-picked Prohibition Commissioner Haynes put out a steady stream of glowing press reports: "The Amendment is being enforced to an even greater extent than many of its devoted friends anticipated" [January 1922]. "[The] home brew fad is taking its last gasp" [December 1922]. "Bootleg patronage has fallen off fifty per cent" [April, 1923]. "There is little open and above-board drinking anywhere" [December, 1923].[23] While the commissioner steadfastly denied reality, his own Bureau of Prohibition plunged ever deeper into corruption. In April 1921, the grand jury for the Southern District of New York reported that, "almost without exception the [Prohibition] agents were not men of the type of intelligence and character qualified to be charged with this difficult and important duty and federal law."[24]

Although Prohibition agents did not need to meet the normal civil service qualifications, they were required to sign an oath that they had never been associated with the wine or liquor businesses. Yet the recommendation of Samuel Koenig, the corrupt Lower East Side Republican boss was sufficient to obtain the appointment another East Side thug, John J. Kerrigan, as a Prohibition agent. Kerrigan later had the gall to state publicly that a Prohibition agent in New York could make from forty thousand to fifty thousand dollars a year. And provided he had enough political pull, even the mighty Wheeler, whose writ on all Prohibition issues usually ran so large, could not fire him.[25]

Employing under-paid and under-qualified dry agents to control a multi-million-dollar illegal industry was the perfect recipe for corruption. In the first eleven years of the Prohibition Bureau, there were 17,972 appointments to the service, 11,982 separations from the service without prejudice, and 1,604 dismissals for cause. One in twelve dry agents was dismissed for bribery, forgery, conspiracy, extortion, theft, or other causes, and this, the Wickersham Committee later concluded, was only the tip of the iceberg. The extensive turn-over in dry agents led critics to claim that the Bureau was nothing but a training school for bootleggers. As Stanley Walker wrote of the dry agents, "as a class, however, they made themselves offensive beyond words, and their multifarious doings made them the pariahs of New York."[26]

Triumphant at the passage of the Eighteenth Amendment, dry reformers were emboldened to launch other campaigns to scrub the country clean of its noxious vices. There was a renewal of the anti-tobacco campaign. There was an anti-profanity crusade. The General Federation of Women's Clubs had sought to ban the tango and hesitation waltz in 1914. After 1920, the list of proscribed dances was enlarged to include the bunny hug, turkey trot, Texas

Tommy, hug-me-tight, fox trot, shimmy dance, sea-gull swoop, camel walk, and skunk waltz. Jazz and Negro music were widely condemned; "Does Jazz put the Sin in Syncopation?" asked the *Ladies' Home Journal* in 1921. The answer was that it did. It was the wrong time to introduce musical prohibitions, however. Reformers could keep the black musicians out of respectable places. They could preach to their young about the dangers of the juke joints; but they could not shut off the radios. Like the internet today, radio in the 1920s was expanding and impossible to control. Radio was the voice of subversion. Listeners could experience the corrupting influence of jazz music in the privacy of their own rooms.

Crusades were taking place in other areas as well. Though often grudging and never shared by everyone, the pre-war United States had tolerated the presence of foreign radicals on its shores. Emma Goldberg and Carlo Tresca had had their troubles with the law. Yet Goldberg and Tresca were passionate, articulate, large-than-life radicals who enjoyed the friendship and support of many of the first progressives. By 1920, however, reform had not only turned in a dry direction; it had become fiercely anti-foreigner. In 1920, Attorney General A. Mitchell Palmer rounded up Red Emma and her associates and had them deported on the steamship *Burford*. It was only the beginning. Radicals in thirty-five American cities were arrested and imprisoned. In New York, more than 650 men and women were taken for questioning at the Department of Justice headquarters on Park Row. Federal attorneys busily wrote out warrants for an even wider dragnet. Accusing them of conspiring against the United States and the State of New York, the New York State Assembly refused to permit the seating of five elected socialist deputies. The drys and the anti-vice leagues had regularly employed arguments from eugenics and the racial purity movement. When Madison Grant published *The Passing of a Great Race* in 1916, his chauvinistic arguments were endorsed in the *Annals of the American Academy*.

With the spread of anti-foreigner sentiment, worse was to come. In 1920, the muckraking journalist, Lothar Stoddard published *The Rising Tide of Color Against White Supremacy*, followed, in 1922, by *The Revolt Against Civilization: the Menace of the Underman*. The Dillingham Commission, followed by the Laughlin Report, recommended that immigration be restricted to people of the "Anglo-Saxon type." The 1921 and 1924 immigration acts were the result of these recommendations.[27]

RESISTANCE

Prohibition certainly did change America. It changed it, however, in ways that few had foreseen and even fewer—certainly none of Prohibition's supporters—could possible have desired. To paraphrase the columnist Heywood Broun, Prohibition changed America from a drinking man's country to a country where the drinking man had to fight his way through a bevy of chattering school girls to get a drink at the bar. As it changed America, Prohibition also presented organized crime with an undreamed of windfall. While other countries chose to deal with the problem of drunkenness by licensing and regulating the traffic in drink, the United States chose to prohibit that traffic entirely. Effectively, albeit unintentionally, the government was deregulating the traffic in drink and then forbidding law-abiding citizens from having anything to do with it. No commission of mafia families, no team of mob lawyers could have come up with a better solution. The history of organized crime in America conventionally starts with Prohibition. It is appropriate, for Prohibition gave organized crime its show-biz break.

The progressive movement had kicked up a national hornet's nest, revealing what Lincoln Steffens called "the sins of the cities." These sins were exemplified by honky-tonk vice, official corruption, and political machines. The urban saloon played a central role in these urban sins; it contributed to the degraded condition of the urban poor and workers, the spread of prostitution, and the political grip of the machines. When the Anti-Saloon League advocated a policy of abolishing the saloon, most urban reformers backed the League.

But the sins of the cities were not the only abuses the progressive movement uncovered. The progressives also revealed, and widely publicized, stock-market swindles, instances of corporate greed and malfeasance, rampant political graft, financial scandals, and the use of trusts and monopolies against the common citizen. These revelations provoked a revulsion against the nation's governing classes—not only against corrupt politicians, but equally against greedy industrialists, bankers, and financiers. These groups were summed up in the pejorative term "Wall Street." During the progressive era—broadly the Roosevelt, Taft, and Wilson years—reformers did much to correct this second set of abuses, enacting an impressive corpus of regulations on a wide variety of issues, as well as the creation of new statutory bodies charged with enforcing the new regulations. These years saw the growth of professional interest and academic study of government, industry, and planning. Yet for many Americans who felt threatened by the flood of immigrants and the cities' growing economic dominance, for those appalled by the revelations of the muckraking journalists, mere technical regulation was not a real solution. The nation's governing classes had been shamed and discredited; they had failed the people. Americans saw a need to impose a higher standard of moral conduct.

The Eighteenth Amendment and the accompanying Volstead Act were careful to specify exactly what was prohibited. The new laws explicitly banned beer. Beer could be brewed, but its alcohol had to be removed. These same laws, however, explicitly exempted hard cider. Cider could be made at home for home consumption; it could not, however, be transported nor sold. These prohibitions and exemptions were not random. Beer was the drink of the industrial workers, often immigrants. Beer was supplied by the iniquitous saloons. Beer was now to be prohibited. Cider, by contrast, was the traditional drink of farmers of the old Anglo-Saxon stock. Cider was made on the farmstead. Cider was still acceptable. The prohibitions and exemptions were aimed at specific groups. During the House debate on the Eighteenth Amendment, New York

Congressman Richard F. McKiniry brought this out when he denounced the Amendment as an expression of the "malicious joy" of rural America in "inflicting this sumptuary prohibition legislation on the great cities. It preserves their cider while it destroys the city workers' beer."[28] Prohibition was class legislation.

Prohibition was aimed at two specific groups—the urban workers and the urban elite. The urban workers needed to be moralized, and, in the case of the immigrants, properly "Americanized." The urban elite needed to be chastised and forced to take their responsibilities seriously. It is not surprising, indeed it is almost poetic justice, that when resistance to Prohibition began to coalesce, and it was a matter of hours rather than months, it expressed itself as a coalition between these two groups. It was the working classes, particularly the Irish, Jews, Italians, and Blacks, who, together with the urban elite successfully defied and finally overthrew Prohibition. It was a rebellion, or perhaps counter-revolution, of the under-privileged and the over-privileged.

The two wings naturally played two different parts. Drys represented drink as a lower-class vice, the curse, as the famous motto went, of the working class. For generations, dry propaganda had insisted that alcohol was poison and that drinking led working men to poverty, disease, crime, and suicide. By radically deregulating the alcohol traffic, Prohibition inadvertently sponsored a national experiment, allowing these venerable old dry contentions to be tested. The result was very surprising. Drink, it turned out, was equally the vice of the urban upper and middle classes. Under radical deregulation, drink also became a fashionable vice. "The Volstead Act," writes Andrew Barr, "helped establish drinking as sophisticated and urbane. In 1930, one survey found that three out of four Hollywood films referred to drinking in some way. The hero drank in two out of every five films and the heroine drank in one out of five. The villain, by contrast, only drank in one out of ten films."[29] Did nine out of ten villains really support the Volstead Act? Perhaps they were just too busy keeping the "Anglo-Saxon type" heroes and heroines supplied in drink.

Al Capone summed it up perfectly: "They call Capone a bootlegger. Yes. It's bootleg when it's on the trucks, but when your host in the club, in the locker room or on the Gold Coast hands it to you on a silver platter, it's hospitality. What's Al done then? He's supplied a legitimate demand. Some call it bootlegging. Some call it racketeering. I call it business."[30] Bootlegging, hospitality, and business—what was bootlegging for the drys still remained traditional hospitality for the wets. And this was what allowed it to become "business" for Capone.

THE OVER-PRIVILEGED OF NEW YORK

This place! Society isn't staying home and entertaining anymore. Society is going out to dinner, out to night life, and letting down the barriers.

—Columnist "Cholly Knickerbocker" in the Ritz-Carlton Bar, New York, 1919[31]

After a short, post-war recession, the gross national product of the United States began to grow at a steady 2 percent a year. From 1922 to the end of 1929, unemployment remained low, averaging 3.7 per cent. In these same years, prices increased by less than 1 percent annually. The 1920s were a period of economic growth, full employment, and low inflation. Other beneficial trends, legacies from earlier progressive legislation, continued as well. Workers worked increasingly shorter shifts, though output per man hour improved. Per capita income, which had already been rising before 1910, continued to increase throughout the 1920s. In the first two decades of the twentieth century, the average income of the American employee rose 25 percent. Between the inauguration of Harding in 1921 and that of Hoover in 1929, however, the pace more than doubled. Average annual income during these years rose by an unprecedented 30 percent.

Who were the beneficiaries of these decades of growth? Workers and employees in 1929 were, in real terms, earning over half again as much as in 1900. They also were spending more. In 1922, American producers turned out around one hundred thousand radios; in 1929 the annual figure had climbed to three hundred fifty thousand. The figures for the production of refrigerators are similar, a 150 percent growth over this period. Motor cars show the same pattern: 1.5 million motor cars were produced in 1922; 4.7 million motor cars were produced in 1929.

But workers and salary earners were not the only beneficiaries. The same years that saw workers' wages increase 30 percent saw company profits increase 62 percent—over twice as fast. Workers and employees were doing well, but corporations were doing even better. Andrew Mellon, treasury secretary under both Harding and Coolidge, cut taxes in 1924, 1926 and 1928. Mellon argued that these tax cuts favored those with incomes under $5,000 per year. Though true, the cuts favored those earning over $100,000 even more. According to Senator George Norris, the wealthy Mr. Mellon got a bigger tax break than "the aggregate of practically all the tax-payers in the state of Nebraska." The Coolidge years were a period of low government expenditure, tax cuts, easy money, and light regulation. Earning far more than they could possibly spend, the rich put their money in the stock market, which, to the delight of bankers, brokers, and investors, was booming. These were good years to be privileged in America.[32]

If workers, employees, and the rich were the winners in the 1920s, who were the losers? After decades of depression, farm incomes had begun to rise in the 1890s, roughly the same years that conditions of non-farm workers had begun to improve. The rise, spurred by a growing urban market, continued through 1913. In the next four years, however, war-time demand caused farm prices to spike by an incredible 82 percent. With America's own entry into the war in 1917, prices rose another 25 percent. Net farm income more than doubled during the war years. The war had been good to farmers. But when peace came, the bubble burst. Wartime U.S. and Allied government purchases had sent the price of wheat to $2.50 a bushel. When wartime purchases ceased in 1920, wheat prices tumbled to less that $1 a bushel. Wool fell from 60 cents to 19 cents a pound, and the price of corn dropped 75 percent. The farmers were victims of their war-time success; when incomes had doubled they had borrowed heavily to invest in land and new machinery. They were also victims of improved technology. Taking advantage of Wilson's Agricultural Extension Service, farmers had begun to use improved herbicides and pesticides, better varieties of seeds and more effective fertilizers, thereby doubling or even tripling their yields. This was fine during the war-time years when hungry Europe needed all the food that America could produce; but when Europe demobilized and resumed farming, American farmers found that they were producing more than they could sell. By 1929, according to the Bureau of Labor Statistics, a family of two adults and two children needed to earn $2,500 a year to ensure a "decent standard of living." In this same year, well over half the families filing income tax returns had incomes of under $1,500. Insofar as these returns are an accurate reflection, over half of America's families were unable to maintain a decent standard of living. Within this class was the majority of America's farmers.[33]

What was the effect of Prohibition on these patterns of wealth and distribution? In a strict sense, the effect of Prohibition was nil. Prohibition was a set of laws prohibiting things; Prohibition neither produced goods nor created wealth. The only incomes generated by Prohibition were the wages that the Bureau of Prohibition paid its employees to enforce Prohibition laws; but so niggardly were these wages that many of these agents were forced to solicit gratuities from the public. If we take Prohibition in a larger sense, however, and include activities that were related to Prohibition, the picture changes. The difficulty here is: how do we define Prohibition-related activities?

Bootleggers bought trucks in large quantities. Indeed, it has sometimes been claimed that bootleggers were the pioneers of American interstate trucking. Thus trucks and trucking might count as a Prohibition-related activity. Bootleggers also bought boats, favoring the speedy and maneuverable little craft that were able to dodger Coast Guard cutters and dock in secluded coves. Obviously, neither truck nor speed boat manufacturers had created their industries to service bootleggers. Truck and speed boat dealers did not knowingly sell their products to those who intended to use them to break the law. Were they to do so, they would have rendered themselves liable to the charge of being criminal accessories. Still, it is hard to believe that speed boat dealers in Coney Island, Montauk Point or Atlantic City really imagined that the hard-faced men in dark suits with bulges under the armpits were about to take up water-skiing. Truck and boat dealers sold their products freely to bootleggers and, if they had any sense, did not ask too many questions.

The catering industry provides a similar case. It has never been any secret that the availability of drink enhances the pleasurability of an evening spent dining out at a restaurant. To put it differently, the lack of drink's availability encourages people to save their money and eat at home. Nor is it a secret, at least among the catering trade, that drink is more profitable than food. These truisms were amply demonstrated in the first months of Prohibition. According to Stanley Walker, "the purveyors of the old type of entertainment lacked vision. Most of them were staid men, had been in business for years, and were completely befuddled by the problems bought about by prohibition. They couldn't untrack themselves." In January 1920 a dry agent walked into Jack Dunston's famous old restaurant on Sixth Avenue in New York and asked for a drink. He got one. He then asked for a half-pint of Scotch, and when he got that, he arrested the waiter and the captain and carted them off to jail. The raid, Walker observes, "was resented because Jack's place was anything but a vicious resort. Indeed it was so respectable that Mr. Dunston was a prominent citizen. And Mr. Dunston was raided again, forced out of business." Walker lists a number of such prominent citizens, whose restaurants served honest food and drink, but who, unable to "untrack themselves," had been forced to close their doors. "During the first three years of prohibition," he remarks, "they took a terrible beating from the Federals."[34] New Yorkers mourned the demise of their favorite eateries.

But younger restaurant owners, or those more agile and astute, soon found that there were ways of coping with these problems. It was simply a matter of bribery. Yet even after the cops and the dry agents had been taken care of, there was still the problem of supply. Anyone who made a living selling alcohol needed a reliable bootlegger. Fortunately, Walker goes on to comment, New York was well-supplied with these. During Prohibition, a well-organized and efficiently-run bootlegging industry in New York was able to cater to the city's every need.

Whether they either anticipated or wished it, during Prohibition the trucking, speed boat and catering industries placed themselves in the service of the bootleggers. Certainly there were many in these industries that wished that it had been otherwise, for if Prohibition introduced legitimate businesses to crime, it also introduced criminals into legitimate business. Bootleggers started by buying trucks and supplying resorts with booze; they ended up buying trucking companies and owning the resorts themselves. They also organized the truckers, waiters, cooks, and any of the other workers in the industries they were involved in. Crime had entered legitimate business, and crime intended to stay.

A more particular case is that of the entertainment industry. Here it is not a matter of entertainers providing bootleggers with services materially needed to smuggle and supply drink. All entertainers provide is entertainment. Yet entertainers provided this entertainment in resorts supplied by bootleggers and resorts where bootleggers hung out. And this was a symptom of a much older pattern: the entertainment business traditionally has associated with the underworld. The industry was a *demi-monde,* a night-time floating world hospitable to other creatures of the night. When Bessie Smith sang, "Any bootlegger is a pal of mine," she was voicing the opinion of the entire entertainment industry.

Entertainers and bootleggers grew up on the same mean streets. This was particularly true of the Jews, who played such a predominant role in both industries. The pioneers and first generation of Hollywood producers and studio owners were all first- and second-generation Eastern European Jews—Goldwyn, Mayer, Fox, Selznick and the Warner brothers. Marcus Loew and William Fox started out in peep shows and penny arcades. Adolph Zukor started in the fur business, then moving into penny arcades and finally film production. The singer and comedian, Eddie Cantor, played his own first role as a scab working for Pork-Faced Sam's gang on the Lower East Side, "I pulled a cap down over my eyes, donned a big red sweater and flourished a bat, looking for all the world like a chief of a gashouse gang, when in reality I was flat-chested, underweight, frightened at my own bluff and ready to be blown over by a breath."[35]

As producers, directors, actors, and singers, these were the Jews who later brought themes and stories of the Lower East Side to Vaudeville and then to the movies. Prowling the streets near Chatham Square, the Bowery Boy was traditionally Irish; his theatrical *doppelganger* dancing and cavorting on the Vaudeville stage was more likely to be a Jew. Even the guy in black-face doing the coon dance on stage was liable to be a Jew. When another set of Jewish boys rose to prominence in the bootlegging profession during Prohibition, they looked to the Jewish entertainers and impresarios for the acts in the gang-run resorts and clubs.

Nor was all the entertainment Jewish. Eddie Cantor and Flo Ziegfield were attracted by Black music and Black performers, as was another of their compatriots, Irving Berlin.[36] Entertainers and bootleggers had no reason to be snobbish, even less to be racist; they were operating in an outlaw culture and had no inhibitions about what went on in the clubs. If the customers wanted striptease, striptease was what they would get; if the customers wanted "Mother Machree," that could be supplied. What the New Yorkers who thronged to the city's new honky-tonk resorts really wanted was fast music they could dance to. Young urban customers wanted jazz music played by Black musicians, and that was what the entertainment and bootlegging industries gave them. New Yorkers rushed to Harlem to hear Duke Ellington, Cab Calloway or to see "Snakehips Earl" Tucker dance. It was Prohibition that introduced urban white America to black culture.

Entertainers were suspected of leading immoral lives; that was what made them so fascinating to the tabloid-reading public. Vaudeville and the early movies were regarded as plebeian forms of entertainment, snubbed by high culture and so devoid of high cultural pretensions. This allowed Jews, Italians, and other immigrants, along with Blacks, to enter these media and shape them in congenial ways. In normal times, such shaping might have proved more difficult. Popular culture is normally policed. In normal times, resorts and popular entertainment are subjected to a regime of vigilance through licensing and inspection. But the Prohibition years were not normal times. Prohibition had created a hiatus, a cessation of normal vigilance, and its replacement by an ineffective regime. But since ineffective vigilance is effectively freedom, Prohibition allowed a new American honky-tonk culture to be born, one centered more on film and music than on sex and gambling, one more attuned to the sensibilities of immigrants and blacks than to rural whites. Significantly, the new honky-tonk culture was also attuned to the sensibilities of urban, middle-class whites who belonged to Fitzgerald's "Lost Generation." Jewish, Italian, and Irish bootleggers and Jewish, Italian, Irish, and black entertainers served middle-class whites in the audience or clubs. Prohibition was mid-wife to more than the hip flask.

The question of what constitutes a Prohibition-related activity is in the end unanswerable. If we take 'Prohibition-related activity' to mean in some way resisting, disobeying or violating the provisions of the Volstead Act, then much of everyday urban activity would need to be included. Transport, catering, and entertainment are all normal activities in a modern society; the fact that they were all pressed into service in the resistance of Prohibition says a good deal more about the abnormality of Prohibition than anything about these activities. In the cities, it was resistance to Prohibition, not Prohibition itself, that became normal. During the fat years between 1922 and 1929, it was anti-Prohibition that grew and prospered, while Prohibition withered on the vine. This was not the way things were supposed to happen. Prohibition was supposed to penalize the workers, the immigrants and the irresponsible white elites. The only target really hit was the first, and here the hit was only partial. In predominantly working class suburbs and working class towns, the saloons were closed, and the workers were indeed deprived of their beer. In larger towns, by contrast, underworld ingenuity soon devised ways of getting the barrels rolling again. Not only did the other two targets, the immigrants and the urban middle classes, escape the trap that the Anti-Saloon League had carefully laid for them; many of them actually cashed in on resisting Prohibition. Prohibition was supposed to be a victory for the Protestant, white, middle-class Americans who supported the Anti-Saloon League. Yet it is hard to see what, beyond moral satisfaction and a touch of anticipatory *Schadenfreude,* bitterly deluded afterwards, they ever got out of it. The claim that Prohibition was responsible for economic growth was always nonsense. Anti-Prohibition contributed more to economic growth than did Prohibition. Nor did Prohibition do anything to help farmers and rural Americans. Their condition only worsened. The invisible hand had bestowed its fruits with a singular lack of impartiality or justice, showering riches on the iniquitous cities while treating the country man with miserly contempt.

Prohibition enforcement "was a joke in most urban America," comments Ann Douglas, "but in New York it was an all-out, full-scale farce. Seven thousand arrests for alcohol possession or drinking in New York City between 1921 and 1923 (when enforcement was more of less openly abandoned) resulted in only seventeen convictions; observers estimated the number of illegal speakeasies, dives and drugstores as somewhere between a monstrous thirty-two thousand and an unbelievable one hundred thousand. "Yankees Training on Scotch" ran the shameless headline of a 1922 story about Babe Ruth's team. Bishop James Cannon, tireless leader of the Anti-Saloon League, referred to New York as "Satan's Seat." Some people during Prohibition, playing on John Winthrop's famous words about the "city on the hill," called New York the "City on the Still."[37]

Before the war, suffragettes had discussed how well-educated women would find their place in a new society of equal opportunities and make their contributions to politics, the professions and culture. There was even talk of sexual equality and freedom. In many ways, the 1920s represented the flowering of the New Woman. Yet it was always supposed that the New Women would bear some resemblance to the old. No one foresaw the cloche hats, bobbed hair and kewpie doll make-up; or that, during the 1920s, the hemline would migrate resolutely upward or that women would roll down their stockings and rouge their knees, a body part visible for the first time in American fashion history. Corset and brassiere sales were plummeting while the sales of lipstick skyrocketed. Women wore shift dress that, one author complained, seemed to weigh no more than a quarter pound. No one had predicted that the New Woman would turn out to be a flapper who kissed and told and petted in the back seats of cars, writing about it in women's magazines, and who danced away the night, either tightly clinging to her partner or, even more horrifying, jerking spasmodically to the jungle rhythms of the Charleston. For old-fashioned sporting gentlemen, the appearance of these flappers, drinking, dancing, and leaving their greasy lipstick smears on cigarette butts and table napkins while they chattered in the night clubs like a flock of noisy magpies, was far more disconcerting than Prohibition itself could ever be.

At the center of these transgressions there was, appropriately enough, another woman. Born Mary Louise Cecilia Guinan in Waco, Texas, probably in the late 1870s, and evolving by stages as ranch hand, bar girl, Vaudeville hoofer and singer and bit-part movie player, and going through three marriages, "Texas" Guinan arrived in New York to rescue it from dullness just in time for the nightclub's first flowering. By the time Edmund Wilson met her in 1925, Texas was already a "formidable" woman, "with her pearls, her prodigious glittering bosom, her abundant and beautifully bleached yellow coiffure, her bear-trap of shining white teeth, her broad back that looks coarse and raw behind its green velvet grating, [and] the full-blown peony as big as a cabbage exploding on her broad green thigh."

Texas was imperious. It was said that by the time she was fourteen years old, she was capable of rounding up one hundred head of cattle. This may have marked her true vocation, for as a hostess she rode roughshod over her customers like a veteran stockyard manager. Texas was possessed with a steely determination that people were either going to have fun and spend money at her place or else become the source of others' amusement. She wheedled corpulent, bald millionaires into playing leap-frog on the dance floor; she ruffled the hair and undid the ties of prominent social leaders and pelted stately dowagers with white, celluloid balls. She greeted her customers with a hearty, "Hello, sucker!" letting them know that getting royally rooked by Texas Guinan was a rare privilege, indeed the only privilege they could expect at her hands. She dominated her audience, ordering them to buy flowers and dolls from the scantily-clad salesgirls circulating from table to table, telling them when to applaud and when to keep silent; she commented on the performances or upon her clients' dress and mannerisms; she threw glasses of water at the occasional customer who dozed off. She generated such an atmosphere of gathering tension and excitement such that, by about four o'clock each morning, fights would regularly break out among her addled but over-stimulated clientele. Texas quickly dealt appropriately with all manifestations of indiscipline. "Brawlers," wrote Edmund Wilson, "are summarily torn up by the roots and quietly put into the streets, with a ruthlessness and dispatch of a Renaissance prince making away with a dangerous enemy."[38]

Texas was also a match-maker. So successful was she at pairing off her singers, dancers, and salesgirls with rich, eligible bachelors that New Yorkers began to speak of "Guinan Graduates" as if her night clubs were some sort of finishing school. But Texas's true genius lay in mixing people. If New Yorkers were stepping out, it was not to meet people of their own class and backgrounds. Night clubs in New York in the 1920s were a honky-tonk territory; socialites, Vaudeville stars, newspapers reporters, politicians and gangsters were all free to enter. The secret of Texas Guinan's unlikely success was that by victimizing her customers indiscriminately, she facilitated the mixing. Texas was acting like an overbearing old school marm whose harshness forges unity in the classroom. Everyone was a worm in the eyes of Texas; everyone was liable to be insulted, over-charged, or bullied. This made it easier for the Social Register scions to sidle up to the underworld, for respectable city fathers to giggle with showgirls, or for society girls to accept the offer of a whirl on the dance floor with gangster Larry Fay. This, as Texas instinctively knew, was what they all wanted anyway. As New York's nightclubbing mayor, Jimmy Walker put it, New York was a city where a prominent debutante could meet a gangster in a night club and feel that she was the privileged one.

Besides the socialites and gossip columnists, regulars at Texas's clubs included leading New York politicians such as Mayor Jimmy Walker, and police officials, and theatre people. Celebrities included Mae West, W. C. Fields, Charlie Chaplin, and the Hollywood evangelist Aimee Semple McPherson. On hand were visiting British aristocrats and deposed crown heads of Europe. Of course, Arnold Rothstein and his gambling friends were there, along with the underworld lawyer William J. Fallon, the city's major rum-runner and bootlegger, Bill Dwyer, as well as Owney Madden. Madden became her partner and a partner in the rival Stork Club. Texas was the subject of one of the first *New Yorker* profiles. She was also a confidant and drinking buddy of Walter Winchell, who plugged her in his columns whenever he got the chance. She was a genuine celebrity with an out-of-town following.

So celebrated had Texas grown that the federal authorities began to plot her downfall. In late 1927, dry agents raided the 300 Club, where Texas Guinan was acting as hostess. As they led her off, the orchestra struck up the "Prisoner's Song." When she arrived at the precinct station, she amused reporters by heckling and insulting the police and federal agents, treating them as badly as she did her own customers.

Wise-cracking Texas Guinan, the queen of the night clubs, was New York's favorite loud mouth. She fought her case by claiming that she was just an entertainer and that it was no business of hers if people wanted to drink while listening to her patter. She added for good measure that she didn't see why the man who spent his money getting silly with a cutie at night was being more antisocial than the man who spent his days dreaming up Wall Street scams. The judge was not amused by this line of defense. The jury, however, saw her point, and Texas won her case.

The chief strategist in the Bureau of Prohibition's new offensive in the late 1920s was Assistant Attorney General Mabel Walker Willebrandt, who was described as "deft and inscrutable." As formidable and resourceful in her way as Texas Guinan was in hers, Walker Willebrandt lit upon a ruling of a court in Butte Montana, later confirmed by the Supreme Court. The Montana court had disinterred a provision from the United States Revised Statutes which allowed the government to confiscate the furniture of anyone who had not paid the excise tax on the liquor they possessed. Walker Willebrandt foresaw that it might be easier to prosecute speakeasies and night club for tax offenses than for breach of the Volstead act. It was the beginning of that process of legal lateral thinking that, in a few years, would enable the government to place both Waxy Gordon and Al Capone behind bars.

Helen Morgan was a different sort of woman. Languorous and sad-eyed, Helen had won fame as the star of *Showboat* on Broadway. Each night, she looked beautifully dreamy as she leaned against the piano and sang tragic songs in her club, the House of Morgan. On December 29, 1927, however, dry agents raided the nightclub, where, acting as they later claimed under direct orders from Washington, they wrecked the place and carried away the furniture. Helen Morgan lacked Texas's sharp tongue. Indeed her romantically disheveled appearance and glazed expression were largely a product of an excessive love of drink. She didn't even appear at her trial; it was, she said, more than she could bear. Still, if Texas was New York's wise-cracker, Morgan became the city's damsel in distress. Starting from the dry agents' claim that they were acting on direct orders from Washington, the newspapers soon concocted a tale of pique and feminine jealousy. Like the Wicked Witch of the West, the envious Mabel Walker Willebrandt had dispatched her axe-wielding flying monkeys to destroy the establishment of *la belle* Helen.

It was all an invention, of course; Washington denied that they had told their axe-men in New York where to strike. The judge practically ordered the jury to condemn Morgan when her case came to court. Once again, however, the jury balked, and, like Texas Guinan, Helen Morgan walked out a free woman. As one of the jury later told the press, "We couldn't take the word of two prohibition agents against Miss Morgan."

In truth, Walker Willebrandt was an unlikely candidate for the role of Wicked Witch of the West. An outspoken women of unconventional, some even said "advanced" views, she had irritated Washington by roundly declaring some unwelcome home truths: Prohibition was a shambles, she said; liquor was freely available. Even United States Senators sometimes came to work drunk. In morality and even in personal appearance, Federal Prohibition Agents compared unfavorably with gangsters. She also stood for women's rights and shocked the staid Coolidge administration by bringing up a daughter on her own. Her championship of the new women may even, indirectly, have contributed to her downfall.

Walker Willebrandt understood that by now even the dimmest of dim-witted night club bouncers could make a dry agent at a hundred paces. What was needed, she decided, was a deep cover operation. Federal operatives needed to penetrate the night-club organizations, find out their network of suppliers, and report it all back to the government. In practice it meant that a new breed of agents, coiffed and attired to resemble Ivy League students, spent night after night at New York's most expensive clubs, all at the tax payer's expense. An example of the New Woman, Walker Willebrandt even encouraged her agents to take their wives along as additional cover. The agents were only too happy to comply. The bar tab at the end of their three-month spree totaled over $75,000, not counting their salaries and other overheads. Yet all that the 1928 Willebrandt raids had to show for all this high-living was $8,400 in seized cash and fines, and fifteen convictions ranging from thirty days to six months. The padlock orders on the speakeasies and night club were usually dismissed or vacated. The decision to bring in the wives drew special flak. The claim that the women who accompanied the dry agents on their nights of whoopee-making really were their wives struck many observers as charitable to say the least. Still, the tale was widely credited in the drier parts of the nation. Though most condemned the raids as another government boondoggle, others cried out in pain for the innocent wives forced by the government to endure the spectacle of vice in these dens of iniquity.[39]

You could get a drink in America in almost any city. When Edna St. Vincent Millay came to Nashville to read her poetry, she was greeted by Ralph McGill, Vanderbilt University student and part-time reporter for the Nashville *Banner*. McGill had been asked by the *Banner* to interview Miss Millay, a request that he accepted enthusiastically. When he first beheld her, she was wearing a "shimmering gold-metal cloth dress" the first that he had ever seen. Entranced, McGill shyly asked the poet if she would grant him an interview. She would be happy to, Miss Millay graciously replied, but first the young McGill would need to supply her with an Orange Blossom. Like a knight charged with a chivalrous quest, McGill dashed out. "It was simple," he later recalled. "At Fouch's (an all-night drug store where newspapermen met in some rooms overhead to witness and discuss politics) the prescriptionist mixed alcohol, oil of juniper and glycerin, shook it, labeled it witch hazel, and I hurried to her suite in the Hermitage Hotel." Nashville, deep in the Southern Bible belt, was a dry town. Yet a Southern gentleman never refuses the request of a lady, especially a lady arrayed in shimmering gold. Happily, the quest was not too arduous. All that was necessary was to pop over to Fouch's (where the boys foregathered in the overhead room to discuss politics and perhaps sample the contents of the witch hazel bottle) and ask the pharmacist to mix the magic potion up. Sometimes not even the drys seemed to take Prohibition enforcement all that seriously.[40]

REBELLION OF THE UNDERPRIVILEGED: JEWS, ITALIANS, AND IRISH

Living in the third floor back, what can you expect,

All the classy people turn me down.

They knock me down.

Where we live you know it's true,

Chances for romance are few.

Papa, we gotta move uptown

With trees around...

—Vaudeville song[41]

The demography of crime is complex and particular in every instance. Yet two general rules stand out as being as close to universal truth as any such observations can be. The first is that the majority of criminals are young men. Women, young juveniles, middle-aged or even elderly men may be criminals too; crime is nothing if not an equal-opportunity employer. Nevertheless, the bulk of the criminal population is consistently composed of males in their late teens and twenties. This is particularly true of crimes involving violence or the threat of violence.

The second rule is that crime is associated with urban slums. Again, this is only a general rule. Crime can take place anywhere. Brigandage and animal rustling are classic forms of rural crime. Nevertheless, more crime takes place in the cities than in the countryside, and within the cities, criminality is likely to be concentrated in poor, overcrowded districts. These zones are difficult to police effectively, where forms of community and familial control function badly or not at all. What is more, as we have already seen, a reliable vector for the emergence of slum criminality is the rise of street gangs. Using these observations, and with the help of studies and statistics provided by the "Kehillah" an umbrella federation of Jewish organizations formed in 1909, Albert Fried makes some interesting observations about the demography of Jewish gangsters in America.

Eastern European Jewish immigration commenced in 1881 and continued until World War I. Not all of America's Jewish gangsters were born in America; indeed, most of the first generation were born in Eastern Europe. Nevertheless, in order to become an effective gangster, it was necessary for a Jewish immigrant boy to spend a significant part of his childhood years in an American city, acquiring English, joining gangs, and getting a feel for the streets. Thus, though the Jews themselves began arriving as early as 1881, the first generation of Jewish gangsters did not emerge until roughly in the years between 1895 and 1905. During these years, this first generation reached early manhood. These would be the Monk Eastman years, the years of his war with the Five Points Gang, the shoot-out under the Rivington Street Arches, and Marty Engel's Jewish brothels. Politically, these were the years of Boss Croker and Mayor Van Wyck, and of the Big Tim Sullivan organization on the Lower East Side. Had everything remained the same, had the Lower East Side Jewish community remained as depressed and overcrowded as ever, and had Tammany and the New York Police Department remained as corrupt and as graft-ridden as ever, we would expect this first generation of Jewish gangsters to be followed by a second generation, tougher and uglier than the first, and so on.

To a limited extent, this is what did happen; the Eastman decade was followed by the Big Jack Zelig decade. The years 1905 to 1915 were marked by Kid Twist and by "Nigger Yoski" and his forty horse thieves. These were the years of Lower East Side Jewish gamblers, the Hesper club, and the murder of Herman Rosenthal. They were also the years of the "schlammers," of strikes and strike-breakers, and of Dopey Benny Fine and his union thugs. Nor does the story of Jewish gangsters end with Zelig. His decade was followed by the decade of Arnold Rothstein and Waxey Gordon, and theirs was followed by that of Dutch Schultz and Lepke Buchalter. Despite this, changes were taking places.

Some of these changes came from above. Police reform dates from the years of Commissioner Roosevelt. In 1902 Charles Murphy took over at Tammany Hall and immediately drove the brothel-keepers out. The 1911 Triangle fire prodded the New York State Legislature into an investigation of working conditions and, eventually, a pioneering series of factory, health, and safety regulations. Other changes, less noted but equally important however, were taking place from below.

At its height, roughly between 1895 and 1910, New York's Lower East Side Jewish community contained more than five hundred thousand Jews. In 1916, however, their number had fallen to three hundred thirteen thousand. By 1925, the number was two hundred sixty-four thousand and still falling. What had caused the halving of the Lower East Side Jewish community in less than two decades? Immigration, to begin with, began to fall after the turn of the century. Immigrants are typically young and hardy, and the decline of immigration deprived the Jewish community of this source of new blood. Yet by itself the decline in immigration explains little. It explains perhaps why an already bad situation did not get much worse; it does not explain why it got better.[42]

A more convincing explanation is suggested by a comparison of the Lower East Side with near-by areas. The Jewish community in Lower Manhattan was declining, but the Jewish community in Upper Manhattan, Harlem, was expanding. Even further north in the Bronx, the Jewish community was growing even more rapidly. So, in fact, was the Brooklyn Jewish community. Jewish communities were even taking root and growing in exotic localities (exotic for Lower East Siders that is) like Long Island and New Jersey. If the Lower East Side's Jewish population was in decline it was because that population was moving elsewhere. If the Jews were moving elsewhere, it was because the housing was better elsewhere, and so was the air they breathed. They were moving to places that were less grimy, less jam-packed, less unsanitary, where the schools were better, where gangs did not roam the streets, and where maybe even the streets had some trees.

So where had they gotten the money to acquire these desirable amenities? They had probably saved it. Jews benefited from the rise in income and improvement in working conditions just like the rest of the American working class. In the wake of the Triangle fire, the city's sweatshop workers struck for better pay and conditions. The strike was long, hard, violent, and nasty. But eventually the ILGWU got much of what they wanted. Orders kept on mounting, and the employers could not deny their seamstresses forever. The war brought a rush of fresh orders. The soldiers in Europe fed by America's farmers were clothed by America's seamstresses. By the close of the war, many Lower East Side Jewish families had saved up enough money to buy themselves a better life.

A Jewish observer, writes Fried, considering the Lower East Side in 1918–1919 might have felt that some modest self-congratulations were in order. The days of the sweatshop and the cold-water tenement flat seemed to be ending. He might even have predicted that, "within ten years of so, Jewish gangsterism, the community's deepest reproach and most awful scourge, would have petered out.[43] Whether Jewish crime was declining in these years is anybody's guess; we will probably never know for sure. But Fried is certainly right in one respect: in 1918–1919 things were looking up for the Jewish community. Had things continued to go in the same direction, the bad old days would soon have been nothing but a bittersweet memory. This was what should have happened, but it was not what did happen. The most momentous change of all was waiting around the corner. With Prohibition, the muse of criminality hit the jackpot.

The demography of Italian gangsterism resembles the Jewish pattern, though with certain important differences. The Eastern European Jews were victims of czarist persecution, but this persecution was always episodic. There were years when the Russian authorities organized pogroms and unleashed the Black Hundreds on Jewish villages and urban ghettos; but these years might be followed by greater or lesser periods when the Jews were left alone and normal life could resume. Jewish immigration to America followed these rhythms, increasing in the bad years and falling when peace returned. If Jewish immigration began to decline after 1900 it was because, both within Russia and without, liberal opinion that disapproved of official anti-Semitism, was effective in campaigning on the Jews' behalf. The South Italians and Sicilians, by contrast, were not fleeing from persecution. They, like an earlier generation of immigrants from Ireland, were rather fleeing from an impoverished agrarian society that held out few prospects of advancement. Economic and social stagnation was a profoundly chronic rather than an episodic problem. Italian immigration did not, therefore, begin to diminish after 1900; instead, it increased, and continued to increase until it was shut off by the war. It would, what is more, surely have continued into the 1920s and 1930s had not the U.S. and Italian Fascist governments (albeit for very different reasons) moved to stop it.

The Jews, who began to arrive shortly before the Italians, were on average better educated and trained. They possessed the skills that enabled them to organize their communities, start small businesses, and pursue higher education in America. The Italians, by contrast, continued to organize themselves in family and kinship networks or on the basis of their homes in the old country. An Italian observer of the Lower East Side in 1918–1919 would have felt less cause for optimism than his Jewish counterpart. To be sure, Italian families were also leaving the Lower Manhattan tenements for better accommodations in the outer boroughs. But things were looking better for the Italians only to the extent that they were looking better for American workers on the whole. Italians were still stuck in lower-paying jobs.

America has inherited its language and much of its culture from Protestant Great Britain, but not its cuisine. It is probably just as well. Cheap food in America has traditionally been immigrant food, food made by and served to the poor immigrant workers. Whoever arrived in America around 1900 was bound to leave their mark on the country's eating habits, and Americans can be thankful that it turned out to be the Jews, the Italians, and the Chinese. Cheap food in turn-of-the-century New York still tended to be Germanic in character, though with Irish and local additions. But this was changing; Jewish delicatessens were spreading out of Jewish areas and, as they did so, adding new dishes to appeal to non-kosher clients. They were hiring non-Jewish workers as well. As Baylor points out, by the end of the 1920s, the local "deli" would seem the New Yorkiest of popular food joints, and though the deli proprietor and maybe the cashier would be Jewish, the cooks and counter guys would typically be Italians. The same was true of mid-priced hotels. In the wholesale and retail clothing businesses many, though not all, of the owners were Jewish, while many, though not all, of the tailors were Italians. Though the neighborhood tavern remained an Irish preserve, the service and retail sectors, which were areas of growth even during the Depression, were dominated by Jews and Italians, with Jews in the position of bosses.[44]

Jews and Italians were finding jobs in the same consumer and service-oriented industries because these were sectors that were expanding at the time. These were also, by a fluke of good fortune, sectors in which Jews and Italians excelled. Jews and Italians make good clothes; they run good hotels, cook good food, sing good songs, and make good movies. Jews and Italians were destined to cohabit these industries anyway; the fact that they also proved talented in these areas probably helps explain why they got along so well together. Nevertheless, throughout the 1920s and 1930s, the relations between the two would remain the same; it was usually the Jews who were employing the Italians rather than the other way around.

All of the patterns held true of organized crime as well. During Prohibition it was the Jews who often owned the beer trucks and the Italians who rode shotgun. In most American cities during Prohibition, Jews and the older Anglo-Irish underworld stood as patrons to the Italians and Blacks. The major exception to this rule—and it was a major exception indeed—was Chicago, which is the subject of the next chapter. Nevertheless, it was the Italian underworld that was on the rise. The Jewish Lower East Side observer might have had reason for deluding himself into thinking that Jewish gangsterism would soon peter out. The Italian observer would have had no reason at all to harbor any such illusion. Italian gangs were moving into their prime.

Bootlegger was never a technical term. During Prohibition it was used for all illegal brewers, rum-runners, smugglers, or retailers. Men like the Diamond brothers, who got their supplies by hijacking other bootleggers might just as well have been described as highwaymen, but they were spoken of as bootleggers. Indeed, anyone who made, transported or sold drink during Prohibition was a bootlegger. When Mark H. Haller made a break-down of the bootlegging profession in New York for the United States Commission on the Review of the National Policy towards Gambling, he thus included both the big shots like Wexler and some small fries like Luciano. His conclusions about the demography and ethnicity of this profession were nonetheless interesting:

> Those who, by the mid-1920s, emerged as leading entrepreneurs tended to be young—born between 1892 and 1900 and thus some 20 to 28 years old when Prohibition began. Prohibition arrived just as the first generation of Eastern European Jewish and Italian young people raised in America were reaching maturity. Data on those who were leading bootleggers in the late 1920s indicate that some 50 per cent were Jewish, some 25 per cent were of Italian background—the rest primarily Polish and Irish in background. Although their previous occupational experiences were frequently, but not universally, in crime, the future bootleggers were by no means prominent in crime prior to prohibition. Many, indeed, graduated from juvenile gangs directly into bootlegging.[45]

Haller's summation is broadly correct, though possibly misleading. Bootlegging could be a rough and tumble business, one that could pose serious risks to life and limb. It was classic young men's work. But bootlegging also depended on a network of connectivity linking manufacturers and suppliers to retailers and individual customers. The younger bootleggers did not create this network. Much of it was there already. Prohibition outlawed the manufacture, transport, and sale of alcoholic beverages and so put countless legitimate entrepreneurs out of business. Yet there were other possible networks that the drinker might rely upon. Bootlegging is simply the name for the black market in alcoholic drink, and black marketing is an underworld specialty. When the underworld fenced stolen goods, and ran brothels and organized gambling, it was creating a black market for customers who were not in other ways criminals. Prohibition created a new black market for the underworld to exploit, a market where, once again, most of the customers were normal citizens. Built upon pre-existing underworld connections, the new black market in alcohol was already organized, at least in its outline. Though Haller includes Johnnie Torrio in his list of prominent New York bootleggers, it could hardly be said of Torrio that he was "by no means prominent in crime prior to prohibition." Torrio already was prominent; by 1919, he had taken over the management of the Colosimo vice empire. Bootlegging at first was a mere sideline for him. Torrio was creating a new string of road houses on Chicago's Far South Side, and these resorts needed to be supplied with girls, gambling equipment, and, of course, drink. Like white slavery, bootlegging simply seemed a part of his core business. The disappearance of a legitimate market in alcoholic drink would not have seemed a major obstacle to someone with Torrio's underworld connections.

Haller is nevertheless right that Prohibition presented a golden opportunity to the graduating crop of juvenile gang members. Since, in 1920, the majority of this class were Jews and Italians, these would compose the great bootlegging army. From their ranks would emerge the eminent gangsters.

We might divide those who resisted Prohibition into two groups: the bootlegging classes and the drinking classes. We know where the Jewish and Italian bootleggers belong; we know where Texas Guinan's customers belong. But in which class do the Irish fall? The answer is both.

Prohibition had put the Irish in an ambivalent position. Almost invariably, the Irish had been the backbone of the nineteenth-century American urban underworld. By the time of the passage of the Eighteenth Amendment, however, the traditional Irish underworld was in decline. In part, this was because the Irish and Germans no longer stood out as foreigners. Jewish and Catholic Eastern Europeans, Italians, and blacks all seemed ethnically, culturally and racially exotic, but the Irish and the Germans no longer did. As a result, Irish criminality only appeared as ethnic criminality in those parts of the city still dominated by Irish gangs. Everywhere else, Irish crime could be glossed as working class crime. In big-city working class districts, the tavern-owners and saloon-keepers were traditionally Irish. It was here that the drys expected that problems of enforcement might arise. What they had not expected was the emergence of a large-scale bootlegging industry dominated not only by the Irish, but also by Jews and Italians. It was the entry of these exotic races into the industry that truly troubled their xenophobic minds.

Yet the drys may have misunderstood the Irish. It was true that traditional Irish criminality was in decline, as second- and third-generation Irish grew more respectable and prosperous. In New York, the Irish community was still nevertheless powerful; it controlled Tammany and had elected Mayor Jimmy Walker and Governor Al Smith; it controlled the NYPD. Had it wanted to, the Irish community in New York could certainly have forced state and local authorities to enforce dry laws more vigorously. But this is not what happened. After some initial hesitation, the Irish community began to push the other way.

Haller's list of prominent bootleggers in New York City includes seventeen names: three are Irish, four are Italian, and nine are Jewish. That makes only sixteen; for in the case of one eminent bootlegger, Haller leaves the ethnicity blank. Owney Madden is given no ethnicity. This seems an injustice against the Irish. Though born in Leeds, England, Madden grew up with the Irish in Liverpool and later in Manhattan.

Madden, we saw, was sent to Sing Sing in 1915, sent up for ten to twenty years for a murder that he did not commit. He fought the sentence for three years. Friends on the West Side started a subscription to pay the costs of an appeal. The three prosecution witnesses recanted their testimony, to no avail. The publicity had turned the Gopher leader into an underworld celebrity, and the Sing Sing warden, Lewis E. Lawes, was anxious to make his acquaintance.

The twenty-year-old Madden turned out to be a model prisoner, keeping strictly to the rules, never asking for special favors, and intervening to sort out disputes between other prisoners. Warden Lawes took a liking to him and, whenever a new underworld celebrity was added to Sing Sing's inmate population, would ask Owney what he thought of the expected guest. "He's a pretty smart fellow," Owney would invariably reply. One day, Warden Lawes stopped Owney and asked him a question. If all these guys were such smart fellows, what were they doing kicking their heels in the gloomy old gray hulk on the Hudson when so many stupid fellows walked free on the street of Manhattan. It started Owney thinking.

In the few years Madden had led the Gophers, he had been arrested forty-five times. He had been shot as well. After quarreling with him during the Election Night Ball at the Arbor Dance Hall at Seventh and Fifty-seventh in 1916, his new wife declared that she intended to turkey-trot, bunny-hug or grizzly-bear with whomever she chose. Owney walked out in a foul mood, coming back later in the night and sitting in the balcony to watch the dancers below. When he turned his head from the dance floor, he found himself surrounded by Gopher enemies, the Hudson Dusters. Still feeling angry and defiant, he told the Dusters to shoot him if they dared. They shot him six times, point blank in the chest. At the hospital the doctors told him he was going to die. When, amazingly he pulled through, he was almost immediately arrested for the murder of Little Patsy Doyle. Now he was in Sing Sing. Maybe he wasn't such a smart fellow after all.

Madden's bullet wounds never healed properly. After his parole in 1923, his health remained somewhat fragile. No longer "that little banty rooster out of hell" as one duty sergeant called him when he fought cops and Hudson Dusters alike in the Battle Rows, Madden left Sing Sing a more serious man. He was thirty-one years old. When he had entered Sing Sing, a *racket* was nothing more than a big shindig with an entrance fee; now *racket* referred to the multi-million-dollar bootlegging industry. He found a job as an industrial consultant for a taxi company; his job was to muscle out the competition. A few months later, he and his old partner, George "Big Frenchy" De Mange, stole two hundred cases of bonded rye whiskey from the Liberty Storage Warehouse on West Sixty-fourth. Several months later, he was riding in a truck the police had pulled over. The truck contained $25,000 worth of stolen whiskey. Owney claimed that he just had hitched a ride and was shocked to discover himself in the company of bootleggers. Though the police could not break his alibi, they had enough to send him back to Sing Sing for parole violations. Nothing happened, however; New York State's Prohibition statutes had just been repealed, and the police liked Owney. The two robberies had given Madden his stake, and he gave up the rough stuff for good.

Madden still had many friends on the West Side; he had made others in prison. These friends stood him in good stead. He had precisely the qualities that the underworld most admires: courage, reliability, and loyalty. He became a partner of Bill Dwyer, longshoremen's leader on the Hudson Docks. The old Gophers had been freight-car thieves, fencing as best they could the goods they stole from the railways. Controlling the West Side docks had enabled Dwyer to amass a bootlegging fortune; he controlled steel plated warehouses, fleets of trucks, and Manhattan's largest brewery. Madden resumed his friendship with Frank Costello who, in partnership with Arnold Rothstein, had built up a trans-Atlantic rum-running empire larger than Waxey Gordon's. Dwyer, Rothstein, Costello, and Madden owned pieces of many of Manhattan's leading night clubs. Gentlemen and their lady friends drank Madden booze in Madden-owned clubs; celebrities sat with him in ringside seats to watch bouts in which Madden-owned boxers fought. They had ridden to the fights in taxis connected to Madden and sent their clothes to be cleaned by Madden's Hydrox Laundry and Dry Cleaners. By 1930, he was, according to Walker, the "Elder Statesmen, the Grand Old Man of the rackets in New York," business manager to the New York underworld, the quartermaster general ensuring that nightclubs, restaurants, and speakeasies were kept supplied with bootleg whiskey, wine and fresh-brewed beer.

Charlie Luciano liked the nightclubs in which Owney Madden and Frank Costello held stakes. Madden backed some of Texas Guinan's ventures and backed the Cotton Club when Duke Ellington was the featured band. Small and trim, with soft blue eyes that looked sad in repose, Madden made his rounds in a well-pressed dinner jacket and sharply-creased trousers that he wore like an army officer's uniform. He would not have looked out of place as a police captain, though Sherman Billingsley, the Stork Club's manager, used to remark that Madden bore an uncanny resemblance to the statue of Civic Virtue in City Hall Park. Though in his later years Billingsley made great efforts to distance himself from his earlier associates, disguising how much he owed his success to the help of Costello and Madden, he had to admit that, whenever he visited the Stork Club, Madden had been a model guest. Usually quiet and wryly good-humored, Madden would now and then startle the company with old tales of the wars between the Gophers and the Hudson Dusters on the West Side. He could grow quite animated on such occasions. During more than one such story-telling evening, Billingsley remembered, his graphic descriptions of past thuggeries had sent the ladies in the company scurrying off to the powder room.

Madden oversaw labor relations as well, finding jobs for managers, bartenders, and bouncers. He made sure that the clubs used gang-owned suppliers, like Madden's own Hydrox Laundry and Dry Cleaners, a racket that Madden complained was far more trouble than it was worth. Madden also made sure that none of his friends or associates became targets for the pickets and stink bombs of Dutch Schultz and Jimmy Hines' phony "Metropolitan Restaurant and Cafeteria Association." Bill Dwyer owned Phoenix Cereal Beverage Company , but their flagship product was called "Madden's No. One," the underworld's tribute to the man who had worked so hard to keep them from going thirsty throughout the difficult years.

The bootleggers appreciated Madden too. When they assembled in Atlantic City in 1929, they decided to offer Madden a token of their esteem—a gold watch. They selected his old partner, Big Frenchy De Mange, to make the presentation. Big Frenchy walked up to Madden, seated as guest of honor in front of his colleagues, and asked Owney to see his watch. Surprised, Madden took his watch off his wrist and handed it over to Frenchy, who then proceeded to drop it on the floor and stamp on it. Then, before the open-mouthed Madden could react, he said, "Gee Owney, I'm sorry I broke your watch, but here's another one for you." If the underworld gave out Oscars for lifetime achievement, Owney would have been first in line to receive one.

The restaurateur Toots Shor got his first job working as a bouncer in one of Madden's many establishments. In an interview in the 1970s, Toots lamented the passing of the gangsters from the New York nightclubs. Madden had been a real boss, Toots claimed. He had class and style. He really knew how to run a joint. The stuff they had in Chicago was, in comparison, "just amateur night. This was New York; this was the big leagues! . . . And in the 1930s the mob had gambling houses all around New York City and Jersey, and you got served the food for nothing. And jeez, it was the best food. Oh boy. You'd go to the crap came and lose $10, and then eat all this beautiful food. These guys hired the best cooks."

"I wish they were back today," Shor concluded sorrowfully.

Toots also lamented the passing of New York's show-girl culture. Throughout the 1920s and early 1930s, the theatres along the Great White Way served up an array of follies and chorus-line reviews, Vaudeville dance numbers and little cabarets on the side streets. On any given night, Shor remembered, the streets of central Manhattan would be packed with beautiful women dressed in expensive clothes in the company of young swains in black ties or old sugar daddies in top hats, all of whom had stood there waiting for their girls, clutching bouquets of carnations or red roses, under the streetlamps outside the dressing room doors. By midnight, taxis were disgorging the glamorous showgirls and their well-heeled escorts into the clubs; there would be shouting for drinks and general raucousness, the sounds of people getting sloshed. Visiting big shots, like Nucky Johnson, in from Atlantic City, would arrive surrounded by a whole entourage of showgirls rounded up by his local hosts.

The underworld were not the only ones who admire courage, reliability, and loyalty. In their old age, ex-Gophers and ex-Dusters sometimes sought out their retired adversaries from the West Side precincts to reminisce and swap war stories. Madden had his admirers in the New York Police Department. They regarded him as tough and straight in all matters concerning business, but generous in his personal relations. He loved pigeons and children. There were ranking officers who, without blushing, would say that Owney Madden was an honest man. Owney reciprocated; he knew a great many cops, and it says nothing to their discredit to add that most of them liked him. Nothing made Owney more furious than two-bit purse snatchers who claimed to the police that they were Madden's boys. If Owney could help the police put these men behind bars, he was happy to be a good citizen. Owney was always on his guard; he was a target and he knew it. There were reckless hoodlums like Vince Coll who would happily shoot him just to make a name for themselves. He was obsessed with the idea that some bent cop or ambitious prosecutor would try to plant evidence or gather false testimony to further their careers. "No strange cop is ever going to arrest me," he told his friends in the detective bureau. By "strange cop" he might have meant gunmen in cop outfits; but he might also have been referring to the dry agents.

In 1923, New York State's own prohibition laws were repealed; and this took much of the pressure off the New York City police. It meant that enforcement of Prohibition was squarely in the hands of the federal dry agents, men who had made themselves thoroughly unpopular in the city. Dry agents continually suffered insults and abuse. When they raided Peter's Blue Hour, an Italian restaurant on West Forty-eighth Street, the patrons pelted them with hard rolls and handfuls of wet spaghetti. Even when they brought off a raid or managed to close a speakeasy with a padlock injunction, their success was often short-lived. Lawyers dreamed up technicalities, and municipal judges, not always sympathetic to Prohibition, would respond favorably by lifting the injunctions and ordering the release of the violators. The NYPD shone by comparison to the dry agents. Pay-offs never stopped during Prohibition; everyone involved in the whole complex business of illegal drinking, from the manufacturers and importers to the club hostesses and bartenders, paid off the police. But it was different now; the police were the honest drinkers' friends. The repeal of state prohibition laws forced the police to improvise. They policed the city by arresting rowdy drunks and breaking up the party when the neighbors complained about too much noise.

They also protected drinkers. Most speakeasy owners tried to provide wholesome enough stuff. The worst that could be said is, that before they sold it to their customers, they, as the saying went, "Gilletted" it, cut it by as much as fifty percent. Some places, however, sold varnish-like concoctions made up of wood alcohol which sent their victims reeling blinded or dying into the street. The alcoholic ward at Bellevue saw a rise in admissions during Prohibition. As a matter of common decency, the police acted against such places. These were also the years when the term "clip joint" came into vogue for establishments which, often with the aid of complicit taxi drivers, preyed on witless outlanders hoping for a night of whoopee in the sinful metropolis. The police, who rarely bothered honest speakeasies and night clubs, took a real pleasure in smashing up the clips that poisoned citizens, fleeced visitors and tarnished the reputation of their city.

Even City Hall played its part. New York's largest brewery was the "Phoenix," located on the West Side at Tenth Avenue between 26th and 27th streets, right in the middle of Hell's Kitchen. The brewery was thinly disguised as a breakfast cereal-making factory, which gave the trucks an excuse to bring in vast amounts of cereal grain. Neither the Walker administration nor Police Chief McNaughton ever moved to shut down the Phoenix. The police did however keep a watchful eye over the Phoenix, in part to safeguard the health of New York's beer-drinking public and in part to protect the brewery from the incursions of rival gangs. The NYPD protected the Phoenix from other predators as well. Several times the police learned of impending raids by federal agencies whose men were waiting in their cars in the pre-dawn hours outside the brewery gates, ready to pounce once the factory opened. McNaughton would order out his squad cars telling them to arrest the dry agents hanging around the Phoenix as "suspicious-looking persons." This gave the brewery workers time to disguise their activities before the dry agents got themselves released.[46]

Prohibition was repealed in 1933; the only time in American history that a Constitutional Amendment has suffered such a fate. Walter Lippmann's 1927 prediction that "the overturning of the Eighteenth Amendment would mean the emergence of the cities as the dominant force in America, dominant politically and socially as they are already dominant economically," had come true. With the repeal of the Eighteenth Amendment, an epic saga of progressivism in America also ended, indeed had ended very messily, in a bitter struggle between wets and drys, urban and rural reformers, Roosevelt Democrats and Hoover Republicans. Prohibition was not defeated by organized crime; Prohibition was a failed reformist project overturned by the cities in a period of economic deflation and massive unemployment. Yet organized crime played a major role in the story of Prohibition. By joining forces with the bootleggers in resisting Prohibition, the cities, the industrial workers, and the urban Democrats had entered into a new partnership with organized crime as it emerged in the late 1920s. Breaking free of this partnership would not prove an easy task. The end of Prohibition was not the end of its consequences. The rise of organized crime during Prohibition is thus a story within a story. And it is to this story that we shall now turn.

Chapter Six

Prohibition in Chicago: Johnnie Torrio, Al Capone, and the Beer War

Bootlegging wars during Prohibition were apt to break out in areas where neither wets nor drys were able to establish a clear dominance. Most of the Eastern Seaboard remained incorrigibly wet throughout the 1920s. Recognizing an anti-Prohibition consensus in their cities, the political authorities in New York, Boston, and Philadelphia quietly declined to enforce the Volstead Act. Here bootleggers supplied drink with a minimum of violence. Large parts of the South and Midwest, by contrast, supported Prohibition. This did not mean that these areas were ever entirely dry; drink seems to have been available in virtually every part of the country during Prohibition. The South, however, regarded drink with the same ambivalence that mid-nineteenth-century Manhattan regarded prostitution: it was condemned in principle as immoral and un-Christian, but so long as it was discretely restricted to white males, it was quietly accepted. The Volstead Act changed little here; the dry areas too remained largely peaceful during Prohibition.

Bootlegging violence was centered instead in a broad band of territory running from Buffalo and Pittsburgh in the East, westward to Detroit and Milwaukee, and southward to Chicago, St. Louis, and Kansas City. There were some special reasons for this. Buffalo, Cleveland, and Detroit are Great Lakes towns through which whiskey was smuggled in from Canada. Some of the violence arose from wars between rival smuggling gangs, yet hardly all of it. Capone smuggled much of his whiskey in trucks from New York, leaving it up to the North Side gangs to supply Chicago with Canadian whiskey.

What is striking is that so much of the violence arose in the industrial belt, in the Midwestern factory towns which had sprouted up like mushrooms in the 1870s and 1880s and which were still expanding during the 1920s. By sucking in large immigrant communities, rapid industrial growth irrevocably altered the social composition of these towns. Nonetheless, their character and politics were still shaped by the character of their founders—Protestant farming families who had trekked during the early and middle years of the nineteenth century. Typically, these families were of Anglo, Scots-Irish, or German origins. They were members of Methodist, Presbyterian, or Lutheran congregations, and they were staunch supporters of the Party of Lincoln. They came from areas that had traditionally opposed slavery, supported universal education, and advocated temperance.

These were the areas of America's Second Great Awakening, the areas where the Methodist Episcopal Church had taken root, where Mother Thompson had led her Women's Crusade, where the Women's Christian Temperance Movement had first emerged, where Frances Willard organized and led, and where Carry Nation wielded her mighty axe. Violence and organized crime thus arose in the Anti-Saloon League's own backyard.

At the heart of these contradictions was Chicago, the town where the motley flock of malodorous miscreants who made their homes in the infamous Levee found themselves confronted by the serried ranks of cherubic do-gooders who drowned out the Charleston and the Dixieland bands with a rousing chorus of "Where is My Wandering Boy Tonight?"

CHICAGO AND THE BLACK LEGEND

We have seen that Chicago always possessed a special reputation for wickedness. Chicago's black legend is something of a myth, however. The city's notoriety is more a result of size and location than of any special vocation for wickedness. Chicago is North America's crossroads. Commerce and industry come together in Chicago. By the 1920s, Chicago had become the economic hub of a vast area extending from the Rockies to the Alleghenies and from the Gulf ports to the Great Lakes and even into Canada. During Prohibition, it was said that Capone's whiskey traveled as far as Moose Jaw, Saskatchewan, Canada. If true, it is really more a tribute to the breadth of Chicago's commercial reach than to the marketing acumen of the Capone outfit.

As capital of the Midwest, a landmass defined by the Great Plains, the Ohio-Mississippi Valley and the Great Lakes, Chicago had also the misfortune of being the greatest city in that part of America that traditionally mistrusted great cities. Already in 1870s, as Chicago struggled to keep a representation in the Illinois General Assembly commensurate with its population, the *Illinois Weekly State Journal*, demanding that Chicago be excised from the state, apostrophized the city thus; "Go thou pestilent, discontented, brawling disturber of the public place, and keep thine own vile sewer [the Chicago River] to thyself."[1] Chicago's problems during the 1920s—unassimilated immigrants, an expanding population of southern Blacks, crime and a dismal tradition of labor relations—were problems it shared with many other cities of the Midwest. There is no reason to suppose that Chicago was relatively more wicked than St. Louis or Pittsburgh or Detroit. Chicago was bigger, however, and Chicago was where it all came together. That made a difference. As capital of the nation's heartland, Chicago's wickedness stood out.

When New York declined to enforce the Volstead Act, Prohibition's supporters, though righteously outraged, were not, perhaps, all that surprised. New York had always been an exception. Judged from the Midwestern heartland, there had always been something un-American about New York. There was nothing un-American about Chicago, however. When Chicagoans showed that they were no more inclined to comply with the Volstead Act than New Yorkers, it seemed a graver matter. It seemed to confirm that vocation for wickedness that had ever seemed to abide in America's second city. Unlike New York, which was just a wicked city, Chicago was a very wicked and very *American* city.

AL BROWN COMES TO TOWN

When I came to Chicago, I had only $40 in my pocket. I went into a business that was open and didn't do anybody any harm.

— Al Capone

When Johnny Torrio left the Lower East Side for Brooklyn in 1908, he left for Gowanus, the home of his friend Frankie Yale.[2]

The Gowanus section of Brooklyn took its name from the canal of the same name. A jagged gash, now partially covered, the canal presently separates the Carroll Gardens district from fashionable Park Slope. Local residents claim that the answer to more than one of Brooklyn's unsolved mafia murders could be discovered beneath the foetid surface of its waters, though few have cared to look. Gowanus is the area of Brooklyn south of the canal, stretching from the naval training station to Brooklyn's port in Red Hook. It included much of present-day Bensonhurst, still the roughest Italian suburb in New York. Immediately below it lies Coney Island, the center of Frankie Yale's business operations.

Coney Island started off as one of New York's arcades or amusement piers. Nineteenth-century amusement parks were typically small areas of parkland which offered rides, games and other amusements. Urban reformers supported the creation of parks, including Manhattan's own Central Park. Disciples of Henry David Thoreau and Frederick Law Olmstead, they venerated nature and imagined that an exposure to even a small patch of wilderness must uplift the spirits of the working masses and turn their minds to higher thoughts. Yet the beauties of nature are hard to preserve, especially after you have invited in the working masses. Rides, games, and working-class amusements were not conducive to the preservation of unspoiled nature; and Manhattan's Republicans had needed to exert themselves repeatedly to block Tammany's attempts to build a race track and other amusements in Central

Park. Central Park was saved as a park, but not Coney Island. Once the developers had started in, there was little prospect that the island would retain its natural setting for long.

A separate community on the outskirts of the yet-to-be-incorporated borough of Brooklyn, Coney Island was allowed to develop the way the developers wanted. It would develop into a commercial honky tonk. By 1900, the developers were luring the New York public in with rides, arcade games, dime museums, nickelodeons, eateries and taverns of every type, and concert halls. There was, of course, every sort of gambling and prostitution too.[3]

Foreseeing the change, and in a good position make a profit, Big Tim Sullivan had invested heavily in the development of Coney Island. He bought shares in Coney Island theatres that presented acts like Eddie Cantor, Jimmy Durante and other Vaudeville stars. Improved transport made it a Mecca for day-trippers from the Lower East Side. With the completion of the new Williamsburg Bridge, Coney Island was only a short drive from Lower Manhattan, something that Kid Twist discovered to his cost in 1908. But Coney Island was still part of Brooklyn, and thus the special playground of the Gowanus boys.[4]

Frankie Yale's origins are uncertain. According to Pilat and Ransom, "Yale was an immigrant from Sicily who saw the statue of Liberty for the first time when he was ten."[5] According to other accounts, he came from Calabria.[6] His real name, Francesco Ioele, would be more typical in the southern part of Apulia than in Sicily. The Ioele and the Torrio/Caputo family became friends in the New World, and when Torrio decided to leave Manhattan in 1908, he moved to Brooklyn, near where Frankie and his brother Angelo had just settled.

Frankie had already had a number of run-ins with the law. He had served a short prison term for his part in an affray, and another for carrying a concealed weapon. He narrowly escaped being convicted on other charges, including one for armed robbery and another for stealing over three hundred dollars worth of sheep and goat skins. In 1916, however, Yale married and reined in his wilder side. Settling down with his new wife in a gloomy, palatial house owned by his in-laws, Yale concentrated his attention on organized protection. He established an ice racket, extending it to Bath Beach. Local residents bought all their ice from Frankie Yale's ice firm, and ice delivery-truck drivers were formed into a union paying their monthly dues to Yale's association.

He manufactured his own brand of cigars, twenty cents apiece and three for fifty cents. No cigar-store owner dared refuse to stock them; though the current phrase "stinks like a Frankie Yale" does indicate a degree of customer disapprobation. Yale's black and white photo adorned every box. His perfectly lozenge-shaped face fitted perfectly into the lozenge-shaped sticker; his jet-black hair is centrally parted and slicked; his unblemished skin has a delicate, almost translucent whiteness; his eyes are round and large and impenetrably dark. The image has the same ethereal quality as those lozenge-shaped photos on crosses in old Italian cemeteries—the faces of the dead staring out at you.

Seeing the face of the very-much-alive Brooklyn boss in a beyond-the-grave portrait reproduced on box after box of cigars must have been chilling. It may have been the real origin of his nickname, the "Prince of Darkness." It probably helped that he extended his protection over funeral parlours. "I'm an undertaker," Yale liked to joke.[7]

Between 1918 and his death in 1928, Yale was also New York president of the *Unione Siciliana*.

An obvious difficulty arises here. Was not the original president of the *Unione* either Giuseppe Morello or Ignazio Lupo, followed by Salvatore D'Aquilo? How could Yale, probably not even a Sicilian, claim such an honor; and how, in particular, could he claim it in Coney Island, a part of Brooklyn dominated by the Neapolitan camorra?

It is probably a matter of dates. Though Yale was a member of a generation that included Torrio, the Morello brothers and the Brooklyn camorra leaders, his rise in the Italian underworld only dates from 1918, a year after the mafia-camorra war ended. Though a racketeer, Yale played no part in that war. As long as he paid the street tax and kept clear of the feud, Pelligrino Morano would not have objected to Yale's rackets in camorra territory. Pilate and Ransom's comment that Yale settled down after he married also seems significant. He had the sense to keep out of the war, to wait matters out. So did Johnny Torrio. Yale and Torrio were neither Sicilian nor Neapolitan, and this helped them from being sucked into an ethnic struggle. There is an Italian saying, "whenever two men fight, a third man enjoys himself." As soon as the Sicilians and Neapolitans finished murdering each other, and as soon as Morano, Lauritano, Vollero, and their gunmen were safely parked in Sing Sing, Yale stepped into the vacum. The dominant power in the Italian underworld in New York was now Ciro Terranova. Yale, whose relations with the Morellos had always been amicable, honoured the Morellos by opening his own branch of the *Unione Siciliana* in Coney Island in 1918. It did not bother Terranova that Yale was not a Sicilian; he was an ally, and that was what mattered. There had long been a branch in Chicago and probably another in Little Italy. There were branches in other cities as well. Later, during the 1920s, when Yale was at the height of his power with bootlegging and gambling connections stretching to Chicago, he would remedy the equivocation by renaming the New York branch of the *Unione Siciliana* the Italo-American National Union. The name was indicative. Terranova's ambitions remained centered on the New York region; Yale's by now were stretching far beyond. By relaunching the old fraternal lodge for immigrant Sicilians as a national union of all Italo-Americans, Yale was declaring his ultimate goal.[8]

In 1916, Yale opened the Harvard Inn in Coney Island overlooking the Atlantic Ocean. The idea for the name came from the College Inn run by Diamond Tony Kelly. There was probably some sort of pun as well. Though the name on the deed was spelled *Uale*, after he bought his new clubhouse, Frankie changed the spelling to *Yale*. Yale's Harvard Inn was a large dance hall with food and girls and an orchestra. There was gambling in back. Next to the bar were billiard tables. The young Al Capone served at the bar.[9]

Born in Brooklyn in January 1899, Alfonso Caponi was the son of recently-immigrated Neapolitan parents. A reasonable student, he maintained a B average until the sixth grade. After that, he was a persistent truant. When his teacher reproved him over this, his volcanic temper erupted, and he hit her. Thrashed by the principal, he quit school. He never returned, for soon he acquired a new mentor—Johnnie Torrio.

After settling in Brooklyn in 1908, Torrio opened The John Torrio Association, an office and rooms above a restaurant on South Brooklyn's busiest thoroughfare, Fourth Avenue, near the Italian markets on Union Street. He bought a share in the numbers racket; and probably shares in brothels, and ran these from the Association.[10] Outwardly, he was respectable; "to the locals, Torrio appeared to be a fairly successful numbers racketeer, quietly tending his part of the so-called Italian lottery."[11] He kept up his links with Paul Kelly, and through Kelly, the Morello gang, the East Harlem underworld, and Jack Sirocco who had taken over his James Street club in Little Italy and his James Street Boys.

The John Torrio Association was only one of a large number of underworld-connected businesses, clubs, and street gangs in Gowanus. Turn-of-the-century Brooklyn's waterfront stretched for five miles and contained sixty odd piers. The piers provided work for many Gowanus families. Like the waterfronts on Lower East Side and Hudson River and the Eighth Avenue railway yards, the Brooklyn docks was a place honest citizens avoided after working hours. The whole area was rough and dangerous; its saloons were underworld hangouts. Smuggling and cargo pilfering had long been rife. Labor on the waterfront had traditionally been controlled by the Irish, just as waterfront crime had been controlled by Irish gangs. By 1900, however, the Brooklyn Italians were fighting their way in. The struggle was long and drawn out, job by job, pier by pier, racket by racket, and the mutual animosity continually expressed it in fist fights, knifings, and occasional murders. Since the newspapers called the Italian gangsters Black Handers, Dennis Meehan named his Irish gang the White Hand.[12]

The Irish youth gangs had names like the Red Hook Rippers, the Garfield Boys, and the Gowanus Dukes. When he quit school at fourteen, Capone joined a gang of boys his own age called the South Brooklyn Rippers. But the Capone family house was close to the John Torrio Association, and Capone's relation with Torrio must also have begun in these years. Quiet, well-dressed, inclined to be chubby, the adolescent Capone had none of that aura of swagger and danger that he was later to acquire. People remembered him as a peaceful lad; the Jewish writer Daniel Fuchs remembered that he was, "something of a nonentity, affable, soft of speech, and even mediocre in everything except dancing."[13] He attracted little attention, a quality that Torrio may have found useful. Capone traveled to the Lower East Side on a number of occasions; Charley Lucania remembered meeting Capone in these years. Lucania was then associated with the Young Five Pointers, part of the original Paul Kelly gang. If Torrio needed a messenger-boy to communicate with Lower Manhattan, he might easily have selected the affable and inconspicuous young Capone.

Torrio's partnership with Yale had barely begun, however, when he received a summons from his cousin in Chicago, Victoria Moresco, asking Johnny to come to Chicago to rescue her new husband, who was being threatened by Black Handers. Torrio made a quick job of it; he left Brooklyn in 1909, returning in a few months. It was his first journey to Chicago but not his last. Between 1909 and 1920, Torrio spent more and more of his time in Chicago. Capone saw him whenever he returned to Brooklyn. When he was back again in 1918, Capone used the occasion to ask Torrio to find him a job. Torrio sent him to Yale, who took the eighteen-year-old on as a bouncer and drinks waiter at the Harvard Inn.

Later that year, while waiting on a table, Capone happened to remark to a young lady among a party of guests, "Honey you have a nice ass, and I mean that as a compliment." Admittedly it was an un-waiterly remark, though probably not really ill-intentioned. Nevertheless, Capone had been pestering the girl all night, and a member of the party, the girl's brother Frank Galluccio, drunk and offended at hearing such words from the lips of the service personnel, stood up and threw a punch at Al. Al responded by swinging a pool cue at Galluccio, who parried with the switchblade that happened to be in his pocket. The result, in the words of a later police dossier, was, "an oblique scar of 4" across cheek 2" in front left ear—vertical scar 2 1/2 on left jaw—oblique scar 2 1/2" under left ear on neck."[14]

When the two men were pulled apart, Capone yelled that he was one of Frankie Yale's boys, and that Yale would see that he got his revenge. Galluccio replied that he had some friends of his own over on the Lower East Side that would soon see to Capone.

The matter was settled in a sit-down at the Harvard Inn. Yale listened as Galluccio's representative from the Lower East Side argued that the incident had been entirely Capone's fault. This representative, it turned out, was Charlie Lucania. Yale listened and told Capone to apologize. There the matter ended. Capone bore no ill-will to Galluccio; a few years later he hired him as a body guard. Nor did he bear a grudge against Lucania for the part he played. Indeed, he used to give Charlie bear-hugs and call him cousin, a habit Charlie never much liked. Charlie found Capone a bit of a loudmouth. He worried about his uncontrolled temper. Capone was simply too Neapolitan for Charlie's tastes.

Yale had merely wanted to settle the squabble. He was evidently impressed with Capone's temper, however, for he started using him as an enforcer. In this capacity, Capone shot and killed Tony Perotta, who owed Yale $1,500. Yale was once again impressed. He now knew that Capone belonged to that category who could, as the phrase went, "do a piece of work" for him. When Capone nearly pummeled to death an Irish White Hand gangster in a bar fight, however, Yale realized that his hot-blooded drinks waiter needed to get out of New York. Wiring ahead to Torrio, he sent him to Chicago.[15]

Capone spent his first year in Chicago as bouncer and later manager at the Four Deuces, a Torrio whore house not far from the Colosimo Café. Its name is a reference to the street address—2222 South Wabash. The first floor of the Four Deuces was a saloon; the second floor was Torrio's offices with a horse-betting parlor; the third floor was a gambling den; the fourth floor was a two-dollar sex mill. Journalist Courtney Ryley Cooper remembered seeing Capone outside the Four Deuces: "I saw him there a dozen times, coat collar turned up on winter nights, hands deep in his pockets as he fell in step with a passer-by and mumbled: 'Got some nice-looking girls inside.'"

But touting and chucking out unruly customers was low-level work. If that is all Capone did, it's hard to explain why he rose so rapidly in the Torrio organization or how he was able to open his own offices on 2146 South Michigan Avenue the following year. It seems more probable that Yale had recommended Capone to Torrio as someone able to "do a piece of work." We get partial confirmation of this from a statement that, in 1931, Mike "de Pike" Heitler gave to the police. There was, Heitler said, a torture chamber in the Four Deuces basement:

> They snatch guys they want information from and take them to the cellar. They're tortured till they talk. Then they're rubbed out. The bodies are hauled through a tunnel into a trapdoor opening in the back of the building. Capone and the boys put the bodies in cars and then they're dumped out on a country road, or maybe in a clay hole or rock quarry.

Adjoining the Four Deuces on South Wabash was an unused store-fronted warehouse. Torrio acquired it and put Capone in charge. Capone stocked the front room with junk; a table with the Bible on top of it featured prominently in the front room. He even had cards printed up "Alphonse Capone, second hand furniture dealer, 2220 South Wabash." He listed himself in the Chicago telephone directory as "A. Capone, Antique Dealer." But the store was never opened; Capone replied to all queries, "We ain't open today;" and the property may well have been used in conjunction with the tunnel and the rough stuff going on in the basement of the Four Deuces next door.

Soon Capone opened his own office on South Michigan, disguising it as a medical office. There was even a waiting room with bottles of medicinal alcohol on display. The police raided the place in 1924, and the found complete listings of everything in the Torrio-Capone empire, including the names of police and prohibition agents on the payroll, itemized incomes from the organization's brothels, names of the organization's breweries, a list of customers, a list of speakeasies, the truck and boat routes used by the bootleggers. The nameplate on the office door read "A. Brown, Md."

When Torrio later put Capone in charge of the Four Deuces, he gave him a cut of the rest of the brothel business. With this, Capone started moving the Capone clan over from Brooklyn. He bought a two-story, red-brick house in a quiet part of town on South Prairie Avenue. Al and his wife, Mae Coughlin, and their infant son, Albert Francis or "Sonny," moved into the seven rooms on the ground floor with Al's mother and two of his sisters. Johnnie Torrio was Sonny Capone's godfather. Upstairs lived the family of his brother Ralph. Al's two younger brothers, Mimi and Matt lived there for a time as well. Al's older brother, Frank, was a frequent visitor, as were his cousins, Rocco and Charlie Fischetti. Though perhaps somewhat crowded, compared to their quarters in Brooklyn, it was sumptuous. Al imported an all-steel master bathroom from Germany, which included a seven-foot tub. There were steel gates blocking the entrance from the alley in back, steel reinforced walls and a screen of steel bars on the windows set close enough to foil the plots of bomb-throwing Black Handers. The claustrophobic effect of all this steel armor was offset by floor-to-ceiling mirrors with gilded cornices in the upstairs parlor. According to Kobler, all the Capone men had "thick, heavy bodies and blunt features." When they united for family councils in mirrored parlor upstairs, they resembled "a small herd of ruminating bison."

Capone's income in 1920 was estimated at twenty-five thousand. With this, he provided for his clan and sent his nephews to private schools. Not bad for a Brooklyn hoodlum who had arrived with just $40 in his pockets.

THE GANGS

In a 1927 study, Professor Frederick M. Thrasher identified 1,313 gangs in the Chicago area. The vast majority were street-corner societies, kids who, left to themselves and having nothing better to do, hung out with each other and committed the sorts of pranks groups of kids often do—fighting, drinking, smoking, vandalism, and petty theft. They gambled and played hooky. Of the 880 gangs in Chicago itself, only forty-five were wholly American. Sixty-three were black and twenty-five mixed black and white. Though 351 were of mixed white nationalities, the number of gangs of solely one nationality was the largest of all—396. Thrasher particularly noted the gangs of Little Sicily, which he described as "a mosaic of Sicilian villages."

The bootlegging gangs were, by contrast, examples of what Thrasher called "master gangs": He found ten to twenty of these groups operating in Chicago,

> "whose names alone are sufficient to strike terror into the hearts of the peaceful residents of the districts where they hold sway. . . . The major interest of the master gangs is probably the illegal manufacture and sale of spirituous liquors, but many of them are not adverse to other types of crime such as the various types of robbery: bank, pay-roll, bank-messenger, jewel, fur and mail. Many of them are also identified with the promotion of other illicit activities such as vice and gambling."[16]

Alongside the Torrio-Capone syndicate there were, among others, the West Side O'Donnells, the Genna family, the Valley gang, the Guilfoyle gang, the

Maddox Circus gang, the Saltis-McErlane gang, Ragen's Colts, the South Side O'Donnells, and, most important, the gang of Dion O'Banion. With the exception of the Gennas, all of these gangs were Irish, Eastern European, or a mixture of the two. These gangs usually owned or controlled a string of saloons. The three O'Donnell brothers—William "Klondike," Myles, and Bernard—and their all-Irish gang owned, for example, a string of saloons on the Southwest Side in the area between Chicago Avenue and Madison Street. They were operating saloons in Cicero as well, just outside the city limits, when the Torrio-Capone forces began to move in. The Saltis-McErlane gang was a criminal organization run by Frank McErlane and centered around the tavern of "Polack Joe" Saltis, also on the Southwest Side. Further south, there was Spike O'Donnell's group, unrelated and unconnected to Klondike O'Donnell's group only a short distance away.[17]

The Ragen Colts from the stockyards district on the South Side were neither exactly a street gang nor a criminal group but a sporting association. Starting out as a baseball team called the Morgan Athletic Club, the association had changed its name in honor of its star pitcher, Frank Ragen. A canny political organizer later elected as one of the city commissioners of Cook County, Ragen enlarged the club, turning it into the center of Democrat Party politics on the South Side. It was said that when Ragen's Colts dropped in on polling day, "everybody else dropped out." Predominantly Irish, their motto was "Hit me and you hit 2,000." Outside of baseball and politics, their main occupation was warring with the South Side's black population. They had a leading part in the July 1919 race riot in Chicago, in which more than five hundred people were injured.[18]

JOHNNY TORRIO PROPOSES A TRUCE

The Torrio-Capone syndicate grew out of the earlier Colosimo-Torrio syndicate, which had its own roots in the old Levee Lords who first arose in the 1880s. The syndicate retained the services of Levee old-timers like the Guzik brothers, Mike "de Pike" Heitler and Charlie Carr. But by 1915 the old Levee had suffered death by reform. When the *Tribune* reporter Henry M. Hyde returned for a visit in early 1916 he found the area neglected and sad; "There are no lights of any color. It is like landing in some remote and ruined city damaged by the plague." He wandered through the once-elegant salons whose floors were now covered with crumbled plaster and broken mirrors. The woodwork, chimney breasts, marble cornices and fixtures had long since been stripped out. Even the lead piping had been hacked out of the walls. On one of the few undamaged buildings he saw a sign, "For Rent Furnished. To Respectable People Only!"[19]

The blight was only temporary, however. As in Midtown Manhattan, brothelization represented a transitional stage, an indication that the area was ripe for intense commercial development. In 1909, architect Daniel Burnham had presented the city with his Chicago Plan, which foresaw, among other things, the radical commercial redevelopment of the area between The Loop and the 1893 White City. From the hodge-podge of brothels, resorts, and remaining residences, a new Beaux-Arts Chicago would arise. Burnham's Chicago Plan indicates that even if Gypsy Smith and his host had never arrived, the Levee was probably doomed. Lake-front property near The Loop was too valuable to remain a honky tonk forever.[20]

Johnnie Torrio and his associates understood that the closure of the Levee did not eliminate Chicago's demand for prostitution. Along with the Guziks, Heitler, and Carr, Torrio began to reconnoiter the suburbs looking for quiet places to re-locate. The town of Burnham, eighteen miles south of the Loop and near the Indiana border, had one thousand inhabitants. Its village president, or mayor, was the twenty-five-year-old Johnny Patton. In early 1920, Patton agreed to sell Torrio an old restaurant and dance-hall called the Arrowhead Inn for $15,000. The Arrowhead straddled the Illinois-Indiana line, protecting it from raids by police from either state. Torrio opened his first suburban brothel here with girls from the old Levee, the first in a string of roadhouses on the southern fringes of Cook County. Torrio hired Johnny Patton as manager, who brought in the Burnham police chief as the bartender and three of the village trustees as waiters. As Burnham was clearly open for business, Torrio opened a new roadhouse, The Barn, nearby.

Jazz musician Mezz Mezzrow was sure that in Burnham "there were more whores per square foot that in any town in the good old U.S.A." an estimated two hundred prostitutes in a town of one thousand.[21] In this way, the Torrio organization gradually opened about a dozen new roadhouses in Chicago Heights, Stickney, Posen, Forest View, Burr Oaks, Blue Island, and Steger and in the Indiana towns of East Chicago, Gary, and Whiting. They were two-dollar houses with eighty cents going to the girl. Torrio also installed buzzer systems in nearby diners and gas stations; if waitresses or station attendants saw police cars cruising down the road to town, they buzzed an alert to the roadhouses.[22] Before becoming bouncer at the Four Deuces, Capone worked briefly as a bouncer at the Arrowhead Inn.

Beer was at first a secondary matter to Torrio. His first brothels were just cribs. It was only later, when they grew bigger and more luxurious, that saloons were attached to them. Eventually some became cabarets with jazz bands and waitresses and roulette wheels and dice games in the back room. Still, at first the girls were the main attraction and the main earners, and the beer business rode piggy-back on the sex trade.

Beer was a bulk commodity. Speak-easies were small businesses like grocery stores. Beer only became profitable when it was shifted in large quantities, but at this point it not only became profitable—it became immensely profitable. It took deep pockets to get into the beer business, however, and, during Prohibition, it took connections as well. With his roadhouses each clearing about $9,000 a week in profit and with Colosimo's network at his disposal, Torrio had both.

In the late summer of 1920, Torrio met with Joseph Stenson, a pre-Prohibition brewer, member of one of Chicago's prominent families and an old acquaintance of Jim Colosimo. Stenson had quietly been keeping one of his breweries running, supplying beer to Terry Druggan and Frankie Lake of the West Side Valley Gang along Fifteenth Street. They had the protection of the Republican committeeman from the Twentieth Ward and Sanitary District trustee, Morris Eller. Torrio proposed that Stenson re-open another two of his breweries and acquire two more in Hammond, Indiana. Torrio and Stenson installed phony boards of directors who would shield them if any of the breweries were raided. By 1924, they had brought in not only the Valley Gang but the O'Banions as well. The accumulated profits of the Torrio-Stenson partnership were estimated at $50 million, of which Stenson pocketed $12 million.[23]

Landesco quotes jounalist Charles Gregston on the relation between Torrio and Stenson:

> A strange pair: Torrio is a native of Italy, a Tammany graduate, a post-graduate pupil of the late "Big Jim" Colosimo. His colleague is the youngest of four brothers who were rich brewers before prohibition. While Torrio was learning the tricks of ward politics in New York and the rewards of sin in the old Twenty-second Street district, and later in Burnham, his twin king of crime was living pleasantly on what is called the "Gold Coast," the son of a wealthy and established family. A common genius for organized crime brought them together soon after prohibition had ushered in the new era of crime through which Chicago is passing.[24]

The arrangements with Stenson were typical. Bootleggers like Torrio worked with two types of silent partners. On the one hand, there were the former brewers, restaurant, and resort owners who had supposedly closed down or surrendered their interests but who, in reality, were happy to re-open their former businesses if they could do so in safety. On the other, there were local politicians and policemen who, for a consideration, ensured that the businesses could indeed continue unmolested. The fragmentation of political authority in Chicago meant that political pay-offs could often be made at the ward level. At the center of it all was Johnnie Torrio who, taking the entrepreneurial risks, received the largest share of the profits.

Sometimes pay-offs would be the responsibility of the Torrio organization; sometimes they would be the responsibility of the organization's associates; more often they would be split between the two. Given the legal problems of Prohibition, this was a sensible arrangement and probably the only way that the beer business could have carried on. Almost everyone involved—the brewery owners, the police, the politicians, and the beer drinkers—were content. They were grateful that the trustworthy, hard-working, clear-sighted little vice king had come to them from Brooklyn and taken this difficult job off their shoulders. Although he made a fortune on whores and drink, Torrio neither drank nor smoked himself; nor was he ever heard to utter profanities. He lived the life of a respectable businessman, and was in the words of his wife, "the best and dearest of husbands." It seemed for a moment that, under Torrio's stewardship, a wet, dirty, and corrupt Chicago would sail peacefully through Prohibition.

Fragmentation of authority in Chicago may have helped hold the price of graft down, but it also made the beer business difficult to run; for the Chicago underworld was itself no less fragmented and disunited. Fragmentation created problems. It made it difficult for anyone to play the role of Owney Madden in New York, enforcing peace in the underworld, linking bootleggers to speakeasy and nightclub owners, and serving as informal back channel to the authorities. It was particularly difficult for Torrio. Not only was Torrio an Italian; he was a New Yorker. Still someone needed to step up. Chicago bootlegging had sprung up almost overnight, bringing with it inevitable problems of order and control. As the rising power, the job fell to Torrio. He had a great deal more business savvy than many of his colleagues. But Torrio had little means of enforcement. This left him with one alternative: diplomacy.

Underworld legend has Torrio summoning the Irish and Eastern European gang leaders to the Four Deuces during the darkest hours of the night like a diabolic school principle summoning truant boys to his office. Here he offered them a treaty. The bootlegging business, he pointed out, promised all of them greater profits with greater security than either safe-cracking or bank robbing. But success in the bootlegging business depended upon peaceful cooperation. Within their own territory, any treaty member was free to run their own breweries or distilleries, or, alternatively, to obtain their booze from any other source they wished. Torrio made a standing offer to supply to anyone in the group beer at $50 a barrel. Cooperation meant, however, that treaty members must refrain from hijacking other members' shipments or encroaching upon saloons in other members' territories. Any gang or gang member who persistently flouted these rules would be declared an outlaw, the common enemy of all treaty members. Torrio offered to broker in territorial disputes, and to adjudicate in the case of complaints.

Unfortunately, though all authorities agree that Torrio brokered some sort of underworld truce at the beginning of the 1920s, we have few concrete details.[25] It seems a safe inference, however. Between 1920 and 1924, an underworld peace more or less prevailed. Chicago itself continued to be plagued by old problems. Labor relations remained bad, and there were bombings, strikes, and acts of industrial sabotage. Race relations remained tense in the wake of the 1919 riot. The murder rate remained high, and there was a worrying increase in the incidence of auto theft. Gang violence, by contrast, did not increase. The annual reports of the official Chicago Crime Commission between 1919 and 1923, though concerned that criminals were becoming more businesslike, have nothing to say about gangs or gang wars. Though the Commission did note that America was "much better able to assimilate the peoples of northern and western Europe than the Latin and Slavic elements," it did not go on to say that these Latin and Slavic elements were currently involved in bootlegging. In fact, the Commission had little to say about Prohibition violations.[26]

The 1922 report echoed the message of Bureau of Prohibition in Washington, claiming that the bootleggers were on the run. The triumphalist tone carries on into the 1923 and 1924 reports. Auto theft was diminishing and the forces of law and order were on the verge of winning the war against drink.[27] Though the newspapers by now knew better, it is still remarkable how well Torrio succeeded in keeping below the radar. Officially at least, Chicago seemed unaware of the bootleggers. Between late 1920 and late 1923 Torrio avoided publicity while he quietly built up his roadhouse and brewery empires. He also avoided fallings out with his underworld colleagues. This was probably the greater achievement, for among these colleagues were Dion O'Banion and the Genna family.

DION O'BANION

In July 1919, the cub reporter Edward D. Sullivan arrived in Chicago to find the city in the grip of the worst race riot in its history. He had hardly gotten off the train from New York when his editor sent him off into the black districts, telling him to get a first-hand story. Perhaps the Chicago *Herald-Examiner* regarded cub reporters from New York as expendable, just so much cannon fodder. No one told Sullivan what a dangerous assignment it was. The black districts were smoldering and about to break out again. Barely an hour before Sullivan and his driver went in, four people had been murdered and a policeman injured. Since no taxi dared to enter these districts, the paper put Sullivan in the sidecar of a motorcycle driven by a cheerful young man from the paper's circulation department.

Sullivan's motorcycle entered the besieged areas, turning into Thirty-first Street. As they did, Sullivan saw a wounded policeman fall to his knees, feebly reaching out for his hat as it fell into the dust before him. Horrified, Sullivan saw the policeman die before his eyes. His thoughts were interrupted by a shot that suddenly rang out beside him. He looked up to see his driver standing in his seat, firing his pistol at a hidden sniper from a near-by rooftop. The driver then sat back down and, gunning his engine, raced up an alley, dodging the bullets fired from a sniper on another rooftop. Almost the moment they entered this alley, however, Sullivan and the driver realized they had made a wrong turn. There was a crowd of about twenty men, some of them armed, all of them angry and drunk, who, hearing the sound of the approaching motorcycle had turned and were coming at them. The driver mounted the sidewalk, and, yanking the motor into reverse, swirled them back out onto State Street. By now Sullivan clearly made out the second black sniper drawing a bead on them from a rooftop as they passed. The driver hurtled by, hugging the curb so as to decrease the sniper's angle of fire, all the while shooting upwards with an automatic pistol.

It took Sullivan most of the ride back to the newspaper office to recover from the adventure. It was only when they arrived that it occurred to him to wonder about the cocky little driver who seemed to be having the time of his life. He must be, Sullivan thought, "one whale of a fellow." What was his name? "Dion O'Banion," the city desk editor replied.[28]

Born outside of Chicago in 1896, Dion's father moved the O'Banion family to Kilgubbin in the western part of the Loop shortly after 1900. Although Kilgubbin had originally been the name of a rough, Irish slum, by 1900 the Sicilians had moved in, turning the district into Little Sicily. With his fine young voice, "Deany" O'Banion had sung in the choir of the Holy Name Cathedral. He joined the Market Street gang with two of his childhood pals, Hymie Weiss and Vinnie Drucci. He was called "Gimpy" O'Banion because of his limp, and under that name he worked as a singing waiter at Chicago's version of McGurk's Suicide Hall, McGovern's at Canal and Erie. Later he worked as a newspaper slugger for the Chicago *Tribune*.

Like the beer wars only a few years later, a newspaper circulation war was a turf war. Gangs of circulation sluggers beat up newsboys selling the wrong paper, vandalized rival delivery trucks and torched rival newspaper stands. Their aim was to force the rival paper off the street, while making sure that their own paper was readily available. O'Banion's exertions on behalf of the *Tribune* attracted the attention of Moses Annenberg, circulation manager at the rival *Chicago Herald and Examiner*. Annenberg offered the promising young slugger a lucrative position as his chief lieutenant and so lured him away from the *Tribune*. Under Annenberg's tutelage, O'Banion became what John Morgan calls the "principle exponent of thuggery in newspaper selling."

By 1909 the twelve-year-old O'Banion had already been sent to the House of Correction for three months on a robbery charge. Two years later, he went up for an even shorter stretch on a similar charge. These were the only occasions, however, for O'Banion became more than the captain of Annenberg's circulation sluggers. His activities attracted the attention of various Democrat Party ward bosses, who had seen possibilities in the cheerful little brute. O'Banion, Weiss, and Drucci organized the Democrat vote at street level. Familiar figures within the Loop and in the lakeshore suburbs of the Gold Coast, the police began to call them the ward boys. When O'Banion appeared in a saloon near election-time, it meant drinks all around. It also meant delivering some voting recommendations which few of the patrons dared ignore. "I always deliver my borough as per requirements," O'Banion boasted.

The *Herald-Examiner* and the Chicago Democrats gave O'Banion and his gang the protection they needed. There was a string of indictments stretching from 1909 to 1922, usually for burglary. But though often charged, O'Banion was never even brought to trial. A 1922 charge for murder was *nolle prossed*. He was even acquitted for the attempted safe-cracking at the Postal Telegraph Building in 1921. Although the police had caught him on his knees jimmying open the office safe with a crow bar, the jury decided that there was not enough evidence to convict him. The jury's scruples were said to have cost O'Banion $30,000.

Like Capone, O'Banion was not a consciously cruel man. Indeed, both were fond of gestures of large-scale generosity. Police sometimes discovered

O'Banion's black limousine prowling through the tenement slums districts on a cold winter's night. They were surprised when Dion, his wife Viola and the boys emerged with turkeys, hams, and baskets of food for the poor inside. Unlike Legs Diamond, who got kicks from double-crossing his friends, a trait that only Arnold Rothstein could admire, O'Banion was a man of strong loyalties. Yet he had a hair-trigger temper; he was ferocious; and, once aroused, he was pitiless and absolutely insensible to pain. Violence put him into a state of euphoria, and he had the unnerving habit of smiling when he killed, his lips parted in a boyish grin, displaying what one psychiatrist called his "sunny brutality." According to Chicago's police chief Morgan Collins, O'Banion was "Chicago's master criminal, who has killed or seen to the killing of at least twenty-five men."

Landesco dismisses O'Banion as "just a superior sort of plugugly;" Allsop regards him as a "case-book psychopath." No doubt he was both, but O'Banion was a psychopathic plugugly with a great deal of charm and street smarts. He was careful; his suits were even tailored to hold three pistols. But he was also reckless and unable to resist the temptation of hijacking other people's trucks.

O'Banion hijacked his first truckful of whiskey in December 1921. He saw the truck momentarily stopped on the street and, acting on impulse, jumped into the cab and pushed the driver out. After a moment's hesitation, he drove it over to his friend Nails Morton's warehouse. A World War I hero, Morton became a gangster and one of Chicago most important fences. Morton gave O'Banion a good price for the truckload, and so, a few months later, Dion had another shot. He and Dan McCarthy, the murderous president of the Plumbers Union, were about to have breakfast at the Sherman House Inn, when the bartender told them there was a truckload of whiskey across the street. O'Banion told the waitress to hold their orders. Then he and McCarthy strolled over to the truck, and, pulling out their revolvers, told the driver to get out of the cab. They were delighted to discover that the truck contained 225 24-pint cases of highest quality, pre-World War I whiskey that Morton was once again happy to take off their hands. Later, in one of Prohibition's biggest coups, the O'Banion gang robbed the Sibley warehouse, carrying off 1,750 cases of bonded whiskey, leaving water-filled barrels in their place.

O'Banion had been a party to the treaty that Torrio had brokered. Torrio still treated O'Banion with restraint. Though less than scrupulous about meeting his obligations, O'Banion was well-connected. He was also useful. Having a base of operations on the North Shore meant that he controlled a supply of good-quality whiskey smuggled in from Canada. Torrio needed access to this supply. The contrast between their two personalities came to light unexpectedly. Police Chief Collins had a tap put on O'Banion's phone, and the Chicago police overheard a conversation between O'Banion and one of his drivers. The driver called to tell O'Banion that he had been stopped by two cops on the West Side who were demanding $300 to let O'Banion's beer through. "Three hundred bucks to them bums!" O'Banion snorted. "Why, I can get them knocked off for half that much." Horrified Collins dispatched a squad of detectives to prevent a massacre. Shortly thereafter, he overheard another telephone conversation between O'Banion and the driver; "I just been talking to Johnnie," the driver said. "And he says to let the cops have the three hundred. He says he don't want no trouble." O'Banion was forced to back off, and when Collins's detectives arrived, the scene was deserted. The crooked cops were probably off celebrating their good fortune, never realizing how close they had come to death or how much they owed to the forbearance of Torrio.[29]

THE TERRIBLE GENNAS

Besides the Torrio-Capone outfit, the only important non-Irish, non-Eastern European gang in Chicago at the opening of Prohibition was the six Genna brothers. Sicilians whose territory started a block north of the Four Deuces and extended to the west along Taylor Street, the Genna family had emigrated from Marsala in 1894 when the oldest brother, Sam, was ten, and the youngest, Mike, was still an infant. The parents died only a few years after arriving in Chicago, leaving their sons to scrounge a living as best they could. They became Black Handers, investing their profits in a cheese and olive importing business. They also ran a poolroom and other gambling concerns.

Among Chicago gangs, the Gennas were exceptional; they had no dealings in beer. In early 1920 they obtained a government license permitting them to handle industrial alcohol, and a three-story warehouse on 1022 Taylor Street, right next to the Maxwell street police station. Discovering that the amount of denatured alcohol they could purchase from legitimate sources was not enough to fill the growing demand, like the Italian gangs on the Lower East Side who, as Rothstein put it, made "rotgut rubbish . . . in their chamber pots," the Gennas turned to alky cookers.

"Few things," the Wickersham Commission sadly had to admit, "are more easily made than alcohol."[30] Traditionally, the production of moonshine whiskey was an artisan's craft. Still owners cooked up a mash made of grains like rye or corn, adding yeast and whatever other ingredients they might fancy, the accepted rule being "The more juicy the garbage, the better the mash, and the better the shine." The potency, palatability, and risk of poison of the resultant product reflected the skill and professional pride of the particular moonshiner. It might equally reflect his greed. As a vast new market opened up before them following the passage of the Volstead Act, greed got the upper hand. The quality of American moonshine dropped precipitously as moonshiners realized that they could sell anything they produced, no matter how toxic, no matter how disgusting the taste. Fortunately, the ingenuity of America's corn farmers, together with the entrepreneurial skills of Sicilian families in the Midwest helped ameliorate this dangerous situation.

We saw that after the Armistice ending World War I, the price of corn plummeted seventy-five per cent. With a glut on their hands, corn farmers began to look for alternative uses. It had been known for a generation that, as a starch, corn could easily be transformed into a sugar. Farmers began turning their surplus corn into a syrup, marketing it as a cheap alternative to maple syrup. Though a promising new outlet and a harbinger for a future, when corn syrup would outsell sugar as America's leading industrial sweetener, there was only a certain amount of corn syrup that America's pancake eaters were able to eat their way through. Fortunately, there was another alternative. The Midwest's beleaguered corn farmers knew that corn syrup could also be distilled into alcohol. Since corn syrup could be legally produced and acquired, industrially-produced corn syrup considerably reduced the risk that the resulting alcohol would be contaminated or would poison the drinker. Though the resulting beverage lacked character, it could easily be enhanced by enterprising and creative bootleggers who doctored corn-sugar alcohol into gin, scotch, bourbon, rye, or whatever else would sell. By 1929, the Prohibition Bureau concluded that about 960 million pounds of corn sugar were being distilled into 70 million gallons of whiskey each year.[31]

Making alcohol from corn syrup simplified the distillation process. Under the aegis of the bootleggers, moonshining changed from a rural artisan's craft to an urban cottage industry, or, more precisely, an urban tenement industry. Families bought, or sometimes rented, cheap home stills—"alky cookers." Bootleggers would supply the families with corn sugar and yeast, charging them around fifty cents a gallon. At the end of the week, when the bootlegger's men arrived with fresh supplies, the family could sell the distilled alcohol for two dollars a gallon. The Gennas persuaded hundreds of tenement dwellers and shopkeepers in Little Sicily to install portable copper stills in their kitchens. They used a system invented by Henry Spingola, a local lawyer and the brother of Lucille Spingola, the fiancee of Angelo Genna. The Genna brothers provided the alky cookers with corn sugar, and paid the keepers fifteen dollars a day to keep the stills running night and day. Compared to what a laborer or shop assistant usually received, fifteen dollars a day was a fortune, and when news of the Genna family's successful industry spread back to Sicily, it set off a minor emigration boom to Chicago.

The Gennas were generous to their friends in office. In 1925 their office manager confessed to federal agents that five police captains were on the Genna payroll. The Gennas also paid around four hundred uniformed police officers, mostly from the Maxwell Street station, a monthly stipend of between $10 to $125 per official, depending upon rank and the type of service they performed. Plain-clothes officers from headquarters and the state attorney's office were frequent recipients as well. There were so many official claimants on the Gennas' bounty that the family found it necessary to keep, in conjunction with the Maxwell Street police, careful records to ensure that extraneous and undeserving police officials did not show up on paydays and falsely claim a share. On paydays, the Gennas' Taylor Street warehouse so swarmed with men in blue uniforms that passers-by sometimes mistook it for the police station.

Even with all this generosity, alky cooking was still a profitable business. A copper still yielded around 350 gallons a week at a cost of fifty to seventy cents per gallon. The wholesale price of this stuff was six dollars a gallon. The retail price — measured in twenty-five-cent shots — was forty dollars a gallon. Even allowing for the approximately 10 percent graft that was probably paid by both the wholesalers and the retailers, plus the money paid by the Gennas to the Maxwell Street police, Asbury estimates their turnover at $350,000 a month, of which $150,000 was pure profit.

By all accounts, however, it was a deadly concoction. The tenements were filled with vermin. Drawn by the reek of the fermenting corn sugar,the animals would tumble into the vats and drown. When Captain John Stege raided Little Italy's tenements, confiscating a hundred barrels of mash, he found dead rats in every one of them. Sometimes the bodies of cats who had chased them were there as well. Still, business was business, and if there were plenty in Chicago willing to pay inflated prices to inflict grievous bodily harm upon themselves, the Gennas were willing to accommodate them.

BIG BILL THOMPSON

By 1923, according to Curt Johnson, Torrio was partner in twelve breweries and handler of output from fifty more, as well as the Gennas' grain alcohol production and that of several other distilleries. He operated fifty whorehouses and one hundred gambling rooms and supplied fifteen thousand speakeasies. "He managed his full-service capitalistic empire to a mighty prosperity, and his own income rose to exceed $15 million a year."[32] These are figures probably from summaries that the Chicago *Tribune* published in a series of articles at the close of the decade. When, in 1924, the police raided Capone's "medical office" on South Michigan Avenue, however, the ledgers only showed that, for the last three years, the Torrio-Capone outfit had made around $3 million a year. According to Walter Noble Burns, police officials nevertheless estimated that the outfit's real profit was closer to $30 million annually. Sixty-five breweries, he wrote, "ran full blast" in the city and its suburbs, many of which Torrio owned; in many others of which he was a partner.[33] In 1926, writes Edward D. Sullivan, United States District Attorney, Edwin A. Olsen, made still another estimate of the Capone outfit's annual profit — $70 million annually.[34]

The estimates, we see, varied considerably. By the second half of the 1920s, Al Capone was an international celebrity, as well-known an American as Charles Lindberg or Babe Ruth. Even European newspaper readers knew about Al Capone and the Chicago Beer War. The government too had begun to take an interest, opening an extensive investigation of Capone's cash flow in order to indict him on an income tax evasion charge. Estimates from this later period have, in consequence, a certain credibility. Estimates from the beginnings of the 1920s, by contrast, are no more than educated guesses. The Torrio-Capone outfit was involved in as many as sixty-five or as few as twelve breweries plus an imprecise, though considerable, number of brothels, gambling houses, and speakeasies. Estimates of the outfit's annual profit ranged from $15 million to $70 million. No one really knew for sure because, in these early years, no one seems to have been paying much attention. Like many other cities, Chicago was at first reluctant to admit publicly that the Volstead Act had been a dead letter from the outset. The reluctance to face the truth was a gift to Torrio, helping him expand without attracting unwanted publicity. It also helped him keep the peace.

Bootlegging was a tide that lifted all boats in the underworld. But the good times would only last so long as the gangs could keep their peace. Gang wars create mayhem, and mayhem creates a public outcry that leads to police crackdowns. Police crackdowns have always been bad news for the vice business. Torrio surely knew all this and hoped that, with the press quiescent, simple monetary greed would help keep the hot-heads in order. The Chicago police were hoping for the same thing.

In 1920, the new Chicago police chief, the young and photogenic Charles Fitzmorris, told the press frankly that the Chicago police could not be expected to eliminate the distribution and sale of liquor entirely. Preoccupied by the anti-Bolshevik crusade, the admission drew little comment at the time. Fitzmorris interpreted Mayor Thompson's pledge to "close the hellholes where liquor and moonshine are alleged and proven to be sold" as a warrant to raid and close down lower-class dives and resorts while leaving middle-class establishments and clubs comparatively undisturbed. It was a tactic sure to win the approval of the respectable press. In 1921 he arrested 550 suspects in Prohibition raids, transferring or suspending fifty-five officers for non-performance; and in 1922 he had the satisfaction of being singled out as "honest, courageous and efficient" by the Chicago Crime Commission.[35]

Fitzmorris's real worry was that Prohibition would spread corruption in his own department. It had happened before; raiding and grafting were anything but mutually exclusive, and the Chicago Police Department had worked hard for the last five years clearing up the messes and scandals following in the wake of the closure of the Levee. Fitzmorris must have known, or at least heard the rumors: breweries were re-opening; Canadian whiskey was coming in from the lake; Little Italy was turning into a distillery; and the Maxwell Street precinct was being paid to look the other way. Still, he held off, not wishing to mount a full-scale campaign against Prohibition violations unless public opinion forced him into it. Like Torrio, Fitzmorris hoped the truce in the underworld would hold. In 1923, however, there occurred the first in a series of incidents that would begin to unravel the whole fragile peace: Mayor Thompson declined to seek a third term.

Lacking a Tammany to ensure peace and stability, Chicago had come to rest instead upon *ad hoc* constitutional, elected monarchies. If New York has provided America with its most infamous political machine, Chicago has provided it with its two most infamous political dynasties—those of Carter Harrison, father and son, and, later, Richard Daley, father and son. Constitutional monarchs do not rule directly; indeed, given the administrative constraints and confusions in Chicago and Cook County, it would be difficult for direct rule to emanate from the mayor's office. Constitutional monarchs rather govern through mediation and representation. Chicago is a jungle of constituencies and partial constituencies, few of which are strong enough to force through any policy on their own. It is the mayor's job to weigh and evaluate the demands of competing constituencies, searching for solutions that are politically viable. Usually the result of this search is a compromise where benefits to one constituency are delicately balanced by favors to another.

The sight of a mayor staggering from compromise to compromise is seldom an inspiring one; and much of the moral opprobrium that the reformist press showered upon the Harrison and later Daley dynasties stemmed from a perception of a mayor whose moral compass led him to stagger aimlessly rather than strike out boldly in a rectilinear fashion. Yet Chicago's social divisions were real; power in the city was monopolized by a narrow white, Anglo-Saxon, protestant (WASP) patriciate. This system was permanently at odds with itself yet united in determination to resist any demand that the immigrant and black workers might place before them. Had the mayor of Chicago followed the rigid course that the WASP patriciate wanted, the city's streets would have run red with blood more often than they did. Fortunately, and contrary to the demands of intellectuals such as S.S. McClure and Alphonso Alva Hopkins, who campaigned for voting restrictions, the United States preserved universal male suffrage. That meant that the poor, the blacks, and the immigrants held onto the vote and, despite all their own divisions, were capable of using it to defend their own rights. The result was that governing the great city of Chicago became a great, though thoroughly unedifying, balancing act. Any other course led to disaster.

In 1915, Chicago's crown fell upon the brows of William "Big Bill" Thompson. A man devoid of conspicuous intellectual accomplishments or interests, Thompson had originally entered politics on a dare from his friends in the Chicago Athletic Club, where he had won fame as "Fighting Bill," the captain of the club's water polo and footballs teams. In 1896, he had coached the Chicago Athletic Club to a national athletic club football championship.

Party politics in Chicago were then in a flux and would remain so until the Depression. In 1915, foreign immigrants composed over 75 percent of the Chicago population. During these years, the black community was expanding rapidly. Chicago WASPs barely comprised 20 percent of the city. They were, however, the richest, most active and most politically influential constituency in the city. Moreover, they were a constituency that regarded a monopoly of political power as their inalienable birthright. This community was nevertheless politically divided. The descendants of the British and Germanic farmers who had migrated from the East traditionally voted Republican. Descendants of southern WASPs displaced by the Civil War often retained their Democrat Party allegiance. Thompson was a WASP, though something of a renegade WASP. His Bostonian father had planned to send him to Exeter and then on to

Yale, but the son rebelled and set out for a cowboy life out West.

He had entered Chicago politics as a Republican. He started as a protégé of William Lorimer, the Republican "blond boss" who had served as congressman from 1894 to 1900 and from 1902 to 1908. In 1909 Lorimer was appointed to the U.S. Senate, though he was expelled in 1912 when the *Tribune* disclosed that he had bought his seat by bribing state legislators.[36] The Lorimer faction of the Chicago Republican Party included Jews and Catholics, who brought it under constant attack from bastions of WASP hegemony, such as the *Tribune* and the *Daily News*.

Thompson was astute enough to realize that, though the WASP vote was insufficient to ensure his election to any major political office, without influential WASP backing he could not even get into the game. As mayoral candidate in 1915, Thompson campaigned for both the WASP and the immigrant vote. To WASP audiences he posed as a reformer, promising progress and good government, pledging his support for vice reform. With other audiences, however, he played on their particular grievances, especially courting the German vote by making much of the fact that his Democrat opponent, Robert M. Schweitzer, despite his Germanic name, was the leader of the Ancient Order of Hibernians. He courted Chicago's neglected black voters as well. It was a strategy of contradictory promises, of posing as all things to all voters, that quickly came to infuriate most of the city's editorial writers. Sullivan described Thompson's 1915 platform as "Wet-Dry—Anti-English—pro-Ally—White Supremacy—Negro—Protestant-Republican—Carter Harrison-Democrat."[37] Yet there was political sense in this seeming incoherence. A man with an unquenchable desire for public adulation and with no fixed ideas of his own, Thompson possessed an uncanny knack of telling audiences whatever they wanted to hear. This is what made him electable.

The mayor successfully ran for a second term in 1919. He had begun to criticize America's prospective entry into the war as early as April 1917. His position, and later attacks on war-time "profiteers," drove the *Tribune* into paroxysms. It accused Thompson of disloyalty, defeatism, pacifism, and anti-patriotism. The editorial on the eve of the election solemnly informed readers that "The Second Front is Here." Southern papers accused Thompson of luring blacks out of the South by defending draft "slackers." None of this did Thompson any harm. The city's large Irish and German minorities were hardly enthusiastic about the war. Southern blacks had their own reasons for coming north. The anti-Thompson press was simply taking pot shots at potentially pro-Thompson voters. The war, in fact, was good to Chicago, and not only for the meat packers and grain merchants. With the war effort underway and with the urban economy bustling ahead full steam, Chicago induced Washington to help finance the Burnham Plan. In 1918, the city began in earnest a far-reaching campaign of center-city redevelopment. Thousands found employment on building sites, and Thompson could run for re-election under his favorite nick-name "Big Bill the Builder."

Thompson's attitude towards the Volstead Act seems to have been little different from Fred Busse's or Carter Harrison Jr.'s attitude towards vice in the Levee. As far as they could, they had avoided the whole issue. Whenever public pressure built up so far as to back them up against a wall, however, they simply turned around and did the expedient. Busse appointed the Vice Commission in 1910; Harrison closed down the Levee four years later. In 1920, Big Bill Thompson issued a statement about the "law of the land;" the following year he made his promise to "close the hellholes where liquor and moonshine" were served. Yet, like Chief Fitzmorris, Thompson probably regarded Prohibition as a nuisance. Though the new law was unenforceable, it carried great potential for mischief. Thompson tried his best to keep both the issue of Prohibition and its relative non-enforcement in Chicago out of the spotlight. He was in good company; it was the same policy that the Jimmy Walker administration adopted in New York City. Indeed, it was the policy of Warren G. Harding's administration in Washington.

What was the relationship between Big Bill Thompson and Johnnie Torrio? The simplest, and most accurate, answer is that there was no relationship whatsoever. Neither had anything to offer to the other. Thompson would not have been interested in Torrio's money; he was independently rich and, for all his other sins, was never accused of pocketing graft. Thompson was not at all like New York's Boss Croker; day-to-day administration bored him. He could never get the hang of it. He had no head for figures. Big Bill liked to be there in the open for ribbon-cutting and corner-stone laying ceremonies surrounded by press photographers. Nor was Torrio in a position to do Thompson any political favors. He never aspired to political leadership in Chicago's Italian community and thus had no constituency that he could swing Thompson's way. For his part, Thompson, who was good at cultivating ethnic voters, had no need to enlist Torrio's electoral assistance.

There was not even much that Thompson could do for Torrio. He did not run the Chicago police. Torrio remained connected to Hinky Dink Kenna, but as a Democrat Party alderman, Kenna played little part in the Thompson administration. In any case, the center of Torrio's operations was no longer the central First Ward but the Far South, on and over the Cook County boundary and the Illinois state line. Torrio corrupted officals and police officers wherever he could, but these were always local officials, the ones who exercised authority on the ground. He had no way of influencing policy in City Hall. As Captain Fitzmorris had feared, under Prohibition, corruption rose from the ground up; it did not spread from the top down.

A relation between Thompson and Capone in this period is even less likely. Capone was a rising gangster, but outside of the Chicago underworld, he was still unknown in 1923. He lacked any sort of political connections whatsoever. Nevertheless, in his influential essay on organized crime in America, Daniel J. Bell wrote that Thompson "helped Capone lay the foundation for all his enterprises." Labor historian, Irving Bernstein observed that "Organized crime, operating with the connivance of the Thompson regime, ruled Cook County as no American metropolis has been controlled before or since."[38]

Any evidence for a relation between Thompson and Capone can only come from Thompson's third, 1927, administration, and we shall look at this later. But by 1927, the Torrio-Capone outfit had already established itself. Therefore, Boorstein's claim that Thompson helped "lay the foundation" for all of Capone's enterprises is simply false. Likewise, Bernstein's claim that under Thompson, organized crime "ruled Cook County" is a piece of unhelpful bombast. Chicago tolerated bootleggers during Prohibition just at it had tolerated the Levee Lords a generation before. But Chicago mayors had not laid the foundation for either the sex or the illegal liquor trades. Both of these businesses had organized themselves with little material help or encouragement from City Hall. The same is true of the Torrio-Capone outfit in Chicago. The contention that any sort of relation existed before 1923 is wholly implausible and lacking in evidence.

More recently, Lindberg has argued that it was Mayor Thompson "who permitted Colosimo and later Al Capone to re-unite the scattered vice elements into an all-powerful crime syndicate."[39] It is true that Thomson allowed both Colosimo and Ike Bloom to re-open their resorts after 1915. But both of these resorts were popular night clubs: Colosimo's Cafe was popular with socialites and the theatre crowd; Bloom's place had long been a watering hole for politicians and the police. Both were shuttered during the anti-vice crackdown, no doubt for good reasons. When they later re-opened, they did so without the bar girls. Allowing Colosimo and Bloom to re-open after 1915 was a normal bureaucratic decision and one that most of the city approved of. As for Capone, during the first Thompson administration, Capone was still a teen-ager in Brooklyn. In January 1923, when Thompson announced that he would not run for a third term, the name "Alfred Caponi" had appeared once in a small newspaper piece concerning drunken driving, assault, and carrying a concealed weapon.

The Chicago outfit would later become the most powerful organized crime syndicate in American history. Torrio and Capone are the Chicago outfit's founding fathers. It is of some interest to know how it all got started. The explanation that it was the step-child of the corrupt Thompson administration is not only factually untrue; it is barking up the wrong tree. Informed opinion consistently interpreted crime from the top down, seeing it as organized by corrupt big-city bosses intent on exploiting the ignorant immigrants and urban blacks. In this way, the immigrants and black are configured as innocent victims. In the same way, vice reformers in both New York and Chicago consistently portrayed prostitutes as the unwilling victims of a mysterious ring of foreign (typically Jewish) white slavers, working in cahoots with corrupt urban politicians.

The story line may be more satisfying told like this, but it happens to be a falsehood. New York did not need Tammany and its white-slaving foreign allies to introduce prostitution; prostitution was there already. Torrio and Colosimo did not need the help of either Chicago's mayor or the Chicago police in running their resorts and keeping them supplied with booze and girls. The two were capable of doing these things themselves. It is an interpretation that refuses to face the fact that organized crime in America, and the Chicago outfit in particular, was not organized or managed by municipal politicians, but by the criminals themselves. The point is not to rehabilitate the reputation of a political blowhard like Chicago's Big Bill Thompson. The point is to understand how organized crime really got started. Neither Torrio nor Capone were connected to, much less directed by, anyone in the the Chicago mayor's office. Neither Torrio nor Capone was wholly welcomed by leaders of the older, predominantly Irish, Chicago underworld. As non-Sicilians from the East Coast, neither was even wholly accepted by Chicago's *Unione Siciliana*. Torrio and Capone had to fight their way to the top against determined opposition from non-Italians and Italians alike.

Had Thompson run in 1923, he might easily have won a third term. He had weathered the storms set off by his anti-war stance. He had kept out of the anti-Bolshevik crusade and the Black Sox scandal. The 1919 race riot was fading into the past. His tone had remained relentlessly up-beat. In the summer of 1921 he hosted Chicago's fifteen-day Pageant of Progress at the Municipal Pier. There were parades, beauty contests, and, as a climax, the release of five thousand "Pigeons of Progress." He wrote the introductory article in *Main 13*, Chicago's first "Magazine for Policemen By Policemen" (In 1916, police officers had been disciplined for attempting a similar publication). In it he told his readers that, as an old football coach, he knew that "Teamwork and you will win the championship—the Greatest Police Department in the World." He even found time to praise the work of the Chicago Crime Commission.[40] With business booming, he could open new building sites and provide more jobs. More jobs and better pay acted as tranquilizers, relaxing labor tensions and soothing old wounds. Thompson was able to patronize the city's black community without roiling the white working classes. There is no reason to believe that, were Thompson permitted to run in 1923, he would not have coasted home to victory. Yet Thompson was not permitted to run. He was dumped by the Chicago Republicans.

Although Thompson had been trading jibes, barbs, and law suits with the *Tribune* and *Daily News* since his anti-war pronouncements in 1917, he had been careful to keep intact remnants of his WASP credibility. Shortly after his re-election in 1919, Thompson appointed the English immigrant, the Methodist Reverend John H. Williamson, to be his special law enforcement commissioner. Williamson used the nomination to launch an anti-crime crusade from his pulpit, announcing his intention of mobilizing twenty-five thousand Christians into a Chicago Law Enforcement Citizens' Commission, though the membership target was quickly downscaled to ten thousand. By 1922, however, Williamson's preaching was becoming a political liability, offending Catholic and black voters and attracting unwanted contributions from the Ku Klux Klan. No stranger to inconsistency, Thompson might easily have ignored all this had his specially appointed law enforcement commissioner actually attained the goal of recruiting ten thousand Thompson-supporting

Christians. But when the new commission gathered in less than half the expected members, Thompson seems to have concluded that the old-fashioned WASP voters had by now either moved to the suburbs or were frequenting speakeasies or simply were not listening. In whatever case, they no longer cared to be wooed by Methodist preachers. With this realization, he promptly dumped Williamson and abandoned the WASP constituency entirely, cultivating henceforth his own particular persona as Big Bill, xenophobe, anti-WASP, and friend of the common man.

Nevertheless, though Thompson was through with the WASP wing of the Chicago Republicans, that wing was not through with him. Having broken with the reformers, and with no record of zealotry on behalf of the Volstead Act, Thompson had left himself exposed.

In January 1923, Thompson's old campaign manager, Fred Lundin, was indicted for his involvement in a school graft scandal. He was indicted, moreover, by the Republican State's Attorney and former Thompson ally, Robert Crowe. An ex-judge, Crowe was politically ambitious, and was serving notice on Thompson that the mayor's non-enforcement of the Volstead Act would be on the agenda during the mayoral elections that year. He may have hinted at other things as well, for shortly after he received information that Crowe had opened a grand jury investigation, Thompson withdrew his candidacy.

If Thompson was quietly dumped by the Chicago Republicans, the party paid a high price. Their 1923 candidate, Chicago postmaster Arthur C. Lueder, proved himself a competent and honest administrator. He was also a political neophyte, unable to divert the voters' attentions from the anti-immigrant, anti-black sentiments perennially festering on his party's dark side. The Democrats won by one hundred five thousand votes, with sixty-six hundred of them coming from the city's black First and Third wards.[41]

For the Democrats, William E. Dever had seemed to be the ideal candidate. He had served four terms on the city council and another three as superior court judge. Though an Irish Catholic, Dever had from the beginning embraced reform; the Congregational minister Graham Taylor had been one of his earliest supporters. He was intellectually serious, well-versed in law and administrative procedures and of proven political competence. Here was a mayor who would finally steer a rectilinear course through the city's many administrative, labor, and ethnic problems.

Nevertheless, Dever's administration turned out a disaster, for it was based on a misunderstanding. Responsible opinion had always held that Chicago's problems stemmed from corruption at the top. Bukowski puts it very simply; "Dever failed because Chicago's problems did not result from government corruption. Rather, they were part of the very fabric of the place." Chicago was a "city with a decentralized and fractious population." Big Bill Thompson had never once tried to resolve any of the issues that divided this fractious population; he had no talent for governing, no capacity and probably no interest in formulating real policies. He simply told every faction what they wanted to hear, pledged his support to all worthy causes, promised everything to everybody, stood in front of the flashing cameras, and then did absolutely nothing. It was a form of total, though sympathetic, indifference that allowed each constituency to believe that their concerns were foremost in their dear monarch's heart. It was a belief that seemed to have a tranquilizing effect on the entire population. By reversing this policy and deciding to become the decider, Dever followed his moral compass's rectilinear course straight through Chicago's many contradictions. This broke the spell and soon brought the fury of nations down upon his beleaguered city.[42]

THE OUTBREAK

One gang had not agreed to Torrio's proposals. They had not agreed because they had not even been consulted—the South Side O'Donnells.

Starting out as small-time thieves and bank robbers, the four O'Donnell brothers had, like other criminal groups in Chicago, acquired patrons and protectors as they expanded. In the years before the war, they had worked as labor schlammers in union disputes and sluggers in the newspaper circulation wars. They had graduated to electoral intimidation. The leader of the group was the elder brother, Ed, commonly known as Spike. By 1920, Spike O'Donnell was a local big shot; his garrulous and faintly whimsical face and trademark polka-dot bow tie were well known in the towns along Chicago's southern border. The face was well-known at St. Peter's Catholic Church as well, where Spike was known as a particularly devout communicant who never missed a Sunday Mass. It may even be that Spike's face was a little too well known, at least for a bank robber. When The Stockyards Savings and Trust Bank was robbed, witnesses had little problem picking Spike as one of the culprits. Thus when Prohibition started, Spike O'Donnell found himself serving the first year of a five-year stretch at Joliet State Prison. Without the dynamic leadership of Spike, the other three O'Donnell brothers—Steve, Walter, and Tommy—began to drift, eventually settling down to work at odd jobs at the Four Deuces under Capone. It was for this reason that Torrio had not thought it necessary to consult them.

Torrio had not, however, counted on the strength of Spike's political connections. Before he even arrived at Joliet, letters were piling up on Illinois Governor Small's desk—six letters from state senators, five from state representatives, and one from a criminal court judge. All of these letters petitioned for Spike's pardon. Governor Small was used to sending hardened felons back onto Chicago's streets with much less solicitation than this. In the summer of 1923, Spike O'Donnell was prowling his old South Side beat again.

Not being a signatory of the *pax torriensis*, Spike O'Donnell felt free to raid the territories of his neighbors, the Torrio-Capone syndicate and the allied McErlane-Saltis gang. He began hijacking their trucks and running his beer into their territories. He reinforced his gang with Harry Hansmiller, a thug imported from New York. He sent Sport Bucher and George Meeghan to persuade saloon owners to buy his beer. According to Walter Noble Burns,

O'Donnell's sales technique was primitive, though persuasive:

> A bunch of high-powered O'Donnell salesmen would storm into a saloon,
> line up at the bar and order beer. When the proprietor had set out the foaming
> glasses the gang leader would take a sip and pull a wry face.

> "This beer is rotten," he would bawl, registering huge disgust, "Who are you
> buying your beer from?"

> "Joe Saltis. It's good beer. My customers are satisfied."

> "It's rotten I tell you. This stuff'll ruin your trade."

> One of the gang would reach behind the bar and turn on the spigot, letting
> the beer run until the barrel was empty, foaming streams flooding out over
> the barroom floor.

> "You'll buy our beer after this. We're your friends. We'll build up your busi-
> ness for you. We'll send you some good beer in the morning."

> That was that. A truck would pull up at the saloon the next morning and
> stock the cellar with O'Donnell beer, and the O'Donnells would call and
> collect.

On the night of September 7, 1923, Walter and Tommy O'Donnell, Sport
Bucher, George Meeghan and a young hood named Jerry O'Connor set out
on just such a beer-selling expedition. The first saloon they visited was that
of Jacob Geis on Fifty-first Street. Geis had already refused the O'Donnells
twice, once throwing the O'Donnell salesman out the door. When the five
O'Donnells walked into the saloon, Geis and bartender Nick Gorysko were
busy serving customers. The O'Donnells grabbed Geis by the neck and
dragged him headfirst across the bar, blackjacking him into unconsciousness.
When Gorysko came out from behind the bar to fight, they blackjacked him as
well, fracturing his skull. Exhilarated by the experience, the five O'Donnells
proceeded to visit five more saloons that had been holding out on them,
smashing up each place in turn. They then retired to Joe Klepka's on South
Lincoln, where brother Spike joined them. Still pumped from the evening's
exertions, they began to celebrate with beer and sandwiches.

Their night's activities had not, however, gone unobserved. Frank McErlane had formed a party of gunmen, and had begun to stalk the O'Donnells,
following them from bar to bar in the wake of their destruction. When they
reached Klepka's, they found the O'Donnells still inside drinking. Danny Mc-
Fall, a gunmen who had come to McErlane from the Ragen Colts, burst in,
followed by three more McErlane hoods.

"Stick 'em up." McFall shouted levelling his .38 caliber pistol at the Jerry
O'Connor, who happened to be nearest.

The two O'Donnells and Bucher and Meeghan dived through exits, leaving Jerry O'Connor caught in McFall's gunsights. They marched him outside where Frank McErlane was waiting for him with a sawed-off shotgun. Klepka, the saloon-keeper, had remained behind the bar. As soon as O'Connor had left the saloon, Klepka heard two shotgun blasts followed by pistol shots. Rushing out, he found Jerry O'Connor stretched out on the sidewalk, the first official casualty of Chicago's beer war.

Ten days later it was Bucher and Meeghan's turn. It was late at night, forty miles outside of Chicago. Bucher and Meeghan were driving in two truckloads of O'Donnell beer when two men brandishing shotguns suddenly materialized over the crest of a hill to block their way. The two armed men forced the drivers to descend from their cabs, disarmed and bound them, and then threw them into the back seat of their car. While this was taking place, the scene was unexpectedly illuminated by the headlights of a passing car. The hijackers swung their shotguns around, yelling for the driver to stop. Instead he pressed down on the accelerator, and was lucky to get away with nothing worse than buckshot craters in his trunk. The driver later recognized the angry little face of Frank McErlane as one of the hijackers. He wasn't sure about the second, but the police reasoned that it was either Danny McFall or Walter Stevens, another hired gun.

As the hijackers' car approached the Chicago city limits, McErlane, who was sitting in the passenger's seat with the shotgun on his lap, turned and fired straight into Meeghan's face. Meeghan jerked backwards against the seat. As Bucher wheeled around to see what had happened to his friend, McErlane emptied the other barrel into the side of his head. Both men were then pushed out of the speeding car into the pre-dawn darkness. The police later said that the close-range blasts had nearly taken their heads off.

Two months later, McErlane hijacked another two truckloads of O'Donnell beer in exactly the same spot. This time the drivers were Morris Keane and Shorty Egan. Miraculously, Egan survived. Bound and gagged in the back seat, and "with the car doing seventy," Egan later recounted that

> the tall skinny guy at the wheel said to McErlane, "What are we going to do with these two birds?" For an answer McErlane shoved the muzzle of his sawed-off within a foot of Keane's face and let her go. As Keane tumbled to the floor, McErlane shifted his gun over onto me and pulled the trigger of the second barrel. I slumped down on top of Keane. As I lay in a daze, I supposed I was dead. When I began to come to, I thought I was a ghost waking up in the other world, and I wondered what it would be like and what old friends I was going to meet. Then I felt Keane's blood on my face and was surprised to find I was still alive. I didn't feel any pain, but was half-blind from the flash of the shotgun and my ears were drumming from the roar. I had sense enough left to know that if I moved or showed any signs of life, McErlane would finish me, and I pretended to be dead.

> I heard the skinny fellow say to McErlane in a voice that sounded far off, "How are we going to get rid of these stiffs?"

"That's easy," said McErlane, and he came piling over the back of the seat and landed on me. He swung the door open—the car was still travelling around seventy—and pitched Keane out. Then he pushed me out after him. I hit the ground on my shoulders and I thought I would never stop rolling. I lost consciousness.

When my senses came back, I was lying in a pool of water, and ice had formed about me. The sky was red, and it was breaking day. I staggered along the road until I saw a light in a farmhouse. I fell from weakness when I got inside the gate, and crawled to the door on my hands and knees. The farmer wouldn't let me in at first. "I'm shot," I said. "Let me in or I'll die." Then he opened the door with a shotgun in his hand. He and his wife cut the ropes and laid me on a bed. They didn't know whether to call a doctor or a priest. But they finally called an ambulance and sent me to a hospital. "Well Shorty," I said to myself when I felt a soft mattress under me, "this is a hell of a lot better than a grave."

Later McErlane's men killed Harry Hansmiller in a running gunfight. The McErlane gang made about ten attempts on Spike O'Donnell's own life, all unsuccessful, though brother Tommy was seriously wounded in one. If Jerry O'Connor has the dubious distinction of being the first official victim in the beer war, Spike O'Donnell holds the honor of being the first gangster in Chicago to be targeted by a Thompson sub-machine gun. Though later the gun became so common that it was nicknamed the "Chicago chopper," it was still unknown in 1925. McErlane's shots went wild; the police were later perplexed at finding bullet holes everywhere. They missed Spike entirely however. "Life with me is just one bullet after another," Spike remarked. "I've been shot at and missed so many times, I've a notion to hire myself out as a professional target." Instead, he left town.[43]

THE CRACKDOWN AND THE REPUBLIC OF CICERO

O'Connor was shot in September 1923, shortly after Dever had taken office. "This town will immediately become dry!" Dever had told the voters. On hearing the news of the murders of O'Connor, Bucher, and Meeghan, he suspended the captain of the New City police precinct. Then he issued a statement:

Until the murders of Jerry O'Connor and the murderers of these two men [Bucher and Meeghan] have been apprehended and punished, and the illegal traffic for control of which they battle has been suppressed, the dignity of the law and the average man's respect for it is imperiled and every officer of the law and every enforcing agency should lay aside other duties and join in the common cause—a restoration of law and order. The police will follow this case to the finish as they do all others. This guerilla war between hijackers, rum-runners and illicit beer peddlers can and will be crushed. I am just as sure that this miserable traffic with its toll of human life and morals can be stamped out as I am that I am mayor, and I am not going to flinch for a minute.

It was the first in a long series of such statements, resolute, long-winded, and sincere, that Dever would solemnly deliver in the course of the next four years over a growing mound of corpses. Though Chicago soon grew tired of hearing them, Mayor Dever never lost his faith in the therapeutic effects of official platitudes.

Dever had appointed Morgan A. Collins as his new police chief, extracting from Collins and State's Attorney Crowe a promise of "a relentless investigation of the beer war." He informed Chief Collins and Chief Detective Hughes that he would assume personal command of the murder investigations. He saw to it that the licenses of two thousand soft drink parlors which were found to have speakeasies in the back were revoked. It was the beginning of a new policy of zero tolerance.[44]

By now, both the police and the papers had heard the story that Torrio had brokered a territorial agreement among the bootlegging gangs. Though Frank McErlane had been identified as the murderer in all three killings, the police reasoned that McErlane would not have acted without Torrio's prior knowledge and approval. They pulled in both Capone and Torrio for questioning, learning nothing. The best the police could do was to get an indictment against Danny McFall. It was worse than useless; although McFall was positively identified as the gunman who had charged into Klepka's saloon and pushed O'Connor out to his death on the sidewalk outside, the same witnesses were equally positive that McFall had brandished a .38 caliber. But O'Connor had been killed with shotgun, not a .38 caliber, and thus McFall was easily acquitted.

Hostilities had now broken out, but hostilities as yet were still limited to a feud between the McErlane-Saltis gang and the South Side O'Donnells. Though the police hypothesis that McErlane would not have proceeded without the approval of Torrio was a reasonable one, it was still only a hypothesis. The police had no evidence linking either Torrio or Capone to the O'Connor killing. It was still possible to hope that the violence could be kept from spreading further. Unfortunately, the police crackdown had further strained an already fragile atmosphere.

The two thousand speakeasies that the police padlocked in the first six months of the Dever administration were all resorts in the city of Chicago itself. Their closure disrupted the territorial arrangements that Torrio and the other bootleggers had drawn up several years earlier, disrupting as well, one must assume, local arrangements between the gangs themselves or between the gangs and the local police. With their customers in the city under attack, the gangs scrambled to find new outlets for their beer and whiskey.

"By 1923," writes Johnson, "Chicago had 20,000 speakeasies, 13,000 more—or almost three times as many—as it had before the Volstead Act took effect. Johnny the Fox Torrio's troops garnered three-quarters of the money made from these 20,000." Torrio, he adds, had at this time roughly eight hundred men on his payroll.[45] Once again, these figures are no more than guesses. That Chicago had nearly three times as many outlets for liquor during Prohibition than before seems doubtful.

Whether U.S. consumption of alcohol declined during Prohibition is a much debated question. Supporters of the Eighteenth Amendment always claimed that consumption had declined dramatically; though others were inclined to be more skeptical. There is no reason, however, to imagine that consumption actually trebled—even in wicked Chicago. The claim that Torrio had eight hundred men under his command in 1923 is possibly misleading. Though Johnson speaks of Torrio as the head of an organization with a military chain of command, Torrio was a businessman, not a war lord. Torrio's varied enterprises might well have provided jobs for eight hundred workers; but these were jobs with the breweries and in the resorts. Torrio never possessed his own, gun-toting, eight-hundred-man-strong private army. Johnson goes on to add that 95 percent of Torrio's workforce was foreign born and in their early twenties and thirties. This is possible; the overwhelming majority of Chicago's workforce at the time was either black or of immigrant stock. Nevertheless, many of the members of the Chicago outfit whose origin we can trace were not foreign-born. They were, like Capone himself, the sons of recently arrived immigrants. How many of them were Italian? We have no precise answer to this question. The best we can say is that, though the brewers, beer-truck drivers and service personnel came from a variety of backgrounds, Torrio recruited most of his muscle from Little Italy and Little Sicily.[46]

In October 1923, Torrio leased a house on Roosevelt Road in Cicero.

Cicero was a town immediately southwest of Chicago, just outside the city limits, though still inside Cook County. More like a small smokestack suburb than a town, Cicero contained about sixty thousand inhabitants, mostly first- and second-generation Bohemians who worked in the steel mills, the Western Electric works, or in the stockyards on the Southwest Side. Though peaceful and law-abiding, Cicero's Bohemians were traditionally partial to good Pilsner beer and had quietly ignored Prohibition. In 1923 they were obtaining their beer courtesy of Klondike, Bernard, and Myles O'Donnell, three brothers who formed the core of the West Side O'Donnell gang, with no relation to Spike and his brothers on the South Side. The West Side O'Donnell brothers worked in partnership with Eddie Vogel, a political boss from the Southwest Side, and supplied beer to Eddie Tancl, a cauliflower-eared ex-fighter who ran a saloon called the Hawthorne Park Café. In exchange for keeping the beer flowing and managing their political affairs, Vogel installed his slot machines in Cicero's saloons, taking a cut of their weekly profits. This was the town's only form of vice. It was a tidy arrangement, and neither Vogel nor the O'Donnell brothers saw any need for Torrio to open a whore house in their town.

With his string of road houses in Stickney and near-by towns, Torrio could easily forego a brothel in Cicero itself. Indeed, what he really seems to have wanted was a toe-hold within the town itself. Eddie Vogel at first ordered the Cicero police to close Torrio's Roosevelt Road resort. When Torrio opened another resort at Ogden and Fifty-second, moving in the six women from Roosevelt Road, Vogel had the police close it too. Vogel's writ evidently ran large in the Cicero police, but Torrio had his own friends. Two days after the second raid, deputy sheriffs sent by Cook County Sheriff Peter B. Hoffman arrived and impounded all of Vogel's slot machines. The message from Torrio was clear: If I can't have my whores, you can't have your slot machines. It was the basis for a deal. A meeting was arranged at the Four Deuces, where the O'Donnell brothers, Vogel, and Torrio hammered out a new agreement. Vogel got his slot machines back, and the O'Donnells were given the resorts along Roosevelt Avenue. Torrio promised not to import prostitutes into Cicero. In return, Cicero was declared an open town, and the Torrio organization was permitted to open gambling houses, pool rooms and saloons in the rest of the city. They were also permitted to use Cicero as their new base of operations. Calculating that an opening up of Cicero was likely to increase their own businesses, Vogel and the O'Donnells were happy to agree to these proposals.

It is possible that, having foreseen the Dever crackdown, Torrio had decided to relocate his base of operation outside the city limits. But with a string of resorts in nearby towns, Torrio was moving in this direction anyway; Torrio may already have had Cicero in his sites. In whichever case, when the Four Deuces was padlocked a short time after the meeting with Vogel and the O'Donnells, Cicero became the Torrio organization's new headquarters. Torrio left arrangements to Capone, who was by now his second in command. Torrio responded to the police crackdown by prudently cashing in some of his chips. He left Chicago on a six-month vacation, carrying with him over $1 million in cash and negotiable securities. He traveled to Italy where he deposited his money in various banks. He brought along his old mother as well, settling her in a luxurious seaside villa near Naples. According to John Landesco, this act made him a hero in the eyes of poor Italian immigrants: "See how Johnnie Torrio takes care of his old mamma; he gives her a villa with fifteen servants."

Capone picked as his headquarters the Hawthorn Inn, a two-story, brown-brick building with white tiles set in its upper façade, not to be confused with the nearby Hawthorn Park Café owned by Eddie Tancl.[47] Capone had bullet-proof steel shutters installed in all the windows. Armed guards watched every entrance. From whom was Capone protecting himself? As the Torrio-Capone outfit had not yet become involved in a bootleggers war, it seems likely that, as with his South Prairie Avenue house, Capone was still worried about Black Handers.

Secure in his new headquarters, Capone turned his attention to local politics. Ed Klovalinka, the proprietor of a soda shop in Cicero, was a small, but rising star in the Cook County Republican Party. He had worked his way from precinct captain to ward leader, and had recently been appointed by Governor

Small as the Republican committeeman from Cicero. Fearing that a Democrat victory in the upcoming mayoral elections would result in the closure of Vogel's lucrative enterprises, Klovinka, on Vogel's advice, decided to ask Capone and the O'Donnells for help. Klovinka approached Capone through Louis La Cava, a Capone gang member friendly with Vogel, and La Cava arranged a meeting with Capone. There were advantages for both sides. If Klovinka held off the Democrat advance, his stock would rise in the Illinois Republican Party. For Capone and the O'Donnells, securing the friendship and gratitude of Republican mayor Joseph Z. Klenha would provide their operations in Cicero with an outer ring of political protection.

Setting to work with his brother Frank, Capone assembled a small army of about two hundred political thugs. Some they borrowed from Ragen's Colts, who had wide experience at electoral terrorism; others were circulation sluggers hired from the O'Banion organization. Already on the eve of the April 1924 election, the forces of the Capone brothers had roughed up the Democrat candidate for town clerk and wrecked his office.

On polling day itself, the armed Klenha forces rolled into town in seven-passenger black limousines. They proceeded to intimidate or slug Democrat voters, kidnap poll watchers, and election officials, even shooting one Democrat campaign worker through the legs and dumping him and eight other Democratic recalcitrants in a basement until the elections were over. When these misdeeds were related to Cook County Judge Jarecki, he called Mayor Dever, asking him to do something. At first Dever responded that there was nothing he could do; Cicero was outside of Chicago's jurisdiction. Yet after a moment's reflection, it occurred to Dever that Cicero was still in Cook County, and, even though there was nothing that he, as mayor of Chicago could do, as a county judge, Jarecki had the authority to deputize a body of citizens to help maintain order anywhere in the county. But how was Jarecki going to find a body of armed deputies at a moment's notice? The obvious solution was to deputize members of the Chicago Police Department.

Dever and Jarecki quickly organized about seventy cops, issuing shotguns to them and dividing them into nine "flivver" squads. Since the cops were acting as citizen deputies, they needed to remove their shields and anything else that would identify them as Chicago police. The flivvers themselves were all unmarked. Though they were led into Cicero by a regular Chicago police car, these flivvers were plain black sedans that looked remarkably like those used by the gangsters, a source of subsequent confusion. The police had been issued descriptions of Al and Frank Capone and told to look out for them. The nine sedans entered Cicero from the East traveling about fifty miles an hour. Speeding down the main street, they recognized Frank Capone, who had just come out of an office building that he intended to rent. The flivver squad screeched to a halt and the police began to jump out. Frank Capone assumed that they were an enemy gang out to shoot him. He reached for his pistol in his back pocket; but before he could draw he was literally riddled with bullets from about forty policemen.

Frank Capone died about at noon on election day. Al and brother Ralph learned of the killing shortly afterwards. The funeral three days later surpassed in splendor even that of Big Jim Colosimo. By noon, the entire Capone house was filled with blossoms from kitchen to attic. By evening, with the floral profusion filling the porch and front terrace, taking up all available space, mourners were forced to drape their wreathes and hanging baskets from the trees and streetlamps up and down the street. Saloonkeepers in Cicero kept their shutters barred and their doors locked for a full two hours. But as the Capone family rode behind the hearse to Mount Olivet Cemetery, the brothers, unshaven to proclaim their grief, at least had the consolation of knowing that Frank had not died in vain; the Klenha ticket had won in Cicero by an enormous majority.

Mayor Klenha now served at Capone's sufferance. Once, when Klenha had failed to do what he had been told, Capone knocked the mayor down the steps of City Hall and kicked him as he struggled to get back onto his feet all in front of a Cicero city cop who was walking by, twirling his nightstick. On another occasion, when the city council seemed about to pass an ordinance that Capone deemed contrary to his interests, his thugs burst into the council chamber, grabbed the council chairman and dragged him out onto the street, clubbing him with their blackjacks.

Vogel came through as well. After the Klenha victory, he helped Capone and the rest of the bootleggers fill Cicero with their resorts. Only Eddie Tancl was dissatisfied. Tancl was an ex-prize-fighter, forced out of the ring and the lightweight championship after he killed another fighter, Young Greenberg, with his deadly knockout punch. He had friends in the Valley gang, however, and eventually settled as manager and owner of the Hawthorn Park Café near the Cicero racetrack at Hawthorn Park. Tancl was by now a respected underworld figure, connected to both the Valley gang and to Ragen's Colts. Klondike and Myles O'Donnell had also started off in the Valley gang. Klondike was old enough to have served in World War I, and was in his late twenties when Prohibition started. He and his younger brother Myles had begun with a string of speakeasies on the west side of the stockyards, extending southwest toward the town of Cicero. Despite the law-abiding inclinations of the town's Bohemian workers, the far south-west was traditional gang territory.

Before the O'Donnell brothers could move into the town, they needed, in classic fashion, to eliminate their predecessors. Billy Clifford, Mike Riley, Cy Cawley, and Tom McElligott were known in Cicero as the "Four Horsemen." Walter Noble Burns suggests that they might have been better named the "Four Hyenas," for they were "cheap skates, small-fry grafters and piker racketeers" who made their living holding up dice games and vice resorts.[48] By 1925, the O'Donnell brothers and their friends seem to have murdered all four of them, along with a number of their associates. With the O'Donnells rising to power, Tancl discovered that he would now be required to buy only O'Donnell beer at O'Donnell prices. Tancl was not happy with this arrangment. Pointing out that he had been in Cicero longer than any of them, Tancl was even inclined to be argumentative. When the O'Donnells began delivering him 'needle beer' (near beer into which pure alcohol had been injected), Tancl refused to have anything more to do with them.

Some sort of truce must have been arranged, for in November 1924, Myles O'Donnell and his friend Jim Doherty were having a long Sunday breakfast in Tancl's Hawthorne Park Café after a Saturday night drinking spree. An argument with the waiter over the check, however, brought Tancl and his bartender, Leo Klimas, over to O'Donnell's table. When O'Donnell threw a punch at the waiter, Tancl stepped in between them. O'Donnell responded by shoving Tancl backwards. Both men then pulled out revolvers and fired simultaneously point-blank into each other's chests. O'Donnell next turned and fired upon the waiter and Klimas, who was coming to disarm him, killing Klimas instantly.

While Myles O'Donnell was busy shooting Klimas, Tancl continued to empty his revolver into O'Donnell's chest. With four slugs in him, O'Donnell turned and lurched out into the street. Stopping just long enough to exchange his empty revolver for a loaded one from behind the bar, Tancl went out after him. Though mortally wounded himself, Tancl managed to stumble after O'Donnell, emptying the second revolver as he went.

About two blocks from the saloon, Tancl at last caught up to O'Donnell, who was collapsing onto the street. With his last reserves of strength, Tancl flung the empty revolver at O'Donnell's head, before collapsing himself only a foot or so away from his intended victim. When the waiter, Marty Simet, ran up to him, Tancl gasped, "Get him. He got me." Simet proceeded to kick the senseless O'Donnell in the head, finally leaving him for dead.[49]

Incredibly, Myles O'Donnell survived, though Tancl did not. The death of Tancl meant that his saloon, the Hawthorne Park Café, was now without a tenant. It had a desirable location in the middle of town. This unexpected demise of the old proprietor forced the landlords to look for a new tenant. Al Capone was happy to take on the lease. By late 1924, wrote Asbury:

> The one-time peaceful streets of downtown Cicero were filled with arrogant, roistering, swaggering gangsters, and crowded with saloons and gambling houses. One hundred and sixty of these places ran full blast day and night, with sidewalk barkers urging passers-by to step in. Among them were the notorious Ship, owned by Capone, and managed by Toots Mondi; the Hawthorn Smoke Shop, owned by Torrio and run by Frankie Pope, where an average of fifty thousand dollars a day was bet on the races; and Lauterback's which operated the largest gambling games in the country, where a hundred thousand dollars in chips frequently risked of a single turn of the roulette wheel. Whiskey sold for seventy-five cents a drink, beer for thirty-five cents a stein, and wine for thirty cents a small glass. Torrio and Capoone owned many of the gambling houses and had shares in others. In every independent resort was posted an agent of the syndicate; his job was to protect the dive and see that Torrio and Capone received their split, which ranged from twenty-five to fifty percent of the gross receipts. The house was also compelled to pay the salary of the agent.[50]

Ralph "Bottles" Capone was put in charge of the Cotton Club, Cicero's version of the famous Harlem nightspot. One thinks of Ade's description of the crowds in the Chicago Levee during the 1890s: "a blaring and glaring and insolent mass held day and night revelry on the very rim of the most highly respectable business section. Everything went, from pitch and toss to manslaughter."[51] Torrio and Al Capone had given Chicago back its honky tonk.

Even if Capone kept his promise and did not introduce prostitutes in Cicero, the town was surrounded by Torrio-Capone brothels. They were more of the syndicates's functional, no-nonsense $2 cribs. In nearby Forest View, popularly known as "Caponeville," however, Torrio opened a sixty-girl brothel. Officially named the Maple Inn, it was better known as the Stockade. An immense old stone and wood structure that had once been an arsenal, The Stockade had a maze of secret chambers behind walls, under floor and above false ceilings where gangsters on the run could hide for weeks and where the girls could be herded in the event of a raid. There were even holes cut in the eyes of the portraits on walls in the gambling rooms, enabling the management to keep tabs on the clientele, a rather kitschy, B-movie touch even in the 1920s.

Forest View had only been incorporated as a town in 1924. Its founders had been World War I veterans and American Legion members. Soon after its incorporation, Al and Ralph Capone asked permission to build a hotel and social club. "I saw no harm," the newly elected police magistrate, John Nosek, later recalled, "because I didn't know just who the Capones were. It looked like a good chance to improve our village." When Nosek realized that a social club meant whores, gamblers and thugs, he ordered the Capones to leave. The next day he ran into Ralph Capone, who told him that if he didn't stop complaining, they would throw him into the village drainage canal. Nosek thought he was joking. The next day two men dragged Nosek over to the village hall. There were seven men waiting for him there. "They told me they were going to kill me. They beat me over the head with the butts of their guns and though I was streaming with blood and dazed from pain they kicked me over the floor. I am not ashamed to admit that I got down on my knees and prayed that they let me keep my life." Nosek had to agree to leave Forest View immediately. Many of the other veterans were forced out soon afterwards.[52] Despite the objections of respectable opinion, the new South Side honky tonk was popular with the roisterers and the gamblers and all those out for a night of whoopee, a not inconsiderable chunk of Chicago's population. Nevertheless, the transformation into a honky tonk could be disconcerting for the former residents.

"TELL THEM SICILIANS TO GO TO HELL"

Apart from the resorts along Roosevelt Road, which, by mutual agreement, were in O'Donnell territory, Cicero was an open city. Neither Torrio nor, later, Capone ever claimed the city.

The older Irish groups like the Valley gang and Ragen's Colts were traditional gangs; they were based on neighborhood associations and youth clubs. With its baseball team, its sponsored events, its politics and its occasional acts of charity, Ragen's Colts resembled the West Side Gophers or even the Eastmans in New York. These gangs were territorial. Local leaders arose to defend their territories against all comers. The mightiest battled their way into the territories of others, playing out an extended game of King of the Castle. Typically, the O'Donnells had shot their way into Cicero. Torrio and Capone, by contrast, had bought their way in. They bought up the leases, installed their roulette wheels and trucked in their beer. The Torrio-Capone outfit was an outgrowth of a vice ring. Neither Torrio nor, to a large extent, Capone were traditional gang leaders; they were criminal entrepreneurs. They were businessmen, and, although neither shrank from violence, violence was not a part of their normal business plan.

Prohibition eventually made the advantages of Torrio's business methods evident even to the most traditional of Irish hooligans. The old Valley gang leader was named Paddy the Bear Ryan. Though this "chubby little man [was] blatant and obscenely profane, full of choler and given to choking rages, he was utterly fearless and of indomitable will." He ran his gang from "a dingy little saloon in South Halstead Street with sawdust on the floor, a slovenly battered old bar, rickety tables with grimy wooden benches beside them. . . ." Paddy the Bear was not a successful entrepreneur, but this hardly mattered. He was a proud warrior chieftain, not a lowly inn-keeper waiting obsequiously upon his customers. His unpretentious saloon on South Halstead was the place where he was king, where, for twenty-five years, he had ruled the roost.

At the beginning of Prohibition, however, Paddy the Bear was murdered by one Walter "the Runt" Quinlan. It was, appropriately enough, over a point of honor. With the death of Paddy the Bear, the Runt went on to open a more luxurious establishment at Seventeenth and Loomis. Here he grew rich selling bootleg beer and rum. It was a favorite hangout of Klondike and Myles O'Donnell. When the police raided the joint, however, they found ten bullet-proof vests, two machine guns and a dozen automatic pistols behind the bar. These and sundry other bits of evidence landed the Runt in the penitentiary, and the Valley gang leadership passed to Terry Druggan and his inseparable companion, Frankie Lake. Druggan finally seems to have seen the light. When he retired at the end of Prohibition, his dinner-service china had his name engraved in gold; his toilet set, all in silver, bore his name as well, a token of gracious living to which even Big Jim Colosimo had not aspired. When not in residence in Chicago, he and Frankie spent their time in their villa in Palm Island, Florida, a short distance away from the vacation home of Capone.[53] During Prohibition, it paid to play by Torrio's rules.

Dion O'Banion had also seen the light. His early career had been one of hooligan, slugger, safe-jacker and free-wheeling desperado. Police Chief Morgan Collins chalked up twenty-five killings, directly or indirectly, to Dion and his friends. Yet, though O'Banion still got a rush from hijacking other bootleggers' trucks or robbing warehouses, he was intelligent enough to see the opportunities for business that Prohibition was opening. Along with Torrio and Capone, and with Druggan, the West Side O'Donnells, and the Saltis-McErlane and Ralph Sheldon gangs, O'Banion had been one of the founding fathers of the gangster republic of Cicero. He had contributed sluggers for the 1924 mayoral elections in Cicero and as payment had been allowed to open his own saloons there. O'Banion persuaded around fifty North Side saloon proprietors who were suffering from the police crackdown in Chicago to relocate in Cicero and by the end of 1924, estimates Pasley, was grossing more than Torrio and Capone. By quintupling his gross receipts in a few short months, however, O'Banion had begun to upset his colleagues. Torrio supposedly offered O'Banion a cut on the Stickney road house in exchange for being cut in on O'Banion's Cicero beer business. "Go peddle your papers, Johnny," Pasley has O'Banion replying.[54]

It might have been wise for O'Banion to show more caution. But this was never O'Banion's way. He further aggravated Torrio by setting him up over the sale of the Sieben Brewery. One of Chicago's largest breweries during Prohibition, the Sieben brewery was located in O'Banion territory on the North Side. Though jointly owned by Torrio, Capone, and O'Banion, its day-to-day management fell to the O'Banion gang. In May 1924, claiming that he wanted to retire with his wife to Louis Alterie's Colorado ranch, O'Banion offered to sell his share to Torrio. Delighted at the idea of finally getting rid of the Irish maniac, Torrio accepted the offer, agreeing to pay O'Banion the half million dollars he was asking.

What O'Banion neglected to tell Torrio was that the Sieben Brewery was likely to be a worthless investment. O'Banion had a network of friends throughout the police and State Attorney's office, and knew ahead of time that the brewery was about to be busted. He had even been told the date of the forthcoming raid—May 19. He told Torrio and Capone to be sure to be at the brewery on the morning of the 19th, in order, he said, to turn their new property over to them and help them expedite their first shipment.

It all took place as O'Banion had foreseen. When the police arrived, the brewery's new owner, Johnnie Torrio, happened to be standing beside thirteen fully-loaded beer trucks talking with the drivers and some precinct cops. A more compromising scene could hardly be imagined. O'Banion was arrested too. Too allay suspicion, he had even brought along Hymie Weiss and Louis Alterie, who were both arrested with him. Still, it was evident that, having just divested himself of the property, O'Banion risked little—a fine at most, which he could peel off the top of the half million dollars Torrio had just given him. Torrio by contrast not only risked his entire investment, he risked serious trouble with the law. He had been fined $2,000 the year before for manufacturing alcohol. Now, as a second offence, Torrio risked a much heavier penalty. Indeed, Torrio later spent nine months in prison as a consequence of the raid. As Torrio learned from his own sources that O'Banion had played him for a fool, his patience with the charming little psychopath grew thinner.

In the end, however, the real instrument of O'Banion's downfall was neither the South Side gangs nor the Torrio-Capone syndicate, but the terrible Gennas. O'Banion had already complained to Torrio that the Gennas were invading his territory with their rot-gut alcohol. The charge was probably true, and Torrio may even have remonstrated with the six brothers over it. There was little that he, or perhaps even the Gennas, could do about it, though. It was simple fact of Prohibition economics that while the Gennas could unload their home-made concoction for as little as $3 per bottle and still make a profit, it was hard for O'Banion to sell his stuff for less that $12 a bottle uncut. Of course, O'Banion was peddling real whiskey and charging accordingly. Anyone who wanted whiskey was well advised to pay O'Banion's prices or simply do without.

Failing to get much satisfaction from Torrio, O'Banion took matters into his own hands; he began to hijack Genna shipments. Had the Gennas followed the tacit rules of engagement in the beer war up to now, they would have responded by hijacking some of O'Banion's own shipments, maybe shooting his drivers in the back of their necks. But the Gennas were Sicilians and not inclined to engage in such puerile foreplay. O'Banion had committed a *sgarro*. At first, Torrio preached restraint; but Torrio's own patience had about run out. The only thing holding the Gennas back was Mike Merlo, the highly respected president of the *Unione Siciliana* after the death of Antonio D'Andrea. Merlo had known O'Banion for years and got along well with him. Merlo was also perceptive enough to understand that a war between the Gennas and the O'Banion gang was sure to be costly and bloody for both sides. As long as Merlo remained in control, O'Banion's life was safe from Sicilian vengeance. But when Merlo succumbed to cancer in November 1924, the last restraint was lifted.

O'Banion had left his job in the Chicago's *Herald-Examiner*'s circulation department in 1920. Since he still needed the cover of a legitimate occupation, he bought an interest in Schofield's flower shop, just opposite the Holy Name Cathedral where he had sung as a boy. There he could be found from nine in the morning to six in the evening, most days, clipping roses and daisies and arranging wreathes and floral bouquets, a sprig of white lily-of-the-valley in his buttonhole.

Dion loved his job. He had a rare ability to lose himself entirely in whatever he did. His wife said that he used to spend his evenings in his slippers, happily fooling with the radio or monkeying around with the player piano. His ambition was always to make the two machines play together. He brought this child-like quality of self-absorption into floral arranging, for which he showed a surprising talent. It was his ability to be so centered, so cheerfully focused, so natural and at-ease with himself in each of the disparate roles he played, that delighted his friends and unnerved his enemies.

On November 3, O'Banion, Weiss, and Drucci went to Torrio's Ship in Cicero, in which they now had one-third interest. As Torrio was handing

O'Banion his cut, Capone remarked that Angelo Genna had lost heavily at the roulette wheel, leaving markers behind for $30,000. Capone suggested that in the interests of peace, O'Banion might agree to cancel the debt. Instead, O'Banion sprang up to telephone Genna, telling him he had one week to pay up. Even Hymie Weiss was taken aback. What was the point of needlessly sowing ill-feeling?

O'Banion shot back, "Tell them Sicilians to go to hell."

A week later, O'Banion received a call at Schofield's shop. It was from city sealer, Carmin Vasco and James Genna, and they were calling to order $750 worth of wreaths for Mike Merlo's funeral. Totally taken up in his floral arrangements, O'Banion jotted down the order, promising the caller that it would be ready when they dropped by the next morning. The next morning found O'Banion hard at work finishing up the orders for the Merlo funeral when the shop bell rang. William Crutchfield, the black janitor described the man he saw enter as "tall, well-built, well-dressed, smooth-shaven." He "wore a brown overcoat and brown Fedora hat." He was accompanied by two Italians, "short, stocky and rather rough looking."

O'Banion came forward from the back room, his left hand gripping a pair of flower shears, his right hand extended in greeting, "Hello, boys," he said. "You want Merlo's flowers?"

"Yeah," said the tall man smiling pleasantly, stepping forward and clasping O'Banion's right hand. Instead of letting go, the tall man yanked O'Banion off-balance, pinioning his arms. Before he could drop the flower shears and reach for one of his pistols with his left hand, the two Italians pumped six revolver shots into him. Two passed through his chest, one through his cheek; two more passed through his larynx. A final shot, the *coup de grace* perhaps administered by the tall man, passed through his brain. O'Banion expired on a blanket of white peonies for the Merlo funeral.

THE O'BANIONITES WADE IN

Big Jim Colosimo's funeral and that of Mike Merlo were bigger and more lavish, for these men were almost public figures. But Deany's funeral had its own special intensity.

The day before, when a special railway express car pulled in from Pennsylvania carrying Deany's specially-ordered casket, crowds were already jamming the railway station. They later jammed in front of the undertaker's window, causing traffic on North Wells Street where Sbarbaro's Undertaking Establishment was located, to back up. When these onlookers were finally admitted, what they beheld was the corpse of the fallen chieftain enclosed in a magnificent silver-bronze tomb with four posts of embossed silver at the corners. The tomb was guarded at its head and foot by silver angels, wings folded and heads bowed in grief, bearing aloft massive, solid-gold candelabras whose flickering light illuminated the dignified gold plaque on the side of the casket that declared simply: "Dion O'Banion, 1892–1924." Behind the angel at the head of the casket, dwarfed by a mountain of fragrant, white lilies glowing in the candlelight, sat the diminutive figure of O'Banion's young widow, veiled and dressed in black, supported on either side by Dion's mother and father. Behind them swelled the sounds of the Chicago Symphony Orchestra, tactfully hidden in a near-by room.

A long procession slowly wound its way past the casket to pay a last homage to the fallen leader. Women in furs and silks dropped orchids into the bier, next to blue-jawed men with well-cut suits and darting eyes. Women in black shawls fell to their knees in prayer before the casket; little girls in tattered dresses, their eyes big in wonder and fear, held candles in their moist hands. There were ragamuffins from Little Hell, newsboys who clutched their newspapers under their left arm as they made the sign of the cross with their right hand, and old beggars who hobbled past on canes and crutches. These had been the recipients of O'Banion's bouts of generosity. They filed past now, craning their necks, standing on tiptoe, determined to catch one last glimpse of their chieftain, visible behind the heavy plate-glass of the casket. He lay in state on a couch of tufted white satin while his left hand stretched out languidly on a special cushion.

But who were O'Banion's people? The Church wanted no part of him: "O'Banion was a notorious criminal," explained a priest from his arch-diocese. "The Church did not recognize him in his days of lawlessness and when he died unrepentant in his iniquities he had no claim to last rites for the dead." These were hard words. Still, at the last moment, after O'Banion's coffin had been lowered into the unconsecrated soil and as the gravediggers were shoveling dirt upon his coffin, Father Malloy, who had known Deany as a choirboy at the Holy Name Cathedral, stepped forward and, defying the ecclesiastical hierarchy, pronounced a Latin prayer followed by Hail Marys and a prayer in English to which the crowd of mourners responded "Amen."

During the service, Hymie Weiss and Louis Alterie were said to have "cried as women might," and Alterie later issued a challenge. If only he had a chance to fight it out with the guys who killed Deany, he told the newspapers, "I would die smiling." "I'd shoot it out with the gang of killers before the sun rose in the morning," he continued melodramatically, "and some of us, maybe all of us, would be lying on the slabs in the undertakers place."

This comment provoked Mayor Dever to issue a declaration of his own, couched in his inimitable rhetorical style. "Are we still abiding by the code of the Dark Ages?" he asked; "Or is this Chicago, a unit of an American Commonwealth?" He announced another crackdown; the police were to disarm the gangsters and jail them or drive them out of town. Instead, the O'Banion killing propelled the Chicago Beer War into a more vicious phase.

Who was fighting whom now? Alterie was an Italian, and so was Schemer Drucci. O'Banion's pallbearers were Weiss, Bugs Moran, Drucci, Alterie, Max Eisen, and Frank Gusenberg. The only friend missing was Nails Morton, who had been killed in a riding accident. It was a collection of Poles, Italians, and Jews. The only Irishman in O'Banion's gang was O'Banion himself.

Nor was the killing even a Torrio-Capone hit. Dion O'Banion's killers were never officially identified. Even so, rumors of their identities spread quickly. According to Walter Noble Burns, writing in 1931:

> According to information gathered by the O'Bannion [sic] leaders, and doubtless authentic, the murder was planned by Torrio and Capone, and the active participants were Angelo and Mike Genna, John Scalisi, and Albert Anselmi. Angelo Genna was the driver of the death car. Mike Genna was the man who shook hands with O'Bannion in the flower shop. Scalisi and Anselmi did the shooting, Scalisi being credited with having fired the final grace shot. Scalisi and Anselmi were said to have been paid $10,000 apiece, and each, it was declared, was presented with a four-carat diamond ring costing $3,000 as a bonus for work well done. Anselmi was said to have sent his ring home to Sicily. When these two precious villains finally fell into the hands of the police, Scalisi was still wearing his ring on a gnarled finger, the headlight solitaire as brilliant as the murderous sparkle of an automatic gun.[55]

Though Torrio and Capone were probably in on it, the murder was a Genna hit. When the Gennas presented Scalisi and Anselmi with their diamond rings it was more than just a pat on the back; it was a public declaration. The Genna family had killed Dion O'Banion and they wanted the rest of the world to know it. The Chicago police also tried to connect Frankie Yale with the murder. Yale had been in town for Merlo's funeral, and had even stopped by to order a two-thousand-dollar wreath at Schofield's. The Cook County coroner's certificate, not issued until years later, read; "Slayers not apprehended. John Scalisi and Albert Anselmi and Frank Yale were suspected, but never brought to trial."[56]

Torrio and Capone attended O'Banion's funeral. Though each had contributed a costly wreath—Torrio had spent $10,000 while Capone, as befitted the second-in-command, has spent $8,000—they wisely kept to themselves. The Genna family was not in attendance. Torrio left for the South almost immediately afterwards, leaving Capone in charge once again. It was a role he loved. Big Al craved celebrity as much as Torrio sought to avoid it. He could seldom resist shooting off his mouth to the press:

> Deany was all right, and he was getting along to begin with better than he had any right to expect. But like everyone else his head got away from his hat. Johnnie Torrio had taught O'Banion all he knew and then O'Banion grabbed some of the best guys we had and decided to be boss of the booze racket in Chicago. What a chance! O'Banion had a swell route to make it tough for us, and he did. His job was to smooth the coppers and we gave him a lot of authority with the booze and beer buyers. When he broke away, for a while it wasn't so good. He knew the ropes and got running us ragged. It was his funeral.[57]

It may not have been wise for Capone to have tried to explain all this to the eager reporters. He might have been wiser to limit himself to expressing his condolences to O'Banion's widow. For by indicating that O'Banion's un-businessman-like shenanigans were running his syndicate ragged, he was also implying that he derived a certain moral satisfaction from O'Banion untimely demise. Those who wished might even infer a certain complicity in the death itself. This certainly seems to have been what the O'Banionites believed. After Deany's death, the atmosphere of jolly free-for-all that had characterized the Chicago Beer War up to now evaporated.

After Deany's death, leadership of the O'Banionites passed to his second-in-command, his boyhood friend Hymie Weiss, a Polish Catholic with finely-cut features and intense dark eyes, whose birth name was Earl Wajciechowski. Weiss started right to work.

When in Cicero, Capone usually ate at Tony the Greek's restaurant above Frankie Pope's. Tony Anton was no gangster, nothing more than a restaurant owner; but he cooked honest food and idolized Al, treating him like royalty. Tony the Greek liked to tell the story of the ragged newsboy who walked in to sell his papers one winter's night when the wind was pounding the sleet against his window panes. "How many you got left, kid?" Capone had asked him. "About fifty, I guess," the boy had replied. Capone fished in his pocket and pulled out a twenty-dollar bill; "Throw them on the floor and run along home to your mother." On a similar winter's night at the beginning of January in 1925, Tony was sitting in a booth chatting with Al. The doorbell rang, and he went off to greet the new customers. He never came back. The next day it was reported in the papers that his body was recovered in quicklime. Weiss was hitting Capone where it hurt most, murdering people guilty of nothing more than being his friends. It was said that when Capone heard the news, he sat down in the booth where he and Tony had been talking and burst into tears.

The next to be targeted was Capone himself. Traveling in his limousine, he was just stepping out to enter a restaurant at State and Fifty-fifth streets in Chicago. His two bodyguards and driver were still in the car. At that moment, another black limousine pulled up alongside them. Leaning out the windows, its occupants — Weiss, Drucci, and Moran — raked the car with automatics and sawed-off shotguns. The two bodyguards flattened themselves on the floor and escaped injury; but Capone's chauffeur, Silvester Barton, was hit in the back.

The attack reduced Capone's car to scrap metal, and he responded by ordering a seven-ton, custom-built Cadillac. He had it equipped with a steel, armor-plated body, a steel-hooded gas tank, the bulletproof glass on the armored car side windows was an inch thick while the front windshield was an inch and one-half thick with gun compartments in the back. The back window was removable, enabling the occupants of the backseat to fire at cars pursuing them. Later, Capone's armored car was inherited by J. Edgar Hoover, a man who, if not exactly a Capone admirer, was at least someone who respected him professionally. Capone now adopted the practice of traveling in convoy — a scout car ahead and touring car full of sharpshooters behind. To avoid the risk of sniper attacks, he adopted the convoy system even when traveling no farther than a block.

With Silvester Barton in the hospital, Capone hired Tommy Cuirnigione as his temporary chauffeur. He quickly disappeared like Tony the Greek. A month later, in mid-February, two boys noticed that their horse refused to drink from the usual cistern. They told a patrolman who, leaning over the edge, thought he sniffed a rotten smell. Eventually the patrolman and the two boys fished the decomposing body of Cuirnigione out of the cistern. They had evidently tortured Cuirnigione, for his body was covered with cigarette burns. Then they put five slugs in his head and, putting a concrete slab against his belly and wiring his wrists tightly to his ankles to hold it in place, dumped his body into the cistern.

In mid-January 1925, Torrio and his wife returned from their trip in time for Johnnie to stand trial in the Sieben Brewery case. Calculating perhaps that, for the moment, he was safer in prison than on the streets of Chicago, Torrio had decided to plead guilty. Before announcing his nine-months sentence, Federal Judge Adam Cliff allowed Torrio five days to settle his affairs.

Torrio spent the first day with his wife shopping on Michigan Avenue. By the time their chauffeur, Robert Barton, the brother of Silvester, had driven them back to their apartment, it was dusk, and no one noticed the big black Cadillac limousine with no license plates and with its curtains drawn that was waiting on the corner. Torrio helped Barton unload the parcels from the trunk, piling them into Ann's outstretched arms. Ann Torrio was so laden with parcels that, as she approached the front door of the apartment building, she had to turn around to push the door open with her back. In this way it was Ann Torrio who first saw that the black Cadillac that had been parked by the corner was now moving slowly towards them. She noticed too that its curtains were being drawn back and that the men inside the car were armed. Too petrified to scream, she failed to warn her husband who, walking with Barton toward the building, was facing in the wrong direction. Thus Torrio had no idea of the ambush until he felt the bullets in his chest and jaw.

Instinctively, Torrio crouched and started to run. But the bullet to the chest had spun him around, and another pair of bullets hit him in the right arm and in the groin. He fell to the ground. Another bullet hit Barton just below the right knee. These bullets had been fired by two men who had jumped out of the car with automatic pistols. Two more men remained in the Cadillac, firing shotgun blasts into Torrio's car, smashing the windows. One of the men with the automatic pistols walked up to Torrio to deal him the *coup de grâce*. He put the gun against Torrio's temple, but when he pulled the trigger, the gun simply went 'click.' He was out of ammunition. He started to reload, but at that moment, the Cadillac driver beeped his horn. He turned and ran back to the car, which sped away. A witness later identified the man as Bugs Moran.

Torrio was sped by ambulance to Jackson Park Hospital. Capone was at his bedside within an hour. He had Torrio moved to a windowless room on the top floor, and posted his own bodyguards to supplement those of the police. During the night the nursing superintendent noticed three carloads of armed men circling the hospital building. She called the police who sent a party of squad cars to disperse the would-be assailants. The police offered to arrest the surviving O'Banionites and bring them in front of Torrio so he could identify, but Torrio told them to forget about it. Speaking with difficulty through his shattered jaw, he told them, "I won't rap any of them. I wouldn't lay the finger, not even on the guilty man." When the police asked Torrio if he knew who shot him, he replied, "Sure I know them."

The police knew them too. Even if they hadn't had witnesses who picked out Moran and, later, Weiss as the men with the automatic pistols and Gusenberg as the driver behind the wheel, the police would have figured it out anyway. "I was sure all along," said Captain William Schoemaker, "that the men who shot Torrio were not Italians. If Italians had tried to kill Torrio, they would have killed him and made sure of the job by stepping up to him after he had fallen and blowing out his brains." It was surely a bad sign for the O'Banionites that even the Chicago police were now labeling them as bunglers.[58]

Police Captain Schoemaker's assertions notwithstanding, recent authors have wondered whether Italians really were entirely extraneous to the attempt on Torrio's life. According to Allsop, Moran may have been one of the gunmen, but the hit itself had been ordered by a group in the Chicago *Unione Siciliana* opposed to Torrio—the Aiello family.

The O'Banionites fared better against the Gennas themselves. Except for the Maxwell Street Police Station, which they owned, the Gennas were never popular with the Chicago police. None of the Sicilian gangs were. They were too clannish and too violent. Angelo Genna had a long string of suspected assassinations behind him, usually involving *Unione Siciliana* business. Nor were the police happy when, following the death of Merlo, Genna simply took over as the *Unione* president. It looked like more trouble to come.

Soon after assuming the presidency of the *Unione*, Genna married. In May 1925, the young couple had found a suburban bungalow that appealed to them. On the morning of the 25th, Angelo climbed into his rakish roadster with cash in his pocket for the down payment. As he drove down Ogden Avenue, a touring car shot out of a side street and began to pursue him. Behind the wheel, according to the police reconstruction, was Frank Gusenberg; in the backseat were Weiss, Drucci and Moran with sawed-off shotguns. Taken by surprise, Genna pressed down on the accelerator. But he misjudged a curve and swerved into a lamppost on Hudson Street. As he struggled to free his car, the touring car came up and slowed to a walking pace. All three gunmen emptied their barrels into the driver's seat window. Genna was buried in an unconsecrated plot in Mount Carmel Cemetery, a few steps away from O'Banion's grave. As a final gesture of defiance, the Genna family made sure that Angelo's casket cost a thousand dollars more than O'Banion's.

With Bloody Angelo taken care of, the O'Banionites turned to Deany's actual killers—Scalise, Anselmi and Mike Genna. They allowed themselves to believe they had come to an arrangement with another *Unione Siciliana* gangster, a foppish musician named Samoots Amatuna, to put the Gennas on the spot. But Amatuna informed Mike Genna, who, with Scalise and Anselmi, snuck up and ambushed them instead. Moran and Drucci were sitting in their car waiting for their intended victims to show up, when Mike Genna's car appeared from nowhere spraying the would-be assassins with a fusillade of sawed-off shotgun blasts. Moran and Drucci were both wounded.

Shortly thereafter, however, as Genna, Scalise, and Anselmi were bowling south down Western Avenue, they noticed that they themselves were being followed by a squad car ringing its gong. Believing perhaps that they had successfully murdered Weiss or Drucci, and not wishing to be caught with recently fired shotguns in their car, the trio tried to flee. In reality, the four policemen in the squad car had no idea about the earlier shooting. Angry about another shooting a week before in which three of their brother officers had been murdered, they had recognized Mike Genna at the wheel of his car and decided to harass him.

Speeding at about seventy-five miles an hour, the two cars careened down Western Avenue for about twelve blocks before the inevitable crash occurred. A loaded truck pulled out in front of the Genna vehicle at Fifty-ninth Street, and, trying desperately to avoid a collision, Mike Genna sent his car into a spin. He crashed it into a telephone pole and his car came to a dead stop with the police car coming to a screeching halt a few yards away.

Knowing nothing about the ambush shortly before, and not understanding why Genna had attempted to flee, Detective Michael J. Conway stepped out and strode towards the wreck.

"What the hell," he shouted out angrily, "Why didn't you fellows stop? Didn't you hear the gong?"

To police eyes, they were arriving at an accident scene. Their instinct was to run to the car and see if anyone was hurt. The last thing they expected was to be greeted by sawed-off shotgun blasts. Scalise's first blast hit Detective Charles B. Walsh in the chest, tearing away the entire left side of his face. It sent him spinning to the pavement. Before the other detectives could even register what was happening, Scalise unloaded his other barrel square into Detective Harold F. Olson as he emerged from the squad car. The range was perfect for a sawed-off shotgun, and both detectives were dead by the time they hit the ground. Neither had time to pull out their revolvers.

Closest of all to the wrecked vehicle, Conway looked aghast into the eyes of Mike Genna as he sat in the driver's seat and drew out his pistol. Conway started to pull out his own weapon, but Genna got there first, plugging Conway before he could get off a shot. Conway plunged forward, falling in front of the Genna car. The only detective left standing was William Sweeney, who, seeing Conway fall, ran around the squad car and began to fire over its roof. Sweeney's volley sent Genna, Scalise and Anselmi sprawling out from the other side of their own car. The entire battle had not lasted more than thirty seconds.

There now followed a eerie silence. Sweeney, behind the squad car, had emptied his revolver. The three Sicilians crouching behind the twisted wreck of their car had not fired a further shot. Perhaps the enormity of what they had just done was beginning to dawn on them—two police officers murdered, one seriously, perhaps fatally, wounded. Around the silence like the eye of a hurricane, a pandemonium was beginning to grow. People poured out of the surrounding shops, garages and factories or leaned out of upper-story windows. Hoping to keep them pinned down until reinforcements arrived, Sweeney reached out and snagged Olson's dropped revolver. As he did so, the Sicilians decided to run. They had seen a weed-filled vacant lot with an alley on the other side, and decided to make for it.

They had not gone more than twenty yards when Sweeney saw them running, Mike Genna striding ahead, Scalise and Anselmi lagging behind, all with shotguns under their arms. Sweeney took out after them. He might easily have caught either Scalise or Anselmi, for they were slow runners; but it was Mike Genna that the four police detectives had recognized and Mike Genna that Sweeney had seen shoot Conway. So, when Scalise and Anselmi wheeled off to their left, Sweeney let them go; it was Mike Genna that he wanted.

Sweeney chased Genna into an alleyway where, suddenly, Genna stopped. He swung around and leveled own shotgun at Sweeney, who was coming up behind him. It may have been just a ruse, for Genna ought to have known that his shotgun was empty. He may have been hoping that Sweeney would turn and flee. Then he heard the hammer clicking harmlessly. Perhaps Mike Genna really had forgotten that his shotgun was empty. The chase was on again.

As he ran, Sweeney had fired several revolver shots at the fleeing Genna as well, though all had missed. He chased Genna through suburban back yards and under clotheslines. He chased him as Genna darted through an open gate at the end of an alley only to find himself charging up the porch steps towards the back door of the house of a certain Mrs. Eleanor Knoblauch. When he realized where he was headed, Genna stopped. He stood still an instant before Mrs. Knoblauch's back door, not knowing which way to go, before he turned and began to race down the steps again to dart off in another direction. It was just long enough to give Sweeney one clear shot. It pierced Genna's left leg eight inches above the knee, nicking an artery. Clutching the wound, Genna rolled off the porch steps. He landed on the grass beside the darkened window to Mrs. Knoblauch's basement. Smashing the glass with the butt of his shotgun, he dived in.

Sweeney stood panting on the back lawn. The bullet that he had sent into Genna's left leg had been his last. As impulsively brave as he had been up until now, the unarmed Sweeney was not about to silhouette himself by crawling through the window into the pitch dark basement when he knew that Mike Genna was probably lying there with several bullets left in his own revolver. Fortunately, reinforcements had begun to arrive. In the company of two other police officers, Sweeney entered the basement through the kitchen. The found Genna lying in a pool of blood, his empty shotgun beside him. As the policeman entered, Genna tried feebly to lift his blue-steel Spanish revolver. But before he could even level his gun, he fainted. He came to momentarily as the ambulance guards were carrying him out in a stretcher. As a medic leaned over to make him more comfortable, Mike's eyes popped open, and he snarled out his dying words; "Take that, you blue-coated bastard," giving the surprised medic a vicious kick. He was dead before the ambulance had traveled a dozen blocks.

Drucci was badly enough wounded in the Genna ambush to spend some time in the hospital; so it is possible that it took some days before he was in any condition to savour the news of Mike Genna's death. When they finally heard, it must have been a consolation to the boy, lying there in a bed of pain and suffering. Still, the thought that the gang had bungled another assassination must have rankled. Had they used this stretch of involuntary repose to think things out calmly and rationally, they might well have concluded that now would be a good time to put away the shotguns for a while. Their victory, such that it was, owed nothing to their own intrigues and designs, and everything to the courage and determination of the fleet-footed Detective Sweeney.

Samoots Amatuna was now on Weiss, Moran, and Drucci's hit list. He had double-crossed them, pretending to betray Mike Genna but had set them up instead. In November 1925, Amatuna found himself in Isadore Paul's barber shop on West Roosevelt Road. He had dropped by to get himself sleeked up for a performance of *Aïda* that evening. Dressed in opera attire with tickets in his pocket for himself and his fiancée, Rose Pecoraro, the sister-in-law of the late Mike Merlo, Amatuna was sitting in the barber's chair, loudly humming Verdi's "Victory March." Two men, coming in from the street, walked up and pulled out revolvers.

Seeing them come, Amatuna vaulted behind the chair, using it as a shield to hide behind. The first assailant, a skinny, young Italian-looking guy, proceeded to fire four shots straight into the back of the chair. The predictable effect of this display of marksmanship was to put four holes into a perfectly good barber's chair. A momentary silence followed while the second assailant looked perplexed at his colleague as he stood there, feet planted, gun arm outstretched, staring defiantly ahead. What did he want to go and murder the barber chair for? Then, with a puzzled shake of his head, the second assailant walked around behind the chair where he found the shaking, but otherwise unharmed, Amatuna cowering in his evening dress, and dispatched him with three quick shots to the body and a mortal shot to the neck that passed next to the spinal cord.

When the police arrived shortly thereafter, they quickly identified the first assailant. Even without the eye-witnesses, they immediately recognized this as the bungled work of Drucci. They were less sure about the second man. He was a taller guy and probably not Italian. According to gangland rumor, however, he was Myles O'Donnell's pal, Jim Doherty.

Angelo and Mike had been the Genna family's warriors. With their elimination, the Genna family was no longer a threat to anyone. The leading figure in the Genna's business operations, older brother Jim, fled to Rome shortly after Mike's death. The family's *consigliere*, Tony the Gentleman Genna, a peaceful, scholarly man more interested in architecture, music, and philanthropic projects in Little Sicily than in the Beer War, was gunned down a month later. By the early summer of 1925, the terrible Gennas were no more.

THE MCSWIGGEN KILLING

Historically, the Chicago underworld was more closely connected to the Democrats than to the Republicans. It was, as John Landesco observed, largely a matter of geography. The wards on the city's eastern side fronted Lake Michigan; here were neighborhoods with a prosperous, middle-class population and with a relatively low rate of crime. The wards in the western half, the river wards, were the city's first slum area, and they were later the zones into which the immigrants poured. They were poorer with higher rates of crime. These were also the areas where corrupt, Democrat ward bosses like Johnny Power, ruled and where the street gangs had emerged. From the 1870s until World War I, the river wards consistently voted Democrat.

By the advent of Prohibition, however, these older divisions had begun to break down. Diamond Joe Esposito was an early follower of Republican Senator Charles Deneen. In 1915, piqued by Carter Harrison Jr.'s closure of the Levee, Big Jim Colosimo announced his support for Republican William Hale "Big Bill" Thompson, and discovered, perhaps as a consequence, that he was permitted to operate his Colosimo Café with little police interference. The exodus of Southern blacks to Chicago further complicated the political balance in the river wards. Especially after the 1919 race riot, these blacks were little disposed to support corrupt, Democrat ward bosses and their hooligan minions. Nevertheless, Landesco observed that remnants of the old Democrat ward machines could still exercise power locally, and used their influence on behalf of the bootlegging gangs. The Saltis-McErlane gang had the support of the labor racketeer and ward politician "Big Tim" Murphy. Murphy had also befriended Colosimo and Torrio, and until he was murdered in 1928, helped look after Capone's interests.[59]

Until 1924, O'Banion had helped keep the Forty-second and Forty-third wards on the North Side solidly Democrat. A common gag at the time was: "Who will carry the Forty-second Ward? O'Banion in his pistol pocket." In late 1924, however, there were rumors that O'Banion was about to switch sides. Alarmed, a group of prominent Chicago Democrats banded together to offer him a testimonial banquet. The gala event was held in the private dining-room of the Webster Hotel, and included, aside from the O'Banion gang, the Democrat candidate for the U.S. Senate; former state's attorney Colonel Albert A. Sprague; along with Democrat notable and mayoral candidate Robert M. Schweitzer. Also present were Chief of Detectives Michael Hughes and Police Lieutenant Charles Egan. Mayor Dever was not present. He had certainly neither been invited nor informed, for the banquet was effectively a plot against him. When he heard about it, he immediately demanded an explanation from Chief of Detectives Hughes, who lamely tried to explain that the moment he noticed the O'Banion gang present at the ceremonies, he had withdrawn. The explanation was not very convincing; Hughes must have known that the party was being held in O'Banion's honor. Anxious to ingratiate themselves with the notorious gang leader, the Democrats presented him with a platinum watch set with rubies and diamonds. Nor was it the last of these "Belshazzar feasts," as a clergyman dubbed them. The plain fact was that the Schweitzer and Sprague wing of the Chicago Democrat Party was running scared.[60]

Mayor Dever, curiously enough, was a wet. Six months into his term, he had told a German audience that he wished Chicagoans could have "good, wholesome beer at a moderate price." What he did not want, he went on, was poison. "The poison," he said, "had found its way into our body politic. It has worked its way into our city, county and state governments."[61] It was something of a mixed metaphor, one that had perplexed the city's voters. What did Dever mean by praising good beer while condemning poison? By late 1924, it was clear that what it meant was no beer and a police crackdown. This is not what many of the voters had wanted. Currents within the Chicago Democrat Party were clearly considering a change of course.

Rumors of dissension in the Democrats' ranks were music to Republican ears. Dever was looking vulnerable in the up-coming 1927 mayoral elections. Robert Crowe had split with Thompson at the beginning of 1923, criticizing his lack of zeal in crime enforcement. As state's attorney, Crowe was well-positioned to lead a law-and-order crusade, and newspapers were suggesting that Crowe might be a strong Republican mayoral candidate. Nevertheless, there was a major blot on Crowe's political horizons: the state's attorney's office had been batting next to zero.

The Chicago police and the federal dry agents had certain successes to their credit. One of Dever's first acts was to close down the inter-racial black-and-tans on the Far South Side, where incidents of "soul kissing" had been reported. "These places are vile to the last degree," Dever had complained. By November 1923, Dever had revoked the licenses of sixteen hundred businesses accused of Prohibition violations, and the police had raided and closed down around four thousand saloons. They had smashed and torched The Stockade. By 1926, an estimated nineteen thousand speakeasies had been forced out of business. The police had begun to kick over the tenement stills in Little Italy; they had busted scores of corrupt police officers; they had filled the prisons with prohibition-law violators, unfortunately killing a few by-standers in the crossfire. What they had not done was to nail any of the big shots—gang leaders, bootleggers or complicit suppliers. Nor had they stemmed the tide of booze and beer.[62]

In the Spring of 1924, Dever ordered a raid at Capone's offices on South Michigan Avenue. Here they found Jake Guzik's ledgers, complete with names of hotels, restaurants, and speakeasies, Canadian and Caribbean suppliers, brewery owners, bordello and gambling houses. There were lists of police and municipal officials on the Torrio-Capone payroll—a complete financial breakdown of the Torrio-Capone syndicate. "We've got the goods now!" Dever declared jubilantly. Yet before the ledgers could be studied, the state's attorney's office decided that, as there had been no search warrant, the material had been illegally seized. Municipal judge, Howard Hayes impounded the ledgers and returned them to Torrio.

The police owed their arrest of Torrio at the Sieben Brewery more to O'Banion's wry sense of humor than to their own efforts. Torrio was given a $5,000 fine and a nine-month prison sentence. Had he been given the maximum, he would have served five years. The sheriff of at the Lake County Jail in Waukegan let him furnish his cell with throw rugs, a radio, a gramophone, wall pictures, and a brass bed with a comfortable mattress. The sheriff allowed Torrio to hold business conferences in his cell or on the sheriff's front porch. Torrio either ate at the sheriff's home or had his meals brought in. The sheriff also installed bullet-proof steel-mesh blinds in the windows of Torrio's cell. This last measure was at least defensible; the real threats to Torrio were not coming from the law. Still, compared to some others, Torrio was serving hard time. Failing to nail them on anything more serious, Cook County magistrates had sentenced Terry Druggan and Frankie Lane to one year for contempt of court. Druggan spent most of his evenings with his wife in their Gold Coast apartment; Lane stayed with his mistress on North State Parkway. They were allowed out for meals, entertainment, shopping, and golf.[63] Mayor Dever may have been serious about his anti-bootlegging crusade; yet there were plenty of magistrates, sheriffs, prohibition agents, and police officials in Chicago who regarded Prohibition as, at best, a sham, and, at worse, a nice way to make some extra money.

Worse, from the perspective of the state's attorney's office, the failure to stem the tides of beer and booze had been the failure to stem the tides of blood and crime. Like Mayor Dever, State's Attorney Crowe was a wet who believed in law enforcement. Yet here the similarities ended, for though Crowe assented to the principle that state officials had a duty to enforce the statutes, he agreed with Chief Fitzmorris that the Volstead Act was unenforceable. Eighty percent of the population of Cook County was wet, he proclaimed, and this included most judges and jurors. Like Fitzmorris, Crowe was concerned that Prohibition was spreading corruption and crime. He had little patience with Dever's vacuous pronouncements about the war against the bootleggers being won.

He was particularly annoyed at the "wordy war" between Dever and United States District Attorney Edwin A. Olson, each claiming credit for drying up Chicago. The fact of the matter, he repeated, was that Chicago was not dry, nor likely to become so. Dever's obsession with the war against bootleggers meant that criminals were literally getting away with murder. Elected as a wet who was willing to get tough on law-breakers, Crowe promised to ignore the beer drinkers and concentrate on real criminals. "Bring 'em in, and I'll prosecute 'em," had been his message to the police. Yet, though each major gangland killing, from Jerry O'Connor onwards, seemed to ratchet the level of violence a notch higher, the state's attorney seemed paralyzed. None of these killing was ever solved. There were few arrests and no convictions.

A month after the Cicero elections, a free-lance hijacker named Joe Howard had slapped and kicked Jake Guzik, who ran to Capone to complain. "I don't see why they call me a hoodlum," Guzik once complained, "I have never carried a gun in my life." Indeed, Guzik was never more than a whoremaster and an accountant. A short little man shaped like a penguin, Guzik had jowls that hung over his shirtcollar like dewlaps. The watery little eyes set back in their sockets and the pouting lips gave Guzik the expression of a sorrowful grouper. It was said that the nickname "Greasy Thumb" derived from his ineptitude as a waiter who couldn't keep his thumb out of the soup. Despite all this, Capone felt a real affection for the wobbly little man. The next day Howard was standing at the cigar counter of Henie Jacob's saloon, a few doors away from the Four Deuces. According to witnesses, when Capone walked in, Howard greeted him and stuck out his hand. Capone grabbed him by the shoulder, demanding to know why he had struck Guzik. When Howard replied, "Get back to your whores, you Dago pimp," Capone emptied his revolver into his head.

The next day, the *Tribune* carried Capone's picture, the first glimpse that Chicagoans had of the man who would soon become their town's most internationally recognized citizen. The killing had been in broad daylight and in front of witnesses, and thus the *Tribune's* caption began, "Tony (Scarface) Capone also known as Al Brown who killed Joe Howard. . . ." The detective in charge of investigations told the reporters, "I am certain that it was Capone." Nevertheless, in the hours between the shooting and the first formal inquest, all of the witnesses suffered memory lapses. Capone himself had vanished. He sauntered into the Cottage Grove police station a month later. Someone, he said, had told him that the police wanted to talk to him about something. "Who, me? I'm a respectable business man, a second-hand furniture dealer. I'm no gangster. I don't know this fellow Torrio. I haven't anything to do with the Four Deuces. Anyway, I was out of town the day Howard was bumped off."[64]

Capone made this statement to Assistant State's Attorney William H. McSwiggen, who announced that he would be bringing an indictment against Capone. The inquest remained open for two and a half months, but in the end could only conclude that Howard's death had been caused by "bullets being fired from a revolver or revolvers in the hands of one or more white male persons."

The handsome young McSwiggen had become the darling of the Chicago press. Brought up on the Irish West Side, McSwiggen had grown up with the future West Side O'Donnell gang—the brothers Klondike and Myles, Jim Doherty and Tom "Red" Duffy. Like Doherty and Duffy, he was the son of a Chicago police officer, Sergeant Anthony McSwiggen. Bill McSwiggen had been a good student, bright enough to work his way through law school. He quickly entered politics, like many of the West Side Irish supporting the wet Republicans. By 1924, as assistant state attorney under Crowe, he had already earned a reputation as a brash, energetic, "hanging prosecutor" who had challenged his first jury to have "the guts to do the right thing, as you promised me to do, and send them [the defendants] to the gallows." He had sought the indictment against Capone for the Joe Howard murder. Later he prosecuted his boyhood associates, Myles O'Donnell and Jim Doherty, for the Tancl-Klimas murders. Again, he was unable to obtain a conviction.

In the middle of a war with rival gangs invading each other's turfs and hijacking each other's beer trucks, Crowe's strategy of prosecuting the gunmen while leaving the honest bootleggers alone proved impossible. The bootleggers and the gunmen were by now the same people. Even more embarrassing, not only were the bootleggers and the gunmen the same people on Chicago's West Side, these same people also tended to be political supporters of Crowe's and McSwiggen's faction in the Chicago Republican Party. Crowe was accused of winning his office through the support and assistance of Diamond Joe Esposito, the Genna family, the O'Donnell brothers and Capone. Whether there was any substance to these charges, it was noticeable that Crowe and McSwiggen had yet to successfully prosecute any of these gangs for anything.

All this might have mattered little if Capone and the O'Donnells had not started shooting at each other. Yet the O'Donnells had begun encroaching upon Capone territory, offering his saloons a better brew at a cheaper price. In the prevailing irrational atmosphere, Capone construed this as a declaration of war.

In reality, Assistant State Attorney McSwiggen had never severed relations with his boyhood friends. His prosecution of Myles and Jim Doherty had been a notable failure. Nor did he neglect to cultivate Capone. Everything that the son of an Irish police sergeant should be, McSwiggen was. He was good-looking, rugged, boisterous, witty, and immensely likeable. He was a pretty fair drinker. Capone later claimed that he had genuinely liked the lad. Whether this was literally true, Capone could point out that he and McSwiggen had drunk and chatted together when McSwiggen had dropped by the Ship in Capone's part of Cicero. In the late afternoon of April 27, 1926, Klondike O'Donnell sent Duffy, Doherty, and brother Myles to the McSwiggen household to invite Bill to come to Cicero with them to "brace up on some good beer. I know it's good beer because I delivered it to the saloons myself." Young McSwiggen accepted the invitation with no hesitation.

About three hours later, joined by a retired police officer named Hanley, the jolly party was driving up to Harry Madigan's "Pony Inn," an O'Donnell hangout a few blocks away from Capone's own "Hawthorne Inn." Capone had been informed of their presence a half hour earlier and had immediately jumped to the wrong conclusion. He had learned of Doherty's involvement with Drucci in the Amatuna murder several months before. He inferred from this that the O'Donnells were now arrayed with the O'Banion survivors against him. The news that a large group of O'Donnells were cruising around

Cicero seemed to indicate an attack was imminent. Capone knew that the party included the two O'Donnells, Jim Doherty and Red Duffy. He didn't know who the other two were, but probably reasoned that they must be other O'Donnell gunsels.

Without a further word, Capone walked over and pressed a button in the wall. A secret panel slid open revealing a cache of Thompson sub-machine guns. Picking out three of them, he formed up a party and led them out the back door. Once outside, he organized a convoy of five cars: a lead car to act as scout; two other cars acting as gunships close behind; his own car about fifty yards behind these; and a tail car at the rear. The purpose of the lead and tail cars was to bottle up the zone of operations, making sure that no other vehicle would enter the zone while the shooting was taking place. Capone would later deny that he was in any of the cars; yet there were three sub-machine guns and three cars of which the third was Capone's own. It seems most likely that Capone himself was shooting from the third car.

The attack took little more than twenty seconds; after that the five cars sped away. McSwiggen, Doherty, and Duffy had been mowed down as they tried to run away. They were all badly hit. The more experienced O'Donnell brothers had known enough to spread-eagle themselves on the ground. They remained unscathed. Hanley, the driver, was still in the car when the shooting started and remained untouched as well. Taking him for dead, Myles and Klondike propped Duffy up against a tree; then they loaded McSwiggen and Doherty into the Doherty's car and took them to Klondike's house in nearby Berwyn. Both were dead by the time they arrived.

Red Duffy, it turned out, was not dead at all. He regained consciousness shortly after the O'Donnells had driven off. "Pretty cold-blooded to leave me lying there," he remarked to the barman of the Pony Inn who had rushed out to help him. They took him to a hospital where he died several hours later.

As soon as the O'Donnells arrived home, they dragged McSwiggen's body into their house. They later claimed that they were trying to save him. But if this had been so, they would certainly have taken him to a hospital instead. It's more likely that they took him there because they didn't know what else to do. They carefully went through McSwiggen's pockets removing everything they found in them, even cutting the labels off his clothes. Then they dragged his body back to their car and sped off again. They drove off to a lonely patch of black prairie outside of Berwyn and unceremoniously dumped their two childhood friends on the side of the road like sacks of potatoes lying atop each other in a jumbled heap.

Terrified that they were about to be implicated in the murder of an assistant state attorney, the O'Donnells had panicked. Their cover-up was pathetic. The bodies of Doherty and McSwiggen were found and identified almost immediately, and their presence in the O'Donnell party quickly established. When the police arrived at the O'Donnell house, they found McSwiggen's blood everywhere. Though the O'Donnells had failed in their attempt to avert suspicion, their frantic activity did, however, manage to sow confusion, and this allowed the Chicago papers to preserve for several months the pious fiction that the dashing McSwiggen had died in the line of duty.[65]

As soon as Capone learned of McSwiggen's death, he panicked as well, leaving Chicago to hide out for three months.

The murder caused a public uproar, and Capone's flight was taken as an implicit admission of guilt. State Attorney Crowe, capitalizing on the outpouring of public sympathy towards the McSwiggen family, deputized raiders who overran the South Side honky tonks, breaking up the slot machines and roulette wheels, overturning the crap tables, axing the beer barrels and smashing case after case of whiskey. They arrested Capone's girls, confiscated his cash and impounded his ledgers. Twenty-five of the thirty-three resorts they attacked belonged to the Torrio-Capone syndicate. Crowe's raiders partially wrecked his biggest brothel, the Stockade in Stickney. The next night three carloads of local vigilantes arrived to finish the job by setting the place on fire. The local fire brigades arrived too, but only to ensure that the fire didn't spread to neighboring houses. When asked why they were standing idly by while the Stockade burned to the ground, one fireman replied laconically, "can't spare the water." When someone asked if there was going to be an investigation, Deputy Chief Stege simply laughed. The Reverend William H. Tuttle of the Citizens' Association was delighted at this turnabout. "I appreciate the wonderful news," he told reporters, his face beaming in the ruddy glow of the vigilantes' work; "I'm sure no decent person will be sorry."

Yet Crowe's flurry of activity raised as many questions as they answered. Why was the state attorney acting only now, in Capone's absence? Why hadn't he done anything when Capone was there? Crowe might well label Capone a cop-killer; he could empanel grand juries and swear that he would track him to the ends of the earth. The truth was that Capone's absence suited Crowe rather well. More than anyone else, it was Crowe who needed to foster the image of Bill McSwiggen as a fallen hero.

Capone remained in hiding until the end of July. His role in the murders may have been an open secret, but as soon as he understood that, despite all the bad publicity, there was no real evidence against him, he surrendered himself to the authorities. "Of course I didn't kill him," he told reporters as he waited for Crowe's deputy to pick him up on the Indiana state line. "Why should I? I liked the kid. Only the day before he was up to my place and when he went home I gave him a bottle of Scotch for his old man." Why then did he flee immediately after the murder, they asked? It's the police, Al replied. They've told "a lot of stories. They've shoved a lot of murders over on me. They did it because they couldn't find the men who did the jobs, and I looked like an easy goat." He denied that there was any bad feeling over the Joe Howard prosecution or over McSwiggen attempts to indict Scalise and Anselmi. Finally, exasperated by the refusal of some of the reporters to believe that McSwiggen would stoop to drinking with a gangster like him, Capone blurted out, "I paid McSwiggen. I paid him plenty and I got what I was paying for." It was an unwise admission; bribing assistant state attorneys is a criminal offence. Still, as embarrassing as the admission may have been for Capone, it was far more excruciating for State Attorney Robert E. Crowe.

Events seemed to move out of control. Beyond the attempts on Capone's own life and the murder of his chauffeur, Tommy Cuirnigione, there had been about a dozen other attacks on the Capone outfit. His boys were clamoring for revenge. On August 10, 1926, four Capone gunmen attacked Weiss and Drucci. Less than a week later, their car was rammed on Michigan Avenue by a sedan who sprayed their cars with bullets. Both times Weiss and Drucci scampered to safety.

The next month it was the O'Banionites turn. Capone and his bodyguard, Frankie Rio, were having lunch at the Hawthorne Inn. It was the day of the big Autumn event at the Hawthorne Race Track, so the place was packed. Suddenly from the outside, a big black touring car, like the ones from the detective bureau, came charging down the street. Like the detective bureau cars, this one had a gong on the left running board which was clanging wildly. From the passenger seat window, someone with a tommy-gun was firing blanks into the air.

Startled by the racket, several of the customers, Capone included, jumped up to see what was going on. Capone was walking up to the door, pushing his way through the other excited customers, when Frankie Rio grabbed him from behind and forced him down.

"It's a stall, boss, to get you out. The real stuff hasn't started."

Rio was right; a moment later a convoy of ten cars commenced their approach. As the first car drew up alongside the restaurant, it began to rake tommy-gun bullets through the plate glass windows. This first car cruised to the far end of the street where it stopped, its gunmen firing all the while. It was immediately followed by a second car, which repeated the procedure, pulling up just short of the first. The second car was followed by a third, and then a fourth, and so on until nine tommy-guns were simultaneously dousing the restaurant like a line of firemen dousing a burning building. After the nine sub-machine gunners had completed the artillery barrage, a man in a khaki shirt and brown overcoat stepped out of the ninth car. He was holding another tommy-gun against his chest. He stopped in front of the shattered window to survey the damage with an unhurried, inspectorial air. As he did so, a tenth car pulled up. Two men with sawed-off shotguns stepped out and positioned themselves on either side of the man in the khaki shirt, who, his inspection evidently completed, knelt down and fired his whole drum into the restaurant. This final formality accomplished, the three men returned to their respective cars. There followed three short horn blasts, and the entire convoy rolled away.

Had they caught sight of Capone, the marauders would probably have shot to kill. But Frankie Rio had pulled his boss down in time, and the O'Banionite caravan had to content itself with a display of firepower. Still, it was an impressive display. The police calculated that the marauders had emptied ten 100-bullet drums. The windows of the Hawthorne Inn, the Anton

Hotel, and the barber shop, laundry and delicatessen beside were all shattered. The woodwork was smashed and the furniture destroyed beyond repair. There were neat rows of .45 caliber bullet holes in the back wall of the Hawthorne Inn. Cars parked along the curb were riddled as well. "This is War," declared the editorial of the *Chicago Herald* the next morning. The "Bootleg Battle of the Marne" Pasley called it. Fortunately the only real casualty was a Mrs. Freeman who, along with her husband Clyde and their five-year-old son were sitting in their car waiting at the curbside. They had just driven up from Louisiana and happened to be parking in the wrong place at the wrong time. As thirty slugs came zinging through their window, Mrs. Freeman was hit in the arm and her right eye was pierced by flying glass from their car window. Capone insisted on paying Mrs. Freeman's hospital expenses and on repairing the damage to his neighbors' properties as well.

"Weiss," a relieved Capone told reporters afterwards, "will never kill me by any such silly stage play in broad daylight. He might as well have come after me with a brass band." It was true; as a hit, the display was noisy rather than murderous. Maybe that was the intention—nothing more than shattered glass and a lot of noise. Still, it had been an attack, and the ball was now in Big Al's court.

Instead of replying, Capone first proposed a truce. He invited Weiss to meet his representative, Tony Lombardo, at the Morrison Hotel. An unnamed police official was also invited as a referee. Capone had instructed Lombardo to offer Weiss exclusive beer sales rights to the entire North Side. It was a generous offer; but Weiss was still in a vengeful mood. He didn't care about the beer territories, he said; he wanted another account settled. What account was that, asked Lombardo. Dion O'Banion's death, Weiss replied. Weiss demanded that Capone give them Scalise and Anselmi as the price of peace. Lombardo shook his head, but agreed to relay the proposal by phone. "I wouldn't do that to a yellow dog," was Capone's answer. With that, Weiss stalked out, leaving Capone with little choice.

Earlier in the month, a young man calling himself Oscar Lundin had approached a North Side landlady, named Mrs. Anna Rotariu, asking if she had a room to rent. Mr. Lundin specifically asked for a room overlooking William Schofield's flower shop on North State Street. Mrs. Rotariu told Mr. Lundin that such a room would become available on October 8. She warned him that it was only a small, cramped room with little in the way of furnishings. Mr. Lundin assured her that it didn't matter; he would be delighted to take it.

That same day, a pretty blond woman calling herself Mrs. Theodore Schultz rented a third floor room at 1 Superior Street, a street crossing North State with an unobstructed view of the back and side of Schofield's flower store.

Although both Mr. Lundin and Mrs. Schultz seemed happy to pay their first month's rent in advance, neither moved in. In both cases their places were taken by pairs of unnamed men, two of whom were described as of Italian appearance. Several days later, further unidentified men arrived to take up residence.

After the O'Banion murder two years before, Hymie Weiss had kept the rooms on the upper floor of Schofield's flower store as his office. In the early part of October, Weiss was working to fix the trial of Polack Joe Saltis and Lefty Koncil for the murder of a minor gangster, Mitters Foley. Although Foley had been gunned down in front of five eye witnesses, Weiss had pulled together $100,000 to convince the jury of his friends' innocence. He spent the morning of October 9 at the Criminal Court Building, four blocks away. When the trial recessed for the day, he called a conference at his place. Besides his driver and his bodyguard, Weiss was accompanied by the leader of the Saltis-Koncil defence team, William O'Brien and a fixer and private investigator from the Twentieth Ward named Benny Jacobs. As the five men climbed out of Weiss's Cadillac in front of Holy Name Cathedral and started to cross the street to Schofield's front door, they were hit by a barrage. The main target, Weiss, was killed almost instantaneously as twelve bullets ripped through him. His bodyguard, Paddy Murray, taking fifteen hits, fell dead beside his boss. The other three men received serious, though non-fatal, wounds.

The shots had all come from the room on North State Street. The police later found three chairs arranged in a semi-circle in front of the window where the shots had been fired, with piles of cigarette butts beside each of the chairs. The killers had been keeping watch for two days; there was a grey fedora on the messed-up bed and bottles of wine on the floor. The police later found a tommy gun a block away, which indicated that the killers had made their getaway through a ground floor window that led into the alley. Weiss had been standing directly in front of Holy Name Cathedral, and the automatic fire had splattered onto the building's face mangling the cornerstone inscription which read: "A.D. 1874 At the Name of Jesus Every Knee should Bow in Heaven and on Earth," a quote from St. Paul's Epistle to the Philippians.

The following morning Capone held an impromptu news conference at the Hawthorne Inn. "I'm sorry Weiss was killed," he told the reporters, "but I didn't have anything to do with it." He said that he'd offered to come downtown, but the police had told him not to bother. "There's enough business for all of us without us killing each other like animals in the street," he continued. "I don't want to end up in the gutter punctured with machine-gun slugs, so why should I kill Weiss?"

Why indeed? "He knows why," Chief of Detectives Schoemacher snorted at the reporters, "and so does everyone else."

"Capone played safe," said Police Chief Morgan Collins, "first by importing killers, expert machine-gunners, and then by hurrying them out of town." Collins claimed that Capone had recently imported fifteen gangsters from New York. Asked if it was true that he hadn't even called Capone in for questioning, Collins replied, "It's a waste of time. . . . He has his alibi."

But reporters who kept arriving at the Hawthorne Inn, found Capone eager to push his own point of view: "Hymie was a good kid," he told one group as he passed out cigars and drinks to them. "He could have gotten out long ago and taken his and been alive today. When we were in business in the old days I got to know him well and used to go often to his room for a friendly visit. Torrio and me made Weiss and O'Banion. When they broke away and went into business for themselves, that was all right with us. We let 'em go and forgot about 'em. But they began to get nasty. We sent 'em word to stay in their own backyard. But they had the swell head and thought they were bigger than we were."

Capone explained that after Torrio was shot, he'd gone over to have a talk with Weiss: "What do you want to do," he'd asked him, "get yourself killed before you're thirty? You'd better get some sense while a few of us are left alive."

Still in tatters from the attack a few weeks before, the Hawthorne Inn seemed liked a war zone. It was an appropriate backdrop for Capone's pleas. In one interview he pulled out a picture of his seven-year-old son, Sonny, "They've all got families too," he said. "What makes them so crazy to end up on a slab in the morgue with their mothers' hearts broken over the way they died?" Weiss was twenty-eight at the time of his murder.

That seemed reasonable enough, at least from Capone's point of view. But Capone's protestations did not convince everyone. Too much blood was dripping from his hands. There'd been too much violence with his signature on it. The city was sick of the Beer War. Nor did his repeated claim that all he wanted to do was live the nine-to-five life of an ordinary businessman even convince the underworld. It sounded too much like an ultimatum.

When their association with Weiss came out after his death, Saltis and McErlane were terrified that Capone would be coming out after them next. Joe Saltis proposed a new, enlarged peace conference. This was held the following month at the Hotel Sherman. Capone and the other major gang leaders attended. Though reporters were excluded, the police sent a detective along. The informal chairman was the elder statesman of the Chicago underworld, Maxie Eisen, the president of the Kosher Meat Peddlars' Association and close friend of both the O'Banionites and the Saltis gang. He got right to the point: "Let's give each other a break," he said. "We're a bunch of saps killing each other this way and giving the cops a laugh." With this, Capone was asked to state his terms.

To everyone's relief, these turned out to be nothing more than a proposal that everyone now bury the hatchet and agree to adhere to the rules Torrio had originally laid out—no violence, no encroachment, disputes to be settled by arbitration, offenders to be punished by their own leaders. Sadder but wiser, the hoodlum assembly was ready to acknowledge that little Johnnie Torrio may have been right all along.

After the meeting the conference delegates repaired to Diamond Joe Esposito's Bella Napoli Café for a gala dinner. It was an emotional scene. Gangsters slapped each other on the backs and howled with laughter as they recounted how they had tried to kill each other:

"Remember that night when your car was chased by two of ours?"

"I sure do!"

"Well, we were going to kill you, but you had a woman with you!"

Later in the evening, with bellies full and the red wine befuddling their brains, the gangsters grew sentimental. "I'd never have had my boys shoot any of yours if it hadn't been for the newspapers. Every time there'd be a little shooting affair the papers would print the name of the gang who did it. Well, when any of my boys got shot up and the papers came up with the right hunch as to who did it, I naturally decided that in honor I'd have to have a few guys bumped myself."

The effusions of good fellowship offended a Chicago reporter sent to observe the festivities. Their maudlin oaths struck him as sheer hypocrisy. When he later wrote it up, he called it "a feast of ghouls." Maybe so, but they were still the ghoulish outpourings of some very frightened men, men suddenly realizing that they had gotten in too deep. The war had reduced these fearsome warriors to shaky cookies, but now Capone was offering them a way out, a general amnesty. Even though it had ultimatum written all over it, they felt so grateful. They only prayed that the good feeling would last. For them the feast of ghouls was Christmas in the trenches, a time to relax and to make amends, to re-assure each other that they were still human and that now maybe everything was going to be okay.

The Return of Big Bill

By now the *Literary Digest* was carrying almost weekly reports on the Chicago Beer War, complete with cartoons depicting swarthy Sicilian gangsters. Like the Hearst papers, the editors of the *Literary Digest* well understood that stories about gangland shootouts, police raids and car chases appealed to their readers. Yet along with the mainstream press, the *Literary Digest* still presented the Chicago Beer War in terms of the struggle between the forces of law-and-order and the forces of crime. Certainly, there were some disturbing aspects to this struggle; for some reason things were not going the way they should. The Houston *Post,* for example, editorialized after the murder of Hymie Weiss, "It is ridiculous to assume that a little group of outlaws can continue to terrorize a great community if the law enforcement agencies are efficient."[66] The newspaper men must have known by now that it was more than just a matter of inefficient law enforcement agencies or a little group of outlaws terrorizing a great community. Yet, though many must have questioned whether the war against the bootleggers could ever be won, they were still reluctant to put their doubts into print. One of the effects of their reportage had been to burnish the image William Dever, mayor of Chicago, as an honest, get-tough mayor determined to run the bad guys out of town. With his national reputation as a reformer, the Chicago Democrats had no choice; they had to renominate Dever for a second term in 1927.

For their part, the Republicans had no obvious candidate. The revelations following the McSwiggen murder had sullied the reputation of Crowe.

Whether he had knowingly accepted help and campaign contributions from West Side bootlegging gangs, his public reputation was in tatters. In 1923, the Republicans had run a lackluster candidate of unimpeachable record and had lost badly, losing important offices in Cook County as well. They were not going to make the same mistake again. Crowe and Thompson had never been friends; they even referred to each other as crooks on a number of public occasions. Still, Crow was a power within the Illinois Republican Party, and a combination of opportunism and tactical expediency now led him to swallow his pride and approach Thompson to run again.

Big Bill did not disappoint. His platform was a simple demagogic one of 'America first, last and always.' He spoke at meetings with isolationist senators in his opposition to the World Court. Above all, he lambasted his respectable Republican opponents. He described Republican senatorial candidate, William McKinley, as a friend of King George of England. When a debate was suggested between Thompson and two other Republican hopefuls, Fred Lundin and Dr. John Dill Robertson, Thompson arrived with two stockyard rats, which he called Fred and Doc, with whom he carried on a lively, if rather one-sided, debate. Outraged, both the *Tribune* and the *Daily News* carried full reports, thus giving Thompson's clowning an even wider publicity. Robertson responded be repeating the emotive question, "Who Killed Bill McSwiggen," going on to accuse Thompson and Chief of Police Fitzmorris of founding a multi-million-dollar crime ring. But railing at the police only made matters worse. In the aftermath of the McSwiggen killing, Chicago had begun to slip its political moorings. Who could the voter trust: the Republican Robert Crowe, said to have taken money from the Genna family, or the Democrat Robert Schweitzer, who had presented Dion O'Banion with a jewel-encrusted watch? Voters wanted an outsider, and though, as two-time mayor, Thompson should hardly have qualified as one, with his Rat Circus, his flag-waving and WASP-baiting and his palpable rage at the Chicago establishment, Thompson seemed just the sort of holy fool that might do the job. He brushed off his Republican challengers with little effort.

Dever was smart enough to know that he was in trouble. His get-tough policies were making him unpopular. At first, he was reluctant to run again. But the Democrats had no other candidate of similar stature, and a failure to renominate Dever might seem a repudiation of his policies. This was a step that the Democrats did not wish to take, for though the party was hemorrhaging working-class support, it hoped that it could pick up middle-class voters who normally went Republican. Republican papers like the *Tribune* and the *Daily News* were by now solidly in Dever's camp. These papers argued that the "decent element" in Chicago would be enough to re-elect "Decent Dever."

Nevertheless, though the Chicago Democrats did not wish to repudiate a mayor celebrated as a hero in much of the nation's press, they were reluctant to support the very policy that had occasioned so much favorable commentary. The police crackdown was unpopular with Chicago's voters, and the Democrats knew it. Though Thompson had been accused of aiding organized crime during the Republican primaries, the Democrats decided to ignore the issue of crime and Prohibition enforcement as far as they could, campaigning instead on the issue of "Dever and Decency." Yet *decency* was a theme linked to older, and more visceral, issues in Chicago politics.

Shortly after the Democratic primary, Democrat boss and senatorial candidate George E. Brennan made a statement that set the tone for the Dever campaign: "I cannot believe that the people of Chicago will repudiate honest and efficient government, and turn the city over to be ruled by the black belt, the gunmen and the hoodlums."[67] In March 1926, Chief Collins arrested one thousand black men in a series or raids on the South Side, justifying the raids by saying that Thompson's nomination meant that "white people didn't dare walk on the sidewalks for fear of being elbowed off." "Decency and Dever" soon became code for "WASPs and the Irish Democrats." When Bill Thompson talked of "America first," said Democrat leader Maclay Hoyne, what he really meant was "Africa first;" party workers circulated a picture of Thompson kissing a black child, with the caption "Thompson—Me Africa First" on the reverse side. Though Dever tried to deny it, it occurred to many that there was a pointed reference in the Democratic campaign song—"bye bye blackbirds." The Chicago Democrats were running a Jim Crow campaign.

With Dever's attempt to center his campaign on the issues of efficiency, incorruptibility, and good government coming off the rails, Thompson had a field day. Referring to the raids on the far South Side, he told his audience, "The Cossacks were trying to bring about a reign of terror. If they do it to Negroes now, how soon before they do it to Jews, to Polacks, to Germans?"[68] It was language that the immigrants could readily understand. If the *Tribune's* talk of the "better elements," and the Democrat slogan of "Decency and Dever" seemed coded references to Chicago's ethnic and racial divisions, Thompson's slogan of "America first, last and always" could be taken as an appeal for popular unity. Dever was supported by the Citizens' Committee, a group of wealthy and influential Chicago businessmen and employers not usually on good terms with the Democrat Party. Their endorsement did not escape the notice of the city's labor unions, who came out for Thompson and the Republicans. The charge that, under Thompson, Fitzmorris had helped the bootleggers was resented in the Chicago police force where Fitzmorris had been a popular chief. When Thompson told his audiences that they should go to the breweries rather than to the station houses when they needed the police, because that was where they would find them, the police took it in good part. In fact, Thompson could say whatever he pleased, because his opponents were doing his campaigning for him. For all his standing as Democrat, Irishman and wet, in theory if not in fact, Dever now looked like a hopeless mugwump.

And a lonely mugwump as well. On election day, Thompson swept into his third term by his biggest margin yet. Will Rogers commented that Dever had tried "to beat Bill with the better element vote. The trouble with Chicago is there ain't much better element." Thompson had characterized the Independent Republicans for Dever as "the Gold Coast committee of absentee landlords" each ready to spend $10,000 a day on anti-Thompson newspaper ads. Speaking no doubt for this better element, the *Tribune* fulminated in its editorial that "Thompson is a buffoon in a tommyrot factory."[69] That might be so; but Thompson was the buffoon that the Chicago electorate wanted.

After the election, the better element consoled themselves with the thought that the election had been bought by Capone. There can be little doubt that the bootleggers preferred Thompson to Dever; Thompson had run on the New Jersey slogan, "as wet as the Atlantic Ocean." Certain gangsters had even contributed to the Thompson campaign. The North Side brothel owner Jack Zuta was a member of the William Hale Thompson Republican Club, and it was reported that he had contributed $50,000. "I'm for Big Bill, hook, line and sinker," he bragged, "and Bill's for me, hook, line and sinker."[70] Capone, it was rumored, had collected $250,000 for Thompson. It was never more than a rumor. Still, Capone had every reason to be pleased with the outcome. Within a month of the election, Capone moved his headquarters back into Chicago to the Hotel Metropole in the First Ward.

As his own, unique contribution to the Thompson campaign, Drucci tried to kidnap a Dever alderman on election day and hold him overnight. It was a pointless endeavor; worse, Drucci botched the whole job. Instead of simply whisking their victim away, Drucci and two of his colleagues stopped to vent their rage by wrecking his office and beating up his secretary. It was only at the termination of this temper tantrum that Drucci actually thought of getting away with his kidnap victim, and he ran straight into the arms of the police.

Freeing the prisoner and relieving them of their .45's, the police took Drucci and his companions into custody. Here they remained for several hours until Drucci's lawyer arranged for an arraignment at Chicago's Criminal Court. The hours spent in the holding cell had done nothing to improve Drucci's mood. It was turning out to be a bad day, and someone was going to have to pay. The police detail that arrived to escort Drucci to the court building included a tough old cop who had once beat up Joe Saltis, a certain Danny Healy. Riding to the Court Building, Healy began to taunt Drucci. This was the limit. "You. I'll get you," Schemer spat out, "I'll wait on your doorstep for you." Healy told Drucci to shut up; but Drucci was too mad to listen. "Go on, you kid copper," he said, "I'll fix you for this."

Now it was Healy's turn to get mad. He told Drucci to shut his mouth; he pulled out his pistol and threatened him with it. This only increased Drucci's rage, "You take your gun off me or I'll kick hell out of you," Drucci screamed. He lunged forward and grabbed Healy's right hand, immobilizing the gun. "I'll take you and your tool!" he cried, "I'll fix you!" Both men were now standing in the police wagon; Drucci's two hands were clasped around Healy's right wrist. Quickly, Healy's left hand shot up. Taking the pistol from his right hand, he lowered it, and fired four slugs into Drucci's mid-section. Schemer Drucci was dead on arrival at the Criminal Court Building.

Drucci's lawyer naturally demanded that Healy be arraigned for murder then and there. What murder, asked the Chicago Chief of Detectives. Drucci had attacked a police officer carrying out his duties, "We're making a medal for Healy," he said.

Capone went to Drucci's funeral; so, among others, did Bugs Moran, Maxie Eisen, Frank and Pete Gusenberg, Joe Saltis, and Frank McErlane. They contributed an arrangement consisting of an empty chair with white and purple flowers woven into it, and ribbon bearing the words, "Our Pal." It was harbinger of the Hotel Sherman Treaty six months later. The bereaved Mrs. Cecilia Drucci, supported by Dion O'Banion's widow, posed a heart of red roses inscribed to "My Darling Husband." "A policeman murdered him," she explained to the press, "but we sure gave him a grand funeral."[71]

The press had expected Capone to indulge in electoral intimidation and ballot-rigging in the 1927 elections. They were wrong. The underworld kept a low profile. The police, who had deputized extra poll-watchers and organized flivver squads for the violence they were sure was going to occur, found themselves witnessing the quietest and straightest mayoral election that Chicago had seen in a generation. Rumors and accusations aside, Capone had no need to intimidate the Chicago electorate. They were going to vote for Thompson anyway. Thompson had won the Black, Italian, and Jewish vote in 1919, though Dever had won them for the Democrats in 1923. In 1927, Thompson not only re-conquered these old constituencies; he increased his 1923 margin. He also made major inroads among Eastern European Catholics, normally a solidly Democrat constituency. When the total came in, Thompson had gathered 516,000 votes to Dever's 433,000, a margin of 82,000. Even had he wished to, Capone could not have bought or intimidated 82,000 Chicago voters.

During the 1927 campaign, Thompson boasted that if ever King George the Fifth showed up on the shore of Lake Michigan, he would punch him "on the snoot." He told another audience that the University of Chicago was "a conspiracy to destroy American history on behalf of the King of England." As mayor, he launched a campaign to burn the contents of the University's library, only relenting when he was informed that the core of the collection had been donated by Queen Victoria as a gesture of sympathy after the Chicago fire. Commentators and editorialists found these irrelevancies confusing, if vaguely amusing.

Bukowski observes, however, that when Thompson spoke of the King of England or the University of Chicago, his immigrant and working-class audience took them as allusions to groups and institutions that had been anything but open and welcoming to them—the rich, the bosses, the millionaires, and absentee landlords on the Gold Coast.[72] It was the world that excluded them. If the Democrats had stumbled into their Jim Crow campaign blindly, Thompson plowed into the WASP Establishment deliberately. Neither Thompson nor the Democrats were really avoiding the issue of Prohibition and crime; they were instead going to the source. Underneath it all, Prohibition had always been about race, ethnicity, and class.

A rebel WASP, Thompson lashed out against the Chicago Establishment with neither shame nor mercy. In doing so, he enjoyed the support of another

WASP rebel, William Randolph Hearst. Hearst's popular Chicago daily, the *Herald-Examiner*, supported Thompson through thick and thin. The similarity seems all too apparent—two big angry men with gargantuan appetites and egos to match throwing themselves upon the public and demanding its applause. Hearst invited Big Bill to stay at his California ranch, San Simeon, where Thompson was suitably impressed. What is more surprising than the tone and content of Thompson's harangues was the fact that Chicago soon began to accept them. With all the killings, revelations, and acrimony, by 1927 a pestilential stink seemed to emanate from Chicago politics. The voters no longer trusted the "better element." Judge Harry B. Miller had remarked, "If Thompson wins, Chicago will have Fatty Arbuckle for mayor."[73] If, dazed by events, Chicago voters really had put Fatty Arbuckle in the mayor's office, at least they got comedy in return.

Al Capone never threatened to punch the king of England in the snoot or to burn the contents of the University of Chicago Library. Like most sons of immigrants, he was far more interested in earning acceptance from the WASP Establishment than in kicking it around. The 1927 mayoral elections marked the beginnings of a period of underworld peace, one that would last until late 1928. Capone spent these months cultivating his image as a public citizen, a flamboyant but loveable beer baron. He presented himself as a hard-working businessman. Given the special nature of his business, the image was true enough. "There are a lot of people in Chicago that have got me pegged for one of those bloodthirsty monsters you read about in story books," Capone complained to the papers:

> . . . the kind that tortures his victims, cuts off their ears, puts out their eyes with a red-hot poker and grins while he's doing it. Now get me right. I'm not posing as a model for youth. I had to do a lot of things I don't like to do. But I'm not as black as I'm painted. I'm human. I've got a heart in me. I'll go as far in my pocket as any man to help any guy that needs help. I can't stand to see anybody hungry or cold or helpless. Many a poor family in Chicago thinks I'm Santa Claus. If I've given a cent to the poor in this man's town, I'll bet I've given a million dollars. Yes, a million. I don't take any credit to myself for being charitable and I'm just saying this to show that I'm not the worst man in the world.[74]

Chicago's problems with labor were endemic, and responsibility for the explosion of racketeering during the 1920s cannot be assigned exclusively to either the Thompson or the Dever administrations. Nevertheless, the police crackdown during Dever's term in office worsened an already dangerous situation. The war against bootleggers had distracted the police and the state's attorney's office. Yet the real problem was not that legitimate authority was devoting insufficient resources to labor racketeering. A far worse problem was that legitimate authority in Chicago was losing the war against the bootleggers, and in so doing, actually losing control of the streets. It was a vicious circle. When legitimate authority loses its effectiveness, it loses its legitimacy as well. As the effectiveness and legitimacy of government authority declined in Chicago, the Capone outfit expanded to fill the gap. Capone's image of himself as an honest, hard-working businessman was more than just a ploy on the part of Capone. Frightened, confused, and increasingly distrustful of existing authority structures, the citizens of Chicago needed someone to turn to. For many, Capone was the most credible power in town.

Capone held court in his new headquarters at the Metropole Hotel in an office beneath portraits of Washington, Lincoln, and Big Bill Thompson. He became a man about town. When Mussolini's Air Force ace, Commander Francesco de Pinedo, landed his seaplane on Lake Michigan, Capone was among the group of official Chicago notables there to greet him. Capone became a leading Cubs fan. He took up golf. He helped sponsor the Dempsey-Tuney rematch. Despite his lack of cultivated manners, Capone had a quick mind, and could rarely resist quipping with reporters.

The press lapped it up. Capone schmoozed with Damon Runyon and let himself be interviewed by Walter Winchell. He talked to the European press. Capone was always news; even those journalists who disapproved of Capone had to take notice of him. Yet the disapprovers seemed to diminish every day. "Some of the biggest 'Drys' in the country buy from me and have for years. So let's stop kidding," he said.[75] America was growing thoroughly sick of Prohibition, sick of its overblown oratory, and frightened by the violence it had unleashed. "So let's stop kidding," seemed a sensible first step. Capone was becoming a mirror of his times, and the press began to dote as slavishly upon Capone as it had doted on the moral reformers a decade before. "Nobody's on the legit," he told the reporters; "everybody's got some larceny in them." It seemed a refreshingly, and reassuringly, honest thing to say.

Capone's truce held from the Hotel Sherman Treaty in October 1927 until the winter of 1928. It was a period of relaxation. As the numerous attempts on his life testify, the armor and the bodyguards and the car conveys were not there for show. When Capone went to the theatre, he sat in the back row with his guards fanned out around him; he adopted similar arrangements whenever he went to a restaurant or nightclub. Like Mrs. Astor in the 1880s, he refrained from sitting or standing near windows. These were necessary precautions, but irksome ones, and Capone and his family were happy to spend more time in Miami.

Yet even here Capone could not let down his guard. Winchell probably got Capone's Miami number from their mutual friend, Owney Madden. Indeed, the interview may have been Madden's idea in the first place. When Winchell dropped in, Capone was playing poker with his gunsels. He waved them away and motioned Winchell to sit down at the poker table. Winchell noticed that Capone kept a loaded automatic pistol in one of the gullies on the table where the chips were kept. He asked Capone why he needed an automatic pistol in a friendly game with his own gang. Capone, who was in a depressed mood, replied morosely, "I have no friends." Winchell had fun interviewing Capone. He returned to his "shack" three times. On one occasion, Capone gave him a racing card already filled out. Winchell placed his bets accordingly and won all his bets—"and what long shots!" he crowed in his column.[76]

Capone wanted to get out of the business. When he was arrested on a concealed weapon charge in 1929, he told the police, "I have a wife and eleven-year-old kid, a boy whom I idolize, and a beautiful house in Florida. If I could go there and forget it all, I'd be the happiest man in the world." He been trying to forge peace in the underworld, he said. "What are you doing now?" the police asked him.

"I'm living on my money. I'm trying to retire."

"You should get out of the racket and forget it."

"I've been trying to, but I can't do it. Once you're in, you're always in. The parasites trail you, begging for favors and dough. You fear death; and, worse than death, you fear the rats who would run to the cops, if you didn't constantly satisfy them with money."[77]

The Chicago Beer War was nearly over and the Capone outfit was the clear winner. There was peace for now, but it was an uneasy peace. Despite his efforts at peace-making, Capone suspected that violence in the American underworld was not about to cease. Beer wars all over the country had produced a shake-out in the American underworld. Only the strongest, the best organized and most ruthless and most intelligent, syndicates had survived the ordeal. By 1929, these surviving syndicates had begun eyeing each other with suspicion. The war was not going to stop here. Even without his troubles with the law, Capone knew that he would not be allowed to pocket his winnings and retire to Miami.

Chapter Seven

The Underworld at War: Part 1—From the Fall of the Gennas to the Aiello Uprising

The Chicago Beer War had unfolded as an underworld turf war. Prohibition had created an opportunity, potentially an immensely profitable black market for the underworld to exploit. Seeking to cash in on the bonanza, Chicago's underworld gangs rushed in, each trying to nail down a piece of the new market for themselves or perhaps also to expand at the expense of their neighbors. The result was a messy gangland dust-up in which hundreds of gangsters were killed or wounded, most of them in circumstances too obscure for even the local papers to speculate over.

Arising from the old Levee vice ring, Johnny Torrio's organization had an advantage from the start. Torrio looked at Prohibition as a business opportunity. The way to make money out of it was not to hijack other bootleggers' whiskey convoys or murder their beer salesmen. Acquiring resorts and supplying them with beer from clandestine breweries in which he was a silent partner was a safer and sounder strategy. By the middle of the decade, the Torrio organization, now under Al Capone, had risen to a predominate position in the Chicago bootlegging underworld.

The violence in Chicago did not abate after the rise of Capone. It did, however, change in character. The struggle in the first years of Prohibition was between rival claim-stakers, each hopeful attempting to seize a place in a market whose contours had yet to emerge. By the middle of the decade, the contours of this market had become more discernable. As early as 1923, bootleggers were able to keep Chicago in beer and spirits, albeit often of doubtful quality. Regular networks of supply and distribution were being laid, and a rough territorial division was coming into force. By 1923, competition was no longer among pioneers setting up stakes in virgin territory; it was between underworld groups struggling to control the new business that had come into being. It was a struggle over market dominance. The underworld war that developed in Chicago after the murder of Dion O'Banion was less an underworld turf war between rival bootleggers than a struggle for control of the underworld itself.

The bootlegging market was an illegal one, however, and this had important consequences. One was that, since the bootlegging business was illegal, the struggle to control it was necessarily illegal as well. It was predictable that this struggle would involve violence.

A similar sequence of events was taking place in other American cities. By the mid-1920s, locally predominant underworld gangs were emerging throughout urban America in the bootlegging business. The very nature of that business, however, meant that rivalries among these gangs could never be kept isolated. Bootlegging was an illegal form of interstate commerce and international trade. Bootleggers had partners in other states and cities and even, when smuggling was involved, in neighboring countries. Since bootlegging was an illegal business, these partners were invariably other underworld gangs. A consequence was the emergence of bootlegging syndicates, interstate crime confederations of allied gangs who bought and sold from each other. And the consequence of the emergence of syndicates of allied bootlegging gangs was that wars involving one member of the syndicate in one city quickly spread to gangs in cities along the chain. Allied gangs were drawn into local wars, thus transforming them into wars among rival crime confederations. At stake was no longer local bootlegging predominance, but a hegemony in American organized crime as a whole, a hegemony that would extend beyond bootlegging to drugs, unions, and other forms of racketeering.

In these wars the Italian underworld, and the Sicilian mafia in particular, seemed to hold all the trumps. Already before World War I, the *Unione Siciliana* had been involved in an interstate counterfeiting racket. Black Hand extortion had also been organized on an interstate basis. The Italian underworld already had a network of connections within Italian communities throughout America, a connection that predated Prohibition by over a decade. These connections helped the Italian underworld dominate the alky-cooking business, which, as we shall see, was a major bootlegging focus during the middle 1920s. By the end of the decade, the Italians emerged as dominant in the American underworld, sometimes allied with other, particularly Jewish, groups. As a result, the war for American underworld control that unfolded in the late 1920s and early 1930s was essentially a struggle among rival Sicilian gangs.

We are now about to tell the story of the American underworld at war. That story is painfully obscure in certain aspects. We can see that the war was complex. Each gang was like a piece in a chess game, whose prospects might alter dramatically with each move, even if the piece itself remained on the same square. Yet, unlike a chess game, we cannot always be sure of the piece's color or even of the number of players in the game. There was nothing inevitable about the outcome, either. From the perspective of 1910 or even the early 1920s, it would have seemed odd that organized crime in America would come to be so dominated by immigrants from a single island in the Mediterranean. For all its obscurities, it is important not to over-simplify the war or take too much for granted.

"PUBLIC SERVICE IS MY MOTTO" — AL CAPONE[1]

"Prohibition is just a business," Al Capone said in one interview. "All I do is to supply a public demand. I do it in the best and least harmful way I can."[2] Honest Al, the plain businessman, compelled to operate outside the law. It was more than just that.

Capone took over from Johnny Torrio, and Torrio had been heir to Big Jim Colosimo, king of the Levee. The old Levee gang had been a vice ring, and though the Levee itself had shut down in 1914 and 1915, the old Levee gang itself had never quite disbanded. If Chicago's drinkers never once went thirsty during Prohibition, it was because older chains of supply were still in operation.

Torrio was not Chicago's first bootlegger. By early 1920, Terry Druggan and Frankie Lake had already taken control of a clandestine brewery, while Jake Guzik was raising cash to buy another. Towards the end of that year, another member of the old Levee vice ring, Mike "the Pike" Heitler pulled off his legendary "coup de hooch," hijacking one thousand gallons of whiskey that he had already sold to Chicago's saloonkeepers, forcing them to buy it back again at twice the price. Guzik, Heitler and other members of the old vice ring remained very much in business, running brothels, gambling houses, and resorts in the far southern and southwestern parts of Cook County, as well as supplying drink to saloons and restaurants in the Loop that managed to remain open. Guzik retailed drink to Colosimo's Café.

It was a profitable business. At the end of 1920, the first year of national Prohibition, the director of the Prohibition Bureau in Chicago, Major A.V. Dalrymple, quit in disgust. Mayor Thompson, Police Chief Garrity, and a number of other top Chicago officials had blocked his every move, he wrote in his final report. Conspicuously lacking in dry zealotry, the second Thompson administration was no doubt guilty of some foot-dragging. Nevertheless, despite lack of official support, Major Darlymple's Prohibition Bureau had still chalked up a fine haul for 1920. It had closed down twenty-five hundred illegal stills and seized more than $4 million of illegal alcohol—a one-year record that neither Dever's Chief Collins nor even Elliot Ness was ever to match. Despite all this, Dalrymple insisted, these closures and seizures were a mere drop in the ocean. Chicago was neither dry nor likely to become so, at least without a dramatic change of heart. Chicago had not closed down, not even for one moment.[3]

The old Levee gang had been, and still was, a vice ring; it organized and operated resorts that offered sex, gambling, and drink. The three vices had always been complementary; resorts that offered sex or gambling usually offered drink as well. The biggest offered all three. Prohibition did not radically change the way men like Guzik or Heitler operated. Drink was now prohibited, which made it more expensive and more difficult to come by, though potentially more profitable. Middle-aged men in the business for decades, Guzik and Heitler were plugged into a vast network of suppliers and customers within Chicago and beyond. They had strategic friendships with police officers and officials throughout Cook County. With these kinds of connections, the Volstead Act simply necessitated an adjustment in operations, concentrating more on the now profitable bootlegging business.

Although the ledgers the police seized in 1924 at the offices of a certain "Al Brown M.D." on South Michigan Avenue could not be used as legal evidence, the police did have an opportunity to peruse them. These contained, as we have seen, listings of the breweries and distilleries supplying the Torrio-Capone organization as well as the names of their customers. There also were accounts from the organization's various sex emporia and gambling houses and the names of police officers and officials receiving pay-offs. There was an unbroken line of continuity running from Colosimo through Torrio to Capone.

Nevertheless, Capone was not a traditional vice lord; he was something less, though at the same time, something much more. In 1924, Capone was still second-in-command in Torrio's revived and reinvigorated vice empire. Second-in-command did not imply, however, that Capone ever managed the Torrio vice ring. Capone was no manager, and the ledgers the police found in the South Michigan Avenue apartment were Jake Guzik's, not his. Day-to-day management fell to Guzik, and would continue to do so after Capone became boss in his own right. His special pleading notwithstanding, Capone was not a businessman, honest or otherwise; he was a gangster. Like Mayor Thompson, Capone was an uncrowned monarch, a political boss concentrating on matters of diplomacy and high policy, who left routine administrative work to others. In Capone's particular case, moreover, diplomacy and high policy included violence and war.

In 1924 and 1925, Torrio began gradually withdrawing from active participation in the Chicago underworld. Bergreen writes that, on his release from prison in 1925, Capone sent a fleet of cars that whisked Torrio out of Chicago. "After several years abroad, Torrio quietly returned to New York, where he eventually lost whatever visibility he had acquired.[4] Yet loss of visibility is not the same as loss of influence.

Before leaving for Naples, Torrio had meetings with Luciano, Lansky, and Costello; these are described in Luciano's not always reliable final testament. No doubt Torrio conferred with others as well, including Paul Kelly, Frankie Yale, Owney Madden, and Longy Zwillman. There are no records of these meetings, unfortunately. Torrio told Luciano that he wanted to establish himself as the American sales agent for top European distilleries and wineries; "This was seven long years before Repeal," Luciano later observed, "and it was almost impossible to believe. Here was this guy predicting that my fucking bootleg business, and everybody else's for the matter, was going to wind up in the shithouse." He later told Charley and his friends, "You gotta get into big politics; you can buy top politicians the same way you bought the law."[5]

Torrio spent the next two and a half years in Naples, returning to New York in early 1928. The accepted theory is that Torrio left Italy fearing for his safety after Benito Mussolini had declared war on the Mafia. Though numerous sources repeat this story, it seems unlikely.[6] Mussolini had declared war on the mafia in Sicily. By "mafia," the fascist government meant groups in Sicily's agrarian interior connected to the pre-fascist political clienteles. The fascists accused these Mafiosi of holding up grain production and skimming agricultural rents from the big landowners in the cities.[7] None of Torrio's Sicilian connections, however, came from Sicily; they all came from New York and Chicago. Torrio was not Sicilian; he had probably never been to the island. He certainly was not involved in grain speculation there.

Johnny and Anna Torrio lived in an elegant apartment in a fashionable Neapolitan neighborhood; they attended the opera in Naples' sumptuous Teatro San Carlo; they spent their weekends on Capri or on the Amalfi Coast. There is no evidence showing that the fascist police took any interest in Torrio, nor any reason why they should have.

Had they been informed that Torrio had served nine months in prison for the crime of owning a brewery, their reaction would simply have been puzzlement. Mussolini's police were dimly aware that, in America, there were first- and second-generation Sicilians who were violating the Volstead Act. But Prohibition in America meant little and mattered less to the Italian police. Mussolini used his police to further his own political agenda, and helping America enforce the Volstead Act or clean up vice rings was not on it. Torrio would simply have seemed a rich Italo-American *signore*, who lived in quiet and respectable luxury with his American wife. He was not a threat to the regime. When Torrio left Naples in early 1928, he almost certainly did so for his own reasons.

With Torrio abroad, Capone kept up relations with old New York friends—Frankie Yale, Owney Madden, Charlie Luciano, and others. We shall see that he made new friends as well, friends in Detroit's Purple Gang, in the Mayfield Road Gang from Cleveland, and St. Louis's Egan's Rats. Indeed, the Capone Outfit had connections in gangs from the East to the West coasts and from Canada to the Gulf of Mexico. In one sense, they were all business connections. The Outfit bought and sold alcohol, and this implied the existence of a network of suppliers, distributors and customers. Since many of these suppliers were smugglers, it is not surprising that the Outfit had contacts in port cities along the Great Lakes, in New York, and in New Orleans. Yet Capone managed neither the chain of supply nor that of distribution. His role in the Outfit was a more special one. Capone looked after security.

Security was no minor consideration. Bootlegging was an illegal business; those involved could neither claim the protection of the law, nor could they sue associates who reneged on their contractual obligations. The only security in the bootlegging business was whatever security the bootleggers could organize for themselves. Capone represented the business interests of the Chicago underworld, of the men making good money from bootlegging and vice, of men who had no desire to see their businesses upset by random hijackings and reckless shootouts. Capone's job was to reduce these distractions, keeping the turbulent spirits in check. Capone took his duties as underworld police chief seriously. He stood in front of the bullet-riddled Hawthorn Inn and declared to reporters that "there's enough business for all of us without us killing each other like animals in the street."

"What do you want to do, get yourself killed before you're thirty?" he had asked Weiss.

"What makes them so crazy to end up on a slab in the morgue with their mothers' hearts broken over the way they died?" he had asked the assembled reporters. As Johnny Torrio's protégé and successor, Capone understood that war in the underworld was bad for business; he mourned the necessity of having to murder those too pig-headed to get the message.

SAMOOTS

Weiss, Drucci and the wild Irish gangs were not Capone's only problem. There was a storm brewing in the Italian underworld. Lasting from 1916 to 1921, the Alderman's War in the 19th Ward had resulted in thirty gangland slayings in the Italian sections. The only thing clear in the whole obscure and bloody business was the involvement of the Genna family in every phase. The Gennas were ruthless and ambitious, using the war between Anthony D'Andrea and John Power to rise within Chicago's Italian community. Keeping the peace in the Chicago underworld required keeping the murderous propensities of the Genna family in check. In this, Torrio was helped by influential figures within Chicago's Italian community—Diamond Joe Esposito and Mike Merlo, as well as, possibly, Frankie Yale in Brooklyn. Highly respected in the Sicilian community, *Unione Siciliana* president Merlo had been a close associate of Torrio and boyhood friend of Dion O'Banion; he was perhaps the one person capable of holding back the Gennas.

As we have seen, when Merlo succumbed to cancer in early November 1924, however, this last restraint evaporated. With Merlo gone, the Gennas felt at liberty to take up their bloody quest once more. Before doing so, however, they needed to liquidate some unfinished business on the bootlegging front. On November 10, 1924, two days after Merlo's death, the Gennas murdered Dion O'Banion.

Merlo's death meant that a new president for the *Unione Siciliana* needed to be found. According to Capone biographer, Laurence Bergreen, "The selection of Merlo's successor provoked Frankie Yale to return to Chicago. As head of the powerful New York branch of the *Unione*, Yale had considerable influence over the selection of who would fill the corresponding post in Chicago. He conferred with Torrio and Capone, and the three men decided to appoint Angelo Genna."[8]

That Yale conferred with Torrio and Capone seems a safe assumption. Yale arrived in Chicago a few days before Merlo's funeral. He attended a gala dinner that Esposito laid on for him; he would certainly have found time to talk with Torrio and Capone too. That Yale, Torrio, and Capone decided to appoint Angelo Genna as the next *Unione* president, however, seems highly unlikely. Neither Torrio nor Capone had the authority to make such an appointment; neither were members of the *Unione*. Yale was president of the New York branch, but his exact position within the *Unione Siciliana* always remained obscure. As criminal boss, Yale's authority never extended beyond South Brooklyn. Nevertheless, both Ciro Terranova in East Harlem and Joe Masseria in Lower Manhattan treated Yale with respect, as did the presidents of other branches of the *Unione*—Frank Milano in Cleveland and Merlo in Chicago. Yale's boast that he was president of the underworld probably had some foundation, though his position was probably more honorary than executive. Yale would have felt entitled to have a say in determining Merlo's successor; indeed, he suggested that the *Unione* accept Torrio as its temporary acting boss while consultations were held and proper elections organized.

If Yale asked Torrio and Capone whom they wanted as the next president, they would not have indicated the unmanageable Angelo Genna. Their choice would have fallen instead upon Tony Lombardo. As a successful wholesale grocer, Lombardo represented the more legitimate face of the *Unione*. Lombardo was also close to Capone, advising him and keeping him well-informed about goings-on inside the *Unione*. Lombardo was recognized as Capone's man and his representative within the *Unione*; and this would have made Lombardo's candidacy unpopular with those members who did not wish to see their *Unione* come under Capone's dominance.

In the end, however, all political maneuvers were otiose; Genna muscled his way into the presidency, and nobody dared to oppose him.

Shortly before Merlo died, one of his lieutenants commissioned a waxen effigy of the beloved leader's head. The sculptor exactly modelled and tinted the leader's face. Deep brown eyes and pepper and salt hair that matched Merlo's own were carefully affixed to the sculpted head, which was then mounted on top of a twelve-foot-high figure made of copper wire and clothed in a suit of blue flowers. This effigy was placed in state on a dais erected in the funeral parlor and later rode on a float that accompanied Merlo's corpse to the cemetery. So imposing did it seem that, as the thousands of mourners entered the funeral parlor to pay their last respects, the newspapers reported that they stopped short. "Fear gripped" when the saw the powerful leader's face gazing down upon them. That was exactly the reaction Torrio and Capone wanted— fear. Behave yourself; do the right thing; Big Brother is watching. The Chicago *Unione Siciliana* had a membership of fifteen thousand, plus another ten thousand in Cook County. The president was an unofficial leader of the entire Sicilian community. Mike Merlo had filled the bill admirably.

Angelo Genna was a different sort of man. The youngest of the Genna brothers, Angelo's way of settling differences of opinion usually involved shedding blood. His ascension did not bode well for future peace.

The Gennas naturally saw matters differently. Angelo's installation as president of the *Unione Siciliana* gave the family a new respectability. In January of 1925, two months after his inauguration as *Unione* president, Angelo married the girl of his dreams. Lucille Spignola was the daughter of a prominent, successful, and highly-respected Chicago Sicilian family. The Genna-Spignola union was a classic celebration of gangster social mobility. Their wedding cake weighed two thousand pounds. It was decorated by a master sculptor who had learned the secrets of his art in Italy itself. It took six immaculately dressed Genna gunmen to wheel the creation into the Ashland Auditorium where three thousand guests sat waiting.

The Genna-Spignola match was more than just a beauty-and-the-bullet alliance in Little Sicily, however. It was a love story as well. The twenty-eight-year-old Angelo Genna adored his beautiful eighteen-year-old bride, who, dreamlike in her white silk, tulle, and orange blossoms, had, in the months before, ferociously defied her parents, who threatened to disinherit her rather than see their family allied with the lowly Gennas. So much did Angelo dote on his bride that he soon began to neglect his duties as president of the *Unione Siciliana* for his new role as patron of the Chicago Civic Opera. Music rather than the booze racket became his preferred topic of conversation, operatic divas and bel canto tenors rather than gunmen his preferred dining companions.

But the newlyweds had barely four months of married life ahead of them. On May 25, 1925, Angelo Genna's car wrapped itself around a Hudson Street lamppost. As he struggled to free himself from the wreckage, Angelo was filled with lead by the O'Banionites .

His mangled body was rushed to Evangelical Deaconess Hospital. As he lay on the operating table, a detective sergeant came up and told him; "You're going to die, Angelo. Tell us who bumped you off." Genna shrugged his shoulders. Lucille rushed in and took his head in her arms. "Who shot you, sweetheart?" she asked. Angelo just shook his head and died. The police questioned the Genna family. The press, eager to hear what they had learned, questioned them about it. Nothing. According to what the Genna family had told him, Captain John Stege remarked sarcastically to reporters; "Angelo had no enemies; everybody liked him." Angelo had served as *Unione* president a bare six months.

Angelo Genna was succeeded as Unione president by Samuel Samuzzo Amatuna, whom everybody called Samoots.

"Samoots Amatuna," wrote Walter Noble Burns, "his name sounds like the chord of a guitar—was musical and murderous, a gay, light-hearted troubadour, and one of the most treacherous and cold-blooded killers in gangland." So particular was he about his wardrobe that once, his pistol waving in the air, he had chased a horse-driven, Chinese laundry truck down a Chicago street when he discovered that the laundry had scorched one of his two hundred monogrammed silk shirts. When he caught up to the truck, he leveled his pistol at the driver, then, changing his mind, lowered it, and shot the horse instead.

Together with Angelo Genna, Samoots had taken part in Labriola, Raimondi, and Esposito hits during the Aldermen's War. He was arrested as one of four musicians who had unsuccessfully attempted to kill the business agent of the musicians' union. The foursome arrived with their weapons hidden in their violin cases—forever establishing a cliché in gangster literature. As Burns describes it in his inimitable Chicago journalese, the quartet entered the union hall where "the business agent stood by in expectation of a soul-soothing harmony. Samoots and his confederates drew sawed-off shotguns from their cases instead of violins and played a buckshot scherzo in G minor."

Immediately after Angelo's murder, Samoots rallied remnants of the Genna faction in the *Unione* and, with the help of his two bodyguards, Bummy Goldstein and Eddie Zio, had walked in and assumed the presidency for himself. In one sense, Samoots was acting as a Genna loyalist, moving to protect the Genna interests within the *Unione*. In another sense, however, Samoots was betraying the Gennas. He was assuming the presidency, and all the rich benefits that went with it, for himself. But by now the Gennas had gotten to thinking of these benefits as belonging to them. Had they been asked, they might have responded that they were not at all sure that they were willing to give a lion's share of these perquisites to their good friend Samoots. But no one asked them. Amatuna had simply waltzed his way into the *Unione* presidency without even consulting his former colleagues.

Samoots had a problem: he needed money. He loved gambling and luxury; he was also known as the most generous of all the boys in the Chicago rackets. When he went to the barber shop, he treated all his friends to a shave and a haircut; if he asked a friend to help him pick out a new suit, the friend could be sure that Samoots would buy him one to match. "He never knew when to stop giving. Those who knew him said his hands were always open and he always had a smile" a friend said. Gambling, luxurious living and open-handed generosity bought Samoots popularity, but it also landed him deeply in debt. Debt may have been one of the reasons Samoots assumed power in the *Unione*. Debt may also have been one of the motives that led him to approach the Gennas' enemies.

The most circumstantial contemporary accounts of Little Mike Genna's death is that of Walter Noble Burns. In the course of his description of the death of Mike Genna, Burns provides us with the following pieces of information:

> Hymie Weiss, Moran and Drucci, still on the trail of O'Bannion's [sic] murderers, had conducted negotiations with Samoots Amatuna to put Scalise and Anselmi on the spot and betray them to the vengeance of the North Siders. Amatuna, a native-born Sicilian, closely allied with the Gennas, was a friend of Scalisi and Anselmi and as bitter an enemy of the Weiss-Moran-Drucci crowd as the Gennas themselves. The North Siders were fighters but unskilled in diplomacy, and their clandestine overtures were as crude and maladroit as they were bold. But the wily Amatuna pretended to fall in with

their schemes and in the end outsmarted them and repaid their treachery with treachery more subtle and crafty. He agreed to have Scalise and Anselmi standing on the corner of Sagamon and Congress streets at nine o'clock in the morning when Moran and Drucci were to drift by in their car and slaughter them. But instead of putting Scalise and Anselmi on the spot, Amatuna, by a double-cross of the classic art, put Moran and Drucci themselves on the spot.[9]

The O'Banion gang had started in Kilgubin, the old Irish suburb that, by the 1890s, was filling up with Italians and Sicilians. Weiss and Drucci had grown up alongside Italian gangs, and must have known, or at least believed they knew, something about the Italian underworld in their city. They certainly knew that Samoots Amatuna had been a Genna torpedo during the Alderman's War. If they believed that Samoots was going to put the Gennas on the spot for them, they must have had their reasons. Certainly, Samoots was not going to betray his friends out of love for the North Siders. Yet he might have done so for hard cash. Samoots needed money and the Weiss gang had been going about telling people that they would do anything to get revenge. Here was surely a deal in the making.

But who was Amatuna negotiating to betray? Burns, we saw in the last chapter, named the participants in the O'Banion murder as Scalise, Anselmi, Mike Genna and Angelo Genna. Weiss, Drucci, and Moran had gotten their revenge on Angelo Genna three weeks earlier. That left Mike Genna and the other two killers. It was Little Mike Genna who was reported furious at the brass-faced effrontery of Samoots in walking into the *Unione* and declaring himself president. His fury was loud and clear, loud enough for Weiss and Drucci to hear it and perhaps to lead them into believing that Amatuna would help them put Mike Genna on the spot. Nevertheless, as Burns tells it, it was not Mike that Samoots sold to the O'Banion gang. The deal was for Scalise and Anselmi only, not for Mike Genna. If Genna was with Scalise and Anselmi on the morning of June 13, it may have been, as Kobler suggests, because Amatuna, coming to his senses, had revealed the plot to Mike, and Mike had devised a counter-stroke.

This is not the only solution, however. According to Capone's first biographer, Fred D. Pasley, Genna was with Scalise and Anselmi because they were taking him for a one-way ride: "The diabolic irony of the situation into which Mike Genna was plunged on that June morning may now be set forth. Actually Scalise and Anselmi were taking him for a ride."

The trap into which Mike Genna had walked with his eyes wide open was divulged by a prominent Italian to a friend at the detective bureau soon after the June 13 shooting. "Mike," he said, "was on his way to execution, when the squad car officers were mistaken for enemy gangsters and fired upon. Momentarily, it upset the plans of Scalise and Anselmi, but in the end it was all right, as Mike was killed anyway."[10]

The account of this unnamed "prominent Italian" is not entirely convincing. When the police squad car turned around to chase the Sicilians, the police began to sound their gong. Though the police did not know about the shooting earlier in the day, the Sicilians must then have realized that the car behind them was a police squad car. After their car had crashed, Mike Genna jumped out and fired both barrels of his shotgun at the advancing officers. He had been armed all day. If Pasley's version is correct, Mike could have had no inkling that Scalise and Anselmi were about to murder him.

What makes the two versions difficult to reconcile is that these discrepancies in detail are symptoms of a more basic disagreement. Scalise and Anselmi, wrote Pasley, were taking Mike Genna for a ride because "Gen. Al Capone" had ordered them to. Previously Al Capone had ordered the two Sicilian torpedos to murder Dion O'Banion—the third man in the O'Banion hit squad being Frankie Yale.

There is a *prima facie* plausibility to Pasley's reconstruction. Torrio and Capone had reason enough for wanting O'Banion dead. So of course did a number of other people. In contrast to the murder of Big Jim Colosimo, finding a motive is not a problem. Nor can the rumors linking Capone and Yale to the O'Banion hit be dismissed as confabulations invented years after the crime was enacted. We saw that the Cook County coroner's certificate mentioned Frankie Yale along with Scalise and Anselmi as the murder suspects; the rumors were thus contemporary. If Yale was the third man, then the O'Banion hit must have been an improvisation. Merlo had died on November 8. Yale arrived in Chicago the following day, in time to learn that Angelo Genna had taken over the Chicago *Unione* and in time to pass by Schofield's to order a two-thousand-dollar funeral wreath for Merlo. He may have visited Schofield's once again on the following day, not to order flowers this time, but to murder O'Banion.

Yale was picked up after the murder, but he had a good alibi. At the time of the shooting, he said, he was having lunch at the Palmer House. The police went to check out this story; they found that waiter Nick Delassandro remembered serving him. The alibi was supported by Yale's dining companion as well—Samoots Amatuna.[11]

There are some difficulties with Pasley's reconstruction, however. John Scalise and Albert Anselmi were part of the Genna gang. They were contract killers recently imported from Sicily by the Gennas. As we shall see, they had little compunction about switching sides when the price was right. Nevertheless, in November 1924, Scalise and Anselmi were working exclusively for the Gennas. Torrio and Capone were no doubt involved in the O'Banion murder at some level; Burns writes that Capone had planned the hit. It was nevertheless the Gennas who carried it out. Whether the third man was Mike Genna or Frankie Yale, the man waiting for them in the car outside was identified as brother Angelo. Scalise and Anselmi were working for the Gennas, and it was the Gennas who paid them, giving them each a diamond ring for a job well done.

Suspicion did not immediately focus on the Gennas, however. The day after O'Banion's funeral, his old friend, Two-Gun Louis Alterie told a reporter, "I have no idea who killed Deany, but I would die smiling if only I had a chance to meet the guys who did, any time, any place they mentioned, and I would get at least two or three of them before they got me. If I knew who killed Deany, I'd shoot it out with the gang of killers before the sun rose in the morning and some of us, maybe all of us, would be lying on slabs in the undertaker's place."[12] Alterie may have just been indulging in some melodramatic posturing. Still, in the days immediately after the shooting, Hymie Weiss and his friends were still unsure about the assassins' identity. They were Italians, that much was clear, but were they Italians connected to the Gennas or to Capone? The failure of the Gennas to attend Deany's funeral was surely taken as an indication of guilt, as was the story that the Gennas had given their two Sicilian torpedos a pair of diamond rings. By the end of 1924, Weiss had decided that both the Gennas and Capone were guilty. He decided to declare war on both of them; it was the only honorable thing to do—a reckless, foolish but somehow heroic gesture.

On January 12, 1925, Weiss, Drucci, and Moran raked Capone's limousine with machinegun fire. Capone had just gotten out, and so was not hurt; his two bodyguards had dropped to the floor and escaped injury too; but his chauffeur, Sylvester Barton, was shot in the back. Barton's replacement, Tommy Cuiringione, was kidnapped shortly after. When his body was later recovered wired to a cement block and thrown into a cistern, it was covered with cigarette burns and other marks of torture. A week later, it was Torrio's turn. In the spring, Weiss and company switched their attentions to the Gennas. Angelo was murdered in May, and Mike followed less than three weeks later.

Capone biographer Robert J. Schoenberg comes up with yet a further twist. Following the murder of Angelo Genna, he observes, the police announced that they thought the occupants of the other car were Weiss, Moran, Drucci and driver Frank Gusenberg. By the time of Mike Genna's death, a short time later, the original police assumption had become a certainty. The Weiss gang had killed Angelo Genna and were planning to do the same to Scalise and Anselmi when they walked into an ambush. Angelo and Mike were the warriors of the Genna clan; the clan's leaders and brains were two of the older brothers, Tony and Jim (Vincenzo). Though Jim Genna was in Sicily at the time, Tony was still in Chicago. On July 8, 1925, less than a month after Mike's death, Tony Genna was murdered. The set-up was similar to the Dion O'Banion murder. Someone Tony Genna knew and was expecting came up to shake his hand. With Tony momentarily immobilized, someone walked up behind him and shot him in the head. The police hypothesized that one of the men involved was Schemer Drucci. In November it was Amatuna's turn. He was murdered, we saw, in a barber shop by two men tentatively identified as Schemer Drucci and Jim Doherty. According to Schoenberg, however, Capone had not only planned and executed the O'Banion killing; he had planned and executed each of the other killings as well—Angelo Genna, Tony Genna, and Samoots Amatuna.

Schoenberg has a point. In only one of these cases can we really be sure of the identity of the killer: Mike Genna's killer was police officer William Sweeney. There were witnesses to the murder of Angelo Genna, however, and from their descriptions, and from the license number of the pursuing car, the police had good cause to believe that the occupants of the second car were the leading members of the Weiss gang. They also had good reason to believe that Drucci and Moran had tried to ambush members of the Genna gang; both were wounded, and Moran's car was badly shot up. In the case of Amatuna's murder, however, all they had to go on was a vague description; the two killers had been a tall guy and a short, Italian-looking guy. Gangland rumor identified the big guy as Jim Doherty; the police merely assumed that the Italian had to be Drucci. In the case of Tony Genna, the police really had nothing at all to go on. The killers were presumably all Italians, and, lacking anything better, the police wondered whether Drucci might have been one of them. The link between Drucci and either Tony Genna's or Amatuna's murder was, at best, tenuous.

Schoenberg's thesis is that Drucci was not involved in any of these murders; they were all Capone killings. Capone had arranged the murder of O'Banion in such a way that both the police and the Weiss gang would assume it was a Genna hit. He had then orchestrated the murder of Angelo Genna in a way that the police and Gennas would assume that the hit had come from the Weiss gang. Having fallen for the bait, the two gangs would then proceed to tear each other to shreds. With the Genna and the Weiss gangs noisily at each other's throats, Capone was free to murder anyone he pleased, secure in the knowledge that the police and the papers would interpret these murders as causalities in the Genna-Weiss war. Diabolical Al.[13]

It is impossible to rule out Schoenberg's theory. We cannot prove that Capone was extraneous to any of these murders. Yet saying we can't prove Capone's innocence is not the same as proving his guilt. Schoenberg may be right; but he may also, as Sherlock Holmes put it, be twisting facts to fit a theory rather than tailoring theory to take account of all available facts. Capone had a motive for murdering O'Banion. The untimely deaths of Angelo and Mike Genna certainly were not unwelcome to him. But Capone had little motive for murdering Amatuna, and no motive at all for murdering Tony Genna.

Despite his bloody past as a Genna torpedo, Amatuna was a rising and well-known figure in the Italian community. Only twenty-six when he died, he had amassed an alky-cooking fortune which he had largely given away in gifts and charitable donations. Amatuna was no doubt buying influence, just as Diamond Joe Esposito had done decades earlier, setting himself up as patron of Chicago's Italian, or, more specifically, Sicilian community. Like Esposito, he had opened a restaurant, the Ciro, which served as his clubhouse. Scalise bought a piece of Amatuna's resort, perhaps using some of the money he had received after killing O'Banion. Amatuna was also a rising power in the *Unione Siciliana*, and special protégé of Merlo. He was visiting the barber shop on the night of his murder to spruce himself up for his date with Rose

Pecoraro, Merlo's sister-in-law.

As president of the *Unione*, Amatuna had taken personal charge of raising the hundred thousand dollars used to defend Scalise and Anselmi for the
murders of detectives Walsh and Olson.[14]

Burns writes that Scalise and Anselmi

> "were making heavy weather in their flight [from the accident and shoot-
> out with the police]. As they ran through the alley they threw away their
> shotguns. This was a matter of no special consequence. But a vagrant little
> breeze — a malicious little breeze — blew off their hats. This was fatal. They
> could have picked them up, of course, but they were in a hurry. Still, if they
> were to avoid suspicion from everyone they passed, they must have head-
> covering of some kind. They went into Edward Issigson's dry-goods store
> on Fifty-ninth and Rockwell streets. They could not speak English, but they
> made signs that they wanted to buy caps. Issigson was no fool. He knew
> at once that these two fellows had been in the battle and were trying to get
> away. He refused to sell them caps.[15]

Later, Issigson flagged down a passing patrol car, and pointed at the two bare-
headed desperados who were trying to jump aboard a street car. The police
dragged them off to detective headquarters. Scalise and Anselmi's vain attempt to procure headgear is confirmed by Sullivan. Evidently bare-headed-
ness was a sure sign of criminality in Chicago. Their guilt seemed evident to
all. Besides the surviving police officers, there were numerous other witnesses
to the car chase and shoot-out. Though the police squad car looked like it had
been used for a shoot-gallery target, the Genna car had but one bullet hole;
there was thus little question of who had fired first. Scalise and Anselmi were
guilty beyond any reasonable doubt. The state, everybody assumed, would
send them on a quick trip to the gallows. Yet with the help of the lawyers paid
for by the money that Amatuna had raised, in the first of three trials, Scalise
and Anselmi, pleading self-defence, were only convicted of manslaughter.
Scalise and Anselmi were released on bail pending their second trial.

When the first verdict was announced, the papers expressed outrage. For
the Chicago police, it was more than outrage. Two brother officers had been
shot down in broad daylight before they had even had a chance to pull out
their weapons, and their killers were free on bail. The Chicago police descended on the tenements around Maxwell Street like furies from hell to kick
over the Italian stills. They had originally been Genna stills. An account book
found in Mike Genna's possession gave full details of how much the Gennas
had been paying the Maxwell Street police. Scalise and Anselmi's lawyer
pulled the book out during the first trial, telling the jury how much the Gennas had paid in police protection, how many policeman had lined up outside
the Gennas' Taylor Street offices to collect their graft each month, how the
Gennas had allowed the police to buy moonshine from them at a discount
and get into the bootlegging racket themselves, how police squad cars used
to accompany the trucks to protect them from hijackers. "The business of the
Gennas was conducted as openly as a department store on State Street, and not

a wheel could have turned except under the protection and permission of the police."[16] This added insult to injury.

But by now, the stills the police kicked over were no long the property of the Genna family; some of them belonged instead to their successor at the *Unione Siciliana*—Samoots Amatuna. Amatuna complained to a friend that he had gone in debt some $22,000 contributing to Scalise and Anselmi's defence fund, and now the police were wrecking his business. "More than half those stills were mine," he told a friend. The friend later explained to the police that the stills "cost him $800 to $1,000, and each time he set one of them up, the police came along and kicked it over again."[17]

Samoots had other enemies besides the police. His takeover of the *Unione* may have irritated Mike Genna, but with Mike gone, Samoots was his natural successor. Amatuna not only inherited many of the Genna stills; he inherited the rest of the gang as well. Frightened and discouraged at the deaths of their leaders, the Genna gang had begun to unravel. Amatuna set to work putting it back together. Rumors of this work soon reached the ears of Hymie Weiss. His gang had not gone to all the trouble of smashing the Genna gang, just to have Samoots Amatuna piece it together. In the second half of 1925, Samoots had dangerous enemies lined up against him—the Chicago police and the North Side gang, together with their allies. For Capone, Amatuna was never more than a minor irritant. He was not Capone's candidate as president of the *Unione*, but he was an improvement over Angelo Genna. Capone had accepted Angelo Genna's presidency; he was prepared to live with that of Amatuna.

After the barbershop shooting, Amatuna was taken to Jefferson Park Hospital. He was fully conscious, and his friends expected that he would survive; the doctors, who had examined the X-rays and seen how the bullets had shattered his spine, knew otherwise. When the police arrived to question him, he yelled for them to get out. Rose Pecorara rushed to his bedside. Their wedding had once been postponed on account of Mike Merlo's funeral; but now they had set the date, even rented the hall and bought the flowers. More than a thousand guests had been invited:

When Samoots was told he was doomed he ordered [his brother] Luigi to call a priest. To administer holy unction? No. To join him with Rose in a marriage that was to be love's victory over the grave. "Rose is going to be my bride before I die," he said. He took her hand in his and lay with a happy smile on his face. The priest came, but Samoots had fallen into a coma. Still holding his sweetheart's hand, he passed from unconscious life to lifeless unconsciousness.[18]

His funeral was sumptuous, not as grand as Merlo's, at which ex-Mayor Thompson, Mayor Dever, and Police Chief Collins had been among the mourners, but still impressive. Amatuna had been president of the Chicago *Unione Siciliana*, an important personage not only in the Italian community, but in the rest of the city as well. Capone no doubt attended. Little Sicily had no doubts about who murdered Amatuna—the Irish. The Gennas had had their admirers both within the *Unione* and within the larger Sicilian community; "The Irish had captured the government, the public officials were Irish, and there were several hundred crooked Irish police sharing the profits of the Italian bootleggers," said one contemporary.[19]

CAPONE AND THE UNIONE SICILIANA

If Schoenberg's theory is true, then Capone had the Gennas set up, hoodwinking the police, the press, and the North Siders, into believing that the Genna family had killed Dion O'Banion when, in reality, it had been Capone himself. But why didn't the Gennas say anything? Why didn't they send messages to the police, the press and, above all, Weiss, setting things straight, proclaiming their innocence, and denouncing the perfidy of Big Al? To do so was certainly in their interest. If it was not the Weiss gang who chased Angelo Genna, murdering him when he emerged from the wreck, if it was just another Capone set up, why didn't Weiss tell the Gennas? Schoenberg's attempt to resolve all the mysteries with one big theory leaves too much unresolved, too many details unexplained. It is better to stick more closely to the texture of the events.

Yet this is not the real objection to Schoenberg's theory. Whether his theory accounts for some of the missing details, it has got the big picture wrong. According to Schoenberg, everything had gone just the way Capone had planned. Setting his enemies against each other, he had eliminated them one by one; now he was moving in on their territories. Now he was in control.

But Capone was not in control. No one was in control. That was the real problem. Nothing had gone according to plan, and the city of Chicago was falling apart. Gang warfare had broken out all over. Some of the gangs in the south and southwest, regarding Capone and the Gennas as their racial enemies, were rallying to Hymie Weiss. Others, frightened by the engulfing tide of violence, were running to Capone for protection. The Ragan's Colts clubhouse was bombed on repeated occasions in a war that had nothing to do with the troubles among Capone, the Gennas and the North Siders.

The Chicago police might shut down speakeasy after speakeasy, imprison drinkers, and kick over as many stills on Maxwell Street as they wanted; they could not regain control. They had never been able to stem the tide of booze; now they could not even protect their citizens. Had Capone really orchestrated all this chaos? Capone could move swiftly, taking advantages of the missteps of others, but Capone was simply reacting to events that neither he nor anyone else could control. Besides, in the swirling paranoia, Capone was prone to commit his own blunders—witness the killing of Bill McSwiggen.

Capone's task would have been much easier if he could have united the rival factions in Little Italy and Little Sicily next door, but the fall of the Genna family had not brought peace to Chicago's troubled Italian communities.

Amatuna had organized the defense fund for Scalise and Anselmi's first trial. He had just launched the fund for the second trial when two assassins brought his fund-raising career to a permanent close. With Samoots's death, responsibility for raising the cash to defend Scalise and Anselmi passed to another *Unione* official, Orazio Tropea.

An ex-Black Hander and Genna killer supposedly able to throw the evil eye, Tropea was described by Burns as "lean, swarthy, with cruel face and black, wintry eyes."[20] Tropea's Black Hand gang included his driver, Ecola "the Eagle" Baldelli, as well as Vito Bascone, Felipe Gnolfo, and Tony Finalli. Tropea was also friends with Giusppe Nerone, known as *Il Cavaliere* on account of his polished manners. Baldelli, Bascone, Gnolfo, and Finalli may have been simple thugs; but Tropea and Nerone were men with some education. Nerone in particular had been to university in Sicily where he later taught secondary-school mathematics. He had been forced to flee Sicily, however, and ended up in America where, under the aliases of Antonio Spano and Joseph Pavia, he became a successful criminal.

By the beginning of the 1920s, he had become part of the Genna gang. First he worked as a bodyguard. Later, when the alky-cooking business took off, the Gennas found that Nerone's mathematical skills were useful. Nerone rose to become the Gennas' business manager. The Gennas tended to be clannish, however, and neither Nerone nor Tropea was ever admitted to their inner councils. Nor were either of them rewarded, or at least rewarded as richly as thought they deserved. "It was my brains that made the Gennas," Burns has Nerone complaining. "If it had not been for me they would still be in the gutter."[21] The murders of Angelo and Mike Genna created vacancies at the top of the Sicilian underworld. Ambitious men, Nerone and Tropea thought that the Gennas' misfortune might be their opportunity.

Anthony Genna, called "Tony the Gentleman" or "Tony the Aristocrat," is usually identified as the Genna family *consigliere*. In reality, Tony Genna was a man averse to violence. He had moved out of the family enclave in Little Sicily, taking an apartment in the Congress Hotel where he lived with Gladys Bagwell, a cabaret pianist and the daughter of a Baptist minister. Tony studied music and architecture. Nevertheless, the Genna family was strictly old school. Though Tony was not involved in gang warfare, he had never for a moment broken with his brothers. Tony was an official in the *Unione Siciliana*, helping manage a project to build low-rent model houses for the immigrant community. The *Unione Siciliana* remained, as ever, a contradictory and multi-faceted organization.

In July 1925, two months after Angelo's murder and a month after Mike's, Tony Genna received a phone call from Giuseppe Nerone. Nerone said that he had important business to discuss. Tony may have suspected that Nerone's business had something to do with his brothers' murders. He accepted Nerone's invitation for a meeting which was set in front of at Cutilla's grocery on Grand Street.

Arriving first, Tony stood waiting in front of Cutilla's store until a car stopped on the other side of the street. Two figures got out and waved cordially to Tony. "Hello Tony," said the larger of the two men crossing over, "how are you?" He reached forward and grabbed Tony's extended right hand. The moment he had done so, the second man drew out an automatic pistol and shot him five times. Dying in County Hospital, Tony whispered a name into the ear of his sweetheart, Gladys. The name sounded like "cavallaro" and this sent the police on a wild-goose chase. Eventually they realized that Tony Genna had been trying to say *il Cavaliere*, Giuseppe Nerone's nickname.

For his part, Orazio Tropea saw the Scalise and Anselmi defense fund as an invitation to take up his career as a Black Hand extortionist once again. Of the $50,000 he raised, Tropea transferred more than half to his own bank account in Sicily. Angelo Genna's brother-in-law, Henry Spingola, was a member of a large and prosperous Sicilian family from the suburb of Oak Park. The family had been in America over fifty years, and Henry and his eight brothers had all been born in America. Henry had gone to law school and was active in the church, the American Legion, and the Knights of Columbus. He knew Amatuna and Tropea well, and had agreed to contribute $10,000 to the first defense fund. When Vito Bascone asked him to contribute to the second fund as well, however, Spingola replied that he had already given enough. When Bascone pressed, saying that Tropea would take offence at his failure to contribute, Spingola finally agreed to write a check for $2,000. Enraged at what he thought was Spingola's lack of respect, Tropea arranged for Spingola's murder in January 1926. Several days later, he arranged for the murder of two other prosperous Chicago Italians who had shown a similar reluctance, Antonio and Agostino Morici. As the Morici brothers were driving home on a cold and blizzardy evening, another car holding three passengers, two with sawed-off shotguns, pulled up alongside them. The two cars careened down Ogden Avenue, skidding and losing each other in the curtains of snow, until the pursuers finally got close enough to let off their guns. Both the Morici brothers were hit, and, losing control, ran their car into a signboard. On impact, the two brothers plunged through the windscreen to their deaths on the sidewalk.

Neither Tony Genna's murder, nor those of Spingola and the Morici brothers were ever officially solved; nevertheless, during the next few months, Tropea, Bascone, Baldelli, and Gnolfo, as well as a number of associates, allies, and innocent by-standers were murdered. The culprits of these latter crimes were never indicated by name, much less arrested. The press, however, assumed that they had all been murdered in reprisal for their involvement in the murders of Henry Spingola and the Morici brothers. This is a reasonable supposition. But, even if revenge was the motive for these latter murders, revenge could not have been the motive for the murders of Tony Genna or Spingola or the Morici family.

Like Amatuna, Nerone and Tropea were men who would be king. The Genna family had been groping their way towards a new legitimacy, assuming a more public role in the *Unione* and allying themselves with the highly respected Spingola family. But Nerone and Tropea had each been marginalized in the family's move towards greater respectability. The slayings of Angelo and Mike, however, changed everything. The Genna business manager, Nerone, moved to take over the alky-cooking racket, killing Tony Genna, who represented what was left of Genna business interests. Tropea used his position in the *Unione* to organize a new type of Black Hand extortion. Spingola and the Morici were victims of Tropea's Black Hand gang. But Nerone's and Tropea's violence had earned them real enemies in Chicago's Italian underworld, and their murders, along with those of their henchmen, in short succession, showed that the Italian underworld was capable of cleaning up its own back yard, exterminating Black Handers and other troublesome vermin.

Securing its own back yard, however, required an understanding between the Italian underworld and the most powerful underworld organization in town—the Capone Outfit. This would not be easy, for the Chicago Italian underworld was perennially divided and at war with itself. There is no indication that Capone was in any way involved in any of these latter killings. These were murders following in the wake of the destruction of the Genna gang, and the actual killers may all have been Sicilians connected to that gang. Nevertheless, the struggle for control of the remnants of the Genna empire was simultaneously a struggle for the control of the *Unione Siciliana* and, with it, the Italian underworld. This was a struggle to which Capone would now increasingly become committed.

The War of Sicilian Succession — the Aiello Uprising

With the death of Amatuna, Capone at last succeeded in installing his *consigliere*, Antonio Lombardo, as president of the Chicago *Unione Siciliana*.

Lombardo was a self-made man, a classic American rags-to-riches story. He had arrived in America, he wrote, with a mere $12 in his pocket. By diligence and hard work he had built up a successful wholesale grocery and cheese importing business in Chicago's Little Sicily. "He was one of the hundreds," Lombardo wrote of himself, "who cheered joyously, when, from the deck of the steamer, they saw the Statue of Liberty and the skyline of New York, their first sight of the fabled land, America. With his fellow countrymen, he suffered the hardships and indignities to which the United States subjected its prospective citizens at Ellis Island without complaint, for in his heart was a great hope and great ambition."[22]

As a wholesale grocer, Lombardo had done well out of Prohibition, prospering as a sugar dealer, a source for the Gennas' alky-cookers. He was an early friend of Capone. When the North Siders asked the Capone Outfit for a peace conference in October 1926, it was Lombardo who stood in as Capone's representative. Still burned up over the murder of O'Banion and a recent ambush of Drucci, Weiss had showed up in a truculent mood. Weiss announced that his first condition for a truce was that Capone place Scalise and Anselmi on the spot, so that his gang could murder them. It was Lombardo who phoned Weiss's demand to Capone, and Lombardo calmly repeated Capone's response, "I wouldn't do that to a yellow dog." When, a year later, the North Siders saw the light, realizing that a cessation of hostilities would be advantageous to all parties, they asked Maxie Eisen to sound out Lombardo, asking him if Capone would consent to a new peace conference. During the talks themselves, Capone sat surrounded by Lombardo, Jake Guzik, and brother Ralph as his three *consiglieri*.

As president, Lombardo re-instated Merlo's policy of making the *Unione* the respected and semi-legitimate representative of Sicilian interests in Chicago, the official voice of the Sicilian community. This was a role that the *Unione* had always played. Most of the important figures in the Sicilian community, particularly those with some sort of political ambition, were members of the *Unione*. It had contacts with unions, city officials, the Catholic Church and other civic bodies. In the words of Alson J. Smith writing in 1954, however, the *Unione*

> acted as an intermediary in the settlement of personal feuds between various members of the Sicilian community who did not wish to take their disputes before the legal authorities. Quite often, these disputes involved extortion, kidnapping, etc., which in the Old World had been the province of the Sicilian Mafia, the old Black Hand. The Unione was also custodian of a set of weird medieval customs by means of which the Sicilian community in America was bound to that back in Sicily, such things as "blood brotherhood" and omertà, the law of silence.[23]

It was Lombardo who, following Yale's recommendation, changed the official name of the *Unione Siciliana* to the Italo-American National Union. Lombardo moved the offices inside the Loop, opened a publishing house, and sponsored a youth program. He hired a professor from New York University to write a history of famous Italians in Chicago. He lobbied the city to find jobs for Italians on the municipal workforce. He even succeeded in forcing Big Bill Thompson to accept a Sicilian "representative" in his administration, appointing *Unione* official and Capone *consigliere*, Dan Serritella, as City Sealer.

Even without his ally as president of the *Unione Siciliana*, Capone's influence was extending in all directions. When Capone re-established himself in Chicago in 1925, taking for himself a suite of eight rooms in the Hotel Metropole, he also rented rooms upstairs for his new entourage. Included was Frank "The Enforcer" Nitti. Francesco Raffaele Nitto had been born in Sicily in 1889 and had emigrated to the United States when he was three. He worked as a barber, then as a fence, and then as gunmen. He was a small, deliberate man with a good head for figures and a talent for organization. He became Capone's second-in-command in charge of the day-to-day operations of the underworld police.

Al's brother, Ralph "Bottles" Capone, was put in charge of the beer operations; he also ran the Suburban Cigarette Services and the Waukesha Waters company, a soft-drink and mineral water bottling concern that supplied fizzy water and mixers to Capone's resorts. Inevitably, Capone felt obliged to find jobs for all his brothers, cousins, and nephews. Aside from Ralph, however, the only Capone cousin who rose to any prominence in the Outfit was Charles Fischetti, who, along with Laurence "Dago" Mangano, organized beer distribution. The Fischetti family long remained members in good standing in the Chicago Outfit. Bert Delaney was in charge of running the Capone breweries, and Joe Fusco, from a prominent Chicago Sicilian family, managed the distribution of hard liquor. Also included were a Sicilian shoemaker's son named Tony Accardo, later known as Joe Batters; a fugitive from Naples called Felice De Lucia, better known as Paul "the Waiter" Ricca; a talented Welsh thief and bunko artist named Murray Llewellyn Humphrys, nicknamed by the newspapers "Murray the Hump" or "Murray the Camel" but called by his underworld friends "Curly"; and finally Capone's loose-cannon chauffeur, Sam "Mooney" Giancana.

Another Capone intimate, Vincenzo Gibaldi, was born in Sicily in 1903, arriving in Brooklyn when he was less than one. When his father was killed by Irish White Handers, his mother married a grocer named Angelo De Mora and moved to Chicago's Little Italy. The oldest in a family of six brothers and half-brothers, Vincenzo did well in school. He did even better in sports, however, winning the school's boxing championship. He joined an amateur athletics club, which, recognizing the boy's potential, put him on the local circuit as a welterweight. Vincenzo chose a suitably Irish ring-name—"Jack McGurn." But boxing was not the only sport for which Vincenzo displayed a precocious talent. His father had been shot while having his shoes shined; he died with the fifteen cents payment already clutched in his palm—three nickels. At the age on nineteen, Vincenzo returned to Brooklyn to hunt White Handers. He wounded the leader and killed two men involved in his father's slaying. In each of their hands he left a nickel. It was to become the McGurn signature.

As a grocer, McGurn's stepfather, Angelo De Mora, sold sugar for the alky cookers. In 1923, however, Angelo De Mora was murdered, probably by the Gennas, who were trying to take over his business. According to underworld legend, McGurn bought a Daisy air rifle, practicing assiduously on Chicago's sparrow population. The police claimed that, trading in his air gun for something more serious, McGurn hunted down and murdered five Genna gang members. McGurn joined the Capone Outfit, becoming Capone's favorite gunmen as well as his favorite golfing partner. Along with some of the other Capone bodyguards, Michael Spranze, Phil D'Andrea, and Frankie Rio, McGurn kept himself in fighting trim skipping rope and working out in the gym that Capone installed for his boys in the Hotel Metropole. McGurn liked wide-checked suits, heavily padded in the shoulders, flower-figured neckties and pointy patent-leather shoes. He slicked his curly black hair back and parted it in the middle in imitation of Rudolph Valentino. Kobler calls him "the complete jazz age sheik, a ukulele strummer, cabaret habitué and snaky dancer."

Capone kept his ties to Cicero too. The diminutive Lou Cowan had started off selling newspapers on a Cicero street corner, though by the time he met Capone he had acquired his own newsstand. Capone trusted Cowan enough to place several million dollars' worth of property in his name. Cowan became Capone's bail bandsman. Every Outfit member had a card with a telephone number on it. The number was to a druggist on Twenty-fifth Street and Fifty-second Avenue in Cicero. If ever an Outfit member found himself arrested, he was to telephone the druggist, giving his name and the precinct to which he had been taken. The druggist would scurry across the street to Cowan's newsstand and relay the message. Cowan would then hop into a limousine that Capone kept on hand for just this purpose, and hurry to the precinct with his property deeds in his pocket. In that way, Outfit members could always be sure of making bail.

Another ex-newsboy, Frankie Pope, managed the Hawthorn Smoke Shop, the headquarters of Capone's gambling operations on the South Side. He looked after the off-track betting on the horses and dogs. The young Johnny Patton from Burnham, who back in 1920 had sold Torrio the Arrowhead Inn for a mere $15,000, remained as Capone's political agent in southern Cook County.

As the new *Unione* president, Lombardo faced the daunting task of guaranteeing order in the most deadly segment of Chicago's underworld milieu— the Italians. Naturally he looked to Capone for help. Acting as patrons of the community, Lombardo and Capone worked to mediate disputes and personal feuds, eliminate extortion and street crime, and, by keeping the police sweet, ensure that the immensely profitable and increasingly Italian-dominated Chicago vice ring kept running smoothly. The alliance between Capone and the *Unione* under Lombardo had its dangers, however. By installing his own *consigliere* as president of the *Unione,* Capone was wading into all the feuds and struggles in Chicago's Italian communities. The alliance meant that enemies of either Lombardo or Capone were now allies in a struggle against the pair of them. Given the turmoil in the Italian underworld, alongside his new friends, Capone was getting himself a bunch of new enemies.

An intimation of the treats in store for him was almost served up by the chef of Joe Esposito's Bella Napoli Café. It was Capone's favorite restaurant. Only a few months earlier, Capone had celebrated the Sherman House Treaty by hosting the notorious "feast of ghouls." Now he learned that the chef had been offered $35,000 to poison him. Tempted by so large a sum, the chef seems to have agreed at first. At the last moment, however, either sympathy towards his most eminent client or a sense of professional pride stayed his hand. The prussic acid was not added to *Signor* Capone's *minestrone.* Al was relieved to hear it. "If I had known what I was stepping into in Chicago," he remarked, "I would never have left the Five Points Outfit."[24] Later, he learned that the poisoning plot had been concocted by Joe Aiello.

Aiello, with his eight brothers and numerous cousins, led their own faction within the *Unione.* Born in Bagheria in Palermo Province in 1890, Aiello emigrated to America when he was seventeen. At the advent of Prohibition, he was a partner in Lombardo's wholesale grocery business, Lombardo & Co. In the early Twenties, Lombardo and Aiello borrowed $100,000 from Capone to set up a wholesale corn sugar business to supply Little Sicily's alky cookers. Both were on good terms with Frankie Yale. Following the death of Merlo, Lombardo and Aiello both had a claim to the *Unione* presidency. Instead, Angelo Genna simply seized the presidency for himself. Lombardo was Torrio's and Capone's candidate; Angelo Genna's little *coup d'etat* at the *Unione* was more of a setback for Torrio and Capone than for Aiello, who had grown close to the Genna family. With Angelo Genna succeeding Merlo, the outlook for the Aiellos seemed bright. With the murders of Angelo, Mike, and Tony Genna, followed by that of Amatuna, however, the Aiellos' prospects took a decided turn for the worse. In late 1925, Joe and Dominic Aiello were trying to pick up the pieces, taking over the Genna faction in the *Unione* and knit the Gennas' alky-cooking empire back together. In their minds, blame for the fall of the House of Genna centered on one man—Al Capone. The Aiello family thus became the leaders of all those in Chicago's Sicilian underworld opposed to the Capone Outfit.

The proud and prickly Gennas had refused to ally with any but fellow Sicilians. Wiser, the Aiellos built up a network of alliances in the Chicago area. They worked with Billy Skidmore and Barney Bertsche, two ex-gambling house owners who now ran a string of resorts with beer and bootlegging concerns, and with Jack Zuta. Skidmore and Bertsch had been allied to the North Siders and continued to do business with Bugs Moran. Capone was not worried about Skidmore and Bertsch. They were traditional Chicago underworld figures, men with an array of political connections and an interest in bail bonding and jury-fixing. They had attended the meeting at the Hotel Sherman and had agreed to pay Capone a percentage of their take. They were businessmen, and, as much as they probably hated paying protection to the Capone Outfit, would not annoy Capone if he did not bother them. If Skidmore and Bertsch wanted to do business with the Aiellos, Capone was not going to stop them. Zuta was a Russian Jewish brothel owner who did Moran's accounts for him. He was not a danger either.

Capone was probably more worried about the Aiellos' approach to Moran. There was bad blood between Capone and the North Siders. Yet Moran was observing the Hotel Sherman agreement and behaving himself. He even bought Capone's whiskey. After the Hotel Sherman meeting and Mayor Thompson's pledge to make Chicago as wet as the middle of the Atlantic, the Beer War in Chicago had begun to wind down. There was continuing violence among the Irish gangs in the South West, but the leading bootleggers were now concentrating on selling drink rather than murdering competitors. Capone's real worries were no longer on the bootlegging front. The real threat now came from the Aiellos, who were trying to raise the Italian underworld against him.

With Lombardo president of the *Unione,* the Aiellos felt out-maneuvered. They took their complaints to New York *Unione* president Frankie Yale. Chicagoans, however, were Yale's best customers; a steady stream of Yale trucks carrying Yale whiskey left Coney Island bound for Chicago, and Yale was reaping a handsome profit. He had no desire to stir up trouble with Capone.

The Italo-American National Union was another matter. That was Yale's pet project. His ambition was to transform the network of loosely-affiliated *Unioni Siciliane* into a unified Italo-American underworld syndicate with himself as president. Lombardo was a Capone man, body and soul. With Lombardo's accession as president of the powerful Chicago *Unione Siciliana* (which, despite the official change, it continued to be called), Yale's influence and prestige suffered a serious blow. Insulated by Capone against any pressure Yale might bring, Lombardo could act independently. Yale temporized; he tried to maintain good relations with Capone while quietly encouraging the Aiellos and turning a blind eye to their machinations.

Capone's new predominance in the Chicago *Unione* was resented in the Sicilian underworld. Capone was a Neapolitan, a whoremonger, an acolyte of that other Neapolitan whoremonger, Johnny Torrio. He worked closely with Jews and Blacks. In meetings with *Unione* members in New York, Cleveland, Milwaukee, Pittsburgh, St. Louis, and Dayton, the Aiellos found pockets of resentment, men who, out of Sicilian pride or from local rivalries, were willing to throw in their lot with the Aiello family. It was the beginning of a national anti-Capone coalition.

Capone had his own allies and spies and was kept informed of the Aiello plot. In November 1927, two of the Aiello family, Robert and Frank Aiello, were returning from a mission to St. Louis when they stopped at a roadside café near Springfield Illinois. Someone knew about their mission. They had followed them to the cafe, and, bursting in with guns, left the two Aiello brothers sprawling face-down in their lunches. The killers were never identified. Though Capone, who took the Aiello threat extremely seriously, might have ordered the killings, it seems more likely that the killers had come from a Capone faction within the St. Louis Italian underworld. After the Springfield murders, six more pro-Aiello members of the St. Louis *Unione* were gunned down in short order.

In May 1927, a body had been found in the rundown area of De Koven and Des Plaines Streets in Chicago. The murdered man was wearing expensive clothing and carrying $1,200 in his pockets. Robbery had not been the motive. He was also wearing a shoulder holster with a gun. Oddest of all, the police found a nickel clutched in his cold right hand. Between May and October, three more corpses were found in a similar condition—money in their pockets, an unfired gun, and a nickel in their right hand. Eventually the police identified the corpses; they were those of Antonio Torchio of New York, Anthony K. Russo and Vincent Spicuzza of St. Louis, and Samuel Valente of Cleveland. Each had tried to take up the Aiellos on their standing offer—"$50,000 to anyone who can show us a Capone notch." Eventually they figured out the meaning of the nickel too, but every time they hauled Jack McGurn in, he had a good alibi.

Knowing that the best defense is a good offense, in the summer of 1927, Capone carried the war into Aiello territory. In six weeks Capone's gunmen got six Aiello notches for themselves: Lawrence La Presta, 1 June; Diego Attlomionte, 29 June; Numio Jamericco and Lorenzo Alagno, 30 June; Giovanni

Blaudins, 11 July; and Dominic Cinderella, 17 July. In each case, the coroner's verdict was "slayers not apprehended." In the Cinderella killing, they went so far as to arrest McGurn and his companion, Orchell De Grazio, then released them "for lack of evidence."[25] McGurn also shot and wounded the Gusenberg brothers, Frank and Pete, in November 1927.

Alarmed at the new spate of gangland slayings, Chief Detective William O'Connor called for police volunteers. He specified that the men he was looking for needed combat experience; he wanted army veterans, men who knew how to handle a machine gun. O'Connor was going to declare war on the underworld. He assembled his new team and invited the newspapers in to hear his pep talk:

> Men, the war is on. We have got to show that society and the police department, and not a bunch of dirty rats, are running this town. It is the wish of the people of Chicago that you hunt these criminals down and kill them without mercy. Your cars are equipped with machine-guns and you will meet the enemies of society on equal terms. See to it that they do not have you pushing up daisies. Make them push up daisies. Shoot first and shoot to kill. If you kill a notorious feudist you will get a handsome reward and win promotion. If you meet a car containing bandits pursue them and fire. When I arrive on the scene my hopes will be fulfilled if you have shot off the top of their car and killed every criminal inside it.[26]

"Turn the streets of Chicago into the fields of Flanders, and make Michigan Avenue a free-fire zone." The speech was in all the papers. The Chamber of Commerce must have loved it. The same day, the armoured squads shot and killed Joe Saltis's bodyguard and arrested forty-five gangsters charged with shootings, stabbings, and bombings. It was all union racketeering stuff, however, and neither the Capone Outfit nor the Aiello family was seriously inconvenienced. Indeed, the presence of armored squad cars filled with machine-gun toting World War I vets patrolling the streets of Chicago rather suited Capone; it served to discourage the Aiellos. Indeed, it may have even given him an idea.

In November 1927, the Chicago police got a tip-off from an underworld source. The police, the stool pigeon said, ought to pay a visit to a house on 4442 Washington Blvd. In an apartment in the Washington Blvd building they found a machine-gun nest directly overlooking Antonio Lombardo's house on the opposite side of the street. Some of Lombardo's friends went over to talk with Joe Aiello about it, but they were told that Aiello was in New York.

The police then got another tip-off about a house ten miles away, on North Western Avenue. At the North Western Avenue address they discovered a cache of dynamite and a box of percussion caps that someone had carelessly left behind. Even more careless, someone had left a registration receipt from the Rex Hotel at North Ashland Avenue. The receipt was in the name of Antonio La Mantio. The police naturally high-tailed it to the Rex Hotel, where they discovered La Mantio, a twenty-three-year old Milwaukee gunman, in the company of four members of the Aiello gang. La Mantio proved quite willing to unburden himself. He told the police that Joe Aiello had hired him to bump off Lombardo and Capone. He went on to describe the trap that he and the Aiellos had laid. They had mounted another gun nest in the Atlantic Hotel at 316 South Clark Street, opposite Hinky Dink Kenna's tobacco shop. When the police arrived at the hotel room, they found high-powered rifles clamped to a window and trained on Hinky-Dink's front door. Capone was an old customer; he sometimes liked to drop in, buy some cigars, and stick around to chat a bit with the old 1st Ward boss.[27]

Capone and Lombardo were brought to the detective bureau on South Clark Street. It was a mere formality. The police knew that they would refuse to identify any of the men arrested in the Rex Hotel. But when Capone discovered that the men were working with Joe Aiello, who was supposed to be in New York, his attitude changed dramatically.

The police arrested Joe Aiello for attempted murder. Within an hour of Aiello's arrival at the detective bureau's lock-up on South Clark Street, the officers on duty there were surprised to see six taxis pull up in front of the station house and disgorge about twenty-five men, some with arms. Some of the men looked Italian, so the duty officers at first assumed that a big raid had gone down, and the detectives were bringing in a bunch of Italian hoods for questioning. Then they looked again. All of them were Italians, and they were coming with guns. Besides, they were not entering the police station, but surrounding it. The astonished station officers next beheld three gangsters calmly walk towards the station house, one of them, Louis "Little New York" Campagna, taking an automatic pistol from his side holster and shifting it into his pocket, probably trying to make it look less conspicuous.

As they stood there, mouths agape, watching the trio approach, the light began to dawn. Capone's boys had arrived to take delivery of `their' prisoner! Capone thought he could deal with the Chicago Police Department as if he were some sort of foreign power. Camapgna was arriving to `extradite' Joe Aiello to Capone.

As soon as the officers understood what was taking place, they seized and disarmed Louis Campagna and his two bodyguards. Curious to see what would happen, they decided to put Campagna in a cell with Joe Aiello. A Sicilian-speaking detective, disguised as a prisoner, was placed in an adjoining cell.

"You're dead, friend, you're dead," the detective heard Campagna growl to Aiello. "You won't get up to the end of the street still walking."

"Can't we settle this," Aiello pleaded. "Give me fourteen days and I'll sell my stores, my house and everything and quit Chicago for good. Can't we settle it? Think of my wife and baby."

"You dirty rat! you broke faith with us twice now. You started this; we'll finish it."

Aiello was booked for conspiracy to commit murder. By the time his lawyer arrived to spring him on bail, a crowd of curious reporters were congregating at the sergeant's desk. They saw Aiello run to Chief O'Connor and ask for police protection. "Sure," O'Connor said, turning to the listening reporters. "I'll give you police protection—all the way to New York and onto a boat. . . . You'll get no police protection around Chicago from me." When he saw that Aiello's wife and son had come to the station, he relented and let a pair of policemen escort Aiello to a taxi. The next day, Aiello disappeared, and three Aiello-owned bakeries closed down. Aiello's lawyer appeared at court and explained that Joe Aiello had suffered a nervous breakdown and could not appear at his committal proceeding. In truth, taking two of his brothers, Tony and Dominic, Joe Aiello had fled to Trenton and remained hidden for the next two years.

The reporters questioned Capone as well. "When I was told that Joey Aiello wanted to make peace, but that he wanted fourteen days to settle his affairs, I was ready to agree," He lied. Then, more truthfully, he continued: "I don't want no trouble. I don't want bloodshed. But I'm going to protect myself. When someone strikes at me, I will strike back."[28]

Some have suggested that the aborted Aiello ambush was a Capone set up all along. Antonio La Mantio was working for Capone; his job was stringing the Aiellos along, setting up hits on Capone, and possibly Lombardo as well, making sure to leave plenty of evidence lying around, including his name and address. When everything was all ready, with Joe Aiello sitting beside the window on South Clark Street impatiently waiting for Capone to come buy his cigar, a stool pigeon called to set alarms ringing with the Chicago police. It is impossible to disprove. It seems odd to have singled out Hinky-Dink's cigar store, though. The "Little Fella" had retired from active politics after closure of the Levee. Though still an elder statesman in the old 1st Ward, Kenna was not that close to Capone.

Bathhouse John Coughlin remained an alderman, however. A couple of years earlier, Capone had asked him to drop by. "Alderman," Capone told him, "you were a good pal of Big Jim's. You stood in with Torrio. Well, they're gone now, and we're running the show, and we don't want trouble with you. Let it get around. I'm telling you because I like you."

It was a piece of friendly advice, and Coughlin, who had feared the worst, felt relieved. "My God," he told his friends after he got back from the meeting, "what could I say? Suppose he said he was going to take over the organization? What could we do then? We're lucky to get a good break as we did!"[29] So much for the theory that Capone was working for Kenna and Coughlin. He scared the pants off the old boodling duo.

THE WAR OF SICILIAN SUCCESSION SPREADS

Whether the Aiellos had been set up, their family was temporarily out of action in Trenton, New Jersey.

After leaving Chicago, Joe Aiello and his brothers visited Yale in Brooklyn. There they complained that Capone had forced Lombardo down the throats pf Chicago's *Unione Siciliana*. Now, with Capone's backing, Lombardo was holding out on Yale too. Lombardo, they said, was not sending him his cut, the dues which, as national president, were owing to him. According to Alson Smith, Yale did not care much who was president of the Chicago *Unione*. If Lombardo and Capone had cheated Joe Aiello out of the presidency, that was Joe's tough luck. Yale wanted his cut though, and he believed what Joe Aiello was telling him: Lombardo was deliberately holding back. Yale, according to Smith, issued an order telling Lombardo to step down and let Joe Aiello take his place.[30] It is hard to believe that Yale would have done anything that stupid; Lombardo was never going to obey such an order, and with Capone running Chicago and the Aiellos in hiding, Yale had no means to force him. There was, however, another course open.

Capone had already begun to suspect that Yale was helping the Aiellos stir up trouble for him in the *Unione*. Now he suspected that it was Yale who was hijacking the whiskey shipments from Brooklyn. It was a common enough practice during Prohibition. A buyer purchased a consignment of whiskey, making part or all of the payment up front. But the whiskey would disappear in transit, the work of unknown bad guys, the supplier would tell his customer. It was an unfortunate incident . . . sorry about the inconvenience. It was the supplier who made the schedules, dispatched the trucks and determined the routes and times, so it was the supplier who best knew how to hijack his own trucks. Nor was there much that the buyer could do about this: bootleggers couldn't sue other bootleggers. They couldn't ask the police to investigate the hijacking. They couldn't take the supplier to court. What made Capone particularly suspicious was that the trucks were being hijacked in Brooklyn, in Yale's own back yard. Frankie, it seems, was not making any great effort to hide what was going on, and Capone felt offended

Nevertheless, killing Yale was a serious matter. Before acting on his suspicions, Capone wanted to make sure. Capone turned investigations over to McGurn, who sent a spy named James Finesy de Amato to Brooklyn. Yale's men observed de Amato making long-distance calls to Chicago from a Brooklyn phone booth, and de Amato was gunned down less than a month after he arrived. Whether de Amato was relaying evidence of Yale's involvement in the hijackings, McGurn was now convinced of Yale's perfidy. McGurn had a flair for the dramatic. He sent Yale an anonymous note: "Some day you'll get an answer to de Amato."

On a sunny mid-afternoon on July 1, 1928, as Yale sped down Borough Parkway in Brooklyn, a closed car with Illinois license plates brushed alongside him. Inside were five men armed with a veritable arsenal of Tommy guns and sawed-off shotguns. Seconds later, Yale's bullet-riddled car was slowly plowing its way through a neighboring gate, careening into a tea party taking place in the back garden. As the women screamed, the children peered in curiously, noticing Yale's lifeless head still lolling in front of the steering wheel.[31]

The Yale murder was the first major gangland hit in New York since 1922. It was also, the papers commented, the first Chicago-style killing in

New York, the first time a Tommy gun had been used on the East Coast. It soon became obvious that it was more than a 'Chicago-style' hit. It was the Yale murder that helped give McGurn his nickname of "Machine Gun Jack."

It was also the occasion for New York's first Chicago-style gangland funeral. "No Supreme Court Justice or venerable saloonkeeper who has been making other men Supreme Court Justices ever went to the grave with quite the fanfare that attended the obsequies of Frankie Yale, the Brooklyn mobster," wrote Thompson and Raymond. His obsequies were attended by two widows, both claiming to be married to the deceased, who were vying with each other in displays of torrential emotion on either side of the grave.

Unlike the Chicago gangsters, Yale had been a communicant in good standing. Frank Yale was listed on a board of the church in which his services were sung, and as a donor to the parish of $1,500 in a single gift. In fact, he had donated a great deal more than this.

Ten thousand of his fellow citizens attended the requiem mass in St. Rosalia's Roman Catholic Church in Brooklyn or followed the cortege to Holy Cross Cemetery. Yale's business partner and successor, Little Augie Pisano, was there. Fellow *Unione Siciliana* notable, Lupo the Wolf Saietta, recently released from custody, was also conspicuous among the mourners. At the ceremony's culminating moment, when the grave diggers had filled their spades and were prepared to spread the first dirt clods over Yale's gleaming silver casket, 112 selected dignitaries tossed red roses into the air, letting them float down into the open grave or onto surrounding grass.

Thirty-eight automobiles were needed to carry the floral offerings. Crosses of blossoms towered fifteen feet high beside the grave, and rose lyres swayed at its foot. Between the arms of the flower lyres were floral clocks made of blue and white violets in which were pasted in gilt paper the hands of time to show the exact hour at which Frankie died, 4:10 p.m. Gauze ribbons in blue and pink and purple and white bore sentimental messages from the bereaved followers.

"We'll see them kid," said the message upon a small, red pillow of roses. Another big floral offering said, "Love, pal," and still others bore the words, "Good-bye, old timer," and "Love from the Boys." There was a ponderous bleeding heart with a dagger made out of lavender and white violets plunged into its center. There was an eighteen-foot floral column of red and white roses, bearing Frankie's initial "Y."[32]

"We'll see them kid," the pillow had proclaimed, and it did not take long.

Lombardo had moved the Italo-American National Union offices to the Hartford Building at Dearborn and Madison streets. He usually spent a few hours each day working there. On Friday, September 7, 1928, Lombardo stepped out from the Italo-American National Union headquarters and into the bustling mid-afternoon crowd of Dearborn Street. A year ago, with the Aiellos on the rampage, he had never stepped outside without a full complement of eight bodyguards. But now, with the Aiellos in Trenton and Yale taken care of, he had begun to relax his guard. Besides, the Hartford Building was inside the Loop; walking around Chicago's business district surrounded by eight torpedos would create a scandal. He would stick out, look just like a Sicilian crime boss. Lombardo was anxious to improve the Sicilian community's image.

So on Septermber 7, Lombardo was accompanied by just two bodyguards, Joe Ferrara and Joe Lolordo. Tony and the two Joes stopped to watch as a small airplane was hauled up the side of the Boston store, one of the city's largest department stores. It was destined to be part of a display, and had attracted a small crowd of on-lookers. Lolordo later testified that, as they turned to walk on, passing the Raklios Restaurant at 61 Dearborn, he had heard someone say, `Why, there they are!' A man in grey stepped out of the restaurant and, walking up behind Lombardo, sent two .38 caliber dum-dum bullets through the back of his head. A tall man, in a dark suit, appearing from nowhere, fired a bullet into Ferrara's back. Lolordo pulled out his pistol and set out after the man in grey. A patrolman grabbed him and wrestled his pistol away, ignoring Lolordo's pleas to let him go.

Although Capone was in residence at the Hawthorne Inn on the day of Yale's murder, he was out of town when Lombardo was killed. By now, he was spending more and more time outside of Chicago. He spent the winters of 1927–28 and 1928–29 in Miami and was negotiating to buy a house on Palm Island where he planned to move his family. He was trying to convince a skeptical Dade County police force that he had left the rough stuff behind him. He returned to Chicago for Tony Lombardo's funeral, though. His friends had advised him to stay in Florida. The press would be looking for him in Chicago, and would get up a rumpus if they found him. Other people, the ones who had killed Lombardo, might be looking for him too. "I will see my pal to his grave," Capone replied. Burns takes the reply as a challenge to the Aiellos; 'If you want to come and get me, I'll be at Tony Lombardo's funeral.' But Capone was loyal to those who were loyal to him. Lombardo had been a good friend, and Capone really wanted to see him to his grave. He took no chances, coming to the funeral surrounded by formidable men — Scalise, Anselmi, McGurn, Frank Rio and Dago Joe Montana. He didn't share his thoughts with the reporters this time, at least directly. He expressed himself instead in a great heart of red roses eight feet high with an inscription worked in white roses; "To my Pal," the inscription read. After the funeral, he went back to Florida.

Capone was not challenging the Aiellos to come and get him because he could not even be entirely sure that it was the Aiellos who had murdered Lombardo. The Aiellos had stirred up the underworld against Capone, but especially after the Yale murder, guns were pointed at Capone from every direction. The Aiellos were doubtless delighted at the news of Lombardo's death; but the hit could have come from a number of sources. Capone may not have even known himself, though he seems to have had some suspicions. On the day after Lombardo's funeral the police found an Italian lying beside a burnt car with a bullet through his head near Benton Harbor, Michigan. Though the police never found out who the Italian was, they did discover that

Capone, McGurn, and Mops Volpe had been at a near-by hotel a few hours before the incident.

A little while layer, the Aiello headquarters at 431 West Division Street was riddled with two hundred machine-gun bullets, and Tony Aiello and Charles Delo were wounded. "Tough Tony" Califiore, of the Aiello gang, was shot. Salvatore Cannelli, another Aiello man, drove home from a visit to his sweetheart in Melrose Park, where his wedding engagement had been announced at a party. He was killed by two men who waited in his garage and almost blew his head off with sawed-off shotguns. Bowlegs Olivieri and Joseph Salmone, two Capone henchmen, took the "the big trip." Automatic pistols broke "the bad news" to Virgilio Aliotta, of the Aiello faction. Joseph Cavaretti, allied with the Aiellos, was "taken for a walk," instead of for a ride, and killed by two men he had supposed to be his friends in front of the Church of God in Little Hell [Little Sicily].[33]

Peter Rizzito was president of Local No 13 of the Chicago *Unione*, and a close friend of Lombardo. He had been having a telephone conversation with his friend just before Lombardo had left his eleventh floor office in the Hartford Building. The conversation had been long enough, some said, to allow his killers to get in place on the street below. Nonsense, others said, it had been a normal business conversation. Rizzito was a true friend, and would make a good president to follow Lombardo. Whatever the truth, Rizzito was murdered the next month by two men with sawed-off shotguns. No one could guess who they were or why they had done it or what, if any, bearing it had on the Capone-Aiello war or the Lombardo killing. All that was certain was that the sad days of the Alderman's War were back in Little Sicily.

The war was taking a terrible toll. The retreat of the Aiellos had brought no peace. Events were spinning out of control. New Black Hand gangs were forming and murdering each other, sometimes blaming it on Capone or the Aiellos. Little Sicily was turning into a wasteland. Wrote Orville Dwyer in the *Tribune*,

> More than 300 families have moved away from here since August 1 [1928]. "Why did they all go?" They were told to go. They got a mysterious telephone call or anonymous letters. And the next day they were gone. A few weeks ago laughter and music came out of these houses, lights twinkled in them in the evening. Now they are empty and their windows stare like blind eyes in the sun. There are hundreds of vacant flats, whole buildings.

> There are 300 to 400 fewer children in the [Edward] Jenner School this year than there were last. St. Philip's has lost more than 200 children. "Do you know that you cannot buy any meat in practically this whole district?" . . . A few weeks ago the butcher shops started suddenly and mysteriously to close down, one by one. They have been closed for several weeks now. The same sinister, inexplicable force.[34]

Tony Aiello, writes Burns, "was a dark, slender young man, with a little black mustache. He was a salesman for the Aiello gang and bustled about the North

Side drumming up trade. He looked quite innocuous. He carried a little black book in which he entered orders, a lead pencil tucked behind his ear." He also carried a 45-caliber automatic pistol in a shoulder holster. Tony stepped out of a barber shop next to the Aiellos West Division Street headquarters, just as Giuseppe *il Cavaliere* Nerone was getting out of his car. The two men looked at each other and did a double take. Then they pulled out their guns. Tony Aiello was just that much quicker; he got off three shots while Nerone only got off one, only shattering the barber shop window. Two of Aiello's bullets had hit Nerone. As he lay writhing on the pavement, an Aiello bodyguard stepped up and finished him off. No one knew what it had all been about; indeed had not the barber's nine-year-old son blurted out what he saw before his elders could hush him up, we would not even be able to place Aiello at the scene. Since no one was going to testify, the police did not even bother to pick up Tony Aiello. The murder probably had nothing to do with the murder of Tony the Gentleman Genna. Nerone had been doing quite well for himself lately, not in anything wholesome, one imagines.[35]

The Underworld at War: Part 2—Many Cities: From the St. Valentine's Day Massacre to the Castellammarrese War

"THEY'RE ALL DEAD"

On the morning of February 14, 1929, three empty trucks were waiting in the warehouse on North Clark. A fourth truck was jacked up in the center of the floor while mechanic Jimmy May was fixing a wheel. Jimmy's dog, a German Shepherd named Highball, sat nearby, tied by his leash to the truck axle. As May worked, six men waited. It was bitterly cold that day, so the men were stomping around with the collars of their overcoats turned up and their hats pulled down. Outside, Bugs Moran was hurrying toward the warehouse. He had brought a friend, Ted Newberry, with him. Another friend, Willie Marks was coming from the opposite direction. As they turned the corner, Moran and Newberry saw what looked like a police car drawn up in front of the warehouse. Assuming that some sort of police shake-down was taking place, they beat it. When they saw Henry Gusenberg approaching, they warned him to get away too. Coming from a different direction, Willie Marks drew the same conclusion and disappeared as well.

We know that there were at least four and at most six killers. Two of them were the men in police costumes. They told Jimmy May and the six other men in the North Clark Street warehouse to turn and face the wall without putting up any sort of resistance. It was just some sort of police shake down, they must have thought. As they turned, at least two other men dressed in plain clothes entered, probably from the back. All seven men were then systematically mowed down by Tommy-gun fire. The killers were methodical, swinging their guns along the line three times—at head level, at chest level, at stomach level. Afterwards the killers carefully blasted any of the fallen bodies still showing signs of life with sawed-off shotguns. The police later found that some of the bodies were almost cut in half, still hanging together with shreds of tattered flesh. After the shooting, the killers in plainclothes raised their hands and marched out to the police car, closely followed by the two men in police costumes, walking behind with their guns lowered.

The noise of the shooting, which some had taken for a pneumatic drill while others had thought sounded like some kind of fast, weird drumming, had brought people to their windows and onto the street. What they now beheld looked like a police action, two men under arrest being led away by two police officers. It was only several hours later that the dog's incessant howling caused a landlady named Mrs. Landesman to send one of her lodgers over to investigate. He soon came running back, sick and pale: "They're all dead," was all he could say.

St. Valentine's Day Mysteries

One wonders if God understands Sicilians.

—Walter Noble Burns

Two months earlier, in the pre-dawn chill of December 5, 1928, Patrolman Frank Osowski of the Cleveland police was pounding his beat when he noticed two touring cars pulling up in front of the Statler Hotel. Curious, he stopped to watch, counting eleven well-dressed men getting out of the cars and walking into the hotel. After hesitating a moment, Osowski stepped across the street and peered into the doorway after them; he saw the men checking in. A rough-looking bunch, "The men looked both ways and pulled their hats down as they entered the hotel," Osowski later testified.[1] He watched as they climbed into the elevators to take them up to their room. As soon as the elevator doors had closed, Osowski walked into the foyer and asked the desk clerk for the registration book, jotting down the names he read there. Later, clocking off from work, he stopped by to drop his list off at the detective bureau.

It was just a precaution; for the names meant nothing to Osowski. But to the Cleveland detectives arriving the following morning and discovering the list waiting for them, the names rang a bell. The list included some of the best-known bootleggers in the country. Interested in finding out what possible motive this motley party of gangsters could have had for convening in their city at such an ungodly hour, the detective drove over to the Statler—though not before taking the precaution of assembling a small army of law-enforcement officials as back-up just in case.

By the time the detectives arrived, the number of suspicious-looking out-of-towners had grown to twenty-three.[2] None of them offered any resistance, nor did any of them seem to be committing crimes. So the detectives just took them to police headquarters to be photographed and fingerprinted. The detectives questioned them as well, though naturally they were unable to learn anything useful. Then they booked all twenty-three on "suspicious persons" charges, posting bonds of $10,000 each.

Several hours later, Cleveland's leading "Sugar Baron," Joseph Porello, walked into police headquarters. He brought with him pledges for approximately $400,000 of real estate in the Cleveland area. With this collateral, all but one of the detainees, a small-time hoodlum from New Jersey wanted on a murder charge, were released pending their hearings.

Who were these twenty-three "suspicious persons" and what were they doing in the pre-dawn hours in Cleveland's Statler Hotel. Unraveling this question will take us, first, into the background of the St. Valentine's Day massacre in Chicago and, from there, into the war that was about to engulf the entire American underworld—the Castellammarrese War.

Among the twenty-three gangsters were seven from Chicago. The Chicago contingent included the new *Unione* president, Pasqualino Lolordo, and his assistant, Joseph Giunta. We can start with them.

Pasqualino's brother, Joe Lolordo, had been one of Tony Lombardo's two bodyguards. After the Lombardo shooting, Joe had dashed south down Dearborn Street with policeman Leslie Finlayson close on his heels. Joe ducked into a shoe store in the Hartford Building, where Officer Finlayson caught up and disarmed him. At first, Joe Lolordo denied that he had anything to do with Lombardo or the shooting. His denials were not believed, however, and Lolordo soon changed his story. He was chasing after one of the assailants, he said, a 'man in gray.' His original denials plus the fact that none of the other witnesses had seen the 'man in gray' made police suspicious. Joe had been standing on Lombardo's left side when the fatal dum-dum blasts had been fired; the bullets had entered Lombardo's brain from the left side. This also seemed suspicious. Nevertheless, Joe Lolordo was still carrying his own revolver when he was stopped; it was not the murder weapon. The police had recovered the murder weapons, which had been thrown away, perhaps by the mysterious 'man in gray.' The recovery of the murder weapons seemed to confirm Joe's story. Suspicions revived however as soon as it was known that Joe's older brother, Pasqualino "Patsy" Lolordo had succeeded Tony Lombardo as *Unione* president. Nevertheless Capone liked the two Lolordo brothers. He trusted Joe and had been happy to see Patsy take over as the new *Unione* president.[3]

Nevertheless, even by the standards of the Chicago *Unione Siciliana*, Patsy Lolordo's tenure in office was to prove brief. On the 8th of January, 1929, Lolordo and his wife Aleina met two well-known but unidentified, gangsters outside of Lolordo's apartment. The two had arrived for lunch. Several hours later, the first two gangsters left, and three other men arrived. Lolordo welcomed them cordially, and took them into his study. Later, from the laundry where she was ironing, Lolordo's wife heard her husband fetch a bottle of wine and some wine glasses; he was evidently going to propose some sort of toast. A few minutes later, as Lolordo was making his toast, two of the guests pulled out .38 caliber guns and emptied both clips into his body.

It was an old trick, like the cordial handshake that suddenly tightened, immobilizing Tony Genna while the assassin slipped out of the shadows and shot him in the back of the head. A man on his feet, glass raised on high, saying a few choice words about peace and good fellowship is effectively immobilized, almost a perfect target. Lolordo's assassins pumped eleven slugs into Patsy without spilling a drop of their wine. It's a swell way of killing someone, though it seems a lousy trick.

It may help to review the chronology here. By late 1927 violence in Chicago resulting from the Capone-Aiello war had begun to spread to the rest of the Chicago underworld. In early November, Jack McGurn wounded Pete and Frank Gusenberg in the cigar store of Chicago's McCormick Hotel. Later that month, Jack Zuta's restaurant on 323 North Ashland was bombed. Three days later, Billy Skidmore's and Barney Bertsch's headquarters at 823 West Adams was bombed as well. November was also the month in which the Aiellos set up gun nests opposite Tony Lombardo's home and Dink Kenna's cigar store.

The war continued through 1928. In early January two more of Skidmore/Bertsch/Zuta resorts were bombed. Two days later, two Capone lieutenants, Phil D'Andrea and Dago Lawrence Mangano, shot up the Pasticceria Bella Palermo, the Aiello Brothers Bakery at 473 West Division Street. During the 1928 Republican primaries, the homes of candidates on both the Thompson-Crowe and the Deneen wings were bombed, while the mayor of Little Italy, Joe "Dimey" Esposito was gunned down. In July of 1928 came the murder of Yale. The murder of Tony Lombardo followed in September 1928. The police issued arrest warrants for Joe and Dominic Aiello as well as Zuta over the Lombardo killing, but the Aiellos claimed to have been in Trenton at the time, and Zuta had a water-tight alibi. Capone was mostly in Florida. The Statler Hotel meeting in Cleveland took place on December 5. Patsy Lolordo was murdered on January 8, 1928, a month before the St. Valentine's Day massacre.

According to newspaper reports, after Patsy Lolordo's murder, his wife, Aleina, told the police that one of the murderers was Joe Aiello. But Mrs. Lolordo refused to testify or talk to the papers. It would, she said, be signing a death warrant for her son, an eighteen-year-old student at the University of Illinois. John Stege, Chicago's deputy police chief, denied that Mrs. Lolordo had ever made any identification, dismissing the reports as a rumor. It turned out that the source of the *Tribune's* report was Dan Serritella, a Capone intimate more than once accused of spreading false tales. Had he deemed it necessary to preserve a news blackout, Captain Stege would not have hesitated to deny that any identification had been made. Nevertheless, the police did not pursue the Aiello connection, speculating instead that Lolordo had been killed by the Gusenberg brothers. Thus the report that Lolordo's wife had identified Joe Aiello as her husband's killer seems part of the Capone Outfit's campaign of disinformation.

The police did find a draft constitution in the Lolordo apartment for a new "North-West Italian-American Club." They surmised that Lolordo was planning some sort of institutional reorganization, possibly the founding of a rival to the *Unione*. Lolordo, in other words, was planning to betray someone, either Capone or Aiello or possibly both. Thus Lolordo's presence at the *Unione Siciliana* reunion at the Hotel Statler a month earlier could be evidence that he was already part of an anti-Capone plot. Still, as Allan May observes, whoever killed Lolordo entered the apartment as a friend. Indeed, the two men who entered for lunch and the three murders who came later, were all admitted and cordially greeted. Some sort of plot was clearly being hatched; but whomever Lolordo was plotting with betrayed him instead. We do not, unfortunately, know the identities or the purposes of any of the five visitors.

Capone biographer Robert J. Schoenberg identifies Patsy Lolordo's murderers as James Clark and the Gusenberg brothers, Pete and Frank. It is not an unreasonable supposition; yet Schoenberg suffers from a compulsion to provide solutions to every mystery whether or not they are supported by any evidence. His identification of Clark and the Gusenberg brothers as the Lolordo murders is no more than a hypothesis. Nevertheless, it is a plausible hypothesis; Schoenberg has got the context right.

Despite inevitable rumors to the contrary, there is no real evidence that Joe Aiello had returned to Chicago in January 1929. But he wouldn't have needed to; others were acting in his stead. The Moran gang, including the Gusenberg brothers, as well as some yet-to-be-identified gangs in Little Sicily were supporting the Aiello cause. If Lolordo was still a Capone loyalist, he counts as one of the fifteen losses the Outfit sustained between mid-November 1928 and mid-January 1929.

Neither Tony Lombardo nor the Aiello brothers were gangsters; they were Sicilian businessmen with racketeering and alky-cooking connections. Lombardo had a long-standing connection with Capone inherited from Torrio. When Angelo Genna succeeded Mike Merlo as *Unione* president, Lombardo moved closer to Capone. It was the Aiellos that now needed protection. They began by trying to enlist the support of Frankie Yale. When Capone had secured Lombardo's election as *Unione* president, the Aiellos complained bitterly to Yale in Brooklyn, telling him that Lombardo had been unfairly elected and that, with Capone's support, Lombardo was holding out on him. Nor was the end of the Aiello's efforts. They also soon found allies in Sicilian gangs connected to the *Unione* in Chicago and other Midwestern cities. By 1925 if not earlier, the Aiellos had formed a grand North-Side alliance in Chicago itself. The alliance with Skidmore, Bertsch and Zuta was a business partnership, or, perhaps, a pact of mutual self-defense against Capone. Although the Capone forces had begun punishing the Skidmore/Bertsch/Zuta group in late 1927, bombing their resorts, they were never the real threat. The real threat came from the remnants of the old North-Side gang, led now by Bugs Moran and financed by the Aiellos and no doubt by the Skidmore/Bertsch/Zuta group as well. "Moran," writes Schoenberg, "was the key:"

Without his [Moran's] backing, [Joe] Aiello could not mount further defiance. . . . Furthermore, the North Side gang, for all their weakness, had been asking for it. In the last year, the Gusenbergs had shot Jack McGurn twice, the second time trapping him in a phone booth, and almost killing him with pistol fire. When the outfit interfered with traffic to Moran's dog track, the Fairview Kennel Club, he retaliated by setting fire to Capone's Hawthorn Kennel Club.[4]

Schoenberg may or may not be correct in his identification of Lolordo's killers; he is, nonetheless, surely right in claiming that, without the Aiellos encouragement and money, Moran would never have dared attack the Outfit's bootlegging operations. In this sense, from the point of view of Capone and McGurn, Moran was definitely "asking for it."

From Capone's perspective, the Aiellos were the aggressors. They had refused to accept Lombardo's presidency and the Outfit's hegemony. Now they were complaining to Frankie Yale, raising the Sicilian clans up against him and enlisting the services of the murderous North Siders, who had their own reasons for disliking Capone. Yet Schoenberg is also right in pointing out that the Aiellos might have had reason to see the war as legitimate self-defense. Capone might have traced a line of legitimate succession from Johnny Torrio back to Big Jim Colosimo, but that didn't give him the right to control the *Unione Siciliana*. From the perspective of Chicago's Little Sicily, Torrio and Capone were the outsiders. They were that pair of Neapolitans Colosimo had imported from New York City. The Aiellos thought they were the rightful heirs to the Chicago *Unione* presidency; but Capone had made them swallow Lombardo instead. They told Yale that Lombardo was protecting the Outfit's interests, and that both the Aiellos and Yale himself were being squeezed out. Lombardo was helping Capone encroach on the Aiellos' sugar and alky-cooking businesses. But Chicago's Sicilian alky cookers, or at least a significant portion of them, remained loyal to the Aiellos. This is what made it so difficult for Capone and McGurn to get at the Aiellos. Joe Aiello and his brothers could hole up in Little Sicily. Capone could neither eliminate Joe and Dominic Aiello, nor even pinpoint their whereabouts. The Moran gang was, by contrast, easier to get at. The North Siders were not as powerful as they were in the days of O'Banion and Weiss. Without financial inducements and logistical support, Bugs Moran would never have dared challenge the Capone Outfit. But now the Aiellos and their Sicilian colleagues were supplying Moran with all the support he needed, and the Moran gang was becoming a serious nuisance. Capone and McGurn may have decided that, as long as the Aiello brothers were hidden, they ought to concentrate on Moran.

The identity of the St. Valentine's Day shooters has never been satisfactorily established. We are not even sure of the number of gunmen involved—four, five, or six. The police found evidence that the Capone Outfit had recently acquired six new Tommy guns. If these were the same guns used in the massacre, this would be conclusive evidence of Outfit involvement and would help establish the number of killers at six. Unfortunately, the police were unable to trace the guns, and thus were unable to determine whether they were the murder weapons. The police did trace the six Tommy-guns as far as a certain James "Bozo" Shupe, a friend of John Scalise, Albert Anselmi, and Joe Giunta. Not for the first time, police arrested Scalise and Anselmi. But they had nothing to hold them on. Even if they were the murder weapons, the guns had since vanished. Nothing linked the Sicilians to the crime scene, so they were quickly released.

A year later, the Michigan police recovered two Tommy guns in the home of a man involved in a police shooting. Both guns tested positive at the Northwestern forensics laboratory, which also established that one of the guns had been used to murder Frankie Yale. In the same home they found a shirt with the laundry marking "FRB." The police guessed that these were the initials of Fred R. Burke, an Egan's Rats gang member currently wanted in Ohio for armed robbery and murder. As a bank robber, Burke and his companion, James Ray, often disguised themselves as policemen. Burke was also missing one of his front teeth. One of the few pieces of material information that the police garnered from eye-witnesses was that the driver of the murder car dressed in a police uniform was missing one of his front teeth. Burke was probably one of the killers.

The murderers' car was a big black Cadillac equipped with gong and gun rack, identical in every respect to a police touring car. Coming down North Clark Street on the way to the rendezvous, the Cadillac was sideswiped by a truck. Horrified at the likely consequences of hitting a police vehicle, the truck's driver, Elmer Lewis, scrambled out of the driver's seat and hurried over to apologize. The two policemen in the front seat merely smiled and waved him away. Relieved, though somewhat bewildered, Elmer Lewis got back into his truck and drove away. A week later, the police recovered the remains of a black Cadillac about three miles from the shooting. Someone had been busily dismantling the car when they had accidentally set the garage workshop on fire. The police recovered the engine serial number, and determined that the car had been bought two months earlier by a man giving a false name and false address. The garage workshop too had been rented under a false name. There was a real address, however; the garage tenant lived in a house adjoining the Circus Café, the headquarters of Claude "Screwy Moore" Maddox's Circus Gang. Maddox was a long-time Capone ally with ties to the Detroit Purples and the Egan's Rats of St. Louis. Even without the Burke tie-in, a connection to the Purples and the Egan's Rats would make sense. Whoever had planned the massacre would not have wanted to use local Chicago shooters; these might have been recognized by the Morans. The police could get no further than this, however. Demolishing a black Cadillac was not a crime.

The police too had heard the rumors that James Clark and the two Gusenberg brothers had killed Patsy Lolordo. When Clark, along with Frank and Pete Gusenberg, were among the St. Valentine's Day victims, the police started looking for Joe Lolordo. Even if Joe had not planned the murder himself, they reasoned, he might have been one of the gunmen. He had served in a machine-gun detachment during the war. But Joe Lolordo had disappeared without a trace.

The St. Valentine's Day Massacre was a professional job. Whoever planned it had the time, connections, and resources to find the killers and organize the police disguises. They had also thought to rent two rooms across the street from the warehouse on North Clark. Ten days before the murder, the rooms had been let to two men claiming to be taxi drivers working the night shift. They insisted on taking front rooms, however, instead of quieter rooms in the back. Whenever the landlady or cleaners entered the rooms, they found the men sitting beside the windows.

Whoever planned it also knew how to bait the trap. The Detroit Purples smuggled Old Log Cabin whiskey from Canada, which they sold to Capone, giving him the exclusive franchise to sell the merchandise in the Chicago area. It proved a popular brand; so popular that after the peace agreement, even Moran became one of Capone's customers. But Capone charged a high price for the stuff, and, hoping to increase his profit, Moran changed suppliers and switched to a cheaper brand. Moran's own customers still wanted Old Log Cabin, however; so Moran was forced to approach Capone and ask him to re-instate his old contract. Capone refused. By now he had sold an exclusive for the brand to Paul Morton, brother of Nails. Morton was a reliable customer who never gave Capone any trouble. Why should Capone cut off Morton's supply just to please Moran, who was both unreliable and extremely troublesome? Rebuffed by Capone, Moran proceeded to demonstrate just how troublesome and unreliable he was by hijacking whiskey shipments destined for Capone. It was evidently this that gave someone in the Outfit an idea for a trap.

Capone arranged for a truckload of his own Old Log Cabin whiskey to be hijacked, and had the hijackers send word to Moran asking if he wished to buy their wares. Moran proved more than willing. The hijackers next informed Moran that they could get a hold of the stuff in larger quantities. Would he be interested in buying a bigger shipment? The price they asked was $57 a case, a bargain from Moran's point of view. Moran readily accepted. The hijackers arranged with Moran to meet them with the goods at his warehouse at 2122 North Clark.

The killers, so far as we can guess, all came from outside the Chicago area. Nevertheless, though the police found evidence of a connection with the Egan's Rats, they issued a Chicago wanted list as well. The names included Claude Maddox, Capone ally and suspected liaison with the Rats, and Outfit members James Belcastro and Frank Maritote. For good measure they even included Joe Aiello on the list. The usual suspects. Leading Outfit members all had good alibis however. Capone was conspicuously in Florida. Jack McGurn was of course on the list. McGurn was probably the one they most wanted to talk to. As Capone's chief of operations, McGurn had managed the war against the Morans for over two years. He had recently been cornered in a telephone booth by the Gusenbergs and nearly killed. If anyone was willing and able to mount such an operation, it was "Machine-Gun Jack" as the papers now liked to call him. But McGurn had an alibi as well. He had conspicuously been in bed.

The police found McGurn two weeks later registered under the name of J. Vincent D'Oro in the Stevens Hotel. With him was "an extravagantly blond lovely" (as described by Schoenberg) named Louise Rolfe. Like McGurn, Rolfe was a tournament golfer. The pair had met on the links, and it was love at first sight. Separating from his wife, McGurn had taken up residence with Rolfe at the Stevens Hotel. When the police asked Rolfe whether she was married to McGurn, Louise had demurely replied, "not yet." McGurn swore that between nine in the evening of February 13 to three in the afternoon on the 14th , he and Louise Rolfe had been alone together in their hotel room. Furious, the state's attorney sought to bring a perjury indictment against him. But in front of the grand jury, Louise confirmed McGurn's alibi. When the angry prosecutor demanded to know how they could possibly have spent so much time alone together, Miss Rolfe sweetly replied, "When you're with Jack, you're never bored." The two were later married.[5]

The operation had gone off almost perfectly. The only slip-up was the failure to get Moran himself. Moran had gotten off to a late start that morning, and was hurrying up when he saw what he took to be a police squad car stopped in front of his warehouse. Had Moran even suspected that the car was being used by rival gangsters, he would probably have burst in, guns blazing. But the disguises worked too well. Moran wanted no trouble with the police, so he turned and slunk off, telling Henry Gusenberg to do the same. Already inside the warehouse along with Clark and the Gusenbergs were Moran gang members Adam Heyer and Albert R. Weinshank. The heavy-set, moon-faced Weinshank could easily have been mistaken for Moran, especially bundled up against the chill. The look-outs on the opposite side of North Clark had seen Weinshank enter the building, and may have mistaken him for Moran, springing the trap too early.

Frustrated at his inability to name the St. Valentine's Day murder squad, Schoenberg tacks to the opposite extreme and questions whether the massacre really was a Capone hit after all.[6] As usual, Schoenberg has a point. There is no material evidence linking Capone or any member of the Outfit to the killings. Nevertheless, there is at least one good reason for believing that the St. Valentine's Day Massacre was planned and executed by the Capone Outfit: this is what the Chicago police believed.

The St. Valentine's Day Massacre was one more stinging black-eye for the Chicago police. Even Luciano was critical. "A real god-damn crazy place," Charlie had commented after a trip to Chicago. "Nobody's safe in the streets."[7] According to the editorials and articles appearing in newspapers and journals around the world after the massacre, the police in Chicago were too inefficient or too corrupt or too scared to keep the streets safe for ordinary citizens. The Chicago police also had some official enemies. Moran was not the only one taken in by the copper outfits. The police disguise also convinced Frederick Silloway, the Prohibition administrator for Chicago. "The murderers were not gangsters," he told the press immediately after the massacre. "They were Chicago policemen." The Chicago police, he explained, were hijacking whiskey from the Moran gang. When the Morans threatened to expose the police, the police ambushed and murdered the gang to keep them from talking.[8] Silloway had the job of stopping Chicago's citizens from drinking, and was exasperated that the Chicago police were not helping him. He assumed that their non-cooperation could only come from the worst reasons. His accusation drew furious denials from the Chicago police, and the police were later cleared of any involvement by ballistic trials at the Northwestern University laboratory. The first laboratory of its type in America, a prototype for the FBI Laboratory, funds for the Northwestern laboratory had been donated by Chicago businessmen. The St. Valentine's Day Massacre was the lab's first case.

Joe "Hop Toad" Giunta succeeded Lolordo as *Unione* president. Giunta had been brought over from Brooklyn four years earlier by Lombardo. He was twenty-two at the time. A slight man with good manners and a dandified taste in dress, his talent on the dance floor had earned him the nickname of "Hop Toad." He seems to have served as private secretary to both Lombardo and Lolordo, becoming president after Lolordo's January 1929 murder.

We know very little about Giunta. Though someone Lombardo trusted in Brooklyn obviously knew and vouched for him, he had no reputation before coming to Chicago. Giunta spent the next four years in Chicago, working largely in Lombardo's shadow. We know that he became close to Scalise and Anselmi. When the police arrested the duo for possible involvement in the St. Valentine's Day Massacre, they arrested little Joe Giunta as well.[9] According to Burns, it was Capone who had Giunta appointed as *Unione* president, nominating Scalise as his number two. Giunta, however, "fell quickly under the domination of the masterful Scalisi [sic] and dwindled into an inconsequential figurehead while Scalisi ruled the under Capone's personal direction." When the national *Unione Siciliana* assembled at Cleveland, Burns continues, the leaders were concerned that the wars in Chicago had brought the *Unione* into disrepute. They tried to negotiated a peace between Capone and the other *Unioni*. But Capone's personal spokesman, Scalise, informed the conference, "I will not agree to peace until I have the men who killed my friends Lombardo and Lolordo."[10]

Burns has mixed up his dates here. The Cleveland conference took place a month before Patsy Lolordo's murder. Lolordo, not Scalise, attended the conference.

There is another problem as well. Both Torrio and Capone had influence in the Chicago *Unione Siciliana;* yet neither of them ever ran the organization. Like Lombardo and Aiello, Lolordo was a sugar baron, a Sicilian making a fortune selling sugar to the alky cookers. He stood in good stead with Capone, who had no objections to his succeeding Lombardo as *Unione* president. Giunta stayed on as well, presumably continuing as private secretary. When Lolordo was murdered, Giunta simply carried on as president. There is no reason to think that Capone, still in Florida, was directly involved in his nomination. Indeed, Capone probably did not give Giunta much thought. Giunta may have become *Unione* president because no one else wanted the job; the last four presidents had been murdered. What does seem sure, however, is that, with Lombardo gone, John Scalise had become Capone's link to the Sicilian underworld.

Like McGurn, Scalise had worked his way up in the Capone Outfit; he had started as a gunmen, becoming a Capone bodyguard. Later he was given a position of responsibility. Scalise was now an important figure within the Outfit; he dressed richly, with plenty of diamonds, gangster style. As Capone's new envoy, the ambassador *in partibus siculorum*, Scalise was an important figure in the Sicilian underworld as well. If anyone nominated Giunta for the job, it would have been Scalise. Word soon reached Capone, however, that all this power was swelling Scalise's head; "I am the most powerful man in Chicago," he reportedly boasted.[11]

Kenneth Allsop adds a significant detail. Despite the power of the Capone Outfit, the Sicilian underworld continued to recognize Joe Aiello as its leader. Aiello held secret conferences with his fellow Sicilians, Scalise and Anselmi, promising that if they would help him eliminate Capone, they could write their own ticket in the Sicilian underworld. It was Aiello who, according to Allsop, told Scalise and Anselmi to approach Capone and tell him that they favored Giunta as a replacement for Lolordo.[12]

According to Allan May, Capone first suspected Scalise and Anselmi of disloyalty when he received word that the twosome had been spotted at a restaurant in Waukegan having lunch with Joe Aiello. A waiter saw them together, and told a friend in the Outfit. Aiello had supposedly told the two gunmen that his offer of $50,000 for a Capone notch still stood. Not only that, Aiello supposedly continued, if they eliminated Capone, he would see to it that they were put in charge of the Outfit. They would have all the profits from the South Side. Aiello would be the boss of booze and vice on the North Side, and the pliable Joe Giunta would remain as *Unione* president.[13] These last details seem dubious. The Outfit was filled with Capone loyalists, men who would never accept Scalise as their leader. The Outfit was also filled with non-Italians; but neither Scalise nor Anselmi could speak English. How were they going to talk with Jake Guzik? Still, whatever Aiello was offering Scalise as inducements for betrayal, the plot fit in with Aiello's long-term goal—putting the Capone Outfit under Sicilian control.

Capone did not at first wish to believe that Scalise and Anselmi had betrayed him, so he devised a test. Some time in April or May 1929, Capone invited them to the Hawthorn Inn in Cicero. During dinner, Capone faked a falling out with his bodyguard Frank Rio. Rio slapped Capone across the face and stormed out. Anselmi and Scalise swallowed the bait; the next day they approached Rio and invited him in on the conspiracy to murder Capone.

Hurt and furious, Capone wanted immediate vengeance. It was Frank Nitti who suggested a different scenario. Nitti suggested a banquet for top Capone lieutenants; Scalise and Anselmi would of course receive an invitation; so would Joe Giunta. The party was held at The Plantation, an old-style Southern mansion, complete with magnolias, that had been converted into a roadhouse. It was located in Hammond, Indiana, just across from Torrio's old Arrowhead Inn in Burnham.

In the movie version, a jazz band is playing in a balloon-draped banquet hall filled with tuxedoed gangsters and glamorous escorts. The atmosphere of champagne, balloons, and merriment is suddenly broken when Capone, baseball bat in hand, confronts the traitors.

Later on that evening, two Hammond police officers saw two large automobiles bound for Chicago. They looked like gangster cars, and so the officers decided to investigate. Exploring the area where they had seen the two cars, they came across a third car abandoned by the roadside. Peering inside, they saw what looked like two bodies covered by a brown blanket. They were the bodies of Anselmi and Giunta. Scalise's body was found a short distance away.

As soon as the names of the victims had been made public, the papers speculated that Scalise and Anselmi had been killed by the Moran gang in reprisal for their part in the St. Valentine's Day Massacre. The speculation was wrong on two counts. First, Scalise, Anselmi and Giunta had not, as far as we can reconstruct, taken part in the massacre. Second, they had not been killed by the Morans. The day after the murder, however, the *Tribune* had come out with a truer version. The slaying had nothing to do with the massacre, the article said; "The three Chicago Sicilians slain near Hammond Tuesday night were the victims of a quartet of their countrymen who, according to police theory last night, aimed in that way to secure peace in the control of the rich booze and vice profits." The article went on to say that "The three were killed because they were reaching out with extortionate hands for the rum running profits and levying tributes on tradesmen in legitimate lines of business." The "police theory" seemed obviously based, as the article itself admitted, on "Sicilian sources." The article even closed with a gallant touch, "The authorities were further informed that the slaying were done in Indiana as an evidence of good will toward the Chicago police."[14]

The article had no by-line, which might well mean, as May points out, that the source was Jack Lingle. If Lingle had provided the information, than its source was certainly not Sicilian, but Neapolitan. Lingle had got it from the Big Fella himself; the *Tribune* story was Capone's version of the events. Scalise, Anselmi, and Giunta had been "reaching out with extortionate hands" and "levying tributes on tradesmen in legitimate lines of business." Capone was telling the world that his victims were nothing but three, low-down old-fashioned Sicilian Black Handers. He was asserting his right to lay down the law and decree punishments in the Chicago underworld. Judge Al.

From the coroner's report, it emerges that the three men were beaten, then finished off. When the "victims fell to the floor," the report concluded, "their assailants stood over them and fired several shots in their backs."

Scalise threw up his hand to cover his face and a bullet cut off his little finger, crashing into his eye. Another bullet crashed into his jaw and he fell from his chair. Meanwhile, the other killers—there must have been three or four—had fired on Giunta and Anselmi, disabling them. Anselmi's right arm was broken by a bullet. When their victims fell to the floor their assailants stood over them and fired several shots into their backs.[15]

ALKY COOKERS AND SUGAR BARONS

Bootlegging unfolded in the Midwest in three overlapping phases. During the first period, much of the whiskey came from pre-existing stocks.

As originally drafted by Wayne B. Wheeler, the Volstead Act regulated national prohibition as narrowly and strictly as possible, closing all foreseeable loopholes. The original draft gave government agents virtually unlimited power to search and seize plus the power to arrest anyone suspected of having consumed alcohol. Before coming to a vote, however, the Act was amended by the House Judiciary Committee and the Senate Judiciary Subcommittee, both concerned to uphold the constitutional amendment protecting citizen from unreasonable searches and seizures. Congress was looking for a compromise in which, though the manufacture, sale, and transport of alcohol would be illegal, the private consumption of alcohol would still be permitted. Under such a compromise, it would be permissible to keep private stocks of alcohol in homes and clubs. Strictly speaking, such a compromise was illogical; if the manufacture and transport of alcohol were prohibited, how were individuals to maintain their private stocks?

The loophole was closed in early 1920, and private stocks of alcohol became illegal. Nevertheless, the hope that individuals could keep their stocks helps explain why, in the months leading up to Prohibition, distilleries were more active than ever. Once Prohibition started, the Act envisioned that most distilleries would shut down, placing all remaining whiskey in government bonded warehouses. The Act foresaw that only some distilleries, those licensed to manufacture medicinal and industrial alcohol, would remain in production. This was what was supposed to happen. It is not what did happen.

Legal access to the bonded whiskey depended on Permits for Withdrawal. These were issued by the Bureau of Prohibition to those using the alcohol for legitimate purposes. One such legitimate purpose was medicinal. Doctors could prescribe and druggist could legally dispense alcohol. By July 1920, before Prohibition was even six months old, more than fifteen thousand physicians and fifty-seven thousand pharmacists had applied for licenses to prescribe and dispense alcohol. The majority were probably individuals who, objecting to Prohibition, were simply taking advantage of a legal loophole to keep themselves and their friends in drink. Others, however, surely saw the loophole as an invitation to make a killing.[16]

During the Harding administration, open sale of permits for withdrawal served as one of the ways that the Ohio Gang in Washington enriched itself at the nation's expense. Harding's corrupt attorney general, the avaricious Harry Daugherty, appointed William J. Burns, of the Burns Detective Agency as head of the Justice Department's Bureau of Investigation (later FBI), with associate and crony, Jesse W. Smith, as his unofficial assistant. The Ohio Gang clubhouse in Washington, the "Little Green House on K Street," was more than a spot where senators, congressmen, and cabinet members might drop by for highballs and no-limits poker. It was also where petitioners met quietly with Jesse Smith and others to negotiate favors for cash.[17] Under Daugherty, the Department of Justice compiled a list of convicted bootleggers who could be sold pardons. Special agent Gaston B. Means later testified that he once collected over $7 million in cash bribes and, finding nowhere else to put it, had stuffed it all into an empty goldfish tank before handing it to a senior Department of Justice official. The first "King of Bootleggers," George Remus, explained to a Senate investigating committee in 1924 that he would set up fake drug companies to request permits to obtain alcohol from the distilleries for medicinal purposes. He made so much money out of this scheme that he eventually bought the distilleries as well.

Depending on the size of the purchase, these permits were on sale at the Little Green House for amounts ranging from $50,000 to $325,000. Jesse Smith assured Remus that, even though he had been convicted of Volstead Act violations by a lower court, "General" Daugherty would see to it that the Justice Department had his conviction overturned. Remus, Smith promised, would never have to spend a day in jail. Remus later observed sourly to the senators, "I tried to corner the graft market, only to find that there is not enough money in the world to buy up all the public officials who demand a share of the graft."[18] If Ohio, the home of the Anti-Saloon League, bears much of the responsibility for bringing Prohibition to America, the corrupt Ohio Gang did its best to strangle the beast in its cradle.

Buying Permits for Withdrawal was not the only method of thwarting Prohibition in the early 1920s. By the middle of 1920, Arnold Rothstein in New York had already established contacts with British distillers, chartered a freighter and commissioned a fleet of speed boats to smuggle the stuff into Long Island coves. Johnny Torrio had already entered into partnership with Chicago's Joseph Stenson to keep the Stenson brewery open and running. Nor was Torrio even the first; Stenson was already selling his beer to Terry Druggan and Frankie Lake of the Valley Gang. By the middle of 1920, whiskey from Canada had already begun to trickle across the Detroit River and Lake Erie. The trickle would later turn into a flood.

The standard price for a permit at the Little Green House was $50,000, however. This was not the sort of money that low-life gangsters were able to afford, at least not at the beginning of Prohibition. Smuggling cost money too, at least when practised on any scale. Smugglers had to invest in boats and trucks and pay the crews and drivers. Smuggling was a business, and needed to be run with a regularity and attention to detail likely to be beyond many low-life thugs. The first bootleggers were often respectable businessmen. Remus was an Ohio doctor, a solid citizen from a middle-class neighborhood. It was easier for a respectable doctor to buy a permit for withdrawal than for a known gangster. A doctor lent the whole operation a touch of deniability; the dry agent could later claim that he had no idea what the good doctor was really up to.

Political pull was another requirement. Even if he had the money, a gangster still needed access to the men with the power to put in the fix. Jesse Smith could put in the fix for you in Washington, but before a bootlegger could bribe Smith, he needed an introduction to him. The Little Green House on K Street did not admit any old riff-raff off the street; they only let in riff-raff that someone had vouched for.

The system worked to the advantage of men like Rothstein and Torrio. Having already made fortunes in the underworld, they were in a position to finance bootlegging from their own accumulated resources. They were well-connected as well. Rothstein had Tammany; he was close to Tom Foley, and even had the ear of Charlie Murphy. Torrio was close to Kenna and Coughlin. In the 20th Ward he worked with Sanitary District trustee Morris Eller. Rothstein and Torrio already had money and pull. They had business experience and an air of plausibility, if not exactly of respectability.

Most gangsters had none of these assets. Before Prohibition, gangsters simply did not have relations—business or social—with respectable citizens. Senior politicians with WASP surnames did not collect graft money from cat houses and pool rooms themselves. They employed intermediaries, often several layers of intermediaries, to do it for them. All this would eventually change, but not immediately. In the early 1920s, the old proprieties were still observed. For aspiring young gangsters this left two choices. They could accept the senior underworld figures as their mentors and role models, as Luciano did with Rothstein or Capone did with Torrio. Failing that, they could take up alky cooking.

In December of 1922, Prohibition commissioner Roy Haynes announced that the "home brew fad is taking its last gasp." By dismissing the alky-cooking stills that had begun to spring up in the slums and immigrant districts of major cities as a "home brew fad," Haynes showed that he had not the slightest clue what was about to hit him. He seemed to be implying that moonshining, a traditional and even folkloric pastime in the Ozarks, had become fashionable in the cities. Alky-cooking, however, proved something more than a passing fashion. Though disorganized at first, the fad for home stills soon reached industrial levels. As it did, it grew better organized, more profitable and more tightly controlled. By 1924, Midwestern bootlegging was already entering its second phase—the alky-cooking period.

Distilling kits, we know, were cheap and were still available from mail-order houses. Some years earlier, the Department of Agriculture had helpfully published a pamphlet instructing farmers in how to turn their excess apples and other fruits into spirits. The pamphlet remained in print during Prohibition. Thus, even relatively poor families had ready access to both the supplies and the know-how to enter the alky cooking business. It was the Italians, however, who transformed alky cooking into a major commercial enterprise. Italians—and Sicilians in particular—had two advantages. Though the traditional American underworld specialized in crime, the Italian underworld specialized in protection. The Italian underworld, that is, did not so much rob banks and jewellers as impose tributes on all those who did. The Italian underworld in fact imposed its tributes as widely as possible, not just on card sharps and bank robbers and jewel thieves, but on butchers and bakers and cigar-store proprietors, and, indeed, on any working Italian immigrant. The Italian underworld was thus in labor management from the start.

It so happened that much of the Italian labor organized by racketeers was connected to the wholesaling, preparation, and retailing of food. Within almost any immigrant Italian or Sicilian community, networks already existed that could supply the tenement stills with corn sugar needed to produce alcohol and supply speakeasies and other outlets with the finished product. The Sicilian mafia and the Neapolitan camorra were already in the business of organizing and controlling people, so when an opportunity to make a fortune through a highly profitable, though illegal, use of labor, arrived, the Italian underworld was already halfway there. In this case, the workers needed little persuasion. The $15 a day that the Gennas paid to keep the stills running full blast for twenty-four hours daily was much better than what the factories could offer. Also, the Genna family had no trouble finding other families in the grocery business who were prepared to act as wholesale suppliers of corn sugar.

The Gennas, of course, had expenses to meet. They supplied the stills with corn sugar, gave the still-keepers their wages, and paid off the Maxwell Street police. An anonymous friend of Samoots Amatuna claimed that it cost Samoots between eight hundred and one thousand dollars to set up a still; so he was understandably vexed that the police kept kicking them over. Even so, by the mid-1920s, when Chicago's Little Italy had begun reeking with fumes from the tenement alky cookers, keeping the cookers supplied with corn sugar became a major worry and expense. It is not surprising that the Gennas struck up an early partnership with the respected Spignola family and with the wholesale grocery firm of Antonio Lombardo & Co., president, Tony Lombardo, vice-president, Joe Aiello. We do not know precisely when Capone made the $100,000 loan to Lombardo & Co. Considering the amount involved, it must have been more than a loan; the Gennas were selling Capone a piece of the game. Dimey Esposito probably held a piece too.

This was the pattern all over the Midwest. Sicilian gangs looked to wholesaler grocers for sugar and business experience and to the established underworld for finance and political protection. The process created new leaders. "Demand," writes Hank Messick, "created a new supply, and new kinds of opportunities. At first there was little organization, little pressure. Development was along community lines, and communities were based on such things as religion and race. In each community a leader arose to dominate the economy and eventually to control it. The serfs—retail sellers, drivers and runners, distillers, and brewers—needed his help to arrange protection from police and competitors. They needed the credit he could supply. The leaders were always men of some business ability and much natural ferocity. They had to be—to be leaders. It was sometimes necessary to fight to retain authority in a given area or, if opportunity offered, to expand at the expense of someone else."[19]

CLEVELAND

Messick is writing of Cleveland, Ohio, whose first sugar baron was "Big Joe" Lonardo. The Lonardo family came from Licata, on the southern coast of Sicily. In the 1880s the four Lonardo brothers still worked as *carusi*, carters and haulers in the island's sulphur mines. Towards the end of the century, however, the four brothers emigrated to the United States, settling in Cleveland's immigrant district, Woodland. They were joined there in 1907 by their boyhood friends and fellow sulphur-mine workers, the seven Porrello brothers. The head of the Lonardo family, "Big Joe," was, like Tony Lombardo and Joe Aiello, a successful retail grocer who had branched out into wholesaling. He also, according to Messick, ran some sort of nickel business. Rich, successful, and immensely portly, Big Joe was recognized as the *padrone*, the boss and leader, of Cleveland's Sicilian community. In 1920, that community still numbered fewer than ten thousand. By 1926, Big Joe Lonardo was dealing extensively in wholesale corn sugar. It was in this year that the Woodland district Italian community was disturbed by a series of unsolved murders.

A certain Louis Nobile was killed in June 1926. Angelo "Chink" Bottaro was murdered about the same time. Chink had stolen a 100-pound bag of corn sugar, with which he intended to set himself up as an independent supplier. A grocer named Luigi Colofato had similar ambitions. He proceeded so far as to buy himself his first diamond ring and first diamond stickpin—a sort of gangster starter kit. Colofato was taken for a ride and dropped off in Shaker Heights, where most of Cleveland's more successful gangsters would eventually buy their homes. Both Messick and criminal writer Rick Porrello argue that these men were victims of the Lonardo/Porrello gang. Some time in 1926, however, the head of the Porrello brothers, Joe, split off from the Lonardos to start his own sugar wholesaling business. Joe Porrello and his six brothers had pooled their money and acquired a headquarters in the upper Woodland Avenue area around East 110th Street. The split seemed amicable, for later that year Joe Lonardo felt confidant enough to visit his relatives back in Licata. He left his closest brother and business partner John in charge. But John Lonardo lacked his older brother's status and business experience. During Big Joe's six-month Sicilian sojourn, the Porrello family moved in to take over the $5,000-a-week corn sugar business that Big Joe had developed. When Big Joe Lonardo returned from Sicily and learned what happened, he confronted the

Porrello brothers. They had stolen his business, he told them, and he wanted it back.

On October 13, 1927, Big Joe and John Lonardo went to Ottavio Porrello's barbershop on Woodland Avenue to talk with the Porrello brothers. It was not their first visit. Relations between the two families were still superficially normal. This time, as on previous occasions, business conversation would be mixed with a friendly game of cards in the back room. Usually Big Joe brought a bodyguard; but this time his bodyguard, Charles Colletti, had been hauled in by the Cleveland police over some business concerning two out-of-town gangsters whose bullet-ridden bodies had recently found tied up with clothesline in Amber Park. So Big Joe and John arrived unguarded. As their host, Angelo Porrello, was ushering them into the back room, two gunmen burst in. They shot both Big Joe and John, and then, standing over Big Joe, fired six more bullets into him to make sure. Though John had been hit twice, once in the left leg and once in the stomach, he was evidently not the main target; he still had enough strength to dash after his attacker, catching up with him in front of a butcher's shop on Woodland Avenue. When the gunmen heard John Lonardo come up behind him, he turned and clobbered him on the forehead with his pistol butt. John Lonardo later died from the skull fracture rather than the bullets.

Porrello involvement in the double homicide has never been demonstrated; nevertheless, both Messick and Rick Porrello assume that the barber shop meeting was a set-up. Their reason for this conclusion is straightforward; with the elimination of the two eldest Lonardo brothers, the Porrello family became Cleveland's leading sugar barons. Joe Porrello's pre-eminence was demonstrated in December 1928 when, as we saw, he appeared at the police station with pledges for approximately four hundred thousand dollars' worth of real estate in the Cleveland area, enough to free the men caught in the raid at the Statler Hotel.

What had prompted this display of bootlegging solidarity on Porrello's part? Even more to the point, why had the twenty-three gangsters come to Cleveland in the first place?

The Cleveland police learned that, before the meeting, some of the arrested had met with the Porrello brothers in their sugar warehouse. The police knew of the Porrello brothers' involvement in alky cooking in Cleveland's Woodland district. They suspected that the Porrellos had been behind the murders of Big Joe and John Lonardo a year earlier. They naturally looked at the Statler Hotel gathering from the perspective of the Porrellos, and reasoned that the family had called an underworld summit to confirm their position as Cleveland's leading sugar barons. The police hypothesis was certainly right, at least as far as it went. Yet the twenty-three gangsters were far from a collection of random bootleggers. Patsy Lolordo and Joe Giunta were not the only Sicilians in the group. So were the other five men from Chicago, the nine from Brooklyn, and the two each from New Jersey and St. Louis. In fact, everyone at the meeting was Sicilian.

Walter Noble Burns, we saw, regarded the reunion as a Sicilian underworld attempt to negotiate a settlement between Capone and the Aiellos. Burns went so far as to invent a defiant, though impossible, speech in which John Scalise refused to make peace until the murder of Patsy Lolordo was avenged. Despite the gaffe, Burns has certainly gotten the context right. The well-informed Allan May even suggests that there "is a high possibility that this was the first national meeting of the *Unione Siciliana*."[20]

Yet even if all those at the meeting were *Unione Siciliana* officials, the late-night reunion at the Statler Hotel was surely something more than a convention. It was a council of war.

Frankie Yale's original project remains shrouded in mystery. There were at least three branches of the *Unione Siciliana* in New York—East Harlem, Lower Manhattan, and Brooklyn. There may have been a fourth branch in The Bronx. Though notionally the president of the *Unione* at the national level, Yale was never president of any of the New York chapters, not even of the Brooklyn branch. We saw earlier that, with the incarceration of Ignazio Lupo Saietta in 1910, the presidency of the *Unione* in New York fell to Salvatore "Totò" D'Aquila.

D'Aquila was a cheese importer with no known criminal record. Presumably his role in the New York *Unione* was similar to that of Mike Merlo in Chicago—representing the more legitimate interests of the membership. As always, the *Unione* had two faces; as president of a large, and seemingly innocuous, Sicilian benevolent society, D'Aquila gave Yale the space where his own, special project might quietly unfold. That product seems nothing less than the domination of the entire Italo-American underworld.

During the early 1920s, both Yale and Torrio traveled extensively. Yale liked horse racing, and was spotted at racetracks in the cities around the Great Lakes. After the Dion O'Banion shooting, Johnny Torrio took Ann on a long vacation. They visited Hot Springs, Arkansas; New Orleans; St. Petersburg; and Palm Beach. They also traveled to Havana and the Bahamas. According to underworld legend, wherever the Torrios went, they were followed by Schemer Drucci, who was determined to avenge O'Banion. But, on each occasion, Johnny "the Fox" gave him the slip. This is the role that underworld legend assigns Drucci; if O'Banion is the chirpy Mad Hatter of Chicago crime, Schemer is the half-cocked March Hare. It would not be surprising if the Torrios made visits to other cities—St. Louis and Kansas City and possibly Louisville, Memphis, and Atlanta. Years before, as a lieutenant in the Colosimo-Van Bever white-slaving ring, Torrio had gone south on business. He had gone to Milwaukee and Detroit as well. If Capone had connections to the criminal underworld in every city with a significant Italian population, it was because Colosimo, Torrio, and Yale had already laid the ground work.

The presumption is that Torrio and Yale were working to unify the Italian underworld. For Torrio, unification may have meant nothing more than business connections. McPhaul's colorful confabulations notwithstanding, Torrio's career as a gunman was limited to the elimination of the Black Hand gangs preying on Big Jim Colosimo. He consented to, and possibly helped plan, the murder of O'Banion, but he himself took no part in the shooting. From the late 1920s on, he was content to play the role of senior underworld statesman, respected and consulted, but out of the headlines. He did not aspire to be king of the underworld.

Yale, by contrast, cherished just such aspirations.

Despite the fact that he was probably not Sicilian, Sicilian gangs throughout the country accepted Yale as the national president of the *Unione Siciliana* or Italo-American National Union. The *Unione Siciliana* in Chicago, however, had been a special case from the beginning. It was the largest such society in America, and one that had been founded by neither Yale nor Torrio. Although both Torrio and Yale had good relations with Merlo, the Chicago *Unione* rejected Yale's suggestion that, following Merlo's death, Torrio be appointed president, if only temporarily. Angelo Genna, a pure-blooded Sicilian, was allowed to assume power instead. The Genna ascension marked the beginning of a Sicilian uprising against Torrio and Capone, an uprising later led by the Aiello family. When the Aiellos tried to enlist Yale's help in ousting Capone's candidate, Tony Lombardo, Yale found himself caught in the middle; and eventually paid with his life.

D'Aquila continued as New York president until he was murdered on the orders of Joe Masseria in 1928. The year 1928 had thus been a fateful one for the *Unione Siciliana*. The deaths of three of the leaders—Yale, Lombardo, and D'Aquila—within a few short months must have weighed on the minds of the Sicilians meeting at the Statler Hotel that December. Nevertheless, even if their meeting had not been cut short by an eruption of Cleveland police, there was little that these men could have done about these events now. They had certainly not met to elect a new president of the Chicago branch, for the new president, Patsy Lolordo, was there with them. Nor had they assembled to find a successor for Frankie Yale. For Yale would have no successor.

By now, Yale's ambition to unify the entire Italo-American underworld under his leadership had become, like Yale himself, a casualty of war. The *Unione* was too battle-scarred to serve as a vehicle for underworld unity any longer. Most of the *Unione* leaders at the Statler Hotel must surely have realized this. If, as May hypothesizes, the Statler Hotel conference was really the first national conference of *Unione Siciliana* leaders, it was almost certainly the last as well. Yet, though Yale's own dream of unifying the Italo-American underworld under his command had died with him, the ambition itself remained alive.

If the meeting were a national, *Unione Siciliana* conference, we should at least expect the president of the Cleveland chapter to be in attendance. Yet the conference host, Joe Porrello, was not the president of the Cleveland *Unione*, nor, as far as we know, even an active member. The president of the Cleveland *Unione* was rather Frank Milano. Frank and Tony Milano had arrived in Cleveland as boys, around 1900, settling in Mayfield Road. In 1902, along with Anthony D'Andrea of Chicago, the Milano brothers began spreading counterfeit money supplied to them by Ignazio Lupo Saietta of New York. Younger than Anthony D'Andrea, the Milano brothers escaped imprisonment until 1911, when Tony Milano was apprehended and sent to prison until the beginning of Prohibition.[21]

The Sicilian gang closest to the Milano brothers and the old *Unione* in Cleveland was the Mayfield Road Gang, led by Alfred "Big Al" Polizzi. Polizzi had also arrived in Cleveland as a small boy from Sicily, settling in the Woodland district. As a boy, Polizzi and his friends, the three Angersola brothers, was recruited by the circulation manager of the Cleveland *News*, Mickey McBride, to battle the toughs from the Cleveland *Plain Dealer* and *Press* during the newspaper circulation wars in the second decade of the twentieth century. With McBride's and Milano's backing, Polizzi started his own profitable wholesale corn sugar business. By 1929, the Mayfield Road Gang was allied with the Milano brothers and also with powerful Jewish bootlegging syndicates in Cleveland and Detroit. Messick, in fact, interprets the December 1928 Hotel Statler meeting precisely as an attempt on the part of Porrellos to forge a grand alliance against the Milano brothers, Big Al Polizzi and their Jewish allies.[22]

Milano and Polizzi were undoubtedly putting the pressure on the Porrello brothers. At the time of the Statler Hotel meeting, Frank Milano had already told Joe Porrello that he wanted a piece of his sugar business. On July 5, 1930, Milano called Joe Porrello to ask him to come over for a conference at his headquarters, a saloon and social club at Mayfield and Murray Hill roads in Cleveland's Little Italy called the Venetian Restaurant. Porrello arrived with his bodyguard and number two, Sam Tilocca. Soon after they entered the club, they were both shot and killed, Porrello with three bullets in the head and Tilocca with five bullets wounds in the body. Tilocca managed to stagger out onto Mayfield Road before collapsing in front of his new car. The police never did find out exactly what had taken place inside; but they did hear that present at the club at the time of the murder were Frank Milano, Big Al Polizzi, John Angersola and Big Joe Lonardo's ex-bodyguard, Charles Colletti. The police arrested all of them, along with club staff members; but they got nowhere. No one had seen anything, nor did any of the staff remember Milano, Polizzi, Angersola or Colletti being in the club. The police were forced to release them all. Three weeks later, James Porrello was killed by a shotgun blast as he bought lamb chops. In February 1932, two other brothers, Rosario and Raymond were killed while playing dominos. A third player was murdered as well as a man who had just stopped by for a soda. By 1932 the Porrello family was virtually eliminated. If the Porrello family had called the Hotel Statler meeting to ask for protection, that protection had either not been forthcoming or had not been effective.

But if Messick is right, and the Hotel Statler meeting had been called by the Porrellos to ask for protection, why had the brothers summoned Sicilians from gangs as far away as New Orleans and Tampa? How could allies like these protect them from a threat in the Cleveland area? Why had the largest contingent of all been nine Sicilians from far-away Brooklyn? Cleveland is a Midwestern city. If the Porrellos felt that they were being threatened or encroached upon in Cleveland, why did they not turn to the organization best able to impose order in the underworld in that area—the Capone Outfit? Of course, it could be that the very people who were bothering the Porrello brothers also happened to be good friends of Al Capone.

There is an early, though ambiguous, indication of Chicago Outfit involvement in Cleveland. In the closing paragraph of Orville Dwyer's 1928 Chicago *Daily Tribune* article on the desolation of Chicago's Little Sicily, quoted in the last chapter, Dwyer writes, "The Sicilian people, unorganized, are peaceful and industrious. Organized, with bad leaders, they are a terrific power for evil. They (Lonardo and the Aiellos) have chased dozen of families out of each other's properties just so these properties would stand vacant and fail to be a source of income."[23]

There is surely some sort of error here—"Lonardo" for "Lombardo." The war in Chicago's Little Sicily was between Tony Lombardo and the Aiello brothers. Big Joe and John Lonardo from Cleveland were not, as far as we know, in any way involved in that war. The two wars were, however, contemporary; and we know that the Aiellos had sent emissaries to Midwestern cities with significant Sicilian populations, Cleveland included, trying to stir up trouble for the Capone Outfit. Though there is no specific evidence tying the Lonardo family directly to the Capone Outfit, we are told that one of the *Unione Siciliana* leaders supporting the presidency of D'Aquila in New York was Big Joe Lonardo.[24] Both Lonardo and Capone also were tied to the Cleveland Syndicate.

The implication seems clear: the extremely murderous, though obscure struggle taking place within Chicago's Italian community had spread to Cleveland's Italian community, where the Lonardo family had become the allies of the Capone Outfit while the Porrello brothers were the allies of the Aiello family. The Hotel Statler meeting in December 1928 was thus not so much a meeting of the *Unione Siciliana* in its entirety, but rather a meeting of the anti-Capone currents within the *Unione*. The fact that present at the meeting were Patsy Lolordo along with Hop Toad Giunta, his successor as *Unione* president as well as victim, along with Scalise and Anselmi, of Capone's wrath a few months later, implies that, not only were the attendees of the Hotel Statler involved in some sort of anti-Capone plot, but that Capone soon got wind of it.

Messick describes Cleveland's Mayfield Road Mob—the Milanos, Big Al Polizzi, and the Angersolas—as the mafia arm of the Cleveland Syndicate. The syndicate itself was centered on four ruthless, though extremely talented, Jewish gangsters, Louis Rothkopf, Morris Kleinman, Samuel Tucker, and Moe Dalitz.

Born in Boston in 1899, though moving to Ann Arbor, Michigan, when he was under two years old, the teenage Moe Dalitz became a member of Joe and Benny Bernstein's Detroit Purple Gang. Arising in the second decade of the twentieth century, the Detroit Purples was one of the most violent gangs in the history of American crime; Carl Sifakis credits it for at least five hundred killings, which, given the geographical limitations of its operations, makes it far more violent than the Capone Outfit. It specialized in larceny, kidnappings, and extortion. The gang became involved in labor racketeering before 1920. After the introduction of Prohibition, the Purple Gang, together with the Mayfield Road Mob, dominated whiskey smuggling from Canada across Lake Erie and the Detroit Rivers.[25] In 1926, the Purples cornered three rival gangsters from St. Louis in Detroit's Milaflores Apartments, and mowed them down with Thompson sub-machine guns. In 1931, the Purples turned their machine guns on the rival "Little Jewish Navy," murdering three of their "admirals" in the Collingwood Manor Apartments. Throughout Prohibition, both Capone in Chicago and Luciano in New York used the Purples along with Egan's Rats in St Louis as guns for hire. It was often convenient to hire outside gunmen as these would not be easily identified by their intended victims or traced by the police. Thus when the Chicago police wanted to know who had taken part in the St. Valentine's Day Massacre, they naturally looked to St. Louis and Detroit.

Even within the underworld, the Detroit Purples had a reputation for being the roughest of the rough. Once, while entertaining a visiting delegation of Purples in his suite, Charlie Luciano was appalled to see those bums from Detroit trying to drag the showgirls that he had invited up to entertain them off into the bedrooms. This was not the way Charlie thought that gentlemen behaved during a social get-together in another gentleman's suite, and he told them so. These are "working girls," he told them; they had to get up in the morning. If his esteemed colleagues from the Midwest wanted prostitutes, that could be separately catered for. Some were even titillated by the Purples' lack of polish. Jazz musician, Mezz Mezzrow, once played at Luigi's Café, an opulent club run by the Purple Gang in Detroit. "It struck me funny how the top and bottom crusts of society were always getting together during the Prohibition era," Mezzrow recalled. "That Purple Gang was a hard lot of guys, so tough they made Capone's playmates like a kindergarten class, and Detroit's snooty set used to feel it was really living to talk to them hoodlums without getting their two-ounce brains blown out."

Dalitz had left the Purples long before the Collingwood Manor massacre, moving to Akron. From there he ran bootlegging operations in Cleveland and Toledo. He remained on good terms with his old gang however, which, along with the Mayfield Road Mob, was smuggling ever larger quantities of Canadian whiskey into the country.

This marked the beginning of the third and final phase of bootlegging in the Midwest—the Canadian whiskey period. Through stealth, fraud, or armed robbery, most of the bonded government warehouses had been cleaned out by the late 1920s: the good whiskey stored inside had by now all found its way onto the black market. The few distilleries still producing whiskey clandestinely could not come close to meeting the country's demand. The U.S.

had by now also become wary of alky-cooked corn whiskey. Though bearing authentic-looking labels supplied by expert Sicilian counterfeit artistes, alky whiskey was apt to contain something watered down, flavored, and doctored with suspicious ingredients by persons not known to be overly fastidious in regard in their customers' well-being. Canadian whiskey, by contrast, was the real stuff, and with the Detroit Purple Gang and the Cleveland Syndicate in charge of smuggling it, the real stuff was arriving in sufficient quantities to make it widely affordable. Dalitz bought it from his underworld friends and made a fortune selling it to suppliers throughout Ohio and as far away as West Virginia and Kentucky. It was very profitable. When Senator Kefauver later asked Dalitz whether his later investments in the gambling and entertainment industry had been funded by the stake he had earned by bootlegging, Dalitz simply replied, "Well, I didn't inherit my money, Senator."

Messick's comment that the Mayfield Road Mob worked as mafia enforcers for the Cleveland Syndicate is accurate enough, provided it is not taken to mean that the Sicilians merely worked as muscle for the Jewish criminal entrepreneurs. Relations went both ways. The Mayfield Road Mob controlled its own alky cooking and the wholesale corn sugar businesses. Though alky cooking was by now the down-market side of bootlegging, it was still a profitable business. The Irish Thomas Jefferson McGinty also worked on terms of equality with the Cleveland syndicate. As circulation manager for the Cleveland *Plain Dealer,* Tom McGinty had squared off against Mickey McBride during Cleveland's circulation wars, both recruiting immigrant kids from the Woodland area to act as circulation sluggers. Later, taking advantage of his connections in both Ohio politics and newspapers and his connections with the immigrant gangs in the Woodland district, McGinty rose to become Cleveland's first king of bootleggers. He continued to be close to the Jewish and Sicilian gangs, even though, by now, they were too rich and powerful to need his tutelage any longer.

Big Al Polizzi's connections to the Jewish syndicate were even more personal. His adopted brother, Albert Charles Polizzi, who liked to be called "Chuck" to distinguish himself from brother Alfred, "Big Al," was born with "Berkowitz" as a surname. His Jewish immigrant parents died, and he was adopted by the neighboring Polizzi family. Messick and Fried speculate that Chuck Polizzi served as the link between the Mayfield Road Mob and the Cleveland Syndicate. Nor is this an isolated example. The Detroit Purple Gang had established allies in Detroit's small Sicilian underworld and even recruited Yonnie Licavoli and his brothers from St.Louis to work for them in Detroit. Another Cleveland Syndicate member, Louis Rothkopf, used Frank Costello as his New York connection. Luciano, who remained close to his New York Jewish roots throughout his career, had no objections to Dalitz or the rest of the Syndicate, nor, of course, had Capone.

By around 1928, there had thus arisen an organized criminal, bootlegging network whose outlines we can trace in some detail. This network extended from St. Louis and Kansas City north to Chicago, and from there to Milwaukee and Detroit. From Detroit, it swung east along the southern shores of Lake Erie to Buffalo, and included not only Cleveland, but smaller, industrial cities like Toledo, Akron, Youngstown, and the lake port of Sandusky. From Ohio and upstate New York, it spread east into Pittsburgh and coalesced with bootlegging syndicates in the New England-Middle Atlantic region from Boston to Baltimore. It was a network with connections to New Orleans and Tampa, to real estate developments in Florida, the Bahamas, and Cuba and probably to the Los Angeles area as well.

The bootlegging network stretched across a map that roughly corresponded to the map of nineteenth- and early twentieth-century urban and industrial development in America. It also corresponded to a map of the Jewish and Italian diasporas in America. Neither of these correspondences is by chance. Prohibition was not so much a noble experiment as a challenge to the entrepreneurial ingenuity of the American underworld. Fortunately for the underworld and America's imbibers, though unfortunately for Prohibition's supporters, industrialization and immigration brought forth the answers to this challenge.

Still, for some it must have been a bewildering experience. There are some things that you are unlikely to encounter in a South Italian village, among them whiskey, beer, Jews, and Irishmen. Yet the immigrants of Italy were all here together in New York, Chicago, and Cleveland, making whiskey, trucking beer, and dealing with Jews and Irishmen at every turn. No wonder not everyone in the Italian underworld approved. Some objected to working with Jews and other non-Italian groups; there were even Sicilians who objected to working with Neapolitans. The Aiellos, from the traditional mafia stronghold of Bagheria in Palermo province, comprised one such family. This is what makes it so interesting that only Sicilians met at the council at Cleveland's Hotel Statler in 1928. Nor were they just any Sicilians. The Milano brothers and members of the Mayfield Road Mob were not among the invited. There were six Sicilians from Chicago, but none of them represented the Capone Outfit. There were nine Sicilians who came from New York, but no one represented Ciro Terranova or Joe Masseria. Envoys came from New Orleans and Tampa; but no one came from Purple-dominated Detroit. If the guest list of the Hotel Statler conference seems to delineate one side of an emerging underworld divide, the list of the names of those not invited seems to delineate the other.

THE CROWN PRINCE OF CASTELLAMMARE

Two of the party of nine Sicilians from Brooklyn were Joe Profaci and Joe Magliocco, both of whom would later become boss of one of New York's five mafia families. Magliocco succeeding Profaci on his death in 1962. Both would be present at the Apalachia convention in 1957. Both would later have a seat on the mafia's national council, where they might encounter their old adversary, Frank Milano. Nor is this the end of the associations between the two men. The Profaci and Magliocco families were linked to each other through marriage. They were linked to other families as well—that of Stefano Magaddino, boss of Buffalo, and that of another boss from Brooklyn, Joe Bonanno. Some of these ties and family alliance had been forged in America. Others had been made before the families left Castellammare, the town on Sicily's northern coast in which they all had been born.

A *castellammare* is a castle facing the sea. Usually a fortress erected upon a rocky promontory, a *castellammare* is positioned to protect a harbor or port entrance. Though the original *castellammare* after which the Sicilian town of Castellammare del Golfo is named was built by the Arabs, the fortress that today's tourist admires was constructed approximately three hundred years later, around the time of the Emperor Frederick II. This fortress has suffered from neglect and from clumsy restorations and changes of use over the centuries. For much of the nineteenth century, it served as a prison.

With Sicily in almost permanent revolt, the Neapolitan government had need of prisons. The police dumped both political prisoners and common criminals into the fortress at Castellammare del Golfo. The fortress remained a prison for a short period after the new Italian government took power in Sicily in 1860 as well and became involved in one of the first rebellions against the new state, the Cutara revolt of 1862.

Garibaldi had been entranced by the spectacle of the nation in arms, an entire people arisen to fight for their natural rights. After liberating Sicily from Naples, Garibaldi had invited the Sicilian partisans to take up their arms again and follow him on his march to liberate Rome. But the Sicilian partisans politely declined. Italy was a foreign country to them; if Italy wanted to be liberated, they thought, then Italians could liberate it themselves. Besides, many had been fighting for decades. They were tired of the war and only wished to return home and enjoy their newly-won freedom in peace.

Wisely, Garibaldi left the matter there. Two years later, however, the new Italian government revived the idea. All able-bodied Sicilian men, the government proclaimed, were to be inducted into the Italian army. The government saw it as a disciplinary measure to help curb the island's growing unrest.

In Castellammare, the reaction was instantaneous. As soon as the town was notified of its draft quota, townspeople assembled in the main piazza shouting, "*Non si parte, non si parte*" ("We won't go. We won't go."). Scuffles with the *carabinieri* broke out, and soon the partisans were digging out their old rifles. They broke open the fortress as well, releasing the prisoners inside.

Men in Sicily were apt to find themselves in prison for any number of reasons, not all of them dishonorable. Prison could happen to anyone; it was a fate that, in Sicily, seemed a misfortune that honorable men faced with stoic courage. Townspeople sympathized with the prisoners locked away in the dark fortresses. Bringing food or gifts to the prison, or just singing songs outside the barred windows, was regarded as an act of charity. There was little shame attached to prison in Sicily. Consequently, whenever a Sicilian town rose up and forced the resident government officials and their police escorts to run for cover, the first things the townspeople did were to burn the official books—the ones that listed the people's debts—and let the poor devils out of the fortresses and lock-ups and tell them to beat it before the troops came back.

The mafia in Castellammare del Golfo retained some of its original charisma, its associations with Sicilian patriotism, resistance to tyranny and protection of the common people. Stories were made up to show the mafia's ancient and noble pedigree, founded, it was said, at the time of the Sicilian Vespers Uprising. While northerners regarded the mafia as a criminal organization, some families in towns like Castellammare del Golfo were proud to associate themselves with what Joe Bonanno calls in his autobiography the "Tradition" (with a capital "T").

By 1900, the mafia was almost a caste in towns like Castellammare. Mafia families were related to each other though blood and marriage, with the same family names showing up over and over again in the records. According to Joe Bonanno, the Bonannos were "the leading family of Castellammare." This may be wishful thinking; for, in the records of Castellammare del Golfo, the names Buccellato and Magaddino crop up most often.[26]

Joe Bonanno's grandfather, Giuseppe, was a landowner. His own father, Salvatore or, in its Sicilian version, "Turiddu," Bonanno was the youngest of Giuseppe Bonanno's four sons. As the baby of the family, Turiddu was his mother's pet, doted on and protected. As often happened to the over-protected youngest sons in land-owning Sicilian families, Turiddu's mother dedicated him to the priesthood at an early age, hoping to save her youngest thereby from the rough-and-tumble world to which his three older brothers already belonged. But the sacerdotal life did not agree with young Turriddu Bonanno; at the age of twenty-one he was expelled from seminary. By now, his father had died; two of his older brothers had left to raise their own families; and the third brother, the feisty and thick-skinned Peppe Bonanno, had been shot in an ambush. A family friend and ally, Stefano Magaddino senior, had stepped in as guardian of Bonanno family interests in Castellammare. It was to the elder Stefano Magaddino that Turiddu Bonanno turned for advice and assistance.

Joe Bonanno strongly hints that his uncle Peppe had been killed by the rivals of the Bonanno and Magaddino families, the Buccellato clan. Soon after his father had left the seminary and put himself under the tutelage of Stefano Magaddino, Joe continues, it so happened that "two members of the Buccellato clan met their death." How had this unforeseen tragedy befallen these two Buccellato soldiers? Bonanno is elusive: "The people of Castellammare had their own ideas as to who was responsible, but they kept it to themselves." He goes on to inform us, however, that, after the murder of the two Buccellatos, Turiddu's standing in the town rose; he "was seen more and more in the town square, in the social clubs, and in the fields." Turiddu also became closer to Stefano Magaddino, celebrating his new intimacy by marrying Don Stefano's niece, Caterina Bonventre.

A little over a year after their wedding, the union was blessed by the birth of their first child, Giuseppe Bonanno, called by his Italian friends Peppino, but better known in America as Joe, or, to the readers of the New York tabloids, "Joe Bananas."

My birth, writes Joe Bonanno, was the cause of much celebration. Wishing it to be the cause of peace as well, Turiddu Bonanno asked his enemy, Felice Buccellato, to stand at the baptismal font as the child's *padrino* or godfather. According to the Magaddino story, Turiddu's friends had advised him to end the war with the Buccellato clan by "cutting off the viper's head," killing Felice Buccellato himself. Instead, Turiddu walked unarmed into the café where Buccellato spent his afternoons, and proposed an armistice sealed at the baptismal font. The Buccellatos and the Bonannos would become *compare*, and the war between them would end. Buccellato agreed to play his part, and thus the people of Castellammare dubbed the little infant the "dove of peace." A more inappropriate sobriquet for the future Joe Bananas cannot possibly be imagined.

It is quite conceivable that one of the stipulations of the peace treaty between the Buccellato and Magaddino clans required Turiddu Bonanno to leave Castellammare and settle in America. By now there may also have been an arrest warrant with his name on it back home. Whatever the case, in 1905, Turiddu did take his family to settle in the Williamsburg section of Brooklyn, at that time the Castellammaresi enclave in New York. But the American sojourn did not last long. In 1911, Turiddu and his family returned to Castellammare, where Joe's father once again became embroiled in local feuds, first with a neighboring rancher and later with the Buccellato clan.

With the outbreak of World War I in early 1915, Turiddu was drafted into the Italian army along with many of the other young men in Castellammare. He was wounded in a battle on the Austrian front that fall, and sent home to recuperate. Other sources speak of him contracting a respiratory disease. He died shortly before Christmas in 1915. With his death, Joe and his mother were adopted into the Magaddino clan.

Joe's legal guardian became Giuseppe Magaddino, brother and *consigliere* to Stefano, the head of the Magaddino clan and patron of Joe's father. But it was Don Stefano Magaddino who now undertook the instruction of young Joe in the notions of honor, respect, and *omertà*, which served as the foundation for the Tradition. It was also Don Stefano who taught young Joe about the feud between the Buccellatos and the Magaddinos. But, although his Uncle Stefano taught Joe the values of a man of honor, it was his ninety-seven-year-old Bonanno grandmother who taught him what a vendetta truly meant. My grandmother, Joe writes, "could often be heard reciting the rosary or talking to herself out loud. Sometimes in the midst of her monologues I would hear the name of a Buccellato that had recently passed away. It was as if she were keeping count of the enemy dead on her rosary." One evening, after a Buccellatto ambush, Joe heard his grandmother muttering over her rosary:

"In a sack, they found him in a sack . . . and now they don't want to open the casket."

Later Joe learned that they had buried his godfather, Felice Buccellato, that day. "They had found his body in a gully," he wrote. "The body was in a burlap sack, hacked to death and too horrible to look at."[27]

It was Uncle Stefano, wrote Bonanno, "who endowed me with a love of our Tradition," telling him that the "Tradition was the bulwark against chaos." Not everyone in Castellammare would have agreed. According to a 1907 report, the town was in the grip of an epidemic of *Mano Nera* extortion. Trapani was a wine-producing region, and Castellammare was an important center for bulking and export. Unlike America, where the Black Handers usually threatened dynamite, the Castellammarese Black Handers threatened the axe, staving in the wine-barrels, thereby ruining the wine and flooding the warehouses and cellars. Once they got started, the gangs did not always stop here; the 1907 report goes on to speak of gangs smashing the tables and chairs, overturning the cabinets and stomping the ripped ledgers into the puddles of wine and muck. Finally `pri u currivu e comu un dispettu' ("just out of spite and as a mark of disesteem") the gang members squatted down and shat in the mess they had made. Behind the Black Hand gangs in Castellammare were rivalries among the merchants themselves, who would set the gangs against their enemies to drive them out of business.

Despite the excitement of the Buccellatos and Magaddinos robbing and murdering each other, life in Castellammare, wrote Joe Bonanno, could still be "very provincial." He craved something more heroic. He decided to become a sea captain, and travelled to Trapani to study in a nautical preparatory school, qualifying after a year for a place at the Nautical Institute in Palermo.

Joe turned out to be a good student. He particularly liked English. What drew him to English as a young student in Sicily was not, however, the prospect of speaking it as a language, but the prospect of reading adventure stories. His textbook was a collection of English sea tales, appropriate for a nautical institute, called *The Boundless Sea*. He liked the story of the Spanish Armada. He was particularly moved by an account of Nelson's death during the Battle of Trafalgar, how Nelson bravely fought on though mortally wounded, continuing until victory was assured, then, as death approached, turning to the chaplain and saying, "Doctor, I have been a *great* sinner."

Bonanno might have fulfilled his ambition to become a sea-farer had not Mussolini's Fascists intervened. Students at his nautical college were required to sing the Fascist anthem each morning. They were told that they were expected to take out memberships in the Fascist Party. Finally they were told to wear Mussolini's black shirt as part of their school uniform. "These measures," writes Bonanno, "offended me, and I protested them vigorously." He helped organize a student protest. Even when the college authorities warned him that he must don a black shirt or be expelled, he held out. Finally, having no other choice, the college suspended him.

This last detail seems doubtful. Bonanno tells us that he left Sicily in the middle of 1924, right after his suspension from nautical college. Yet in 1924 the Fascist organization of power in Sicily was still two years away. Cesare Mori's anti-mafia campaign took place a year later, in 1927. It is hard to imagine students being expelled in Sicily for refusing to wear a black shirt in 1924.

There is another way at looking at Bonanno's departure. During World War I, with many of the young men in the Castellammare area serving in the Italian armed forces, the war between the Buccellatos and the Magaddinos went into temporary abeyance. Only when these men had returned home after discharge did the war start up in earnest again.

In 1920 or 1921, Stefano Magaddino and one of his younger nephews, Pietro Magaddino, were trapped in a Buccellato ambush. Don Stefano survived, but Pietro did not. After Pietro's murder, there was a renewal of hostilities and a string of casualties, mostly, Bonanno assures us, on the Buccellato side. Even so, the Bucellattos were still dangerous. That same year, Stefano Magaddino sent two of his remaining nephews, Stefano junior and Antonino, all the way to New York. Yet even here they were not safe. Stefano Magaddino junior and a friend named Gaspar Milazzo were ambushed in Brooklyn by Buccellato family affiliates shortly after they arrived. The Buccellato ambush went badly wrong, however, and, instead of killing Magaddino and Milazzo, two innocent by-standers were killed. Rallying his fellow Castellammaresi, Magaddino struck back, killing two of the New York Buccellatos in return.

That same year, 1921, Joe Bonanno was sent away to naval college. Don Stefano may have supported his nephew's ambition to become a merchant marine captain. But Stefano senior may also have seen it as a way of getting Joe out of Castellammare and out of danger. Only sixteen years old, Joe was too young to have taken much part in the war against the Buccellatos, yet he was still a possible target for their reprisals. If his Uncle Stefano forced him to withdraw for the next three years, it was either because he feared that Joe was still in danger or because he had other plans for him. The former seems the stronger probability. The decision on Joe's final destination seems to have been made by Joe alone. He spent several months enjoying himself, staying first with a Magaddino uncle in Tunisia and then with a Bonanno cousin in Paris. Both urged Joe to make his home with them. Joe, however, was determined to go to America, even if it meant entering clandestinely.

Together with another Magaddino cousin, Joe sailed from Le Havre to Havana, Cuba. From there, they found a small fishing boat to smuggle them in through Tampa, Florida. Their luck almost ran out on them; two immigration guards spotted Joe in the Jacksonville railway station, and Joe and his cousin were placed in a detention center. Fortunately, Joe was almost as well-connected in America as he was in Sicily. From the detention center, Joe called his uncle, Pete Bonventre. Bonventre contacted Stefano Magaddino in Buffalo, who sent his friend, Willie Moretti down to rescue them.

THE CASTELLAMMARESE ALLIANCE

Some time after the murder of Pietro Magaddino in Castellammare, his two surviving brothers, Stefano junior and Antonino, also emigrated to the large Castellammarese community settled in the Williamsburg section of Brooklyn. There were by now Castellammarese colonies in Brooklyn, Detroit, Buffalo, and nearby Endicott, New York, and each was roiled by the vendetta between the Magaddino and Buccellato clans. In August 1921, Stefano Magaddino was arrested as a fugitive over the killing of a Buccellato in Avon, New Jersey. In 1922, Stefano Magaddino and another Magaddino Castellammarese, Gaspare Milazzo, were ambushed outside a grocery store in Brooklyn. Magaddino and Milazzo both left Brooklyn, probably fleeing arrest warrents.

Stefano Magaddino went to Buffalo. Between 1913 and 1921, there had been a gang war within the Sicilian communities on both the southern and northern shores of Lake Erie that had accounted for nineteen victims. Many of the murders were attributed to a Buffalo gang named the "Good Killers." This name may come from the old sectarian name, "*Buona Gente*" or "Good People," a term by which the mafia in Sicily often identified members of their organizations. The modern American term, "Goodfellows" probably derives from "*Buona Gente*." These "Good Killers" were also involved in Detroit's gang wars, which claimed eleven victims between 1916 and 1921.

Magaddino succeeded Joseph Peter Di Carlo as boss of the Buffalo mafia in 1923, remaining Buffalo's highly respected mafia boss and doyen of the American Castellammaresi until his death in 1974.[28] Di Carlo had been forced to flee to Miami, where he later set up a successful gambling organization. Magaddino took over Di Carlo's gambling, loan sharking, and protection rackets, and united the Castellammarese clans in Buffalo, Endicott, and possibly Hamilton, Canada, organizing highly profitable smuggling and alky-cooking businesses. Magaddino's own network also included towns in upstate New York and upstate Pennsylvania. There had also been a representative from Tampa, Florida, at the Statler summit. A city with a large Cuban population, the Tampa underworld was under the influence of both New Orleans and Havana. It can hardly be a coincidence that, wishing to enter the U.S. illegally, Joe Bonanno and Peter Magaddino traveled from Havana to Tampa.

Joe Bonanno later claimed that the Aiello family was on the side of the Magaddino Castellammaresi from the start, though it is also possible that, before the murder of Gaspare Milazzo in Detroit, Stefano Magaddino was not tied to the Aiello family by anything more than common interests. Magaddino did business with the Lonardo family in Cleveland during the middle years of the decade. By the end of the decade, however, the interests of the Aiellos in Chicago and those of the Castellammaresi in Buffalo and New York had begun to coalesce. The Castellammaresi from Buffalo and Brooklyn sent representatives to the December 1928 Hotel Statler meeting. Though Kobler speculates that Pasqualino Lolordo and Joseph "Hop Toad" Giunta were representing Capone at the Statler meeting, by now Lolordo may have been plotting some sort of double-cross. He was murdered a month later. Capone discovered Giunta's ties to the Aiello family shortly thereafter. Capone had not been informed of the Statler meeting; and so it seems probable that Lolordo and Giunta were representing Joe Aiello instead.

Gaspare Milazzo, by contrast, traveled to the small Castellammarese colony in Detroit, where he went under the name of Gaspar Scibilia. Though we do not know whether the Magaddino and Buccallato clans were involved in the series of Good Killer murders in Buffalo, Frank Buccellato had been running a Buccellato clan gang in Detroit since 1915. We are not sure of the date of Milazzo's arrival in Detroit. Most sources state that Stefano Magaddino and Gaspare Milazzo left Brooklyn after surviving a Buccellato ambush in 1922. Detroit journalist, Mario Machi, states that Milazzo was in Detroit a year earlier, in 1921, and had already been accepted as the leader of the Magaddino faction of Detroit's Castellammaresi. In whichever case, it is certain that, as soon as he had established himself, Milazzo did more than declare war on the Buccellato gang; he launched a bid to take over Detroit's entire Italian underworld. In this endeavor, he was encouraged not only by Stefano Magaddino in Buffalo, but, towards the end of the 1920s, by Joe Aiello in Chicago. Though the Aiello clan would have had little interest in the Magaddino-Buccellato vendetta as such, he would have been delighted to support Milazzo in his attempt to take over the Italian underworld in Capone-allied Detroit. It was an ambitious project, however. Not only was most of Detroit's Italian underworld cooperating with the Capone Outfit, but the Outfit was on good terms with both Detroit's Purple Gang and the Cleveland Syndicate. Indeed, seeing trouble brewing among the Italian gangs, the Purples had sought to reinforce their position by bringing in Italian muscle from St. Louis.[29]

The St. Louis mafia was, as one police officer told the St. Louis *Post Dispatch* in 1997, "strictly minor league." It lacked the power and influence of John Lazio's Kansas City mafia. Nevertheless, the St. Louis mafia had been firmly tied to Chicago since the time of Torrio, and this makes it interesting that the St. Louis mafia were *Stoppaglieri*. The original *Stoppaglieri*, we saw, had been founded in Monreale, Sicily, in the 1870s; for several decades the Monreale *Stoppaglieri* had been involved in a war with the *Fratuzzi* of Bagheria. This may well have seemed ancient history; but the mafia had a long memory, and part of explanation why the *Stoppaglieri* of St. Louis became such firm allies of the Capone Outfit and the Detroit Purples may have been the fact that the Aiello family came from Bagheria.

The St. Louis mafia, locally nick-named "The Green Ones," was founded in 1915 by three *Stoppagliere* refugees from Sicily, John and Vito Giannola and Alphonse Palizzola. The three men each settled in separate cities, John Giannola in Chicago, Vito Giannola in St. Louis, and Alphonse Palizzola in Springfield, Illinois. Several years later, however, Vito persuaded brother John and Palizzola to come to him in St. Louis, where they imposed a tax in the city's Italian community on all goods sold. In 1923, Vito moved to take control of the city's wholesale meat industry as well. By the middle of the decade, the Giannolas and Palizzola had set up an alky-cooking business. Alky-cooking was highly profitable during the middle years of Prohibition, and the Giannolas' operations were soon challenged by other gangs—Egan's Rats and a gang called the Cuckoos. The result in St. Louis was similar to that in Chicago, Cleveland, and a number of other cities—thirty gangsters murdered and eighteen wounded.

Alphonse Palizzola was the first to be murdered. On September 9, 1927, four gunmen blasted away at Palizzola on Tenth Street. A ten-year-old boy was also killed by one of the ricocheting bullets. Vito Giannola was the next to die. He was found hiding in the house of Augustina Cusumano on December 28, 1927. Giannola had scared away Augustina's husband and had moved in with her. Two men, claiming to be police officers, came to the house and, after finding Giannola hiding in a secret compartment upstairs, shot him thirty-seven times. John Giannola went into hiding after the death of his brother and was never again a factor in St. Louis. He was said to have died peacefully in his sleep in 1955. Among the wounded during the war was James Licavoli, a future boss of the Cleveland Mafia. Licavoli was shot by police as they attempted to arrest Joseph Bommarito, another associate of The Green Ones. Interestingly, another associate of Licavoli, Giovanni Mirabella, was arrested at the Statler Hotel meeting in December 1928. What he was doing there is a mystery. For, as Mario Marchi, Allan May, and Charlie Molino comment in their article on St. Louis, The Green Ones of St. Louis had been all but eliminated. Nevertheless, members of both the Giannola and Licavoli families turned up in Detroit at the end of the 1920s where they were allied with the Purples and other Italians against Milazzo's Castellammarese faction.[30]

JOE BONANNO MEETS HIS MENTOR

Shortly after his own arrival, Joe Bonanno celebrated his twentieth birthday in the little house in south Brooklyn of his Bonventre uncle and aunt. It was his new home in America. He was at loose ends. "I don't know of any jobs for nautical students," his Uncle Petrino casually mentioned to him one day, "but I can teach you how to be a barber."

The offer, Joe knew, was well-meant. Still, he was horrified. His father's last words, clutching his ten-year-old son to his breast, had been; "Your name is Bonanno. Always be proud of your name." The Bonannos were Men of Honor; they did not gain their living cutting other people's hair.

Bonanno described his neighborhood in Williamsburg as having two or three stills on every block. Soon he was working for the Di Gregorio brothers, whose still was hidden in a basement, and connected to a neighboring garage by a secret tunnel. The young Joe Bonanno had made enough money to buy himself snappy clothes and a big, fast dark-gray Hudson, with special compartments for stashing gallon cans of alcohol. But when the Di Gregorio "alchemist," brother Giovanni, fell asleep at the still, blowing up the basement, the still, and himself, Joe found himself unemployed again. He went to the movies a lot that year, as often as he could, and even began fancying himself a matinee idol, a new Rudolph Valentino, star of the silent screen. He signed up for acting classes in an old studio off Union Square. "You're a natural, Peppino," the professor exclaimed when he saw him walk across the studio floor, "Never change that walk." The Professor said that he would cast him as a tough guy and sometimes a lover. Joe was pleased; he was just doing what came naturally to him, he thought. But though acting the role of a tough guy and sometime lover was more commensurate with his destiny as a Bonanno than barbering, it was still not enough. Joe wanted to be that tough guy. He heard that Salvatore Maranzano had arrived from Castellammare. For Joe Bonanno, it was not a moment too soon.

As a boy in Castellammare, Joe had known Maranzano, a member in Uncle Stefano Magaddino's gang. He was connected to the Trapani mafia as well, married to the sister of certain "man of respect" in Trapani, Don Totò. He later moved to Palermo, where he opened a successful food business. Joe always called him "Don Turiddu." When Uncle Stefano dropped by Palermo to visit Joe at Nautical college, he usually took him to lunch at Don Turiddu's house.

Soon after his arrival in Brooklyn, Maranzano quickly took over bootlegging and alky cooking in the Castellammarese section of Williamsburg and Little Italy. The move was unopposed, for Maranzano had an air of natural authority about him. He was handsome, Joe remembered, "He could make his face smile sweetly, or he could look severe enough to make you tremble."

Maranzano was a gentleman. "He liked fine clothes," Joe continued. "He dressed like a conservative businessman, preferring grey or blue suits, soft pinstripes on the blue."

But what really made Maranzano a commanding figure was his voice. It had "an entrancing, echolike quality. When Maranzano used his voice assertively, to issue a command, he was the bellknocker and you were the bell."

Maranzano had graduated from seminary. His priestly training gave him an air of decorum and formality in his manners. To Bonanno, he seemed to possess the solemn bearing of an archbishop. Maranzano had acquired a taste for study while in seminary; he read Latin well and owned a library of books on theology and history. His favorite was Roman military history, however. He liked to compare the mafia to the Legions of the Emperor Julius Caesar, a role he clearly coveted for himself. Indeed, Maranzano was the closest thing to an ideologue, an intellectual apologist, that the mafia ever produced.

Joe first encountered Maranzano at the welcoming dinner that the Castellammarese community gave for him in 1925. Maranzano immediately picked the young Joe Bonanno out from the crowd:

"When your father was alive, I always followed him."

"Yes, Don Turiddu."

"And your Uncle Stefano was my teacher."

"Yes, Don Turiddu."

"Peppino, you understand me."

"Don Turiddu, I . . . I . . . yes, Don Turiddu."[31]

Bonanno was mesmerized; "I suppose it was like falling in love," he observed decades later. He was barely twenty-one and Maranzano was forty.

Maranzano would probably have sought out Stefano Magaddino's nephew anyway. There was a strong Sicilian connection. But what he came to value especially in Joe was his higher education. Maranzano could lecture Bonanno about the role of the Tradition in Sicilian history, reveal to him his ambition to remodel the American mafia on the model of Caesar's legions. He could explain these things to Bonanno without needed to stint on his words or recast his teachings into simple images that the uneducated could understand. It was a solace to have the companionship of this intelligent youngster.

"Only you understand me," Maranzano told Joe one evening.

"Yes, Don Turiddu."

For Joe Bonanno, it must have seemed that destiny itself had come to kiss him on the cheek.

Joe Bonanno introduced Maranzano to the movies, and Don Turiddu soon became almost as enthusiastic about the silent screen as Joe himself. He especially liked the westerns. Sometimes the friends would duck in to one of the movie houses along the Bowery. Later in the evening, they would pace the street of Lower Manhattan, earnestly discussing Sicilian history, their plans to dominate the New York underworld, and the westerns they had seen.

Chapter Nine

The Underworld at War: Part 3—New York

ARNOLD'S BOYS

"His longish face, often weirdly pale, reminded me of that of a clown on holiday. On the other hand, the long lashes fringing his cold eyes softened the hard lines of his face, so that but for his hooked nose he appeared almost handsome, particularly when he laughed, which was often."

—Nat Ferber on Arnold Rothstein[1]

Like the Midwestern gangs, during the first two years of Prohibition, New York gangs such as the Diamond brothers, the West Side Gophers, or Dutch Schultz bought or forged permits for withdrawal or bribed or broke their way into the government-bonded warehouses where liquor destined "for medicinal purposes" was being stored. Much of what they obtained found its way to the curb exchange next to police headquarters on Mulberry Street. By the middle of the decade, however, whiskey from Great Britain had begun to arrive in quantity. Freighters stopped at rendezvous points outside the three- (later twelve-) mile limit. They were met by the "sunset fleet," the bootleggers' motor launches. Cases of whiskey, tied up in burlap sacks, were lowered into the launches, often in darkness and high seas, and taken to coves and beaches on Long Island and along the New Jersey shore where the bootleggers' trucks were waiting. Given the quantity of the merchandise arriving and the problems of trans-shipment, the larger bootleggers soon began investing in storage facilities in Cuba and the Bahamas.

Around 1924, Frank Costello made his own deal with the mayor of St. Pierre, the capitol of a group of rocky little islands off Newfoundland, one of the few French possession left in North America. In return for storing Costello's whiskey, St. Pierre took $2 for every case that went through, eventually earning for itself more than $4 million. Prohibition was not only a bonanza for the American underworld: the British West Indies invested their earnings in overhauling and upgrading their port facilities. The Cuban Tourist Agency ran an ad showing American tourists, drinks in hand, thumbing their noses at Prohibition officials in Miami. The success of Scottish distillers in keeping New Yorkers in drink meant that for succeeding generations, Scotch rather the American whiskey would become the sophisticated set's tipple of choice.

Traditionally the most under-funded and neglected of United States services, the Coast Guard seemed powerless. Even with better boats and better gear and with captains and crews receiving instruction in naval combat, there was little the Coast Guard could do to stop the flow either across the Atlantic or, later, across lakes Erie and Ontario. By then the bootleggers had deep pockets. As the government began to re-equip the Coast Guard cutters and retrain their crews in 1924, Bill Dwyer and Frank Costello stepped in with a campaign of bribery on a massive scale. Captains or officers were wined and dined, ending the evening in a luxurious apartment in the company of a Broadway cutie. In the morning the offer would arrive: All this can be yours, the sailor would be told. All we want is a little cooperation. Dwyer and Costello suborned entire cutter crews that way, using them to run liquor for them. Sometimes they posed as Coast Guard cutters themselves, and even had to interrupt bootlegging occasionally to mount rescue operations for boats in distress. The blatant bribery and the hi-jinks on the high seas became so notorious that both Dwyer and Costello were eventually arrested, though they managed to beat the rap in their 1926 trial.[2]

The middle years of the decade were a time of underworld peace in New York itself. Bootleggers might battle gangs of marauding hijackers on the wooded back roads from Montauk to Atlantic City; there were acts of piracy as rival gangs chased each others' speed boats from cove to cove; but the city was spared the gang violence of Chicago, Cleveland, or Detroit.

Arnold Rothstein never aspired to be a gang leader himself, not in the sense of Paul Kelly or Johnny Torrio. Rothstein was a white-collar criminal and swindler. More than anything else, however, he was a gambler. When Nat Ferber was investigating stock-market swindles for the Hearst *Daily American*, he found that the stock-market bucket-shop firm of Fuller & McGee had regularly been making out checks to Rothstein. The checks were to cover Eddie Fuller's gambling debts, Ferber later discovered. Though the firm of Fuller & McGee bilked their unwary clients for over $5 million in phony stock deals, Eddie Fuller was a lush and a compulsive gambler; and so much of the firm's illegal profits eventually found their way into Rothstein's pockets. "There was a night that he and Fuller stood on Broadway outside of Lindy's, betting on the odd and even number of license plates on cars turning onto Broadway from near-by streets. As much as $10,000 was wagered on a single number and Rothstein won consistently. He won because he had the cars "stacked" and by a system of signalling was able to produce the odd or even tag desired."[3]

No wonder Rothstein characters regularly pop up in Damon Runyon's stories.

Rothstein was a gambling-house proprietor who moved in fashionable circles. For years he played weekly poker with New York *World* editor, Herbert Bayard Swope. He ran a bail bonding operation in conjunction with Tammany boss Tom Foley. Politically and socially well connected, he liked to prey on people. "I have known him to take $5,000 to fix a man from a rap," wrote Ferber, "hold the money and do nothing for about ten days: then phone him to announce that he had spent $4,000 in vain, and to come get the remaining $1,000."[4] Though "almost handsome" when he laughed, the laughter was usually at someone else's expense. What was a man like Rothstein doing courting young hoods like Costello, Lansky, and Luciano?

Rothstein had grown up with gangs; he had been picked up by Big Tim Sullivan, had known Herman Rosenthal, Monk Eastman, and the Five Pointers. Though not a gangster himself, he knew the ways that gangsters could be useful. They were a sort of underworld lumpenproletariat, an underworld labor force. Rothstein had the money, the connections and the grand schemes. The young hoods had the hustle and the muscle on the streets. Some were hungry and eager to rise.

One of Rothstein's protégés was Irving Wexler, better known as Waxey Gordon. Born in 1886 (or 1888) to a poor Polish-Jewish family on the Lower East Side, Waxey dropped out of public school at an early age, taking to the streets where he became a pickpocket. The usual explanation is that he earned the nickname *Waxey* through the deftness of his pickpocketing technique. His fingers, they said, were as slick as wax. But wax is not particularly slick, nor would waxy fingers or, even less, fingers of wax be of much use to a pickpocket; so it is possible that 'Waxey' is just a shortening of Wexler. The story behind the other part of his name is much simpler. *Gordon* was an Anglo alias that Waxey adopted. He used others as well, but for reasons that have not survived he was particularly attached to the name *Gordon*.

Waxey first came to public attention as a strike-breaker working for Dopey Benny Fine's gang. In May 1914, Pinchy Paul, another strike-breaker, was murdered by Nigger Benny Snyder on the orders of "Joe the Greaser" Rosenzweig. Paul, it seems, was trying to undermine Rosenzweig's standing in the Furriers' Union. Paul was an enemy of Fine as well, or, more precisely, an ally of Fine's arch-enemy, the later Five Points gang leader, Jack Sirocco. Fine had tried to ambush Sirocco's men outside the Arlington Dance Hall. In the confused melee that followed, all of Sirocco's men escaped unharmed while a city official named Frederick Strauss was accidentally murdered. On learning the news, Purroy Mitchell vowed, as mayors are bound to do, to destroy the organized gangs and the gangsters once and for all. The police responded by hauling in as many Jewish gangsters as they could. Benny Fine was among the arrested, but not Joe the Greaser, for Joe was already in jail. He was there because the half-witted Snyder had told the police about the Paul murder.

The police cared little about the murder of Pinchy Paul. Pinchy, Joe the Greaser and Nigger Benny were minor hoodlums, hardly worth the trouble of arresting. Frederick Strauss, by contrast, was a well-liked city official. Even the mayor had taken an interest in his murder. So though Joe the Greaser was already in the tank, the detective pulled him up for questioning again. Asked if he had heard any rumors about the Strauss killing, and perhaps told that things would go easier for him were he to prove helpful, Rosenzweig replied that he had he had in fact witnessed the murder. He gave the police a list including Benny Fine and nine of his gang members. Now the uncorroborated testimony of an accused murderer incriminating his enemies is worth nothing in court. Still, it was something for the police to go on. Eventually they were able to make a case for two of Fine's men, Isidore Cohen, better known as "Jew" Murphy, and Waxey Gordon. After a lengthy trial, however, both were acquitted.[5]

Gordon was by now a major criminal. In his 1933 tax evasion trial, he confessed that already by 1910 he had amassed over $100,000 from gambling and other illicit activities. According to a Kehillal report, Gordon took over as leader of Fine's gang in 1914. By 1917, he had become a major cocaine dealer as well.[6]

In 1920, Gordon was approached by a Detroit hoodlum named Big Maxie Greenberg. Greenberg had started out as a member of Egan's Rats. William "Jellyroll" Egan was a St. Louis gangster-politician. His gang had started, like some of the Chicago gangs, as a group of Irish thugs that Egan used to control his ward. In the pre-war years, however, as municipal politics and the demography of St. Louis evolved, Egan's gang expanded to include Italians and Jews. Egan's gang also became involved in unions and strike-breaking. In 1917, Greenberg was arrested on the charge of grand larceny and sentenced to a ten-year stretch in prison. His boss, Jellyroll Egan, still had powerful Democratic connections, however, and in 1919 was able to wrangle a presidential pardon for Greenberg. It was probably unwise for Big Maxie to return to St. Louis, so he went to Detroit instead. Here, gazing perhaps at Windsor, Ontario, just across the Detroit River, he may have beheld the future.

Greenberg had been one of the first to realize Prohibition's potential for illegal profits. He had already smuggled several loads of liquor across the river from Canada. Now he wanted to go big time. He wanted Gordon to front him for $175,000. Gordon told Big Maxie that he did not have that much to lend. He added however that he knew someone who might be able to help him out. Waxey took Greenberg's proposition to Arnold Rothstein, who told Waxey that he would be happy to discuss the matter with Greenberg in person. They met the next day on a bench in Central Park. Greenberg explained that big-time smuggling required investments in trucks and warehouses. He was worried that his Canadian suppliers, aware of what he was doing, were going to jack up the price if he didn't act soon. If Mr. Rothstein would simply lend him the necessary capital, he would soon be able to repay his debt with interest.

Rothstein simply listened as Greenberg set out the proposal. Then he suggested that Greenberg drop by his office on Fifty-seventh Street the next day. When Greenberg arrived for the second meeting, he found that Rothstein had considered his proposal carefully and wanted to make a counter-offer. If the Canadians were trying to gouge him on their prices, he asked, why not go elsewhere? Why not ship in the booze directly from England?

Greenberg was taken aback. Transporting alcohol across the Detroit River was one thing, transporting it across the Atlantic Ocean was another. How could all this be managed for $175,000?

Rothstein replied that he was not thinking of $175,000. He would stake Greenberg his hundred seventy-five grand, taking the trucks and properties he owned in the Detroit area as his collateral. Greenberg would pay Rothstein the high interest as agreed. But this was not the end of Rothstein's interest. Once Greenberg had awakened him to the potential profit in liquor smuggling, Rothstein was not going to rest content in the role of banker.

Some of Rothstein's colleagues in the Wall Street bucket shop swindles had fled to Europe to avoid prosecution. Through Dandy Phil Kastel, Rothstein contacted Harry Mather, who had earlier acted as Rothstein's agent in his dealings with Swiss banks and with Amsterdam diamond merchants. Rothstein told Mather to buy twenty thousand cases of Scotch whiskey. Mather rapidly assembled the desired merchandise, adding a few hundred cases of ale on his own. He also found a Norwegian ship under a libel in England, and arranged to have the outstanding bill against it lifted so that the ship might sail.

While Mather was arranging for the merchandise to be loaded and shipped from England, Rothstein was figuring out how all this stuff could be landed and sold once the ships reached the U.S. His first step was to contact a boat-builder in Bayonne, New Jersey, who put together for him a small fleet of specially built speed boats, able to carry between seven hundred and one thousand cases of whiskey each. Next he sought a location where the whiskey could be landed. In the years spent running his exclusive club in Hewlett, Long Island, Rothstein had made friends with local politicians and law enforcement officials. So in answer to the question of where he could marshal his little rum-running armada and where they could unload their precious cargo, Rothstein's thoughts naturally turned to Long Island.

This was just the first of eleven crossings made by the Norwegian freighter in the space of a year. Each time it carried approximately a half million dollars worth of smuggled liquor. Rothstein smuggled in diamonds this way as well. He smuggled so many uncut diamonds from Amsterdam that he soon glutted the market. He also began importing opiates. Although the market for heroin was still in a protean stage, it was to become a market that no supplier could ever glut.

Though Rothstein had quit rumrunning as early as 1922, Greenberg and Gordon remained involved. Gordon had his own rum-running steamship called the Nantisco. In 1925, while bound for the Astoria Docks in Queens, however, the Nantisco was intercepted by the Coast Guard. When Coast Guard Agents found a large consignment of scotch in the hold, the captain, Hans Fuhrman, agreed to turn state's evidence. Fuhrman's information led to a raid on Waxey's headquarters at the Knickerbocker Hotel. Gordon was not present at the time, but Big Maxy Greenberg unluckily was. Big Maxey had just fallen out with his old boss, Jellyroll Egan, in St. Louis. Egan had ordered four thousand cases of whiskey to be smuggled up the Mississippi. When they failed to arrive, Egan accused Maxey of hijacking them. The accusations touched off a bootlegger's war in which Egan was slain and Big Maxey forced to hide in New York.

In Waxey's headquarters, the dry agents discovered incriminating maps, codes, and charts, plus the names and addresses of prominent customers. Fortunately for Waxey, the prosecution's star witness, Captain Fuhrman, was murdered shortly before the trial began. He had been put in a hotel room where he was closely guarded by the police. Unable to otherwise explain the death, the police weakly claimed that it had been a suicide. Though the explanation seemed lame, the prosecution was unable to prove an alternative cause of death. As a result, Waxey was acquitted as he had been in 1914.

With two murders and a number of other misdeeds chalked up on his ledger, the New York police now regarded Gordon as a criminal kingpin. Knowing this, Gordon must also have realized that he would be subject to surveillance and harassment if he stayed in town. He certainly could not remain in a luxurious suite at the Knickerbocker. He moved to Jersey City, where he placed himself under the protection of the powerful, corrupt, and bilious mayor, Frank Hague.[7]

In Paterson, Gordon started the Eureka Beverage Company, a large brewery which pumped its beer through a series of underground pipes to a bottling and barreling plant several blocks away. New Jersey, was probably the best place for him to be. Aside from Mayor Hague's protection, Prohibition enforcement in New Jersey was notoriously lax. New Jersey helped supply New York City with beer. By 1929, the state had even managed to expel its fourteen prohibition administrators. The New York *Times* made up a little piece of doggerel to celebrate the Garden State's achievement:

One by one they interfere

With those Jersey tides of beer;

Manfully, they face the flood,

Then, alas! Their name is mud.

Heroes for a little day,

One by one they pass away.[8]

Gordon was at the center of a syndicate of nine men controlling thirteen breweries supplying beer to New York, New Jersey, and Pennsylvania. Eight of these men were Jewish gangsters who had started their careers as racketeers and petty gamblers. They were named the "Jewish Syndicate." Nor were they the only Jewish group in operation. Gordon's activities put him in conflict with Meyer Lansky, and this resulted in a bloody underworld war. In 1928 and 1929, Gordon and his friends pooled their resources and expanded their operations, shipping their beer in freight cars to the West Coast. By now, Waxey Gordon and his Jewish Syndicate were perhaps the country's leading producers of beer. To protect themselves from hijackers and rivals, the group had formed two strong-arm squads. One was headed by someone the police merely identified as "Abe," but whom Block identifies as Newark gangster Abner "Longie" Zwillman. Zwillman had muscled his way into Gordon's operations, demanding a cut. Reasoning that it was safer to have the Newark gangster as an ally than an enemy, Gordon and his friends agreed to let him in. The other strong-arm squad was formed by New Jersey mafia leader Willie Moretti. Among those working with Moretti were Charley Lucciano and Vito Genovese. The police dismissed the Moretti group as "small fries." Their report adds however that "They were kept on the brewery payrolls to avoid trouble for the breweries."[9] Hijacking was a constant risk, and either Zwillman or Moretti were capable of hijacking the Jewish Syndicate's beer trucks. It was better to hire the potential hijackers to guard these trucks instead.

By the end of the 1920s, Waxey Gordon had built an empire. He owned hotels, breweries and distilleries. He had swank apartments on West End Avenue and Central Park West; a summer house on Bradley Beach, N.J.; and a personal fleet of Lincolns, Pierce-Arrows, and Cadillacs. He kept a library with expensively-bound, first editions of Dickens, Thackery, and Sir Walter Scott. To entertain his guests, the book cases swung open to reveal a fully-stocked bar behind. He also became a theatrical angel, financing such Broadway hits as *Strike Me Pink* and *Forward March.*

Rothstein had an eye for underworld talent, spotting virtually every future gangland leader at a tender age. He needed them, for he had seen the future. He took young Meyer Lansky out to dinner in 1920 and explained to him that "It's going to be the chic thing to have good whiskey when you have guests." He had already made the necessary contacts in London and Edinburgh, he told Lansky. At this point, he leaned forward and began to speak in the first person plural; "*We'll* have crews *we* can trust and ships to bring it across the Atlantic. *We'll* avoid running risks by unloading the cargo at sea and by taking delivery outside the U.S. three-mile limit. *We'll* have to hire or buy a fleet of small, fast speedboats and that type of thing, so the cargo can be distributed at night to special places *we'll* set up on the coast. Either they can let us have the whiskey on the ocean that way, or *we* can take delivery from one of the nearby Caribbean islands—Cuba may be a good place. It will be your job to smuggle the Scotch into the United States so *we* can distribute it."[10] All these "we's" seduced Little Meyer.

Lansky was convinced; "I felt I had nothing to lose. He knew I was working with Charlie Lucania, as he was still known, and that we could call upon our friends, the mixture of Jews and Italians who were loyal to us."[11]

Another of Rothstein's first recruits was "a frail, white-faced, handsome, sadistic former package thief" named John T. Nolan.[12] Though Nolan came from North Philadelphia, he seems to have gravitated to Manhattan's West Side some time before the war, working with the Gophers. Stealing from the railway yards, he earned there the name by which he became better known—Legs Diamond.

Legs became Rothstein's special bodyguard and kept an eye over his floating crap games. Sometimes he followed the winners home at night, relieving them of their winnings. "It became the thing at Police Headquarters," wrote journalist Stanley Walker, "when a gambler was found murdered with all his pockets empty, to ask, 'Did Legs takes him home?'" Only Rothstein could have found this trait amusing.

In 1920, Rothstein formed Legs and his brother Eddie, along with jewel thief named Gene Moran, into an escort to accompany his whiskey shipments in from Long Island. They were so effective that Rothstein sometimes rented them out to other bootleggers. In 1921, the Diamond brothers told Rothstein they wanted to turn independent. They were not interested in setting up their own bootlegging operations; they wished instead to prey on the operations of others. By now the Diamond brothers had seen what was coming into New York. Prohibition meant boom times for smugglers. Along with the Scotch, trucks laden with silks and spices, rich jewels and furs, cocaine, morphine, and other banned or highly-taxed goods were wending their way through the woods off Montauk Point. Fat priors and tax gatherers were wandering through Sherwood Forest by night. Just to think about it made Legs' cruel mouth water. He had already recruited two more eager, young marauders into his gang—Salvatore Lucania and Arthur Flegenheimer, later known as Dutch Schultz. Mr. Rothstein gave the undertaking his blessing. He would help the gang fence their rich booty.

Friendship with Charlie Lucania was probably one of the motives behind Rothstein's impromptu dinner invitation to Meyer Lansky. The year before, the Sicilian boss, Joe Masseria, had broken up one of Lansky's games the year before, and Meyer's friend Charlie Lucania had helped straighten things out. To someone of Rothstein's caliber, Masseria and his *Unione Siciliana* were still only small fries; their chamber-pot stills in the tenements were supplying a market that he did not care to cultivate. These small fries were, nevertheless, an inconvenience, and whenever they tried to throw their weight around, they could be a real nuisance. Charlie Lucania was part of a younger generation of Sicilians who, though still connected to the *Unione Siciliana,* maintained friendly contacts with Jewish and Irish gangsters as well. Rothstein thought it might be useful to know some of these younger Sicilians.

Despite the fact that Lucania would one day become Charley Lucky or Lucky Lucciano, the supreme leader of the Italian underworld, he never liked the mafia. Charlie had no sympathy for the old dons. He disliked the way they stuck their fingers into every aspect of immigrant life, their insistence that everyone in the community, rich or poor, young and old, had to show respect and pay their little tributes. There was something un-American about the old dons.

"I remember that once a neighbor of ours by the name of Forzano had a little penny-ante poker game in his kitchen once a week" he later told Martin Gosch. "Would you believe it that them dirty Dons sent one of their boys to draw off a dollar a week from the pot for expenses."

Lansky brought Lucania over to meet Rothstein. If Lansky's six-hour dinner with Rothstein represented an epiphany, a glimpse into the future, for Lucania the meeting represented something much stronger. Just as Lucania had recognized Lansky as his spiritual blood brother, he now saw Rothstein as his new spiritual father. It was, at least on Charlie's part, love at first sight.

Charlie began to spend his spare time with Rothstein, imitating his manner of dressing and pestering him with questions about proper etiquette. Charlie was still in his early twenties, and Rothstein seemed to enjoy the young Sicilian's adulation. Sometimes, however, it could get embarrassing. One afternoon, when Charlie had an important date, Lansky overheard him ask Rothstein "how to behave when I meet a classy broad." This was too much. The idea that Rothstein, who, like many Jewish gangsters, was rather restrained in his sexual behavior, was supposed to transform Lucania into a suave lady-killer had sent Rothstein into fits of laughter.

Still, Lansky and Lucania were useful. Rothstein introduced them to Waxey Gordon, and soon Lansky and Lucania were dealing directly with Nucky Johnson, the Atlantic City boss who controlled a large stretch of beaches on the Jersey shore where rum-running skiffs could make their landings. They made contacts with Moe Dalitz and Johnny Scalise of the Mayfield Road gang in Cleveland, and later with the Purple Gang of Detroit. These controlled the landing points on the Great Lakes where Samuel Bronfmann's and Lewis Rosenstiel's Canadian booze was brought in. They met Solly Weissman of Kansas City. These were all big-time names, men who would never have let the two New York youngsters in the door were they not acting in the name of Arnold Rothstein. Lansky and Lucania spent the next few years as Gordon's trouble shooters, contacting suppliers and arranging transport and distribution. Often they rode shotgun, escorting the shipments into New York, variously accompanied by the Diamond brothers, Legs and Eddie, Dutch Schultz, as well as Meyer's brother Jake or his inseparable pal Benny Siegel.

Lansky continued to learn from his new mentor: "Rothstein taught us that mass production of cars would revolutionize many things in America. I realized myself how important it could become in our particular kind of business." Just as the demand for alcohol acted as the stimulus for the bootlegging industry, so the needs of bootleggers themselves were acting as a stimulus for car and truck manufacturers and rental agencies. During the 1920s, a single room at the fashionable Waldorf-Astoria cost six dollars a day; but daily car rentals started at fifteen dollars. Meyer Lansky saw the light, and soon a Lansky-Siegel garage and rental agency was operating on Cannon Street under the management of Moe Sedway.

Rothstein's fascination with the automotive industry also brought home another lesson to Lansky and Lucania; "We were in business like the Ford

Motor Company. Shooting and killing was an inefficient way of doing business. Ford salesmen don't shoot Chevrolet salesmen. They try to outbid them." As in the sale of whiskey, quality and reliability equaled customer satisfaction equaled success. Lansky and Lucania preferred growing rich; it seemed the American way.

Rothstein had another reason for valuing Lucania's assistance—he knew his way around the drugs world. Rothstein had seen that the bootlegging industry opened the way to other forms of smuggling. He set Waxey Gordon and Lucania to work developing the drugs market. They discovered an untapped demand in every city they approached, and many of their big-time contacts Lansky and Lucania owed as much to drugs as to booze. They sold to "King" Solomon in Boston, to "Nig" Rosen in Philadelphia and to Johnny Torrio in Chicago.

Drugs were responsible for Charlie's second, and near fatal, bust. In 1923 he sold a packet of heroin to a buyer on East Fourteenth Street in Little Italy. Several days later, he sold another packet to the same buyer. The buyer, however, turned out to be a federal agent, named John Lyons, who, searching Lucania, found several more packets of pure heroin in his pockets. Lucania later claimed that he was just doing a favor for a friend of Vito Genovese named "Big Nose Charley" Lagaipa; "With one junk conviction already on my record, and with everyone knowing my puss, it looked like I was going up for a long stay in the federal pen. I tried everything; I offered them three bastards everything they could name." But these were federal narcotics agents, and neither Charlie's nor Frank Costello's friends in the police department or among the Prohibition agents could help; "they wouldn't even look at me." Having no intention of going to prison, Lucania offered to show the agents his supplier. He gave them an address at 164 Mulberry Street, telling them where the cache was. When it turned out that he had led them to the right spot, they let him walk away a free man. It was an expensive lesson. Charlie not only lost the $75,000 that was to be his share of the deal, but he had to reimburse Big Nose Lagaipa for the drugs he had lost. Worst, he had acquired a reputation as a stool pigeon.

Charlie was crushed. Three years had been invested in social mobility—improved manners and new clothes, smart new friends, the classy broads he squired to expensive clubs. All seemed to go up in smoke. He was no better than a crumb.

> I was really ashamed to face all the friends I made in society, guys I played golf with. All I could think about was how to get clean again in front of those legit people. Besides, for the whole summer I was being grilled every five minutes by the police, or else I had to go and see a psychiatrist every day for two hours, which was one of the conditions they made when they dropped the charges. I didn't want to go and make any deliveries up on Park Avenue; I wouldn't even go to the speaks that had a better class of customers. I was like a hermit.

The situation was saved by his friend Meyer Lansky, who came up with a new wrinkle on Lansky's Law: "Right now you want to impress a lot of people . . . Give them something they want bad enough, and they'll even buy horseshit and molasses."

"What are you talking about?" Charlie wanted to know, "You want me to give away our best Scotch?"

"Who's talking about business? There's a fight coming up next month; a pair of tickets are harder to get than a good set of counterfeit plates. Don't that throw you an idea?"

Lansky was referring to the Dempsey-Firpo fight scheduled for September 14. at the Polo Grounds. He was right too about good tickets being hard to come by. Nevertheless, by now Lansky and Lucania had cash to spread around. With a campaign of lavish expenditure plus some discrete help from Arnold Rothstein who asked his friends to help the young fellows out, Lansky and Lucania acquired two hundred seats in the first five rows. Shortly before the big night, Rothstein bestowed on Charlie a further mark of favor: he took him out shopping. "Charlie," he told him, "I'm going to turn you into another Francis X. Bushman."

Charlie was as temperamental as a young maiden at her debutante season. He wanted his new suits to be tailor-made, with special, flashy modifications of his own devising. No, Charlie, Rothstein told him gently, "I want you to wear something conservative and elegant, made by a gentile tailor."

"My tailor's a Catholic," Charlie replied sulkily.

He was mollified when Rothstein presented him with a dozen French, silk ties, explaining that French silk was the best. Charlie was enchanted with the gift; for the rest of his life he swore by French silk shirts, underwear and pajamas.

> So the night of the fight I had on a beautiful double-breasted dark oxford grey suit, with a plain white shirt, a dark blue silk tie with little tiny horse-shoes on it, which was Arnold's sense of humor. I had a charcoal grey her-ringbone cashmere topcoat, because it was a little cool, and a Cavanagh grey fedora.

He held court in Row A seat 1 throughout the preliminary bouts:

> It's what I had always dreamed about, that some day the biggest people in New York would come up to me to say hello, to say thanks for the ring-side seats that their big-shot friends couldn't get for love or money. It was a pretty big thing when Dick Enright, the police commissioner of the whole city, came over to see how I was feeling. And right with him was Bill Lehey, the police chief.

Charlie and Meyer had discussed their guest list for weeks. They invited Jimmy Hines and Al Marinelli, the two bosses allied with them from Tammany. They invited other bosses from both the Democrat and Republican parties. They invited showbiz people, like the impresarios Flo Ziegfeld and Earl Carroll. They invited Boss Jim Pendergast who came all the way from Kansas City in his private railway car, picking up guests from Chicago on the way. They had given Capone a dozen seats to spread around the Chicago crowd, but somehow Capone had forgotten to give a seat to Johnnie Torrio. So Lucania gave Torrio a seat next to him in the front row, while putting the Chicago crowd in the third row. "My two hundred seats mixed up everybody from whores to politicians, from society to Delancey Street. I had made up my mind I was going to make friends from everywhere."

For Charlie, it was his coming-out party.[13]

JOE THE BOSS

Before 1920, Italian underworld activity had been limited to Italian communities. This changed very quickly with the advent of Prohibition. As in the Midwest, pre-Prohibition liquor on the East Coast had been put into U.S. Government bonded warehouses, where it was available for medicinal purposes. East Side and Irish gangs forged permits or bribed customs officials or simply broke into the warehouses. Though many of the warehouses were on the West Side—Irish territory—the whiskey itself found its way to Little Italy. For two years after 1920 a curb exchange in whiskey flourished in Lower Manhattan on Kenmare, Broome, and Grand Streets, and on Elizabeth Street as well. Though the curb exchange was a market open to everyone, it was still in the territory of Joe the Boss Masseria, the president of the Lower Manhattan branch of the *Unione Siciliana*. Masseria put Tommy "the Bull" Pennocchio in charge. Pennocchio possessed diplomatic and managerial skills, and the curb exchange became the nerve center for the entire New York bootlegging underworld. It was next to the Mulberry Street headquarters of the New York Police Department, however, and this eventually proved so embarrassing that the police were forced to shut it down.[14]

Masseria had started as a gunmen working for Ciro Terranova. Indeed, some sources claim that the Masseria family had come from Corleone, and the Joe the Boss's father had been among the founders of the Morello-Lupo gang. By 1920, Joe Masseria at approximately thirty had established himself as *Unione* boss in Lower Manhattan under acting Manhattan president, Totò D'Aquila. Late in 1920, another member of the *Unione* in East Harlem, Umberto Valenti, confided to Nick Gentile that, with the support of D'Aquila, Masseria was trying to kill him. Valenti ran a speakeasy on the Lower East Side, and Masseria's men had already gunned down a Valenti bootlegger named Salvatore Mauro on Chrystie Street. Declaring war on Masseria, in the next eighteen months Valenti and his gunmen murdered six of Masseria's men.

In May 1922, Valenti killers ambushed Vincent and Ciro Terranova in Vincent's East Harlem office on 116th Street. Ciro escaped unharmed, but Vincent was killed. A few hours after killing Vincent Terranova, Valenti's killers murdered a prominent *Unione Siciliana* official, Joseph Peppo, while he was standing at the Broome Street corner of the Mulberry Street police station. That same evening Masseria and two of his henchmen hid themselves in a doorway at 194 Grand Street, near the southern corner of the Mulberry Street station. Soon they saw Umberto Valenti and his bodyguard, Silva Tagliagamba, walking along Mott Street. The pair turned into Grand, walking towards Mulberry where the Masseria trio were waiting for them. When they reached 190 Grand Street, Masseria gave the order to open fire. The result was a disaster. By now darkness had fallen, and the street had filled with the evening speakeasy crowd. Four people — two men and two women — were in the line of fire and felled. Valenti and Tagliagamba were not hit. They drew and returned fire. Then they fled.

When they heard the shots, the police came racing out of the Mulberry Street station. Masseria fled up Mulberry with two detectives behind him. They saw him throw away his pistol, a .38 caliber automatic. Then he gave himself up.

Valenti was jubilant. Masseria was finished, he thought. Not only was he stupid enough to set up an ambush a half block from the police station; the ambush itself had been a miserable failure. Four innocent passers-by had been seriously wounded. Valenti expected to see Masseria arrested and tried immediately. But somehow Masseria's case kept getting postponed. Two years into Prohibition, Masseria had already grown some powerful friends among the New York magistrates.

By August, Valenti lost patience and decided that if he wanted Masseria eliminated he would have to do it himself. Masseria lived in a house on the corner of Second Avenue and Fifth Street. Early one morning, Valenti sent four of his torpedos over. The boys decided to wait under cover until an unsuspecting Masseria opened the door to come out. The moment he did, they decided, three of the gunmen would fan out, blocking all possible avenues of escape. The fourth would then run directly at him, pistol lowered, firing as soon as he got in range. Even if the first shots missed, whichever way he ran, Masseria would immediately be caught up in a deadly crossfire. Masseria was obese. Even if he made a break, they could quickly run him down.

There's a widespread misconception about fat men that they cannot run very fast. They cannot run very far. But they can be quick. Had Masseria tried to outrace the killers, they certainly would have run him down. But he was not thinking about running the New York Marathon. The moment he saw the first gunman running at him, Joe jumped, dodging the bullet speeding towards him. When he turned and saw three other men closing in on him, he continued to bob and weave. He faked a move in one direction, then, as the guns swerved, he sped off in the other. The next thing the four killers knew was that Joe Masseria had disappeared into Heiney's Millinery Shop on 82 Second Avenue.

The proprietor, a Mr. Fritz Heiney, was just setting up behind the counter when he heard the burst of shots. He was about to go and see what all this ruckus was about when he was suddenly confronted by his first customer of the day in the form of his neighbor, Mr. Masseria, who seemed agitated. It quickly became Mr. Heiney's turn to become agitated when Masseria's appearance was followed by those of four gunmen. One of them strode in to confront Masseria who seemed to be doing some quick-motion dance routine in the back of the store with Mr. Heiney's hats. The man fired three shots at close range, but, amazingly, the fat little Sicilian was able to jump away each time, clearing the counter and running back out the door. The only result was two bullet holes in Mr. Heiney's front window. With these shots, the first torpedo had emptied his pistol. He ran out of the shop and jumped into the waiting car, which sped off.

Nor was this the end. The assassins' get-away car swung into Fifth Street, where it ran smack into an International Ladies Garment Workers Union demonstration. This sudden confrontation may have surprised the gangsters more than it did the lady demonstrators, who were accustomed to having goon squads arrive to break up their meetings. The four Valenti torpedos could have stopped to explain that they weren't that sort of goons. Unfortunately, having just humiliated themselves in Heiney's Millinery Shop, the thugs were now in a foul mood and didn't care to explain anything to a bunch of protesting ladies. Instead they opened fire on the unionists to clear a pathway for themselves. The gunmen felled five of the workers and ran over another two, one of the wounded later died as a result.

The police later burst into Masseria's apartment and found him sitting on his bed soaking his feet in a tub of water. He grimly showed the officers his new straw hat with two bullet holes in it. Yet he remarked that the only injury he had sustained was to his feet which had become sore from all the running around and dodging.

Masseria sent Valenti an invitation to a peace conference. Valenti accepted. While Valenti and Masseria walked to a spaghetti joint on East Twelfth Street, two of Masseria's henchmen approached; one covered Valenti's bodyguard while the other opened fire. Valenti ran off diagonally towards a taxi. One of Masseria's boys followed him to the middle of the street, stopped, and pumped the full load of his automatic into his back as he was trying to get into the taxi. Valenti died, one hand on the taxicab's door, as he turned, pistol in his free hand, to fire back.

Once again, innocent by-standers were caught in the fray—a twelve year-old girl walking with her four year-old sister and a street cleaner. Fortunately, both survived.

Joe the Boss seems to have learned his lesson. A successful boss does not take pot shots at his enemies from the corner of the police station; nor does he murder innocent by-standers. After 1922 Masseria disappeared from the newspapers until, at the end of the decade, he was forced to deal with a more lethal set of adversaries.[15]

CHARLIE LUCIANO

Possibly because Charlie took such pains to deny it, many authors have assumed that Charlie Luciano spent the mid-1920s as a soldier in Joe the Boss's regime. As Reppetto puts it, before 1927, "to Rothstein and other mobsters Luciano was just another hired hand."[16] He was, after all, still in his early twenties when he met Rothstein, lacking in polish, grammar, and überworld contacts. Yet Luciano, Lansky, and Costello were more than hired hands. Rothstein had helped each of them set up. Luciano went into a bootlegging partnership with Frank Costello as early as 1921. Just as he had done with Lansky and Costello, Rothstein went out of his way to cultivate Charlie. Of the three, it was Charlie that came to regard him with real affection:

> He taught me how to dress, how not to wear loud things, but to have good taste; he taught me how to use knives and forks, and things like that at the dinner table, about holdin' a door open for a girl, or helpin' her sit down by holdin' the chair. If Arnold had lived a little longer, he could've made me pretty elegant; he was the best etiquette teacher a guy could have—real smooth.[17]

In 1920, Charlie Luciano was only twenty-three and still known as Salvatore Lucania. He met an eighteen-year-old Neapolitan named Giuseppe Antonio Doto. Doto had already restyled himself Joseph A. Adonis—Joe A for short. Some time in 1920, Joe A had gone to Philadelphia to see the Neapolitan flyweight Frankie Gennaro fight. There he had met fight promoter Boo Boo Hoff, who introduced him to bootlegger Waxey Gordon. Gordon took an instant liking to little Joey A, and offered him a carload of bottled-in-bond rye whiskey for $10,000. But Joe A did not have that much cash. So the following day he traveled back to New York and asked his friend Charlie for a loan. Charlie suggested that they both return to Philadelphia.

The next morning Charlie and Joe A took the morning train south. It was Charlie's first long train journey and the first time he had ever breakfasted in a dining car. He was impressed with the white table cloths and the men in business suits with brief cases reading the papers. "They were really elegant, like old money, and I said to myself, 'That's for me.' Then I remembered that Joe and I was sittin' there carryin' guns and that I got thirty-five grand in my pocket to buy booze with down in Philly, just so guys like them could pay through the nose for it."[18]

Charlie does not say where he got the thirty-five grand, whether it was his own or something he borrowed from Rothstein. Happy, he ordered himself corn-beef hash with a poached egg on top, and liked it so much that he had two more helpings. He later tried to tell his mother how to cook American food for him, but all she did was stare at him.

He bought the carload of whiskey that Waxey Gordon had offered Joey A. It was the first of a series of deals between Charley and Waxey; "I never had a real problem with Waxey Gordon from the day we met down in Philly.

We shook hands and in about a half an hour, it was all settled—prices, splits of goods, profits, the whole deal."[19] Over the next few years, Gordon landed Scotch whiskey at Atlantic City, and with Nucky Johnson's help, trucked it to Camden and then over the bridge to Philadelphia. In Philadelphia, Waxey had set up distilleries making 100 proof alcohol. Waxey either sold his Scotch uncut, or, for a lower price, cut with alcohol and water. Charlie bought both the cut and the uncut whiskey, eventually setting up his own cutting plants. He sold mainly to Midtown speakeasies. The garment district especially was always filled with buyers, often women, and the ready-to-wear manufacturers always offered them hospitality, typically trying to dazzle the out-of-towners with a bottle or two of premium Scotch "just off the boat." Often it was Charlie's Scotch.

MR. MARANZANO INTRODUCES HIMSELF

According to Joe Bonanno's account, Salvatore Maranzano emigrated from Sicily in 1925.[20] According to Luciano, however, Maranzano had arrived in New York shortly after the war, and took the lease on an apartment on Second Avenue and Fourteenth Street on the Lower East Side. The location was symbolic, almost within sight of Masseria's own headquarters. Maranzano protested that his intentions were peaceful; he had no desire to encroach on Joe the Boss's territory. Weren't there Castellammaresi in Lower Manhattan as well as in Brooklyn? Maranzano just wanted to claim dominion over his rightful subjects. Joe the Boss didn't believe Maranzano for a minute.

During the winter of 1922–23, Maranzano became a familiar figure on the Lower East Side, where, according to Charlie, he "would come round the neighborhood once and a while and hold up his hands, spread out like he was a Pope giving the people on the street a blessing."

Charlie describes two meetings with Maranzano in 1923. Recognizing Charlie as a potentially valuable ally, Maranzano invited him to lunch in the back room of a small restaurant called Il Palermo, just off Minetta Street in Little Italy. He tried to win Charlie with a display of effusive charm:

> When I walked into the room, Maranzano comes over to me with his arms in the air—and there he goes doing the fucking Pope routine again. He puts his arms around me and says that his name is Salvatore just like mine, that I'm his namesake, the "Young Caesar." Then he starts quoting Julius Caesar to me in Latin for chrissake! If he had something nice to say to me, why in the hell couldn't he have said it in English. So I told him that, and he started to laugh. And I'll never forget what he answered. He said "My son, words of praise are only meant for the great, and you will do great things." Shit. I could've spat in his face.

Undeterred, Maranzano pressed on: "I understand that you now like to be called Charlie," he said. "Somehow, I find it difficult to think of you as anything but Salvatore. Tell me, is my name not good enough for you to keep? Is there something about it that shames you."

Luciano thought of mentioning that he didn't like being nicknamed "Sally," but then kept it to himself. Maranzano could have had no idea what it was like to being nine-year-old Sicilian boy called "Sally" by your second-grade classmates. Maranzano was beginning to sound just like his parents. His mother had blackmailed him with a "Why do you renounce the name of your Savior, my son?" routine. Luciano liked the name *Charlie*; it had the right ring to it. Maranzano's censorious remarks about the "Jewish company" he was keeping offended him as well.

Maranzano's charm offensive failed on Luciano for exactly the same reasons it would later succeed with Bonanno. Joe Bonanno identified with Admiral Nelson and the great heroes of history. He remembered his father's last words—be proud that you're a Bonanno, proud of our Tradition. Bonanno was just waiting for someone to play upon his vanities, someone to call upon him to step forward and, invoking the names of his nation and his illustrious ancestors, take up that heroic role that destiny so obviously held in store.

Luciano's vanity worked in a different direction. He was no Salvatore; he was Charlie, pure New York street-child, a mutt with no pedigree, no illustrious ancestors and no advantages other than his own determination never to be a crumb. Unlike Bonanno, who pictured himself as a sanctified hero, an armor-clad warrior, painted in stained glass, standing in the window of a Memorial Chapel, Luciano saw himself as arising from the dust, as being no one but himself. Luciano was a new man, entirely self-invented, with no forbearers, family connections or even mother and father. Luciano loved America because it gave him the opportunity to succeed in his own way and on his own terms. Luciano was never going to warm to Maranzano's talk about Sicilian pride and Olde Worlde Traditions. Luciano was making up his own edition of the hero's life; unlike Bonanno's, Luciano's story included a "virgin birth."

Nevertheless, Maranzano made him feel insecure: "Maranzano was a guy with plenty of education; he spoke five languages and really knew a lotta culture. And me, just because I had no good schooling, I made myself feel like dirt every time I had any contact with him. Of course, he helped."

Charlie refused Maranzano's first offer of alliance. Afterwards, acting impulsively, he sent Maranzano over a case of King's Ransom Scotch. It was the best that money could buy, and Charlie knew that Maranzano would appreciate his gesture of "saluting the health of the King." It was expensive, costing Charlie nearly $2,000. But afterwards he felt elated, almost light-headed, that he had dared to make the gesture.[21]

At their next meeting, Charlie was feeling more self-assured. Maranzano spotted Luciano sitting in the front row of the Polo Grounds for the Dempsey-Firpo fight, and had come over to greet him. Proud as a peacock in the new finery that Mr. Rothstein had made him buy, Charlie was flattered that it had been Maranzano who had come over to greet him. The two men shook hands, exchanging greeting and making small talk. Then, when the crowd's cheering rose to a deafening roar as Jack Dempsey strode down the aisle beside them,

Maranzano took Luciano by the shoulders and whispered in his ears:

"I have a business proposition for you."

"You mean like the last one."

"No, no. It's a better deal. You'll see."

"I'm listening."

"Good. We meet then?"

"Where?"

"At my club, if that is agreeable."

Two days later, bringing Frank Costello along with him, Luciano met Maranzano at his club, near his Lower East Side apartment. Once again, Maranzano was all cordiality; taking the two into his back room and pouring them drinks. He launched into a speech about the evils of unbridled competition. Torrio and Lansky had always argued that competition was healthy in principle; but Maranzano now took the opposite line. Competition, he said, would only lead to pointless bloodshed; "As things now stand, we are interfering with each other. We are competing for the same whiskey markets, and, unfortunately, killing each other's men. This is foolish, and it costs us both too much money and too many good men. This should come to a stop."

Maranzano's proposal was the he and Luciano should go into partnership. Luciano and Costello would put their Jewish and Irish bootleggers at his disposal. He, in recompense, would cut them in on the alky cooking, protection rackets and gambling interests that the Castellammaresi controlled: "I would like you to join the great Maranzano family," he told Charlie. "You would be like my son, like a favorite son. I am prepared to be very generous. You will be like my own *bambino*."

Charlie didn't want to be anybody's *bambino*. Still, Maranzano's terms were interesting. A guaranteed cut of Maranzano's takings would probably amount to even more than any of them was now making. Costello was impressed; "It's a helluva deal Charlie," Frank said, arguing that, if they accepted it, they would become the equal of the established mafia dons.

Still, in his gut, Charlie distrusted Maranzano. He was hoping that it was a feeling that his friends would share. But most of them seemed enthusiastic. Only Little Meyer was against the proposal. But all he had to say was, "It stinks."

At this, Charlie remembered, everyone started yelling at Meyer, until, suddenly, Vito Genovese saw the light. In the eyes of Maranzano, he said, Luciano, Costello, Adonis, and he were a bunch of young Italian punks who happened to have some good connections with the Jewish and Irish syndicates—

connections that made Maranzano hungry. What the young hoods lacked was the influence and prestige of the older dons. In exchange for these contacts, Maranzano was thus offering to absorb them into `the great Maranzano family' holding out the prospect of high rank, prestige, and untold riches to come. But, Vito continued, that was where the catch came in. Once the four of them were inside the Maranzano organization, Maranzano had no incentive to keep his side of the bargain. Once they were inside his family and he had their contacts, Luciano, Costello, Genovese, and Adonis became four nobodies. Why should Maranzano want to place them over his own Castellammarese troops?

Why should Maranzano even let them remain alive? Who was going to complain if he had them bumped off. "What's wrong with you guys?" Lansky asked his four Italian friends. "Don't you know the deal won't last two days. You don't have to be a big brain or adding machine or nothing else to know that the minute we join up with Maranzano that fat old son-of-a-bitch will have us knocked off."

Luciano politely responded to Maranzano the next day. The time, he said, was not yet quite ripe.[22]

A few days after the Demspey-Firpo fight, two of Charlie's shipments were hijacked in New Jersey. About the same time, federal agents raided his warehouses in Upper Manhattan. Suddenly Charlie had orders to fill and no supplies. Nucky Johnson had heard about the New Jersey hijackings; when he called to thank Charlie for the fight tickets a few days later, he commiserated with him. It was a piece of bad luck. Maybe Charlie and Joe A ought to drop by and see if there was anything he could do to help them out.

Nucky Johnson had always observed strict neutrality in the underworld wars, especially in the wars between the Italians; but Nucky was always very hungry. Charlie sensed that Nucky was curious to hear what Charlie might offer him for helping him out of a jam. Charlie and Joe A drove the hundred and forty miles from New York to Atlantic City in a little over three hours. They met Nucky in the secluded bungalow that Nucky kept for just such private meetings. Charlie blurted out his proposal immediately; "Look Nucky, I don't want to beat around the bush, and I'm not looking to chisel a sharp deal. I need all the Scotch I can lay my hand on, and you know everything that's coming in and out. Now I want a better deal than the fair shake you've been giving everybody. I'll make you a partner."

Charlie's proposal was to give Nucky a cut of all his rackets.

Nucky evidently had been expecting such an offer, for he replied immediately, "I'll give you an exclusive on my beach. Nobody else can land any stuff there. I'll give you protection all the way to the Camden ferry across from Philly. I'll let Costello bring in all the slots he can handle. You can run gambling spots that we'll decide on, near the big hotels. Now, Charlie, what do I get?"

Before answering, Charlie explained that he needed some good Scotch right away. Was anyone making a shipment?

"Maranzano," Nucky answered. "A boatload, two trucks, of uncut stuff will come in at Ventnor two nights from now. It's going to be cut by Waxey Gordon and Bitsy Bitz in Philadelphia."

Johnson pulled out a map and showed Charlie the route that Maranzano's two trucks would be taking. It passed through Egg Harbor, New Jersey, by a back road.

"After getting that information, I shook hands with Nucky on the deal. That day I gave him ten per cent of everything as long as the Volstead Act remained the law; everything from my outfit, that is. But the rest, including Costello, Lansky, Siegel, and Adonis all chipped in, so it wasn't too big a bite for any one of us."

The deal was huge; Charlie and his friends were offering ten percent of everything they had for an exclusive on Johnson's beach and gambling rights in the city, offering to go into an exclusive partnership with the acknowledged kingpins of the American bootlegging world. If the deal worked out, they would all make millions. Nucky complimented Charlie on his aplomb. He told him that he liked the way he handled himself. So did Joe Adonis driving back in the car; "That's the smartest move you ever made. It's worth millions."

Two nights later, on the back road into Egg Harbor, two trucks laden with cases of uncut Scotch whiskey were stopped by a fallen tree. When the two men riding shotgun got out to clear the debris, Lansky and Siegel stepped out of the shadows and opened fire. One of the guards was killed, while another fell wounded. With that, Charlie, Joe A, and six more armed men appeared surrounding the two trucks; "and the rest of 'em gave up right there. But that didn't do them no good, because we took their guns away from 'em and give 'em a good beating before we took off with the trucks. Maybe the best thing about it was that none of 'em recognized us because we was all masked."[23] Luciano began to bring the Scotch he landed in Atlantic City to Waxey Gordon's, and later his own, plants in Camden and Philadelphia where it was cut with 100 proof alcohol and re-bottled.

JOE THE BOSS MAKES CHARLIE AN OFFER

"Joe Masseria had decided he didn't like the Sicilians born in Castellamare del Golfo. Therefore, they must be executed."

—Frank Costello[24]

According to some accounts, Joe the Boss Masseria's father, Giuseppe senior, came from Corleone with Giuseppe Morello and Ignazio Lupo Saietta. If this is true, Joe the Boss might count himself as a member of one of the founding families of the *Unione Siciliana* in New York. This makes his failure to attend Frankie Yale's funeral stand out. Nor was his the only notable absence. Another founding member conspicuously missing was Ciro Terranova. In 1922 Umberto Valenti had murdered Ciro's brother, Vincent Terranova at the *Unione* headquarters on 116th Street. If Ciro suspected that Yale or the Brooklyn chapter of the *Unione* had something to do with Vincent's murder, his absence would be more than comprehensible. Most of the mourners in fact came from Brooklyn. The only important representative from the Manhattan underworld was Ignazio Saietta, but Lupo the Wolf no longer played an active role in the *Unione*. The Manhattan Sicilians stayed away. In context, this could not have been a message of good will.

Yale had been known as the "Prince of Darkness;" he had a cunning, silky charm all his own. An arch-plotter, he needed to persuade, to flatter and bend people's wills. All this was foreign to Joe the Boss's nature. Masseria was not sentimental; he was not even affable. Usually he was about as charming as a dyspeptic grizzly bear. Nevertheless, though incapable of sentiment, guile, or charm, Joe the Boss was able to recognize the enemy when he was staring him right in the face.

Whenever Joe the Boss Masseria thought about Maranzano, his hackles rose. He began to snarl. Masseria ran into Charlie several times in 1922 and 1923. He obliquely sounded him out through Gaetano "Tom" Reina, the *Unione* boss in the Bronx. Reina was an old ally of Masseria. When he invited Luciano and Genovese to the Claridge Hotel in Midtown Manhattan, it was partly, as he said, to meet the young Sicilians making their way in the underworld, and partly to ask Charlie and Vito what they thought about working for Masseria. Charlie liked Tom Reina, so he was cordial but non-committal. A few months later Charlie was having diner with Benny Siegel in Jack & Charlie's 21 Club when Masseria and his lieutenants breezed in with a party of showgirls. Charlie treated Joe and his party to some of his private stock of uncut Scotch. Later Charlie went to meet him in his offices over a restaurant, not a half-dozen blocks from Maranzano's own club. Whenever Masseria looked out the window in the direction of Maranzano's club, his face contorted with rage. Charlie had just told him about Maranzano's ambition to become a new Julius Caesar:

> He's gonna kill himself with that crap—Masseria growled—When are you going to wake up? Don't you know the only reason he didn't knock you off, and all them punk kids with you, is because he needs you? Get smart. Come in with me, and then you can be the first lieutenant of the real Sicilian boss of this whole fucking city, of the country. You want money? I'll make more money for you than you can count. Just say the word.[25]

Luciano has little to say about his life in the mid-1920s. He describes the meetings with both Masseria and Maranzano in 1923, as well as the story of his partnership with Nucky Johnson. The story then jumps 1927 when he was summoned again by Joe the Boss. All Charlie tells about the four intervening years was that he was busy buying cops.

In 1925, Johnny Torrio, on his way to Italy, announced that Prohibition would eventually be repealed and that his friends ought to be buying legal options from European distillers and wine producers. Lansky, also at the meeting, agreed; "The only way to get legitimate is to move in with legitimate people," he commented. To do this, however, Torrio cautioned, you needed to buy some friends; "You've gotta get into big politics; you can buy top politicians the same way you bought the law." Soon Charlie was paying two Tammany bosses, Albert C. Marinelli from Little Italy and Jimmy Hines, Owney Madden's and Dutch Schultz's political connection on the West Side. Charlie's English was not good enough to read the New York *Times;* so he read the *Daily News* and the *Mirror* instead. He would pick up the early morning editions after he knocked off from work, usually shortly before dawn, going home to his Murray Hill apartment. "I'd lay there and read that stuff and it all looked so legit I couldn't even believe that I done it, that it was my muscle that put them 'very respectable' guys where they was. . . . I had personally helped elect more than eighty guys over a short time, all votin' my way, aldermen, councilmen, mayors, congressmen, even senators. They were mine. I picked 'em. I elected 'em. They belonged to me lock, stock and barrel."[26]

In late 1927, Joe the Boss contacted Red Levine, a contract killer and driver that both he and Charlie used, and gave him a message. Masseria told Levine that he wanted to see Luciano and his boys right away. They could find him, he said, in his suite at the Hotel Manger on Seventh Avenue. The message wasn't an invitation; it was an ultimatum. If Charlie didn't go, Joe the Boss would take it as a declaration of war and act accordingly. Charlie and his friends assembled in Moe Ducore's drugstore across the street from the hotel, sending Red Levine and Nick Gentile over to case the place and make sure that Masseria wasn't planning some sort of ambush.

What did Masseria want? Lansky opened the meeting; "It's gotta be yes or no," he said. "Either Charlie goes with Joe the Boss or there's going to be a lot of blood spilled."

These were the only options. Not that the prospect of spilled blood necessarily troubled them. Indeed, Benny Siegel immediately proposed to kill the "fat old bastard." "Bugsy," Charlie later recalled, "was the only nut I ever knew who had real ice water and absolutely no fear in them days." Still, Masseria was powerful and dangerous, and Luciano and his friends didn't need to be spending their time ducking bullets.

> I was sure that sooner or later Maranzano and Masseria would have a war. The two fucking Sicilians would never be happy until one of them got rubbed out. To me, the whole thing was a matter of organizing a business; for them, it was pride that came first—who was going to be Boss of Bosses. I figured—and this was one time I was dead wrong—that Masseria would wind up on top.[27]

So Charlie and Adonis walked over to the Hotel Manger and took the elevator up the Masseria's suite. They found Masseria sitting in his room stuffing himself. He was in front of a table loaded with antipasto, prosciutto, salami, shellfish, toasted peppers plus a tureen full of pasta with sauce and cheese.

There was enough on table for a banquet and I kept figuring that any moment Masseria's mob was going to show up and sweep down on the table. But nobody showed. I think Masseria ate half of all that food by himself, most of it with his fingers—and if he didn't look like a pig on two legs, I never saw one.

The only other person in the room was a dour-faced young Sicilian named Joe Catania, also known as Joe Baker, Ciro Terranova's nephew, and Masseria's current bodyguard. Joe the Boss kept eating for a while, taking no notice of Charlie or Joey A. Finally, he asked Charlie if he'd brought his piece. Charlie replied that this was supposed to be a friendly meet, whereupon Joe sent Catania over to frisk them. Assured that they were both unarmed, he turned to them and announced menacingly, "Now you have a chance to be my friend or the both of you are dead men."

Charlie told him that they had indeed come to join up. He would be Masseria's new number two, giving him a piece of everything he had, except, he added, "not one fucking drop of whiskey."

At this, Masseria exploded. With gobs of half-masticated food spurting from his mouth, he erupted from behind the table, grabbed a crystal lamp and hurled it into the wall on the other side of the room. He smashed the dishes still piled with half-eaten food and then stomped off shouting and cursing and looking for other bits of hotel furnishing to pound into smithereens. Catania backed away intimidated, while Charlie and Joe A stood by and waited.

Suddenly Masseria stopped in mid-rampage. He turned to Charlie and said; "You dirty, skinny son of a bitch! You're the only *paisan* in this whole fucking town that ain't afraid of Joe the Boss." Then he broke into a big grin, "Come here, Charlie Lucania, you just made yourself a deal," he said. Then he walked over and gave his new business partner a great big greasy bearhug.

Charlie and Joe A walked back over to Ducore's drugstore where the boys were waiting for them. They were all relieved that some sort of accommodation had been reached. Nobody would call Joe the Boss a sharing person. He was more like the psychotic toddler at the birthday party who bites the other kids and grabs all the ice cream, cake, and prizes for himself. When Charlie and Joe recounted the scene, not one of them imagined that the partnership would last too long.[28]

Charlie dates his association with Masseria's crime family to 1927. Not everyone has accepted this version. Masseria, they argue, was the boss of the Sicilian underworld in Manhattan's Little Italy, a boss whose influence extended all the way to East Harlem and Brooklyn. As a Sicilian and ex-Five Pointer working in Lower Manhattan, Charlie Luciano could not have avoided the concupiscent eye of Joe the Boss for long. If Charlie was making money in Manhattan, Masseria would have wanted his cut. Joe Bonanno, for example, states that Charlie Luciano was a lieutenant in the Masseria regime until Maranzano persuaded him to switch sides. But Bonanno's perspective is too narrow. He fails to consider Charlie's connection with Rothstein. More especially, Bonanno fails to mention Charlie's Scotch.

Alky-cooking existed in New York. As early as 1918, Tammany Boss Murphy and the Corn Products Refining Company were involved in a scheme to sell malt dextrine (an ingredient in beer-making) to the British government.[29] During Prohibition, there was alky-cooking in the tenements of Little Italy and the Castellammarese section of Williamsburg. Typically, New York's tenement alky-cooking industry was under the protection of Italian crime bosses such as Masseria or Maranzano. Nevertheless, along the East Coast, the 'home brew fad,' never became predominant in the New York bootlegging industry. There were no major sugar barons in New York; nor were there wars as in Chicago and Cleveland. The availability of Scotch whiskey in quantities shaped both the bootlegging business along the East Coast and the evolution of the bootlegging underworld. It was a business, moreover, from which older mafia bosses like Masseria and Maranzano were still largely excluded.

Bonanno's account also fails to take into account Luciano's connection to Albert Marinelli.

In 1921, a young Tammany-connected magistrate in Little Italy, Albert C. Marinelli, demanded that the Italian community have a greater voice in the Hall. A protégé of Rothstein and election district captain under Tom Foley, Marinelli was appointed port warden in 1921. His duties were to patrol the East Side docks, guarding them from bootleggers and rumrunners. During his tenure as port warden, however, no shipment of contraband alcohol was ever seized at the docks, nor were there many arrests for burglary, pilferage, or smuggling. At first, much of the whiskey arriving at Marinelli's docks found its way to the nearby curb exchange. Later, when the exchange was closed, Marinelli opened a truck rental business at Kenmare and Mulberry. Most of his customers were bootleggers. Though he later did business with Masseria and even Yale, his best customers, and probably partners as well, were Luciano, Lansky, and Costello.[30] He was an important man to know; and Luciano showed his gratitude by giving Marinelli one of the precious tickets to the Dempsey-Firpo match. Charlie does not mention giving Joe the Boss a similar ticket.

TOMMY LUCCHESE

A small man, barely five two, Gaetano "Tommy" Lucchese was missing one of the fingers on his right hand. When he was arrested in 1923 for car theft, one of the cops fingerprinting him yelled out, "Hey it's Tommy Three Fingers." The reference was to the baseball pitcher, Mordechai "Tommy" Brown, who was similarly missing one of his digits. Tommy Lucchese eventually got used to the name Tommy Brown but always detested being called Tommy Three Fingers or Three Fingers Brown. During the late 1920s, Tommy Lucchese was part of the family of Bronx boss, Gaetano "Tom" Reina.

Like the Morello and Terranova families, Reina had emigrated from Corleone to East Harlem in the opening years of the twentieth century. He was one of the founding fathers of the *Unione Siciliana* in New York. Unlike the Morello-Terranovas in East Harlem, Reina spent his career quietly in the Bronx, prospering through his control of ice deliveries there. Reina kept out of the *Unione* struggles, keeping himself strictly to his trade unions. Though he managed to avoid the attention of either the papers or the police, Reina still ran his own Family. One of his most important captains, Gaetano "Tommy" Gagliano, ran the plasterers union. Tommy Lucchese, started as a soldier in Gagliano's crew.

Masseria had asked Tom Reina to sound out Charlie Luciano in 1923. Charlie had then refused to be drawn into a commitment. Both Corleonesi, Reina and Masseria were old allies. Recently, however, Reina had become troubled by Masseria's campaign to wipe out the Castellamarresi. Reina wanted peace and good relations with all the leaders of Sicilian underworld in New York—including Maranzano. Another ex-seminarian like Maranzano, Reina had met Don Salvatore when he arrived in New York from Castellammare del Golfo. The old don had taken to Maranzano, and the two men had become friends, a fact that made Masseria distinctly uneasy. When he heard from Terranova cousin Pete Morello that Reina and Lucchese had continued to confer with Maranzano, he decided to have his old ally eliminated. He decided to throw in Tommy Lucchese for good measure.

> Reina was no little potato—Luciano recalled. He was a boss. And under the old-time rules, a boss don't get hit—pop! just like that. But in the case of Tommy Lucchese, that was different. It was all I could do to convince Joe that Tommy went with Reina to find out what was going on and report to me. If Joe hadn't bought the story, Tommy was as good as dead. But the whole situation seemed to turn Masseria into a raving maniac. He used to call me from all over New York about a half dozen times a day with a new name of some guy he wanted to bump off. It was driving me crazy.[31]

Charlie was now Joe Masseria's underboss, while Lucchese was number two in Gaetano Gagliano's crew. The two friends kept each other up to date concerning the plots and counter-plots that were hatching in the opposing camps. Both of them wanted to keep their back channel under wraps. "Tommy and I was friends from the old neighborhood," Charlie commented, "but for a lotta reasons we didn't play that up: we used to meet in private most of the time, and it wasn't for a time that a lotta guys knew we was close."

Maranzano, Charlie learned, was offering Reina a share of Masseria's Lower East Side rackets as inducement to join with the Castellammaresi. In 1929, Reina seems to have come to his decision. "Tommy come to me and he told me the whole story," Charlie recalled. "He said that Reina forced him to go with him to a secret meeting with Maranzano, and Tommy was surprised that Reina seemed to like Maranzano's deal." Neither Charlie Luciano nor Tommy Lucchese could see any use in an underworld war. Masseria and Maranzano, they thought, had brought the idea of vendetta with 'em when they came to America. I never seen nothin' like it. It was like in the hills of

Kentucky, with families knockin' each other off for some fucked-up reason that maybe goes back a hundred year and nobody remembers why no more.

> All us younger guys hated the old mustaches and what they was doin'. We was tryin' to build a business that'd move with the times and they was still livin' a hundred years ago. We knew the old guys and their ideas hadda go; we was just markin' time. The way we looked at it was that getting' rid of a Masseria or a Maranzano was no different from some bank tearin' down an old buildin' so they could put up a new one. For us, rubbin' out a mustache was just like makin' way for a new buildin' like we was in the construction business."[32]

By late 1929, Charlie, Tommy, and their associates in the younger generation, had decided that a major redevelopment in the New York City underworld landscape was overdue.

MR. MARANZANO MAKES A COUNTER-PROPOSAL

In the summer of 1929, Luciano had his hands full with his bootleg Scotch business. He took the consignments in South Jersey, smuggling his cargo into Nig Rosen's warehouses in Philadelphia, where most of it would be cut and re-bottled. It meant that he worked nights and was out of Manhattan much of the time. This infuriated Masseria. Early one morning, Joe the Boss called his hotel room. Where in the hell had Charlie been the last few days, he wanted to know. Delivering Scotch to Philadelphia, Luciano replied, and what in the hell are you doing calling me at this hour in the morning.

Masseria told Luciano that a "couple of punks" had "got themselves picked up on West End Avenue last night and now they're in the can. I want them out—loose—right now. I need them." The two "punks," it turned out, were Abraham "Bo" Weinberg and Charlie "The Bug" Wokman, two of the Dutchman's top contract killers. If Masseria needed Weinberg and Wokman sprung, it could only mean that Masseria had an urgent job for them. The thought made Charlie uneasy.

> It's your district—Joe yelled down the receiver—and you're the one us- ing my money to pay off the cops there. When I need your muscle, you ain't around no more. You ain't never around lately. You're always off on your own fucking business. That's gotta stop, and it's gotta stop right now. I wanta see you, right now—and we're gonna get this thing settled. You understand, Mister Salvatore Lucania?[33]

Charlie said he'd get Costello to take care of Weinberg and Wokman. He then suggested that Masseria drop by. It was a breach of etiquette; bosses summon their underlings, not the other way around. But when Joe immediately ac- cepted Charlie's invitation, Charlie knew that some sort of confrontation was brewing. "Come alone," he added.

When Masseria came storming in a little later, Luciano had Frank Costello beside him. Charlie tried to placate the angry boss; but Masseria cut him short: "Stop the horseshit! I don't buy this crap from you anymore. From now on you work for me twenty-four hours a day. And everything you got goes into my pot. You don't like it? Well that's just too fucking bad."

Masseria was obviously referring to the Scotch shipments, and Charlie reminded him that they had made a deal and shook hands.

"The whiskey belongs to me!" Masseria shouted. "And if I want to, I'll drink it all myself. I break the handshake!" With that, he strode out of the room.

Siegel, Torrio and Adonis had been waiting in foyer. As soon as Joe the Boss left, they came up. Charlie called in Lansky and Genovese as well. Within a half hour, the seven were having a council of war. Losing the Scotch was unthinkable. It was not just a matter of money; Torrio and Lansky had earlier convinced Charlie that, by buying options on overseas brands, Luciano and Costello could emerge as legitimate businessmen at the end of Prohibition. Costello had already obtained an option for King's Ransom Scotch. The end of Prohibition would turn importing Scotch into a legitimate business. Nothing, however, could make alky-cooking legitimate. The end of Prohibition would eliminate the demand for the alky-cookers' insalubrious product. It was therefore essential that Luciano and Costello keep their Scotch business out of Masseria's hands. This left Charlie with one alternative. He called Lucchese and asked him to arrange a meeting with Mr. Maranzano.

Lucchese soon relayed Maranzano's reply. The Castellammarese boss had been deeply grieved when he heard that Luciano had joined forces with Masseria. Nevertheless, his offer to take Luciano into the "Great Maranzano Family" still stood. But first, Luciano would have to undergo a test to prove his loyalty. He would have to kill Joe the Boss.

According to Joe Bonanno's version, Luciano visited Maranzano at his Brooklyn address. It was the first time Bonanno and Luciano had ever met, and Bonanno was struck by Luciano's refusal to speak Sicilian. Luciano would listen to Maranzano's well-turned speeches in Sicilian or Italian, but would only reply in American street slang. Not that Bonanno remembers Luciano as having that much to say:

"Do you know why you're here?" Bonanno has Maranzano asking Luciano.

"Yes."

"Then I don't have to tell you what needs to be done."

"No."

"How much time do you need to do what you have to do?"

"A week or two."

"Good. I'm looking forward to a peaceful Easter."

Though Bonanno does not give the date of the meeting, from Luciano's remark that he could do the job in a week or two, from Maranzano's remark that he was looking forward to a peaceful Easter, and from the fact that Masseria was eventually killed in mid-April, 1931, we can infer that the meeting must have taken place either in the Spring of 1931, or, at the limit, the end of 1930.

Luciano gives a radically different account. According to him, the meeting took place in early October 1929, before the great stock market crash.

This is hardly the only difference between the accounts of Bonanno and Luciano. Charlie described the meeting as taking place under the cover of darkness on a shipping pier in Staten Island. When Maranzano told Charlie that he was to kill Masseria, he had gone on to specify, "I mean you. You, personally, are going to kill Giuseppe Masseria." Charlie bluntly refused. No sooner had the words escaped his lips, then someone blackjacked him from behind.

When Charlie came to, he "felt someone splashin' water on my face, and I was tied up and hangin' by my wrists from a beam over me, with my toes just reachin' the floor. There were some flashlights shinin' at me and I could make out maybe a half-dozen guys with handkerchiefs coverin' their faces so that I couldn't tell who anybody was." He saw Maranzano, unmasked, standing in front of him. Charlie yelled in his face, "I ain't goin' to do it." With this, Maranzano set the masked men to work; "they did a pretty good job, with belts and clubs and cigarette butts—until I passed out again."

When he regained his senses, Maranzano began to beseech him:

> Charlie, this is so stupid. You can end this now if you will just agree. It is no big thing to kill a man, and you know he is going to die anyway. Why do you have to go through this, Charlie? Why are you so stubborn? All you have to do is to kill him, kill him yourself. That you must do, kill him yourself. But Charlie, I promise you, if you do not do it, then you are dead.

Instead, Charlie lashed out with his feet, kicking Maranzano in the groin. Maranzano doubled up in pain, falling to his knees and shouting out, "Kill him! Kill him!" Staggering back onto his feet, Maranzano grabbed a knife and slashed Charlie's right cheek to the bone. He slashed again, this time opening a deep gash along Charlie's chest. Suddenly, regaining his calm, Maranzano stopped. He stepped back and said "No! Let him live. He'll do what has to be done or we will see him again."

Maranzano's men cut Charlie down and threw him into the back seat of a car. They drove part way into town, and dumped him by the side of the road, where he was found by a cruising police car.[34]

"Until he related the story in 1961," Richard Hammer observes, "Luciano had never given a satisfactory explanation of that October night." He had unquestionably received a serious beating from someone. He had needed fifty-five stitches to repair the wound. The knife slash along the right cheek

had severed a muscle, giving him a rather louche, sinister look for the rest
of his life. From whom? Rumors have long swirled around the incident, and
most commentators are reluctant to accept Luciano's melodramatic account.
About one of the incident's consequences, however, there has been less disagreement. Charlie, his underworld colleagues all told him, had been lucky
to survive, so lucky, in fact, that his friends made up a new nickname for
him—Lucky Luciano.

Why did Charlie refuse to kill Masseria? Richard Hammer adds a note
that in the "tradition-laden Sicilian underworld you cannot kill the leader personally, and then succeed to his throne." If Charlie had killed Masseria, he
would have been ineligible to lead Masseria's family. It is the Sicilian underworld version of the poison pill provision. Does such a rule really exist in the
Sicilian underworld? It is a question much debated on mafia Websites.

Whether Luciano's account of the incident is believable, his sequence of
events is more plausible. Luciano probably re-initiated contact with Maranzano in the late summer of 1929, shortly after he had fallen out with Masseria
over the Scotch business. For the next year and a half, Luciano was thus leading a double life. Still officially an underboss in Masseria's regime, he was, in
fact, plotting Joe's downfall.

It was a delicate period. Luciano and Reina were simultaneously negotiating with Maranzano. Though Luciano's betrayal was still a secret, Pete
Morello had told Masseria what Reina was considering, and Masseria's reaction had been predictably murderous. Joe's first idea had been to murder
both Reina and Tommy Lucchese. But Charlie needed Tommy as his contact
with the Maranzano family, so Charlie convinced Joe the Boss that Tommy
was on the level. At this point, both Charlie and Tommy wanted to keep war
from breaking out. Charlie had teamed Lucchese up with the Jewish labor
racketeers Lepke Buchalter and Gurrah Shapiro, and the three had begun to
organize the entire garment district. It was turning into a fantastic racket. If
a war broke out, however, the threesome would have to split up. Lucchese
would be forced to side with the Castellammaresi while Lepke and Gurrah, as
friends of Charlie's, would side with Masseria.

Luciano urged Lucchese to prevent Reina from joining with Maranzano
until Luciano was ready to move. Events, however, were getting ahead of
him. In January 1930, Masseria told Charlie that he had new proof that Reina
was planning to betray him. Reina must have had his own sources inside the
Masseria regime, for that evening Tommy Lucchese told Charlie that Reina
had discovered that Masseria had given orders to murder two important Castellammarese underbosses, Joe Profaci and Joe Bonanno. Neither Luciano nor
Lucchese wanted Profaci or Bonanno murdered; they were part of the younger
generation of Sicilians.

Six months earlier, Charlie and Tommy had worked to preserve the peace;
by now, however, after Masseria had taken Charlie's Scotch business and had
called for a pre-emptive strike on the young Castellammaresi, war seemed
unavoidable. "We all agreed then that there was no way to stop the war. The

only thing we should think about was how we could win it. That's when we suddenly realized we had to switch our old plans around—that Masseria had to go first instead of Maranzano."[35]

"Now when you're dealing with a Sicilian," Charlie observed, "you gotta think like a Sicilian, or you ain't got a chance." If Masseria was planning hits on Profaci and Bonanno, and if he was keeping these plans from his number two, Charlie Luciano, there could only be one explanation: Masseria wanted the responsibility for the hits to fall on Charlie. If the hits went down as planned and Maranzano swallowed the explanation, than Maranzano would blame Charlie and "would come after me with everythin' he had." Charlie would be trapped in the Masseria regime with no room for maneuver.

> The minute I explained it, Bugsy Siegel said. "We're always wastin' time. You Italian bastards are forever chewin' it over and chewin' it over until there's not a fuckin' thing to swallow. There's only one way to go—we gotta knock off Reina as soon as possible and Tommy's gotta pass the word to Maranzano that it was a hit from Masseria. And we gotta make sure than notin' happens to Profaci and Bananas."[36]

If Maranzano believed that Reina's murder had been ordered by Masseria, he would become all the more anxious to enlist Charlie and his young friends.

"I really hated to knock off Tom Reina," Charlie commented a little sanctimoniously, "and none of my boys did either. Reina was a man of his word, he had culture, and he was a very honorable Italian. He practically ran the Bronx. . . . But he had to be eliminated so I could keep on living and keep on moving up." He gave the job to Vito Genovese.

According to the reconstruction of Thomas L. Jones, every Wednesday, Reina had a date he never broke. He would leave his home at 3138 Rochambeau Avenue, near the Woodland Cemetery in the north Bronx about 5:30 p.m., and drive the five miles south to the house of a favorite aunt who lived at 1522 Sheridan Avenue, just across from Claremont Park. The two of them would have dinner together and chat for two or three hours. On a cold winter's night, on February 26, 1930, Reina went for his last supper.

At about 8 p.m. he kissed his aunt goodbye and stepped out of her house. As he stepped onto the sidewalk, a figure moved out of the shadows behind a parked automobile. Reina recognized the figure. "Vito told me that when Reina saw him he started to smile and wave his hand. When he done that, Vito blew his head off with a shotgun," Charlie remembered. Vito fired both cylinders at almost point blank range. The shots blew most or Reina's head off, sending his lifeless body flying back against the stone wall that fronted the property before it crumpled to the ground. Lowering the shotgun, Vito Genovese quickly stepped into a waiting car and disappeared into the night.[37]

As Luciano had calculated, Maranzano believed that Masseria had called the Reina hit. Maranzano in fact suspected Joe Catania. Masseria made things worse by trying to seize control of the Reina Family himself, handing it over it over to Joseph Pinzolo, whom Luciano described as even "fatter, uglier and dirtier than Masseria was." Most of the rising soldiers in the Reina Family were young guys who looked to Luciano as their leader. How could Masseria think these guys were going to put up with a mean old mustache Pete? In fact, Pinzolo only lasted until September. Tommy Lucchese lured Pinzolo into an office near Times Square. While he was busy checking receipts, either another friend of Luciano's, Dominic "The Gap" Petrilli, or his friend, Girolamo Santucci, known under his ring name of "Bobby Doyle," walked in behind Pinzolo and placed two bullets in the back of his head.[38] Pinzolo, Charlie remarked, didn't even get a regulation *Unione Siciliana* funeral.[39]

ATLANTIC CITY

In the beginning of 1929, leading bootleggers from the Northeast assembled for a meeting in Atlantic City.

As Allan May observes, depending on whose account you read, the idea for the Atlantic City convention came from Charlie Luciano, Meyer Lansky, or Frank Costello. Costello's claim seems the best; he certainly was one of the organizers in1929, as he would be in New York in 1934 after the fall of Prohibition. Some of the Jewish bootleggers as well as Johnny Torrio no doubt helped in the organization. Luciano claims that he chose Atlantic City because Lansky, who had taken out his naturalization papers in October 1928, was getting married the following May. Meyer's friends decided it would be nice to hold the convention in a city where Meyer and Anna could enjoy a sort of prenuptial honeymoon.[40]

The Jewish bootlegging syndicates were represented by Moe Dalitz and Louis Rothkopf from Cleveland, Charles "King" Solomon from Boston, Waxey Gordon from Jersey City, Longie Zwillman from Newark, Dutch Schultz from the Bronx and Max "Boo Boo" Hoff and Harry "Nig Rosen" Stromberg from Philadelphia, and a number of Detroit Purples, including Abe Bernstein. Luciano arrived with Lansky, Costello, Adonis, Genovese, Frank Scalise, Albert Anastasia, and Vince Mangano. Bonanno came from Brooklyn. Owney Madden came with Big Frenchy and Johnny Torrio. Al Capone came with Frank Nitti and Jake Guzik and bodyguards Frank Rio and Tony Accardo.[41]

Conceived in the 1850s as a large-scale version of New York's Coney Island, Atlantic City, whose broad avenues running parallel to the beach were named after famous oceans and seas of the world—Pacific, Atlantic, Arctic, Baltic, Mediterranean and Adriatic—and whose cross avenues were named after states—Pennsylvania, Connecticut, Kentucky, and others—ended at its famous Boardwalk. The town's first pier, 650 feet long, floated away in a nor'easter two months after its opening. Another quickly arose in its place, only to be wrecked when a storm-tossed schooner crashed through it. Finally, in 1887, a one-thousand-foot iron pier was constructed that lasted until 1944. The pier was purchased by H. J. Heinz, who installed a gigantic, neon '57' (for 57 varieties). The unearthly glow illuminated the entire town by night, defining Atlantic City in the same way that the gigantic smoking Camel cigarette billboard defined Times Square. "Atlantic City is not for the introspective," wrote James Hunecker in the *New Cosmopolis* in 1915. "It is all on the surface; it is hard, glittering, unspeakably cacophonous, and it never sleeps at all. Three days and you crave the relative solitude of Broadway and Thirty-fourth Street; a week and you may die of insomnia."[42]

These were years of anti-vice crusades, the time when reformers in New York and other older cities campaigned to suppress prostitution, gambling, Sunday drinking, and late-night roistering. Atlantic City, by contrast, was a new town, and one, moreover, specifically designed to cater to a working class clientele. Salt-water taffy, sex, gambling, drinking, and late-night roistering were the town's only industries. Thus like Coney Island, Atlantic City fought hard to keep the anti-vice campaigners from shutting down its honky tonks. Nevertheless, in 1910, the new governor of New Jersey, Woodrow Wilson, visited Atlantic City and declared that it was living under "a reign of terror." "It is a question," he continued, "of emancipation from everything that is disgraceful and rotten." Wilson's relentless anti-vice campaigns over the next two years put a number of state politicians behind bars. Among Wilson's targets were Atlantic City Republican bosses Smith E. Johnson and his son Enoch "Nucky" Johnson, who alternated with each other as the town's sheriff and deputy sheriff, thereby circumventing a New Jersey state law that prohibited sheriffs from serving two terms in a row. Though Nucky was charged with electoral fraud, he was popular with Atlantic City's large black community, one which consistently voted Republican and helped Nucky secure an acquittal. The run-in with Governor Wilson also taught Nucky a lesson. The governor's anti-vice crusade had incriminated many of the state's most prominent Republicans; Nucky found it wiser to remain in the background. When the New Jersey Republicans offered him the state party chairmanship, Nucky replied, "Let someone else have the throne. I'll take a seat at a ringside table."[43]

Although Nucky Johnson kept a low profile politically, he was personally anything but a shrinking violet. Six months after the death of his wife in 1912 (when Nucky was only thirty), he "threw the first of his infamous "annual parties," distinguished by an astonishing intermingling of high society, politicians, underworld racketeers, and several dozen Broadway "cuties" Nucky hired through a chorus girl agency in New York. The parties were usually staged at the Ritz-Carlton, taking over a couple of floors, with a dozen bottles of champagne and cracked ice in the bathtubs of every bathroom."[44]

It was Prohibition, however, that transformed Nucky Johnson from the corrupt local boss of a sea-side resort into a major underworld power. As early as 1922, Atlantic City had become a center of bootlegging. Nucky's unrivalled grip on Atlantic City meant that the rum-runners' speedboats could land their merchandise on the Atlantic City beach with little fear of arrest or harassment. His control of the New Jersey Republican Party meant that he could also ensure that goods landing on the beach could make their way safely to the Pennsylvania border at Camden or the New York border at Newark.

For all this, Nucky charged a ten percent tariff on the imported alcohol. It was enough to make him almost unbelievably rich, and to finance ever more extravagant wing dings at the Ritz Carlton, night-clubbing sprees, a collection of limousines including a powder-blue Pierce-Arrow and Manhattan apartments for his favorite cuties.

Bootleggers too were happy with Nucky's "fair shake," for it allowed them to conduct business in a safe and predictable way. They competed for Nucky's favor, which allowed Nucky to choose the gangs he wished to do business with. He picked the biggest and the best, from the Purple Gang and the Capone Outfit in the Midwest to the major Jewish and Italian bootleggers on the East Coast. In the northern part of New Jersey, Nucky's friends included Longie Zwillman, who had extended his own bootlegging empire from Newark to include Fort Lee and parts of western Long Island. It also included Waxey Gordon, who had extended his operations south to the Philadelphia area, which he shared with Nig Rosen and Boo Boo Hoff. It included King Solomon of Boston, who ran bootlegging in southern New England. Together with bootleggers operating in the New York area—Owney Madden, Charlie Luciano, Frank Costello and Bill Dwyer—these men formed a loose consortium of smugglers and suppliers along the northern half of the East Coast.

Masseria and Maranzano were not invited to Atlantic City in 1929. Luciano, Costello, Adonis and even Schultz, all major figures in the distribution and retailing of alcohol in New York, attended the conference, while Masseria and Maranzano, whose involvement was limited to alky-cooking in the Italian tenements, did not. Alky-cooking interests had not been invited.

The contrast is revealing. When Luciano, Costello, and Adonis joined the Masseria regime in 1927, they joined as leading figures in a segment of the bootlegging industry from which Masseria and Maranzano were largely excluded—the whiskey business. Masseria and Maranzano each longed for a piece of that business, the richest prize of all. But when Joe the Boss told Luciano and Adonis that "now you have a chance to be my friend or the both of you are dead men," Luciano had responded that he could have a piece of everything, but "not one fucking drop of whiskey." If Joe the Boss became somewhat agitated at Charlie's spirited reply, it is no doubt because Scotch whiskey was what he really had his eye on all along. But if Joe then relented, giving his Sicilian *paisan* an unwelcome bear hug, it may have been because Joe realized that declaring war on Luciano, Costello, and Adonis would drive them and their whiskey business straight into Maranzano's embrace. That was the last thing he wanted. Far better to have Luciano and his friends as allies; even if he was not getting Charlie's whiskey business, he was at least getting a line to Charlie's whiskey-smuggling allies—non-Sicilians like Costello and Adonis as well as Jews like Lansky, Siegel, and Zwillman. In the event of war, these were the right allies to have. For his part, and regardless of whatever the exact nature of the relationship between Lucaino and Masseria before 1927 may have been, Luciano understood that, as much as he hated the "greedy old dons," he would need to ally with one of them if he wanted to stay alive. Yet he and all his friends also realized that, as Meyer had put it so perspicaciously several years earlier, once either one of the old dons got hold of his whiskey business, "the fat old son-of-a-bitch will have us knocked off." Luciano and his friends had to keep the whiskey business out of their hands. When Joe the Boss then broke his handshake with Luciano, Charlie thus knew what the gesture meant and what he had to do.

The meeting was a genuine business convention; Nucky Johnson presented fur stoles to the wives and girl friends of the conference guests. When the conventioneers arrived, they found that their host, Nucky, had booked suites for all of them in the Breakers Hotel using a set of invented WASP-sounding names, as the hotel had a policy of admitting only white Protestants. At first, everything went according to plan. But then a cigar-chopping Al Capone, clad in a purple jacket and white pants and surrounded by a small army of thugs, tramped into the Breakers' lobby. It was too much. The Chicago contingent was promptly barred from the place. Nucky Johnson quickly tried to find alternative accommodations for the Capone Outfit in the somewhat less WASPy President Hotel. But Capone was having none of it. When Capone spotted Johnson with his trademark red carnation, he stormed up to him. According to Luciano,

> Nucky and Al had it out right there in the open. Johnson was about a foot taller then Capone and both of them had voices like foghorns. I think you could have heard them in Philadelphia, and there wasn't a decent word passed between them. Johnson had a rep for four letter words that wasn't even invented and Capone is screamin' at me that I made bad arrangements. So Nucky picks up Al under one arm and throws him into his car and yells out, "All you fuckers follow me."

The motorcade wound up at the Ritz, behind which loomed Johnson's own mansion. Capone, still enraged, stormed into the lobby and started ripping pictures off the wall and throwing them at Johnson. "So everybody got over bein' mad and concentrated on keepin' Al quiet. That's the way our convention started."[45]

Al soon got over his pique, for the local papers later photographed Nucky Johnson and Al Capone nonchalantly strolling down Atlantic City's famed Boardwalk—another pair of celebrities enjoying the sea breezes.[46]

Nucky Johnson and many of the others present wanted to talk about the future of the bootlegging industry. Al Smith had run against Prohibition in the 1928 presidential election. Though he had lost to Herbert Hoover, many still foresaw that the end of Prohibition was only a matter of time. It was the Italians, particularly Torrio and Costello, who led the meeting off on another direction. Torrio had recently returned from Europe and had been given an earful by his New York friends about recent events in Chicago. Torrio was upset; this was no way to run a business. Concern changed to horror when the St. Valentine's Day Massacre was splashed, in screaming headlines, across the nation's newspapers. Capone's recklessness was making trouble for everyone.

The bootlegging consortium, called the Group of Seven asked Torrio to open one of the meetings. Torrio told the convened gangsters that they needed to organize themselves, recognize each other's rights and interests, respect each other's territories and work together to prevent outsiders from muscling in. After this short speech, he turned the meeting over to Costello.

The Atlantic City conference was Frank Costello's coming out party. As Torrio's spokesman and chief of staff, he naturally assumed control of the meetings, showing a style that would later earn him the nickname of Prime Minister of the Underworld. The next day it was Costello who the reporters featured as that out-of-town celebrity promenading on the boardwalk in the company of Nucky Johnson.

Costello said bluntly that he wanted to stop the sort of stuff that was happening in Chicago. As long as they stuck to bootlegging and gambling, ordinary people were on their side and they could make a pile.

"But if you make the people afraid of you, then they're going to turn the other way and start yelling at the government to clean us out. That means the Internal Revenue boys, the FBI, the narcos, and every DA in the country. It ain't worth it."

With this introduction, Costello began to outline his proposal:

From now on nobody gets killed without a commission's saying so. Johnny and I have a little piece of paper we want to show you. We want to have a national commission with every family represented, twenty-four by our count. No boss will be attacked unless the commission says he has to go. And no button-man gets hit without a hearing from his own boss.

The old way—killing a guy who bugs you, or who's in your way—is no good any longer. If we run our thing like a business, we'll get respect and all the dough in the world. If we keep the fireworks going, we'll be out of business in a year.

At this point, according to some accounts, Capone stood up and expressed his agreement. Costello then sat down, turning again to Torrio. Johnny Torrio slowly rose to his feet and looked down the table at Capone. He bore the sorrowful look of a doctor about to give his patient some bad news; "You're going to jail, Al," he said softly.

"To what?" said Capone, still smiling.

"To jail," Torrio replied, "We have to smooth things out right now. You go back to Chicago after the Valentine Day shoot-out, and the O'Banion boys will be at war—and the heat will grow higher and higher. We think you need a vacation, Al."

Capone stared at Torrio. "Tell me when I'm supposed to laugh," he said.

"This ain't a joke, Al," interjected Costello. "We got too much invested in you to ruin the gravy train. Make it easy on yourself. Think of a way. But we need you off at 'college' till things cool off."

Capone stormed out of the conference. He went back to his hotel, where he sat alone in his room to cool off and think. Up to then, the convention had gone well for him. He had met Moses Annenberg, circulation manager for the Hearst newspapers, while strolling on the Boardwalk. Capone and Annenberg soon cooked up a scheme for a national wire service for horse racing. The wire service would be centered in Chicago and managed by one of Costello's assistants, Frank Ericson.

Capone also remembered a detective on the Philadelphia police force, a James "Shooey" Malone. The two of them had gotten friendly on the Hialeah race track the year before. Capone called Philadelphia and talked to Malone. After the final day of the conference, Capone and his bodyguard, Frank Rio, drove to Philadelphia. The two went to see a movie at a theatre on Market Street. When they came out two hours later, Malone and another detective, John Creedon, were there waiting for him;

> "You're Al Capone, aren't you?" said Malone, acting out his part in the charade.

> "My name's Al Brown," Capone replied. "Call me Capone if you want. Who are you?"

> The two detectives flashed their badges.

> "Oh, bulls eh? All right. Then here's my gun."

Capone handed over his .38. By doing so he established that he was carrying a concealed weapon. He prodded Rio, who handed over his gun as well. Malone and Creedon took them down to the station and booked them on a concealed-weapons charge.

Later that evening, Capone was questioned by Philadelphia's director of public safety, Lemuel B. Schofield. Capone seemed relaxed and, as was often the case during these years, in an expansive and philosophical mood. It was the last thing that Schofield expected. "I had a most interesting conversation with Capone on the rackets in the United States," he later told the press. "He was in a reminiscent mood and seemed to be at the point where he was anxious to be at peace, not only with gangsters, but with the law. In a quiet, gentlemanly manner, he told me that he was on an errand of peace when Detectives Creedon and Malone grabbed him."

Part of Capone's relaxed mood stemmed from a belief that he was facing no more than three months. Yet the next morning, Judge John E. Walsh of the criminal division of the municipal court gave Capone and Rio the maximum—one year in prison. Still, it was hardly hard time. The warden gave him a cell to himself and allowed him to furnish it in any way he pleased. For his work assignment, Capone drew the prison library. He spent his year pleasantly enough, reading books and newspapers, chatting with the reporters who kept flocking to interview him, and growing pudgy on the stodgy prison diet and his lack of exercise. In this way, Capone sat out the climax of the war.

Chapter Ten
The Underworld at War: Part 4—The Endgame

The End of Joe the Boss

In Luciano's account, the final meeting with Maranzano took place in early 1931 at the Bronx Zoo. Luciano brought Tommy Lucchese and Joey Adonis along with him. He also brought Benny Siegel so that Maranzano couldn't pull the "exclusive Sicilian" routine on him. It was late afternoon, and the meeting was set in front of the lion's cage. Luciano, who always dreaded dealing with Maranzano, had worked himself up into a state of adolescent resentment. "I hope you appreciate that the lion is supposed to be the king of animals," he grandly announced to Maranzano.

The remark was designed as some sort of put-down, but Maranzano just burst out laughing. He walked over and put his arm around Luciano's shoulder. This made Charlie furious. "Maranzano," he said, pulling himself away, "there's been something I've been waiting to tell you a long time. My father's the only one who calls me *bambino*."

It was a somewhat irrelevant observation. Maranzano had yet to open his mouth. But Charlie was simmering. Maranzano looked hurt, then said softly that he didn't understand; what had he done to make Charlie resent him so? But Luciano cut him short again; "Let's stop the horseshit and get down to business. If we work everything out, then we'll be friends. That's it."

Maranzano quickly agreed to Luciano's terms; he would not interfere with Luciano's business, nor with that of Costello, Adonis, Lansky, and Siegel. Luciano and his friends would enjoy complete autonomy within the Maranzano regime. He once again, expressed his regret. He was saddened that Charlie felt so provoked.

"Never mind," Charlie told him curtly. "I'm ready to forget it. Look ahead."

But as Charlie turned to go, Maranzano couldn't resist stretching out his hands and placing them on his shoulder. "Whether you like it or not," he intoned, "Salvatore Lucania, you are my *bambino*."

To an outside observer witnessing the scene taking place in the gathering dusk in front of the lion cage of the Bronx Zoo, it might seemed that a Catholic priest was engaged in admonishing one of his more unruly young parishioners. It made Charlie sick with fury.[1]

On the morning of April 15, 1931, Luciano visited Masseria at his headquarters on lower Second Avenue. Having just bumped off several Maranzano soldiers, Joe the Boss was in an ebullient mood. "old Joe was beaming and laughing like he could taste Maranzano's blood out of a gold cup." Luciano had told him that he had worked out plans for a new series of hits, and when he described them to him, Masseria leaped out of his big leather chair, "and he starts to dance in the middle of the office. The only time I ever saw anything like it was in the newsreels during the war when they showed Hitler doing a dance like that when he beat France. It reminded me of Masseria—two fruitcakes in search of a brain."

Charlie suggested that they drive down to Coney Island and have lunch at the Nuova Villa Tammaro. It was a mob favorite, and the owner, Gerardo Scarpato, was a friend of theirs. Go ahead and enjoy yourself, Charlie told Joe when the got there. Order up a feast. This is a victory celebration. He wanted to make sure that Joe was still stuffing himself after all the other patrons had gone.

By about 3:30, the restaurant had emptied out, and the waiters were going home. Joe was just finishing up his cream pastries and drinking his espresso, when Charlie suggested a card game to help him relax and digest the heavy meal. Okay, Joe agreed, but he reminded Charlie that they had to get back to the office to work out the details of the plans. Charlie nodded then went off to get a deck from Scarpato. Soon Joe was so engrossed in his hand that he failed to notice that the doors of the black limousine outside—the black limousine that had tailed them from Manhattan—were opening.

Charlie noticed it though. He quickly excused himself, saying that he had to go to the bathroom. Joe the Boss poured himself another glass of wine and sat sipping it, alone now in Scarpato's cavernous dining room when the limousine's passengers, Vito Genovese, Joey Adonis, Albert Anastasia and Bugsy Siegel, marched in through the front door. They pulled out their revolvers and fired twenty shots. Masseria took six of them squarely in the midsection, collapsing face down on Scarpato's white tablecloth as his blood gushed over his shoes and onto the floor. The papers later said that he was holding the ace of diamonds in his hand.

As soon as his friends had departed, Charlie sauntered out of the men's room and over to the phone. He phoned the police, reported the murder and waited for them to arrive. Did he see what had happened, the police wanted to know. No, Charlie replied. Did he have any idea who the shooters were? No, and Charlie couldn't think of anyone who might want to harm his old pal Joe. The police were a little suspicious. How come he hadn't noticed anything? How was it that he had spent three hours with the victim, but then, at the fatal moment, been away? "I was in the can taking a leak," he replied. "I always take a long leak."

This, at least, is the canonical version; the one that Luciano insisted was in all the papers the next day. In his biography of Meyer Lansky, however, Robert Lacey points out that, "there is no mention in the police record, nor in contemporary newspaper reports, of Luciano, or of any other material witness being found at the scene of the crime." Luciano, Lacey continues, was a well-known gangster by 1931. It's hard to imagine him doing something as dumb as standing beside Masseria's body waiting for the police to show up. Even if they couldn't make him for the murder itself, the police would have held him as a material witness. It's impossible to believe that, after excusing himself from the table, Luciano did anything but open the back door and keep on walking.[2]

Even the detail of the ace of diamonds clutched in Masseria's dead hand turns out to be bogus. It was placed there later by a news photographer who thought it made the scene look more dramatic. The detail lives on in underworld lore, however, where the ace of diamonds is still considered an unlucky card.

The driver of the limousine was Ciro Terranova, who probably thought that killing Tom Reina was a lousy way for the Lower East Side to show its respect for the Bronx. Luciano and Joe Valachi both place Terranova at the wheel of the black limousine, but Valachi gives a somewhat different line-up. He drops Siegel and includes Joe Stretch and someone called "Cheech" in the murder party. He also has both Luciano and Ciro Terranova shooting Masseria. According to both Luciano and Valachi, Terranova was so rattled after the murder that he couldn't start the car.

THE CASTELLAMMARESE VERSION

Joe Bonanno gives us the same events from the Castellammaresi perspective. According to this account, Frankie Yale was "a group leader in Masseria's Family," who wished to send one of his soldiers, Al Capone, to help Torrio in Chicago. Before doing so, however, he naturally sought to clear it with his leader, Masseria. Joe the Boss proved willing, and indeed gave his "blessings" to Yale's project. And so Capone was duly sent to Chicago. Once he arrived, however, he immediately began to misbehave, encroaching on the territory of the city's leading Family, the Aiellos of Castellammare.

There are a number of oddities here. Capone had never been a soldier in Masseria's Family. He was a Neapolitan from Brooklyn who, on the strength of Torrio's recommendation, had worked in Yale's Harvard Inn. Nor were the Aiellos the leaders of the Chicago underworld; they were not even the leaders of the Chicago *Unione*. Besides, it was the Aiellos, not Capone, who initiated the War of Sicilian Succession.

Bonanno's account continues that the Aiellos put up with the incursions of the impudent young Neapolitan thug as long as they could. Eventually, however, they complained to Masseria, inviting him to come to Chicago and reprimand his trouble-making lieutenant, Capone.

> In 1929, Joe Masseria went to Chicago at [Joe] Aiello's invitation to hold a clarification parlay. Also in attendance was Gaspar Milazzo, the Castellammarese stalwart from Detroit. . . . Aiello told Masseria that he considered Capone an intruder in his city. Masseria offered a typically stupid response. He offered to check the ambitious Capone in return for the rights to the east side of Chicago. Aiello would retain his sphere of influence over the west side of Chicago and everything west of the city.[3]

Bonanno calls Masseria's offer "ludicrous". What, he asks rhetorically, would Aiello "want with Dubuque, or Sioux Fall?" Joe Aiello thus sent Masseria packing, all the way back to Lower Manhattan. Once he got there, smarting from the insult, Joe the Boss contacted Capone and ordered him to make war against the Aiellos. Masseria even promised to recognize Capone as father of his own family if he won.

The account seems back to front. Capone and Torrio stood for the underworld establishment in Chicago. It was the Aiellos and the Castellammaresi— Stefano Magaddino, Gaspar Milazzo, and Salvatore Maranzano—who were the intruders. Capone and Masseria were, at best, bootlegging connections. By the late 1920s, both were suffering from the problems in their respective Sicilian underworlds, the Aiellos in the Midwest, Castellammarese clans on the East Coast.

Bonanno resumes his account: Not only did Masseria order Capone to make war on the Aiellos, he approached Gaspar Milazzo in Detroit, offering to divide the entire country with him, if he would just betray the Aiellos. Milazzo, writes Bonanno, was "deeply shocked" by the suggestion. Milazzo had stood at the baptismal font as godfather to Aiello's youngest son. This is a significant detail. If, as Bonanno tells us, Joe Aiello and Gaspar Milazzo had become *compari* to each other, the inference is inescapable that the Aiellos and the Castellammaresi had formed a united front. Nor was the common front limited to Detroit. Offended at Masseria's dishonorable suggestion, Milazzo sent Masseria a disdainful reply. Then he traveled to Buffalo to seek the advice of Stefano Magaddino.

When Joe the Boss learned that Milazzo and Magaddino were conferring, his rage knew no bounds. "So the Castellammaresi are conspiring against me now!" he thought. Arrogantly, Masseria demanded that both Gaspar Milazzo of Detroit and Stefano Magaddino of Buffalo come to see him in New York. But:

> Gaspar and Stefano refused to kowtow to him, and this infuriated Masseria all the more. He vituperated against all the Castellammaresi calling us un-

ruly and thick-skulled.

Up to now, Masseria had been keeping his insults on the personal level. Now he was disparaging the honor of Castellammare itself.

Who did this fat man think he was?[4]

Bonanno's story that Masseria tried to broker a peace between Capone and the Aiellos, and that, later, that he approached Gaspar Milazzo in Detroit is not accepted by most writers. The story does not appear, for example, in any of the biographies of Capone nor in either Kurt Johnson's or Virgil Peterson's accounts of organized crime in Chicago. Nevertheless, as Bonanno was an actual participant in the war, his account cannot be dismissed out of hand. If Masseria did indeed visit Chicago, it may have been because he was troubled by the Yale murder—troubled less by the elimination of Yale than by the fact that Chicago-style killings were spilling over into New York. The claim that Masseria next approached Gaspar Milazzo in Detroit is likewise unsupported by sources other than Bonanno. Nevertheless, Bonanno does give an interesting perspective on the events that were about to take place in Detroit.

In 1930, Bonanno continues, Masseria decided to launch a pre-emptive strike against the Castellammaresi in Detroit:

Early in 1930, Gaspar Milazzo was assassinated in a Detroit fish market. The bereaved followers of Gaspar cried out for revenge. . . . In New York City, the biggest tinderbox of all, the air crackled with static electricity. A sense of foreboding gripped the Castellammaresi in the city. We had no doubt that Masseria was responsible for Milazzo's slaying. But what could we do about it? Masseria was a formidable enemy. In terms of resources, manpower and allies, Masseria had a huge advantage over the scattered Castellammarese clans. He was Goliath and we were David.

In Brooklyn, the Castellammaresi held a Family meeting. The head of our Family was Cola Schiro, a compliant fellow with little backbone. Stefano Magaddino had used Schiro as a sort of puppet ruler in Brooklyn. . . .

[The prospect of] War frightened Cola Schiro. At our Family meeting, Schiro therefore spoke in favor of neutrality. . . .

Maranzano, with whom I attended the meeting, winced at Schiro's attitude. He had already told me he considered Milazzo's slaying as being tantamount to a declaration of war against all Castellammaresi.[5]

A Castellammarese from Brooklyn, Sasa Parrino, had been with Milazzo in the fish market when the murderers had burst in. He was killed in the gunfire. Many, however, thought that Sasa Parrino's death was just bad luck: "What am I to think," Sasa's brother Joe asked during the meeting. "My brother's death was an accident. Sasa happened to be with Gaspar in the fish store and they both got shot."

At this, Maranzano, who had remained broodingly silent up until now, rose to his feet. A hush fell upon the room:

"I want to point out that according to my information Gaspar's body had five bullets in it."

(Pause.)

"But Sasa's body," Maranzano continued, leaning forward now, his eyes fixed on Joe Parrino, "had six bullets in it."

(Another pause.)

"It was no accident!"

(gasps, coughing, oaths, mutters)

Slowly, Maranzano straightened his body, then, looking upwards, his eyes half-closed, threw his chest forward, inhaled deeply and cried out: "É una sporca macchia sull'onore di Castellammare" ("It's a black mark on the honor of Castellammare.")

It was as if he were sounding our battle cry.

"What shall we do now, don Turiddu?" peeped the voice of Cola Schiro cringing in a corner.

"Why ask me?" Maranzano replied. "I'm just a soldier."[6]

It is a magnificent scene. Maranzano's modest reply, `Why ask me? I'm just a soldier,' seems straight from the pages of Plutarch.

Prohibition, which became state law in Michigan in 1918, had sparked a violent war among the Black Hand bands in Detroit. The Adamo, Vitale, and Giannola gangs fought themselves to near extinction between 1918 and 1921. Exhausted by the three-year war, the surviving Italian gangs could do little to stop the Purple Gang from seizing control of all of Detroit's more lucrative rackets during the 1920s. With most of the older Black Hand gang leaders already dead by late 1920, leadership of the Sicilian underworld passed to the grocer and influential elder statesman, Sam Catalonotte, who managed to preserve Italian underworld peace in Detroit until his death in 1930. Many of the younger Italian gangsters either ended up working for the Purples and other gangs in the Cleveland-Toledo region or working for the allied River Gang, operated by the Licavoli brothers of St. Louis.

At the time of Sam Catalonotte's death in 1930, the remaining Sicilian gangs in the Detroit area were the Eastside gangs of Angelo Meli, "Black" Leo Cellura, William "Black Bill" Tocco and Joseph Zerilli, and the Westside Mob made up of Sam Catalonotte's surviving brothers, Joseph Tocco (brothers of Black Bill) and, most important, Chester W. "Ches" LaMare.

Born in Chicago in 1884, Ches LaMare had worked closely with Tony Lombardo in Chicago in the years immediately before Prohibition. He had arrived in Detroit in 1915 and had worked his way up the ranks of the Giannola gang as a gunman. In 1921, LaMare opened the Venice Café in Hamtramck, an industrial town within the Detroit city limits. Hamtramck had become Detroit's version of Chicago's Cicero, a new honky-tonk district in the industrial suburbs. Hamtramck had four hundred "soft-drink" licensees (whose drinks were anything but soft), one hundred fifty around-the-clock brothels, breweries, stills, and numerous pool rooms and gambling houses. In 1923, following the irate demands of concerned Michigan citizens, the Michigan State Troopers simply suspended the Hamtramck city council, taking on municipal duties themselves. The crackdown lasted from 1923 to 1927.

As Hamtramck's leading gangster, LaMare's various interests suffered greatly during the mid-1920s police crackdown. Ches's own rap sheet showed eighteen arrests on such counts as extortion, armed robbery, Prohibition law violations, carrying concealed weapons, and white slavery. Nevertheless, in 1927, after promising Federal Judge Charles E. Simmons that he would go straight, Ches was let off with a $1,500 fine and released on probation. Judge Simmons' leniency was undoubtedly influenced by the fact that LaMare was now working for the Ford Motor Company as a consultant on labor problems.

Confidant that his connection to Ford would now protect him from further troubles from the law, LaMare began to muscle in on the Detroit rackets of Meli, Cellura, and Black Bill Tocco. When the Eastsiders responded by threatening war, LaMare suggested a peace conference. The conference was to be held at the grocery and fish market of Philip Guasetello on 2739 Vernor Highway in Detroit. Guastello, however, was a LaMare ally, and his fish market was in LaMare territory. Fearing an ambush, the Eastside Mob sent Gaspar Milazzo (better known in Detroit as Gaspar Scibilia or Sciblia) and his assistant Sasa Parrino.

Milazzo and Parrino had reputations as underworld peacemakers, and Meli hoped that this would be enough to ensure their safety. On May 31, 1930, Milazzo and Parrino drove to the Vernor Highway fish market in Milazzo's expensive new car. They were ushered into the living quarters behind the market, seated and served lunch. Shortly after noon, however, two gunmen burst in and began firing. Milazzo was killed instantly, but Parrino survived long enough to be taken to the hospital and questioned in Italian by a Detroit policeman.

Although the police learned nothing from the dying Parrino, they already knew of the feud between the Meli and Lamare factions. The war ended in February 1931 when Angelo Meli persuaded three of Ches Lamare's bodyguards to kill their boss. The Detroit police heard from their informants that one of the two killers was Ches Lamare's bodyguard, Joe Amico. After Lamare's murder, Meli was finally able to consolidate his position, allying himself with the Tocco and Zerilli families as well as with the Partinico faction, a group of Detroit families from Partinico in Palermo Province. This, in brief, is the origin of the Detroit Family.

Municipal police forces interpreted crimes in the context of their municipalities. The Chicago police understood little of Aiello's plotting in Detroit and Cleveland, nor could the police in Brooklyn imagine why a party of killers had arrived all the way from Chicago to murder Frankie Yale. So it is possible that the Detroit police missed some of the larger implications in the murders of Milazzo and Parrino. Nevertheless, in 1930 the Detroit underworld was dominated by the Purple Gang, not the mafia. Milazzo was not even a major figure in the Detroit Italian underworld. The police attributed his and Parrino's murders to Ches LaMare's gang. The explanation seemed sufficient.[7]

Joe Aiello spent some of his time in hiding under the protection of Gaspar Milazzo in Detroit. In late 1929, however, he sought refuge in Buffalo, where he lived, as the Castellammarese pretender to the Chicago throne, under the protection of Stefano Magaddino.

Like Milazzo, Aiello were murdered in 1930. With Capone in jail, he had returned to Chicago where he was murdered by a party of gunmen staked out in an apartment in front of Aiello's hiding place. Virtually all authors assume that the murderers were Outfit members. According to Luciano, however, Aiello was machine-gunned down by the Brooklyn gang leader Al Mineo. The hit, Charlie said, had been ordered by Joe the Boss as a favor to Capone.[8] It seems unlikely. The Chicago Outfit was the most efficient killing machine in the American underworld. If the Outfit had needed extra guns or unknown faces, they would probably have turned to their friends in Detroit or St. Louis rather than Brooklyn.

It is difficult to know what was really at the back of Maranzano's mind. Did he actually believe that Masseria was sending his gunmen to the Midwest to pick off Castellammare leaders, and that this had left a "black mark on the honor of Castellammare"? Or was the "question of honor" merely a ruse, an excuse to launch the war that he had been planning for years? Maranzano was undoubtedly looking for a *causus belli*, a plausible justification for a war against Masseria. Raising the murder of Milazzo to a question of honor allowed Maranzano to shame the Brooklyn Castellammaresi into backing him in his war against Masseria.

According to a tradition that re-surfaces in organized crime Websites, Salvatore Maranzano had come to the U.S. as the emissary of the Sicilian mafia's *capo di tutti i capi*, Vito Cascio Ferro. Don Vito's scheme was that Maranzano would unify and organize the disparate parts of the Italian underworld in America, placing it under his personal command.[9] The enigmatic and mysterious Cascio Ferro plays the role of the *Gran Vecchio* in any number of mafia legends, and few scholars have taken the story seriously. How could Cascio Ferro have imagined, they wonder, that he might manage the entire Italo-American underworld from New York to Chicago while he was sitting somewhere in Sicily? Nor is this the only objection. Despite the fact that, lying on Sicily's northern coast, Castellammare del Golfo is in easy reach of

Palermo, the town is still in Trapani province. Vito Cascio Ferro, however, hailed from Bisaquino, near Coreleone, in the interior of Palermo province. In terms of the classic Sicilian mafia, the mafia as it existed before the 1960s, Maranzano and Cascio Ferro came from two different countries—Trapani and Palermo—with separate mafia hierarchies. Even granting that Cascio Ferro was the top boss of the Palermo mafia and had concocted some scheme for seizing control of the American underworld, he would have sent as his emissary someone from Palermo, someone he knew and trusted like Joe Morello from Corleone. He would no more have sent an emissary from Castellammare than from Timbuktu.

Yet even if, for practical reasons, the Cascio Ferro story seems improbable, there is no reason to doubt that when Maranzano stepped off the boat to America, his mind was filled with grand ideas. Unifying the American underworld into a single instrument under his control may have been an impossible dream, but who is to say that Maranzano did not dream it? Salvatore Maranzano may have been a criminal; but he was a criminal with a grandiose vision of the future. It is this that is so striking about the first generation of mafia bosses in America—the mustache Petes. They had a sense of history. Like their predecessors, the sectarian revolutionaries of the early nineteenth century, and, even more, like their true prototypes, the great barons of Sicily from the Middle Ages to the sixteenth century, they thought in terms of dominance.

The first generation of mafia leaders were more warring barons than criminal entrepreneurs. They were men of honor who thought in terms of territory, personal control, and dynastic alliances. And since honor could be won by struggle, they naturally thought in terms of war as well. "In my world," Bonanno tells us, "according to the old Tradition, a man fights for personal honor and he feels patriotism for his family. Our fighting is personal, direct, man-to-man." He adds a little ruefully, "You call this a feudal notion."[10]

It certainly seemed a feudal notion to Luciano, Costello, and Capone. Through their insane quest for absolute underworld dominance at whatever cost, Masseria, Maranzano, and Joe Aiello were making it hard for criminal entrepreneurs to earn a dishonest buck. There's plenty for everybody, Capone repeated throughout the Chicago Beer War, why can't we all work peaceably together? This had been Johnny Torrio's philosophy, and it would eventually become dominant in the American underworld. It was a new, and specifically American, philosophy, but one that Bonanno despised. "When the old-style Sicilians talked of honor and respect, it was all so much cant and blather" to Luciano. "Without a tradition to guide him, Charlie Lucky fell back for his system of values on the most primitive consideration: making money. His conversation was not laced with idealistic words such as 'honor' and 'trust' but with mundane ones such as 'outfit' and 'syndicate.'"[11]

War would only cease, Maranzano had explained to Luciano in 1923, when one man rises victorious from the heap and finds himself acknowledged as leader by all other men of honor. Unfettered and unconstrained, the new leader would initiate an epoch of wise and just rule, eliminating strife and competition and ensuring peace for all. It was a role for which destiny had marked him. Charlie and his friends were inclined to be skeptical. Masseria and Maranzano seemed two warmongers; if today they were at war with each other, tomorrow they would be at war with someone else. Charlie did not believe in Maranzano's bright vision of a harmonious underworld under the benign dictatorship of Salvatore Maranzano. Masseria and Maranzano looked like pint-sized versions of Mussolini and Hitler, and Luciano did not believe in thousand-year Reichs. When he later saw the photo of Hitler dancing his jig at the defeat of France, he was perspicacious enough to recognize the analogy. The only way that war could be ended, Charlie decided, was by eliminating the warmongers.

LIFE IN THE GREAT MARANZANO FAMILY

They were so honorable that no one in the mafia ever trusted anyone else.

—Meyer Lansky

Tom Reina's killing at the end of February 1930, and Masseria's ham-handed attempt to take over his Family afterwards, had brought Gaetano "Tom" Gagliano and most of the younger Reina soldiers over into Maranzano's camp. Gagliano contributed $140,000 to purchase cars and machine-guns and to rent apartments.

Before attacking Masseria, however, Maranzano needed the approval of the supreme leader of the Castellammarese alliance, Stefano Magaddino. After the Brooklyn meeting, Maranzano took Bonanno to Buffalo. Bonanno's cousin, Don Stefano, was hesitant, less daunted perhaps at the thought of a Castellammarese defeat than that of a Maranzano victory. If Maranzano did succeed in eliminating Joe the Boss, Brooklyn would become an independent bastion of power. Maranzano would then become a rival rather than an ally. Still, eliminating Joe the Boss seemed the first priority. Thus Magaddino agreed that Maranzano would be "supreme commander in the New York theatre of war." Furthermore, the Castellammarese strongholds of Detroit and Buffalo "would supply Maranzano with money, arms, ammunition, and manpower." Magaddino and Aiello each agreed to contribute $5,000 a week throughout the course of the war, though Chicago's contributions ceased with Aiello's death in October 1930. Maranzano also received the support of Joe Zerilli, the new Castellammarese leader in Detroit.[12]

Pietro Morello, "Don Petru," was Masseria's bodyguard and constant shadow. Nicknamed "the Clutching Hand," Morello was a dour old Corleonese, tough as old leather and able, in the words of Albert Anastasia, to "smell a bullet before it leaves the gun." Maranzano regarded Morello as Masseria's chief-of-staff, a man who could stay on the mattresses for years, subsisting on onions, bread, and hard cheese, and still come out as tough and mean as ever. Maranzano regarded the elimination of Morello as a top priority. But before he even got a chance, Morello was murdered, either by two of Charlie Luciano's friends, Albert Anastasia and Frank Scalise, or by someone in the Maranzano group. They had followed him to his office in East Harlem where Morello and a Masseria collector were counting up the proceeds from Morello's loansharking operations. Anastasia and Scalise shot down the pair of them and then swept up the money from the table. It came to over $30,000.[13]

Seeking reinforcements, Maranzano "opened the books," taking new recruits into the mafia. Among these new recruits were Joe Valachi, his friends Salvatore "Sallie Shields" Shillitani and Nicky Padovano.

Valachi later described his initiation. It had taken place in Maranzano's farm at Wappinger Falls in upstate New York in November 1930. Joe, Sally, and Nicky had arrived and had been left in the anteroom for several minutes; "After a time, a guy, I forget who, comes to the door. He waves at me and says, 'Joe, let's go.'":

> I'd say there were about forty guys sitting around the table, and everybody gets up when I come in. The Catellammarese and those with Tommy Gagliano are all mixed up, so they are one. I don't remember everybody. There was Tommy Brown—you know, Tommy Lucchese. . . .

> I was led to the other end of the table past them, and the other guy with me said, "Joe, meet Don Salvatore Maranzano. He is going to be boss of all of us throughout the whole trouble we are having." This was the first time I ever saw him. Gee, he looked just like a banker. You'd never guess in a million years that he was a racketeer.

> Now Mr. Maranzano said to everybody around the table, "This is Joe Cago," which I must explain is what most of the guys know me by. Then he tells me to sit down in an empty chair on his right. When I sit down so does the whole table. Someone put a gun and knife on the table in front of me. I remember that the gun was a .38 and the knife was what you would call a dagger. After than, Maranzano motions us up again, and we all hold hands and he says some words in Italian. Then we sit down and he turns to me, still in Italian, and talks about the gun and the knife. "This represents that you live by the gun and the knife." Next he asked me, "Which finger do you shoot with?"

I said, "This one," and I hold up my right forefinger.

> I was still wondering what he meant by this when he told me to make a cup of my hands. Then he put a piece of paper and lit it with a match and told me to say after him, as I was moving the paper back and forth, "This is the way I will burn if I betray the secret of this Cosa Nostra," All of this was in Italian.

Next, Maranzano explained the significance of the oath to Valachi and told him the Cosa Nostra's rules. Then he told everyone to rise again:

> "Throw a finger from zero to five." So all the guys around the table threw out their right hand at the same time. Some of them had no fingers out; some had

two or three, the limit, naturally, being five. When all the fingers are out, he starts adding them up. I forget what it was. Let's say it came to forty-eight. So Mr. Maranzano starts with the first man on his left and keeps counting around the table, and when he got to forty-eight, it fell on Joe Boanno, also known as Joe Bananas. When Mr. Marazano saw where the number fell, he started to laught and said to me, "Well, Joe, that's your *'gombah'*" — meaning he was kind of me godfather and was responsible for me.

So Joe Bananas laughs too, and comes to me and says, "Give me that finger that you shoot with." I and him the finger, and he pricks it with a pin and squeezes until the blood comes out.

When this happens, Mr. Maranzano says, "This blood means that we are now one Family."

After the initiation ceremony, Maranzano treated his new members to a banquet. At the end, after the coffee, Maranzano stood up and made a short speech:

"We're here together because Joe Masseria has sentenced all the Castellammaresi to death. At the same time you other guys started at your end because he had Tommy Reina killed without justice. So now we are all one. We're only a few here, but in a month we'll be four or five hundred. We have to work hard. The odds are against us. The other side has a lot of money, but while they're enjoying themselves, we'll eat bread and onions."[14]

"'We few, we happy few, we band of brothers,' Sally, Nick and me," Valachi recalled, "being the new members, talked among ourselves — mostly about how great it was to be in the mob and how we were going to put all our hearts into the 'trouble.'"

Maranzano gave each of them photos of Masseria and posted them as look-outs in flats rented near the places where Masseria and his heavies had their homes and businesses. Valachi was sent to Pelham Parkway in the Bronx to stake out the home of Steve Ferrigno, a ranking officer in the Family of Al Mineo. In the beginning of November 1930, after over a month's fruitless waiting, Valachi was about to enter his apartment when he saw a car pulling up in front and Masseria and Ferrigno step out.

Ferrigno noticed Valachi standing there. He may have caught Valachi's jaw dropping, or simply, as Valachi himself suggests, "You got to understand, this is a Jewish neighborhood, and they can see I ain't no Jew." Ferrigno and Masseria were immediately suspicious. They not only followed Valachi into the building, but stepped into the elevator with him as well. To throw them off, Valachi rode all the way to the sixth floor. As soon as he got out, he dashed back down the back stairs to his apartment, on the second floor, yelling, "Joe the Boss! Joe the Boss! I just seen him!" The next morning, Valachi's friends managed to pick off Mineo and Ferrigno as they left the apartment. They had missed their major target, however. Masseria had prudently decided to wait several minutes after his meeting with Mineo and Ferrigno had broken up. He had heard the shots and been able to melt away.[15]

According to Virgil Peterson, Maranzano's army numbered around six hundred men by the end of 1930. These included both the original Castellammaresi soldiers and Tom Gagliano's troops as well as the defectors and new recruits. Bonanno insists that it was still a story of David and Goliath however. The Masseria forces outnumbered and out-gunned the Castellammaresi. This means that, during the winter of 1930–31, there were as many as fifteen hundred Italian underworld soldiers patrolling the streets of New York or waiting for their prey from look-out points in rented flats. They were prowling the streets in touring cars as well. "Maranzano and his personal staff rode in armored cars," writes Bonanno. These cars, two Cadillacs outfitted especially for us in Detroit, had special metal plates on the sides and bulletproof windows. Maranzano's Cadillac was always proceeded by the other Cadillac. Sometimes a third car would ride his car, making it nearly impossible to ambush our leader."

"We carried pistols," Bonanno continues, "shot guns, machines guns and enough ammunition to fight the Battle of Bull Run."[16] But it never came to that. What was supposed to be a gangland Armageddon turned into nothing more than an Arms Race. Either these fifteen hundred soldiers were very unlucky or very near-sighted, for until the hit on Masseria took place, Morello, Mineo, and Ferrigno were about the only major casualties in the entire New York theatre of war.

The moment the big hit had taken place, however, the heavy armament was no longer necessary. With Masseria face down in a Coney Island restaurant, the war seemed over, at least in New York. The troops could demobilize, come off the mattress, and go home. This is what many now hoped.

To the Castellammaresi, the elimination of Joe the Boss seemed a stunning feat of arms. When he heard the news, Joe Bonanno almost danced with glee. Maranzano immediately set about consolidating his power. Neither man paused in their excitement to consider what Luciano's real motives might have been.

Shortly after the Masseria murder, Joe Valachi remembered,

Mr. Maranzano called a meeting. I was just notified. I don't remember how, but I was notified. It was held in the Bronx in a big place around Washington Avenue. The place was packed. There was at least four or five hundred of us jammed in. There were members there I never saw before. I only knew the ones I was affiliated with during the war. Now there were so many people, so many faces, that I didn't know where they came from.

We were all standing. There wasn't any room to sit. Religious pictures had been put up on the wall, and there was a crucifix over the platform at one end of the hall where Mr. Maranzano was sitting.[17]

Crucifixes, Luciano remembered, were indeed very much in evidence: "The whole joint was practically covered with crosses, religious pictures, statues of the Virgin and saints I never heard of. Maranzano was the biggest cross nut in the world—he wore a cross around his neck, he had them in his pockets, wherever he was, there was crosses all over the place."[18]

Maranzano had rented the banqueting hall at the Grand Concourse in the Bronx for the occasion. According to Charlie, along with the banqueting hall, Maranzano had rented a large throne-like chair from a theatrical prop warehouse and placed it in the middle of the dais. He had rows of chairs arranged on either side of his throne. These he reserved for his barons, the bosses and captains that had fought on the Castellammarese side. They had been summoned to do homage and pledge their fealty to their new overlord, and, in exchange, receive at his hands their patents of nobility as bosses, under-bosses and captains of the newly-founded *borgate*, as Maranzano in Italian referred to the Families. Below the dais stood the hoi-polloi, the simple mafia soldiers like Valachi, called upon to testify as mute witnesses to the great pageant taking place before their wondering eyes.

The crosses, the rented hall, the phony throne, the trumped-up medieval investiture ceremony, reeked in Charlie's nostrils. His was the place of honor, the chair at the right hand of Maranzano. He sat there like the young Prince Hal, drumming his fingers, just waiting for the farce to conclude.

Mr. Maranzano now addressed the assembly. He read out the accusations against Joe Masseria, listing the names of the people and organizations he had unjustly shaken down. He told how Masseria had sentenced bosses and soldiers to death without cause, how he had sentenced the Castellammaresi to death and declared an unjust war upon them. Speaking in Italian, he listed the charges in the cool and detailed manner of a prosecuting attorney. More allusively, lowering his voice to a bare whisper, he spoke of "Chicago," accusing it of interference and of aiding the enemy. But now, he said, stretching out his arms in his familiar gesture of benediction, a new day was dawning.

Mr. Maranzano told the assembly that he would no longer be leading his own Family. Instead, he was assuming the position of *Capo di Tutti i Capi*, "Boss of All Bosses." As the supreme commander he would be entitled to a share from each of the Families, adding that he would later be explaining to each of the bosses exactly how much their tribute was going to be.

Maranzano outlined a new power structure for New York. Luciano would take charge of the former Masseria Family; Vito Genovese would serve as his under-boss. Tom Gagliano would be Father of the Reina Family in the Bronx with Tommy Lucchese under him. Vince Mangano and Frank Scalise would take over the Mineo Family in Brooklyn with Albert Anastasia as his under-boss. Joe Bonanno would be the Father of the Castellammarese clans. Joe Profaci would run his own Family in Staten Island with Joe Magliocco under him. The key to this structure, Maranzano insisted, was iron discipline and a clear chain of command. The five fathers would be directly responsible to him. The appointed lieutenants would be responsible to the bosses and under-bosses; they had the duty of organizing the common soldiers into ten-man crews, appointing a *capo-decine* as the leader of each crew. This new hierarchy, Maranzano told the assembly, was based on Caesar's Roman Legions.[19]

Maranzano's model of the Roman Legions was not original. It was part of the legacy of the old *Carboneria*, the secret societies of early nineteenth-century Sicily, and had been wide-spread in the Sicilian mafia for decades.

Maranzano not only considered himself the supreme commander of the five Families of New York, but also as *capo* of the entire network of Castellammarese clan and allies stretching across the country. Shortly after the Bronx assembly, he called another assembly, a congress of the entire Castellammarese alliance. It was held at a resort near his farm at Wappinger Falls in May 1931 and attended by approximately three hundred bosses and delegates from around the country. Above the resort a plane circled in the sky, keeping watch for police cars and other uninvited guests.

Maranzano had ordered that all the exits from the main room be boarded shut, leaving only the front door left open. Here Maranzano stationed an honor guard of four soldiers, guns at the ready, who frisked the guests as they arrived, asking their names and Family affiliations. The guests were informed that, once the meeting had gotten started, they would not be permitted to leave the room. If someone needed to go to the bathroom, they were to ask one of Maranzano's guards to escort them. The guards told the most important bosses to seat themselves at the room's long table. The others were told to remain standing.

As soon as the guests were assembled and the bosses were all seated, Maranzano appeared outlined in the front doorway. With all eyes had turned upon him, he strode into the room and seated himself at the head of the table. He remained there, not saying a word, scanning the faces of the seated guests. In the strained silence the droning of the plane motor became increasingly audible until it seemed to fill the room.

"The plane is circling the grounds," he announced. "It is armed with machine guns and bombs. Please remain in your seats. The meeting is about to begin."

Maranzano was just being theatrical. Joe knew that. He wanted to impress his guests, and perhaps intimidate the waverers. It was all for show. Still, Maranzano's extravagant behavior was beginning to trouble Bonanno: "In front of me—Maranzano began again, leaning back in his chair—I see many nice people with good expressions on their faces. I also see people with pale, frightened faces. I don't want anyone to fear me. If you don't want to stay here, raise your hand, and you'll be allowed to leave. If you remain here under false pretenses, then you're not worthy to be at this meeting and you deserve to die.

He waited a moment for these words to sink in. Then he arose from his seat and slowly began to pace the length of the table. As he passed each leader, he stopped and closely examined their face. When he had finished his inspection, he told two men to rise. Then he re-seated them, each in an assigned place. When this was accomplished, he resumed his own seat. From the outside the monotonous buzz of the aircraft engine continued.

"So," he announced when he had resumed his seat, "on my right side is the honest line. And on my left side is the dishonest line."

Protests and exclamations burst out from both sides of the table. A frightened little boss placed on the left side began to bleat piteously, "Don Turiddu, I'm honest! Don Turiddu, I'm honest."

"All right," said Maranzano, suddenly cutting them short. "That's enough! Sit down all of you, it doesn't matter where. Only your conscience knows which side you're really on. But what's past is past. What's important now is peace."

The peace Maranzano had in mind involved a further extension of Castellammarese power. In his speech, he carefully reviewed the events of the war, and then turned to his plans for the future. These centered around Chicago, where Maranzano planned to hold his first national convention. This required an understanding with Capone.[20]

According to Bonanno, he, Maranzano, and Luciano traveled to Chicago at the end of May, stopping on the way to pick up Stefano Magaddino, and Joe Montana. Luciano, he adds, insisted on bringing Meyer Lansky along. Although Bonanno calls Capone "a rather jolly fellow," saying that he was "an extravagant host . . . [who] picked up the tab for everyone's accommodations and provided the food, the drink and the women," and who presented Maranzano with a gold watch studded with diamonds, he is rather guarded about the details of the meeting. Maranzano, he tells us, gave a speech. It started with a justification for his conduct during the war. But now, Maranzano claimed, he just wanted "peace and the enjoyment of a society of friends." He then spoke glowingly about Capone, who, predictably, he insisted on referring to as "Alfonso," and his activities in Chicago. Maranzano finished by implicitly recognizing Capone as the head of the Chicago Family. "All clapped," remarks Bonanno.

Capone then "gave a speech praising Maranzano. We all applauded, acclaiming as much the man as what he stood for. . . . We hailed Maranzano."

But Bonanno knew that Maranzano was becoming unhinged. At the Wappinger Falls meeting he had gone out of his way to torment and humiliate his allies. He seemed like the mad Roman emperor who introduced his horse into the Senate, forcing the Senators to accept it as one of their members. Maranzano had started the war as a Julius Caesar, a tough-minded, dedicated warrior-leader, but the taste of power had transformed him into a Caligula or a Nero. Joe Bonanno discovered that he had some pressing personal business to attend to. After the Chicago meeting he began to see less and less of his boss. By August, he had even stopped going to Maranzano's office. Sometimes he phoned to touch base, sometimes he didn't.

Bonanno had conveniently absented himself, and so could not serve as a witness to the next part of the story. He'd heard rumors though. Maranzano was becoming ever more erratic and dictatorial. He would fly into rages at subordinates, accusing them of holding out on him. Maranzano was under great pressure, Bonanno says. The calculated outbursts and accusations, he explains, were all parts of the great man's sense of theatre. But where were these theatrics going to lead?

Like all mad emperors, Maranzano saw conspirators everywhere. He resented Magaddino, calling him a *rustic*, a country oaf. He summoned him from Buffalo, then made him wait for over an hour outside his office door. "Who does he think he is?" Magaddino growled to his cousin Joe and Joe's close friend, Gaspar Di Gregorio.

"Many people are upset with him," said Magaddino pointedly.

Bonanno knew that he was being sounded out. He stood still and remained expressionless.

"Will someone please tell me what's going on," Gaspar demanded

"The three of us," Stefano said meaningfully, "can't betray each other." He paused and waited.

"It's understood," Joe finally mumbled almost inaudibly.

"We can't betray each other," Stefano repeated.

"I'm in the dark," Gaspar exclaimed, "What's all this about."[21]

After the talk with Magaddino, Bonanno found lots more business to keep him away from Maranzano's office.

Magaddino and Bonanno were not the only ones. By the end of September 1931, Joe Valachi had a grievance. He'd been at a banquet in Brooklyn, and seen the envelopes that the dons from all over the country were placing in Maranzano's hand, the kind of envelopes that were stuffed with cash. It hadn't been the only time. But none of the soldiers had yet seen a penny of their reward. He wanted to ask about this, but "Mr. Maranzano wasn't somebody you just started telling what to do." He would never have dared bring it up himself. But, guessing his feelings, Maranzano had asked him to drop by his house in Brooklyn.

"Joe," said Maranzano, "I hear you're wondering why you didn't get a bigger piece of the take from the banquet."

Maranzano was right, of course; but Valachi didn't want to say so.

"Don't worry," Maranzano went on, "you'll get your share and more. But we are holding on to the money right now because we have to go on the mattress."

Valachi was surprised to learn that a new war was about to be launched. He pricked up his ears:

I'm listening as he explains why. He said, "I can't get along with those two

guys"—he was talking about Charlie Lucky [Luciano] and Vito Genovese—
"and we got to get rid of them before we can control anything." He talked
about some others who had to go too—like Al Capone, Frank Costello,
Willie Moretti from Fort Lee, New Jersey, Joe Adonis and Charlie Lucky's
friend from outside the *Cosa Nostra*, Dutch Schultz.

Gee, I wanted to say, who wants to control everything? But you got to remember that it's just a few months since we are at peace. All I wanted was to
make a good living. But naturally I dared not say anything.[22]

Valachi was not a man of vision. Still, Maranzano's news frightened him.
It was not so much the prospect of a new war, but the fact that Maranzano
should be telling all this to him, a simple soldier. If Maranzano had told him
that he was planning to rub out Charlie and Vito, who else, Valachi worried,
might be in the know?

Maranzano told Valachi to go home and go to bed, and to show up at the
office at a quarter to two. But Valachi couldn't get to sleep; he "spent the night
tossing and turning." The next morning he called the office. He was relieved
to be told that everything was all right. Then his friend Dominic "The Gap"
Petrilli happened to call, "Hey, I've been looking all over for you," The Gap
said. "I've got a couple of new girls over in Brooklyn." Thus, instead of going
to the office as he had promised, Valachi and Petrilli "went over to Brooklyn
and fooled around with the girls until about midnight." And so Valachi happened to be absent as well.

If little Joe Valachi knew what Maranzano was planning, Charlie Luciano must have known as well. But by now it hardly mattered much. Charlie
was deep in his own plans. The Castellammarese alliance turned out to be
more brittle than it appeared. The young Castellammarese leaders thought like
Charlie. They wanted to run their businesses. They had no problems dealing
with the Purple Gang or with Dalitz or with Capone, but they didn't want to
be squeezed by Maranzano, and they didn't want a new war. Luciano met
with some of them in Cleveland. None of them were going to worry if Charlie
bumped off their supreme commander.

The only problem was how. Only Maranzano's trusted bodyguards were
allowed to bear arms in his office. Anyone else, especially an Italian, was
bound to be patted down and carefully searched before entering. An Italian
hit was impossible.

Once again it was Lansky who came up with a solution. Concerned by
Capone's troubles with the Internal Revenue Service, Maranzano had been
striving to get his books in order. He had become a legitimate taxpayer lately,
bragging to Charlie that now he could even invite a Treasury agent in to in-
spect his records. The remark gave Meyer an idea. The assassins, he said, had
to look like tax inspectors, specifically non-Italian tax inspectors. The ideal
assassin, Meyer commented, would have thick glasses, better if he were wearing a yarmulke under his hat. Charlie and Meyer looked at each other and then
nodded—Red Levine. Meyer and Benny Siegel got in touch with Levine; they

also contacted Schultz's hit man, Bo Weinberg. They found two more suitable looking candidates, and put them through a quick crash course in tax accounting, enough at least to fool Maranzano's guards.

Luciano also knew something that Valachi didn't know. Bonanno's under-boss, Angelo Caruso, had told Charlie's Philadelphia bootlegging partner, Nig Rosen, that Maranzano had already hired the Irish gangster, Vince Coll, to kill Luciano and Genovese. Rosen had immediately passed the information along to Costello.

One cannot help wondering. Caruso was close to Bonanno. If Caruso knew, than Bonanno must have known as well. Luciano says that Caruso had spilled out the information when drunk, but Sicilians do not get drunk very often. Luciano had once saved Bonanno from a Masseria hit; perhaps Joe was finding a way of returning the favor.

At about 2 p.m. on September 10, 1931, Tommy Lucchese showed up unexpectedly at Maranzano's office one the eighth floor of the Grand Central Building at Park Avenue and Forty-sixth Street. He had some urgent business with Maranzano, he said. Couldn't it wait? asked Maranzano from the inner office. He was expecting a visit from Charlie and Vito. It was strictly a private matter; he didn't want Lucchese hanging around. It'll only take a minute, said Lucchese; it's a message from Tom Gagliano. Lucchese took Maranzano by the arm and started to walk with him into his private office.

At that precise minute, four owlish men in business suits suddenly appeared in the doorway. "We are looking for a Mr. Salvatore Maranzano," they said, "Would any of you be the gentleman corresponding to that name?"

"It's him," replied Lucchese, indicating Maranzano in the inner office. He turned to Maranzano. On second thought, he said maybe the message from Tom Gagliano wasn't all that important. Maybe it could wait. Maybe you better see what these new arrivals wanted. He sailed blithely out the front door.

"It's about your taxes, sir," said one of the four men, waving some official-looking documents. He walked up to the desk of Maranzano's secretary clumsily fumbling with the lock of his bulky briefcases. Maranzano's five bodyguards gathered around the reception desk, leaning forward, concentrating on the briefcase, when suddenly they noticed that one of the other men was holding a Tommy-gun in their face. "Stand up against the wall, all of you," he barked.

While one held the Tommy-gun keeping them covered, a second frisked the five bodyguards, removing their weapons. The remaining two walked into Maranzano inner office. The Grand Central Building was at the heart of midtown New York; the station below was crawling with cops who would come running at the sound of gunfire. The four assassins could easily be bottled up on the eighth floor. Luciano and Meyer had not wanted the hit to attract attention. They had decided that Maranzano was to be murdered in silence—with knives. But Maranzano was strong; he fought back hard, crying out and batting away the slashing knives with his arms. Finally the two killers had to reach in their briefcases and pull out their pistols. They left him at last with six stab wounds in the chest and body and four bullets in his head. They cut his throat for good measure.

The two killers raced out of the inner office and out the front door closely followed by their two partners. Maranzano's five bodyguards came running after them. They were not giving chase. They hadn't even stopped to pick up their weapons. They just wanted to get out of the office and out of the building before the police arrived and picked them up as material witnesses. Standing outside in the corridor, Tommy Lucchese was last to leave. He walked into the inner office to make sure that Maranzano was truly dead. Satisfied after a cursory examination, Lucchese turned to go and walked straight into a wide-eyed Bobby Doyle, a Maranzano soldier who had heard the shooting and run into the office. "Better get out of here, Bobby," said Lucchese over his shoulder as he walked to the elevator. Doyle stared disbelievingly at the lifeless body of the dead *capo*, then, turning, he ran straight into the arms of the police.

Walking down the staircase, Red Levine and his companions ran into Vincent Coll. He had an appointment with Maranzano to make the final arrangements about Luciano's and Genovese's murders. Maranzano had paid him $25,000 in advance. "Get out of here, Vince," Levine told Coll, "the place is crawling with cops." Professional courtesy.[23]

THE COMMISSION

Luciano saw that Maranzano got a regulation funeral—the train of black limousines, the flowers, tears, and eulogies, the whole works. Then he boarded a train to Chicago for the national convention that Maranzano and Capone had agreed to several months before. During the first afternoon, he had a series of meetings with underworld leaders:

> I knew they wanted to hear from me, direct, face to face, not in an auditorium. I explained it to them that all the war horseshit was out, that each outfit in each city could be independent but there would be a kind of national organization to hold it all together. I told them that we were in a business that had to keep moving without explosions every two minutes. Knocking guys off just because they come from a different part of Sicily and that kind of crap was giving us a bad name, and we couldn't operate until it stopped. Masseria and Maranzano had been our real enemies—that was the way I put it—not the Law. We could always handle the Law; we were doing it everywhere. But how can you handle the crazy people.[24]

Like old Saturn, Maranzano had been set to eat his children. It seemed only right that the demented parent should have been killed by his own "*bambino*." The bosses offered Luciano the usual tribute of cash-stuffed envelops. Wisely he refused; "I don't need the money. I got plenty, and besides why should you be paying anything to me when we're all equals."

Luciano also moved on Torrio and Costello's project. He proposed a commission. At first he wanted to keep it as loose as possible, an informal forum bringing all the syndicates together. He wanted it to be an open forum, combining Italian, Jewish, and other outfits. It was Lansky who objected. Charlie was doing right to keep in touch with his Jewish and Irish colleagues, Meyer said; but the Italians, especially the Sicilians, had their own traditions. Maranzano had organized them into their separate Families, appointing bosses and underbosses over them. Charlie would do well to keep the Sicilians where they were, leaving arrangements as Maranzano had left them. This meant letting the Sicilian Families have their own commission, their own *Cosa Nostra*. Lansky, Charlie observed, must have had a Sicilian wet-nurse; he understood the Sicilians better than the Sicilians themselves. He agreed to Meyer's suggestion, only stipulating that, from now on, the position of *Il Capo di Tutti i Capi* was eliminated. Instead, he created the position of the *consigliere*, an advisor to the bosses as well as a tribune for the common soldiers. Soldiers were allowed to bring their grievances to the *consigliere* who, in his turn, could take them up with the bosses with no fear of reprisals. Luciano appointed Lansky as his own *consigliere*.

This is the birth of the Cosa Nostra National Commission as Luciano tells it, and the simple truth is that we do not have a better, or even an alternative, version. It had been Maranzano who had, a year earlier, divided the New York Cosa Nostra into five Families or *borgate*. Bonanno, we saw, would succeed Maranzano as head of the Brooklyn Catellammarresi; his underboss was originally his old friend Gaspar Di Gregorio, later followed by Carmine Galante. Bonanno's friend, Joe Profaci continued to run the Staten Island Family with Joe Magliocco as his underboss. When Magliocco died in 1963, he was succeeded by Joe Colombo.

We also saw that after the murder of Reina in 1930, and after the short interregnum of Joseph Pinzolo, leadership of the Bronx mafia passed to Thomas Gagliano with Gaetano "Tommy Brown" Lucchese as his underboss. Lucchese succeeded Gagliano after Gagliano's death in 1953, dying himself in 1967. The Family of the Masseria allies, Alfred Mineo and Steve Ferrigno, both murdered in 1930, was taken over by two Brooklyn gangsters, Philip and Vincent Mangano, closely associated with Albert Anastasia. When the two Magano brothers disappeared under mysterious circumstances in 1951, murdered, according to underworld rumor, on Anastasia's orders, Anastasia himself became boss, remaining in power until his own murder in 1957.[25]

These divisions reflected the balance of power in the Sicilian underworld of New York at the close of the Castellammarrese War. In a larger sense, they mirrored the Sicilian diaspora itself. Though Mulberry Street remained the symbolic center, Lower Manhattan's Little Italy was no longer home to the biggest Sicilian community in the city, much less in the country. The Sicilian community in Brooklyn and possibly even East Harlem was bigger. It is hard to be exact; census data does not distinguish Sicilians from Neapolitans or Calabrians, and the various communities were beginning to dissolve. Charlie spoke for the majority when he said, "knocking guys off just because they come from a different part of Sicily and that kind of crap was giving us a bad name."

Nevertheless, traditionalists, High Tories like the Bonanno Family, long continued to arrange marriages among their offspring and the offspring of allies and *compaesani*. It was the *homines novi* like Torrio, Costello, and Capone, none of whom were Sicilian, who married the girl down the block, even if she did not happen to be Italian.

The early *Cosa Nostra* Commissions remained informal. Though their bid for power had ended in defeat, the Castellammarresi retained a significant presence. As a senior statesman in the Castellammarese clans, Stefano Magaddino from Buffalo was a regular at the council table. So were representatives of the Capone Outfit. Torrio, Capone, Nitti, and Ricca had all come from Brooklyn, and so, in this sense, the Chicago Outfit was a daughter colony of Brooklyn. Even if the Capone Outfit had become a fully separate and independent organization, for at least a generation the Outfit continued to treat New York with a degree of filial deference. Frank Milano from Cleveland and Joe Zerilli from Detroit had each played their role in the underworld war, and so, along with Buffalo, Cleveland, and Detroit had the right to direct representation on the Commission. Though the Hudson River is an administrative boundary and political frontier, northern New Jersey had long been part of the New York metropolitan economy. Longy Zwillman from Newark and Willie Moretti were part of the Commission.

The Bonanno, Profaci and Mangano Families came from groups of inter-related clans in the closely-knit Italian enclaves of Brooklyn and the outer suburbs. Vince and Phil Mangano's Family came from the Red Hook and Sheepshead's Bay area in Brooklyn. It centered around work at the Brooklyn docks. These were traditional communities, long accustomed to the paternalistic sovereignty of organizations like the *Unione Siciliana*. They paid their required tributes. The three Brooklyn Families were more than just criminal organizations; they were neighborhood patriarchies who naturally looked at the *Cosa Nostra* Commission as a sort of underworld senate where the Godfathers could wheel and deal with each other. And this is precisely what they were apt to do, often at great length. Electing Frank Mangano as their chairman and Joe Profaci as secretary, Charlie Luciano was dismayed to find the Brooklyn Godfathers taking up entire Commission meetings with neighborhood disputes and the personal problems of obscure Brooklyn soldiers. Charlie, who had never revised the unfortunate impression that an enforced sojourn at the Brooklyn Truancy School in 1911 had left him of that borough, found such proceedings tedious.

In fact, Luciano took little interest in *La Cosa Nostra*'s internal affairs. Though technically the boss of the ex-Masseria Family, the role of an old-style Godfather, with all the formality and constricting ceremony, didn't interest the free-wheeling Charlie. It was too traditional, too Sicilian. Nor did it quite suit Costello. Costello was another independent free-wheeler, with gambling and property interests throughout the country. Even though most sources list him as an underboss in the Luciano Family, his role was much closer to that of Torrio, with whom he maintained a long friendship. The voluble Costello did enjoy the meetings, however. Later described as "prime minister of the underworld," he took on the role of moderator or chairman of the board at Commission meetings. The role of traditional Godfather suited Don Vito better. Luciano's Italian lieutenants had already gotten into the habit of reporting directly to Vito Genovese, and Charlie was happy to leave the day-to-day running of his Family and management of his soldiers in Genovese's hands. So it was Don Vito who often represented Luciano on the Cosa Nostra Commission.

Though the Bonanno, Profaci, and Mangano Families were the traditionalists of the Cosa Nostra Commission, the meetings might even be trying for the young Joe Bonanno. When he became Father of the Brooklyn Castellammaresi, Joe Bonanno was not yet twenty-eight. Though he had had a real affection for Salvatore Maranzano, he couldn't, in spite of himself, help liking Charlie Lucky as well. Charlie Lucky was a genuine American democrat, a person with no regard for tradition, a person who would consort with whomever he wanted to consort with. Besides, both Charlie and Joe were both movie fans. It's tempting to imagine them skipping out on another interminable Commission meeting, sneaking off to an afternoon matinee instead— two young criminal overlords watching a film and enjoying a box of popcorn together.

APPENDIX: DIXIE DAVIS TELLS A TALE

In the summer of 1939, J. Richard "Dixie" Davis wrote an article for *Collier's* magazine.[26] It was about the murder of Salvatore Maranzano, and the so-called "Purge Day" or 'Night of the Sicilian Vespers' murders that supposedly followed. According to Dixie Davis, the Purge Day murders had been carefully organized by Charlie Luciano. Concerned that a backlash or loyalist uprising might materialize when the news of Maranzano's murder spread through the American mafia, Luciano had taken the precaution of drawing up a list of potential opponents within the mafia. As soon as he assured that the Maranzano hit had taken place, Luciano moved with characteristic ruthlessness. Davis estimated that, throughout the United States, as many as ninety suspected Maranzano loyalists were executed.

On his own, Davis would hardly be counted as a reliable source. Though he knew the rackets, he had no first-hand knowledge of the Italians. He was rather Dutch Schultz's lawyer and advisor. Guilty, among other things, of perjury, he spent time in prison and was eventually disbarred. His source for the Purge Day story was Schultz's own bodyguard and lieutenant, Abraham "Bo" Weinberg. According to Davis, Weinberg told him that, "at the very same hour [as the Maranzano murder] there was about ninety guineas knocked off all over the country." It was, Weinberg continued, the way that the mobs were "Americanized."

Bo Weinberg was certainly qualified to speak as an authority on the Salvatore Maranzano killing. He and Red Levine were part of the hit squad. But he may not be such a reliable source about the other ninety killings. Although Davis cites Weinberg as his source, he fails to tell us where Weinberg got his information. By the time the *Collier's* article appeared 1939, Weinberg had been dead for several years, murdered by the Dutchman in one of his fits of suspicious rage, dunked in cement, and then dumped in the East River. Weinberg was not giving interviews to anyone. So, assuming that Davis was not making the whole thing up, there's no way of finding out where Weinberg got his information about the "ninety guineas" who got "knocked off all over the country."

Despite the lack of confirmation, the next year the story of the ninety murders passed from the *Collier's* article into Craig Thompson and Allen Raymond's *Gang Rule in New York*. From here it found its way into other articles and books, including King's County (Brooklyn) Assistant District Attorney, Burton Turkus's account, *Murder Inc.* The story had the simplicity of a "just-so" story; it was an explanation of how, in Weinberg's words, "we Americanized the mobs," how the American mafia got to be the way that it was. In a single, concerted action, Luciano and his followers supposedly re-organized the American mafia, eliminating the "Mustache Petes," the old-style Sicilian dons, and putting in their place a new generation of modern, American-style leaders like Luciano himself. The action represented, as Turkus wrote, a "mass extermination of mafia executives;" it shone as "a remarkable example of planning."

So satisfying was this image of the elimination of the old greaseball generation, and their replacement by a new, Americanized breed, that no one bothered to check the facts. In 1976, however, the historian Humbert S. Nelli published the result of his examination of newspaper reports across America for the months surrounding the Maranzano killing. He discovered that, compelling as the Purge Day story may be, it does not happen to be true; "available evidence indicates that not ninety, or forty, or twenty, or even five murders were carried out across the United States in conjunction with, or as a consequence of, Maranzano's death." Purge Day was a myth.

Nelli's findings were welcomed by criminologists and academic sociologists who had never been happy with popular accounts of the mafia and their exploits. Nelli's findings seemed to confirm suspicions that stories about the mafia, their exotic customs, and arcane initiation rites were all made up. The fact that the Purge Day story was later repeated by gangsters themselves, in Joe Valachi's 1960s confessions for example, simply showed that gangsters too were bamboozled by what academic writers called the mafia mystique.

But who would invent such a preposterous tale—journalists, dime novelists, grade-B Hollywood film scriptwriters? Such people do, no doubt, bear a certain responsibility; the press photographer who placed the ace of diamonds in Joe the Boss Masseria's dead hand was, like others of his profession, capable of gilding the odd lily when he thought he could get away with it. Nevertheless, blaming the media for the Purge Day story will not do, for it is clear that the media learned this particular tale from the gangsters, not the other way around. The media may have spread the story; they may, on occasion, even have embellished it a little. But they did not make it up. They were rather reporting a story that originated with the gangsters themselves.

So who made up the story? Some have suspected Luciano, who, in his last testament, circulated some pretty tall tales. Nevertheless, when journalists asked him about the Purge Day story in the 1960s, Charlie expressed his own bewilderment. He'd heard the story, of course, but couldn't understand it. After murdering Maranzano, he said, he'd gone to meet the bosses of other outfits around the county. He'd gone to explain his actions and put an end to hostilities. What else was he going to do? The last thing he wanted was a new round of blood-letting.

A better candidate might be the Schultz gang. Weinberg was murdered in 1935. Davis presumably heard the Purge Day story from him in that year or in late 1934. In the back of both Weinberg's and Davis's mind, there may have been another set of events, ones that had taken place several months earlier. In the summer of 1934, bowing to the demands of the German Army, Adolf Hitler liquidated his old brawling partners, the Storm Troopers, the S.A. of Ernst Roehm. To accomplish this gruesome task, he picked soldiers from Himmler's S.S., a new, thoroughly modern, and far more sinister formation, together with units from Goering's police. Along with hundreds of Storm Troopers murdered in the purge, dozens of other Hitler enemies and old associates, scattered throughout Germany, were yanked from their beds and summarily shot. The event came to be known as the Night of the Long Knives.

Weinberg had killed for Joe the Boss Masseria. He knew Luciano as well, knew him well enough indeed to arouse Dutch Schultz's suspicions. But as a Jew, Weinberg would also have known about the Night of the Long Knives. He may have seen it as an appropriate analogy. Hitler had seized control of his outfit, purging out the trouble-making rowdies; in the same way, upon his own taking control, Luciano had decided to whack out all the old Mustache Petes. Weinberg was not blaming Luciano over this. Indeed, from Weinberg's rather feral perspective, it probably seemed the smart thing to do. Weinberg probably told the Purge Day story to Davis as a token of the admiration he felt towards his friend Charlie Luciano.

Any reader glancing at the last chapters' footnotes will be aware that in reconstructing the final stages of the Castellammarese War, I have drawn heavily on three sources—Luciano, Bonanno and Valachi. Each of these sources has been subjected to criticism, and indeed each is problematic in its own way. It is worth looking at these sources. Valachi is the simplest case.

Joe Valachi is usually presented as the first member of the American mafia ever to sing, ever to give testimony about that enigmatic organization. The claim is not strictly true. Valachi may have been the "canary that sang," but the untimely death of the "bird that flew," Abe "Kid Twist" Reles, while in custody awaiting trial deprived the Kefauver Committee of an opportunity to learn more about Albert Anastasia. Nonetheless, as a figure involved in organized crime for over forty years, Valachi was a walking history book. He was close to the major events in the history of organized crime, some of which he witnessed himself.

But how reliable is Valachi's testimony? In his history of organized crime in New York, Virgil W. Peterson devoted the entire second half of his study to a critical examination of Valachi's evidence. Peterson can claim to be the dean of the history of organized crime in America; his knowledge of the subject is unparalleled. Peterson has little difficulty in revealing numerous inconsistencies and errors of fact in Valachi's testimony before the McClellan Commission. A "relatively insignificant underworld character," Valachi, according to Peterson, was a man of "limited intelligence" currently in prison for murder. One day in 1960 while in the Atlanta Prison yard, crime boss Vito Genovese had seized Valachi's hand and kissed it. Valachi took the gesture as the kiss of death. According to the prison psychiatrist, Valachi then fell into a paranoid state characterized by "delusion of persecution."[27]

These may be good enough reasons for doubting Valachi's reliability in general. Nevertheless, Peterson's examination reveals where the specific source of Valachi's inaccuracies lay. The author of the 1967 President's Commission report on organized crime, Donald Cressy, opened his report with a much-quoted comment: "Our knowledge of the structure which makes 'organized crime' organized," he wrote, "is somewhat comparable to the knowledge of Standard Oil which could be gleaned from interviews with gasoline station attendants."[28] A lower-echelon soldier in various crime families, Valachi was indeed the humble gas-station attendant struggling to make sense of the boardroom struggles of Standard Oil, or, perhaps more accurately, the veteran soldier trying to explain the entire war from his own battlefield recollections and the stories of his old GI buddies.

Not merely a man of limited intelligence, Valachi was also a man whose first-hand knowledge was limited to the New York area. Nevertheless, as the best witness the authorities could produce, the senate investigators peppered Valachi with specific questions, many of which he was in no position to answer. As a Senate sub-committee witness, testifying under bright lights with television and news cameras whirring about him, Valachi was visibly overwhelmed. When Senator Curtis of Nebraska asked him whether the Cosa Nostra was active in Omaha, Valachi hesitated before replying. He leaned over and whispered something in the ear of a Justice Department official sitting next to him. Then he replied, "Senator, I never heard of Omaha, and I never heard anything about Omaha." Senator Curtis pressed on; "Well what about Des Moines then?" "Where is that, Senator?" Valachi replied. "That is in Iowa," he was informed. "I never even heard of that," Valachi replied. Newspaper accounts later mentioned Valachi's whispered conference before answering. Surely Senator Curtis had hit some sort of nerve, and Valachi had been too frightened to reply. What he had actually said to the official, it turned out, was "Where the hell is Omaha?"[29]

Valachi's inconsistencies stemmed from his ignorance and habit of repeating to the senators whatever underworld scuttlebutt happened to be lodged in his memory. These inconsistencies naturally crop up wherever Valachi strays out of his natural depth. Valachi's account of the Castellammarese War, by contrast, is based on his personal recollections. These recollections are clear and consistent, and thus Peterson's reservations no longer apply. Nor does the Atlanta prison psychiatrist's diagnosis that Valachi was suffering from a paranoid fear of Vito Genovese seem relevant. Many underworld figures nursed just such a fear in regard to the treacherous Don Vito; not to do so would have seemed to them evidence of a lack of sanity rather than the opposite. Peterson further comments that Valachi's personal recollections have been rejected by a number of major criminological authorities. This criticism seems fatuous. Valachi may have been no genius; but who was present at these events, Joe Valachi or the eminent criminologists?

If Valachi's banal recollections are neither guileful nor self-serving, the same could never be said of the accounts provided by Bonanno and Luciano. Bonanno's account, especially, is an extended exercise in self-justification.

Bonanno considers Sicilians, and the *picciotti* from Castellammare del Golfo in particular, to be God's gift to organized crime in America:

> In the New World the numerous Sicilians soon began to dominate affairs among fellow Italian immigrants. Our superiority rested just as much on social structure as on numbers. Our clan system gave us great solidarity and afforded us advantages in our enterprises. Many outsiders tried to copy the Sicilian ways, but since they didn't fully understand our Tradition, the result was usually a caricature. Neapolitans, for example, went in for loud clothes, rough-house and maudlin outbursts of violence. The archetypical Sicilian, in contrast, is stoic, self-possessed and given to violence only to restore order, not out of display.

So superior were the Sicilians of Bonanno's Tradition that, according to him, wherever they landed, they simply took over. Leadership was their natural right, an entitlement, a recognition of their natural superiority and the superiority of their clan system and their Tradition.[30]

Bonanno pauses in his account to ridicule the story of Valachi's initiation. "Valachi was a stranger to our Tradition," he comments, "recruited because the war needed fresh bodies, new faces." Valachi, he adds meaningfully, "whose parents, I believe, were from the Naples region," was never in a position to understand. "To expect Valachi to act as a reliable guide to our Tradition," he concludes grandly, "was like asking a new convert to Catholicism in New Guinea to explain the inner workings of the Vatican."[31]

Maybe so. But why should Valachi, not an imaginative man, have inserted these bizarre details into his otherwise mundane and factual account? The ritual he described is a mafia classic, an oath of brotherhood that has survived intact and almost unchanged from the early nineteenth-century *Carbonari*. The piece of paper that Maranzano set in Valachi's cupped hands and set alight would, in all probability, have born the picture of a saint, probably the Virgin of the Annunciation. The Annunciation symbolized the dawning of a new day and, for the candidate member, a new life. Maranzano would have known and understood the symbolism, and no doubt would have reveled in it. Bonanno may dismiss this all as mumbo-jumbo; but it was Maranzano's brand of mumbo-jumbo not Valachi's.

Though Bonanno denies, or at least minimizes, the first Wappinger Falls meeting described by Valachi, he is our only source on the second Wappinger Falls meeting, when Maranzano began to behave like a mad emperor.

Joe Bonanno also points out that he had never undergone a similar initiation. For him to become a member of Maranzano's crew, Bonanno wrote, a simple dinner invitation had been sufficient. This is no doubt true. But then Joe was not only from Castellammare del Golfo, he was also a Bonanno, related to the Magaddinos and the Bonventres. That made him special. As Joe's son, Bill Bonanno, later tried to explain to his young fiancée, the uncomprehending and thoroughly alarmed, convent-educated daughter of Joe Profaci, Rosalie, there was family and then there was Family. As the son of Joe Bonanno, Bill qualified on both counts. No one was going to prick a Bonanno's trigger finger and make him swear an oath. The Bonannos were to the manor born. Initiation ceremonies were for people who were not family, for common soldiers like Valachi; initiation were designed to impress upon these simple souls the solemnity and gravity of the Sicilian Tradition they were about to enter. Indeed, it was in the time of Maranzano that a new name for Sicilian organized crime in America began to be used—*La Cosa Nostra*.

The death of Joe the Boss and the Staten Island beating are not the only suspicious tales in Luciano's 'Last Testament'. His account is larded with fairy stories waiting to trap the unwary reader, or perhaps the unwary interviewer.

In 1961, Charlie Luciano was living in exile in Naples. He had become something of a local celebrity, signing autographs for U.S. sailors in his California restaurant and chatting with newspapermen looking for a story. Charlie claimed, not very convincingly, that he was now going straight, and, indeed, he had made a number of legitimate business investments. Yet Charlie also had suffered a number of setbacks. Along with Meyer and others, Charlie had invested in Cuban casinos. In 1959, however, the young Fidel Castro had overthrown the Battista dictatorship and soon closed all the casinos. The following year, the mafia Commission in New York decided to reduce Charlie's monthly pension. Worst of all, Charlie next heard that his ex-number two, Vito Genovese, had put a contract out on his life. One result of these reversals was a massive coronary occlusion that hospitalized Charlie. The doctor told him to take it easy; he was under too much pressure and ought to cut down his business responsibilities. Charlie decided that the time had come to retire.

Charlie had earlier met Martin Gosch, who had described himself to Charlie as a Hollywood producer and screenwriter. Gosch had cooked up a movie project. It was to be loosely based on Charlie's life but, in the manner of Ben Hecht's *Scarface*, would contain allusions to more recent underworld events—the shooting of Frank Costello and the murder of Albert Anastasia. The project appealed to Charlie's vanity, and he and Gosch set to work on the script. Soon Gosch was telling him that he had found backers in London and Paris, and had even lined up Dean Martin to play the role of Charlie. Charlie was delighted. Then the boom fell: Genovese's number two, Tommy Eboli, told Charlie to drop the movie. It was not a request; it was an order. The Apalachin meeting in 1957 and the popular televison serial *The Untouchables* had been giving Italo-American crime too much publicity lately. Charlie's projected movie would only make things worse. If Charlie did not drop the project, New York would stop all payments to him.

Faced with financial decline, a deteriorating heart and the distinct possibility that Vito Genovese's gunmen were behind every Baroque column, Charlie called up Gosch. The movie had to be called off, Charlie said. When Gosch began to protest, Charlie cut him short. "I know how these guys thinks," he told him; "if you go ahead, they'll kill me, then they'll kill you and maybe some other guys for good measure." What he now had in mind was a different project. "Marty, would you be willin' to take down my whole life story. I mean it. I've been thinking about it for the last three days. I want somebody to know my life."[32]

Stupified, Gosch could only stammer, "You're playing games with me, Charlie."

"No, I swear to you, I'm not. The condition is only this. I'll give it all to you. I won't hold back notin'. But you gotta promise you won't use it, no part of it, for ten years. And I mean ten years after I die."

Later Charlie added another condition; "You can't use anythin' I'm gonna to tell if Tommy Lucchese is still alive, even if the ten years are up. He's one good friend I don't want to hurt."

For the next three years, until he died of a heart attack on the pavement outside of Naples' Capodichino Airport, Charlie Luciano and Martin Gosch were inseparable companions.

But was Gosch really a Hollywood producer and screenwriter? The truth was that Gosch was something of a fraud. Aside from a single involvement in producing an Abott and Costello movie, he had neither a major production not a single script to his credit. Though Charlie gave him masses of material, Gosch was unable to do anything with it. In 1972, as the ten-year date drew near, Martin Gosch contacted another writer, Richard Hammer. The two came to an agreement that, using Gosch's notes, Hammer would write a book entitled *The Last Testament of Lucky Luciano*.

But Gosch and Hammer soon fell out. Gosch had begun interfering, trying, as Hammer put it, to "rewrite my writing." The disagreement, however, was not over matters of style. "He never wrote a word," Hammer scornfully told Allan May. "He couldn't. He could hardly write his own name!" Gosch had found the task of writing quite beyond him. Gosch was rather objecting to the way that Hammer was treating Charlie.

Hammer had been chosen because he was knowledgeable; he was involved in a *Playboy* series on underworld crime. Certainly he was more knowledgeable and able than Gosch. But Hammer had never known Luciano. He did not feel any sympathy for him or loyalty. Gosch, by contrast, had been Luciano's shadow during his last three years, and had grown to know and like Charlie. Neither a historian nor an investigative journalist, he had done no research on organized crime. But this had never been part of the project. Gosch had simply agreed to take down what Luciano said and to sit on it for ten years. At the end, he was supposed to weld these notes into a life of Charlie Luciano in Charlie's own words.

An investigative journalist with a reputation to make, it frustrated Richard Hammer that he had never been able to interview Luciano face to face, never been able to put to him pointed, hard-ball questions like *Time* magazine's Mike Stern a few years before. Gosch's project forced him into the role of a passive amanuensis, unable to demonstrate his own journalistic prowess. It irked the hell out of him.

Hammer feared, quite realistically, that by presenting Luciano's autobiography without critical commentary, he was laying himself open to a roasting from his contemporaries—he specifically mentions Nick Gage and Nick Pileggi. The strain is visible in the writing. It is clear from Charlie's own quoted words that he was talking to a sympathetic listener; but it is equally clear from the surrounding editorial commentary that the sympathetic listener was Gosch, not Hammer, the editor. Indeed, Gosch seems to have intervened, trying to re-write Hammer's commentary whenever it became too pointed.

It would be nice to check Hammer's version against Gosch's notes. As Allan May discovered, however:

> While writing the story Hammer had access to all of the notes, which Gosch demanded back. When asked about the story that Gosch's wife destroyed the notes, Hammer remarked, "I knew her very well. When he died she had the apartment on Crescent Drive, in Beverly Hills, and she couldn't stay there so she was going to live with her niece in Las Vegas. She had an apartment full of stuff that she didn't know what to do with. I knew her well enough to know, and my wife knew her well enough to know, that indeed, she never discussed it with anyone, she just told the superintendent, 'I'm moving. Take all the stuff and throw it in the incinerator.' She didn't think it was worth anything."[33]

Hammer knew that Charlie's statements were full of factual inaccuracies great and small. He was able to edit away some of the errors, and occasionally comments on doubtful points. Yet he never challenges Luciano's account directly. Nor, we can hope, does he invent or otherwise doctor Luciano's words. Slippery, self-serving and mendacious as these words may be, they are Charlie's words, not those of Martin Gosch or Richard Hammer.

Just as Hammer had feared, the appearance of the book was greeted by a front-page lambasting in the New York *Times* by Hammer's colleague and former friend, Nick Gage.[34] Gage had showed Luciano's version of his 1936 trial to his lawyer, Moses Polakoff, and Polakoff had discovered numerous errors in that version. Luciano had certainly embellished his account and sometimes even re-arranged the facts to make a better story or to present himself in a better light. Nevertheless, many of these errors concerned procedural details of a trial that happened thirty years earlier. They were errors over matters that Polakoff would have understood and remembered far better than Luciano. Gage moreover used Polakoff because Polakoff provided him with a reliable source against which Luciano's statements could be checked. The approach is understandable, but unfortunately the parts that can checked against reliable sources are by far the least interesting parts of Luciano's story. The most interesting and valuable parts are the stories for which Luciano and his underworld colleagues are our only sources. These include the story of the Castellammarese War. Without the accounts of Luciano, Bonanno, Valachi, and others, the murders of Joe the Boss Masseria and Salvatore Maranzano would be just two more unexplained gangland slayings.

Accepting the eminent gangsters' accounts as historical evidence is not the same as accepting these accounts at face value. Luciano and Bonanno give contradictory accounts of the Castellammarese War. Unwilling to see themselves represented as interlopers and aggressors, the Castellammaresi suppress certain key facts while sharpening or embellishing others. In the resulting version, the Castellammaresi re-emerge as traditional men of honor responding to an intolerable affront. Throughout his career, Luciano, gave conflicting accounts of the beating he received in Staten Island in 1929. Though the fact of the beating was never in question, the context and the identity of his tormentors are changed to suit Charlie's convenience. In bringing his story up to the present, Luciano also grows increasingly bitter over the betrayal of Vito Genovese. Did Genovese really murder Tom Reina, or is it an example of Luciano seeking to heap yet more obloquy on the venomous Don Vito? Capone may have been sincere when he expressed remorse over the killing of Bill McSwiggen, but does that mean we believe him when he tells us that he was not in one of the murder cars?

The eminent gangsters are, in short, imperfect sources. Their accounts are self-serving, their tales filled with embellishments and outright fabrications. But where are our perfect sources? The recollections of the eminent gangsters resemble—differ only in degree from—the recollections of other eminent personages, eminent politicians, eminent sports heroes, and eminent film stars. There is a problem of historical truth that resides in all autobiography. The world as the eminent personage recollects it, and the image that this eminent personage wishes to project onto posterity, so often collide with the historical truth as the historian unearths it. It is a problem inherent in writing history from sources, and, as such, a problem that all historians must confront. Failure to confront the problem is not a mark of methodological virtue, it is merely a cop out.

Chapter Eleven
The Fall

"Was it not wonderful?" Charlie Luciano asked Martin Gosch. When he and his family arrived in America, Sicilians were the lowest of the low, the bottom of the food chain. Destiny seemed to have consigned him to a life as a crumb. Yet here he was, at the end of the 1920s, living in his own suite in the Waldorf Towers. America, he told John Davis in the 1950s, truly was the land of opportunity.

The Prime of Charlie Lucky

Charlie had gone apartment hunting in 1928. He'd always liked the feel of grand hotels, he decided—their crowded lobbies filled with scurrying bellhops, obliging porters, and chambermaids willing to run errands for tips. Big hotels had banks of phones, dark oak-panelled rooms, restaurants, coffee shops and quiet little corners tucked behind the potted palms. They were marketplaces, busy yet anonymous, stylish yet private, the perfect cover for any kind of business meeting. Charlie's first thought had been to move into the Park Central where Arnold Rothstein had rooms. But when Mr. Rothstein was shot there, Charlie began to regard the place as somehow jinxed. Besides, he had decided that he really wanted to see trees from his windows. So he rented a spacious apartment at the Barbizon Plaza on Central Park South, with a panoramic view of Central Park.

Right across the street from Charlie's apartment was the St. Moritz, where Walter Winchell had his own suite. The two men could wave to each other from their windows. Winchell didn't like it and told his friends so. Charlie soon heard what Winchell was saying; "I said to myself, 'Fuck him.'" What right had Winchell to act so high and mighty. Charlie was paying for his apartment at the Barbizon in cash while Winchell was getting comped by the St. Moritz, getting his rooms for free for occasionally mentioning the joint in his column. So who was calling whom a racketeer? "Sometimes I'd take a walk down Central Park South and once in a while I'd see Winchell. I'd wave to him and say, 'Hi, neighbor.' It burnt him to a crisp."

Still, Luciano and Winchell went to the same night clubs and had Owney Madden as a mutual friend. Winchell needed to keep in touch with the gangster world and did so through Texas Guinan, Larry Fey, and others. But he depended on Madden more than anyone else. Since Charlie could often be found at Owney's table, Winchell must have been on sociable terms with Charlie. Sometimes the pair would even drop in on the columnist. One of Winchell's editors, Emile Gauvreau, complained that he found Madden and Luciano loafing in the news rooms, feet on the news desks, waiting to have a chat with Winchell.[1] Though Winchell couldn't afford to be seen too publicly with Luciano, he couldn't afford to dismiss him either.

Charlie admired Madden. He liked his nightclubs, liked to drink whiskey at Owney's table. Even after the stock market crash, there was always something happening at Owney's clubs, some out-of-town big shot coming in for the night, doing the town and anxious to meet the young comers like Luciano and Costello. Madden was happy to arrange an introduction. The restauranteur, Toots Shor, got his first job working as a bouncer in one of Madden's many establishments. In an interview in the 1970s, Toots lamented the passing of the gangsters from the New York nightclubs. Madden had been a real boss, Toots claimed. He had class and style. He really knew how to run a joint. The stuff they had in Chicago was, in comparison, "just amateur night. This was New York; this was the big leagues!"

"I wish they were back today," Shor concluded sorrowfully.

Toots also lamented the passing of New York's show-girl culture. Throughout the 1920s and 1930s, the theatres along the Great White Way served up an array of follies and chorus-line reviews, with Vaudeville dance numbers and little cabarets on the side streets. On any given night, Shor remembered, the streets of central Manhattan would be packed with beautiful women dressed in expensive clothes in the company of young swains in black ties or old sugar daddies in top hats, all of whom stood waiting for their girls, clutching bouquets of carnations or red roses, under the streetlamps outside the dressing room doors. By midnight, the glamorous showgirls and their well-heeled escorts would be disgorging into the clubs, shouting for drinks, getting raucous and getting sloshed. Visiting big shots, like Nucky Johnson, in from Atlantic City, would arrive surrounded by a whole entourage of showgirls rounded up by his local hosts.

It was an atmosphere Shor loved. Toots had gotten used to seeing Luciano in the clubs where he worked. What did Luciano look like, the interviewer asked Toots. "He looked like he was a nice guy," Toots shot back. Then he continued, "He laughed, he had fun. He was a good fellow to me. He picked up a check—in those days you were looking for a guy to pick up your check, you didn't have anything. And he was liberal to his people that worked for him. He was a nice guy."[2]

By 1928, Charlie had found a showgirl of his own. Her name was Gay Orlova. When Charlie first met her, Orlova was lead dancer at the Hollywood Club. The two of them soon became inseparable, and their friends kept expecting Charlie and Gay to get married. It was only natural, they thought; Gay was a nice girl, and Charlie was obviously crazy about her. Why shouldn't Charlie want to settle down?

There were wedding bells all over gangland in those years. Joe Bonanno couldn't wait for the Castellammarese War to end so that he could marry his sweetheart, a nice Castellammarese girl from Brooklyn, and settle down. Vito Genovese got married as soon as the Castellammarese War was over too, though in his case it was his second marriage. His first wife had died, and Vito arranged a convenient widowhood for his prospective second bride. Vito got married alongside his best friend, Anthony "Tony Bender" Strollo. It was a double ceremony in March 1932, where each acted as best man for the other. Meyer Lansky wed in 1929; the Atlantic City convention doubled as a honeymoon for the newly-wedded Mr. and Mrs. Meyer Lansky.[3]

These wedding bells were followed by more than a few Winchellesque "blessed events," for, as Charlie observed, there seemed to be "some kind of Italian law that [a guy] had to bang out a million kids." "Joe Adonis bought a place out in Jersey and he finally wound up with a couple of kids. Willie Moretti built a place in Jersey that was like a fort, and he raised a family."

The gossips of gangland fully expected that Charlie and Gay would follow suit and tie the knot. Why shouldn't Charlie, now that he had everything he wanted? But Charlie didn't want to become a husband. Settling down was the first step on the road to becoming a Godfather, becoming like Masseria or Maranzano. Charlie shunned marriage, saying, "I always figured that some day I was going to wind up on a slab, and I didn't want to leave a widow and kids crying over me."

For men with such unconventional lifestyles, gangsters could be remarkably conventional in their views on sex and marriage. Capone prided himself on being a good family man. He took special care of his mamma, and sent his nieces and nephews to private schools. He was devoted to his wife Mae and their boy Sonny. Yet Capone was a great, indeed an obsessive, consumer of women, holding firm to the opinion that when a guy no longer falls for a broad, he's "all washed up." When he took up golfing afternoons with Jack McGurn, the boys with machine guns in their golfbags pretending to be their caddies used to install little surprises on the course—whores in the sandtraps as late afternoon pick-me-ups.

None of this was for Charlie Luciano. In his own mind, he was not a criminal or underworld leader; he was a playboy, a fashionable and elegant man about town. Playboys, he thought, don't settle down; they keep on playing. Playgirls too. If Charlie didn't want to transform himself into a Godfather, he didn't want to transform his partner, the willowy, dark-eyed Gay Orlova, into another mob mamma with a brood of bawling little mafiosetti on her knees.

The role of playboy and fashionable man about town not only required money; it also required considerable *savoir-faire*. Charlie was honest enough to admit that he was still somewhat lacking in this department. This is where Gay came in. She was a class act. She was fluent in Russian and French, which mightily impressed Charlie, who still struggled not to sound like he was just off the boat. "There was nothing cheap about her," he remembered. "She understood that I was always trying to improve myself. I could let my hair down with her and we got along great. She was meant for good times and that was all I was looking for in them days."

The search for good times and self-improvement meant mornings shopping for clothes together. Charlie had become fanatical about his silk shirts and underwear, his custom-tailored suits and his hand-made shoes. Gay had excellent taste, and knew all the places where Charlie could get the things he wanted. During the racing season, Charlie and Gay might spend their afternoon at the track. They traveled up to Saratoga.

Charlie also had particular, if idiosyncratic, tastes in food. As a professional bootlegger, Charlie prided himself on his knowledge of imported whiskeys and his taste in French wine. Maranzano, he observed cattily, knew nothing about wine. Charlie liked eating at the Villanova restaurant on West Forty-fifth Street with friends from Vaudeville like Jimmy Durante. But he also liked the small family bistros in Little Italy where he ate with Lucchese and Anastasia. His favorite course was always desert. Wherever he ate, the meal would end with a trip to an ice cream parlor in Little Italy; "I loved that stuff—spumoni, tortoni, Italian ice. But not like they made it in the fancy joints. Only the old guys in the little places knew how to make real ice cream."

Charlie kept an office at Claridge Hotel, but only used it for very private business. Usually he met with his associates in two rooms across from his old hang-out at Moe Ducore's drugstore on Broadway near Fifty-first Street. He'd shifted his business away from Ducore's though; he preferred the food at Dave Miller's Delicatessen a few doors away. When Charlie's friends came over for a business conference, he'd take them over there. "Davey," he'd shout as they walked in, "close up the joint, we're having a meet." Miller would close the blinds and hang a "closed" sign on the door. Then he'd set up his long table with plates of Charlie's favorites—corned beef, pastrami, dill pickles, potato salad, cole slaw, black Greek olives, sliced rye bread, and pumpernickel. The gangsters would make their own sandwiches and get their drinks directly from the cooler. Charlie remembered it as "one helluva Kosher ball." When he walked out, Charlie would deposit one, maybe two, C-notes in the register. Years later, exiled in Naples, it got Charlie's mouth watering just thinking about all that delicious food in Dave Miller's Delicatessen.

Like most gangsters, Charlie was a confirmed night owl. He and Gay made the rounds of the nightspots, another pair of bright young things partying until dawn. He called it the "midnight jamboree". Before setting off, Charlie liked to take in a film; "the best way to clear my mind," he said, "was

to see a movie." The last stop before turning in was usually Dave's Blue
Room, an all night restaurant and demimonde hangout. He'd drop in for a bite
and a talk with Tommy Lucchese, who'd arrange to meet him there. Charlie
and Tommy were in loan-sharking together, and needed to talk business. One
night their conversation was interrupted by the arrival of Dave Rubinoff, an
orchestra leader who played the violin on the Eddie Cantor radio show. But
Rubinoff was also a compulsive gambler, and into Lucchese for ten grand.
Charlie remembered,

> Lucchesecalled him over and said, "How are ya' Ruby? Where ya been?"
> Rubinoff just stands there and starts to shake.
>
> "Ruby, you owe me money. When are you going to pay me?"
>
> "Tommy, listen to me—you don't understand. I'm a little short right now."
>
> Lucchese reached out and took hold of Rubinoff's left hand and began to
> massage the knuckles gently. "You got a nice hand there, Ruby. It makes
> beautiful music. And it makes a lot of money too. Now you don't want noth-
> ing to happen to that hand, do you Ruby?"
>
> Right then and there, I saw that Tommy wasn't kidding. He was really going
> to let Rubinoff have it. Not kill him, but maybe bust his knuckles, like on his
> right hand, not the good left hand that he picks the notes out with.

It was late at night and Charlie was sleepy. He'd hardly been listening to the
conversation. Instead, he realized that what he'd actually been hearing was the
sound of Rubinoff's voice. It was thick and soft, almost furry with its heavy
Russian accent. Just like the sound of Gay's voice he'd been thinking, except
deeper. Suddenly he knew that he couldn't let Tommy go ahead and break this
poor yid's knuckles. He startled Lucchese by breaking into the conversation.
"Get the hell outta here," he told Rubinoff; "and take care of the payment
before noon tomorrow." Fortunately for Charlie's friendship with Lucchese,
Rubinoff managed to get an advance on his salary from Eddie Cantor the next
morning.[4]
   When he left the Blue Room, he often went over to Gay's apartment to
spend a few hours alone with her. She never asked any questions then or made
any demands, never tried to nag him into marrying her. But she was always
good to be with, so Charlie just kept coming back. They remained together, on
and off, for over ten years. She came to visit him in prison. Later he wanted to
take her into exile with him, but it turned out that she was an illegal immigrant
and couldn't get a passport. Still, she came to the pier to wish him bon voyage, and, best of all, bought him a new traveling wardrobe. "I was probably
the best-dressed guy that ever come over from America; I had a different suit
for every day of the month and my underwear, shirts, and pajamas all had the
same little initials on them—real class. I found out later that Gay had it done;

she was nuts about initials, the same as Arnold Rothstein."

Charlie later came to realize that what attracted him about Gay was not only her beauty and class, but also her mystery. She never talked about her past, never even told Charlie where she came from. He didn't even know whether Gay Orlova was her real name. Maybe some guy had just hung it on her, he mused, somebody who thought it was a good name for a showgirl—"Gay All Over." She certainly was that, Charlie said. She was the good-time girl, the one who only lived for the present. She sure loved to drink. And he never really knew anything about her. But wasn't Charlie the little boy from nowhere himself? His favorite story was not the adventures of Admiral Nelson; it was *Oliver Twist*. Not knowing where Gay came from allowed him to fantasize, turning her into his exotic Russian princess or his good-time fairy godmother who was there when he needed her, always ready with just the right gift—pairs of silk boxers with little monogrammed "CL"s.

Charlie may have needed the monograms to remind him who he was in those days. His own name was in a constant state of flux. He officially became Charlie *Luciano* when a precinct house desk sergeant, finding *Lucania* hard to pronounce, slipped out with Luciano instead. That was in 1928, the same year that he checked into the Barbizon. Here he had called himself Charles Lane, choosing a respectable, easy to pronounce, Anglo name, while still making sure that his monogrammed CL pajamas and undies got back to him from the laundry.

Charlie never particularly liked *Lucky* as a nickname. He always thought of himself as Charlie. He particularly disliked being called Lucky Luciano, though this is what the newspapers began to call him. The name was never used by his underworld colleagues. His friends still called him Charlie Luciano or even Charlie Lucania. His soldiers addressed him as "Mr. Luciano." When they were talking about him, however, they began to use a new name, one that soon became common throughout the underworld—*Charlie Lucky*.

As boss, Charlie decided that it was time to up-grade his accommodations once again. He heard that the penthouse suite atop the St. Moritz Hotel was vacant and thought that he might like to lease it for himself. But Walter Winchell raised a stink, telling the management that if they let Luciano into the penthouse suite, he'd move out. Not only that, he said he'd write a column telling his readers why he did so. When the St. Moritz deal fell through, Charlie decided to go all the way and rent an apartment in the Waldorf Towers, the private annex to the Waldorf-Astoria Hotel.

At the time, the $800 per month that it cost to rent a suite in the Waldorf Towers seemed an astronomical sum. At these prices, tenants were hard to find in the depths of the Depression. Charlie was offering cash in advance. He wasn't making any difficulties either. When the management asked him how he wanted it furnished, he was wise enough to distrust his own taste and told them to fix up the place as they saw fit—just so long, he added, as they made it look "classy." Along with smooth," "classy" was his favorite term of approbation. He signed the lease under the name of "Mr. Charles Ross."

I didn't have no trouble with them until some idiot in my outfit came to see me one day. He didn't know what number my apartment was, so he asked the desk clerk. But he didn't ask for Mr. Ross—he asked for Charlie Lucky. The clerk came up to see me later in the afternoon. He said they were getting all kinds of complaints from other people in the building about a notorious gangster living there. Well, I knew the Towers wasn't going to throw me out. After all, I was paying my rent regular, which was more than they could say for some of the bluebloods that was freeloading there. So I figured it was pay-off time. I didn't even ask the clerk how much he wanted. I just reached in my pocket and peeled off two C-notes. And from then on, I gave him two hundred every month, just for himself. I didn't have no trouble after that.[5]

The Towers, he said, was "the best class address in New York." Still, he missed the view from his window at the Barbizon. He missed looking down onto Central Park. He missed the water, "missed watching the people skating on the park and even the ducks swimming on the lake." When he had first moved into the Barbizon, it had been winter. As he walked up to his window for the first time, he had been amazed to see Central Park Lake stretched out below him—covered with ice. There were crowds of skaters moving upon it. The motions struck Charlie as graceful and random, like shifting abstract patterns sketched out in a frigid silence. It was "smooth." They spoke directly to Charlie's mind: "Whenever I had a tough problem, I could stand at my window and watch the skaters—the little kids and their mothers—and it made me feel very peaceful; it cleared my head."[6]

How deeply was Charlie in the ice palace then? He'd been dealing for years. But was he skating too?

When they first examined him in 1936, the doctors at Dannemora classified Luciano as a heroin addict. Prison doctors are known to make bad diagnoses, but not about something like this. They see too much drug addiction, and the signs are hard to miss. Charlie admitted that he had taken a lot of pain-killers in the wake of the Staten Island beating and hints that he might have used narcotics at other times as well. The year of 1936 was awful for Charlie. First there'd been the arrest and then the long, costly, and humiliating trial. By early summer, he was in a holding cell in Manhattan, waiting to be transferred to Dannemora. They'd taken everything away, his money, his expensive suits, his custom shoes. He couldn't control anything anymore, not even his own thoughts. Sitting alone in the hot cell with his head in his hands, he felt he was going out of his mind. He'd been into the stuff pretty heavily for the last few months. Of course they'd taken that away too. And that didn't help. He could use the icy feeling now, the cool flush, the clear head, the detachment, the smoothness—what he had felt long ago watching the small, dark gliding figures gyrating against the clear, gray ice, tiny and distant when made out through the black filigree of barren branches seen from his window high above at the Barbizon.

DRUGS AND THE DEATH OF ARNOLD ROTHSTEIN

Luciano was not the only gangster to use heroin. Gangsters had been smoking dope in Chinatown joss-houses for generations. It had been legal then, or at least not specifically outlawed or controlled. It was in the years before World War I, the time of the reformers and their clean-up campaigns, that new laws limited or prohibited the sale or use of narcotics. The first national law, the Harrison Act, which prohibited the sale of narcotics without prescription, was only passed by Congress in 1914. Back then however, the use of narcotics had not seemed a serious social problem—not like liquor.

To be sure, the opium dens themselves were exotically dangerous, but they were located in the wrong part of town. They attracted only the fallen: "Cheap actors, race track touts, gamblers and the different types of confidence men took to it generally," wrote Hart Crane in 1896. Prostitutes and showgirls sought their solace in hop-houses too. But respectable people did not consume drugs in Chinese opium dens. They consumed them in the privacy of their own homes.

Opiates were freely available, often disguised as cordials or nerve tonics. They were sold in pharmacies and drugstores, usually without a prescription, for medicinal purposes. "At the turn of the century, writes George E. Pettey, patent medicines containing opiates in some form were sold in every drugstore in the country. They were offered for relief of headaches, general aches, various pains, the "misery" and that "tired feeling." School children could go to a local soda fountain and buy a medicated drink containing cocaine."[7] In 1900, according to Mark Sullivan, "the total volume of the business was $59,611,355. The patent medicine manufacturers comprised, at that time, the largest single [national] user of advertising space in newspapers."[8] At its simplest, opium was made into laudanum, an alcohol-based tincture, and dispensed with an eye-dropper. Cocaine could be treated in the same way. Relief usually came in a little, dark-glass stoppered bottle. There was something homely about the dear little stoppered laudanum bottle, especially in comparison with the big bottle. It could be clutched in the palm of the hand or secreted away in a purse. Whiskey and beer were the tipples of choice for the trouble-making classes. But the little stoppered bottle promised respite and surcease rather than presaging any outbreak of violence. Users simply became sedated. At worst, they might wander about the house in wraith-like trances, whimpering pathetically. This still seemed infinitely preferable to disturbing the neighbors with raucous screaming and the breaking of crockery, the predictable result of drunkenness. Overdosing, of course, could be dangerous. Most of the bawds that did themselves in at McGurk's Suicide Hall used some form of patent medicine. Nevertheless, the little stoppered bottle still seemed the more genteel way of getting blotto.

Luciano's only previous conviction had been for selling doses from the little stoppered bottle. It was in 1916, only two years after the Harrison Act, and he was only nineteen, still only Salvatore Lucania. He'd had a near miss in 1923, when he only got off by rolling over on his source. By now, the authorities were growing alarmed. The opium parlor habitués had once seemed like the living dead, souls lost beyond any hope of redemption. But it now appeared that there was a much larger class out there, one which wished to try opiates and, increasingly, cocaine and cannabis resin as well, for what we would now call "recreational purposes."

Katcher assumes that Rothstein learned about narcotics from his young protégé, Salvatore Lucania. It seems possible, though there is no way of proving the assumption; we simply do not know who first alerted Rothstein to the potential in drug smuggling. It was Big Maxey Greenberg who opened Rothstein's eyes in the fall of 1920 to the potential profits in whiskey. At some time, he began to smuggle opiates as well.[9]

Late in 1921 Rothstein stopped his rum running operations. We can only speculate why. Not only would a seizure have proved costly, it would probably have resulted in a trial and bad publicity too. Publicity was what Rothstein most wished to avoid. He was currently at the center of all sorts of shady operations, operations that could easily have become unstuck if he became the object of serious investigations. Rothstein's role as underworld deal maker depended on his keeping his name out of the spotlight. He had made good money during his stint as a bootlegger, but he was a gambling man, one who prided himself on his ability to calculate the odds and see around the corner. Rothstein may have looked at these odds and decided that the risks were just too great.

Nevertheless, even if Rothstein ended his bootlegging career after eleven voyages, he hardly severed his connections with the bootlegging world. He continued to provide funds and connections for other bootleggers—Waxey Gordon, Big Bill Dwyer, and Frank Costello—as well as investing in their clubs and resorts. This was a behind-the-scenes activity which, though less lucrative, carried less risk. He also continued to use connections in the bootlegging world to smuggle in uncut diamonds, stolen objects d'art and, increasingly, drugs. Whether it was Luciano who had first alerted Rothstein to the potential of the drugs business, it was certainly Rothstein who provided Luciano with the network of contacts, suppliers, and outlets that Luciano built into a drug empire.

Shortly before 11 p.m. on the night of November 4, 1928, the operator of the service elevator at the Park Central Hotel at Seventh Avenue and Fifty-sixth Street heard the footsteps of a man staggering in the corridor. The operator went up and asked, "Are you sick?" The man pulled out a one-dollar bill, "Get me a taxi. I've been shot."

The elevator operator ran down to the lobby where he found the hotel detective. According to the detective's later statement:

> I was in the lobby when young Kelly, who works the service elevator, comes running in. He sees me and tells me that a man is shot or sick or something in the service stairway. I go with Kelly and I see this man. He is hanging on the banister with one hand and he is holding his belly with his other. He says,

"Call me a taxi, I've been shot."

I send Kelly to look for a cop. I take a good look at this fellow. . . . Sure I recognize him. Everybody knows Arnold Rothstein. About then, the cop on the beat comes in.[10]

The beat cop in question, Patrolman Davis, first called the station house, "like the book says. Then I go to the hotel. I get one look and I know who he is. I ask him who shot him, and he says, 'Get me home. The address is 912 Fifth Avenue.'"[11]

Rothstein had kept himself out of the headlines, but not entirely out of the limelight. Everybody on Broadway knew who Rothstein was, the house detective, the cop on the beat, the doctor in the ambulance, the hotel maid who tried to clean the room in which he was killed, the waiters at Lindy's where he had been sipping a cup of coffee an hour before the fatal event. His shooting hit the front pages the next day. Everyone in New York now knew that the notorious Arnold Rothstein had been shot, and that he had insisted on calling a taxi and on being taken home, an insistence he repeated for the next two days as he lay dying in the hospital.

The police, of course, knew who Rothstein was. Although they went through the usual stonewalling routine, claiming it was a normal murder case, saying that investigations were well in hand, decrying the undue publicity that the popular press had attached to the case, it was clear that the case had immediately been shunted up to the highest level. There the investigations were stalled. Just three days after the shooting, the *Daily News* complained of the "strange lassitude hampering the activities of the detectives seeking to solve this crime." The "wise ones" along Broadway, the paper continued, had begun to shake their head and wonder who it was who had put in "the fix."

The hand of the police was forced on November 9, when lawyers representing the Rothstein family demanded that the district attorney's office take into its protection all of Rothstein's "books, records, ledgers and any paper having to do with Arnold Rothstein's business and financial affairs." The Rothstein family members were the presumptive heirs, and their concern was understandable. Though rumored to be rich, even fabulously rich, no one had ever known the real contours of the secretive Rothstein's fortune. The Rothstein family wished to ensure that the details of their deceased member's financial empire were placed in safe hands where they would not be tampered with. Yet it was no less obvious that the Rothstein papers might contain other pieces of interesting information. They might, for example, contain clues concerning who killed Arnold Rothstein and why. Despite this, the police had failed to secure these papers at the outset of their investigations. It seemed one example of the "strange lassitude" on their part. The Rothstein family lawyer, William H. Hyman, noted this reluctance and also the reason for it. The papers could provide more than just clues to the Rothstein murder, he said. They could provide insights into ten years' worth of crimes and dirty dealings in New York City. It was essential that the papers be secured immediately, he announced solemnly, for "If those papers are ever made public, there are going to be a lot of suicides in high places."

District Attorney, Joab H. Banton, defended the police, saying that his office had every intention of securing the Rothstein papers. But, in order to protect the value of the estate and the interests of the heirs themselves, he was waiting for Rothstein's employees to go through these papers themselves, many of which were necessary for their businesses. It was a strange way of ensuring their integrity. Rothstein's employees were being allowed to shift though the evidence at their leisure and without supervision. It was especially odd considering that one of these so-called "employees" was Charlie Luciano, who may well have used the opportunity to subtract from the mass any reference to his involvement in the narcotics business. Indeed, newspaper photographers recorded at least a dozen people entering Rothstein's studio and going through the papers before District Attorney Banton decided to take a look himself. When he finally went in, he announced to the press that there had originally been around forty thousand pages of documents, but that now some of these documents had unaccountably gone missing.

Not all of the incriminating evidence was lost however. Federal attorneys had begun to interest themselves in Rothstein's drug empire two years earlier. A few days after the shooting, United States Attorney, Charles H. Tuttle, obtained a federal warrant to go through Rothstein's papers. As Tuttle later explained, for over a year federal agents had been convinced that "the dope traffic in the United States was being directed from one source. More and more, our information convinced us that Arnold Rothstein was that source." Armed with a federal warrant, Tuttle was able to uncover evidence to make major drug seizures in New York, Buffalo, and Chicago and, at the French Line pier on the West Side. Federal agents valued the seized drugs in the millions.[12]

The newspapers were less interested in the drugs than in the usual questions: Who was covering up? Who was holding out? Who was blocking the investigations? The papers were filled with revelations, declarations, and wild theories for months. It was all something of a sham, however. The police knew perfectly well who had killed Arnold Rothstein, as no doubt did the wise ones along Broadway. The problem was simply that they couldn't lay their hands on George McManus.

Six weeks before the fatal shooting, Rothstein had taken part in a poker game. The game had been organized by McManus.

Like everyone else in the New York gambling world, McManus knew who Rothstein was. They had played poked together, and McManus knew that Rothstein was a high roller. So when two high-rollers from out of town blew in and told him that they were looking for a game, McManus thought of Rothstein. Rothstein had no objections. When the game commenced on the night of September 8, it included, along with Rothstein, McManus and the two out-of-towners, three more players from New York.

With his usual modesty, Rothstein probably assumed that he would take the out-of-towners to the cleaners. It had happened this way many times before. But not that night. The game started slowly with pots of several hundred dollars; but the pots rose quickly into the thousands. Rothstein had brought little cash with him that night, playing instead with markers—little slips of paper with a figure in dollars scrawled on them, and with the initials *A.R.* at the bottom. Losing consistently, Rothstein kept writing out fresh markers and throwing them down on the table. The other players collected these markers themselves, throwing them back into the pot to make their own bets. As they did so, cash began to disappear from the table. Pots now consisted of nothing more than piles of white slips of paper lying at the center of the green felt cloth. Stubbornly, Rothstein tried to buck his bad luck, betting on long odds and only digging himself further into a hole. Finally, after more than thirty-six hours, when all the exhausted players insisted on calling it quits, Rothstein challenged one of the out-of-towners to cut a high card for $40,000. The stranger agreed; he was already up by almost $200,000, though most of it was merely in slips of paper. The two men cut and Rothstein lost. The stranger added another A.R. marker to his fistful of confetti.

Early on the morning of September 10, the moment of settling up came. Rothstein collected all his markers, totaled the amounts and announced the results. Then he tore them all up. It was not an entirely unusual procedure; gambling was illegal, and gamblers did not like to walk about with incriminating evidence in their pockets. Still, Rothstein's debt was a large one, around $250,000, and Rothstein's behavior made the strangers uneasy. "Don't worry about it," McManus told them. 'That's A.R. Hell, he's good for it." He told them that Rothstein would get in touch with them in a few days.

But A.R. didn't get in touch with them in a few days, or even a few weeks. Instead, he told his friends that he had no intention of paying. The game had been rigged, he said. His friends demurred: they doubted that the game had been rigged. Even if it had been, they added, Rothstein was still obliged to pay. When columnist Damon Runyon heard the rumors, he went to see Rothstein. "Are you welshing on your bets," he wanted to know.

"I never welsh," Rothstein told him. "I'm just making them sweat a little."[13]

Sweating most was George McManus. As the game's organizer, he acted as the host and guarantor. He was not responsible for Rothstein's debts, of course, but, as the one who had introduced the out-of-towners to Rothstein, he was the one to whom these out-of-towners turned to make sure they got paid. But there was little way that McManus could put pressure on Rothstein. He tried sending Tammany boss Jimmy Hines over to talk to him. Hines was powerful, with connections both in the underworld and at the Hall, but he was not as powerful and well-connected as Arnold Rothstein. Hines could only plead with Rothstein; you're putting poor old McManus in a bind, he said. I'll pay when I'm good and ready to, Rothstein told him, and not one moment before.

Did Rothstein just want to make McManus and the out-of-towners squirm a little? It wouldn't have been very sporting of him. But Rothstein never had any use for good sportsmanship. A good sport, he once remarked caustically, is just a sap who makes a habit out of losing like a gentleman. It is quite possible that Rothstein was making McManus sweat just out of pique. But it is also possible that Rothstein himself was temporarily short of cash.

The narcotics seized after U.S. Attorney Tuttle had taken a look at Rothstein's papers were valued at about $4 million. Official estimates of the street value of seized drugs are notoriously unreliable, and, in whatever case, the profits would have been divided between Rothstein and an army of intermediaries. Nevertheless, the sums involved were very large, enough to pay off the gambling debt several times over. How much Rothstein had spent on acquiring the drugs is something we will never know. Nor will we ever know how much of what Rothstein agreed to pay was cash up front. International drug dealers are not renowned for their trusting dispositions, however, so it seems unlikely that Rothstein had acquired the entire consignment on credit. He had probably been forced to pay for much of it in hard cash. It is thus possible that, at the time he was shot, much of Rothstein's working capital was tied up in drugs, and he was indeed short of cash. If he was holding out on his gambling debts, it was not—or not just—out of pique and congenital bad sportsmanship. He didn't have the money, and wouldn't have the money until his drugs were sold.

Throughout October, his creditors kept hounding him. He confessed to his estranged wife that he had dropped a lot of money in a card game. But he wasn't going to tap himself out to pay it back, he said. He'd done a lot of waiting in his time; now it was his creditors' turn to wait. Carolyn Rothstein was still worried. "If you'd like to make your monthly payment [to me] less, Arnold, I'll understand," she told him a few days before the fatal shooting. He patted her hand and told her not to worry. "Even the Treasury runs short once in a while," he joked. The next she saw him, he was dying in a hospital bed.

Immediately after arriving at the Polyclinic Hospital, Rothstein was wheeled into the operating room where the surgeons extracted the bullet. There had been massive internal bleeding. After the operation, he was sedated and put to bed in a guarded room. The first person he saw on waking was Detective Patrick Flood.

"Hello, Paddy," he said, recognizing him.

"Hello, Arnold. Who shot you?"

"I won't talk about it. I'll take care of it myself."

Flood stood up. "Get well quick, Arnold," he said. He walked out into the corridor and told the assembled reporters that Rothstein had told him nothing. It was the extent of police questioning.

Later Carolyn Rothstein rushed in. By now, Rothstein was drifting in and out of consciousness. Three times Rothstein came to. Each time he looked for

Carolyn and asked her to take him home. Why the concern for getting back to his apartment? Rothstein would surely have kept some record of his drug deal back home. It is only speculation, but it is possible that he wanted to get home and destroy the evidence before someone else found it.[14]

McManus was probably drunk when he shot Rothstein. He'd been drinking and working himself up for days. Still, dead men don't pay gambling debts. Had McManus been sober, he would never have shot Rothstein. Rothstein knew that too, and so he had not expected to be shot. But he hadn't wanted to rile the big, angry Irishman either. That is why he gave his revolver away before setting off to meet McManus. McManus had probably swaggered and threatened Rothstein the moment he came through the door. Rothstein, who despised drunks, would have said something cold and sarcastic. It was too much for McManus. He shot Rothstein one time, at close range. McManus, who at six feet two was much taller than Rothstein, probably just fired blindly. The bullet hit Rothstein in the stomach and then sped downwards, ripping its way through internal organs as it went.

Frank Costello's biographer, Leonard Katz, writes that, after the death of Rothstein, his surviving heirs split up his empire among them. Lepke took over the unions; Dutch Schultz took the numbers racket; Frank Costello took the rest of the gambling. But Charlie Lucky, he tells us, got the drugs. It is an over-simplification. Rothstein did deals; it was not in his nature to bequeath anything to anyone. Besides, neither the gambling nor the drug rackets were ever exclusively Rothstein's to bequeath. Luciano was not the only one of Arnold's boys to launch himself in the drug world. Waxey Gordon and Lepke Buchalter became major drug dealers, though Lepke's real accession dates from after Rothstein's death. After 1925, Rothstein began supplying drugs to the Torrio-Capone Outfit in Chicago, King Solomon's syndicate in Boston, and Nig Rosen's syndicate in Philadelphia. After he retired from bootlegging, Rothstein retained the service of Henry Madden, using him to supply drugs from Europe. Later Madden was joined by Dapper Dan Collins, Jacob "Yasha" Katzenberg and Sid Stajer. By 1927, Rothstein had become big enough to seek suppliers directly in Asia, sending Katzenberg and Stajar to China and Hong Kong, where they were later joined by George Uffner. By now, the distribution network was broadening at home as well, and Rothstein brought in Costello's partner, Phil Kastel. After Rothstein's death, Luciano and Lepke continued to deal directly with these suppliers, using Yasha Katzenberg as their main Chinese connection. Katzenberg was later joined by egregious labor thug and Lepke associate, Curly Holz. Had he lived long enough to see it flower, Rothstein might have discovered that drugs were destined to become the most profitable racket of them all.[15]

UNCLE FRANK

Among the interesting tidbits that the New York police eventually dredged from the mountains of papers in Rothstein's apartment was an IOU for

$40,000, signed by Frank Costello. But Costello had never made any attempt to hide his association with Rothstein. Costello acknowledged that the marker was indeed his. Though he declined to explain what the particular marker was for, it later turned out that he needed the money to buy a brewery. Rothstein's lawyers considered the marker a legitimate debt, an opinion that Costello never contested. Rothstein's estate was able to collect in full. Unlike Luciano, who frequently faded into the darkness, the better to hide his criminal activities, the jovial Costello emerged into the sunlight.

When Luciano moved into the Astoria Towers in 1931, he acquired some new neighbors. Benny Siegel and Frank Costello each maintained suites at the Waldorf-Astoria Hotel.

Like Charlie, Costello loved grand hotels. Even when he was staying in his apartment on Central Park West, Frank would show up every morning at the Waldorf barbershop for a shave, trim, massage, and manicure. It was his little ritual, his way of starting his business day. As he sat there, he chatted with his lieutenants, Frank Erickson or Dandy Phil Kastel, who sat in the chairs next to his. He socialized with his more legitimate friends, the ones who knew that, first thing in the morning, they could always find Costello in the Waldorf barbershop. "They gave Costello a face like a baby's ass," Luciano remembered. Charlie, whose taste in self-indulgence tended more towards silk underwear than towards facials, thought Frank was "nuts." "I wouldn't let a barber get a razor that close to my face," he opined.

After spending his morning relaxing, and talking in the barber's chair, Costello liked to retire to the Peacock Alley, off the main lobby, for lunch. The hotel reserved a special table for him. Here he got down to serious business. During racing season he would sometimes entertain J. Edgar Hoover.

Benny Siegel was increasingly on the West Coast. He was well-liked there. Robert Lacey notes that "people who got to know Benny Siegel personally have countless tales of his warmth and charm. It is difficult, in fact, to find much evidence of his ever doing a mean deed in his life—with the exception of breaking the noses of people who called him Bugsy, and killing the people who really upset him." When Siegel was in residence in New York, he liked to invite Meyer Lansky and his wife over for lunch. Unlike Costello, however, Siegel and the Lanskys preferred the kitschy Wagnerian splendour of the Waldorf's Norse Grill. Their table was close to that of ex-president Herbert Hoover, another of the Waldorf-Astoria's distinguished residents.

Costello was now a very rich man. With Rothstein's backing, Costello and Bill Dwyer had grown into New York's biggest bootlegging team. Costello had even arranged for his shipments from Europe to be stockpiled in St. Pierre and Miquelon, turning these two tiny, French-owned islands at the mouth of the St. Lawrence Seaway into his own private discount liquor warehouse.

In the mid-1920s, Costello started to embark on another career. We saw that, leaving Chicago for Europe after his nine-month prison stretch in 1925, Johnnie Torrio had stopped in New York and paid a call on his young friends Luciano, Costello, and Lansky. When he predicted that Prohibition would eventually be repealed, adding that, while in Europe, he intended to buy the U.S. distribution rights for all the best Scotches while they were still going cheap, Charlie was dumbfounded. Here was Torrio in 1925 predicting that "my whole fucking bootleg business, and everybody else's for that matter, was going to wind up in the shithouse." Charlie never moved on Torrio's proposal; but it set Frank and Meyer thinking. Torrio also gave his three friends one more piece of useful advice; "You gotta get into big politics. You can buy top politicians the same way you bought the law." It was this last piece of advice that Costello took most seriously.

Like Charlie and Meyer, Costello had started out as one of Rothstein's boys. Rothstein himself had been Charles Murphy's secretary for underworld affairs with special responsibility for gambling pay-offs. Rothstein thus served as the conduit between Tammany and the underworld. Like other bootleggers, Costello, Luciano, and Lansky were sometimes arrested. But Rothstein saw that their charges always ended up marked "dismissed." The fix went in at the preliminary hearing, before the case got to the newspapers and stirred up publicity. Assistant district attorneys suddenly discovered that they had insufficient evidence. Important witness somehow never showed up. Police officers suffered sudden lapses of memory; they were no longer so sure that they'd seen what they thought they had seen. Most Prohibition violations in New York ended up this way—fixed before committal proceedings. "Of the 6,902 liquor law cases called," reports Katcher, "6,074 were dismissed at inception." Of the remaining cases, another four hundred never made it to trial. All told, seven out of every eight cases of Prohibition violations never made it past the Magistrate's Court.[16]

When Murphy died and was succeeded by lesser men, Tammany's control over Rothstein weakened. Rothstein went independent, becoming a rogue fixer and underworld busybody, still connected to Tammany through Foley, Hines, and Marinelli, but accountable to none of them. He had become New York's king of bailbonding, as well as the man who could probably quote you the going price for most of the magistrates and assistant district attorneys in the five boroughs—many of whom were beholden to Mr. Rothstein for the offices they held.

Rothstein was, as Katcher reports, the solvent that continued to hold Tammany and the underworld together in the second half of the 1920s. It was a position on the doorstep that gave him an immense power. After Rothstein's death, Costello inherited more than his gambling empire; he inherited the role of solvent, bonding the under- and überworlds together. Frank Costello was soon buying important friends as fast as Charlie Lucky was buying silk pajamas.

Rothstein was a creature of shadows, a man, in Gene Fowler's memorable phrase, "who dwelt in doorways. A mouse standing in a doorway, waiting for his cheese." Rothstein shunned publicity and hid his underworld associations. Costello, by contrast, thrived on light. He seemed to have emerged from the Italian underworld and stepped out into the überworld and legitimacy. Shor described those days like this:

> Jimminy Cricket, it was a different era then. In those days you'd walk into Moore's Restaurant, and you'd see all the politicians, men like Jimmy Walker and Jim Farley. You'd see all those guys. You'd see Frank Costello sitting at one table and Charley Sherman, who was supposed to be a tough guy, sitting at another. You'd see them all sitting around talking to one another."

> Then you'd go to the Plaza Theater, and you'd see Owney Madden and those fellows, all those judges and politicians and the other side. They'd say hello to each other. Or you'd go to the Palace Theater. It was a Vaudeville house, and it was a big thing to go on Sunday nights. Then you'd go to the Cotton Club, and you'd see the same people at all those places. You'd see Frank Costello and his wife and these different fellows and their wives, all the gamblers and bootleggers. All they ever did was gamble and bootleg.[17]

THE FALL OF CAPONE

The prison surgeon who took out Al's tonsils told the press that he had never seen a prisoner "so kind, so cheery and accommodating." Capone, he continued, "has brains. He would have made good anywhere, at anything. He had been an ideal prisoner. I cannot estimate the money he has given away. Of course, we can't inquire where he gets it. He's in the racket. He admits it. But you can't tell me he's all bad after I've seen him many times a week for ten months."[18]

Not everybody was so scrupulous about inquiring "where he gets it." In 1927, the Supreme Court supported Mabel Walker Willebrandt's campaign against the bootleggers by ruling that, regardless of how he gets it, a man still has to pay a tax on his income. The government, in short, had a legal right to collect taxes on illegal money. With this ruling, the Internal Revenue's Enforcement Branch set up shop in Chicago.

The tax inspectors started with the Druggan-Lake gang. They turned next to Al's brother, Ralph. After exhausting all the delaying techniques his lawyers could think of, Ralph was fined $100,000 in early 1930 and sentenced to three years in prison. They turned to Jake Guzik next. On the strength of the testimony of the messenger Guzik used to convert his cash take into banker's checks, Guzik was fined $17,500 and sentenced to five years in prison. In December 1930, Frank Nitti pleaded guilty to evading $158,823 in taxes and was sentenced to eighteen months in prison and a $10,000 fine.

The investigators had started their investigations of the Big Fella as early as 1928, methodically tracking down every item of expenditure of Capone and his household. They planted spies in his outfit. They shifted through the mound of evidence from police seizures after the 1926 McSwiggen killing. By late 1930 they were closing in. They had turned up Lou Shumway, the bookkeeper at Capone's betting establishment in Cicero, the Ship. Possibly Shumway had offended the Chicago Outfit in some particular, for he was not at all anxious to be publicly identified. In exchange for a promise of police protection, Shumway made a deposition to the grand jury.

These were the years that had brought Capone accolades of sorts. In 1930, along with Albert Einstein, and Mahatma Gandhi, Al Capone was voted on of the ten "outstanding personalities of the world" by Chicago's Medill School of Journalism. In the following year, the Chicago Crime Commission, which had once regarded Capone as Public Enemy No. 1, dropped him from their roster entirely. It was now official; whatever the government might say, Al Capone was no longer a public menace; he was simply a major celebrity.

Big Al played the part. When he walked out of Philadelphia's Holmesburg County Prison in March 1930, the New York stock market had crashed, and America was entering the Depression. Beneath a sign reading "Free Food For The Workless," Capone was soon financing a soup kitchen on the Chicago's South Side that served one hundred twenty thousand meals in six weeks. Capone, his brother Ralph claimed, fed three thousand unemployed every day. On Thanksgiving Day, Capone donated an extra five thousand turkeys. He threw a huge Christmas party in Little Italy, where one old woman knelt before him and kissed his hand. Capone the philanthropist.[19]

There were other Capones as well. The treasury agents who discovered Shumway working as a cashier at the Biscayne Kennel Club also observed Capone at the near-by Hialeah Racetrack. He was "greeting a parade of fawning sycophants who came to shake his hand—a veritable Shah of Persia." Mr. and Mrs. Alphonse Capone threw elegant soirees in their Palm Island residence to which Miami society and show business personalities were invited. The Hawthorne Inn in Cicero, or "Capone's Castle" as the tour-bus guides called it, was becoming an impromptu national monument. A whole literary industry was springing up around Capone. In Hollywood, the 1930 success of First National's *Little Caesar* with Edward G. Robinson was followed by the Warner Brothers' *Public Enemy*, starring James Cagney, and Howard Hughes's *Scarface*, starring Paul Muni. While "Rico," the character played by Edward G. Robinson, was a generic Italo-American gangster, the movie-going public had little difficult in identifying Hymie Weiss in Jimmy Cagney's character and Al Capone as the gangster played by Paul Muni.

Damon Runyon covered Capone's 1931 tax evasion trial for the Hearst press, giving his readers the latest on Capone's inexhaustible wardrobe. When he arrived at the Federal Court Building on the morning of June 16 to fix the date of his hearing, he wore a suit of banana yellow. He was clad in white-bordered black silk pajamas when he talked with the reporters in his Hotel Lexington suite on the hearing's eve. When the trial got underway in October, the reporters noted, not only did Capone wear eleven different outfits on eleven consecutive days, but eleven different color combinations. These are the touches we lose in the black-and-white photos. For the summations on October 17, we learn that Capone wore a grass green suit. For the sentencing a week later, he wore heater-purple pinchback suit. Capone the fashion plate.

But all these Capones finally collapsed in 1932 when, appeals exhausted, Al Capone simply became prisoner no. 40822 in the Atlanta Penitentiary, serving out a ten-year sentence for tax evasion.

BRING ON THE FEDS

Failing to file a personal income tax form is a *federal* crime. Capone had been targeted by *federal* agencies—the IRS and U.S. attorneys. He was sentenced by a *federal* judge in a *federal* court.

The Bureau of Prohibition was also a federal agency, of course. But it had failed miserably in its task and was by now an object of near-universal derision. Nor did it seem likely that state and local authorities would step in to fill the breach. Dimly perceiving perhaps that strict enforcement of the Volstead Act was not what the voters, at least the urban voters, really wanted, elected officials hesitated before committing tax-payers' dollars to putting more armed policemen on the streets, especially since the immediate result of such a policy was likely to be more officials "on the pad," more citizens in prison and, quite probably, more citizens shedding their blood on the city streets. By now, state and local officials were quietly cutting back their enforcement efforts instead of ramping them up. That left the federal government.

In 1929 the new Hoover administration had made a show of its earnestness and good intentions. One manifestation of the new get-serious policy was Elliot Ness and his legendary "Untouchables." Ness began his operations in Chicago while Capone was serving his sentence in Philadelphia. Declaring war on the bootleggers, the incorruptible Norwegian-American did succeed in temporarily disrupting the Outfit's operations.

Yet by now the Outfit had seen that Prohibition's days were numbered. As Ness was moving in on their speakeasies, the Outfit was moving out, expanding into trade unionism and other "legitimate rackets," some of which they found to be even more profitable than the over-crowded bootlegging industry. Indeed the problem of how to enforce Prohibition was no longer even the real question, for by now it was apparent that Prohibition was unenforceable.

With New York City, Chicago as well as the state legislations in New Jersey and Connecticut openly refusing to cooperate with the Bureau of Prohibition and the Democrat Party advocating its repeal, it must have been clear to even the most moss-backed Methodist preacher that the Noble Experiment was dead as a dodo. Redoubling the enforcement efforts would not bring Prohibition back to life. The real problem was, by now, quite a different one: it was organized crime. The failure of Prohibition had given bootlegging syndicates a free hand, a vacuum to grow into. After nearly a decade's experience in running the bootlegging business, crime had become bigger, more entrepreneurial and more business-like. In a word, it had become more organized, not just at a municipal level but at interstate levels as well. Organized crime had put down roots. Prohibition legislation might come and go, but organized crime intended to stay. What the government truly needed was a policy to combat organized crime, and this policy, by its very nature, needed to be coordinated at a federal rather than a municipal or state level. Thus starting with the Hoover administration in 1928 and continuing under Roosevelt, the fight against organized crime would be led by the "Feds" or the "G-men."

In principle, the fight against organized crime was everyone's business; it was a struggle that united federal and local agencies. Or at least it ought to have. The reality was rather more complicated. The Constitution vests police power largely in state rather than in federal hands. The Bureau of Prohibition, an experiment in federal police power, had been exceptional in this respect. It had also been a failure. The problem was now one of extending federal police power effectively into the states and cities without violating Constitutional law and, equally important, without setting off debilitating turf wars between federal and local authorities. One of the advantages of using treasury officials to prosecute gangsters for income tax evasion was that, since state and municipal police forces were ill-equipped to conduct such investigations, the possibility for conflict was less. Still, a potential for conflict remained, and was, indeed, exacerbated by a common misperception.

Back in the 1890s reformers had laid the blame for what Lincoln Steffens called "the sins of the cities," notably prostitution, gambling, and drunkenness, on the corrupt municipal machines. The Rev. Dr. Charles Parkhurst coined the term *organized crime* in 1892 to describe the relation between prostitution, the New York police, and Tammany.[20] The diagnosis was substantially true at the time, at least in regard to prostitution and gambling. It was no longer true, however, in regard to bootlegging in the 1920s. We saw that Capone gave Bathhouse John Coughlin a friendly warning to keep out of his way. Coughlin and Kenna were from the horse-and-buggy days of municipal corruption; Capone was now running fleets of trucks in from New York and over from Canada. He was conducting war operations in Detroit and Cleveland. The last thing he needed was a couple of old-style boodlers bumbling all over the battlefield. Nevertheless, the perception remained. Big Bill Thompson, the Chicago *Tribune* proclaimed, was behind the Capone Outfit. Admittedly, Big Bill was never much of an asset in the fight against organized crime in Chicago; he let fester bureaucratic rivalries between the police and the state attorney's office. Yet he had no interest in protecting Capone or fostering any of the Outfit's activities. Tammany in New York was later accused of protecting Costello. But, as Daniel Bell astutely observes, the relationship was really the other way around. With Franklin Roosevelt in the White House and Fiorello La Guardia in Gracie Mansion, the political roar of the once almighty Tammany tiger had dwindled to a faint meow. Costello could have run his games anywhere he wanted. He agreed to use Tammany clubhouses because, that way, his old friends at Tammany could pay the heating bills and keep their clubs open at night.[21]

Criminal syndicates in Chicago and New York still practiced bribery and corruption on a massive scale, but they were no longer managed by the political machines. They managed themselves. Organized crime had evolved; it had kept up with the times. Often for partisan political reasons, contemporaries were often reluctant to acknowledge this fact.

THE COUNTER-OFFENSIVE IN NEW YORK

If New Yorkers continued to vote Democrat during the 1920s, it was not out of love for Tammany. Boss Murphy had hoped to save the Hall by adopting a reformist course; but the attempt could never be more than a partial success. Tammany Hall was a patronage-dispensing machine; the machine functioned to manage the political status quo. Nevertheless, under Murphy's leadership, Tammany had supported reformist candidates, candidates who, once elected to office, could exercise reformist leadership. Murphy's strategy came to fruition with the election of Al Smith as New York State governor in 1919. Proving an able governor, Smith devoted his attentions to administrative and legislative reform. Political credit for Smith's success, however, redounded primarily to Smith and his associates and to the New York Democrats rather than to Tammany. New Yorkers voted Democrat because they liked Smith.

New Yorkers also liked their Tammany "night mayor," the high-stepping, dapper little Jimmy Walker. Walker had defeated the Hearst mayor, "Red" Hylan, and had won a second term in office in 1929. During the campaign, his Fusionist-Republican adversary, La Guardia, accused him of spending his nights in "whoopee joints," leaving $200 tips to the hat-check girl. More damaging, he accused the Walker administration of dragging its feet on the investigation of Rothstein's murder for fear of the dirt that would inevitably come out. He flourished a letter from Rothstein's files showing that Judge Albert H. Vitale, a Tammany judge campaigning for Walker, had an outstanding marker for $19,940 with Rothstein. It was all in vain. Walker embodied the spirit of the times and won re-election easily.

The following year, however, Mayor Walker and his girlfriend, the showgirl Betty Compton, were caught in a raid on a red carpet joint in Montauk, Long Island. Walker ducked out the moment the police burst in, and later persuaded the assistant sheriff of the Montauk police to pretend he hadn't seen him. But his girlfriend Betty, in the back room winning heavily at the roulette wheel, got caught. When she and the other patrons were marched out through the kitchen, she glimpsed Mayor Walker, sitting at the table with a waiter's apron on, trying to look inconspicuous as he ate a plate of beans with the kitchen staff. Understandably, Betty felt peeved. First she'd lost her winnings, and now her escort had deserted her, sneaking off, leaving her to spend the rest of her evening waiting for the magistrate to show up at night court in deepest Long Island. Nor could the escapade remain secret very long. Governor Franklin Roosevelt later questioned Walker about his ungallant behavior. Walker replied that he didn't want to tempt fate "by showing up in a rural hoosegow."

Beau James could still get away with pranks like these. It had been Walker who, as mayor, had instructed the NYPD to protect Owney Madden's West Side Phoenix Brewery, while it had been Governor Al Smith who had repealed the Mullen-Gage Act and had run as a Wet for the presidency. The New York Democrat Party was heroically leading the fight against Prohibition, and the city's voters backed them all the way.

In 1929, however, trouble erupted within the New York Democrat Party itself. In August of that year, Governor Roosevelt asked the appellate division of the First Judicial Department to authorize an investigation into instances of alleged misconduct in the city's magistrate courts. The appellate division nominated a reformist Democrat, Judge Samuel Seabury, as referee. A Tammany adversary of long standing, Judge Seabury's three successive investigations lasted until 1932 and threw an ugly spotlight first upon the magistrate courts, revealing the venality and sheer incompetence of many of the political hacks whose only qualification for their seat on the bench was loyal service to Tammany. It was the Seabury inquiries that forced the resignation of Walker and gave the mayor's office to the Fusionist-Republican candidate, Fiorello La Guardia.

At five foot two inches tall, and with a voice as rough and nasal as Costello's, the distinctly rotund, frequently disheveled and irrepressibly bumptious La Guardia was hardly anybody's notion of what the mayor of America's largest city ought to look like. Throughout the 1929 campaign, Al Smith's advisor, Frances Perkins, thought him an improbable candidate. Standing next to the elegant Jimmy Walker, she said, La Guardia "looked like a lump."

Nor had La Guardia ever been the Repubican candidate of choice. Traditionally the more disciplined of the two parties, for many New York Republicans the uncontainable Italian was a morsel far from easy to digest. Yet La Guardia looked like he might be a winner, and the party badly needed a winner; it hadn't had one since Purroy Mitchel. Franklin's Roosevelt's landslide victory in 1932 crushed any illusions that the Republicans in New York might have nursed that the party of Herbert Hoover would reap benefits from Jimmy Walker's fall. The party needed a candidate that didn't look like other Republicans. The feisty congressman was at least technically a Republican. So in 1933, it was La Guardia or nothing. Still, it was never more than a temporary agreement. The Republicans would support La Guardia until a real Republican came along.

Over one issue, however, there was no disagreement. La Guardia, the Republicans, and the anti-Tammany Democrats all wanted to put the gangsters out of business. Shortly after his election, La Guardia took to the radio to tell his fellow citizens his policy towards racketeers. The theme was, in La Guardia's own words, "let's drive the bums out of town." He began with Costello.

Vending-machines that dispensed candy or soft drinks were all legitimate. Machines that were used for gambling were illegal. But what about pin-ball machines, which, as gaming machines, might be used for gambling? What about vending machines that also allowed gambling? Costello fixed his fruit machines so that every time a nickel was put into the slot and the handle pulled, a little packet of mints dropped into the tray below. In this way, his fruit machines could be classified as vending machines. If the fruit machine also came up with a winning combination—three cherries or three bars or whatever—the machine would throw out some slugs as well. These slugs could be used for re-plays or redeemed for cash. Costello came up with this gimmick in 1930, and even founded his own confectionery company, the Triangle Mint Company, to supply him with the mints.

By 1931 Costello had installed more than five thousand of these doctored machines in speakeasies, stationary stores, and candy stores in New York. When the candy store was near a school, he thoughtfully installed little ladders so the kiddies would not be left out. It is hard to estimate how much he made out of the operation. In the first place, it was franchised. Costello, Luciano, and the other bosses gave their friends and the soldiers in their Families the stickers for a definite number of machines—usually around twenty. It would be up to the franchise-holder to place the machines and see to their upkeep.[22] It was like the franchising of stills during Prohibition. The franchise-holder was expected to kick a certain fixed amount upstairs every week. Costello took care of most of the ice, bribing policemen and judges.

Leonard Katz estimates that Frank's daily gross from slot machines was about $50,000, which came to over $18 million a year, tax-free. Most of this, of course, went toward overhead. Costello not only had to pay his employees and franchise-holders; he was icing dozens of politicians and judges and seemingly about half of the NYPD. Still, even if he only managed to keep 10 percent himself, $1.8 million per year was an incredible take in the first years of the Depression. It was, as Leonard Katz puts it, "a lovely racket."

Costello certainly loved it. His police tail, Rudolph McLaughlin, remembers that during the slot-machine days, Frank would walk between five and seven miles each day, uptown, downtown, all over New York. It was not that Costello couldn't afford a cab. He could have bought a whole cab company with just a week's take on his machines. It was just that Frank loved walking. He liked sunny days on the streets of New York; he liked people recognizing him, waving to him, running up to ask him for a favor or a racing tip. He liked to pop into the places where his machines were, run his hands over them, check that the little pink triangular sticker was in place, and exchange a few pleasantries with the proprietor. He was happy to hear about other people making money from his rackets. He never seemed to get tired. His bodyguard, Big Jim O'Connell, may have felt otherwise. Big Jim had served as a skipper in Costello's "Sunset Fleet" of rum-runners. He was beefy, red-faced man of over 250 pounds, occasionally foot-sore, it seems, from having to follow Frank around all day. McLaughlin, who tailed the pair of them, sympathized with Big Jim. O'Connell, he discovered, was less a bodyguard than a companion and buffer: if you wanted to talk to Mr. Costello, you had to go through Big Jim. Indeed, sometimes McLauglin got sucked in as well, becoming less Costello's police tail than part of his posse.

In October 1934, La Guardia organized a press photo-op. Standing on a police tugboat loaded with confiscated slot machines while the photographers crouched with their flash cameras on the pier alongside, La Guardia took off his jacket, grabbed a sledgehammer and started pounding away on Costello's machines. "A picture like this," he announced to the press, "is worth a thousand indictments."

"I hate to say this, Mayor La Guardia," shouted one of the newsmen standing on the pier, "but what you're doing is illegal."

"That just makes it more fun," replied La Guardia, pounding away.

It would not remain illegal for long. Costello's lawyers had obtained a ruling enjoining the police from tampering with his slot machines. La Guardia's Fusion administration fought the injunction all the way up to the Supreme Court. In May 1934, they obtained a ruling that allowed them to amend the state penal code in such a way as to give the state clear title to seize and destroy anything it considered a gambling machine.[23]

In 1935, La Guardia grabbed the headlines once again. He told Commissioner of Market, Fellows Morgan, to meet him at his home at 6 a.m. on December 20, "the shortest and coldest day of the year," as Morgan recalled years later. La Guardia was plainly up to something. As the two men journeyed to the Bronx Terminal Market, Morgan noticed that the mayor was bringing a set of rolled-up notices. When they arrived, he further noticed that the mayor had arranged a company of police buglers to be standing in front of the market restaurant. So cold was the morning that before they could blow their call, the buglers had to be taken inside the restaurant to thaw out. Having resolved this minor glitch, Morgan watched as the mayor climbed a platform and, as the bugles blew their call, unrolled one of the notices. It was a proclamation. Under an obscure clause in the city's archaic charter, the mayor had the power to ban the distribution of foodstuffs. By the power vested in me as Mayor of New York, La Guardia grandly announced, I am henceforth banning the distribution of artichokes. He handed copies of the proclamation to the police and told them to post them around the market.

The meaning of the spectacle was lost on no one. The distribution of artichokes in New York was controlled by the Union Pacific Produce Company, and the Union Pacific Produce Company was controlled by Ciro Terranova, New York's "artichoke king."

"I want it clearly understood," La Guardia told the assembled porters, truckers, and distributors, "that no bunch of racketeers, thugs, and punks is going to intimidate you as long as I am mayor of the City of New York."

The stunt received enormous publicity, even if some of it was, to say the least, bemused. Do we really need the mayor making a spectacle of himself as the "protector of the virtue of artichokes," inquired the *Herald Tribune*. Distributors had a right to distribute artichokes, the *Post* thundered, and the mayor had no right to rule the city by proclamations. The mayor was unperturbed; the point of theatrics is after all to make publicity, even bad publicity. The mayor was publicizing his determination to fight racketeers, thugs, and punks, and in this endeavor he had succeeded brilliantly.[24]

Early in his first term, La Guardia had selected a comparatively low-ranking police official, Lewis J. Valentine, as police commissioner because Valentine had the reputation of being a tough but honest cop. It was Valentine who issued the famous "muss 'em up" order. When he noticed a gunman in the day's police line-up impeccably dressed in a Chesterfield coat, he told the officers, "When you meet men like that, don't be afraid to muss 'em up. Blood should be smeared all over that man's velvet collar. . . . With killers, racketeers, and gangster's the sky's the limit." Cops on the beat should treat them as a breed with no civil rights, "You can club them with impunity."

Responding to criticism of Valentine's statement, La Guardia publicly sided with his new police commissioner, announcing "It's about time we gave honest people a break." The result once again was mixed publicity. The *Times* supported the mayor while the *Herald Tribune* worried about civil rights violations. La Guardia took no part in the ensuing debate; once more he had made his point. He and Valentine were declaring open season on gangsters.[25]

La Guardia was not the only man in New York hoping to establish his credentials as a gang-buster. The post of district attorney is an elective one. This could mean that in New York City the five boroughs' district attorney's offices were, like the New York magistracy, filled by Tammany nominees. The Seabury inquiries into the magistracy soon spread over into the district attorney's office. Hoping to avoid further scandal, the Democrat Governor, Herbert Lehman, decided to appoint a special prosecutor. He provided District Attorney Dodge with a list of four men, all prominent Republican jurists, ordering District Attorney Dodge to appoint one of the four to the post. But when Dodge called upon the four men, he discovered that each had pressing reasons for not accepting the nomination. Instead, the four issued a press statement urging Dodge to appoint the one man that Tammany least wanted to see in the job—Thomas E. Dewey.

Raised in Owosso, a small town in the farming belt of central Michigan where, as he later put it, "it wasn't quite respectable to be a Democrat," Dewey had come to Manhattan as an aspiring young lawyer and immediately joined the Young Republicans. He attracted the attention of George Medalie, a prominent lawyer influential in the Republican Party. When Medalie was nominated U.S. attorney in 1930, Dewey came with him as his chief assistant, leading in the well-publicized investigations into the activities of Waxey Gordon and Legs Diamond.

Dewey had carefully studied the Capone case. The federal prosecutors had not bothered with the question of how Capone had gotten his money; they concentrated instead on whether he had paid his taxes. To prove that Capone had been earning far more than he had declared, Elmer L. Irey, chief investigator for the Treasury Department, had meticulously gone through every record of the expenditures of Capone and his family. It was an investigation that demanded painstaking work by a team of skilled investigators, one that had demanded the resources of the federal government. As assistant U.S. attorney for the Southern District (which included most of New York), Dewey was able to obtain the assistance of Irey and his Treasury agents as well as of federal lawyers and FBI and Narcotics Squad agents. He even obtained the cooperation of federal postal inspectors, who were empowered to snoop on the mails. With their help, Dewey extended the investigations into Waxey Gordon and Dutch Schultz.

Six months later during his prosecution of Gordon, Dewey was relentless. Before the jury he carefully reconstructed the eminent gangster's lifestyle—the limousines, the maids and chauffeurs, the expensive private schools for his children, the silk shirts and underwear, the closets bursting with tailored suits, the furnishings, and the bookshelves lined with Morocco-bound collections of classics of English literature. Dewey toyed with Waxey on the stand, making him squirm and wiggle, catching him in inconsistency after inconsistency, permitting him to plead and seek to justify himself in his thick, Lower East Side accent. The jury took only fifty-minutes to reach the verdict of guilty. Congratulating Dewey, the judge sentenced Waxey to ten years' imprisonment.[26]

Working with Medalie on the Waxey Gordon case, Dewey knew the value of the tax statutes. He knew that racket-busting was also an exercise in public relations. The public wanted the racket-busters to go after the big shots, the big racketeers and gamblers whose names had come out in the Seabury inquiries. In 1934, J. Edgar Hoover had named Dutch Schultz as the FBI's Public Enemy No. 1. This was now Dewey's obvious target.

THE DUTCHMAN

Born and raised in the Bronx, Arthur Simon Flegenheimer served his first and only prison term at the age of seventeen for burglarizing a Bronx apartment. Sent to Blackwell's Island (today's Roosevelt Island) in the East River, his behavior there was so uncouth that he was transferred to the tougher prison, from which he managed to escape. Captured a bare two hours later, he had a month's extension of jail time tacked on for each of his hours of freedom. Released in 1920, he returned to his old Bergen Avenue gang with his prestige enhanced and with a new name, chosen after a member of the legendary Frog Hollow Gang—Dutch Schultz.

Schultz spent most of the 1920s in comparative obscurity. He was used for any sort of "heavy" work in New York, usually supplying extra muscle for bootlegging runs, eventually rising to the position of beer-truck driver, where he met Luciano, Lansky, and the Diamond brothers. In early 1928, Schultz and his childhood friend, Joey Noe, began setting up their own beer business in the Bronx, making up for their late start by their ruthless sales technique. The gang expanded southwards towards Harlem and the Upper West Side—encroaching on the territory of Legs Diamond.

The Diamond gang responded by cornering Noe outside the Chateau Madrid, a nightclub on West Fifty-fourth, in October 1928. Despite the bullet-proof vest he was wearing, Noe was hit in the chest and lower spine and later died. He had been Schultz's only real friend, the only one, Paul Sann wrote, who called him Arthur, just like the days when they were street kids on Bergen Avenue together. Noe was the only one Schultz ever took along when he went to see his mother. When Noe died, Schultz was distraught.

Wanted by the police, Legs Diamond had been hiding out in an apartment in Albany. His one contact with the outside world was his mistress, the dancer Kiki Roberts. Tailing Kiki, Schultz's enforcer, Bo Weinberg, found out where that apartment was. On the night of December 18, 1931, Legs returned to his hide-out after beating a murder rap in New York City:

> Jack (Legs) Diamond, laughing in alcoholic glee at his latest victory over the law, marched from the arms of the titian-haired Kiki Roberts into the fatal revolver blast of Manhattan assassins, detectives determined tonight. . . . Three times in the last four years his enemies tried to put him on the spot. Each time Legs went to a hospital. Each time he cheated death. But after his last miraculous recovery it was declared that his body was so full of lead that it would sink in Salt Lake. . . . Three soft-nosed bullets had ripped through Diamond's head. All entered on the left side and from the deep powder burns about the wounds detectives decided that the death weapons had been pressed against their target.[27]

Kiki Roberts didn't even go to Legs's funeral. She had gone into hiding in Boston. When she re-emerged, she used her fame as the moll of the notorious Legs Diamond to promote her "personal appearance" in burlesque and vaudeville shows in New York and New Jersey. When Legs's legitimate wife, Alice Schiffer, learned that Kiki was making money off her husband's name, she set off on her own burlesque tour. She and Legs had lived high in the 1920s. At their country estate in Accra, New York, Alice had installed a model of the Sing Sing electric chair in her living room. "Go ahead, take a seat," she liked to tell Legs and his pals, "guys like you ought to get used to sitting in it." Anyone witless enough to take up the invitation was surprised when Mrs. Diamond pulled the switch on them. Fortunately, the shock was non-lethal.

Schultz knew that the U.S. attorney for the Southern District of New York was after him, knew that, as soon as Medalie and Dewey had disposed of Gordon, they would be turning their attentions to him. But first they had to find him.

Dewey had a warrant out on Schultz. But Schultz had gone into hiding, and the police did not know where to find him. The police may not have been looking too hard, for the Dutchman evidently spent all of 1931 in Harlem and the Bronx. He visited Midtown Manhattan as well, bragging to Luciano that he dropped by Polly Adler's whore house three times a week. Charlie was not impressed. Schultz once looked at Charlie and told him that only queers wear silk shirts. Charlie looked back at Schultz, standing there truculently in his cheap, rumbled suit. His idea of a big splurge, Charlie said, was to spend two cents on a newspaper so he could read about himself. Manhattan's premier madam, Adler, was not impressed either. She later observed that "he seemed to have no more warmth or need for human companionship than a machine.

Yet I think that he knew that no one liked him and tried to con himself into believing it didn't matter, that money and power were what counted."[28] Schultz may have figured all the angles of the policy and the union rackets, but he couldn't figure out other people. He couldn't deal with them, couldn't make friends. "Like everyone else who knew him, I disliked him intently," remembered the bank robber Willie Sutton.

Schultz had become part of Charlie's inner circle during the early 1930s. During these years, Charlie and Frank were trying to establish a common fund for paying off the police and the district attorney's office. Each racketeer was expected to contribute. Charlie had invited his friends to the Waldorf to discuss the scheme. Although Schultz had the flu and had been told by his doctor to stay in bed, he came too, but sat by himself in the corner so that the others wouldn't get his germs. "Everyone else—Anastasia, Scalise, Moretti, Dutch Schultz . . . they all said yes." Only Joe Adonis kept stalling.

> I remember Joe Adonis standing across the room, looking in the mirror and combing his hair like he always did. It was his way of stalling. . . . We all sat there looking at Joe's back while he kept running a comb through his hair. Finally, he turned around with a big smile and said, "The star says yes." . . . [On hearing this] Dutch ran across the room and grabbed Joe's head in a hammerlock and breathed right in his face saying, `Now, you fucking star, you have my goims.'"[29]

Decades later, Charlie still remembered the way Dutch Schultz pronounced "germs."

When Medalie and Dewey resigned following Roosevelt's victory in 1932, Schultz felt the danger had passed. He could come out of hiding, give himself up and stand trial. Still, he decided not to give himself up to the Feds in New York City, choosing Albany instead. His trial was held in Syracuse and resulted in a hung jury. For his new trial, Schultz's attorneys arranged for a venue even further north, in the small community of Malone on the northernmost border of the Southern District. Here, half-way to Canada, Schultz, who had recently converted to Catholicism, played the role of the little guy, some poor sap who, whatever he may have done, did not deserve to have the entire weight of the federal government coming down upon him. The stratagem worked, and Schultz won a complete acquittal. Judge Bryant bawled the jury out; "you have rendered a blow against law enforcement and given aid and encouragement to the people who would flout the law."

Schultz's acquittal took his friends by surprise as well. Before his second tax evasion trial, Schultz's chief lieutenant, Bo Weinberg, and his lawyer, Dixie Davis, had taken council. If, as seemed likely, Schultz was convicted in the re-trial, his rackets would be at risk. With Schultz in prison, the East Harlem mafia might descend on them like a flock of ravenous vultures. To protect against such an eventuality, Weinberg suggested that the Schultz empire, lock, stock, and barrel, be placed in the safekeeping of Longy Zwillman. Weinberg traveled to Newark to discuss the proposal with Zwillman. Longy agreed that, without the Dutchman in control, his empire might indeed become unstuck. He worried, however, that East Harlem might be suspicious if he simply moved in to take over. Zwillman did not want to offend the sensibilities of the mafia; so he suggested that Weinberg first talk to Luciano, to ask Charlie to sound out his Italian friends. Luciano listened to Weinberg and Zwillman's proposal, and then responded with his own suggestion. The Jewish and Italian underworlds ought to guarantee the integrity of the Dutchman's rackets together, placing them under their joint tutelage. That way, he thought, no one would feel left out. Costello and Lansky would take over the gambling and policy rackets, Adonis the liquor business, and Lepke and Lucchese the unions. Zwillman and Moretti would split the business in New Jersey. Luciano would take a cut off the top. "I felt like a grave-robber," he later recalled, "here we was talking about cutting up Schultz, and he wasn't even in the can yet."[30]

Everyone seemed satisfied with this arrangement but Schultz. At the time, this hardly seemed to matter. Luciano had brokered the deal on the assumption that the Dutchman was actually going for the fall. Everybody made that assumption. It's what they all wanted to believe. Schultz was a troublemaker. When he heard that Schultz had given himself up in 1934, Charlie had remarked "We've seen the last of that loud-mouth." But, contrary to expectations, Schultz beat the rap. And soon he was knocking at the door at Charlie's Waldorf Towers suite, saying "May I have my rackets back please?"

Charlie was the consummate underworld diplomat. "Of course you can have your rackets back!" he explained to his agitated underworld colleague. The transfer had only been an interim arrangement, he explained, one designed for the Dutchman's own protection, a sort of caretaker government while Schultz attended to other matters. According to Charlie, "The Dutchman was so happy that we'd all been so nice to him that he almost started to cry." He also announced to Charlie and Vito that he was converting to Catholicism, and wanted to know about going to confession. That floored Vito. For years he'd been asking Charlie when he planned to start going to synagogue; now here was Dutch Schultz telling him to be sure to go to Mass.

This is Charlie's version. Whatever Schultz's true feeling towards Charlie may have been, he was less than grateful to Weinberg. Weinberg had evidently failed to inform Schultz that he was offering all his rackets to Zwillman, and Schultz interpreted this oversight on the part of his second-in-command in the worst possible light. He ordered his men to stake out Longy Zwillman's home. According to Luciano, when he caught Weinberg leaving the grounds, Schultz killed him with his own hands. According to other accounts, Schultz stuck Weinberg up to the knees in a tub of wet cement. As soon as the cement had set, he threw Weinberg and the tub into the East River.

Weinberg was not the only lieutenant accused of disloyalty in time of need. Schultz and Julius Modgilewsky, "Modgilewsky the Commissar," better known as "Jules Martin," had been expanding into the restaurant business, taking over the waiters union in Manhattan and then setting up their Metropolitan Restaurant and Cafeteria Owners Association. It was a messy business involving violent goons, phony picket lines and stink bombs of valerian or butyric acid.

In March 1935, the suspicious Schultz decided that Modgilewsky was skimming on him. Dixie Davis was there for the showdown. Schultz and Modgilewsky were drinking heavily and arguing. When Modgilewsky admitted to using $20,000 from their bank account to invest in a factory, Schultz pulled out the pistol he wore tucked inside his pants under his vest, right next to his belly:

All in the same quick motion he swung it up and stuck it in Jules Martin's mouth and pulled the trigger. It was all as simple and undramatic as that—just one quick motion of the hand. The Dutchman did that murder just as casually as if he were picking his teeth.[31]

Later Davis was surprised to read that the body of Martin had been discovered with twelve stab wounds. Why was this, he asked Schultz. "I cut his heart out," Schultz replied

By the end of 1935, Schultz learned that the new special prosecutor for New York, Thomas E. Dewey, was drawing up fresh indictments for tax evasion. It was also rumored that Dewey was planning to indict Schultz for the murder of Julius Modgilewsky.

Relations between Luciano and Schultz were not perhaps as rosy as Luciano wished to paint them. Perhaps the interim arrangements were never really meant to be as interim as all that. *My rackets, my precious rackets,* he moaned to himself. *Charlie Lucky's not going to let me have my precious rackets back.* Luciano and Lansky feared that Dewey might make a bargain with Schultz, asking him what he knew about the operations of Luciano and his friends in exchange for a reduction in the charges or for the elimination of the murder charge. Schultz feared that Luciano was plotting behind his back, passing incriminating tidbits of information to the Dewey investigation, just like he and Lansky had done to Waxey Gordon. According to Feder, Schultz accused Luciano of this straight to his face; "First you stole my rackets, now you're feeding me to the law."

There was only one possible solution, Schultz thought—kill Dewey. If Luciano didn't want to feel the wrath of the Dutchman, he had to agree to hit Dewey before he could bring his indictments. Schultz had already asked Albert Anastasia to case Dewey for him.

Technically speaking, Albert had decided, the hit was possible. Dewey, he discovered, always traveled with two bodyguards. He left his building at the same time, early every morning. At the same time he walked into a drugstore a few blocks away to make a phone call. Dewey later explained that he needed to alert his office, and didn't want to wake his wife by calling from his apartment. Anastasia's caser borrowed a tricycle and a five-year-old kid to ride it. It was a perfect decoy, a proud father watching his kid ride on the sidewalk before going off for work, sometimes strolling past the two bodyguards into the drugstore to buy the kid a candy bar. After four days, Anastasia had it all set up. He'd contacted the assassins and clipped a car for them to use. Everything, he told Schultz, was ready to go. "I'm going to kill Dewey myself in forty-eight hours," Schultz announced then to Luciano.

That, observed Luciano, was against the rules. The underworld didn't just knock off the Law. Killing the special prosecutor would result in a pubic outcry. "I suppose they figured that the National Guard would have called out, or something like that, if Dewey had been killed," remembered one Dewey assistant, Frank Hogan, "and they wouldn't have been far wrong."[32]

Luciano called a council meeting. As Luciano's *consigliere*, Lansky took the chair. The meeting, Luciano remembered, went on for hours. Everybody had something they wanted to say. Schultz had told Luciano that killing Dewey was the only solution, the only way out of the impasse. There was, however, another and equally obvious solution staring them in the face. In the end, the vote was unanimous.[33] Luciano gave the job of organizing the Schultz hit to Lepke. Lepke passed the job to his lieutenant Mendy Weiss, who chose the contract killer Charlie "The Bug" Workman.

About 10 p.m. on the night of October 23, 1935, a black sedan carrying Workman and Weiss and a driver only identified as "Piggy" pulled up in front of the Palace Chop House in Newark. According to Turkus, Charlie the Bug walked into the resort while Mendy Weiss waited by the front door. Workman walked the length of the bar, spotting Schultz's table at the back. There were three men sitting there, counting policy slips. Workman had expected to see four men—Schultz, Abbadabba Berman and the two bodyguards, Lulu Rosenkrantz and Abe Landau. He was too far away to be sure who the three at the table were, and didn't want to get any closer in case they might spot him. He walked into the men's room. Someone with his back to him was washing his hands at the sink. Taking him to be one of the bodyguards, the Bug plugged him in the back of the neck.

Though he hadn't realized it, Workman had just shot Dutch Schultz. The three men at his table may have heard the shot from the bathroom and turned, drawing their guns. Looking in the direction of the bathroom, they may not have seen Mendy Weiss come up on them from the other side. They were thus caught in a cross-fire between Weiss and Workman. This is hypothetical, but it would help explain why Rosenkrantz, Landau, and Berman were shot sixteen times while neither Workman nor Weiss were even scratched. Although both Rosenkrantz and Landau got to their feet after the shooting started, according to the police reconstruction of the crime scene, the three men had all been sitting at the table when the firing started. They had, in short, all been taken by surprise.

At some point, Workman must have realized that none of the three men at the table was Schultz. It was then he remembered the man in the men's room. He ran back and found him slumped over the urinal. Workman rifled his pockets for change, and possibly added another shot for good measure.

While Workman was busy going through the Dutchman's pockets, Rosenkrantz and Landau were on their feet shooting. Shooting wildly, Landau made it as far as the street outside before collapsing, falling backward and ending up sitting in a garbage can. Who were Rosenkrantz and Landau shooting at? If it was Mendy Weiss, then it is possible to reconstruct what happened next.

Weiss ran out onto the street with Landau chasing him. Weiss had lost sight of Workman before the shooting had even started; he had no way of knowing that the Bug was in the men's room going through Schultz's pockets. He didn't feel like going back into the chop house to look for Workman. He didn't feel like waiting around at all. Instead, he jumped into the car and sped off with Piggy.

It hadn't taken Workman long to go through Schultz's pockets. He'd come out of the bathroom in time to exchange shots with Landau before Landau ran out after Weiss. Workman may have paused for a second to take stock: Schultz was in the bathroom; Berman was collapsed at the table; Rosenkratz was crumpled on the restaurant floor; Landau had gone outside. Then he went out himself. Nothing. No gunfire, and, more important, no getaway car.

Back in the chop house, Dutch Schultz managed to stagger out of the bathroom. Testimony of the bartender:

> First thing I noticed was Schultz. He came reeling out like he was intoxicated. He was having a hard time staying on his pins, and was just hanging onto one side. He didn't say a cockeyed thing. He just went over to the table, put his left hand on it to steady him, and then he plopped into a chair, just like a souse would. His head bounced on the table, and I thought this was the end of him, but pretty soon he moved. He said, "Get a doctor, quick."

In the meantime, the Bug had started to walk. He followed the train tracks from Newark and through a tunnel under the Hudson to Manhattan. When he made it back, the buzz on the streets was that Mendy Weiss had just killed Dutch Schultz. The Bug's name wasn't even in the papers. This made him mad. He went to see Lepke, who told him that if he wanted to rifle his victim's pockets for small change, that was his problem. He couldn't expect Mendy to wait up for him. Furious, the Bug went to Miami where Luciano was staying. When he saw Luciano he began to complain about Mendy. Luciano gave him the money for the hit and warned him to stop mouthing off.

Schultz was taken to the Newark City Hospital. Still coherent, he asked for a priest. Father Cornelius McInerney arrived in time to baptize Schultz as a Catholic and administer the last rites.

Around 2 p.m. on the next day, Schultz began to grow delirious. The Newark police chief sent a stenographer and sergeant Luke Conlon for what he hoped might be a death-bed confession. Instead, Schultz told them, "a boy has never wept . . . nor dashed a thousand kim. . . ."

For two hours, as Sergeant Conlon vainly questioned him, Schultz spouted haunting, free verse: "Please crack down on the Chinaman's friends and Hitler's commander. All right, I am sore and I am going up and I am going to give you honey if I can. Look out. We broke that up. Mother is the best bet and don't let Satan draw you too fast."

He told Conlon,

"I know what I'm doing with my collection of papers, for crying out loud. It isn't worth a nickel to two guys like you or me, but to a collector it is worth a fortune; it is priceless. I am going to turn it over to. . . .

Come on, Max, open the soap duckets. Frankie, please come here. Open the door, Dumpey's door. It is so much, Abe, that . . . with the brewery. Come on. Hey, Jimmy! The Chimney Sweeps. Talk to the Sword. Shut up. You got a big mouth! Please help me up, Henny. Max, come over here. . . . French-Canadian bean soup. . . . I want to pay, let them leave me alone.

These were his last words. A more coherent message lay on the table beside him. It was a telegram from Madame Queen, Stephanie St. Clair: "As ye sow, so shall ye reap," it read.[34]

THE TRIAL OF LUCKY LUCIANO

La Guardia and Dewey stood as a team in the 1935 mayoral elections, La Guardia for mayor, Dewey for district attorney. The two men had little in common, and kept out of each other's way as much as possible. La Guardia must have been known that Medalie and the GOP regulars, who had never much liked him in the first place and were now particularly annoyed at him for his support of Roosevelt's New Deal. They were grooming Dewey to replace him as soon as the time was ripe. Nevertheless, for New York's voters, LaGuardia and Dewey were the city's leading gangbusters. It seemed a dream ticket.

Mary Stolberg writes that the murder of Schultz, just four months after he took office, presented Dewey with a "public relations problem." That is putting it mildly. Dewey's appointment had been accompanied by immense fanfare. His appeal to the public had been broadcast simultaneously by the city's three largest radio stations. The press followed his every move. Expectations were sky-high. Dewey had every confidence; he calculated that he would have the Dutchman's head in a few months time. The murder of Schultz that October threw his whole game plan for a loop.

Shortly after the Schultz murder, Dewey seized the headlines with raids against twenty-seven loan sharks. Dewey presented the loan sharks as major racketeers. Fortunately for him, they were not. Had they really been major racketeers, witnesses would have been too frightened to testify against them. Instead, they were independent operators, and enough witness came forward to ensure Dewey an easy prosecution and a string of quick convictions. The loan sharking cases gave Dewey the necessary breathing room. By the following year, 1936, Dewey had found his new centerpiece, someone who could take Dutch Schultz's place. On April 1, 1936, April Fools Day, Dewey issued a statement proclaiming Charlie "Lucky" Luciano as the new Public Enemy No. 1.

Why had Dewey chosen Luciano? Dewey later claimed that, when he started his investigations, he did not know who Luciano was. In the course of his investigation of the prostitution racket, however, he found that Luciano's name kept coming up. Dewey was being a little coy; we know that Dewey had already gathered information about Luciano during his investigation of Al Marinelli. This may provide a clue.

Dewey, we saw, accepted the argument that the best way to take down racketeers was to convict them of tax evasion. Dewey also accepted that, for reasons of public relations, the special prosecutor should concentrate on big-name gangsters, the ones whose names had come up during the Seabury hearings. Dewey and La Guardia both wanted Dewey's investigations to uncover further scandals involving Tammany. La Guardia hated Italian gangsters passionately; he had personally gone after Costello and Terranova. This left Marinelli.

Though little remembered today, Marinelli was much in the news at the time. In 1929 he was behind an attempt to hush up a faked robbery involving Magistrate Albert Vitale. Vitale was already linked with the underworld, particularly with Rothstein, to whom he had written an IOU for almost $20,000. La Guardia obtained the incriminating evidence and used it during his 1929 mayoral campaign. Vitale and his friends were held at gunpoint at the Roman Gardens restaurant in the Bronx by a group that included Terranova. Vitale later arranged to have the stolen goods returning, explaining that the unfortunate incident had resulted from a misunderstanding with Marinelli. Tammany leader in the Second Assembly District on the Lower East Side, in 1932 Marinelli was elected city alderman. In that year, he secured the appointment of his lieutenant, Patrick J. Lupo as deputy commissioner of records in the city court.[35] Dewey would have known all this and would have discovered in the Seabury hearings or from his own contacts that Marinelli was connected to Joe the Boss Masseria as well as a number of younger and lesser-known Italian hoods—Luciano, Adonis, Genovese, Socks Lanza and Davey Betillo.[36]

Marinelli was a perfect target for Dewey. Dewey did make a preliminary investigation about Marinelli, but then he dropped it. We do not know why. Possibly Dewey could not obtain the evidence to make the sort of case he wanted.

To make a tax case, Dewey did not need to prove that the man he was prosecuting was a racketeer; he just had to prove that he was a tax cheat. To do this, it was necessary to show that the defendant, though demonstrably very rich, had never paid his taxes. It helped, however, if the jury also believed that the tax cheat was a major racketeer. In that case, the jury would be willing to recommend the sort of exemplary sentences Dewey sought. A jury will convict a tax cheat, but it will not, all things being equal, seek to inflict a particularly severe sentence upon him. The technique had worked perfectly in the cases of Al Capone and Waxey Gordon. They were each well-known gangsters; they were each demonstrably rich, and neither had paid their taxes.

It backfired in the case of Dutch Schultz. Schultz's lawyers had the trial removed to a little upstate town where Schultz's reputation as a gangster was not well known. Unless one knew just how violent he was, and this was not the sort of information that could be introduced in a tax case, Schultz came across as an unprepossessing nebbish. It was hard to demonstrate that the miserly Schultz was rich; he wore cheap suits and was sometimes too mean to buy his own newspaper. The Malone jury may have convinced itself that the federal prosecutors were exaggerating. Al Marinelli had a reputation as a corrupt politician with Italian gangster connections. He was, however, an alderman; he had a salary, and, no doubt, submitted a tax return. It would have been hard to nail Marinelli for tax fraud. Dewey might have chosen Johnny Torrio; but Torrio too was cautious. He had legitimate fronts, and probably submitted tax returns as well.

Luciano might have seemed a better bet. Even if Dewey did not really know much about him, he had certainly seen his name in police reports. What made Luciano such a juicy prospect, however, was his address. Here was a man with no visible means of support, who always paid in cash, but who lived in a suite in the Waldorf Tower! Yet as special prosecutor Dewey was operating under the laws of New York State. Income tax evasion is a federal not a state crime. Dewey worked closely with the Treasury and could have arranged to try a tax case in a federal court. But Dewey preferred to connect Charlie with some sort of racket.

Among Dewey's assistants was a remarkable black woman named Eunice Hunton Carter. Working as an assistant district attorney under Dodge, Carter had been disturbed by a new pattern of fixing in lower court prostitution cases. Since Judge Seabury's investigations into the abuses of the police vice squads, the NYPD had ceased taking pay-offs to protect whore houses. As an unintended consequence of this withdrawal, Carter suspected that the underworld was now moving in to take their place. Carter told Dewey of these suspicions; but Dewey was at first unmoved. In his radio address, Dewey had told New York that he would focus on the major racketeers; he would not, he promised, try to grab headlines by rounding up whores and two-bit gamblers. Even if Carter's suspicions were correct, Dewey didn't see how busting a network of pimps and procurers was going to help him nail Luciano. Dewey was still hoping to establish some connection between Luciano and gambling rackets. Nonetheless, he told Carter that she could follow up her hunch and see what she came up with. With the permission of Judge McCook, he ordered the bugging and wire-tapping of dozens of the city's brothels.

The results of the continued investigations were both promising and disappointing. They were promising in that they substantiated Carter's hunch: hoodlums were indeed moving in on prostitution. They were disappointing in that the names that Carter was coming up with were not ringing any bells: no well-known underworld figures could yet be linked to the racket. Carter uncovered a ring of 'bookers' who, like Chicago's white slavers, circulated a stable of girls into various brothels, usually for one-week stints, splitting the take with the girls and the madams. Unlike the Chicago pimps, the New York bookers also forced the girls to pay a certain percentage of their earnings into an insurance fund that would provide bail and lawyers' fees in the case of arrest. Carter was confidant that, if she were allowed to dig deeply enough, she would eventually come up with major names. But Dewey did not have time to wait. As special prosecutor, he enjoyed ample resources but had little time. He was under tremendous pressure to get results fast. So Dewey decided to force the pace.

On January 31, he swept up sixteen of the most important bookers. The next night he rounded up the whores. To prevent tip-offs, he kept the police in the dark until the last possible moment. New police teams were formed and sent to unfamiliar locations. Each was issued with sealed orders, which they were instructed not to open until five minutes before the raids were scheduled to begin. Instead of using patrol wagons; Dewey instructed the police to take the whores by taxi to the service entrance of the Woolworth Building, and ride up to Dewey's headquarters in the service elevator. More than one hundred prostitutes were ferried up that night; "I've never seen so many prostitutes before or since," remembered one staff member. "The rooms were crawling with them."

The women were confused. They were accustomed to being arrested, but not arrested like this. They waited for their lawyers to arrive to work out the fix. But their lawyers didn't show up that night. Instead, at 5 a.m. they were confronted with Judge McCook who informed the women and the sixteen men arrested the day before that were being held as material witnesses. Their bail was set at $10,000 apiece. They were escorted to prison where they were refused permission to notify their lawyers or contact their families.

Why all the secrecy? Why were they being locked up without being allowed to talk to anyone? What was Dewey up to? The prisoners were bewildered, and not a little terrified. This is exactly what Dewey wanted. The whores were questioned individually by Dewey staff members—nice-looking, well-spoken young men in suits, not at all like the old vice squad cops the whores were used to. The staff members were polite; they were sorry about the arrests, sorry about the conditions. Things could be sorted out, the restrictions lifted; all that was necessary was a little cooperation.

Dewey had wanted to throw a little fear into his prisoners, for he needed to disarm them. But he didn't want to terrorize them too much, for he needed their cooperation too. Though they didn't know this yet, the women had been assigned an important role in the drama that was to follow. They were the victims. It was up to them to point accusing fingers at the men who had enslaved them. The special prosecutor's own role was that of redeemer. It would be the special prosecutor who rescued the women from bondage; restored to them their dignity; and gave them the courage to tell of their degradation in open court. The trick was to induce the prostitutes to play it according to the special prosecutor's script. That is why he kept them from their lawyers as long as he could; he didn't want anyone cooking up alternative scenarios.

Dewey needed the women to come to him, to play their assigned parts convincingly. And this is why he was offering to be nice to them now. "It's not you we're really after," the assistants told the prostitutes. "Cooperate with us, and everything will get a lot easier for you." Indeed it did. Prostitutes who cooperated were allowed to receive visitors and packets. They got better food and were allowed to wear their own clothes. Some were even escorted to the movies by Dewey's staff members or taken out for martinis and dinner. Cooperation, of course, meant telling everything they knew, naming names, and agreeing to testify as they were instructed in open court. It was an effective strategy, straight out of the "prisoners' dilemma" gamebook.

Dewey needed some solid information as well. He hoped that as soon as he got the prostitutes talking, they would supply him with more names and leads. He also wanted to use the prostitutes to put pressure on the pimps, madams, and bookers. Dewey probably already had enough evidence on them to get convictions; but they weren't his real targets. He kept these intermediaries stewing, letting them know that the prostitutes were talking about them. Then he came down hard. "Give us the names of your underworld connections," he told them, "the guys in charge of the racket, and we'll grant you immunity. Hold out and we'll see that you get the maximum."

Unfortunately, this part of his strategy was still producing little of value. The prostitutes and intermediaries were willing enough to provide names; but they were the names Dewey already knew. One major booker, Nick Montana, was already serving time. Others like Jack Eller and Al Weiner were running independent operations. There were no connections to Luciano. It began to look as if the prostitution racket ended with these men.

Dewey's argument was that Luciano's men were muscling in on the bookers' operations. They were putting the squeeze on the other bookers and on the independent operators, forcing them to join their organization. To back up their threats, they used Luciano's name. A Brooklyn madam, Molly Leonard, said that when she asked the booker, Peter Balitzer, who was behind the new combination, Balitzer had replied, "Lucky is behind it." Balitzer, who was granted immunity and testified as a prosecution witness, said that when one of the brothels in the combination had been robbed, Jimmy Fredericks had smacked the robber in face saying, "Didn't I tell you to stay away from these joints that are bonded; that they belong to Charlie Lucky." Another booker, David Miller, told Dewey that he heard that the whole racket was controlled by Luciano. Dewey cut Miller a deal, getting his wife off the hook, and Miller proved very well-informed about the workings of the racket. But Miller was just a small-time booker; when Dewey pressed him, Miller admitted that he had never even seen Luciano. These stray connections to Luciano were nothing more than hearsay and rumor, and all from very dubious sources.

Within the booking racket there were three men that the police could connect to Luciano's outfit—Tommy the Bull Pennocchio, Little Davie Betillo and Ralph Liguori. Pennocchio and Betillo were soldiers inherited by Luciano from the Masseria Family. Liguori was a small-time hood and pimp. They worked with a collection of bookers and bondsmen within the racket, as well as outside muscle provided by Jimmy Fredericks (Frederico). If Dewey was going to make a connection with Luciano, it would have to come through one of these three. But obviously none of the three men were going to testify against Luciano. This forced Dewey to work the connection by other means.

Nancy Presser, whose real name was Genevieve Fletcher, had run away to New York in 1928 when she was sixteen years old. She found work as a model in the garment district, entertaining out-of-town buyers in the evenings. Attracted to gangsters, within a year of her arrival she had become involved in the Waxey Gordon mob. Indeed, the blonde in bed with Waxey the night that Big Maxie Greenberg and Jimmy Hassell were murdered in New Jersey was said to be Nancy Presser. From the Gordon gang, Nancy also picked up the habit of smoking opium.

In 1931, Nancy met Ralph Liguori, a chunky little hold-up man who pimped on the side. Nancy accompanied Ralph on his heists, carrying his gun for him in case the police stopped him and patted him down. As the number of speakeasies and restaurants paying protection money to Schultz grew larger, the lives of independent hold-up men became more precarious. So Liguori signed up as a $50-per-week Schultz's gunman instead. But the salary was not enough. Liguori gambled heavily, and was deeply in debt to the shylocks. To cover his debts, Liguori began running other girls on the side. Both Liguori and Nancy were heavily addicted to heroin now, another big item on the family budget; and Liguori had started dealing drugs.

Nancy had continued to work as a call girl, earning from $10 to $20 a night. But Liguori didn't like her working independently. He became violent, accusing her of holding out and of chippying for free. In 1935, he booked her into a Harlem brothel, where she turned up to three hundred $2 tricks a week. This was less than she could earn as a call girl; but at least she stayed put and Liguori could keep an eye on her. By now Liguori had joined the booking racket, and was running girls and protecting brothels full time. Life between the two of them was growing nasty. Liguori threatened Nancy with a knife. Shortly before she was caught in the February 1936 roundup, Liguori had beaten Nancy up.

Several years older than Nancy Presser, Florence "Cokey Flo" Brown had run off from a mining town outside Pittsburgh when she was fifteen and found work in a Cleveland speakeasy. Like Nancy, Flo was attracted to gangster life. She worked as a call girl in Chicago, moving to Duluth in the company of a bootlegging lover, following him first to Hot Springs, Arkansas, and later to New York City. With the money she had saved, she set herself and another girl up in a luxury Upper West Side brothel charging $5 a trick. When the Depression hit, she was forced to lower her prices and find more girls. When Flo's joint was pinched in 1933, she had to borrow from the loan sharks the $500 she needed to bail her girls out. This experience taught her the wisdom of joining the booking racket, which, for a fee of $10 a week per girl, promised to provide bail money for all their clients.

The representative of the booking racket was Jimmy Fredericks, and Flo and Jimmy lived together through 1934 and 1935. In January 1936, Flo was pinched again. The cops not only arrested her girls, but found her opium and morphine set ups. Flo was charged with prostitution and drug violation. Her bail was set at $2,800. Fortunately Fredericks and the combination came through with about half; the rest came out of Flo's savings.

On January 31, Fredericks was arrested in the first Dewey roundup, and Flo, just out on bail herself, was left alone and without money. Convinced that the police were about to haul her back in, Flo hid out. She got a job as a companion to an elderly female writer, and earned $25 a week. It was enough to live on but not enough for her morphine habit. In early May 1936, she was arrested for soliciting in front of her apartment on West Seventy-fifth.

Flo tried to get a message out to the bookers, but got no reply. She believed that some of the other girls arrested in the Dewey round-up were getting money from the racket. "They had sent money in to some of the witnesses to try to keep them from talking by being nice to them. Jimmy knew I was in jail, broke and sick, but he hadn't tried to send anything in to me, had he?" In reality, Jimmy Fredericks was in no position to help anyone. But Flo still felt betrayed. "None of them had ever given me a second thought, not even Jimmy," she later recalled.

Drug addicts in the Women's House of Detention got a five-day reduction treatment. It was short and cheap and sheer murder. It was the fifth day of the treatment, when the drug devils were at their worst, that Flo wrote to the Dewey team.

That evening, Dewey assistant Sol Gelb came to see her. What, he asked, did this shaky, emaciated figure in a gray prison uniform know.

"I know Charlie Lucky," said Cokey Flo.

"Oh yeah?" said Gelb, barely concealing his excitement.

Dewey prosecuted Luciano brilliantly. He denied that Luciano had been his target when he had set out. Luciano's name, he claimed, had been forced to his attention. It just kept cropping up during the investigations. Still, the trial was given a big build-up in the press, giving Dewey and his allies plenty of opportunity to characterize Luciano in the blackest colors. Well before the trial started, New York had learned that Luciano, the evil criminal mastermind skulking in the shadows, was now revealed as the city's overlord of vice as well.

For three weeks in the late spring of 1936, the attention of New Yorkers was riveted by the collection of low-life exotica that Dewey displayed before the jury. Still, it was upon the testimony of the twenty-eight prostitutes that the bulk of Dewey's case lay. The prostitutes spoke of their own lives—running away from home, getting caught in bad marriages, being left with small children. Almost all were poorly educated; many were drug-addicts. They described their lives as whores, how the booking ring had begun to squeeze them, depriving them of their independence, gouging them, increasing their cut, and threatening them if they resisted or complained.

Dewey had also anticipated the reaction of the defense councilors. These whores, the defense pointed out, had been arrested, kept in isolation, held in prison for months and threatened with three-year prison terms until a group of twenty-eight among them was finally selected and groomed into witnesses for the prosecution. What possible credibility could such a group of witnesses possess? The answer lay in the performance of the prostitutes themselves.

Dewey questioned his prostitutes with care, showing them every sympathy on the stand, allowing them, often against the strenuous objections of the defense councils, to recount the stories of their lives in their own words. "Why, sometimes to hear Mr. Dewey qualify his witnesses," snorted one attorney, "you would think they were virgins as they took the witness stand." But the prostitutes responded positively to his solicitousness. Instead of showing hostility towards Dewey or even resentment over their lengthy incarceration, some showed gratitude. Dewey had rescued them from a life of degradation. He was their savior rather than their persecutor. When Dewey's behavior in giving special privileges to cooperative prisoners was questioned, Dewey could blandly respond; "With each of these witnesses when they have told the truth, we have done our best to make life in a prison where they are kept as comfortable as possible." Confess and be forgiven. It was as if his major concern was the moral and spiritual well-being of the prostitutes rather than winning the case. His show of sanctimonious concern infuriated the defense councils; "There are no wings on your shoulders," one of them shouted at him. Yet Dewey's performance and those of his prostitutes themselves convinced most of the New York press, and probably won the jury as well.

The central moment of trial came with the link to Luciano. Cokey Flo's first interview with Sol Gelb had gone badly. Gelb tried to interrogate her, but Flo was too jittery with her withdrawal symptoms to respond properly. Later that night she met with another of the Dewey team in the prison psychiatrist's office. They didn't try to interrogate her this time, letting her tell her story her own way. She had met Luciano late one night, she said. She had accompanied Jimmy Fredericks to a Chinese restaurant on 130th Street. Luciano was sitting there with Tommy Bull Pennocchio and Little Davie Betillo. Most of the conversation, she remembered, was in Italian; but at one point Little Davie asked in English about the whorehouses that were holding out. Luciano had responded, "Well, can't you get them together?"

Other times, she remembered, she and Jimmy drove to garage on the Lower East Side. Jimmy always told her to stay in the car while he went inside; but sometimes, bored and curious, she eavesdropped.

A week later, Gelb returned to talk to Flo. This time he brought Dewey with him. Dewey quickly went through the interview notes with her. Then he told her that she'd be on the stand the next day.

The phrase the papers used to describe the emaciated Cokey Flo who walked up to the witness stand the next day was "waif-like". She wore an old blue dress that now seemed two sizes too big for her. Her hair was disheveled and her eyes sunken. She walked with a kind of shuffle. Dewey treated

her with great kindness, and when, during her testimony, she told Judge Mc-
Cook that she had black spots in front of her eyes and asked if she might
have a drink of brandy, the judge quickly agreed. Luciano's two attorneys,
George Morton Levy and Moses Polakoff, began shaking their heads. The
jury seemed mesmerized, staring intently at Cokey Flo, hanging on her every
word. How were they going to beat a performance like that?

Four days later, Dewey called Nancy Presser to the stand. Nancy was in
better condition. The night they brought her to the Woolworth Building, she
had been strung out on dope. She was diagnosed as suffering from gonorrhea
and syphilis. She was bruised in the side where Liguori had beaten her up.
But during her four months in prison she had been well cared for. "Nancy had
been many a man's darling for the moment," Hickman Powell remarked, "but
now she was a precious package for the People of the State of New York." She
was clean now, she said, and she publicly thanked special prosecutor Dewey
for helping her give up the habit.

She had first met Charlie Luciano in 1930, she said. Joe the Boss Masseria
used to threw big parties in his Lower East Side penthouses, and Nancy and
her friends liked to drop in. Charlie Luciano went to these parties too. Nancy
spotted him there and learned who he was, though she had not really gotten to
know him yet. She saw him again at a party given by Waxey Gordon's mob,
and again at Kean's Tavern, a mob hang-out near Madison Square Gardens.
Two years later, she saw him at Kean's Tavern again. By now, however, both
of their lives were different. Charlie had become the big boss, but Nancy had
started her downward slide. She was living with Ralph Liguori, addicted to
heroin and turning cheap tricks in Schultz-controlled Harlem. She played up
to Charlie that night, reminding him that they'd met at Joe the Boss's parties.
Finally, as she was leaving, she slipped him a note with her phone number.

Nancy described her life with Liguori. Ralph had been acting crazy,
threatening her, forcing her into Jimmy Russo's cheap Harlem whorehouse.
Sometimes she said that Ralph would come to the house and bang on the bedroom door while she was in there with a client. Finish it up, he'd yell, there's
others waiting. Then, at the lowest moment of her life, she got a phone call.
It was Luciano.

She'd first gone to his place at the Barbizon. Then, the following year,
he'd invited her to the Waldorf Towers. She'd gone there seven or eight times.
Charlie wasn't at all like Ralph, she said. Charlie offered her champagne. She
told Charlie about her troubles with Ralph, and Charlie had listened sympathetically. He generously offered her money. I t was to keep her out of the
cat-houses he told her.

What else had she and Charlie done together, Dewey wanted to know.

"When Charlie called me over, he'd give me a hundred dollars, but we'd
just talk. That's all. We never went to bed together. Charlie couldn't. You
know what I mean?"

Sitting at the defence table, Charlie suddenly saw crimson, "All I knew
was that I had to hit someone. . . . "Moe Polakoff saw me start to move, so he

grabbed me by the arm and ground his foot right on top of mine. My right foot was so sore that I couldn't have moved if I wanted, and I let out a yell because he hurt me so bad. The whole courtroom turned around and looked at me and it took a couple of minutes before it was quiet again."

The counselors presented their closing arguments, and Judge McCook charged the jury late on Saturday night, June 6. It was almost ten when they started their deliberations. Though most people went home, a few reporters hung around, waiting for the jury. Others went over to the Woolworth Building with the Dewey team. Dewey himself had loosened his tie and snatched a few winks on his office couch. Dewey had been impressive, the newsmen agreed; but they still rated it a toss-up. About 5:30 a.m., someone came in to wake Dewey. The verdict was in, they told him.

After deliberating for six hours, the jury found the accused guilty on all counts. Luciano was declared guilty of fifty-six counts of enforced prostitution. "You need have no doubt about the righteousness of your verdict, I am sure;" Judge McCook told the jurors.

Ralph Liguori received a sentence of from seven and one-half to fifteen years. With two prior felonies, Jimmy Fredericks and Tommy Bull Pennocchio drew twenty-five years each. Little Davie Betillo drew a term between twenty-five and forty years. Luciano got between thirty and fifty years.

The papers agreed with Judge McCook. So, of course, did Mayor La Guardia. The reporters who had worried about the conduct of the trial kept their doubts to themselves for now. Court officials and members of Dewey's own staff quietly wondered how the case would hold up on appeal. No one, outside of the underworld, as yet went so far as to say that Luciano had been framed.

Luciano was a criminal. He had done far worse things in his life than run prostitutes. In that sense, the thirty-to-fifty-year sentence that Judge McCook gave was no more than he deserved. He got what was coming to him. Still, the question remains of whether in his 1936 trial Luciano was guilty as charged.

The trials of Capone, Waxey Gordon, and Dutch Schultz had all been elaborate decoys. Supposedly on trial for income tax evasion, in reality, each was on trial for being an eminent gangster. There was a tacit agreement between the jury and the prosecution: you bring in a guilty verdict, we'll see to it that the bum is put away for a long stretch. If the stratagem worked in the cases of Capone and Gordon, it was because the prosecution convincingly demonstrated the defendants' guilt by showing that their declared income in no way matched their luxurious tenor of life. If the stratagem backfired in the case of Schultz it was because Schultz lived like a cheapskate and the federal prosecutors never demonstrated the original charges. At that point, the fact that the federal agents acted in an arrogant and high-handed manner towards the citizen jurors of a small, upstate New York town clinched the matter for the defense. Had the prosecutors been able to bring forward evidence that Schultz was a bloodthirsty sadist, the jury might have proved more cooperative. But evidence of bloodthirsty sadism had no bearing in a tax evasion case.

Ideally, Dewey probably would have liked to try Luciano on a tax evasion charge. His chances would have been good. Although Charlie liked to present himself as a gentleman gambler and *bon viveur*, he actually looked and sounded like a gangster. Dewey had been careful to establish this, blackening Luciano's reputation, describing him to the press as a vice lord and syndicated crime boss. Well before his trial, the *New York Daily News* had called him, "The Droopy-eyed Czar of the Oldest Profession."[37] Looking and sounding like a gangster would have had, of course, no direct bearing in a tax evasion case, but combined with Charlie's lavish tastes and palatial penthouse suite in the Towers would certainly have predisposed a jury to believe that he was cheating on his income tax. Yet in 1936 Dewey was no longer a federal prosecutor but Manhattan District Attorney. So Dewey had to pick some other charge. He came up with pimping.

Dewey in fact never presented clear evidence that Luciano was materially involved in the booking racket. He did present evidence that Luciano underlings like Tommy the Bull Pennochio and Little Davey Betillo were trying to take over the booking racket in Manhattan for themselves. He argued that since Luciano was their superior, he was responsible for what they did. Morally, Dewey had a good case; whether Luciano was criminally responsible under New York State law as it existed in 1936 is, however, another matter. Recognizing this, Dewey tried to improve his case in this respect by introducing evidence that Luciano was indeed directly involved in the booking racket. This is where the prostitutes came in.

Nancy Presser's testimony was never very credible. She had very little real information, only a few telephone conversations she said she'd overheard in Luciano's suite. While she knew some details of Luciano's apartment in the Waldorf Towers, she didn't know how the hotel lobby was laid out or where the elevator was. "She's not an interior decorator," Dewey had snapped. But Nancy later revealed that, while the prosecutors had shown her pictures of Luciano's suite, they had neglected to explain anything about the lobby to her.

What was much more interesting was the role Nancy cast for herself. A genuine gangster groupie, she claimed to have had had sex with most of the Waxey Gordon gang, Schultz, Terranova, Adonis and even Joe the Boss Masseria. This part of her testimony may have been true; she had indeed seen Charlie at Masseria's penthouse and later on at Kean's Tavern. But those were the days before she had met Liguori and gotten herself into all that trouble. She may even have seen him again at Kean's and slipped him the note with her phone number on it. But after that it was all make-believe: Charlie never phoned back.

Nancy later said that the Dewey team told her that they had her on check-kiting, prostitution and drug possession charges. They could send her away for ten to twenty years if she didn't play ball, they told her. Nancy's claim was confirmed by another inmate. Still, the story about the kind man in the suite in the Waldorf Towers who gave her champagne to drink, listened to her sad stories and gave her money to mend her ruined life was certainly never part of the prepared script. That was Nancy fantasizing about the man she longed to meet. She obliged Dewey by nailing Luciano for him, but while she was at it, also transformed him into her personal Prince Charming. Why did she want to deny having sex with Prince Charming? Re-elaborated, twisted, and misquoted, Nancy's statement, "Charlie couldn't. You know what I mean?" has become an on-going underworld dirty joke. What did she mean by it? She never gave an explanation.[38]

Dewey certainly knew that Nancy was an unreliable witness. He may have calculated that the press would love Nancy's romantic confabulations, giving them the widest possible publicity. He may also have reasoned that it would take the defense two days of cross-examination to demonstrate that Nancy had gotten the lay-out of Luciano's penthouse all wrong, thereby inadvertently fixing in the jury's minds that Charlie did indeed live in a fabulous penthouse.

Cokey Flo Brown's testimony was more convincing. She had not been part of the original haul of prostitutes brought in as material witnesses, though her lover, Jimmy Fredericks, had been arrested among the pimps and bookers brought in on the night before. When Cokey Flo heard that Fredericks had been arrested and was being held in connection to a certain Lucky Luciano, Cokey Flo had called her lawyer to ask who this Luciano character was and what she could say to get her sweetheart off the hook. A month later, however, she herself was picked up for soliciting and told she was facing a ten-year sentence for drugs and prostitution. Cokey Flo felt betrayed; the lawyer was connected to the combination, but the combination had done nothing. They hadn't helped Jimmy, now they hadn't helped her.

Racked by the brutal drug withdrawal program, she had stopped eating. She didn't see how she was going to get through a ten-year stretch. Having heard from friends that Dewey arranged for charges to be dropped against helpful witnesses, she wondered whether it was worth a try. She later said she felt badly about committing perjury, but "it seemed to me and everybody else, all the girls there, that the defendants didn't stand a chance. I thought it over, the more I thought that if I gave them a statement, maybe it wouldn't do any harm, and I could help myself."

The prostitutes and other material witnesses spent four months in confinement. Those who proved uncooperative were kept in the Women's House of Detention directly behind the Women's Court at Jefferson Market. Built in 1934, it "copied architecture reminiscent of totalitarian themes of European fascism." It was, according to Ellen Poulsen, a "monstrosity," a "sad depository for lost women;" it was especially hard on women like Presser and Brown who were forced to undergo the drug reduction program.[39] More cooperative material witnesses, those who Dewey's staff had persuaded to tell the "truth," were given much better treatment. Some were moved to apartments uptown, where they were kept in comfort, taken on shopping expeditions and wined and dined and taken to the movies at the expense of taxpayers. Not surprisingly, one of the policemen in charge of the witnesses later testified that the prostitutes began asking him who this Luciano character was anyway, what did he look like, and what was he supposed to have done. These prostitutes were not so dumb. They were certainly bright enough to figure out what Dewey wanted to hear from them and to calculate that things would go a lot easier for them if they decided to tell the "truth." Cooperation with the prosecution in exchange for a reduction or elimination of charges is legitimate plea bargaining. But agreeing to perform like a cage full of birds, singing the tune that the prosecutor has written out for them is more than plea bargaining; it is perjury. Dewey did a brilliant job of prosecuting Luciano, but it helped that he could set all the rules.

Conclusion
Why Do We Need Organized Crime Anyway?

"This American system of ours, call it Americanism, call it capitalism, call it what you like, gives to each and every one of us a great opportunity if we only seize it with both hands and make the most of it."

—Al Capone

The successful prosecution of Luciano did not mark the end of organized crime in America. It did not even mark the end of Charlie Luciano.

In 1946 the New York governor pardoned Luciano on the condition that he be immediately deported. The governor who demonstrated such unexpected clemency happened to be the same Thomas E. Dewey whose stellar performance as prosecuting attorney at Luciano's trial a decade before had helped propel him into the governor's mansion in Albany. The irony was not lost on Charlie nor, one suspects, on Dewey himself.

Thus Charlie left New York City in the same way he had arrived there nearly forty years before—on a boat. This time, however, he made the trip in style rather than in steerage. His buddies all braved the early morning chill on the West Side Piers to see him off. Brushing aside the objections of the federal marshals accompanying Charlie, and despite the early hour, they threw him a farewell party with champagne and big bouquets of flowers in his stateroom. His long-time lover Gay Orlova came too, with a fresh supply of monogrammed silk underwear and pajamas.

Dewey's pardon was part of a deal cooked up between the wartime government and the underworld. Use your influence, the underworld had been told, and keep your eyes and ears open; if you find out anything about sabotage or enemy action, report it us. Pardoning Luciano was part of the government's side of the bargain. Governor Dewey, who played no part in the negotiations, now just wanted to get rid of Luciano as quickly and quietly as possible.[1]

The government's worries over the loyalty of the Italian underworld had turned out to be misplaced. Southern Italians, Sicilians in particular, had no love for Mussolini and his fascist government; their colleagues in the Jewish underworld had even less affection for Adolf Hitler. The underworld served their country loyally during the war. The sons of Southern and Eastern European immigrants, the ones whose parents had arrived at the turn of the century, now thought of themselves as true Americans. When the war put their patriotism to the test, the sons of immigrants passed with flying colors. Their service in war further accelerated their assimilation. So did the years immediately thereafter. On a far more massive scale than the returning World War I veterans, the soldiers returning form World War II chose to abandon the unhealthy tenements of the big-city immigrant ghettos and work and raise their families in the suburbs. So the old Jewish and Italian neighborhoods began to disappear. The East Harlem of Ciro Terranova, the Morello gang, and Frank Costello's childhood, where Vince Coll later earned his unfortunate nickname of "Baby killer," was transformed into Puerto Rican Spanish Harlem.

Luciano's own outfit had hardly been inconvienced by his incarceration anyway. Even before his arrest, the day-to-day management of the Luciano Family had been in Vito Genovese's hands. Tommy Lucchese continued to look after their trade union business while Meyer Lansky managed their casinos and racetracks. The re-arrangement of the New York mafia into the Five Families had been the work of Salvatore Maranzano, an achievement that survived its founder's violent demise. It survived Charlie's less violent removal as well. The arrangement in fact proved robust enough to continue on over the years, despite innumerable changes on top and in the ranks. In the end, the removal of Luciano had no more effect on New York crime than the removal of Capone had on the Chicago Outfit.

As they bid him *bon voyage,* Charlie's friends had little to complain about; it was a good time to be a crime overlord. Meyer was spending more time in Cuba these days. Acknowledging that they didn't even know how to run a crooked roulette wheel, Cuba's Battista government did the sensible thing and called in the boys who did know how. Little Meyer helped the Cubans re-organize their racetracks and their off-track betting industry. Benny Siegel, followed by Moe Dalitz, had a dream of transferring the night clubs and casinos of Havana to the hot sands of the American West. The dream was called "Las Vegas," though Benny Siegel did not survive to see it realized.

Frank Costello, by contrast, remained behind in New York. His exile from the city had been brief, and by the late 1940s he was quite the affable man about town. Costello helped his friends at Tammany, advised Mayor William O'Dwyer, recommended candidates for preferment, and raised funds for worthy causes beside Catholic bishops and municipal magistrates. He held court at the El Morocco club. Like Meyer, Frank was a major stakeholder in gambling concerns all over the country. He still kept his suite at the Waldorf, still hung out with Walter Winchell, and still gave racing tips to J. Edgar Hoover.

The United States had emerged from World War II victorious and, seemingly, more politically unified than the nation had been for decades. At the same time, the country was more than a little awe-struck at waking up to discover that it was now an international superpower. Anxiety over internal criminal enemies was replaced by anxiety over external threats and over the imagined emissaries of foreign powers hiding under our beds.

Winchell maintained his close association with Hoover, built up during the gangbusters' era. The newsman received juicy tidbits of agency scuttlebutt in exchange for plugs in his columns and broadcasts featuring the heroic "G Men" and their ever-vigilant director. But Winchell was discovering a new hero for post-war America—Senator Joe McCarthy. When the diva Josephine Baker decided to end her self-imposed exile and return to New York from Paris, Winchell denounced her in his column as a communist.

Therefore, much as it may have altered the personal histories of Dewey and Salvatore Lucania A.K.A. "Lucky Luciano," the Dewey prosecution did little to alter the course of American history. Forged during Prohibition and in the early years of the Depression, America's organized crime syndicates and the American mafia in particular flourished long after Prohibition and the Depression had faded into historical folklore. In one sense, however, the Dewey prosecution did mark a watershed. Emerging from the turn-of-the-century immigrant street gangs, America's organized crime syndicates were forged by Prohibition and the underworld wars of the late 1920s and early 1930s. Only the strongest, the best connected and the best organized survived the cull, and by the mid-1930s they had all left their bootlegging days behind and were expanding into new territories. For the half century that would follow, their future would lie in organized labor. But that, as the storyteller would say, is another story. By the time of the Dewey prosecution the process of formation was complete. Organized crime in America had come of age, punctuating the end of the era told in this story.

We began this narrative by asking two questions: First, why was organized crime necessary? Second, why is the crime story in America so intimately associated with the immigrant story? We might conclude by trying to provide some answers to those questions.

It may seem deliberately provocative to ask why organized crime in America was necessary. Crime is, by definition, a form of deviancy and, therefore, anything but necessary. Ideally, crime does not exist in a well-run community. Nevertheless, it is no apology or justification for the criminal to simply observe that, if a sizeable portion of a community persistently demands illegal goods or services, a supply of such goods or services will surely materialize. That supply, moreover, will be managed by businessmen who know how to operate in an illegal market — that is, criminals. This is all we mean by speaking of "the necessity" of organized crime: given enough demand, entrepreneurs emerge to arrange for its supply, whether the demand be legitimate or not. To paraphrase William Blake, the tigers of desire are stronger than the horses of organized repression.

The sense that organized crime is business in an illegal marketplace is reflected in the Federal Bureau of Investigation's own definition. According to the FBI, organized crime is "any group having some manner of a formalized structure and whose primary objective is to obtain money through illegal activities." The definition goes on to specify that, in pursuit of their illegal gains, criminals in organized crime typically employ "actual or threatened violence." They also "corrupt public officials" and have recourse to "graft, or extortion." They "have a significant impact on the people in their locales, region, or the country as a whole."[2] The FBI's definition is, on the one hand, comprehensive, while on the other, vague. What is "some manner of formalized structure" supposed to mean? Precisely what sort of "significant impact" do these activities have on "their locales, region and country as a whole?" There is a good reason for this lack of precision, however: organized crime is opportunistic. Organized crime arises to cater to a demand for illegal things, and this demand changes over time and circumstances. The business of crime is an open-ended one that cannot be pinned down by any specific activity. Organized crime is shape-shifting; any definition based on what it is today risks being out of date tomorrow.

For law-enforcement purposes, however, an open-ended definition will not do. To put a gangster behind bars, prosecutors need something solid and specific. But here another difficulty intervenes. An individual who employs violence, actual or threatened, in pursuit of illegal gains, or who corrupts public officials and practices extortion is *ipso facto* a criminal. He is a criminal moreover whether he is organized or not. Legal definitions of organized crime thus seem a bit superfluous, unless, of course, membership in an organized crime association happens itself to be a crime. This can raise a problem.

The problem lies in the contradiction between organized crime regarded as business and organized crime regarded as criminality. As a business, it is integrated into the economic fabric of the community, while as a criminal intrusion, it threatens the integrity of that same community. Should we regard the activities of today's drug cartels as part of the national economy, which in a real sense they are, and should their profits be taken into account in calculating the GNP? Or should they be regarded solely as a destructive, external force, which in an equally real sense they are as well? The honest answer is that they must be regarded as both. Regarding them solely as an external, anti-social force neglects to consider how much the business of crime is connected to other, legitimate businesses. As satisfying as this may appear from a moral perspective, it makes the nature of organized crime seem needlessly mysterious.

We can illustrate this contradiction with a story. In September 1920, Big Jim Colosimo's old lieutenant, Mike "the Pike" Heitler, barely out of Leavenworth for a Mann Act violation, managed to get himself a legal permit for sacramental wine. Armed with this, Heitler was able to order 1,000 gallons of whiskey currently held in a bonded warehouse at the Old Grand distillery in Louisville Kentucky, paying the distillery with a bank draft for $31,000. Even before it had arrived in Chicago, Heitler had already sold the whiskey to Chicago saloonkeepers for a hefty $200,000.

Heitler's whiskey was scheduled to arrive in Chicago at the Gresham Station, near 83rd and Vincennnes. Waiting for the precious cargo, Heitler had assembled a crew of thirty men to unload the freight cars. Along with Heitler overseeing the operations were twenty uniformed Chicago policemen who sipped whiskey from hip flasks that Heitler had thoughtfully provided. Soon after midnight a convoy of unmarked trucks was rolling out of the freight yards, bound, it was assumed, for the saloonkeepers who had paid Heitler so much for their whiskey. But the convoy never arrived. Somewhere between Gresham Station and the Loop, the entire shipment of 1,000 gallons was hijacked. The saloonkeepers demanded their money back. Heitler demurred; he was, he protested, a victim along with everyone else. Yet the word on the streets was that Heitler had hijacked his own shipment, storing it in a secret warehouse, then peddling it to the same saloonkeepers at twice the price.

The aggrieved saloonkeepers complained to the police.

Legally everyone involved in what would go down in Chicago underworld history as the "coup de hooch," Heitler, his men, his customers and the complicit police, were all guilty of Prohibition Law violations. Yet ignoring the fact that the merchandise was a prohibited substance, the police tried to convict Heitler and his associates for commercial fraud. They hoped to prosecute some of the complicit police officers as well. Heitler, however, proved uncooperative; he refused to implicate anyone. In the end, Heitler and five of his associates were sent back to Leavenworth, though for less than a year. Detective Sergeant George Harris, who had been in charge of the detail, was indicted though later acquitted. The director of the Prohibition Bureau in Chicago, Major A.V. Dalrymple, resigned in disgust.[3]

Anyone reading contemporary press accounts of such events might be forgiven for thinking that it was all a matter of corruption. It was the venal and corrupt officials who were thwarting the success of the Volstead Act. Remove these corrupt officials, the rotten apples, the reasoning went, and replace them with honest ones who would do their duty and lock the criminals up, and the violations would cease. Prohibition would become a reality. Yet even at the time, thoughtful commentators understood that this was an oversimplification. The Volstead Act was floundering, neither because bootlegging gangs had descended upon the town nor because officials in Chicago were corrupt. The act was floundering because Chicago was refusing to obey it. The refusal was creating a vastly lucrative market, an economic niche that criminal entrepreneurs hastened to fill. So lucrative was this niche, this illegal market, that the criminal entrepreneurs soon had ample means to bribe officials to look the other way or even guard their whiskey convoys. Corruption was the end product. It was not the *cause* of the Volstead Act's failure; it was instead the *result*.

It was thus the demand for illegal goods and services that begat the bootlegging gangs. These gangs were groups, as the FBI put it, "whose primary objective is to obtain money through illegal activities." As these groups organized their businesses, they then, in their turn, begat the corrupt public officials as well as the graft or extortion. Nor did the chain of begetting stop here. Although corruption was more a result of illegal markets than its cause, once corruption had taken hold, it set off its own vicious circle that led to more commerce in illegal goods and ever more corruption. This is what had a "significant impact" on the community involved—Chicago.

How had it all gotten started? Why was the Chicago police (or any other municipal police force) so corrupt? We might suggest five reasons:

1. They were venal.

2. They didn't think much of Prohibition.

3. They believed that a sizeable proportion of their fellow Chicagoans didn't think much of it either.

4. They had never really enforced anti-vice laws anyway.

5. They had never imagined that their fellow Chicagoans really expected them to enforce these laws.

These reasons are, of course, cumulative rather than alternative. We might even throw in a sixth: Realizing that the bootleggers' convoys were liable to be hijacked by other bootlegging gangs or perhaps harassed by the local police, they felt someone ought to protect them. Besides, the thoughtful Mr. Heitler was offering to pay them for their services and provide some free refreshment as well. Given the real, as opposed to the ideal, situation in Chicago as many of the local cops may have perceived it, they were only doing their duty in guarding Heitler's whiskey consignment, getting a chunk of overtime pay in the bargain. Who were they hurting? But when Heitler then hi-jacked his own whiskey, the Chicago cops felt he had made chumps out of them all. And that made them sore.

Like New York under Tammany, municipal government in Chicago was traditionally based on a double standard. A narrow WASP ruling oligarchy enacted statutes banning not only prostitution but also horse racing, prize fighting, dog fighting, public dancing, cursing. Also banned was any form of sports, roistering, or drinking on the Sabbath. Few outside this oligarchy (and by no means everyone within it) regarded these statutes as enforceable or even took them all that seriously; yet few cared to admit this for fear of calling down moral opprobrium.

The result was that the police were left to enforce the so-called "Blue Laws" at their own discretion. This meant, first, attempting to confine vice and conceal it from public view, and second, levying tributes upon it. We saw that in the 1890s the New York police had tried to justify the first aspect of their policy by arguing that, though it was impossible to eradicate vice, it was at least possible to segregate it and keep it out of respectable areas. Whether this claim was strictly true, it was widely accepted at the time. In respect to the second part, it was further claimed that the tributes on the vice resorts constituted a form of alternative taxation on a part of the urban economy that would not, otherwise, pay any taxes at all. This second claim was not so readily accepted. Critics perceived that, by becoming dependent on the tributes they levied on the vice resorts, the police made themselves ultimately accountable to the owners and managers of these resorts, the underworld, rather than to the public. Forcing the public to pay bribes for permissions, licenses, and other municipal services, corrupt politicians are able to provide further bribe-garnering jobs for their clients and cronies at little cost to the municipal payroll. Endemic corruption in New York and Chicago, as in many Third World countries today, evolved into a form of alternative system of municipal employment, a form of government-on-the-cheap, a jobs-for-the-boys scheme that paid its own way.

It was Rev. Dr. Charles H. Parkhurst, reform leader and early progressive, who first spoke of *organized crime*. In a sermon in 1892 in which he referred to the Tammany mayor Hugh J. Grant and the rest of the city's political leaders, as "a lying, perjuring, rum-soaked, and libidinous lot of polluted harpies" who were "feeding night and day on [the city's] quivering vitals."[4] He also told his listeners that Tammany represented "the organization of crime," while the New York police represented "organized municipal criminality."[5] For him, the business or crime and official corruption were strictly complementary. In order for the business of crime to grow and expand, it was necessary for it to corrupt officials, thereby setting in motion the vicious circle in which crime, now under discrete official encouragement, could grow so rich and powerful that it was ultimately able to seize the thoroughly corrupted municipality "by the throat." Parkhurst was convinced that the damage caused to New York by a corrupt NYPD was far more serious than the damage resulting from vice itself; "The guilt of the proprietors [of vice resorts] is not nearly so great as the guilt of the police system that tolerates and fosters guilty proprietorship," he wrote the Police Commissioners in January 1892. "It is our police system that is the supreme culprit."[6]

The difficulty in eradicating the business of crime always stemmed from the fact that this business is economically embedded in an extensive network of clients, customers and other beneficiaries as well as politically protected by a network of corrupt and complicit officials. Vice, corruption and organized crime, we saw the chief of police telling the mayor in New York, was part of the system, a significant factor in the municipal economy; eliminate vice and corruption, he had said, and the whole political system would buckle. There was never any secret about this. Whatever their private views about vice, corruption and organized crime may have been, America's urban voters seem to have had few illusions and seemed prepared to tolerate a certain level of all three, thereby allowing the business of crime to grow so rooted in its community that the elimination of even major criminals like Capone or Luciano has very little effect. This is not, of course, to say that vice, corruption and organized crime had little effect on urban America. As John Landesco would later say of Chicago, "For many years Chicago has been under the domination of the underworld. For many years Chicago has tolerated vice, and now the underworld and vice have it by the throat."

Once municipal voters in America had woken up to the real costs of corruption, they began to support reform with an enthusiasm that they had never shown for anti-vice campaigns. By re-orienting the priorities away from vice itself and towards the municipal corruption that it engendered, progressives like Dr. Parkhurst were able to achieve far more in a few years than in a century's worth of anti-vice campaigning. By the onset of Prohibition, reform had notched up an impressive series of victories. Chicago's old Levee, already under assault by 1910, was subjected to repeated scourgings by anti-vice crusaders. They succeeded in shutting down Hinky Dink's and Bathhouse John's notoriously seedy Derby, ran the elegant Everleigh sisters out of town, and transformed Big Jim Colosimo into an honest night-club proprietor. By 1915 the resorts were shuttered, and the old First Ward Levee looked like a ghost town scheduled for urban renewal, as set out in the 1909 Burnham Plan. Nor was Chicago in any way exceptional. New Orleans closed down Storyville in 1917. Albert Fried commented that a Jewish observer on New York's Lower East Side in 1918–1919 might have predicted that, "within ten years of so, Jewish gangsterism, the community's deepest reproach and most awful scourge, would have petered out." The first two decades of the new century had indeed transformed America's municipalities. Corrupt machines were reformed or driven from office, honky tonks were shut down, and the complex ties linking machine politicians, police officials, vice lords, and street gangs were pruned back. Though, especially in the Midwest, streets gangs and remnants of the old vice rings still existed, when the Eighteenth Amendment presented a new illegal market to exploit, organized crime still had to re-build their organizations almost from scratch. In this way, one unexpected consequence of reformist success earlier in the century was that, under Prohibition, independent, interstate crime syndicates emerged and replaced the municipal political machines as the organizers or organized crime.

We saw that the investigations of Judge Seabury at the end of the 1920s revealed that the New York police were still levying tributes on prostitutes. One consequence of the crack-down resulting from these investigations was that, with the police off their backs, prostitutes were able to keep a much larger percentage of their earnings. Here was an illicit market waiting to be exploited. Whether Charlie Luciano was directly involved in this exploitation, there is no reason to dispute Dewey's point of departure. Based on the findings of his investigator, Eunice Carter, Dewey discovered that the New York Italian underworld was attempting to organize prostitution in New York, moving in to levy tributes upon it. In other words, the New York mafia was taking over a role formerly played by the NYPD. With the decline of Tammany as the managers of organized municipal criminality, the mafia was stepping in to take their place. This was not perhaps exactly what Daniel Boorstein was thinking of when he spoke of the "ethnic succession" in organized crime.

The idea of ethnic succession was always a blunt tool for analysis. There undoubtedly was some sort of ethnic succession in the story of organized crime in America; but it was not a simple demographic process. We must not think of it as the Jews and South Italians riding up on an escalator with the Irish a step above them and the Puerto Ricans a step below. Nothing so straightforward ever occurred.

As the American economy began rapidly expanding in the first years of the twentieth century, the Great Lakes Basin, where much of the industrial expansion was taking place, sucked in vast quantities of foreign workers. The majority of these workers came from Eastern and Northern Europe. After English and then German (which declined rapidly after America's entry into World War I) the major languages spoken here were Polish and Swedish. There was immigration from Southern Europe as well, and Greek, Levantine Arabic, and Hungarian could all be heard on the streets of Chicago or Detroit. There was Italian immigration too, of course, but Italians were never the majority of Chicago's or Detroit's immigrant population. They were dwarfed in number by the Poles and the Swedes, and by the older Irish and German populations as well. In Chicago, taken by size, the Italians came in about tenth, just behind the Norwegians. So how does ethnic succession explain the emergence of the Capone Outfit in Chicago? Even more insignificant numerically, the Jews had at first seemed simply an exotic element within the Germanic and, later, Eastern European immigration streams. The Italians always outnumbered the Jews. So why was organized crime in Detroit dominated by the Jewish Purple Gang, leaving the Italians to play second fiddle?

In spite of their numbers, the Jewish and Italian immigrants were highly visible. Arriving in the 1880s and 1890s, they had made their homes in Manhattan's Lower East Side and Chicago's River Wards, often occupying formerly Irish poor working-class districts, usually just a short walk from the city's commercial and financial heart. Scandinavians and Eastern European Slavs arrived in large numbers a few years later but were often shunted off to work camps or factory towns where they were less visible. In their new homes in the older urban ghettos, the Jews and Italians took to commerce, becoming the city's tailors and seamstresses, barbers, cheap clothing sellers, short-order cooks, sandwich counter guys, waiters, barbers, push-cart vendors, organ grinders and much else besides. But these urban ghettos were the same areas where Tammany and corrupt Chicago bosses like Johnny Power had traditionally recruited their followers, the areas where vice resorts and honky tonks were tolerated and where the first gangs had formed. The Jews and Italians took to these activities as well, joining gangs, working in the honky tonks and for the corrupt machines. We discover a large number of Jewish names in lists of resort owners in the Lexow and Mazet reports in New York in the 1890s and of Italian names in the 1911 report of the Chicago vice commission.[7] A polemic blew up about Jewish, or Jewish-Italian domination of the vice industry and of the existence of international Jewish white-slavery rings. The influence of Jewish and Italian commerce, already powerful in legitimate retailing, was making itself felt in illegal businesses as well.[8]

As reformist campaigns broke apart the links between political machines and the vice resorts in the honky tonks, the police were no longer able or permitted to manage these resorts. In Parkhurst's words, they were no longer able to play the role of the organizers of municipal criminality. It was a void that Jewish and Italian criminal entrepreneurs were able to step into. It was in this sense that a succession took place. It was not precisely an ethnic succession. It was not that Jewish and Italian criminality succeeded Irish criminality; it was rather that Jewish and Italian criminal entrepreneurs succeeded the political machines as the organizers of organized crime. The older Irish gangs like the Whyos in New York or the O'Banionites in Chicago had been brawlers, yeggmen (bank robbers), and sluggers for hire. They had never managed vice resorts; it would never have appealed to their romantic sensibilities. The Jews and Italians, by contrast, did become criminal entrepreneurs; and though the wilder elements of Chicago criminality were reluctant to see the light, with the enactment of national prohibition, this was the direction that American criminality had to take. Johnny Torrio had been right all along.

Within the larger story of the decline of the old urban machines with their links to their respective vice rings and the emergence of relatively autonomous crime syndicates, there is the particular story of the rise to dominance of the mafia. The Sicilians and Neapolitans had held the best hands from the start; they were better organized. Organized protection rackets were part of their tradition. The FBI, we saw, defined organized crime as a group having some manner of a "formalized structure." This is about as far as the FBI is willing to go in acknowledging that the American mafia has its own tradition along with a formal organizational structure, with grades, rules and initiation ceremonies. The FBI has always been reluctant to admit that the mafia possesses such attributes. In part, treating the mafia as a real organization with some degree of institutional stability contradicts their preferred representation of organized crime as a hostile, predatory force impinging on ordered society from the outside. Besides, representing the mafia as the American development of a sect with roots in Sicilian culture seems to confer a certain legitimacy upon it. Rather, the preferred model is to present organized crime as a malignant, antisocial force, with the FBI cast in the role of the nation's guardians, protecting our shores from alien predators. As much as this may flatter our self-image, it ignores an important truth: illegal businesses cannot thrive without clients and customers. Organized crime exists because we invite it in.

Maybe it's no more than intellectual laziness to think that things could never have been other than the way they were, that organized crime might never have developed in America. Or maybe it's the movies. Maybe what was really necessary all along were gangster films. They tell us so much. In the first critical essay ever written on these films, the young film critic Robert Warshow wrote in 1948 that the celluloid gangster, "is the man of the city . .

. not the real city, but that dangerous and sad city of the imagination which is so much more important, which is the modern world." The "dangerous and sad city of the imagination," however, is the dystopic counterpart of that other American cultural archetype, the shining City on the Hill. And we cannot, it seems, explain the one city without the other. That is why we need the gangsters; for they, as Warshow points out, are the residents of that sad and dangerous, bad city of the imagination. It is not where they want to live. Gangsters want to live in the good, but erqually imaginary, City on the Hill. That is the city of the good life, the city they their parents came to America to find. And they are bound there too; they just have to get there, pull off the last big job, dodge the law one last time, and then get out for good. The American dream will be theirs. But it never is. They are destined to fall in the final reel. And their fall is bittersweet. For the fall of the celluloid gangster is never simply the story of the triumph of justice; it is the story of the loss of innocence and the shattering of illusions as well. Not for nothing Warshow called his essay, "The Gangster as Tragic Hero."

Tragedy, Warshow observes, has no place in the American way of life. It has been written out of the plot, banished. That is where the gangster as tragic hero comes in. "The real city . . . ," Warshow concludes, "only produces criminals; the imaginary city produces the gangster: he was what we want to be and what we are afraid we might become."[9]

Notes

INTRODUCTION

1. Martin Gosch and Richard Hammer, *The Last Testament of Lucky Luciano* (1974), 12 (hereafter *Luciano Testament*).

2. The total number of immigrants admitted to American ports between 1880 and 1919 was 23,462,630, of which 17,097,640 entered through New York. Philadelphia was a distant second, followed by Boston and Charleston. Figures cited in Kesner 1977, 5.

3. Jacob Riis, *How the Other Half Lives: Studies Among the Tenements of New York* (1888), 18–19.

4. See Daniel Bell, *The End of Ideology*, 1962. See also Francis A.J. Ianni, *The Crime Society: Organized Crime and Corruption in America* (1974), and Francis A.J. Ianni and Elizabeth Resuss-Ianni, *Black Mafia: Ethnic Secession in Organized Crime* (1974).

CHAPTER 1

1. Cited in Aldo Maria Viola, 'l'attività cospirativa in Sicilia nel decennio della restaurazione Borbonica (1849–1860) in *Nuovi Quaderni Meridionali* 22.87/88 (1984): 223–47.

2. For the origins of the *Carbonari* and political sects in Sicily, see Fentress 2002, *Rebels and Mafiosi, death in a Sicilian Landscape*, 21–35.

3. Ibid., 63.

4. Ibid., 92–93.

5. Ibid., 139–46.

6. Antonio Cutrera, *La Mafia* (1900).

7. T. Tommasi-Crudeli, *La Sicilia in 1871 Florence* (1871).

8. Napoleone Colajanni, 'La delinquenza in Sicilia e le sue cause' Palermo (1885).

9. Fazio, *Memorie Giovanili* (1901).

10. G. Mosca, 1980: "Mafia" in *Uomini e cose di Sicilia* Sellerio, (originally series of articles for *Corriere della Sera* in 1905).

11. The story was used by Michele Amari in his 1830 account of the Sicilian Vespers and repeated in his popularized and much shortened version, published in Palermo on the six hundred-year anniversary of the Vespers in 1882. Amari was careful to observe that the story was to be taken as true in spirit rather than literally true.

12. On the *Fratellanza* see Colacino, Tommaso 1885, "La Fratellanza: associazione di Malfattori" in *Rivista di Discipline Carcerarie,* 1885, 79–89, Fentress 2002, 214–21.

13. On the *comparatico* in America, see Richard Orsi 2002, *Madonna of 115th Street,* 91, 226.

14. Emanuele Scalici 1883, *La mafia siciliana*; republished 1988.

15. Fentress 2002, 198–200, cf. Notes to Morani report.

16. Cited in Amelia Crisantino 2000, *Della segreta e operosa societa',* 200.

17. Ibid., 201–3.

18. Ibid and Reid 1952, *The Mafia,* 278. See also Pezzino 1990, *Una Certa Recipriocita di Favori,* 172–73.

19. Nelli 1976, *The Business of Crime,* 24–28.

20. On the Leone band, see G. DeMenza 1877, *Le Cronache d'Assise di Palermo.*

21. David Leon Chandler 1975, *Criminal Brotherhoods,* 40–45, Nelli 1976, 28–30.

22. Tom Smith 2007, *Crescent City Lynchings,* 57.

23. Asbury 2000, *The French Quarter,* 407. Pasquale Corte's statement was reprinted in the *American Law Review,* May-June 1891.

24. Nelli 1976, 30.

25. Ibid., 37–38.

26. Tom Smith 2007, *Joseph P. Macheca and the Birth of the American Mafia,* 68–69.

27. July 20, 1890, cited in Nelli 1976, 41.

28. Nelli 1976, 47–66, Gambino 1988, 1–22.

29. Nelli 1976, 50–51.

30. Gambino 1998, 20.

31. Smith 2007, 57.

32. Ibid., 103–5.

33. Captain A. Kalinski; see Gambino 1998, 76.

34. Ibid., 57, 62–66.

35. On the aftermath of the lynching, see Nelli 1976, 1–66, Gambino 1998, 78–88.

36. Nelli 1976. The exception is Chandler 1975.

37. Nelli 1976, p. 64.

38. Gambino 1998, 60.

39. Asbury 2000, 406. This "co-partnership," Asbury claims, was the origin of the *Stoppaglieri.* This is unlikely, the *Stoppaglieri* in New Orleans were probably founded some time after 1875. Nevertheless, it is interesting to discover that some form of Sicilian organized crime existed in the city before the *Stoppagliere* arrival. Asbury further claims that by 1869 this new criminal group had defeated an even earlier group of Sicilian criminals from Messina. Perhaps 1869 was instead

the date of the Provenzanos entry into New Orleans.

40. Cutrera 1900; reprint 1996, 137. The brackets are Cutrera's gloss. Don Simone was Giuseppe Cavallaro's son, see Fentress 2002, 241.

41. Ibid.

42. Louie Armstrong, *Satchmo: my life in New Orleans* (New York: Prentice Hall, 1954; James Bezou, *Horn of Plenty* (New York: Allen, Tourne and Heath, 1947.

CHAPTER 2

1. Sonnino Sidney and Leopoldo Franchetti 1876, *L'Inchiesta in Sicilia*, 12.

2. U.S. Department of Commerce, Bureau of the Census, *Historical Statistics of the United States, Colonial Times to 1957*, 56–57.

3. Robert A. Caro 1975, *The Power Broker: Robert Moses and the fall of New York*, 60.

4. On the end of Tweed, see Alexander B. Callow Jr., *The Tweed Ring*. The citation is from E. L. Godkin, writing in *The Nation*, November 9, 1871.

5. Callow 1969, 32. The citation was quoted in the New York *Times*, November 29, 1870.

6. Oliver E. Allen. 1993, *The Tiger*.

7. New York *Telegram*, May 20, 1921. Cited in Callow 1969, 152.

8. Callow 1969, 152.

9. December 29, 1870.

10. Callow 1969, 152–60.

11. Eleventh Census, 1890, part 1. The figures for the rest of the New York area are similar. For discussions cf. Baylor 1988, *Neighbors in Conflict, the irish, Germans, Jews and Italians in New York City, 1929–1941*, 5–44.

12. Nathan Glazer and Daniel P. Moynihan: *Beyond the Melting Pot: The Negroes, Puerto Ricans, Jews, Italians and Irish of New York City*, 2d ed. (Cambridge, Mass.:MIT Press, 1970), 221.

13. "In New York City, Tammany bosses Fernando Wood and William Marcy Tweed naturalized 9,207 immigrants per year between 1856 and 1867. The pace of naturalization soon quickened. In 1868, Tammany naturalized 41,112 foreign-born in order to swell the ranks of Democratic loyalists and win the crucial gubernatorial contest in that year, freeing the city of state Republican control. The Wigwam hired the New York Printing Company, which Tweed owned, to print 105,000 blank naturalization applications and 69,000 certificates of naturalization. Immigrants fresh off the boat were given red tickets, allowing them to get their citizenship papers free. Tammany paid the required court fees and provided false witnesses to testify that the immigrants had been in the country for the necessary five years." Steven P. Erie, *Rainbow's End, Irish-Americans and the Dilemmas of Urban Machine Politics, 1840–1985* (Berkeley, Calif.: University of Califonia Press, 1988), 51.

14. Moynihan and Glazer 1970, 218.

15. M.R. Werner 1928, *Tammany Hall*, 276.

16. David C. Hammack 1987, *Power and Society, Greater New York at the Turn of the Century*, 161.

17. London *Reviews of Reviews*, October 1897.

18. For Sullivan's career see Daniel Czitrom, "Underworlds and Underdogs: Big Tim Sullivan and Metropolitan Politics in New York, (1889–1913)" in *Journal of American History* 78 (June–September 1976), 536–58.

19. Plunkett's musings were often recorded in the papers. They have since been collected and published in Theodore Riordan 1961.

20. Leo Katcher 1959, *The Big Bankroll, the life and times of Arnold Rothstein.*

21. New York *Times*, March 9, 1900.

22. Ade 1931, *The Old Time Saloon*, 8.

23. Lexow Committee, vol. 1.

24. Erie 1988, 55.

25. See resumé in *Lexow Committee*, vol. 1, 1–76.

26. Ibid., 36.

27. Gilfoyle 1992, *The City of Eros*, 251–52.

28. Lardner and Reppetto 2000, 92–93. The story of the meeting between Mayor Hewitt and Commissioner Murray is often repeated. Lardner and Reppetto, who give no source, are perhaps drawing on Lincoln Steffens. Gilfoyle remarks that Hewitt's activities in suppressing vice were connected to his need to enlist the support of the anti-vice leagues in his struggle against Henry George, Gilfoyle 1992, 195.

29. Asbury 1928, *The Gangs of New York*, 206–15. Asbury also includes what are probably mug shots of nine members of the gang. Piker Ryan's price list, which dates from the 1880s, is also included in Harlow and others.

30. Asbury 1928, 206.

31. Sante 1992, *Low Life*, 211, 214.

32. Sante 1992 and Virgil Peterson 1983, *The Mob, 200 Years of Organized Crime in New York*.

33. Kibbe Turner cites Byrnes' statement in "Daughters of the Poor: A Plain Story of the Development of New York City as a Leading Center of the White Slaving Trade in the World," *McClure's* Magazine, November 1909, 45–61.

34. Asbury 1928, 255–56.

35. Ibid., 254. See also the descriptions in Harlow 1931, Peterson 1983 and Humbert S. Nelli 1974, *The Business of Crime*.

36. Peterson 1983, 101.

37. Alfred Henry Lewis 1912, *The Apaches of New York*, 74.

38. Sante 1992, 222–24.

39. Craig Thompson and Allen Raymond 1940, *Gang Rule in New York*.

40. Werner 1928, 771–73; Lothar Stoddard 1931, *The Rising Tide of Color Against White Supremacy*, 243–46.

41. Sante 1992, 219–22.

42. Laurence Bergreen 1994, *Capone, the man and his era*, 35.

43. O'Connor 1958, *Hell's Kitchen: The Roaring Days of New York's Wild West Side*, 49.

44. Ibid., 25.

45. Ibid., 17.

46. Asbury 1928, 225.

47. Ibid., 236.

48. On Stephen Crane see Stansell 2000, 25–26. Typically, Stansell's rather breathless history of Bohemian culture in turn-of-the-century New York has nothing to say about the low lifes. Yet one has only to read Crane or O'Neill to see that the writers themselves noticed, and were indeed attracted by, them. In this respect, Albert Parry 1933 or Hutchins Hapgood 1965 (copyright 1902) are better sources.

49. Asbury 1928, 315–16. See also Peterson 1983, 102, and Nelli 1974.

50. Curt Johnson 1998, *Wicked City:Chicago from Kenna to Capone*, 98–99.

51. New York *Times*, March 31, 1939.

52. Jack McPhaul 1970, *Torrio: First of the Gang Lords*, 45–47, 51.

53. Luciano testament 1974, 6–7.

54. Ibid., 11.

55. Leonard Katz 1973, *Uncle Frank, the biography of Frank Costello*, 45–46.

56. Graham Nown 1987, *The English Godfather*, 47.

57. Peter Maas 1969, *The Valachi Papers*, 63.

58. Nown 1987, 52, 72–78.

59. Dennis Eisenberg, Uri Dan, and Eli Landau 1980, *Meyer Lansky, Mogul of the mob*, 55.

60. Ibid., 42–46.

61. Luciano testament, 18.

62. Eisenberg, Dan and Landau 1980, 62–63.

63. Ibid., 66.

64. Luciano testament, 33. In Lansky's version, it's Siegel who cases the bank, and reports back to his friends, "I'm not putting any of my money there, anybody can bust in and steal every dime." Eisenberg, Dan, and Landau 1980, 89.

65. Katz 1973, 48–49.

66. Luciano testament, 25.

CHAPTER 3

1. San Francisco *Examiner*, Nov. 28, 1878. In Nelli 1976, 69–70.

2. See Salvatore Salomone-Marino, "Le pompe nunziali ed il corredo delle donne siciliane nei secc XIV, XV, XVI," in *Nuove Effemeride siciliane*, 4 ser 3 (1876): 43–80; *Archivio storico siciliano* 1 (1876): 209–40, "Una festa nuziale celebrata in Palermo nel 1574 e descritta da una contemporaneo," Palermo 1877.

3. September 29, 1902, cited in Nelli 1976, p. 72.

4. Thomas Pitkin and Francesco Cordasco 1977, *The Black Hand*.

5. Pitkin and Cordasco 1977, Nelli 1976 and John S Kendall, "Who killa de Chief," in *Louisiana Historical Quarterly*, vol 22 (1933): 492–530 all give examples of Black Hand letters.

6. Chicago *Daily News*, March 25, 1913, cited in Kobler 1971, *Capone*, 43.

7. *Cosmopolitan*, June 1909, in Nelli 1976, 85.

8. Nelli 1976, p. 88.

9. Petrosino "The Black Hand Scourge," in Nelli 1976, 87.

10. *Times* May 8, July 25, 1908; Frank Marshall White, "The Black Hand in Control of Italian New York," *Outlook* Magazine, 104, (August 16, 1913): 858–59. In Nelli 1976, 90.

11. McAdoo 1906, 154, cited in Peterson 1983, 108–9.

12. Gangrule.com/gangs.php?ID=2.

13. *Times,* Oct 16, 17, 22, 1888; March 27, 30, April 2, 3 1889, cited in Pitkin and Cordasco 1977, 34. Also William J. Flynn 1919, *The Barrel Murder*.

14. Petacco 2001, *Joe Petrosino, l'uomo che sfido' per la prima volta la mafia italoamericano,* 8. This detail is not in other accounts.

15. Gangrule.com/gangs.php?ID=3.

16. Pitkin and Cordasco 1997, note on 234.

17. It was never clear how and when Petto had disappeared. Petacco has his own interpretation of the event, 2001, 19–21.

18. Q uoted in Pitkin and Cordasco 1977, 55.

19. Gangrule.com/gangs.php?ID=2.

20. Petacco 2001, 57–60.

21. Quoted in Flynn 1919, 199–202.

22. Ibid., 208–9. Both the oaths and the letters have been badly translated, and remain obscure in a number of points. Flynn simply refers to the East Harlem group as, among other things, a "Black Hand gang." This is certainly not what the gang called itself.

23. On Cascio Ferro, see Fentress 2002 and Anton Blok 1975, *The Mafia in a Sicilian Village,* and Petacco 2001, 101–11.

24. Petacco 2001, 105.

25. Ibid., 106.

26. Flynn 1919, 208–9.

27. There were these sorts of letters in contemporary Sicilian papers as well, cf. Gaetano Falzone 1975, *Storia della Mafia*.

28. *Tribune* April 27, 1903, in Pitkin and Cordasco 1977. It's not clear when this editorial was written.

29. Ibid.

30. According to Nelli, Giosue Gallucci had emigrated from Palermo instead (1976, 30). Most other authorities, however, agree that after his brother, Gennaro, had escaped from a Neapolitan prison, the two made their way to New York. Gennaro was murdered in East Harlem shortly after arrival.

31. Ibid.

32. New York *Herald* May 18, 1915.

33. Peterson 1983, 127; Sifakis 1999, *The Mafia Encyclopedia*. See entries "murder stable,". 263 and "Lupo the wolf," 228; Asbury 1928, 248.

34. Gangrule.com/gangs.php?ID=4, ID=5.

35. 2001, 66. Petacco claims that he is quoting from a police statement.

36. Nelli 1976, 130.

37. Ibid., 133–34.

38. Kobler 1971, 34.

39. Asbury 1940, *Gem of the Prairie*.

40. Gangrule.com/gangs.php?ID=5.

41. Nelli 1976, 132.

42. Ibid. and Nelli 1976, 130–34.

43. Gangrule.com/gangs.php?ID=5.

CHAPTER 4

1. 1961, 10–11.

2. William Stead 1894 (1972), *If Christ Came to Chicago,* 172.

3. In Douglas Bukowski 1998, *Big Bill Thompson, Chicago and the Politics of Image,* 17.

4. In Stephen Longstreet 1973, *Chicago 1880–1919,* 101.

5. Richard C. Lindberg 1996, *Chicago by Gasllight,* 186–87.

6. Bukowski 1998, 20.

7. Johnson 1998, 18–19.

8. "He never held office but he ruled the city with an iron hand. He named the men who were to be candidates for election, he elected them, and after they were in office they were merely his slaves." Chicago *Record-Herald's* obituary, August 18, 1907, quoted in Nelli 1969.

9. Longstreet 1973, 96–97

10. Longstreet 1973, 202, 287. For Carter Harrison's role in the Haymarket riot, see Lindberg 1996, 27–45.

11. Peterson 1952, *Barbarians in our midst, a history of Chicago Crime,* 84.

12. For Coughlin and Kenna see Asbury 1940, *Gem of the Prairie: An Informal History of Chicago Crime;* also Lloyd Wendt and Herman Kogan 1944, *Lords of the Levee, Bathhouse John and Hinky Dink.*

13. Perry Duis, introduction to Asbury 1940.

14. It was the economics of prostitution that most impressed the Vice Commission. Officially, prostitution was considered a marginal activity, a handful of fallen women recruited from the dregs of society. Not so, the Commission discovered; prostitution was a major business, one of the biggest in the city. It was a business, moreover, whose extent and profitability were consistently underestimated in official sources. The Chicago Police Department had provided the Vice Commission with their list of known houses of ill-fame. But the number was a mere 192. After a few months' research, the Commission found 514 not on the list. The Chicago Police Department estimated that a little over one thousand prostitutes worked in their list of houses. The Commission soon augmented this list to over four thousand. But even this, they added, was probably nowhere near the true figure. There were more houses of ill-fame operating clandestinely in the city. There were the street walkers who took their clients to cheap hotels and assignation apartments. Neither the police nor the Commission had any way of knowing how many of them there were. Besides this, the Commission added, the figures took no account of the legions of part-time or semi-professional prostitutes, girls who worked in factories or department stores at between $4 to $6 per week, but who might double their wages by hustling on week-ends. A true estimate of the number of prostitutes working in Chicago was likely to be in the range of fifteen thousand. At this point, the Commission endeavoured to translate these statistics into dollars and cents. Using as base the number of known prostitutes—five thousand—the Commission asked how much illicit sex this number represented. That of course depended on how many times a prostitute had sex each working day. The Commission calculated that the average working brothel accommodated between fifty to seventy men per day. This again was a conservative estimate, for the Commission reported that one prostitute had told them that she and her partner had,

for years, been receiving between 350 and 400 men each week. Records seized from one brothel showed that, between August 1906 and June 1908, the house had contained anywhere between twelve to twenty-four girls, who, between the above dates, had entertained 179,599 men. Taking these and other records together, the Commission estimated that the average prostitute had sex with approximately fifteen customers each day. Even judging by the gross underestimates of the police, this, the Commission calculated, would mean that 5,540,700 acts of illicit sex were taking place in the metropolis each year. Using their revised estimate of the number of prostitutes in the city, the figure of annual illicit sex acts rose to 27.375 million. But even this, of course, was based on ultra-conservative estimates of both the number of prostitutes and the number of men they accommodated. If the Commission's suspicion were correct, the real illicit sex-acts per annum figure would be closer to 80 million. This, in turn, meant that the annual turnover in Chicago's illicit sex business was somewhere between $15 million and $50 million.

The implications of these figures are rather interesting. Chicago's population at the time was something over 2 million, of which about half were male. This means that a little over one million Chicago males were indulging in eighty million illicit sex act per year (perhaps a little less when the transient trade is taken into consideration). But this is a figure that includes all the males—the toddlers, the babes in arms, the infirm, the decrepit and all those who, for some reason or another, were unwilling or unable to participate. Clearly there were sections of Chicago's male population who were contributing more than others. One can't help but be reminded of the publicity once appearing on McDonalds Hamburger franchises of "Over X Million Sold." As long as it could be provided conveniently and rapidly, and, most important, at a price they could afford to pay, there were sections of Chicago's male population whose appetite for this product was virtually insatiable.

15. Lindberg 1996.

16. *The Social Evil*, 1911, 160.

17. On vice and the Levee, see Asbury 1986, 242–80 and *passim*. Longstreet 1973, 293–303, 401–7. Johnson 1998, 71–79. See also Lloyd Wendt and Herman Kogan 1944.

18. John Landesco 1928, *Organized Crime in Chicago*, 25–43.

19. Asbury 1986, 279–80.

20. Johnson 1998, 10.

21. Ibid., 278. See also the descriptions in Longstreet 1973, 345–53 and in Wendt and Kogan 1943.

22. Lindberg 1996, 130–34.

23. On the padrone system of recruited labor, see Nelli 1969.

24. Johnson 1998, 87–88. The figures are no more than an educated guess.

25. Ibid., 89.

26 Longstreet 1973, 399; also Asbury 1986, 239.

27. Nelli 1976, 125.

28. *The Truth about the Mafia and Organized Crime in America*, 1962. I am citing Allan May as I have been unable to locate this book. May comments that Schiavo's book "seemed to have come right from the public relations department of Mafia Inc."

29. Richard Orsi 2002, *The Madonna of 115th Street*, 122, 131.

30. On D'Andrea, see Johnson 1998, 135, Nelli 1976, 125, 134–36, Kobler 1971, 91–94, May in AmericanMafia.com. Kobler states that Roosevelt pardoned D'Andrea after thirteen months in Joliet. Other sources state that the pardon came in 1908.

31. Landesco 1928, 121.

32. Kobler 1992, 93.

33. Landesco 1928, 123.

34. Allan May AmericanMafia.com, Kobler 1971, 91–95.

35. Asbury 1940.

36. Kobler 1992, 44-5. Lindberg 1996 and Johnson 1998 repeat this evidence.

37. Asbury 1986, 267–69.

38. Johnson 1998, 87. Johnson forgets that income tax was only introduced in 1913. Colosimo was liable to fines but not taxes.

39. Johnson 1998, 84–90; Lindberg 1996, 125–26; Krober 1992, 43, 115.

40. Peterson 1952, 81.

41. Johnson 1998, 78.

42. Ibid., 102; Asbury, 1940, 297–98.

43. Kobler 1971, 33.

44. Lindberg 1996, 141–42; Asbury 1940.

45. Kobler 1992, 38–39.

46. McPhaul 1970, 112–13. McPhaul merely asserts that "the theory was that Vanilla fired the initial shot," but that "Vanilla's weapon was not to be found." He is basing his account on the *Tribune's* accounts from July 15.

47. Peterson is uncharacteristically equivocal, ". . . a gang of hoodlums connected to the vice trust. . ." shot Birns. Since the only hoodlums that contemporary sources mentioned were Vanilla, Torrio and Fitzpatrick, why didn't Peterson simply say that Birns was murdered by Vanilla? The answer is that Peterson stops short of saying something that he does not know for a fact, though he is not above implying it. Besides, Peterson mistakenly identifies Birns as a Morals Squad officer when all the sources agree that he was a regular police detective. 1952, 95.

48. Landesco 1928, 850. Hoyne did not, however, claim that Vanilla had shot Birns.

49. Kobler 1992, 39, 52.

50. Kobler 1971, 51; Johnson 1998, 100.

51. Johnson 1998, 100–1. McPhaul 1970, 74–7 gives a highly embellished version. Indeed, the stories of how Colosimo eliminated three Black Handers and how Torrio eliminated three Black Handers seem suspiciously similar.

52. Kobler 1971, 65–66, Schoenberg 1992, 60–1; Johnson 1998, 106–7, 117–19; McPhaul 1970, 132–51; Asbury 1940, 314–15.

53. Schoenberg 1992, 70–71.

54. Ibid., 72.

55. Schoenberg 1992, 61–62, 62–63.

56. Kobler 1971, 210. MacAdams 1990, 128, Ben Hecht, 128, Burns 1931, 17–18.

57. Landesco 1928, 124–25.

CHAPTER 5

1. Quoted in Barr 1999, *Drink: A Social History of America*, 237.

2. Howard Lee McBain 1928, *Prohibition, legal and illegal*, 61.

3. Walter Lippmann, *Men of Destiny*, New York, 1927, cited in Sinclair 1962, *Prohibition: The Era of Excess*, 5.

4. 1948, *The age of reform*, 187–88.

5. 1989, *Blood and Power*, 12.

6. Sinclair 1962, 14–15.

7. For Leuchtenburg, 1914 represented the "zenith" of the Progressive movement. "In 1912, when social reform was at floodtide, the chief leaders of the movement were Roosevelt, Wilson, La Follette, Bryan and Debs. By 1920, these leaders and their followers were snarling enemies, hopelessly divided by the issues of war." William Leuchtenberg 1958, *The Perils of Prosperity, 1914–1932*, 121.

8. Arthur Schlesinger Jr. 1957, *The Crisis of the Old Order*, 98–99, Richard Hofstadter 1948, *The Age of Reform*, 203.

9. In Sinclair 1962, 88.

10. In Kobler 1973, 198.

11. New York *World*, May 1919, in Sinclair 1962, 71.

12. George Ade 1931, 8.

13. Sinclair 1962, 95.

14. Frederick Lewis Allen 1931, *Only Yesterday: An Informal History of the 1920s*, 245–46, 247–48.

15. In Walker 1960, *The Nightclub Era*, 3–4.

16. Barr 199, 247.

17. On the enforcement of Prohibition, see Merz 1931, *The Dry Decade*, F.L. Allen 1931, Leuchtenburg 1958, Sinclair 1962, Gusfield 1963, and Barr 1999.

18. Sinclair 1968, 90, 167.

19. Kobler 1971, 221, 274.

20. F.L. Allen 1931, 249–50.

21. Ibid., 251.

22. Merz 1931, 59–61.

23. Kobler 1973, 274.

24. Ibid., 275.

25. Ibid., 275–78.

26. Sinclair 1968, 184; Walker 1960, 79.

27. Sinclair 1968, 405, 460-61.

28. In Sinclair 1968, 169.

29. 1999, 238.

30. In Kobler 1971, 306.

31. Neal Gabler 1995, *Walter Winchell, gossip, power and the cult of celebrity*, 184.

32. Michael Parrish 1992, *Anxious Decades, America in Prosperity and Depression*, 30–31, 54–55.

33. Ibid., 81–84.

34. Walker 1999 (1930), 2–53, 81–82.

35. Fried 1993, *The Rise and Fall of the Jewish Gangster*, 39–40.

36. Ann Douglas 1995, *Terrible Honesty, mongrel Manhattan in the 1920s,* 100.

37. 1995, 24.

38. Edmund Wilson, September 1925, reprinted 1996, 32–35.

39. Walker 1999 (1933), 63–68, Kobler 1993, 233, 272–73.

40. Ralph E, McGill, *The South and the Southerner*, p. 123.

41. In Gabler 1994, 6.

42. Figures from Fried 1993, 87.

43. 1993, 89–90.

44. Baylor 1988.

45. Mark Haller 1979, cited in Block 1983, *East Side–West Side*, 131–32.

46. For Owney Madden's career, see especially Nown 1987 and Walker 1999 (1930). Also see Robert Lacey 1991, *Meyer Lansky and the Gangster Life*; Pietrusza 1991, *Rothstein*; Katcher 1994 (1959); and Gabler 1994. Toots Shor's are from the Columbia Oral History Project.

Chapter 6

1. In Bukowski 1998, 19–20.

2. McPhail 1970.

3. John F. Kasson 1978, *Seeing Coney Island,* 4.

4. Ibid. For Sullivan and Coney Island's development, see Czistrom 1976, Oliver Pilat and Jo Ransom 1941, *Sodom by the Sea*, 57.

5. Pilat and Ransom 1941, 272.

6. Kobler and Peterson claim a Sicilian origin. See Kobler 1992, 33; Peterson 1983, 149. Bergreen and Schoenberg claim he was Calabrian, and supplies a birth year—1893. See Bergreen 1994, 44, Schoenberg 1993, 28. As Yale was close to Ciro Terranove and was later president of the Unione Siciliana, it is natural to assume a Sicilian origin. But connection to the Unione Siciliana did not necessarily imply Sicilian origin.

7. Pilat and Ransom 1941, 57.

8. Kobler 1992, 33–35, Bergreen 1994, 44–45.

9. Pilat and Ransom 1941, 274.

10. Schoenberg 1993, 27–28.

11. Bergreen 1994, 31.

12. Schoenberg 1993, 31.

13. Quoted in Bergreen 1994, 39.

14. The incident is described in all accounts of Capone's career. I am drawing on Bergreen 1994, 47–48, and Kobler 1992, 36.

15. Bergreen 1994, 48–50

16. Kobler 1971.

17. Frederic Thrasher 1927, *The Gang: A Study of 1313 Gangs in Chicago,* 432–34.

18. See also Landesco 1928, charter 5.

19. Lindberg 1996, 153–54.

20. Bukowski 1998, 13, 38–40.

21. Johnson 1998, 105.

22. McPhaul 1970, 116–19. See also Allsop 1961, *The Bootleggers,* and

Johnson 1998.

23. *Chicago Daily News,* 17 November 1924, passing into the Wickersham Report 4.372. See also McPhaul 1970, 157–59; Sinclair 1962, 221; and Allsop 1961, 46–47.

24. In Michael Woodisiss 2001, *Organized Crime and American Power,* 186.

25. See, for example, Sifakis's account in his *Mafia Encyclopedia* under the entry 'Torrio'.

26. Bukowski 1998, 138.

27. Annual reports, Chicago Crime Commission, 1919–1924.

28. Edward D. Sullivan 1929, *Rattling the Cup of Chicago Crime,* 1–7.

29. Landesco 1928, chapter 5. See also Fred Pasley 1930, *Al Capone, the Biography of a Self-Made Man,* 46.

30. Summary, 33.

31. Sinclair 1961, 202.

32. 1998, 137.

33. 1931, 37.

34. 1929, 33.

35. Bukowski 1998, 137–38.

36. Bukowski 1998 and Richard C. Lindberg 1991, 99. 127–43. Both are drawing from Kogan and Wendt 1944.

37. 1930, 191

38. Daniel Bell 1973, p. 83; Michael A. Bernstein 1970, *A Perilous Progress,* 297. Cited in Bukowski 1998, 3.

39. Lindberg 1998, 143.

40. Bukowski 1998, 123–25.

41. Ibid., 149.

42. Ibid., 149–50.

43. Walter Savage Burns 1931, *One Way Ride,* 46–51. Allsop 1961, 50–53.

44. Allsop 1961, 52–53.

45. 1998, 145.

46. *Ibid.* Members of the Torrio-Capone outfit at this time included Ralph and Frank Capone and the Capone cousins, the Fischettis; the Guzik brothers; the LaCava brothers; Pete Penovich, Jimmy Mondi; Tony "Mops" Volpi; Peter Payette; Louis Casentino; Frank "the Enforcer" Nitti; and the gambler and ex-king of the newsboys, Frankie Pope. See Kobler 1992, 112.

47. The Hawthorn Inn was at 4833 22nd Street; the Hawthorn Park Cafe was at 48th and Ogden Avenues.

48. Burns 1931, 67.

49. Ibid., 71–74.

50. 1986, 335.

51. Ade 1931, 8.

52. Kobler 1971, 121–23.

53. On Paddy the Bear Ryan and Terry Druggan, see Burns 1931, pp. 71-79. See also Allsop 1961, pp. 289 & 312-13.

54. 1930, 48–49.

55. Burns 1931, 102–3.

56. In Pasley 1930, 103.

57. In Allsop 1961, 83–84.

58. Burns 1931, 109–13.

59. Burns 1931.

60. Landesco 1928, 176–78.

61. In Bukowski 1998, 159.

62. *Tribune* April 23, 1926. See also Asbury 1986 and Bukowski 1998, 158–60 and footnotes.

63. Johnson 1998, 177.

64. Allsop 1961, 49–50.

65. Kobler and Allsop both provide accounts of the McSwiggen killing.

66. In Bukowski 1998, 61.

67. Ibid., 180.

68. Ibid., 186.

69. Ibid., 185.

70. Kogan and Wendt 1943, 269.

71. Allsop 1961, 124–25.

72. 1998, 5–6.

73. Allsop 1961, 204.

74. In Kobler 1971, 229.

75. Sullivan 1930, 158.

76. Gabler 1994, 120.

77. Kobler 1971, 260.

CHAPTER 7

1. "Whatever else they may say, my booze has been good and my games have been on the square. Public service is my motto. I've always regarded it as a public benefaction if people were given decent liquor and square games." In Kobler 1971, 209–10.

2. In Sullivan 1930, 205.

3. Lindberg 1991, 165. After resigning from the Bureau, Dalrymple found a lucrative job in the booming Texas oil business.

4. Bergreen 1994, 175.

5. Luciano testament, 82.

6. In Rick Porrello's-Americanmafia.com.

7. Christopher Duggan 1998, *La Mafia durante il Fascismo*.

8. 1994, 158.

9. 1931, 120.

10. 1930, 107–8.

11. Johnson 1998, 172.

12. In Kobler 1992, 131–32.

13. Schoenberg 1992, 130–36.

14. Burns gives the figure as $100,000, 1930 137. Other authorities give differing figures.

15. Burns 1930, 128. See also Sullivan 1929, 63. Sullivan mentions a fourth gangster in the car.

16. Burns 1930, 139.

17. Allan May, Americanmafia.com.

18. Burns 1930, 144–45.

19. Allsop 1961, 230.

20. 1930, 145.

21. 1930, 132–33. As always, such instances of reported speech are to be taken with due skepticism. Burns reports that Nerone "had had a university education in Sicily and had taught mathematics in a college in Palermo." I am taking "college" here to refer to a secondary school.

22. In Kobler 1971, 162.

23. *Syndicate City: The Chicago Crime Cartel and What to Do About It*, Chicago (1954), cited in Allan May, Americanmafia.com. The "weird medieval customs" were, we saw, not medieval at all, deriving instead from Free Masonry modified to fit Sicily's tradition of god-siblinghood.

24. Johnson 1998, 244–45. He gives the figure of the proffered bribe as $10,000. The figure $35,000 comes from Kobler 1971.

25. Allsop 1961, 126–27.

26. Kobler 1971, 205–6.

27. Ibid., 128–29.

28. Versions of these events are given in Kobler 1971, Allsop 1961, Johnson 1998, and Burns 1931. I am following Allan May in americanmafia.com.

29. In Johnson 1998, 197–98. The meeting probably took place in 1925.

30. In Allan May Americanmafia.com. Burns also states that Yale overturned Lombardo's election, nominating Joe Aiello as Chicago *Unione* president.

31. Wolf 1974, 85. Wolf is giving Frank Costello's version.

32. Craig Thompson, and Raymond Allen 1940, 116–17.

33. Burns 1931, 232–33.

34. Cited by Allan May in Americanmafia.com.

35. 1931, 234–35.

CHAPTER 8

1. In Messick 1967, *The Silent Syndicate*, 39.

2. Allan May AmericanMafia.com. Kobler and Schoenberg give the number as twenty-seven (Kobler 1971, 255, Schoenberg 1992, 232–33).

3. Allan May Americanmafia.com. During the inquest, assistant state's attorney Samuel Hoffman questioned Lolordo's story, especially after Lolordo claimed that he had never been Lombardo's bodyguard. Police Captain John Stege, Chicago's specialist in organized Sicilian crime, did not believe in Lolordo's guilt and convinced Hoffman. When people realized that Joe Lolordo was the brother of the new *Unione* president, Patsy Lolordo, the theory naturally re-appeared.

4. Schoenberg 1992, 206. The "he" in the last sentence probably refers to McGurn rather than Capone, as McGurn now seems to be in charge of operations.

5. Most accounts claim that McGurn married Rolfe so that she couldn't testify against him. Since Rolfe volunteered to testify for McGurn, this seems unlikely. If anything, McGurn and Rolfe were forced into marriage because the state's attorney, out of chagrin, was contemplating indicting McGurn for violating the Mann Act when he took her to Miami for one of Capone's house parties. They also, in their pique, wished to indict Louise Rolfe as well. Though legally

possible, the charge was somewhat odd. Rolfe was accused of crossing a state line for the purpose of self-debauchery. Marriage voided all these problems.

6. 1992, 228-29.

7. In Kobler 1971, 185.

8. Burns 1930, 267–68.

9. Burns 1930, 272.

10. Ibid., 275. Burns also claims that the Gusenberg brothers killed both Lombardo and Lolordo, and that Scalise took part in the St. Valentine's Day Massacre in which the Gusenbergs were, of course, slaughtered. These matters are somewhat like chess problems; it is impossible to move one piece without thereby changing the potentialities of all the others.

11. Ibid., 281.

12. 1961, 141, 270. Allsop naturally does not accept that Scalise and Anselmi took part in the St. Valentine's Day Massacre. Allsop also put the boast about being the biggest man in Chicago into Giunta's mouth.

13. Allan May, americanmafia.com.

14. May 9, 1929.

15. Report of Dr. Eli S. Jones, coroner, Lake County, Indiana.

16. Merz 1931, 65.

17. "The Little Green House slumbered not, nor slept. It was open for business by day and for pleasure mingled with business by night. Greeks came bearing gifts. Also Italians, Armenians, Jews, Germans, Swedes, and native-born Americans—all the internationale of bootleggery." Lewis Allen, *The Lords of Creation,* cited in Messick 1967, 18–19.

18. Sinclair 1962, 185. Messick 1967, 17–19.

19. Messick 1967, 32.

20. Allan May in Americanmafia.com.

21. Nelli 1976, 103, 124–25, 207.

22. 1967, 39–40.

23. In Allan May, AmericanMafia.com.

24. The information was posted in a comment dated February 22, 2005, by a writer who identifies himself as "ShoNuff" on Rick Porrello's Website, AmericanMafia.com.

25. Sifakis 1999. See entry on "The Purple Gang."

26. The account of Joe Bonanno's youth is provided in Bonanno 1983, *A Man of Honor,* 19–57.

27. Ibid., 41.

28. See the entry for Stefano Magaddino in the American mafioso lisiting at geocities.com and the article on the Buffalo mafia by Mario Machi, Allan May, and Charlie Molino in AmericanMafia.com.

29. Mario Machi article on Detroit mafia in AmericanMafia.com

30. Mario Machi, Allan May, and Charlie Molino, in article on St. Louis mafia in AmericanMafia.com.

31. Bonanno 1983, 70.

CHAPTER 9

1. Ferber 1939, *I Found Out*, 195–96.

2. Wolf 1974. Edward Behr 1996, *Prohibition: 13 Years that Changed America*.

3. Ferber 1939, 142.

4. Ibid., 197.

5. I am here following Fried 1993 for convenience, though similar accounts can be found in other sources. The earliest versions are those of Katcher 1959 and Messick 1967.

6. See Block 1995, 133–34. Block is drawing on a report from the Bureau of Social Morals, which was part of the Kehillal. The date it gives when Gordon supposedly takes over from Fine in the garment industry, 1914, is surely wrong. In 1914, Gordon was on trial for murder, and Fine, though under close surveillance, was still free. The year 1915, when Gordon had been acquitted and Fine was in prison, would be a more likely date.

7. Fried 1993, 1000. On Hague, see Fox 1989.

8. Quoted in Sinclair 1962, 186.

9. Block 1995, 136. Block is quoting from a report from Thomas E. Dewey's files.

10. Lacey 1991. Also cited in Pietrusza 2003, 197–99.

11. Eisenberg and Dan 1979, 82–84.

12. Katchen 1994, 239.

13. Luciano testament 54–59.

14. Thompson and Raymond 1940.

15. Ibid. Humbert Nelli writes that Masseria challenged Umberto Valenti, the Morello-Terranova gang, and Totò D'Aquila for leadership of the Manhattan mafia, interpreting the murder of Vincent Terranova as a Masseria hit. But Masseria and Ciro Terranova seemed to remain on good terms until the Terranova gang was virtually eliminated during the Catellammarese War, Nelli 1976, 197–98.

16. Reppetto 2004, 134.

17. Luciano testament, 41.

18. Luciano testament, 34.

19. Luciano testament, 42.

20. Bonanno 1984, 70.

21. Luciano testament, 46.

22. Ibid., 59–62

23. Ibid., 66–68.

24. In Wolf 1974, 92.

25. Ibid 65.

26. Luciano testament, 81–83.

27. Ibid., 88–89.

28. Ibid., 89–92

29. Allen 1993, 229.

30. Katcher 1959, 259–60.

31. Luciano testament, 102.

32. Ibid., 110.

33. Ibid., 112–14.

34. Ibid., 116–19.

35. Ibid., 126. It's not entirely clear who the "we" refers to. At least it must include Siegel and Lucchese.

36. Ibid., 127.

37. Did Vito Genovese really kill Tom Reina? The story is not included in either Dom Frasca's or David Hanna's, admittedly rather limited, biographies of Vito Genovese. Nor does Joe Bonanno attribute Reina's murder to Genovese (Bonanno 1984, 106). Many writers have doubted Genovese's involvement. In the 1950s, Genovese, acting boss of the Luciano family in New York, broke with Charlie. By the time he gave his interviews, Charlie believed that Vito had spent much of the '40s and '50s plotting against him. In revenge, Charlie blackened Vito's name by telling Martin Gosch that drugs were Vito's life, and that Vito had even arranged that Vito's friend, Tony Bender, murder the reformer and journalist Carlo Tresca in Manhattan on behalf of Benito Mussolini.

38. Maas 1970, 80.

39. Authorities who do not accept Genovere's responsbility in the Reina murder, often assume that the real murderer was Pinzolo. If so, this would be an exception to the supposed rule that the boss's murderer cannot succeed the boss.

40. Luciano testament, 105.

41. The list varies in different accounts. Not all accounts list Vito Genovese or Joe Bonanno. All lists agree, however, that neither Masseria nor Maranzano were present.

42. Jonathan Van Meter 2003, *The Last Good Time*, 11–29.

43. Ibid., 40–42.

44. Ibid., 44.

45. Luciano testament, 105–6.

46. The photo appeared in the New York *Evening Journal*. Nucky later claimed that the photo had been faked. Van Meter 2003, 54.

CHAPTER 10

1. Luciano testament, 129–30.

2. Robert Lacey 1991.

3. Bonanno 1983, 88.

4. Ibid., 84-88.

5. Ibid., 93–94.

6. Ibid., 94.

7. Paul R. Kavieff 2001, *Detroit's Infamous Purple Gang*, 5-71.

8. Luciano testament, 129.

9. See also John H. Davis 1993, *Mafia Dynasty, the Rise and Fall of the Gambino Family*, 34.

10. Bonanno 1983, 299.

11. Ibid., p. 162.

12. Ibid., 96–97,

13. See conflicting accounts in Luciano 1974, 128 and Maas 1970, 80.

14. Maas 1970, 87–89.

15. Ibid., 83–84.

16. Bonanno 1984, 104.

17. Maas 1970, 85.

18. Luciano testament, 133.

19. Maas 1970, 95–97: Luciano 1974, 133–35.

20. Bonanno 1984, 125–26.

21. Ibid., 134–35.

22. Maas 1970, 99–100.

23. Luciano testament, 138–42.

24.Ibid., 145–46.

25. I am following Gage 1972, *The Mafia is not an equal opportunity employer*. Other accounts give similar lists, sometimes with minor alterations.

26. *Colliers* Magazine, August 1939, "Dixie Davis tells about the Mob."

27. Peterson 1983, 359–60, 394.

28. Jay S. Albanese 1995, *Organized Crime in America*, and Maas 1970, 43.

29. Organized Crime Hearings, 205–6. Cited in Peterson 1989, 417.

30. Bonanno 1983, 155–63.

31. Ibid., 118–19.

32. Luciano testament, vii.

33. "'The Last Testament of Lucky Luciano'—Revisited," in Allan May in AmericanMafia.com at americanmafia.com/Mob_Report/9-2-02_Mob_Report.

34. December 17, 1974.

CHAPTER 11

1. Emile Gauvreau 1941, *My last million readers.*

2. Columbia Oral History Project: interview with Toots Shor.

3. The Lanskys were married the week before the Atlantic City meeting.

4.Luciano testament, 155.

5.Ibid., 148–56.

6.Ibid., 110.

7. George E. Pettey, *The Narcotic Drug Diseases and Al lied Ailments,* in Katcher 1994, 288. The drink in question was, of course, Coca Cola.

8. Katcher 1959. 289–90.

9. Ibid.

10. Pietrusza 2003, 112–13.

11. Katcher 1959, 4-5.

12. Pietrusza 2003.

13.Katcher 1959, 8.

14. Ibid., 7, 298–99.

15.Ibid., 292–94.

16.Ibid., 249.

17.Columbia Oral History Project: Toots Shor.

18. Kobler 1971, 251.

19. Regarding Capone's soup kitchens, see Bergreen 1994.

20. In his 1892 sermon, he had told his listeners that the police represented "organized municipal criminality," while Tammany represented "the organization of crime." See Gilfolyle 1992, 300. This use quickly spread to the reformist press. William Stead in 1898 frequently used the term in this sense in Chicago.

21. Bell 1966, 144–45.

22. See Valachi's description in Maas 1969.

23. Charles Garrett 1961, *The La Guardia Years, and Reform Politics in New York City*.

24. David Critchley 2008, *The Origin of Organized Crime 1851-1931: the New York City Mafia*.

25. Lewis J. Valentnine 1946, *Nightstick*, 117–19.

26. Fried 1993, 179–81.

27. New York *Daily News*, December 19, 1931.

28. Adler 1953, *A house is not a Home*.

29. Luciano testament, pp. 79-80

30. Ibid., 76–82.

31. Davis 1939.

32. Fried 1975, 189.

33. The most circumstantial account is in Turkus, Burton and Sid Feder 1951, *Murder Inc.*, 133–45. For Luciano's account, see Luciano testament.

34. Paul Sann 1971, *Kill the Dutchman*.

35. Peterson 1983, 165–66, 182–83. The robbery may have been faked to recover evidence concerning the murder of Frankie Yale a year earlier.

36. Thompson and Raymond 1941, 363–65, 394.

37. Ellen Poulsoen 2007, *The Case Against Lucky Luciano* 125. The quote is from the edition of May 12, 1936.

38. The most detailed accounts are in Stolberg 1995, *Fighting Organized Crime: Political Justice and the Legacy of Thomas E. Dewey*, and Richard Norton Smith 1982, *Thomas E. Dewey and his Times*. See also Luciano's own account. For an earlier account, see Hickman Powell 1940, *Ninety Times Guilty*.

39. 2007, 107.

CONCLUSION

1. Rodney Campbell 1977, *The Luciano Project: The Secret Wartime Collaboration Between the Mafia and the U.S. Navy*.

2. From the Federal Bureau of Investigation Web site at fbi.gov/hq/cid/orgcrime/glossary.

3. Lindberg 1991, 163–65.

4. New York *Times*, February 13, 1892.

5. Gilfoyle 1992, 300. This use quickly spread to the reformist press. William Stead in 1898 frequently used the term in this sense.

6. Parkhurst to Police Commissioners, Jan 16, 1894 in "Mayor's Papers," New York City Municipal Archive and Records Center, cited in Gilfoyle 1992, 185. Parkhurst wrote this a month before delivering his famous sermon.

7. American Vigilance Association 1911, *The Social Evil in Chicago: A Study of Existing Conditions with Recommendations by the Vice Commission of Chicago*, see particularly chapter 4. See also Asbury 1940, Landesco 1928 and Longstreet 1973.

8. The accusations of Jewish involvement in crime are to be found in Commissioner's Bingham 1908 article in *Colliers* Magazine. See particularly George Kibber Turner; "Daughters of the Poor: A Plain Story of the Development of New York City as a Leading Center of the White Slave Trade of the World under

Tammany Hall," Vol. 34.1 (November 1909): 45–61. For a modern study, see Edward J. Bristow1983, *Prostitution and Prejudice: The Jewish Fight Against White Slavery, 1870–1939*. Around 1900 the Jews had become particularly associated with New York's Lower East Side prostitution. Though this was, and still is, understandably, a contentious issue within the Jewish community, research confirms that the problem was widespread. Fried mentions the *Year Book of the University* (New York: Settlement Society of New York, 1899). There was also a study done by the US Immigration Commission on the origins of prostitutes in 1909. The study is rather flawed, for in a great many cases the information that the Immigration Commission was seeking turned out to be unavailable. Still, the Commission found that Jewish women were the largest category in both American born and foreign born prostitutes. See Albert Fried 1993, 8.

9. Republished in Robert Warshow 2001, *The Lived Experience*.

Index

Breinigsville, PA USA
02 September 2010
244736BV00001BA/2/P

9 780761 852155